Lecture Notes in Computer Science   8522

Commenced Publication in 1973
Founding and Former Series Editors:
Gerhard Goos, Juris Hartmanis, and Jan van Leeuwen

Editorial Board

David Hutchison
  Lancaster University, UK

Takeo Kanade
  Carnegie Mellon University, Pittsburgh, PA, USA

Josef Kittler
  University of Surrey, Guildford, UK

Jon M. Kleinberg
  Cornell University, Ithaca, NY, USA

Alfred Kobsa
  University of California, Irvine, CA, USA

Friedemann Mattern
  ETH Zurich, Switzerland

John C. Mitchell
  Stanford University, CA, USA

Moni Naor
  Weizmann Institute of Science, Rehovot, Israel

Oscar Nierstrasz
  University of Bern, Switzerland

C. Pandu Rangan
  Indian Institute of Technology, Madras, India

Bernhard Steffen
  TU Dortmund University, Germany

Demetri Terzopoulos
  University of California, Los Angeles, CA, USA

Doug Tygar
  University of California, Berkeley, CA, USA

Gerhard Weikum
  Max Planck Institute for Informatics, Saarbruecken, Germany

Sakae Yamamoto (Ed.)

Human Interface and the Management of Information

Information and Knowledge in Applications and Services

16th International Conference, HCI International 2014
Heraklion, Crete, Greece, June 22-27, 2014
Proceedings, Part II

 Springer

Volume Editor

Sakae Yamamoto
Tokyo University of Science
Department of Management Science
Kagurazaka Shinjuku-ku
Tokyo, 162-8601, Japan
E-mail: sakaeyam@jcom.home.ne.jp

ISSN 0302-9743   e-ISSN 1611-3349
ISBN 978-3-319-07862-5   e-ISBN 978-3-319-07863-2
DOI 10.1007/978-3-319-07863-2
Springer Cham Heidelberg New York Dordrecht London

Library of Congress Control Number: 2014940076

LNCS Sublibrary: SL 3 – Information Systems and Application,
incl. Internet/Web and HCI

© Springer International Publishing Switzerland 2014

This work is subject to copyright. All rights are reserved by the Publisher, whether the whole or part of the material is concerned, specifically the rights of translation, reprinting, reuse of illustrations, recitation, broadcasting, reproduction on microfilms or in any other physical way, and transmission or information storage and retrieval, electronic adaptation, computer software, or by similar or dissimilar methodology now known or hereafter developed. Exempted from this legal reservation are brief excerpts in connection with reviews or scholarly analysis or material supplied specifically for the purpose of being entered and executed on a computer system, for exclusive use by the purchaser of the work. Duplication of this publication or parts thereof is permitted only under the provisions of the Copyright Law of the Publisher's location, in ist current version, and permission for use must always be obtained from Springer. Permissions for use may be obtained through RightsLink at the Copyright Clearance Center. Violations are liable to prosecution under the respective Copyright Law.
The use of general descriptive names, registered names, trademarks, service marks, etc. in this publication does not imply, even in the absence of a specific statement, that such names are exempt from the relevant protective laws and regulations and therefore free for general use.
While the advice and information in this book are believed to be true and accurate at the date of publication, neither the authors nor the editors nor the publisher can accept any legal responsibility for any errors or omissions that may be made. The publisher makes no warranty, express or implied, with respect to the material contained herein.

Typesetting: Camera-ready by author, data conversion by Scientific Publishing Services, Chennai, India

Printed on acid-free paper

Springer is part of Springer Science+Business Media (www.springer.com)

Foreword

The 16th International Conference on Human–Computer Interaction, HCI International 2014, was held in Heraklion, Crete, Greece, during June 22–27, 2014, incorporating 14 conferences/thematic areas:

Thematic areas:

- Human–Computer Interaction
- Human Interface and the Management of Information

Affiliated conferences:

- 11th International Conference on Engineering Psychology and Cognitive Ergonomics
- 8th International Conference on Universal Access in Human–Computer Interaction
- 6th International Conference on Virtual, Augmented and Mixed Reality
- 6th International Conference on Cross-Cultural Design
- 6th International Conference on Social Computing and Social Media
- 8th International Conference on Augmented Cognition
- 5th International Conference on Digital Human Modeling and Applications in Health, Safety, Ergonomics and Risk Management
- Third International Conference on Design, User Experience and Usability
- Second International Conference on Distributed, Ambient and Pervasive Interactions
- Second International Conference on Human Aspects of Information Security, Privacy and Trust
- First International Conference on HCI in Business
- First International Conference on Learning and Collaboration Technologies

A total of 4,766 individuals from academia, research institutes, industry, and governmental agencies from 78 countries submitted contributions, and 1,476 papers and 225 posters were included in the proceedings. These papers address the latest research and development efforts and highlight the human aspects of design and use of computing systems. The papers thoroughly cover the entire field of human–computer interaction, addressing major advances in knowledge and effective use of computers in a variety of application areas.

This volume, edited by Sakae Yamamoto, contains papers focusing on the thematic area of human interface and the management of information, addressing the following major topics:

- E-learning and e-education
- Decision support

- Information and interaction in aviation and transport
- Safety, security and reliability
- Communication, expression and emotions
- Art, culture and creativity
- Information and knowledge in business and society

The remaining volumes of the HCI International 2014 proceedings are:

- Volume 1, LNCS 8510, Human–Computer Interaction: HCI Theories, Methods and Tools (Part I), edited by Masaaki Kurosu
- Volume 2, LNCS 8511, Human–Computer Interaction: Advanced Interaction Modalities and Techniques (Part II), edited by Masaaki Kurosu
- Volume 3, LNCS 8512, Human–Computer Interaction: Applications and Services (Part III), edited by Masaaki Kurosu
- Volume 4, LNCS 8513, Universal Access in Human–Computer Interaction: Design and Development Methods for Universal Access (Part I), edited by Constantine Stephanidis and Margherita Antona
- Volume 5, LNCS 8514, Universal Access in Human–Computer Interaction: Universal Access to Information and Knowledge (Part II), edited by Constantine Stephanidis and Margherita Antona
- Volume 6, LNCS 8515, Universal Access in Human–Computer Interaction: Aging and Assistive Environments (Part III), edited by Constantine Stephanidis and Margherita Antona
- Volume 7, LNCS 8516, Universal Access in Human–Computer Interaction: Design for All and Accessibility Practice (Part IV), edited by Constantine Stephanidis and Margherita Antona
- Volume 8, LNCS 8517, Design, User Experience, and Usability: Theories, Methods and Tools for Designing the User Experience (Part I), edited by Aaron Marcus
- Volume 9, LNCS 8518, Design, User Experience, and Usability: User Experience Design for Diverse Interaction Platforms and Environments (Part II), edited by Aaron Marcus
- Volume 10, LNCS 8519, Design, User Experience, and Usability: User Experience Design for Everyday Life Applications and Services (Part III), edited by Aaron Marcus
- Volume 11, LNCS 8520, Design, User Experience, and Usability: User Experience Design Practice (Part IV), edited by Aaron Marcus
- Volume 12, LNCS 8521, Human Interface and the Management of Information: Information and Knowledge Design and Evaluation (Part I), edited by Sakae Yamamoto
- Volume 14, LNCS 8523, Learning and Collaboration Technologies: Designing and Developing Novel Learning Experiences (Part I), edited by Panayiotis Zaphiris and Andri Ioannou
- Volume 15, LNCS 8524, Learning and Collaboration Technologies: Technology-rich Environments for Learning and Collaboration (Part II), edited by Panayiotis Zaphiris and Andri Ioannou

- Volume 16, LNCS 8525, Virtual, Augmented and Mixed Reality: Designing and Developing Virtual and Augmented Environments (Part I), edited by Randall Shumaker and Stephanie Lackey
- Volume 17, LNCS 8526, Virtual, Augmented and Mixed Reality: Applications of Virtual and Augmented Reality (Part II), edited by Randall Shumaker and Stephanie Lackey
- Volume 18, LNCS 8527, HCI in Business, edited by Fiona Fui-Hoon Nah
- Volume 19, LNCS 8528, Cross-Cultural Design, edited by P.L. Patrick Rau
- Volume 20, LNCS 8529, Digital Human Modeling and Applications in Health, Safety, Ergonomics and Risk Management, edited by Vincent G. Duffy
- Volume 21, LNCS 8530, Distributed, Ambient, and Pervasive Interactions, edited by Norbert Streitz and Panos Markopoulos
- Volume 22, LNCS 8531, Social Computing and Social Media, edited by Gabriele Meiselwitz
- Volume 23, LNAI 8532, Engineering Psychology and Cognitive Ergonomics, edited by Don Harris
- Volume 24, LNCS 8533, Human Aspects of Information Security, Privacy and Trust, edited by Theo Tryfonas and Ioannis Askoxylakis
- Volume 25, LNAI 8534, Foundations of Augmented Cognition, edited by Dylan D. Schmorrow and Cali M. Fidopiastis
- Volume 26, CCIS 434, HCI International 2014 Posters Proceedings (Part I), edited by Constantine Stephanidis
- Volume 27, CCIS 435, HCI International 2014 Posters Proceedings (Part II), edited by Constantine Stephanidis

I would like to thank the Program Chairs and the members of the Program Boards of all affiliated conferences and thematic areas, listed below, for their contribution to the highest scientific quality and the overall success of the HCI International 2014 Conference.

This conference could not have been possible without the continuous support and advice of the founding chair and conference scientific advisor, Prof. Gavriel Salvendy, as well as the dedicated work and outstanding efforts of the communications chair and editor of *HCI International News*, Dr. Abbas Moallem.

I would also like to thank for their contribution towards the smooth organization of the HCI International 2014 Conference the members of the Human–Computer Interaction Laboratory of ICS-FORTH, and in particular George Paparoulis, Maria Pitsoulaki, Maria Bouhli, and George Kapnas.

April 2014   Constantine Stephanidis
                                            General Chair, HCI International 2014

Organization

Human–Computer Interaction

Program Chair: Masaaki Kurosu, Japan

Jose Abdelnour-Nocera, UK
Sebastiano Bagnara, Italy
Simone Barbosa, Brazil
Adriana Betiol, Brazil
Simone Borsci, UK
Henry Duh, Australia
Xiaowen Fang, USA
Vicki Hanson, UK
Wonil Hwang, Korea
Minna Isomursu, Finland
Yong Gu Ji, Korea
Anirudha Joshi, India
Esther Jun, USA
Kyungdoh Kim, Korea

Heidi Krömker, Germany
Chen Ling, USA
Chang S. Nam, USA
Naoko Okuizumi, Japan
Philippe Palanque, France
Ling Rothrock, USA
Naoki Sakakibara, Japan
Dominique Scapin, France
Guangfeng Song, USA
Sanjay Tripathi, India
Chui Yin Wong, Malaysia
Toshiki Yamaoka, Japan
Kazuhiko Yamazaki, Japan
Ryoji Yoshitake, Japan

Human Interface and the Management of Information

Program Chair: Sakae Yamamoto, Japan

Alan Chan, Hong Kong
Denis A. Coelho, Portugal
Linda Elliott, USA
Shin'ichi Fukuzumi, Japan
Michitaka Hirose, Japan
Makoto Itoh, Japan
Yen-Yu Kang, Taiwan
Koji Kimita, Japan
Daiji Kobayashi, Japan

Hiroyuki Miki, Japan
Hirohiko Mori, Japan
Shogo Nishida, Japan
Robert Proctor, USA
Youngho Rhee, Korea
Ryosuke Saga, Japan
Katsunori Shimohara, Japan
Kim-Phuong Vu, USA
Tomio Watanabe, Japan

Engineering Psychology and Cognitive Ergonomics

Program Chair: Don Harris, UK

Guy Andre Boy, USA
Shan Fu, P.R. China
Hung-Sying Jing, Taiwan
Wen-Chin Li, Taiwan
Mark Neerincx, The Netherlands
Jan Noyes, UK
Paul Salmon, Australia

Axel Schulte, Germany
Siraj Shaikh, UK
Sarah Sharples, UK
Anthony Smoker, UK
Neville Stanton, UK
Alex Stedmon, UK
Andrew Thatcher, South Africa

Universal Access in Human–Computer Interaction

Program Chairs: Constantine Stephanidis, Greece, and Margherita Antona, Greece

Julio Abascal, Spain
Gisela Susanne Bahr, USA
João Barroso, Portugal
Margrit Betke, USA
Anthony Brooks, Denmark
Christian Bühler, Germany
Stefan Carmien, Spain
Hua Dong, P.R. China
Carlos Duarte, Portugal
Pier Luigi Emiliani, Italy
Qin Gao, P.R. China
Andrina Granić, Croatia
Andreas Holzinger, Austria
Josette Jones, USA
Simeon Keates, UK

Georgios Kouroupetroglou, Greece
Patrick Langdon, UK
Barbara Leporini, Italy
Eugene Loos, The Netherlands
Ana Isabel Paraguay, Brazil
Helen Petrie, UK
Michael Pieper, Germany
Enrico Pontelli, USA
Jaime Sanchez, Chile
Alberto Sanna, Italy
Anthony Savidis, Greece
Christian Stary, Austria
Hirotada Ueda, Japan
Gerhard Weber, Germany
Harald Weber, Germany

Virtual, Augmented and Mixed Reality

Program Chairs: Randall Shumaker, USA, and Stephanie Lackey, USA

Roland Blach, Germany
Sheryl Brahnam, USA
Juan Cendan, USA
Jessie Chen, USA
Panagiotis D. Kaklis, UK

Hirokazu Kato, Japan
Denis Laurendeau, Canada
Fotis Liarokapis, UK
Michael Macedonia, USA
Gordon Mair, UK

Jose San Martin, Spain
Tabitha Peck, USA
Christian Sandor, Australia

Christopher Stapleton, USA
Gregory Welch, USA

Cross-Cultural Design

Program Chair: P.L. Patrick Rau, P.R. China

Yee-Yin Choong, USA
Paul Fu, USA
Zhiyong Fu, P.R. China
Pin-Chao Liao, P.R. China
Dyi-Yih Michael Lin, Taiwan
Rungtai Lin, Taiwan
Ta-Ping (Robert) Lu, Taiwan
Liang Ma, P.R. China
Alexander Mädche, Germany

Sheau-Farn Max Liang, Taiwan
Katsuhiko Ogawa, Japan
Tom Plocher, USA
Huatong Sun, USA
Emil Tso, P.R. China
Hsiu-Ping Yueh, Taiwan
Liang (Leon) Zeng, USA
Jia Zhou, P.R. China

Online Communities and Social Media

Program Chair: Gabriele Meiselwitz, USA

Leonelo Almeida, Brazil
Chee Siang Ang, UK
Aneesha Bakharia, Australia
Ania Bobrowicz, UK
James Braman, USA
Farzin Deravi, UK
Carsten Kleiner, Germany
Niki Lambropoulos, Greece
Soo Ling Lim, UK

Anthony Norcio, USA
Portia Pusey, USA
Panote Siriaraya, UK
Stefan Stieglitz, Germany
Giovanni Vincenti, USA
Yuanqiong (Kathy) Wang, USA
June Wei, USA
Brian Wentz, USA

Augmented Cognition

**Program Chairs: Dylan D. Schmorrow, USA,
and Cali M. Fidopiastis, USA**

Ahmed Abdelkhalek, USA
Robert Atkinson, USA
Monique Beaudoin, USA
John Blitch, USA
Alenka Brown, USA

Rosario Cannavò, Italy
Joseph Cohn, USA
Andrew J. Cowell, USA
Martha Crosby, USA
Wai-Tat Fu, USA

Rodolphe Gentili, USA
Frederick Gregory, USA
Michael W. Hail, USA
Monte Hancock, USA
Fei Hu, USA
Ion Juvina, USA
Joe Keebler, USA
Philip Mangos, USA
Rao Mannepalli, USA
David Martinez, USA
Yvonne R. Masakowski, USA
Santosh Mathan, USA
Ranjeev Mittu, USA

Keith Niall, USA
Tatana Olson, USA
Debra Patton, USA
June Pilcher, USA
Robinson Pino, USA
Tiffany Poeppelman, USA
Victoria Romero, USA
Amela Sadagic, USA
Anna Skinner, USA
Ann Speed, USA
Robert Sottilare, USA
Peter Walker, USA

Digital Human Modeling and Applications in Health, Safety, Ergonomics and Risk Management

Program Chair: Vincent G. Duffy, USA

Giuseppe Andreoni, Italy
Daniel Carruth, USA
Elsbeth De Korte, The Netherlands
Afzal A. Godil, USA
Ravindra Goonetilleke, Hong Kong
Noriaki Kuwahara, Japan
Kang Li, USA
Zhizhong Li, P.R. China

Tim Marler, USA
Jianwei Niu, P.R. China
Michelle Robertson, USA
Matthias Rötting, Germany
Mao-Jiun Wang, Taiwan
Xuguang Wang, France
James Yang, USA

Design, User Experience, and Usability

Program Chair: Aaron Marcus, USA

Sisira Adikari, Australia
Claire Ancient, USA
Arne Berger, Germany
Jamie Blustein, Canada
Ana Boa-Ventura, USA
Jan Brejcha, Czech Republic
Lorenzo Cantoni, Switzerland
Marc Fabri, UK
Luciane Maria Fadel, Brazil
Tricia Flanagan, Hong Kong
Jorge Frascara, Mexico

Federico Gobbo, Italy
Emilie Gould, USA
Rüdiger Heimgärtner, Germany
Brigitte Herrmann, Germany
Steffen Hess, Germany
Nouf Khashman, Canada
Fabiola Guillermina Noël, Mexico
Francisco Rebelo, Portugal
Kerem Rızvanoğlu, Turkey
Marcelo Soares, Brazil
Carla Spinillo, Brazil

Distributed, Ambient and Pervasive Interactions

Program Chairs: Norbert Streitz, Germany, and Panos Markopoulos, The Netherlands

Juan Carlos Augusto, UK
Jose Bravo, Spain
Adrian Cheok, UK
Boris de Ruyter, The Netherlands
Anind Dey, USA
Dimitris Grammenos, Greece
Nuno Guimaraes, Portugal
Achilles Kameas, Greece
Javed Vassilis Khan, The Netherlands
Shin'ichi Konomi, Japan
Carsten Magerkurth, Switzerland

Ingrid Mulder, The Netherlands
Anton Nijholt, The Netherlands
Fabio Paternó, Italy
Carsten Röcker, Germany
Teresa Romao, Portugal
Albert Ali Salah, Turkey
Manfred Tscheligi, Austria
Reiner Wichert, Germany
Woontack Woo, Korea
Xenophon Zabulis, Greece

Human Aspects of Information Security, Privacy and Trust

Program Chairs: Theo Tryfonas, UK, and Ioannis Askoxylakis, Greece

Claudio Agostino Ardagna, Italy
Zinaida Benenson, Germany
Daniele Catteddu, Italy
Raoul Chiesa, Italy
Bryan Cline, USA
Sadie Creese, UK
Jorge Cuellar, Germany
Marc Dacier, USA
Dieter Gollmann, Germany
Kirstie Hawkey, Canada
Jaap-Henk Hoepman, The Netherlands
Cagatay Karabat, Turkey
Angelos Keromytis, USA
Ayako Komatsu, Japan
Ronald Leenes, The Netherlands
Javier Lopez, Spain
Steve Marsh, Canada

Gregorio Martinez, Spain
Emilio Mordini, Italy
Yuko Murayama, Japan
Masakatsu Nishigaki, Japan
Aljosa Pasic, Spain
Milan Petković, The Netherlands
Joachim Posegga, Germany
Jean-Jacques Quisquater, Belgium
Damien Sauveron, France
George Spanoudakis, UK
Kerry-Lynn Thomson, South Africa
Julien Touzeau, France
Theo Tryfonas, UK
João Vilela, Portugal
Claire Vishik, UK
Melanie Volkamer, Germany

HCI in Business

Program Chair: Fiona Fui-Hoon Nah, USA

Andreas Auinger, Austria
Michel Avital, Denmark
Traci Carte, USA
Hock Chuan Chan, Singapore
Constantinos Coursaris, USA
Soussan Djamasbi, USA
Brenda Eschenbrenner, USA
Nobuyuki Fukawa, USA
Khaled Hassanein, Canada
Milena Head, Canada
Susanna (Shuk Ying) Ho, Australia
Jack Zhenhui Jiang, Singapore
Jinwoo Kim, Korea
Zoonky Lee, Korea
Honglei Li, UK
Nicholas Lockwood, USA
Eleanor T. Loiacono, USA
Mei Lu, USA

Scott McCoy, USA
Brian Mennecke, USA
Robin Poston, USA
Lingyun Qiu, P.R. China
Rene Riedl, Austria
Matti Rossi, Finland
April Savoy, USA
Shu Schiller, USA
Hong Sheng, USA
Choon Ling Sia, Hong Kong
Chee-Wee Tan, Denmark
Chuan Hoo Tan, Hong Kong
Noam Tractinsky, Israel
Horst Treiblmaier, Austria
Virpi Tuunainen, Finland
Dezhi Wu, USA
I-Chin Wu, Taiwan

Learning and Collaboration Technologies

Program Chairs: Panayiotis Zaphiris, Cyprus, and Andri Ioannou, Cyprus

Ruthi Aladjem, Israel
Abdulaziz Aldaej, UK
John M. Carroll, USA
Maka Eradze, Estonia
Mikhail Fominykh, Norway
Denis Gillet, Switzerland
Mustafa Murat Inceoglu, Turkey
Pernilla Josefsson, Sweden
Marie Joubert, UK
Sauli Kiviranta, Finland
Tomaž Klobučar, Slovenia
Elena Kyza, Cyprus
Maarten de Laat, The Netherlands
David Lamas, Estonia

Edmund Laugasson, Estonia
Ana Loureiro, Portugal
Katherine Maillet, France
Nadia Pantidi, UK
Antigoni Parmaxi, Cyprus
Borzoo Pourabdollahian, Italy
Janet C. Read, UK
Christophe Reffay, France
Nicos Souleles, Cyprus
Ana Luísa Torres, Portugal
Stefan Trausan-Matu, Romania
Aimilia Tzanavari, Cyprus
Johnny Yuen, Hong Kong
Carmen Zahn, Switzerland

External Reviewers

Ilia Adami, Greece
Iosif Klironomos, Greece
Maria Korozi, Greece
Vassilis Kouroumalis, Greece

Asterios Leonidis, Greece
George Margetis, Greece
Stavroula Ntoa, Greece
Nikolaos Partarakis, Greece

HCI International 2015

The 15th International Conference on Human–Computer Interaction, HCI International 2015, will be held jointly with the affiliated conferences in Los Angeles, CA, USA, in the Westin Bonaventure Hotel, August 2–7, 2015. It will cover a broad spectrum of themes related to HCI, including theoretical issues, methods, tools, processes, and case studies in HCI design, as well as novel interaction techniques, interfaces, and applications. The proceedings will be published by Springer. More information will be available on the conference website: http://www.hcii2015.org/

General Chair
Professor Constantine Stephanidis
University of Crete and ICS-FORTH
Heraklion, Crete, Greece
E-mail: cs@ics.forth.gr

Table of Contents – Part II

E-learning and E-education

Decision Support

Information and Interaction in Aviation and Transport

Safety, Security and Reliability

Communication, Expression and Emotions

Art, Culture and Creativity

Information and Knowledge in Business and Society

Table of Contents – Part I

Visualisation Methods and Techniques

Knowledge Management

Information Search and Retrieval

Supporting Collaboration

Design and Evaluation Methods and Studies

E-learning and E-education

The Effects of Using Kit-Build Method to Support Reading Comprehension of EFL

Mohammad Alkhateeb[1,2], Yusuke Hayashi[1], and Tsukasa Hirashima[1]

[1] Graduate School of Engineering,
Hiroshima University, Japan
[2] Faculty of Mechanical and Electrical Engineering,
Tishreen University, Syria
{Mohammad,Hayashi,Tsukasa}@lel.hiroshima-u.ac.jp

Abstract. In this paper, we describe the effects of using Kit-Build concept map (KB-map) method as a supportive tool for the reading comprehension of English texts as EFL reading. Reading comprehension is the ability to read text, it is intentional, active, interactive process in all the stages of study for the students and in the daily working activities. One of the most common research points in this field is the English as Foreign Language (EFL) reading comprehension. We have conducted an experiment composed of six experimental reading comprehension sessions. We found that there is no significant difference in the comprehension between the two conditions groups just after the experimental using, but there is noticed difference in the comprehension two weeks after. It shows that the using of KB-map building helps learners to keep their information for long time, and we can say that the using of KB-Map help the students to use and recall, after two weeks, most of the information that are included in their student map.

Keywords: Kit-Build, comprehension test, Delayed comprehension test, reading comprehension, Mother Language ML.

1 Introduction

Reading comprehension is one of the important learning activities and it needs a special ability from the learners to gain the goal of it. Reading comprehension has many problems as slow reading, insufficient comprehension and bad recalling. There are many researchers try to support this learning activity by proposing methods or strategies. The main goal is to boost comprehension skills in the target subject area, or when they are deployed in the language courses, the main aims are to improve students' reading comprehension skills and contribute to the acquisition of the target language [3].

The reading comprehension of "English as foreign language" EFL is special case of reading comprehension; it is highly complex, dynamic, multi-componental and multi-dimensional task in the learning process. We can explain it as a multiple interactions between the reader background and knowledge in his Mother Language (ML)

S. Yamamoto (Ed.): HIMI 2014, Part II, LNCS 8522, pp. 3–11, 2014.
© Springer International Publishing Switzerland 2014

and in the foreign language. In generally, the reading comprehension of EFL is same as the ML reading comprehension but it is slower and less successful than ML reading [2]; this can be explained that the reading process depending on many factors as the level of reader' language proficiency, type of text, text difficulty and task demands.

In this research we are trying to support this complex learning task by using our KB-map method to improve the student's reading ability [5]. We have been developing learning tools to help both the students and the teachers in the learning process. One of these tools is Kit-Build concept map (KB-map), we found that it is a very useful tool for learning the sciences for the students of the mother languages [5], and we found that this tool has good effects for the teachers and students; by the way KB-map is a special kind of concept map and the using of KB-map need a lot of concentration to recognize the two concepts that can be connected by a relation.

To investigate the effects of using KB-map, we design experiment, in this experiment we are comparing the selective underlining strategy for reading comprehension with our KB-map method, and as known the selective underlining is a flexible strategy that may be tailored to fit various types of information, and different skill-levels. As students study, selective underlining helps them learn to pay attention to the essential information within a text.

1.1   EFL Reading Comprehension

The comprehension definition is "the ability to understand something" as the oxford dictionary and the definition of Cambridge dictionary is "the ability to understand completely and be familiar with a situation, facts, etc." from these two definitions we can define the reading comprehension in our research as" the learner's ability to understand completely and memorize the important information that included in the text that he is reading". Also Reading comprehension is defined as the level of understanding of a text/message. This understanding comes from the interaction between the words that written and how they trigger knowledge outside the text/message [5].

In generally the reading comprehension is a very difficult task for students in all the stages of study and especially when they are reading text in a foreign language, the EFL reading" (English as foreign language) is one of the most common research topic in the learning field .

There are many researches tried to solve this problem by proposing methods and strategies to help the students in this task but most of them had slightly significant improving in the students' comprehension just after doing the methods or the strategies. Some of these strategies are selective underlining strategy [10-11], Note-Taking Skills Reading [12], SQ3R (Survey, Question, Read, Recite, Review) [13] and PORPE (Predict, Organize, Rehearse, Practice, Evaluate) [14]. Several investigations of reading comprehension strategies have specifically addressed challenges related to reading expository text. Positive outcomes have been found for students who were taught strategies to help students identify main ideas.

1.2   Selective Underlining

Selective underlining is one of the important classroom strategies and also it is probably the most used; it is used to help students organize what they have read by selecting what is important. This strategy teaches students to highlight/underline only the key words, phrases, vocabulary, and ideas that are central to understanding the reading [10-11] .it is very useful for comprehending the text because it is a flexible strategy that may be tailored to fit various types of information, and different skill-levels. This strategy can also be integrated with the use of technology and electronic information such as eBooks. As students study, it helps them learn to pay attention to the essential information within a text [10]. In generally this strategy is focusing on the vocabularies and comprehension of the text during the reading time, it help the reader to identify the important points of a text, Helps him to pay close attention to what he is reading and also allow greater learning and deeper comprehension.

In the selective underlining strategy, the learner start by reading the text to understand the main topic of the text, after that he reread and begin to underlining the main ideas and their supporting details, then he selects the important facts and the key vocabularies. By using the underlined part of the text, the learner can give a summary for the important information in the text that he has read.

This strategy requested the learner to capture the main ideas, key concepts and the details; also it helps by reducing the needed information in text so it reduces the studying time and in the same time strengthens the reading comprehension.

2   Kit-Build Method

We have been developing learning tools to help both the students and the teachers in the learning process. One of these tools is KB-Map, we found that this tool is very useful for learning the sciences for the students of the mother languages, and we found that this tool has good effects for the teachers and students [4-5-8-9]. In this research we are trying to use this tool to support the reading comprehension of EFL students.

2.1   Overview of Kit-Build Concept Map

As a definition of KB-map we can find "a framework to realize automatic diagnosis of concept Maps built by learners and to give feedback to their errors in the maps" [5]. KB-map is a special kind of concept map, in generally the concept map creation consists of two steps: the extraction of the concepts and the relations from the text and the second one is to select the responsible relation that connects two concepts together. In KB-map the supervisor does the first step by creating the goal map from text and after that he can generate the kit from the goal map by dividing the goal map to the concepts and the relations, and provide the learners with this kit, after that the task of the learner is to find every two concepts that can be related and try to select the responsible relation for them until he finish all the kit.

2.2   KB-map System

We have already developed a system based on the KB-map explained in the previous section. This system is called as "KBmap System". It is a web application with two client systems: "KBmap Editor" and "KBmap Analyzer", and a server system: "KBmap DB". KBmap Editor provides an environment for teacher, or supervisor, to make a goal map, a kit, and for learner to make a learner map. This system has been implemented by Java (version 1.6). KBmap Analyzer has functions to gather learner maps online, generate a group map and diagnose the maps. This system has implemented by Flash and supports version Flash Player 10. KBmap DB has a function to store and share maps. This system was developed by Ruby (version 1.8.7) on Rails (version 1.2.3) and MySQL (version 5.1.30) [5].

3   Experiment Methodology

We are trying to investigate the effects of using KB-map building method as a supportive tool for the reading comprehension task by comparing them with the effects of the selective underlining strategy from two points of view:

1. for the short term: we are measuring the understanding of the participants just after the using of our tool, and compare it with the understanding of other participants who use classical learning tool (selective underlining) with the same conditions.
2. for the long term: we are measuring the remembered information of the participants two weeks after the using of our tool, and compare it with another participants' information who use classical learning tool (selective underlining) with the same conditions.

In this chapter we introduce 2 points of our experiment: the participants, the procedure of whole experiment.

3.1   Participants

The participants of our experiment are 8 Japanese students of 3rd grade of information engineering faculty. Their scores of TOEIC exam are different from 430~625 so they have different reading abilities of English text; we prepare an aptitude test to check their abilities in the reading comprehension. By using the information of their TOEIC records and the scores of the aptitude test, we grouped them into two groups A and B, which are almost commensurate with the reading ability.

We have done our experiment in 6 sessions and the two groups are changing the conditions alternately. For every participant he was three times with the experimental conditions and three times with control conditions.

3.2   Procedure of the Experiment

We planned to do this experiment in six sessions as reading comprehension task for 6 different English texts; firstly we introduced to the participants the strategy of this experiment, the procedure of every session and KB-map system. For the others session we started with the delay comprehension test of the previous session, after that we did a learning activity to improve the English level of participants and in the last 30 minutes they did the session, finally we did questionnaire at the end of the last session of the experiment. During this experiment every group do it with the experimental conditions for three times and with control conditions three times too. We try to make balance between the different texts of this experiment.

4 Experimental Use

This experiment was done in 6 sessions with two group of participants (A, B) both of them has almost the same reading ability. For each group they use the KB-map method for 3 sessions and the selective underlining for 3 sessions too. In this chapter we introduced 2 points: the preparation of the used materials and example of the materials that used in the experiment.

4.1 Materials Preparation

The participants of this experiment are students of 3rd grade faculty of information engineering, so they are interested in the topics of information engineering, so firstly we select a text from Wikipedia in the information engineering field, and check it for the grammatical and semantically error. After that we create the corresponding KB-map (Goal map) that covers the main concepts and relations of the text, after that we do the selective underlining for the important and essential phrases in the text. We prepare the comprehension test. And we check all of the material again to be sure that materials did not contain any error. Finally we check if the answers of questions of comprehension test are covered by the KB-map and the selective underlining to marking the questions that not covered.

4.2 Example of Experimental Material

In this section, we introduce one example of the materials that was used in the third session of our experiment. Fig 1 shows a part of the text that was used as the original text which learners try to comprehend it.

A language is typed if the specification of every operation defines types of data to which the operation is applicable, with the implication that it is not applicable to other types. In most programming languages, dividing a number by a string has no meaning. Most modern programming languages will therefore reject any program attempting to perform such an operation. In some languages, the meaningless operation will be detected when the program is compiled ("static" type checking), and rejected by the compiler, while in others, it will be detected when the program is run ("dynamic" type checking), resulting in a runtime exception."

Fig. 1. Sample of the used text in the third session

The participants requested to read and comprehend this text within 10 minutes and they have the ability to use online dictionary to translate the complex and unknown words to help them in understanding the whole text. After that, the experimental conditions group tried to build learner's map, within 10 minutes, by using the kit that provided by the system which generated it from the corresponding goal map. Fig 2 shows the goal map of the text that was prepared by the supervisor, it contains most of the information of the original text, this goal map is divided by the system to generate the kit that shown in Fig 3.

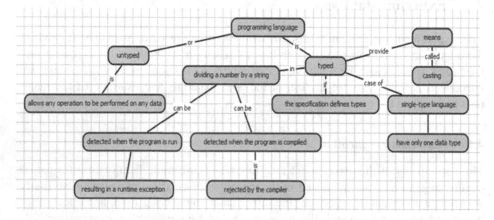

Fig. 2. The Goal map of third session

In the same time, the control conditions group tried to do the underlining for the important sentences in the text within 10 minutes too. The underlined text contains the important information of the text. Fig 4 shows one example of the underlining of the same paragraph.

After that all the participants did the same comprehension test within 5 minutes which is a set of multi-choices questions. All of these questions are asking about information included in the original text, some of them are included in the goal map and some are not, and for the underlined text all of them are included. Fig 5 shows a part of the comprehension test of this session.

By the end of this test they finished the experimental use of that day and 2 weeks after they did the comprehension test again as a delayed comprehension test.

A language is typed if the <u>specification of every operation defines types</u> of data to which the operation is applicable, with the implication that it is not applicable to other types. In most programming languages, dividing a number by a string has no meaning. <u>Most modern programming languages will therefore reject any program attempting to perform such an operation.</u> In some languages, <u>the meaningless operation will be detected when the program is compiled</u> ("static" type checking), and <u>rejected by the compiler</u>, while in others, it will be <u>detected when the program is run</u> ("dynamic" type checking), resulting in a <u>runtime exception.</u>

Fig. 3. Sample of the Underlining of the used text

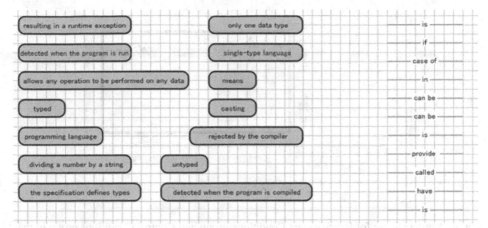

Fig. 4. The kit of third session

Q2: with typed languages, if the error of types of data did not discovered in compiling can we discover it?

   a. can   *b. cannot.*

   c. can with conditions   *d. I don't know.*

Q3: In the untyped languages can we do operation with two types of data?

   a. can   *b. cannot.*

   c. can with conditions   *d. I don't know.*

Fig. 5. Samples of the comprehension test

5 Results and Discussion

We do our experiment with 8 students, we did our experiment in 6 sessions, every session we had 4 students as experimental condition group and 4 as control conditions group, and for the next session they were exchanging the two conditions.

So we have 24 scores as experimental conditions and 24 scores as control conditions, by analyzing these results we can show the effects of using KB-map in the learning process which is presented in this section.

By comparing the results of the Comprehension Test (CT) scores and the Delayed Comprehension Test (DCT) for the both conditions, for the Experimental Conditions Group (EC) we found that the average difference between the DCT and the CT is +3.1 and for the Control Conditions group (CC) we found that the average difference between the DCT and the CT is -20.02.The next figure shows that the using of KB-map building helps learners to keep their information for long time.

From Fig 6 we can notice that there is no significant difference in the results of the comprehension test between the two conditions scores but there is noticed difference in the delayed comprehension test.

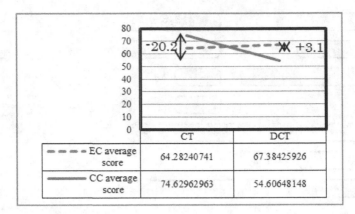

Fig. 6. Average Score for Experimental Conditions group and Control Conditions group in the Comprehension Test and in the Delayed Comprehension Test

In generally, the using of Kit-build concept map need a concentration in reading the text and need to read with attention to distinguish the two concepts that can be related and to find the corresponding relation that connect them together, in the same time this process required the learner to understand the information in the text deeply and required him to comprehend the text in whole. So we can explain our result by the required high load on the learner memory to comprehend deeply the whole text to complete the student map, this load force the learner's memory to keep most of the information that he has already comprehend.

We conducted questionnaire at the end of last session of our experiment, we found that the participants think that the using of KB-map is same as underlining for comprehension test but it is more useful to remember information after a while and it is more difficult to carry out, and they like to use it in reading comprehension task but they need more time to do it.

6   Conclusion and Future Work

In this paper, we describe the effects of using KB-Map method as a supportive tool for the reading comprehension of English texts as EFL reading. We have conducted an experiment composed of six experimental reading comprehension sessions with 8 3rd grade Japanese undergraduate students of faculty of engineering. In the experiment, every student attended three sessions with control condition (selective underlining which is very popular and standard strategy in the reading comprehension task) and 3 sessions with experimental condition (KB-map), and for every session we had a different text. So in generally, we have we have 24 scores as experimental condition and 24 scores as control condition.

In the experimental use, we are comparing the effects of using KB-map method and the effects of selective underlining strategy in the reading comprehension process; we are measuring these effects from two points of view, just after the using and after a while. The process of one session consists of 4 steps:

Overall, from this experiment we can say that the using of KB-map as learning supportive tool for reading comprehension is good as underlining in the short term, but it better for the long term.

Our next step goal is to design a new experiment to compare our KB-map with the scratch concept map for reading comprehension supporting and developing more attractive environment to support this special kind of learning activity.

References

1. Phakiti, A.: Theoretical and Pedagogical Issues in ESL/EFL Teaching of Strategic Reading, vol. 1, pp. 19–50. University of Sydney Papers in TESOL (2006)
2. Anderson, N.: Exploring Second Language Reading: Issues and Strategies, pp. xi + 129. Heinle & Heinle Publishers, Boston (1999)
3. Keith, R., Foorman, B., Perfetti, C., Pesetsky, D., Seidenberg, M.: How Psychological Science Informs the Teaching of Reading. Psychological Science in the Public Interest 2(2), 31–74 (2001)
4. Funaoi, H., Ishida, K., Hirashima, T.: Comparison of Kit-Build and Scratch-Build Concept Mapping Methods on Memory Retention. In: Proc. of ICCE 2011, pp. 539–546 (2012)
5. Sugihara, K., Osada, T., Nakata, S., Funaoi, H., Hirashima, T.: Experimental Evaluation of Kit-Build Concept Map for Science Classes in an Elementary School. In: Proc. of ICCE 2012, Main Conference E-Book, pp. 17–24 (2012)
6. Manoli, P., Papadopoulou, M.: Graphic Organizers as a Reading Strategy: Research Findings and Issues. Scientific Research 3(3), 348–356 (2012)
7. Novak, J.D., Gowin, D.B.: Learning how to learn. Cambridge University Press, New York (1984)
8. Hirashima, T., Yamasaki, K., Fukuda, H., Funaoi, H.: Kit-build concept map for automatic diagnosis. In: Biswas, G., Bull, S., Kay, J., Mitrovic, A. (eds.) AIED 2011. LNCS, vol. 6738, pp. 466–468. Springer, Heidelberg (2011)
9. Yoshida, K., Sugihara, K., Nino, Y., Shida, M., Hirashima, T.: Practical Use of Kit-Build Concept Map System for Formative Assessment of Learners' Comprehension in a Lecture. In: Proc. of ICCE 2013 (2013)
10. http://www.adlit.org
11. http://www.readingquest.org
12. Piolat, A.: Thierry Olive and Ronald T.keelllogg: Cognitive Effort during Note Taking. Proc. Applied Cognitive Psychology 19(3), 291–312 (2005)
13. Huber, Jennifer, A.: A Closer Look at SQ3R. Proc. Reading Improvement 41(2), 108.5–112.5 (2004)
14. Ngovo, J., Bernard, L.: Study Strategies for Narrative Texts: PORPE and Annotation. Proc. Journal of Developmental Education 23(2), 24–28 (1999)

Development of a Learning Support System for Source Code Reading Comprehension

Tatsuya Arai[1], Haruki Kanamori[1], Takahito Tomoto[2],
Yusuke Kometani[1], and Takako Akakura[2]

[1] Graduate School of Engineering, Tokyo University of Science,
1-3 Kagurazaka, Shinjuku-ku, Tokyo 162-8601, Japan
{arai_tatsuya,kanamori_haruki,kometani}@ms.kagu.tus.ac.jp
[2] Faculty of Engineering, Tokyo University of Science,
1-3 Kagurazaka, Shinjuku-ku, Tokyo 162-8601, Japan
{tomoto,akakura}@ms.kagu.tus.ac.jp

Abstract. In this paper, we describe the development of a support system that facilitates the process of learning computer programming through the reading of computer program source code. Reading code consists of two steps: reading comprehension and meaning deduction. In this study, we developed a tool that supports the comprehension of a program's reading. The tool is equipped with an error visualization function that illustrates a learner's mistakes and makes them aware of their errors. We conducted experiments using the learning support tool and confirmed that the system is effective.

Keywords: Programming Learning, Problem Posing, Reading Program, ICT.

1 Introduction

This paper describes the development of a support system that facilitates the process of learning to write computer programs by reading computer program source code. In this study, we define reading source code as working backward from the code to determine the original requirement that led to the program. The process of reading code consists of two steps: reading comprehension and meaning deduction (see Fig. 1).

Information technology has spread throughout society, but there is a shortage of information engineers, and so it is necessary to train many more. There has been extensive research on how computer programming can be learned through the construction of computer programs [1]. However, obtaining deep understanding of programming requires learners to read source code in addition writing programs [2].

Programming experts are highly skilled at reading code because this skill is essential for debugging programs and inferring their purpose [3]. Reading code is an also important activity for gaining a deeper understanding of programming. Furthermore, posing problems is often useful in understanding the scope of a computer program [4]. Accordingly, we developed a support system that facilitates the process of learning to program by reading source code. The target learners are programming beginners.

S. Yamamoto (Ed.): HIMI 2014, Part II, LNCS 8522, pp. 12–19, 2014.
© Springer International Publishing Switzerland 2014

2   The Process of Programming

In previous research, the process of programming has been considered to consist of two steps: algorithm design and coding. Algorithm design is the step in which structures, such as flow diagrams, are used to construct the abstract process from the program's requirements. This processing flow is independent of the programming language. In contrast, coding is the step in which the abstract flow is converted into source code, which necessarily depends on the programming language. In learning to program, learners are often given problems in the form of requirements and asked to write the appropriate source code by first considering the abstract processing flow.

Our research group considers reading code to be an important skill that adds to the process of programming. We previously proposed that the process of reading code consists of two steps: reading comprehension and meaning deduction [6] (see Fig. 1). Reading comprehension is the inverse of coding, and meaning deduction is the inverse of algorithm design. In reading comprehension, learners are required to convert source code into an equivalent abstract processing flow. In meaning deduction, learners are required to deduce a requirement from the abstract processing flow. We developed a learning support system for meaning deduction [6]. However, reading comprehension was still not supported. Thus, in this study, we design a learning support system to foster reading comprehension, and we evaluate the effectiveness of the system.

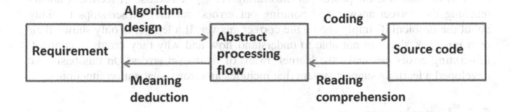

Fig. 1. The process of programming

3   Learning by Using a Flowchart

During the reading comprehension step, learners construct flowcharts from given pieces of source code. A flowchart has the advantage of making a problem (here, a requirement) more likely to be discovered by representing it visually. Figure 2 shows the process of constructing a flowchart. A learner chooses a series of flowchart blocks and populates each block with one of several available statements. Next, they populate each empty rectangular box with concepts. Finally, they connect the flowchart blocks with lines. By reducing the degrees of freedom in the answer, it is easier to convey the intent of the program.

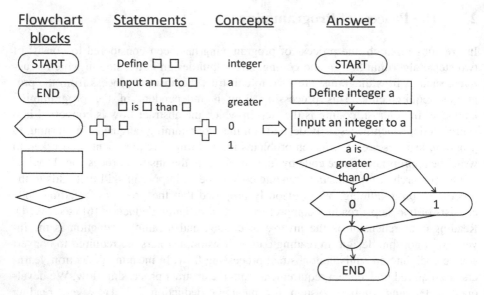

Fig. 2. How to write a flowchart

4   Error Visualization

Error visualization is the process of illustrating error [5]. The use of feedback allows teaching the correct answer and pointing out errors, but the learner stops thinking about the problem if simply shown the correct answer. If a learner is only shown their own mistakes, they are not able to understand how and why they erred. In contrast, illustrating errors can make the learner aware of their own errors. On this basis, we developed a learning support system that includes an error visualization function.

5   Experiments

We conducted two experiments with two different objectives: the objective of Experiment 1 was to examine the reading skill level of learners; the objective of Experiment 2 was to examine the influence of reducing the degrees of freedom of an answer.

5.1   Experiment 1

In Experiment 1, we spent 10 minutes explaining the principles of writing a flowchart to 62 second-year university students who were attending a programming course. The students were asked to solve 4 reading comprehension problems in 20 min, 4 algorithm design problems in another 20 min, and 4 coding problems in a final 20 min. Problems were given in a free-response format, and the maximum possible score for each problem was 2 points.

Table 1 shows the results of Experiment 1. The average score on individual problems was 1.20 for the reading comprehension exercise, 1.21 for the algorithm design exercise, and 1.69 for the coding exercise. From these results, we can conclude that reading comprehension and algorithm design were difficult. Although algorithm design is often considered to be more difficult than coding, reading comprehension was found to be as difficult as algorithm design.

Table 1. Experiment 1 Results

	Average score per problem	Standard deviation
Algorithm design	1.21	0.52
Coding	1.69	0.39
Reading comprehension	1.20	0.38

5.2   Experiment 2

In Experiment 2, we explained the principles of writing a flowchart to 12 fourth-year university students for 10 min. After the explanation, the students were asked to solve 6 reading comprehension problems in 30 min, followed by 6 meaning deduction problems in 15 min. The types of answers permitted are shown in Sections 3 and 4. The maximum score for each problem was 2 points.

Table 2 shows the results of Experiment 2. The average score on individual problems was 1.21 for the reading comprehension exercise and 0.64 for the meaning deduction exercise. From these results, we can conclude that the effect of reducing the degrees of freedom of the answer was small, and that the meaning deduction exercise was a difficult task. From Experiments 1 and 2, we confirmed the need to develop a support system that facilitates the process of learning to program by reading code.

Table 2. Experiment 2 Results

	Average score per problem	Standard deviation
Reading comprehension	1.21	0.55
Meaning deduction	0.64	0.21

6   Learning Support System

6.1   Learning Screen

Figure 4 shows the learning screen of the learning support system. The learner uses flowchart blocks, statements, and concepts to construct a flowchart. First, a learner presses a flowchart block button, which makes that flowchart block appear in the center panel of screen. Next, the learner presses a statement button, which brings that statement (with blanks) to the answer column of the selected flowchart block. Next, the learner presses a concept button and selects a blank entry in a statement, which inserts the selected concept into the selected blank space. When the learner has completed an answer, he or she presses the answer button. If the answer is correct, a message of "Correct answer" is displayed; if the answer is incorrect, the system shows the feedback screen (see next section).

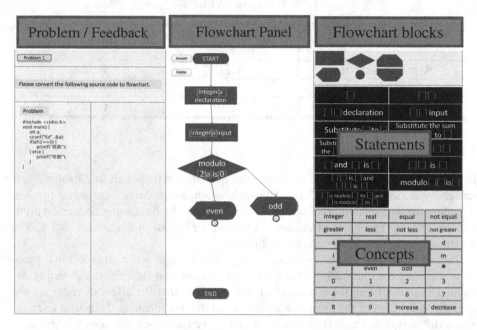

Fig. 3. Learning screen

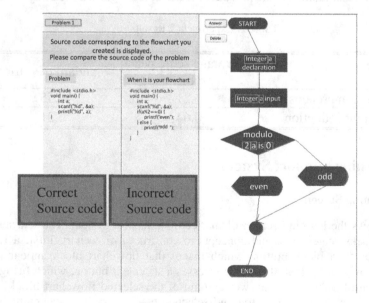

Fig. 4. Feedback screen

6.2   Feedback Screen

Figure 4 shows the feedback screen. If a learner reads the source code incorrectly, the system generates incorrect source code from the incorrect flowchart data, and the learner then looks for mistakes by comparing the incorrect source code to the correct source code.

7   Assessment Experiment

To ascertain the usefulness of the learning support system, we conducted an assessment experiment. In the assessment experiment, we administered a pre-test and a post-test to all participants (6 second-year university students). They are programming beginners. The pre-test and the post-test are identical. There are no feedback of test results to participants.

In the pre-test, after explaining the principles of writing a flowchart for 10 minutes, the participants were asked to solve 6 reading comprehension problems in 15 min. Next, the participants were divided into two groups: an experimental group (4 students) and control group (4 students). We spent 5 min explaining to the experimental group how to use the system.

The experimental group learned by solving 10 reading comprehension problems within 60 min using our system. In the control group, the participants were asked to solve the same problems as the experimental group by pen and paper in 60 min. The control group was allowed to view the correct answer. After this, participants of both groups were asked to take a post-test.

The 6 questions used in the pre-test and the post-test are as follows.

Q1: Flowchart with condition blocks. Basic if-else is included.

Q2: Flowchart with iteration blocks. A normal while loop is included.

Q3: Flowchart with condition blocks and iteration blocks. Both blocks from Q1 and Q2 are included.

Q4, Q5, Q6: Flowchart with nested structures combining condition blocks and iteration blocks.

Table 3 shows the coincidence between participant's answers and correct source codes. Although differences can be seen by comparing pre-test results and post-test results, there was no significant difference between control group and experimental group. Thus, we confirm the contents of the answers.

Table 3. Coincidence between participant's answers and correct answers

Group	participants	wholly coincident			partially coincident (%)		
		pre-test	post-test	pre-post difference	pre-test	post-test	pre-post difference
Control	A	3	4	1	0.56	0.80	0.24
	B	1	3	2	0.31	0.75	0.44
	C	0	0	0	0.26	0.58	0.32
Experimental	D	3	4	1	0.46	0.67	0.21
	E	0	3	3	0.38	0.72	0.34
	F	1	1	0	0.43	0.50	0.08

Subjects A, B (control group) and D (experimental group) gave correct answers with regard to the questions that they can answer within the time limit both in pre-test and in post-test, except for caress mistakes. Therefore, it is assumed that the improvements in test scores of A, B, D depended on their improvements in answer speed.

Subject C, in the pre-test, was not able to use the appropriate flowchart block for the while statement or if statement. In addition, C was not able to describe the appropriate sentence in the flowchart block. For example, when describing "Output an integer" or "Input an integer", C did not describe the variable name specifically. In addition, C was not able to describe the nested structure combining if statements and while statements. In post-test, C became possible to write more specifically the content of the block except for formulas. Furthermore, C was able to use the appropriate flowchart block with respect to the while statement. But still, C was not using the conditional branch block and didn't describe the structure of the conditional branch.

Subject E, in the pre-test, was not able to accurately describe the structure of if statements and while statements. For example, E wrote only one arrows from if block, and didn't write junction blocks. As for while statements, E described pre-determined condition as a post-judgment of iterations. In addition, E didn't describe formulas with natural languages. However, in the post-test, after conducting learning using the learning support system, E became able to write accurate structure of the conditional branch. In addition, E was aware of the structure of the while statement. Furthermore, E was able to explain properly the contents of the formula with natural languages.

In the pre-test, subject C and subject E was not able to adequately describe the flow chart of if and while statements. In the post-test, C was able to correct the error of the while statement for simple problems such as Q2. However, C did not adequately describe the while statement in a complex nested structures such as Q4. Furthermore C did not correct the error on the flow chart of if statements. In contrast with C, subject E who had used the system was accurately describe both if and while statements.

Table 4 shows the percentage of partially coincidence between correct source code and the source code corresponding to flowchart created by subjects. In Q4, the flowchart included both if statements and while statements and had nested structures. The score of Q4 by subject C decreased from 0.36 to 0.29, and the score of Q4 by subject E was improved from 0.64 to 0.86. This result shows the visualization of error using the learning support system are useful for learners in understanding to the flow of processing, such as conditional branches and iterations.

Table 4. Results of partially coincidence

Group	participants	pre-test							post-test						
		Q1	Q2	Q3	Q4	Q5	Q6	avg.	Q1	Q2	Q3	Q4	Q5	Q6	avg.
Control	A	1.00	1.00	1.00	0.36	0.00	0.00	0.56	1.00	1.00	1.00	1.00	0.78	0.00	0.80
	B	1.00	0.60	0.29	0.00	0.00	0.00	0.31	1.00	1.00	1.00	0.86	0.65	0.00	0.75
	C	0.38	0.40	0.29	0.36	0.09	0.04	0.26	0.88	0.90	0.57	0.29	0.78	0.08	0.58
Experimental	D	1.00	1.00	0.50	0.29	0.00	0.00	0.46	1.00	1.00	1.00	1.00	0.04	0.00	0.67
	E	0.38	0.50	0.50	0.64	0.26	0.00	0.38	1.00	1.00	1.00	0.86	0.43	0.00	0.72
	F	1.00	0.70	0.50	0.36	0.00	0.00	0.43	1.00	0.80	0.71	0.50	0.00	0.00	0.50

8   Conclusions and Future Work

In this study, we developed a learning support system to provide guidance on reading comprehension, and evaluated the effectiveness of our system. From the results of the assesment experiment, we confirmed that it is necessary to support learning of reading comprehension, and that our system is effective for doing so. However, the assessment experiment did not include many participants, and the number of participants should be increased in future experiments. Additionally, we did not develop a learning support system for guidance on both reading comprehension and the meaning deduction process, but we believe such a system should be developed in the future.

References

1. Matsuda, N., Kashihara, A., Fukukawa, K., Toyoda, J.: An instructional system for constructing algorithms in recursive programming. In: Proc. of the Sixth International Conference on Human-Computer Interaction, Tokyo, Japan, pp. 889–894 (1995)
2. Corbi, T.A.: Program understanding challenge for the 1990s. IBM Syst. J. 28(2), 294–306 (1989)
3. Uchida, S., Kudo, H., Monden, A.: An experiment and an Analysis of debugging process with periodic interviews. In: Proceedings of Software Symposium, Japanese, vol. 98, pp. 53–58 (1998)
4. Lyn, D.: Children's Problem Posing within Formal and Informal Contexts. Journal of Research in Mathematics Education 29(1), 83–106 (1998)
5. Hirashima, T.: Error-based simulation for error-visualization and its management. Int. J. of Artificial Intelligence in Education 9(1-2), 17–31 (1998)
6. Kanamori, H., Tomoto, T., Akakura, T.: Development of a Computer Programming Learning Support System Based on Reading Computer Program. In: Yamamoto, S. (ed.) HCI 2013, Part III. LNCS, vol. 8018, pp. 63–69. Springer, Heidelberg (2013)

EA Snippets: Generating Summarized View of Handwritten Documents Based on Emphasis Annotations

Hiroki Asai and Hayato Yamana

Waseda University, 3-4-1 Okubo, Shinjuku-ku, Tokyo 169-8555, Japan
{asai,yamana}@yama.info.waseda.ac.jp

Abstract. Owing to the recent development of handwriting input devices such as tablets and digital pens, digital notebooks have become an alternative to traditional paper-based notebooks. Digital notebooks are available for various device types. To display a list of text documents on a device screen, we often use scaled thumbnails or text snippets summarized through natural language processing or structural analyses. However, these are ineffective in conveying summaries of handwritten documents, because informal and unstructured handwritten data are difficult to summarize using traditional methods. We therefore propose the use of emphasis-based snippets, i.e., summarized handwritten documents based on natural emphasis annotations, such as underlines and enclosures. Our proposed method places emphasized words into thumbnails or text snippets. User studies showed that the proposed method is effective for keyword-based navigation.

Keywords: Digital Ink, Annotation, Summarization, Thumbnail, Snippets.

1 Introduction

Tablet and digital-pen devices that accept handwriting inputs have grown more common, and they are used as alternatives to traditional paper-based notebooks [1]. When digital notebooks replace paper-based notebooks, handwritten data will change from off-line to on-line formats. On-line handwritten data obtained by handwriting input devices, in addition to brushstroke coordinate information, include time-series data and pressure factors. As the number of on-line handwritten documents increases, the ability to search for information from such documents should be developed. One of the key ability in document search is how fast we can grasp the summary of each listed document. When we search document, we find the desired document effectively to scan through the summary list of documents called snippets, which is possible to grasp the summary of documents without scanning the contents. This paper presents a new summarized snippets of on-line handwritten documents which improve searching own or others handwritten documents, such as thumbnails and summarized text required in search systems.

Displaying scaled thumbnails (scaled pictures of original content) is an effective way to scan through lists of documents (e.g., thumbnails are effective for Web

S. Yamamoto (Ed.): HIMI 2014, Part II, LNCS 8522, pp. 20–31, 2014.
© Springer International Publishing Switzerland 2014

searches [3][7]). For example, Web image-retrieval services such as Google Images and Yahoo! Image Search output scaled thumbnails in a list view of the search result pages. From these thumbnails, users can see an outline of the original image. However, we cannot use traditional scaled thumbnails to understand a summary of handwritten documents since the text size is too small to read on small device screens.

In addition, text snippets, i.e., portions of original text, are commonly used in a list view of search result pages. For instance, search results from Google Web Search display text snippets, which are constructed by extracting a series of words including the query word. In handwritten documents, however, the accuracy of recognizing handwritten characters is as low as 92.77% [10], resulting in a difficulty in adopting natural language processing to summarize handwritten documents.

To the best of our knowledge, no research has been conducted on navigational views of handwritten documents, although some research does exist on search views of images and Web pages. In our previous work [2], we proposed the extraction method of emphasized words in handwritten notebooks. In this paper, we propose handwritten-document views called "EA Snippets" based on natural emphasis annotations, such as underlining and enclosures, and not based on natural language processing by using our previous work. Two types of EA Snippets are shown:

- Image EA Snippets consisting of important words or graphs, where the text is expanded for easier readability.
- Text EA Snippets consisting of both summarized text and a scaled thumbnail, where summarized text consists of important words listed in order of importance.

Furthermore, we investigate the performance of these proposed snippets types when users search for information in handwritten documents.

2   Related Work

In this section, we refer to researches on thumbnails of images and Web pages, and investigate a method to generate a thumbnail from important parts of a document, which is same approach with our method. Our proposed method generates EA Snippets consisting of important handwritten objects; however, to date there is no research concerning the generation of thumbnails for handwritten documents. Consequently, we look to apply research concerning thumbnails for images [1][4][11], and thumbnails for Web pages [9][12][13] to generate our handwritten thumbnails.

2.1   Thumbnails of Image

Several studies have investigated how to improve the thumbnails of pictures. Amurutha et al. [1] proposed an intelligent automatic cropping technique for pictures. Cropping is used to extract the rectangular area containing the attention objects. Prior to shrinking an image, they used Regions of Interest (ROIs) to crop objects from images. Their experiments showed that thumbnails efficiently increased the performance of context-based image retrieval (CBIR). Suh et al. [11] proposed two automatic cropping techniques; the first detects salient portions of images, while the other is a method of automatic face detection. They generated thumbnails by cropping these detected areas. Their user study shows that these methods resulted in small thumbnails that can be easily find through visual search. Avidan et al. [4] proposed an image resizing method, called Seam Carving, which supports content-aware image resizing. Seam Carving creates the energy map of an image, and then shrinks the image by removing the minimum energy path from left to right, or from top to bottom. Because Seam Carving does not discriminate between attention and other objects, the attention objects become distorted as the image shrinks.

2.2   Thumbnail of Web Pages

Other studies aimed in improving thumbnails of Web pages. Teevan et al. [12] extracted title-texts, logo images, and salient images from Web pages, and produced thumbnails by compiling these component pieces. Their experiments showed that in re-finding tasks, their thumbnails enabled users to find Web pages faster than snippets of text and traditional thumbnails. Woodruff et al. [13] proposed textually enhanced thumbnails of Web pages. These enhanced thumbnails were created by enhancing screenshots of Web pages with query words. In their study, participants searched faster using the textually-enhanced thumbnails than when using the plain thumbnails and text summaries. Lam et al. [9] proposed a thumbnail enhanced with readable text fragments. In their user study, when participants used the proposed thumbnail interface, they could find the area containing the target content in Web pages approximately 41% faster, and with 71% lower error rate, compared to traditional interfaces.

These related studies described in 2.1 and 2.2 proposed methods for detecting important objects, and producing as outputs summarized thumbnails of images and Web pages. We propose a method to detect important objects in handwritten documents by detecting emphasis annotations. Next, based on the results of previous related studies, we use the detected enhanced objects and summarize handwritten documents with EA Snippets.

3   Emphasis Annotations

In this section, we describe natural emphasis annotations used in notebooks. First, we defined some frequently used natural emphasis annotations, which are often used in notebooks. We then performed two investigations: 1) how often emphasis annotations are used in notebooks, and 2) under which situations they are utilized.

We collected 278 handwritten pages from the notebooks of eight university students in their 20s, studying such subjects as mathematics, physics, chemistry, and programming for six months to 1 year. The notebooks were written in Japanese, and our analysis shows that they include three types of natural emphasis annotations: 1) enclosing words, 2) underlined words, and 3) colored words. In addition, we found that emphasis annotations were performed 3.4 times per page on average. Table 1 shows the number of occurrences for each emphasis annotation.

Table 1. Type of emphasis annotation and the number of occurences in collected data

Emphasis Annotation	Number of occurrences
Enclosing Words	345
Underlined Words	304
Colored Words	296

We also interviewed the students to confirm when such emphasis annotations were performed. As a result, we found the following three types of situations:

1. Emphasizing important words or equations
2. Highlighting titles or topics
3. Highlighting a summary of the contents

Furthermore, the participants stated that they also emphasize titles or topics in the index area of the notebook instead of using emphasis annotations.

From the results of our survey, we found that the emphasized words indicate keywords, topics, or a general summary. We therefore assumed that we can easily understand a summary for extracting words and figures based on emphasis annotations and the index area. In addition, our previous work [2] calculated emphasis strength, which represents the importance of the emphasis annotation, each emphasis annotations in Table 1 from the questionnaire survey. We also use the emphasis strength to calculate the importance of handwritten objects.

4   Implementation

In this paper, we proposed two types of snippets based on emphasis annotations: 1) Image EA Snippets (see Fig. 1 (d)) and 2) Text EA Snippets (see Fig.2).

Our system detects both emphasis annotations and words in the title index area of notebook. Then, emphasis annotations are extracted followed by calculating emphasis scores by the method proposed in [2]. Emphasis scores represent the strength of the author's emphasis. Following the calculation of the emphasis scores, our system generates thumbnails or text snippets based on the emphasis annotations of authors.

4.1   Text/Non-text Classification

To detect handwritten diagrams and emphasis annotations, our system classifies all the input strokes into either text strokes or non-text strokes by applying an SVM. We use the following four stroke features as inputs to SVM after reducing the noise of handwritten strokes by using Gaussian filter:

1. Stroke length
2. Stroke curvature

3. Long side length of the stroke's bounding box
4. Number of crossing other strokes

4.2   Emphasizing/Graph Classification

After text/non-text classification, non-text strokes are further classified into emphasis strokes and graph strokes. Emphasis strokes consist of both underlined and enclosing strokes. On the other hands, graph strokes consist of non-emphasis strokes like diagrams and illustration.

Here, a stroke is classified as an underlined stroke when the height of the stroke's bounding box located under the word's bounding box, is within the height of the word's bounding box. Specifically, non-text strokes satisfying the following two conditions are categorized as underlined:

1. Shape condition

$$\begin{cases} 2W_{WordAve} < W_{Stroke} \\ H_{WordAve} > H_{Stroke} \end{cases}$$

2. Neighborhood character count condition

When two or more neighborhood characters satisfy the following conditions:

$$\begin{cases} min(X_{Stroke}) < X_{WordG} < max\,(X_{Stroke}) \\ Y_{WordG} - H_{WordAve} < min\,(Y_{Stroke}) \\ max(Y_{Stroke}) < Y_{WordG} \end{cases}$$

Variables $H_{WordAve}$ and $W_{WordAve}$ are the average height and width of the characters in the page. Variables H_{Stroke} and W_{Stroke} are the height and width of the target stroke. Variables X_{Stroke} and Y_{Stroke} are the sets of x- and y-coordinates of the target stroke. Variables X_{WordG} and Y_{WordG} are the x- and y-coordinates of the median point of the characters' bounding box.

Conversely, the enclosing stroke is extracted if its bounding box encloses the word's bounding box. Specifically, non-text strokes satisfying the following two conditions are categorized as enclosing:

1. Shape condition

$$\begin{cases} 2W_{WordAve} < W_{Stroke} \\ \frac{1}{2}H_{WordAve} < H_{Stroke} \end{cases}$$

2. Comprehension character count condition

The bounding box of the target stroke contains the center point of character, and the number of characters in the bounding box of the target stroke is greater than or equal to

$$max\left(2, \frac{S_{Stroke}}{\alpha S_{WordAve}}\right)$$

Variable S_{Stroke} represents the bounding box area of the target stroke. $S_{WordAve}$ is the average bounding box area of the characters in the page. Variable α is the threshold of the character's density, which we set to 6.0 to maximize detecting accuracy.

4.3 Recognizing Emphasized Words

After emphasizing/graph classification, we detect which part of the text is emphasized by the author, and which patterns of emphasized expression are present in the text. First, our system splits text strokes into character groups. We use .NET Ink Analyzee for the character grouping. After grouping, we detect underlined and enclosed words by using the spatial relationships between character groups, and the underlined and enclosing strokes we extracted from non-text strokes.

Underlined words are located above the underline stroke. Thus, our method detects underlined words by extracting the words satisfying the following conditions:

$$\begin{cases} \min(X_{Underline}) < X_{WordG} < \max(X_{Underline}) \\ \min(Y_{Underline}) < Y_{WordG} \\ Y_{WordG} < \max(Y_{Underline}) + \frac{3}{2}H_{WordAve} \end{cases}$$

Variables $X_{Underline}$ and $Y_{Underline}$ represent the sets of x-and y-coordinates of the underline strokes we extracted from non-text strokes. Conversely, enclosed words are located within the area enclosed by the enclosing stroke. Thus, our method detects enclosed words by extracting words whose median points are within the bounding box of the enclosing stroke.

4.4 Calculating Emphasized Scores

When a word is classified as an emphasized word, we calculate its emphasis score, indicating the importance of the word. First, our system groups strokes by the kind of handwritten object to avoid displaying handwritten strokes discretely. We sequentially check strokes ordered in a time series. Two strokes adjacent in a time series are grouped together if the distance between the center gravities of the strokes is less than the threshold value and the type of emphasis of the adjacent strokes is the same. After grouping handwritten strokes, the score is calculated based on the emphasis strength, calculated from questionnaire survey in [2], each group.

4.5 Generating Image EA Snippets

Compared to traditional scaled thumbnails for images, we should take into account when used for handwritten documents:

- The text in a scaled thumbnail is too small to read.
- The amount of text, i.e., the amount of information, in a scaled thumbnail is not reduced compared to the original data. Due to this, the cognitive load of understanding contents is not reduced.

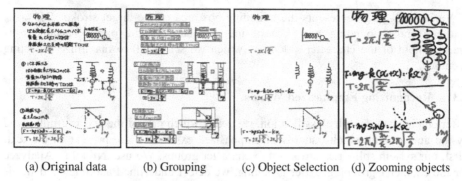

(a) Original data   (b) Grouping   (c) Object Selection   (d) Zooming objects

Fig. 1. The process of generating proposed Image EA Snippets

Therefore, we propose "Image EA snippets" summarizing the intended emphasis of authors. Our proposed method summarizes the contents of handwritten data based on emphasis, such as underlines and enclosings, and increases the size of text in the contents of the thumbnail. Fig.1 shows the process to generate Image EA Snippets.

First, our system groups handwritten strokes, then calculate their emphasis scores by applying the method proposed in [2] (see Fig.1 (b)). Second, the number of text stroke groups is decreased by removing the groups whose emphasis scores are under a threshold (see Fig.1 (c)). Note that non-text stroke groups, such as diagrams, are not removed. The adopted threshold is the maximum value satisfying the following condition;

$$\sum_{n=1}^{N_{SG}} S_{group}(n) B_{thres}(n) < \beta S_{org}$$

where N_{SG} represents the number of stroke groups, and $S_{group}(n)$ returns the area of the bounding box of the nth stroke group. If the emphasis score of the nth stroke group is more than the threshold, $B_{thres}(n)$ returns one, otherwise it returns zero. The scaling rate of the thumbnail is denoted by β, and the area of the original contents is denoted by S_{org}.

Finally, the stroke groups are reallocated and expanded by using the Seam Carving method [4]. Using this method, we can scale down a handwritten document by removing blank spaces, removing contents below the threshold, and maintaining the alignment of stroke groups. Fig. 1(d) shows our proposed thumbnails scaled by the Seam Carving method. From this thumbnail, we can understand the summary of the contents.

Fig. 2. Text EA Snippets generated by our method

4.6 Generating Text EA Snippets

Here, we present a method to generate "Text EA Snippets" based on the intended emphasis of authors. First, our method applies a handwritten recognition method to text stroke groups. Specifically, we use the .Net Ink Analyzer for handwritten recognition. Next, we sort text stroke groups by their emphasis scores, and clip at a maximum the 80 top-ranked words. Finally, our method displays scaled thumbnail to help users understand the layout and graphs of the contents in addition to the 80 top-ranked words. Fig.2 shows our proposed Text EA Snippet summarized by the emphasis annotations. From the text snippet, we can understand the keywords in the contents.

5 User Study

5.1 Collecting On-line Handwritten Data

Compared to traditional paper-based notebooks, digital notebooks enable us to collect on-line handwritten data consisting of a time series of strokes, pressure, and writing speed. Using digital notebooks, we can analyze handwritten data in more detail because we have more information than using traditional off-line handwritten data. Our method uses on-line handwritten data to detect the intended emphasis of authors. Hence, we have developed an experimental system for Windows (using the pen tablet WACOM Cintiq 12WX) to collect on-line handwritten documents.

We have developed our system in Visual C# equipped with a pen tablet device to enter inputs by handwriting. We collected 42 pages (consisting of 38,416 handwritten strokes) of on-line handwritten notebook data written by eleven university students majoring in computer science. We gave them a document containing common topics and current events, and informed them about the important words in the documents. Participants were instructed to create a note summarizing the documents. Note that participants were not forced to follow any format, i.e., participants could emphasize important words using any emphasis expression they wanted, and were allowed to use the notebook in any way they chose.

5.2 Recognition of Emphasized Words

First, we evaluated the recognition performance of our detection method for emphasized words. Here, words in the title index and colored words were successfully detected from on-line handwritten data by using their color and their written area.

We investigated 38,416 strokes contained in the handwritten documents. The manual classification of the documents resulted in 16 enclosings and 72 underlines. Our method detected all the enclosings in the documents with no errors. Conversely, our system detected underlines with 85.71% precision rate, and 96.43% recall rate. We found that text written by hand above the ruled line was falsely recognized as underline. In addition, some underlines could not be detected, because the underline was located far from handwritten text.

5.3   Search Performance

We conducted a user study to compare the search time required for handwritten documents using both traditional thumbnails and our proposed EA Snippets. To measure the search performance, we developed an evaluation application that shows various views of handwritten documents and operates on various device types. We used an iPhone 3GS, and a screen capture of our experimental system is shown in Fig.3. In this study, we compared the following four view types:

1. Traditional Scaled Thumbnails, which are reduced versions of the original image (see Fig.3 (a)).
2. Traditional Head Text Snippet + Scaled Thumbnail, which are generated by recognizing the first 80 characters of handwritten text in a document. A scaled thumbnail is also presented (see Fig.3 (b)).
3. Proposed Image EA Snippets, which are summarized based on their emphasis scores (see Fig.3 (c)).
4. Proposed Text EA Snippets + Scaled thumbnails, which are also summarized based on their emphasis scores (see Fig. 3 (d)).

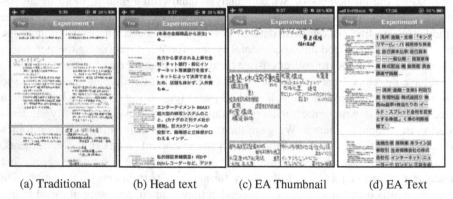

(a) Traditional   (b) Head text   (c) EA Thumbnail   (d) EA Text

Fig. 3. Screen shot of experimental system

On the same screen, four pages are displayed together for 1) and 3). On the other hand, 2.5 pages are displayed for 2) and 4). The goal of this study is to verify which snippets enable us to find information more easily.

We conducted three types of evaluation in our user study. On the first study (described in "1)"), we performed the comparison of the search time of four snippets types to answer the fill-in-blank question, on condition that the keyword of the question is included in the proposed view. After the first study, we also conducted the additional studies in addition to the first study because the first study leaves the two questions; a) we did not consider the situation in which the users searched document by using proposed snippets which is not include the keyword of the question, and b) there is no consideration of document's author, that is to say we did not consider the difference of the performance searching in own documents or other's documents. We conducted the two additional user studies to evaluate the two questions (described in "2)" and "3)").

Search Performance (Emphasized Words Include Search Keywords). First, we evaluate the search performance. We invited twenty participants to participate in our user study, including eleven who were authors of the collected handwritten documents. All participants were university students in their 20s, two of them women. We performed the user study using the four snippets types shown in Fig. 3, and measured the time required to finish answering the questions from each view. In each experiment, all participants were given twenty pages of handwritten documents each from the collected data, along with five questions. All participants were given the same questions and handwritten documents. The participants were required to answer the questions by navigating using the views generated from the documents. The questions were fill-in-the-blank types, and the answers were written directly on the original handwritten documents. In addition, the keywords of each question were indicated using emphasis annotations.

Fig.4 shows the average search time and the standard error. In addition, we performed a Kruskal-Wallis test, and conducted a pairwise comparison of the results. The results show that, on average, our proposed Image EA Snippets result in the best search time among the four snippets types. Compared with the traditional scaled thumbnails, we found that our Image EA Snippets enable users to search 42% faster ($p < 0.001$) on average. On the other hand, compared to traditional head text snippets, our Text EA Snippets also enable users to search faster on average, although the difference is not statistically significant ($p > 0.1$). Moreover, the results show that our Image EA Snippets help users search faster than do our Text EA Snippets ($p < 0.0001$).

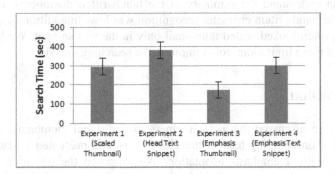

Fig. 4. Results of search performance in user study

Search Performance (Emphasized Words Include No Search Keywords). For the above task, the users could search for answers based on the emphasized keywords. In other words, we did not consider situations in which the users searched for information not based on the emphasized words. We therefore conducted another user study ($N = 10$) for searches not based on the emphasized keywords. Herein, N is the number of subjects used. The results show that the proposed Image EA Snippets enable users to search 24% faster on average than traditional scaled thumbnails, although the difference is not statistically significant ($p > 0.1$), while Text EA Snippets enable only a

9% speed increase (p > 0.1). After this study, some participants commented that they could find the page if they can imagine the keyword from the words which include in the snippet. From these results, we found that our proposed snippets is effective when we can imagine the information we want to know from the words or graph showing in snippet.

Comparison of the User's Own Notes and the Notes of Others. In addition, we also investigated the difference between searching one's own notes and the notes of others (N = 4). The results show that, using traditional scaled thumbnails, the users found the answer 206% slower on average for notes other than their own (p < 0.05). In contrast, there are no statistical differences between searching one's own notes or the notes of another student for Image EA Snippets and Text EA Snippets (p > 0.1). From these result, we found that our proposed snippets is effective for navigating pages of handwritten documents to find information regardless of the authors.

Discussion. After the user study, we discussed with the participants our proposed snippets. Some of them commented that they could not understand what was written in traditional scaled thumbnails, because characters were too small to read. Conversely, they could guess the contents in our proposed Image EA Snippets, and our proposed image snippets often helped them in searching for information in handwritten documents. Participants also reported that if the exact search keyword was not included in the thumbnail, they had trouble determining the contents of the thumbnail. On the other hand, some participants reported that Text EA Snippets occasionally did not help them understand the summary of the handwritten documents, because the accuracy of the handwritten character recognition was low. In addition, some of them said that they often looked scaled thumbnail only in the text snippet. We believe that the removal of these limitations could improve the searching speed.

6   Conclusion

In this paper, we discussed the ineffectiveness of traditional thumbnails in information retrieval when targeting handwritten documents, and presented a new approach, i.e., detecting natural emphasis annotation. We proposed the use of EA Snippets summarized by emphasis annotations. In the user study, we conducted that our proposed snippets are effective for navigating in handwritten documents. In addition, we found that thumbnails are more effective than text snippets for searching handwritten documents because handwritten data are hard to recognize that results in defective structural analysis.

References

1. Amurutha, I.S., Shylaja, S.S., Natarjan, S., Balasubramanya Murthy, K.N.: A smart automatic thumbnail cropping based on attention driven regions of interest extraction. In: Proc. ICIS 2009, pp. 957–962. ACM (2009)

2. Asai, H., Yamana, H.: Extraction of Emphasized Words from On-line Handwritten Notebooks DBSJ Journal. DBSJ 10(1), 67–72 (2011) (in Japanese)
3. Aula, A., Khan, R.M., Guan, Z., Fontes, P., Hong, P.: Comparison of visual and textual page previews in judging the helpfulness of web pages. In: Proc. WWW 2010, pp. 51–60. ACM (2010)
4. Avidan, S., Shamir, A.: Seam carving for content-aware image resizing. In: Proc. SIGGRAPH 2007, Article 10. ACM (2007)
5. Brandl, P., Richter, C., Haller, M.: NiCEBook: supporting natural note taking. In: Proc. CHI 2010, pp. 599–608. ACM (2010)
6. Chen, M., Sun, J.-T., Xeng, H.-J., Lam, K.-Y.: A Practical system of keyphrase extraction for web pages. In: Proc. CIKM 2005, pp. 277–278. ACM (2005)
7. Dziadosz, S., Chandrasekar, R.: Do thumbnail previews help users make better relevance decisions about web search results? In: Proc. SIGIR 2002, pp. 365–366. ACM (2002)
8. Hinckley, K., Zhao, S., Sarin, R., Baudisch, P., Cutrell, E., Shilman, M., Tan, D.: InkSeine: In Situ search for active note taking. In: Proc. CHI 2007, pp. 251–260. ACM (2007)
9. Lam, H., Baudisch, P.: Summary thumbnails: readable overviews for small screen web browsers. In: Proc. CHI 2005, pp. 681–690. ACM (2005)
10. Nakagawa, M., Bilan, Z.: On-line Handwritten Japanese Characters Recognition Using a MRF Model with Parameter Optimization by CRF. In: Proc. ICDAR 2011, pp. 603–607. IEEE (2011)
11. Suh, B., Ling, H., Bederson, B.B., Jacobs, D.W.: Automatic thumbnail cropping and its effectiveness. In: Proc. UIST 2003, pp. 95–104. ACM (2003)
12. Teevan, J., Cutrell, E., Fisher, D., Drucker, S.M., Ramos, G., André, P., Hu, C.: Visual snippets: summarizing web pages for search and revisitation. In: Proc. CHI 2009, pp. 2023–2032. ACM (2009)
13. Woodruff, A., Faulring, A., Rosenholtz, R., Morrison, J., Pirolli, P.: Using thumbnails to search the Web. In: Proc. CHI 2001, pp. 198–205. ACM (2001)

Kit-Build Concept Mapping for Being Aware of the Gap of Exchanged Information in Collaborative Reading of the Literature

Yusuke Hayashi and Tsukasa Hirashima

The Department of Information, Hiroshima University, Japan
{hayashi,tsukasa}@lel.hiroshima-u.ac.jp

Abstract. This paper reports a result of the trial use of the kit-build method in a lesson conducted in a graduate school. The purpose of the lesson is that students understand the content of a book collaboratively. The problem to be addressed here is that it is difficult to acknowledge the discrepancies between a presentation and their own understanding. To solve it this study uses Kit-build concept mapping. Through collaborative reading of the literature with kit-build concept mapping in classroom students could find the problems in their own presentation and tried to refine it with concrete information about the others' misunderstanding.

Keywords: E-learning and e-education, concept map, collaborative knowledge building.

1   Introduction

Collaborative knowledge building activity deepens understanding of the participants of the activity [2]. For example, in constructive collaborative problem solving activity, participants are required to explain their own understanding to the others and to compare it with ones of the others. These activities help them to grasp their own understanding and induce reflection on it. This is collaborative knowledge building activity and contributes to making understanding deeper [3]. Consequently, they build knowledge to solve the problem collaboratively.

Here, it is considered that one of the most important factor for successful is to share information related to the problem. If they couldn't share information about the problem, they wouldn't have a basis for thinking to solve the problem. This study aims at improving the quality of information exchange for collaborative knowledge building. As the first step of that, this study investigates the effectiveness of a method to build concept map against being aware of the gap between information of a provider and receivers in exchange of it.

This study uses a special method to build concept map called Kit-build concept mapping [4]. In this method concept maps cannot be built freely. An information provider makes a concept map as the correct answer. This is called goal map. And then, this is decomposed into separated nodes and likes. These parts are provides to

S. Yamamoto (Ed.): HIMI 2014, Part II, LNCS 8522, pp. 32–41, 2014.
© Springer International Publishing Switzerland 2014

receivers and they make a concept map with the parts to represent their understanding. This method doesn't allow freedom to build concept maps. Instead, an information provider can grade maps of receivers with consistency as the degree of the same parts as the gal map. The degree can be an important indicator of the gap between understanding of a provider and receivers.

This paper report a result of the trial use of the kit-build method in a lesson conducted in a graduate school. The purpose of the lesson is that students understand the content of a book collaboratively. Each student reads a part of the book and provides the contents of the part to the others. Through this activity students can obtain information of the contents of the whole of the book.

This lesson adopts the jigsaw method [1] for making groups of students in order to that learners divide task to read a book and understand the content collaboratively. The characteristics of this method are to make students develop a feeling of responsibility and to facilitate them to examine a relationship between the contents. In this lesson each student is assigned to a chapter and has a feeling of responsibility to explain it to the others. Only after they finish to explain their parts each other they get information about the whole contents of the book.

When students explain the contents their assigned chapter, students play two roles of provider and receiver by turns. For example, there are three students, LA, LB and LC. In the first turn LA is the provider and the rests are the receivers. In the following turns LB and LC become the providers and the rests in each turn become the receivers respectively. All the students become provider more than one time in this manner. In this lesson each student plays provider twice.

The purpose of these activities is to let the students be aware of the gap between provider's understanding and receiver's one. After a provider makes a presentation to the others in his or her group, receivers make a concept map with a kit of a map. In the first turn, this is a task for receivers to organize information that they are provided and also is a task for provider to be aware of the gap between what he or she want to tell to the others and what the others understand from his or her presentation. This is a collaborative knowledge building activity for the contents of the books. And then, by the second turn the provider improve his or her presentation with other students assigned the same chapter. They exchange information of problems happened in their explanation about their assigned chapter and discuss solution about it. This is another collaborative knowledge building activity for way of presentation. Finally, the provider presents the same contents with modification again in the second turn and judge the modification by himself or herself.

As the result, some students are aware of the gap between what he or she explains and what the others receive. And based on that they try to improve their presentations or goal maps.

2   Kit-Build Concept Mapping in Collaborative Reading

The main purpose of this study is to investigate the effectiveness of kit-build concept map system in collaborative reading of the literature in classroom. The supposed lesson style is that students read an assigned part of the literature and make a presentation to explain it. This is a typical lesson in Japanese university. Through this process students share the content of the literature.

This study aims at enables students be aware of the gap between information providers and receivers. When a person tells something for other people, it is not true that they receive it as it is. There could be discrepancies between them. The goal of this lesson is to share the content of the literature. It is preferred that the presenter perceives the state of achievement of the audience and gives feedback for correcting misunderstanding of them effectively. The problem is that it is difficult to acknowledge the discrepancies in a presentation.

This study adopts two methods to conduct effective collaborative reading of the literature in classroom. One is the jigsaw method that is a cooperative learning technique in which learners are divided into two types of groups, jigsaw and expert, and learn through collaboration between the types of groups. The other is kit-build concept mapping that is a special method to build concept maps from a kit provided by a teacher.

The system for kit-build mapping is called "KBmap system". This is composed of two client systems: "KBmap editor" and "KBmap analyzer", and the server system "KBmap DB" [5].

There are two types of KBmap editor that work on desktop and tablet computers. The KBmap editor on desktop computers is for both teachers and learners. Teachers can make goal-map and kit for learners and learners can make their map from a kit on the desktop version. On the other hand, tablet version is only for learners. Figure 1 shows KBeditor on tablet computers and Figure 2 shows the screenshot. The left side shows a kit that includes separated nodes and links. The right side is a KBmap made from the kit. The characteristic of the tablet version is portability. It can be used in not computer rooms but normal classrooms. In this study lessons were done in a normal classroom with Wi-Fi network.

Fig. 1. KBeditor on tablet computers

KBmap analyzer work on only web browsers and can work on tablet computers. In this study students used KBanalyzer on tablet computers in the classroom in order to analyze KBmaps made by other students. The characteristic of KBanalyzer is to show the group map that that overlays learner-maps. On this map the more learner set a link between particular concepts, the thicker the link is displayed. Figure 3 shows a screenshot of KBanalyzer. On the window links many learners set are displayed as thick and high-colored lines and links few learners set are displayed as narrow and light colored lines. In addition to that, KBanalyzer shows each link made by learners. With this information a teacher can identify which links in goal-map are difficult for learners to set　when they make their maps from a kit [6].

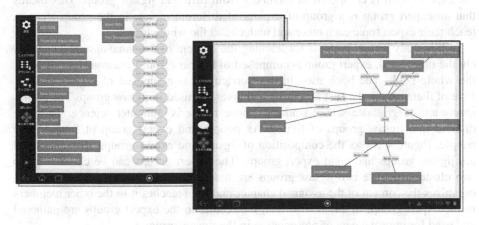

Fig. 2. The screenshot of KBeditor on tablet computers

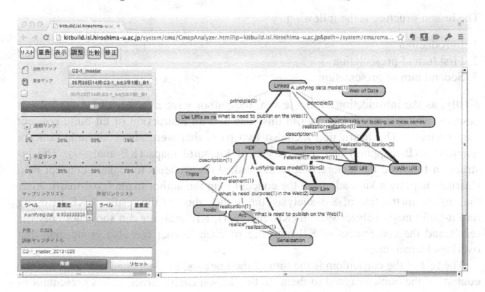

Fig. 3. A screenshot of KBanalyzer

3   Collaborative Reading of the Literature with Kit-Build Concept Mapping in Classroom

This course has two purposes; to understand the subject domain and to polish up presentation skills of students. To achieve them, This study adopts jigsaw method. This is a cooperative learning technique in which learners are divided into two types of groups, jigsaw and expert, and learn through collaboration between the types of groups.   In a jigsaw group, learners learn the same topic together. This is the preparation for the group work in an expert group. The goal of the jigsaw group is that each learner understands the topic well because they join different expert group separately. An expert group is composed of members from different jigsaw group. This means that an expert group is a group of experts of different topics. In the group learners teach their expert topic each other and understand the whole topics.

In this study jigsaw group is for learning the content of the same assigned chapter. On the other hand, expert group is composed of learners from jigsaw group and cover the whole book. The book used in this curriculum is composed of seven chapters. Five of them except the first and the last chapter are used in jigsaw group. The participants are 41 graduate school students whose major is computer science. They are divided into jigsaw groups of five or six people and expert group of four or five people. Figure 4 shows the composition of jigsaw and expert groups. This class had ten jigsaw groups and eight expert groups. The expert groups can be classified into two clusters because two jigsaw groups are made for each chapter.   Each student organizes the content of the assigned chapter and then teaches it to the other members in the expert group. In addition to that, the results in the expert groups are gathered and used for improvement of presentation in the jigsaw group.

The lesson structure is the following:

1. Introduction
2. First turn of presentation
3. Second turn of presentation

Firstly, as the introduction to this lesson, the author gave a lecture about the subject domain, which is the linked data in this case and an instruction of kit-build concept map system.   The instruction included two parts that were about kit-build concept mapping (KB-mapping) and the analysis of kit-build maps (KB-analysis). The instruction followed the lecture. The author asked the students to make a concept map (learner-map) by a kit made from the concept map the author made (goal-map). After that, as the instruction of KB-analysis, the author showed the result of KB-mapping on kit-build map analyzer system (KB-analyzer). KB-analyzer can show not only the result and the correctness of KB-mapping of each learner but also group-map that overlays learner-maps.

The rest of the curriculum is the turn of the learners. Learners had exchanges of the content of the book assigned to them. In this lesson each learner makes presentations twice. They organize the content of assigned chapter and make a goal-map and a presentation. The goal-map becomes the criteria to evaluate the others' understanding of a presentation as well as a guideline to make the presentation. In the first and second turns, learners give presentation to the other group members and check their understanding by KB mapping with the goal-map each other. In addition to that each learner reflects on his or her presentation with the result of KB-mapping and then improve his or her presentation for the second turn.

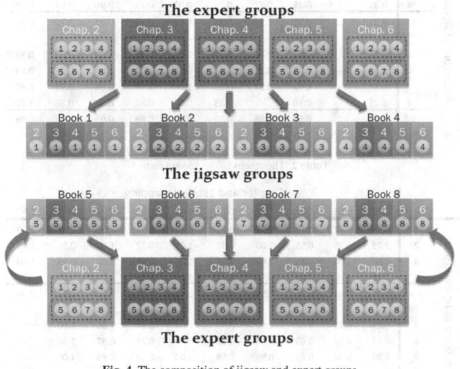

Fig. 4. The composition of jigsaw and expert groups

4   The Results and Consideration

Table 1 shows the change of map score of students. For each chapter from second to sixth each excepting one he or she made a presentation to the others, students basically made two KBmaps in each of the first and second turns. However, in the first turn of the second chapter, all the students made only one KBmap. It is because that it takes much time for students to be familiar with this style of lesson so that there was no time to make KBmap again. In the second turn of the sixth chapter some students also made KBmap only once. There is another reason for that. In this case the students were able to make the correct KBmap on the first attempt so that there was no need to make KBmap again.

From Figure 5 (A1) to (B2) Illustrate the change of map-score of student chapter by chapter. These data is classified by goal map and turn of presentation. For each

Table 1. The scores in the first turn

		C2-1	C2-2	C3-1	C3-2	C4-1	C4-2	C5-1	C5-2	C6-1	C6-2
Ave. score of Jigsaw group	1	0.40	-	0.13	1.00	0.26	0.81	0.63	1.00	0.79	0.91
	2	0.28	-	0.78	0.94	0.37	0.85	0.56	0.71	0.50	1.00
	3	0.23	-	0.75	1.00	0.44	0.85	0.81	1.00	0.64	1.00
	4	0.35	-	0.38	0.82	0.29	0.97	0.79	0.96	0.87	0.89
	1-4	0.31		0.51	0.94	0.34	0.87	0.70	0.92	0.70	0.95
	5	0.24	-	0.57	0.81	0.31	0.87	0.93	1.00	0.95	0.93
	6	0.41	-	0.57	0.81	0.41	0.95	1.00	1.00	0.95	0.95
	7	0.14	-	0.67	0.97	0.53	1.00	0.70	0.88	0.95	0.95
	8	0.25	-	0.50	-	0.33	0.51	0.82	0.93	0.86	1.00
	5-8	0.26		0.58	0.86	0.39	0.83	0.86	0.95	0.93	0.96

Table 2. The scores in the second turn

		C2-1	C2-2	C3-1	C3-2	C4-1	C4-2	C5-1	C5-2	C6-1	C6-2
Ave. score of Jigsaw group	1	0.58	0.97	0.15	0.97	0.71	0.79	0.94	1.00	0.93	1.00
	2	0.75	0.79	0.55	1.00	0.81	1.00	0.77	1.00	0.91	1.00
	3	0.88	1.00	0.45	1.00	0.78	0.88	0.81	1.00	0.93	1.00
	4	0.83	1.00	0.24	0.98	0.73	1.00	0.93	1.00	0.89	0.95
	1-4	0.76	0.94	0.35	0.99	0.76	0.92	0.87	1.00	0.92	0.99
	5	0.69	0.75	0.62	1.00	0.90	1.00	0.94	1.00	1.00	-
	6	0.63	0.81	0.65	0.87	0.68	1.00	0.79	0.97	1.00	-
	7	0.70	0.78	0.82	0.96	0.58	1.00	0.88	0.93	1.00	-
	8	0.56	0.85	0.96	1.00	0.70	0.88	0.97	1.00	0.86	0.80
	5-8	0.67	0.83	0.68	0.96	0.72	0.96	0.89	0.98	0.95	0.89

chapter two jigsaw group were made in this course. And more, as mentioned above, each student made KBmaps in two turns. The second turn was done five weeks later from the first turn.

These graphs shows similar tendency in the two jigsaw group categories. From Fig. 5 (A1) and (B1), in the first turn, the score in the first map-making increased with progression of the course. There might be some reasons for this phenomenon. The students could be familiar with the topic and the style of lessons and learn from others' presentation and feedbacks. It is difficult to distinguish and identify the reason from the data obtained in this study. On the other hand, the score in the second map making was not changed through the chapters. This is just the effect of feedback. The presenter gave feedback to the other members based on the information on KBanalyz-er. However, the style of feedback was not regulated completely so that some students almost directly told correct answers to the other members.

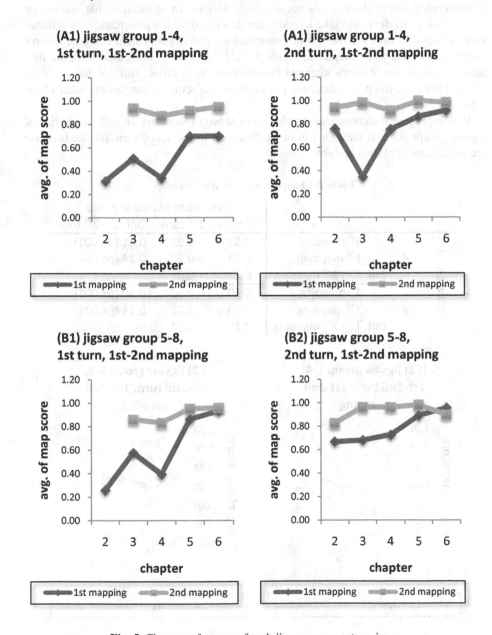

Fig. 5. Changes of scores of each jigsaw group categories

From Figure 5 (A2) and (B2), in the second turn, the score even in the first map making was not changed through chapters. Especially, from the second to fourth chapter, the scores are basically increased from the first turn. This could be the effect of reflection on the first presentation with KB analyzer. Students were allowed to use KBanalyzer between the first and second presentations. In addition to that, the author gave a task to students to make a report that described which information on KBana-lyzer affected to improve the second presentation. The improvement could be always successful. At the third chapter in Figure 5 (A2) the score is decreased from the first turn. Although the students changed presentation to improve, this led the negative effect. However, the group succeeded to increase the score as long as the other chap-ters.

Finally, Figure 6 summarizes the change of score of students. In both categories of jigsaw groups score is increased from the first turn to the scone turn. All the increase are significant as shown in Table 3.

Table 3. Change of score in jigsaw group

| | | | Ave. score of Jigsaw group | | |
			1st turn	2nd turn	Diff. 1st -2nd turn
Jigsaw group	1-4	1st mapping	0.51	0.92	0.41 (p<.001)
		2nd mapping	0.73	0.97	0.24 (p<.05)
		Diff. 1st - 2nd mapping	0.22	0.05	
	5-8	1st mapping	0.60	0.90	0.30 (p<.001)
		2nd mapping	0.78	0.92	0.14 (p=.073)
		Diff. 1st - 2nd mapping	0.18	0.02	

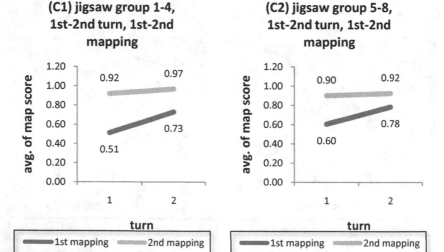

Fig. 6. Change of score in jigsaw group

5   Conclusion

This paper reports the effectiveness of kit-build concept map system in collaborative reading of the literature in classroom. The purpose of the lesson is that students understand the content of a book collaboratively. In such class it is difficult for students as audiences to acknowledge the discrepancies between a presentation and their own understanding.

To solve it this study uses Kit-build concept mapping. Through collaborative reading of the literature with kit-build concept mapping in classroom students could find the problems in their own presentation and tried to refine it with concrete information about the others' misunderstanding.

The result shows in each turn students as presenters could find which part is difficult for the others to understand and give feedback to them. In addition to that, presenters could refine their presentation based on the result. Of course, the increase of the score might mainly come from the presentation is the second time. On the other hand some students, in their reports, stated that they had improved their presentation based on the result of the first presentation and had been confident of success in the second presentation. This shows there could be a possibility of KB concept mapping to be aware of the discrepancies between a presentation and understanding of the audience. It is necessary to identify the scope and the extent of the effect of this style of lesson and improve it further more in the future.

References

1. Aronson, E., Blanney, N., Sephan, C.: The jigsaw classroom, Beverly Hills. Sage Publications, CA (1978)
2. Bransford, J.D., Brown, A.L., Cocking, R.R.: How people learn: Brain, mind, experience, and school. National Academies Press, Washington, DC (1999)
3. Chi, M.T.H.: Self-explaining: The dual processes, of generating interface and repairing mental models. In: Glaser, R. (ed.) Advances in Instructional Psychology, Educational Design and Cognitive Science, vol. 5, pp. 161–238. Lawrence Erlbaum, Mahwah (2000)
4. Hirashima, T., Yamasaki, K., Fukuda, H., Funaoi, H.: Kit-build concept map for automatic diagnosis. In: Biswas, G., Bull, S., Kay, J., Mitrovic, A. (eds.) AIED 2011. LNCS, vol. 6738, pp. 466–468. Springer, Heidelberg (2011)
5. Sugihara, K., Osada, T., Nakata, S., Funaoi, H., Hirashima, T.: Experimental Evaluation of Kit-Build Concept Map for Science Classes in an Elementary School. In: Proc. of ICCE 2012, Main Conference E-Book, pp. 17–24 (2012)
6. Yoshida, K., Sugihara, K., Nino, Y., Shida, M., Hirashima, T.: Practical Use of Kit-Build Comcept Map System for Formative Assessment of Learners' Comprehension in a Lecture. In: Proc of ICCE 2013, pp. 892–901 (2013)

Triplet Structure Model of Arithmetical Word Problems for Learning by Problem-Posing

Tsukasa Hirashima, Sho Yamamoto, and Yusuke Hayashi

Graduate School of Engineering, Hiroshima University, Japan
{tsukasa,sho,hayashi}@lel.hiroshima-u.ac.jp

Abstract. We have been investigating and developing several interactive environments for learning by problem-posing targeting arithmetical word problems. In this paper, we describe "triplet structure" of an arithmetical word problem that is composed of two "single quantity sentences" and one "relative quantity sentence", as the base model of the design of these learning environments. We also report practice use of the interactive learning environments in usual class room by using tablet PCs.

Keywords: Triplet Structure Model, Learning by Problem-Posing, Arithmetical Word Problem.

1 Introduction

Learning by problem-posing is well known as an important way to promote learners to master the use of solution methods [1, 2]. We have investigating technology-enhanced learning environment for learning by problem-posing [3-10]. Learners are required to make arithmetical word problems by combining several sentence cards provided from the environment. We call this kind of problem posing "problem posing by sentence integration". Because the meaning of each sentence can be described formally, it is possible for the environment to diagnose the problems posed by the sentences. We call this automatic diagnosis facility "agent-assessment" in contrast with "self-assessment", "teacher-assessment", and "peer-assessment" [11].

We believe that this problem-posing method is not only worth for realization of agent-assessment by system, but also is valuable for learning for learners. One benefit of the problem-posing of sentence integration is that it enables learners to concentrate learners to construct the structure of problem. In problem-posing with natural language, learners often take much time to write sentences themselves and don't use enough time to think about problems themselves. One more benefit is that the combination of sentences expresses the problem structure of arithmetical word problems explicitly. So, it is expected that to deal with the sentences directly contributes to learn the problem structure.

In this paper, as a model to problem structure of arithmetical word problems, we describe "triplet structure model" that is composed of two "single quantity sentences" and one "relative quantity sentence". We also introduce interactive learning environment for problem-posing and its practical use in usual classroom with tablet PCs.

S. Yamamoto (Ed.): HIMI 2014, Part II, LNCS 8522, pp. 42–50, 2014.
© Springer International Publishing Switzerland 2014

2   Triplet Structure Model

An arithmetical word problem that is solved by one arithmetical operation is composed of three quantities: operand, operant and result quantity. Triplet structure model is a model of these three quantities considering meaning of the arithmetical word problem. In this model, all word problems that are solved by one of the four basic operations are composed of two "independent quantity sentences" and one "relative quantity sentence". Then, depending on combination of them, role of each sentence is changed. In this section, this model is introduced with examples. Relation between an arithmetic story and other problems are shown in Figure 1.

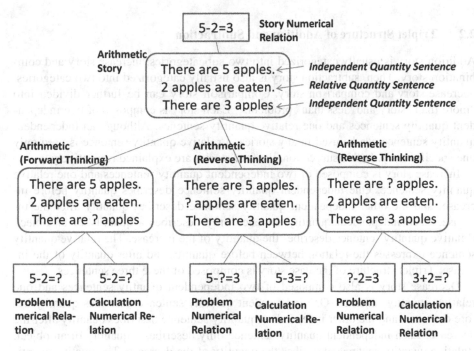

Fig. 1. Relation between Arithmetic Story and Problems

2.1   Story Numerical Relation and Calculation Numerical Relation

By using an answer of an arithmetical word problem, it is possible to make a numerical relation and a cover story composed of all known quantities. We call this cover story "arithmetical story" and this numerical relation "story numerical relation". Then, the numerical relation in the problem including unknown quantity is called "problem numerical relation". As one more numerical relation, there is a numerical relation used in calculation. We call this numerical relation "calculation numerical relation". In this framework, a problem is generated from a story by changing a known quantity to an unknown quantity.

Following is a typical arithmetical problem that is expressed by the triplet structure model.

{There are "?" apples. 2 apples are eaten. There are 3 apples.}

In this problem, the answer is 5 and calculation to derive the answer is 2+3. So, in the above framework, the story numerical relation is "5-2=3", the problem numerical relation is "?-2=3" and the calculation numerical relation is "2+3=5". Then, the arithmetical story is {There are 5 apples. 2 apples are eaten. There are 3 apples.}. In this problem, story numerical relation and calculation numerical relation are different. We call this kind of problem "reverse thinking problem". Reverse thinking problem is much harder than "forward thinking problem" where story numerical relation and calculation numerical relation are the same ones.

2.2   Triplet Structure of Addition and Subtraction

Addition story is usually categorized into two subcategories: increase story and combination story. Then, subtraction story is also usually categorized into two categories: decrease story and comparison story. Comparison story can be further divided into "more than" story and "less than" problem.   Each story is composed of two independent quantity sentences and one relative quantity sentence. Although an independent quantity sentence can be used in any stories, a relative quantity sentence is used only one specific story. In this subsection, the four stories are explained respectively.

Increase story is composed of two independent quantity sentences and one relative quantity sentence. One independent quantity sentence describes quantity before increase, and the other independent quantity sentence describes quantity after the increase. Each independent quantity sentence only describes a quantity of an object. Relative quantity sentence describes the quantity of the increase. The relative quantity sentence expresses the relation between before quantity and after quantity of the increase. Triplet structure of increase story is composed of these three sentences.

Decrease story is also composed of two independent quantity sentences and one relative quantity sentence. One independent quantity sentence describes quantity before decrease, and the other independent quantity sentence describes quantity after the decrease. Each independent quantity sentence only describes a quantity of an object. Relative quantity sentence describes the quantity of the decrease. The relative quantity sentence expresses the relation between before quantity and after quantity of the decrease. Triplet structure of increase story is composed of these three sentences.

Composition story is also composed of two independent quantity sentences and one relative quantity sentence. One independent quantity sentence describes the number of an object, and the other independent quantity sentence describes number of another object. The relative quantity sentence expresses total number of the two objects. Triplet structure of combination story is composed of these three sentences.

Comparative story is also composed of two independent quantity sentences and one relative quantity sentence. One independent quantity sentence describes the number of an object, and the other independent quantity sentence describes number of another object. The relative quantity sentence expresses difference of the two objects. Triplet structure of comparative story is composed of these three sentences.

In these triple structures, although a relative sentence is specific one to each story, all independent quantity sentences has the same expressions and their roles in the stories are decided depending on other sentences. Framework of "learning by problem-posing as sentence integration" is designed based on this model. Multiplication and division story are also defined with the triples model composed of two general independent quantity sentences and one specific relative quantity sentence. In this paper, we also introduce an explanation of problem-solving and problem-posing process based on this model.

In Figure 2, one independent quantity sentence "there are 6 apples" is used in several stories with difference roles in each story. In the increase story, it is used as a smaller number of the apples in the story. In the decrease story, then, it is used as a larger number of the apples. By using with "there are 3 oranges", "there are 6 apples" are use in a combination story, more than story and less than story. The independent quantity sentence is also used in multiplication by combining with relative quantity sentence of multiplication as shown in Figure 2.

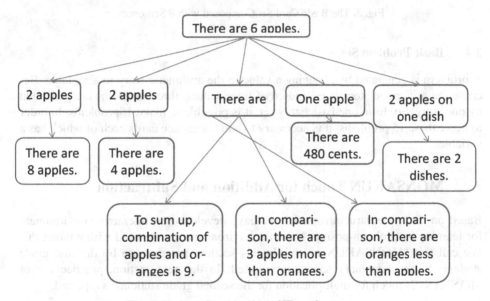

Fig. 2. Various Combination of Three Sentences

2.3   Basic Story Set

The four stories of addition and subtraction can be generated by 8 sorts of sentences because independent quantity sentence can be shared in difference stories. The set of seven sentences are composed of three independent quantity sentences and four relative quantity sentences. The set of sentences is shown in Figure 3. By changing object and numeric numbers, it is easily make many stories with the same characteristics in arithmetic.

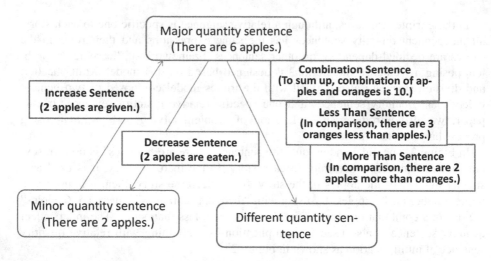

Fig. 3. The Basic Card Set Composed with 8 Sentences

2.4 Basic Problem Set

A problem is generated by changing a value in the arithmetic story to a variable. Because the arithmetic story is composed of three values, three problems are generated by one story. So, from one basic story set, it is possible to make 15problems. In order to make these 15 problems, it is necessary to add 7 sentence cards each of which has a variable.

3 MONSAKUN Touch for Addition and Subtraction

Based on the triplet structure model, we have developed an interactive environment for learning by problem-posing. Now, the environment can be used with a tablet PC. We call this "MONSAKUN touch". In this section, practice use by the first grade students in an elementary school is reported. In the next section, practice use of MONSAKUN touch for multiplication for the second grade students is reported.

3.1 Interface of Problem-Posing of MONSAKUN Touch

In Figure 4, interface of problem-posing of MONSAKUN touch is shown. In the upper left side of the interface, a calculation numerical relation and arithmetic story are shown. A learner is required to pose a problem that can be solved the calculation numerical relation and belongs to the specified arithmetic story by using sentence cards provided in the right side of the interface. The set of sentence cards includes not only necessary ones but also unnecessary ones. The unnecessary sentence cards are called dummy cards. In the lower left side, there are three blanks where a leaner puts sentence cards in order to complete a problem. In Figure 4, two cards have been put in the blanks. In this case, required problem is composed of {"Tom has 3 pencils." "Tom buys several pencils." "Tom has 7 pencils."}. The scene of using MONSAKUN Touch is shown in Figure 5.

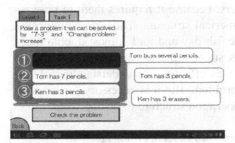

Fig. 4. Interface of MONSAKUN   **Fig. 5.** Scene of Using MONSAKUN

3.2   Procedure of Practical Use of MONSAKUN Touch for Addition and Subtraction

In this experiment, 39 students in the first grade of an elementary school were subjects. Arithmetic word problems that are solve by one addition or subtraction are usually taught in the first grade of elementary schools, but the problem structures are not taught explicitly. In this practice, the problem structure of arithmetic word problems used in MONSAKUN Touch were taught explicitly by a teacher and problem-posing exercise with MONSAKUN Touch was carried out as an exercise to operate the problem structure. This practice composed of nine lesson times (45 minutes per lesson, 3 weeks, 9 days). The students took pretest before the practice period, and took posttest and questionnaire after the period. Each test took 45 minutes. Problem-posing exercises divided into 6 levels. The levels categorized by (1) forward-thinking or reverse-thinking, (2) story operation stricture given or calculation operation structure given, and (3) cover story. In a level, students were required to pose problems following provided story operation structure or calculation operation structure and cover story. Cover stories were excerpted from several textbooks. Also, if the student finishes problem-posing exercise in a level in a class, he/she repeats the same level exercise.

In this practical use, students used the MONSAKUN Touch as an introduction of new level problem-posing (5-10 min) at the beginning of a class. The students, then, are taught the problem structures by the teacher on blackboard (20-35 min). Finally, they used the MONSAKUN Touch as confirmation of teaching (5-10 min).

In pre- and post-test, we used the same problem solving test and problem-posing test. Problem solving test used to assess the students problem solving performance. In problem-posing test, the students are required to pose four problems by composing several sentence cards provided beforehand. This test is used to examine the student's problem-posing performance.

3.3   Log Data and Questionnaire

The number of students that finished posing problems in each level is shown in Table 1. The students performed level 1 and 2 during the 3rd day from the 1st day, level 3 and 4 during the 6th day from the 4th day, and then, level 5 at the 8th day. The teacher has taught the problem structure corresponding to level 5 in detail in the 7th day. The task in level 5 is very difficult for learners, because it requires them to pose reverse-thinking problems from calculation numerical structure. Then, problem-posing with MONSAKUN was not carried out in the 7th day and took almost double times for the exercise on the 8th day. These results suggested that teaching method about the task to present story operation structure was effective for understanding of forward thinking problem and reverse thinking problem. But it is necessary for teaching method about the task to present calculation operation structure to be improved.

Table 1. Number of Student who Finished Each Level of Posing Problems

Level	1	2	3	4	5	6
Number of students	39	39	39	38	39	23
Number of not finished students	3	1	11	0	17	16

The results of the questionnaire are shown in Table 2. Almost all students agreed that problem-posing exercise by using MONSAKUN and effective to learn, but, we supposed, because of level 5, many students answered the problem-posing is difficult. The teacher agreed that it is easy to teach problem-posing using a tablet PC in the general classroom, and he said that he want to use the MONSAKUN in his class. But, also he suggested that it is necessary to improve the sentence of feedback and to expand the kinds of feedback.

Table 2. Results of Questionnaire

	Strongly Agree	Agree	Disagree	Strongly Disagree
1.Do you enjoy posing problems in arthmetic?	35	3	0	0
2. Are arithmetic problems easy to pose?	8	7	19	4
4.Do you think that posing problems made it easier to solve problems?	20	17	1	0
7.Would you like to attend arithmetic classes where problem posing is used?	36	2	0	0

3.4   Pre-test and Post-test Comparison

The results of pre- and post-test are shown in Table 3. The full mark of problem-posing test is 4. The full mark of problem-solving of forward-thinking problems is 9 and the full mark of problem-solving of revers-thinking problems is 8. In the scores of problem-solving test shown in Table 3, there was a significant difference in the scores between pretest and posttest of reverse thinking problems (two sided p-values from

Wilcoxon matched-pairs signed-ranks test with correction for ties, p=.009), and effect size is medium ($|r|$=.45). These results suggest that explicit teaching of problem structures was effective to understand the reverse thinking problem. In problem-posing test, there was a significant difference in the between pre-test and post-test as for the number of correct problems at reverse thinking problems (two sided p-values from Wilcoxon matched-pairs signed-ranks test with correction for ties, p=.0006), and effect size is medium ($|r|$=.39). In contrast with this, the number of correct problems at forward thinking problems decreased. These results suggested that the students would be aware of the difference between the reverse thinking problems and forward thinking problems. Based on these results, we have judged that this teaching method with MONSAKUN Touch is a promising way to teach arithmetic word problems.

Table 3. Results of Problems Test (*1% significant)

		forward thinking problem	reverse thinking problem
pre-test	M	8.82	7.13*
	SD	0.6	0.65
post-test	M	8.71	7.66*
	SD	0.39	1.28

4   Conclusion Remarks

In this paper, as a model to problem structure of arithmetical word problems, we describe "triplet structure model" that is composed of two "single quantity sentences" and one "relative quantity sentence". We have developed an interactive learning environment for learning by problem-posing: MONSAKUN and we used it practical. In the practical use, the first grade students in an elementary school use the environment for 8 class times. By comparing pre-test scores and post-test scores, we have confirmed that learning by problem-posing with MONSAKUN is useful learning method.

References

1. Polya, G.: How to Solve It. Princeton University Press (1945)
2. Ellerton, N.F.: Children's made-up mathematics problems: a new perspective on talented mathematicians. Educational Studies in Mathematics 17, 261–271 (1986)
3. Nakano, A., Hirashima, T., Takeuchi, A.: Problem-Making Practice to Master Solution-Methods in Intelligent Learning Environment. In: Proc. of ICCE 1999, pp. 891–898 (1999)
4. Hirashima, T., Nakano, A., Takeuchi, A.: A Diagnosis Function of Arithmetical Word Problems for Learning by Problem Posing. In: Mizoguchi, R., Slaney, J. (eds.) PRICAI 2000. LNCS (LNAI), vol. 1886, pp. 745–755. Springer, Heidelberg (2000)
5. Nakano, A., Hirashima, T., Takeuchi, A.: An evaluation of intelligent learning environment for problem posing. In: Cerri, S.A., Gouardéres, G., Paraguaçu, F. (eds.) ITS 2002. LNCS, vol. 2363, p. 861. Springer, Heidelberg (2002)
6. Hirashima, T., Yokoyama, T., Okamoto, M., Takeuchi, A.: Learning by Problem-Posing as Sentence-Integration and Experimental Use. In: Proc. of AIED 2007, pp. 254–261 (2007)

7. Hirashima, T., Kurayama, M.: Learning by problem-posing for reverse-thinking problems. In: Biswas, G., Bull, S., Kay, J., Mitrovic, A. (eds.) AIED 2011. LNCS, vol. 6738, pp. 123–130. Springer, Heidelberg (2011)

8. Yamamoto, S., Kanbe, T., Yoshida, Y., Maeda, K., Hirashima, T.: A Case Study of Learning by Problem-Posing in Introductory Phase of Arithmetic Word Problems. In: Proc. of ICCE 2012, pp. 25–32 (2012)

9. Yamamoto, S., Hashimoto, T., Kanbe, T., Yoshida, Y., Maeda, K., Hirashima, T.: Interactive Environment for Learning by Problem-Posing of Arithmetic Word Problems Solved by One-step Multiplication. In: Proc. of ICCE 2013, pp. 51–60 (2013)

10. Yamamoto, S., Kanbe, T., Yoshida, Y., Maeda, K., Hirashima, T.: Learning by problem-posing with online connected media tablets. In: Yamamoto, S. (ed.) HCI 2013, Part III. LNCS, vol. 8018, pp. 165–174. Springer, Heidelberg (2013)

11. Yu, F.-Y., Liu, Y.-H., Chan, T.-W.: A Web-based Learning System for Quesetion-Posing and Peer Assessment. In: Innovations in Education and Teaching International, vol. 42(4), pp. 337–348 (November 2005)

Training Archived Physical Skill through Immersive Virtual Environment

Taihei Kojima, Atsushi Hiyama, Takahiro Miura, and Michitaka Hirose

Graduate School of Information Science and Technology,
The University of Tokyo, 7-3-1, Hongo, Bunkyo-ku
113-8656, Tokyo, Japan
{kojima,atsushi,miu,hirose}@cyber.t.u-tokyo.ac.jp

Abstract. The basic of training physical skills is to imitate instructor's motion. Observation is the very first step to copy the motion of instructor when at the beginning of learning sports of artisanship. However, beginners face difficulties in imitating at the start since they do not have somesthetic image of the movement. In order to help learning physical skills, we propose Immersive virtual environment using head mounted display that indicates 3D motion of instructor super imposed on learner's body. By using this system, learners try to match its own form to instructor's 3D model to imitate instructor's motion from first person view in virtual environment. At the early stage of this research, we tried to transfer pitching skill in baseball. We evaluated the effectiveness of proposed system by measuring throwing distance.

Keywords: Skill transfer, Augmented Reality, Immersive virtual environment, Head mounted display.

1 Introduction

Training systems that transfer physical skills of experts are become more important as the trend of demographic composition changes by falling birth rate and aging. In industry, traditional arts, or sports, it makes training process more efficient if we can project one's somesthetic image to another by using virtual reality technology. In most cases, beginners do not have such somesthetic image so that they cannot mimic the motion of experts' effectively. Many researches had been done to develop the system using virtual reality technologies that support beginners to learn experts' motion for the application of artisanship. Most of them present experts' motion from the first person view of expert through head mounted display and those studies achieved to accelerate the learning speed of beginners.

On the contrary, in field of sporting activities, it is difficult to understand whole motion of instructors from the system that shows instructors motion from the first person view. Sport activities relatively require fullbody motion compared with

S. Yamamoto (Ed.): HIMI 2014, Part II, LNCS 8522, pp. 51–58, 2014.
© Springer International Publishing Switzerland 2014

artisanship. Thus this difficulty is caused by restricted viewing angle of first person view. Learners are not able to image whole movement of such fullbody motion.

In this study, we proposed to design a first person view learning system using head mounted display. The difference between conventional first person view physical skill learning systems is that proposed system allows learner to step away from first person view to third person view seamlessly. Additionally, 3D motion model of an instructor in proposed system is interactively triggered to play back according to the posture of the learner.

This paper first discusses related works (Section 2), followed by proposed methodology (Section 3). Then, we provide an overview and an implementation of a proposed training system in immersive virtual environment (Section 4). We prepared two different conditions of prototype interfaces and conducted exploratory experiments (Section 5). With these results, we discuss the design of integrated systems (Section 6).

2   Related Works

In this section, we introduce and discuss relevant researches on physical skill training using virtual reality technologies.

Nawahdah et al. proposed a system that interactively changes the viewpoint of learner and shows the motion of instructor in 3D virtual environment and suggested the system improves learning efficiency [1]. Anderson et al. Introduced the system that teaches full body motion by using augmented reality mirror and visualizes the difference between instructed motion and learners' motion. The system made a better performance in learning efficiency compared with conventional video learning [2]. Rector et al. developed a system to teach the motion of yoga. Their system captures the motion of learner by Kinect and feedback the difference between instructors posture by audio interface [3]. In terms of auditory feedback, Kapur et al. suggested that it is possible to support understanding the motion of dance by audio interface [4]. Chua et al. implemented virtual reality learning system of Tai Chi. The system displays both captured learner's and expert's motion in 3D virtual environment. Learner is able to compare the difference from an expert visually. Nevertheless, they reported that the system did not make a significant improvement to learn the exact motion from third person view compared with conventional method [5]. Yang et al. introduced a ghost metaphor that super imposes the instructor's motion to learner's body in computer graphics. The system aimed to support learner to subjectively understand the motion from third person view. The system was named "Just Follow Me" and they improved the learning efficacy in calligraphy learning by the system [6]. Hiyama et al. developed a wearable learning system that enables to experience multimodal information of an expert from first person view (Fig. 1). and improved the skill of making Japanese traditional papermaking [7].

Aforementioned works focused on developing the system that compare and visualize the difference of the motion between expert and learner. These works made successful achievements in transferring physical skills like artisanship, which does not includes locomotion, by displaying the information from first person view using virtual reality technologies. However, the effective system that supports learning dynamic motion in sport activities from first person view is yet to be examined.

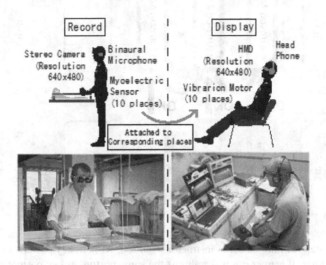

Fig. 1. Wearable recording system and displaying system [7]

3   Methodology

Tracing the instructor's motion displayed 3D through head mounted display is an effective use of immersive virtual environment. Although, it is difficult to train physical skills include fullbody motion or locomotion through such system. In this section we propose a method to apply this kind of system to training physical skills in sport activities. The proposed system designed to allow learner to step away from first person view to third person view seamlessly to overcome abovementioned problem.

There is one additional problem that makes it difficult to follow instructor's motion is the quickness of the motion in sport activities. In order to solve this problem, we adopted key posture method. Key posture method helps learner to mimic a set of movements step by step (Fig. 2). By using this method, learner is able to imitate the instructor's form interactively in accordance with her/his learning speed.

As an example application for sport activity we chose pitching motion in baseball. Instructor's pitching motion is captured by Microsoft Kinect and visualized as 3D model illustrated in Fig. 3. We divided pitching motion into 17 steps. Instructor's 3D motion model is displayed as red model and learner's 3D body is displayed as white model. While learner is trying to mimic the posture of instructor's body, body parts of learner's, which successfully matched to instructor's posture, turn to change its color to yellow (Fig. 4). Certain number of learner's body parts turn to yellow, next key posture is presented to learner.

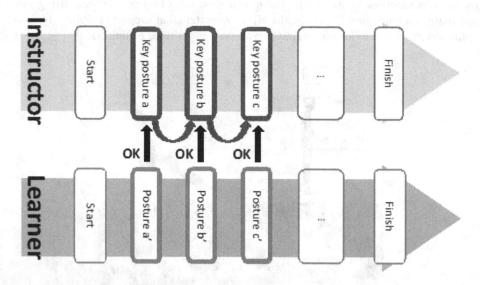

Fig. 2. Step by step learning model of instructor's motion. At first, key posture a of instructor is presented to learner. If learner can make almost the same posture as key posture a, key posture b is presented to learner for the next step.

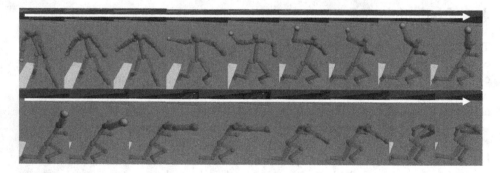

Fig. 3. Instructor's pitching motion captured by Microsoft Kinect. Instructor's pitching motion is divided into 17 steps.

4   Developed System

Fig. 5. illustrates the developed system configuration. Learner trains her/his pitching motion by observing the difference between herself/himself and instructor through head mounted display. Learner's viewpoint is fixed onto the head of learner's 3D model. Lerner's 3D model is captured by Microsoft Kinect in real time.

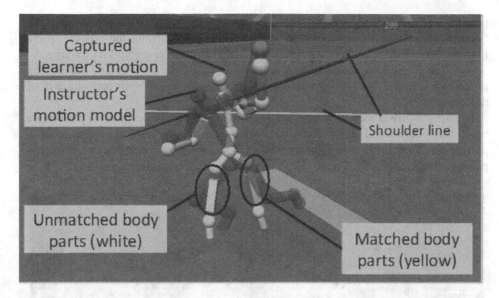

Fig. 4. Visualized difference of the posture of instructor and learner in virtual environment

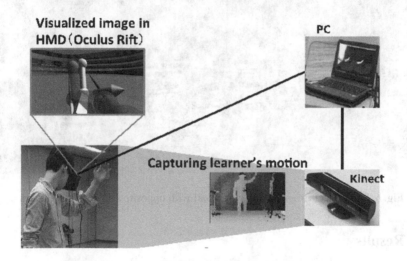

Fig. 5. System configuration

5   Experiment

We conducted an experiment in order to evaluate the efficiency of developed physical skill training system. For an evaluation we compared three different learning methods. As a conventional learning method we used video of instructor's pitching motion (video). As proposed methods we prepared two different parameters for evaluating the conformation of the posture of learner and instructor. First one compares all the part of learner's body parts strictly with instructor's targeted posture (fullbody). Second one relatively put weight on shoulder line for matching the posture (part). Participants of the experiment are randomly chosen whichever method for training.

We had 17 participants, in the age of early 20s, for the experiment. Experiment procedure is as follows. Participants are asked to throw a ball with opposite arm of dominant arm.

Pitching ability is measured by average throwing distance calculated by throwing a ball 5 times before and after training with whichever training method for 7 minutes. 6 participants used fullbody condition, 5 participants for part condition, and 6 participants for video condition. Fig. 6. shows an image of an experiment.

Fig. 6. Experiment image of throwing a ball with opposite arm of dominant arm

6   Results

Fig. 7. shows the result of measured improvement of throwing distance of participants in each condition. Only participants used part condition for training made a significant improvement in throwing distance (p<.05).

From the result that participants used part condition for training made a significant improvement, effectiveness of proposed method for training physical skill in a sport activity has been proved. For the training of fullbody motion, it is more effective to let learners to pay attention to certain points of the body that whole body movement at the early stage of training.

We also made an interview after the experiment. Some participants used fullbody condition for training mentioned that if they had more time for training, they could improve the pitching ability. It requires a further experiment but if we conduct an experiment for a longer time period, effectiveness of fullbody condition may be shown in the result.

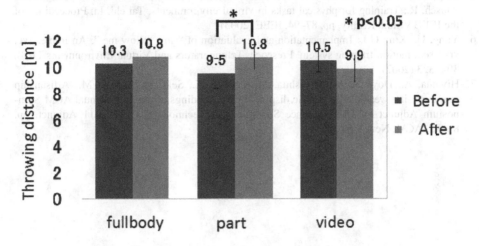

Fig. 7. Training effect results

7   Conclusion

In this research, we proposed a first person view physical skill training system in immersive virtual environment using head mounted display. As a training method for sport activity, we designed step by step learning model that allows learner to observe instructor's motion according to learner's training speed. We conducted an experiment of training pitching skill and compared proposed method and conventional video learning, and proved an effectiveness of proposed method.

Acknowledgments. This research was partially supported by Japan Science and Technology Agency, JST, under Strategic Promotion of Innovative Research and Development Program.

References

1. Nawahdah, M., Inoue, T.: Motion adaptive orientation adjustment of a virtual teacher to support physical task learning. Journal of Information Processing 20(1), 277–286 (2012)
2. Anderson, F., Grossman, T., Matejka, J., Fitzmaurice, G.: Youmove: enhancing movement training with an augmented reality mirror. In: Proceedings of the 26th Annual ACM Symposium on User Interface Software and Technology, pp. 311–320. ACM (2013)

3. Rector, K., Bennett, C.L., Kientz, J.A.: Eyes-free yoga: an ex-ergame using depth cameras for blind & low vision exercise. In: Proceedings of the 15th International ACM SIGACCESS Conference on Computers and Accessibility, p. 12. ACM (2013)
4. Kapur, A., Tzanetakis, G., Virji-Babul, N., Wang, G., Cook, P.R.: A framework for sonification of vicon motion capture data. In: Conference on Digital Audio Effects, pp. 47–52 (2005)
5. Chua, P.T., Crivella, R., Daly, B., Hu, N., Schaaf, R., Ventura, D., Camill, T., Hodgins, J., Pausch, R.: Training for physical tasks in virtual environments: Tai chi. In: Proceedings of the IEEE Virtual Reality, pp. 87–94. IEEE (2003)
6. Yang, U., Kim, G.J.: Implementation and evaluation of " just follow me ": An immersive, vr-based, motion-training system. Presence: Teleoperators and Virtual Environments 11(3), 304–323 (2002)
7. Hiyama, A., Doyama, Y., Miyashita, M., Ebuchi, E., Seki, M., Hirose, M.: Artisanship training using wearable egocentric display. In: Proceedings of the 24th Annual ACM Symposium Adjunct on User Interface Software and Technology, UIST 2011 Adjunct, pp. 81–82. ACM, New York (2011)

An Improved Teaching Behavior Estimation Model from Student Evaluations

Yusuke Kometani[1], Takahito Tomoto[2], Takehiro Furuta[3], and Takako Akakura[2]

[1] Graduate School of Engineering
and
[2] Faculty of Engineering, Tokyo University of Science,
1-3 Kagurazaka, Shinjuku-ku, Tokyo 162-8601, Japan
{kometani,tomoto,akakura}@ms.kagu.tus.ac.jp
[3] Nara University of Education, Takabatake-cho, Nara City, Nara 630-8528, Japan
takef@nara-edu.ac.jp

Abstract. Many universities conduct student evaluations. Their purpose is to encourage improvement in teaching. However, the evaluations are merely subjective assessments by students, meaning that instructors cannot necessarily easily relate evaluations to areas for improvement in teaching. To address this issue, we suggest a teaching behavior estimation model that can estimate teaching behaviors from student evaluations of each lesson. In previous research, we built a model on the assumption that teaching behaviors are not correlated with other behaviors and that student evaluation items are uncorrelated to other evaluation items. However, this assumption could not be verified. Our research suggests a new teaching behavior estimation model that represents the correlation between factors of teaching and factors of student evaluations. To analyze this, we conducted canonical correlation between two kinds of factors and obtained correlations. This result shows that it is possible to construct a teaching behavior estimation model based on factors of teaching behavior and factors of student evaluations.

Keywords: Student evaluation, Lesson improvement, Teaching behavior, Teaching behavior estimation model.

1 Introduction

Student evaluations of teaching are a typical method for supporting lesson improvement by instructors. At present, student evaluations are used by many universities. However, these evaluations are subjective assessments by students, such as "a lesson is incomprehensible." Therefore, it is difficult for university instructors to discern concrete areas for improvement from student evaluations.

We previously proposed an approach that aims to support improvements in teaching [1]. We proposed a model (teaching behavior estimation model) that presumes teaching behavior can be measured from student evaluations and developed a function (teaching behavior estimation function) to identify teaching behaviors in the model

S. Yamamoto (Ed.): HIMI 2014, Part II, LNCS 8522, pp. 59–68, 2014.
© Springer International Publishing Switzerland 2014

that can be improved. In this research, analysis intended to improve the teaching behavior estimation model is conducted. Specifically, we increase the variety of teaching behaviors subjected to analysis and propose a model that yields the relation between the factor of teaching behaviors and the factors of student evaluations. The purpose of this research is to show that it is possible to build the model.

2   Related Works

Students' evaluation feedback methods and student reactions to support teaching improvement have been studied in the past. Stalmeijer et al. explored whether feedback effectiveness improved when physician teachers' self-assessments were added to written feedback based on student ratings [2]. The physician teachers considered the combination of self-assessment and student ratings more effective than either self-assessment or written feedback alone. The authors concluded that self-assessment can be useful in stimulating teaching improvement. However, there was no evidence that the teachers grasped points for improvement of teaching behaviors by reviewing students' evaluations. Thus, our proposed method additionally involves an objective evaluation of the teaching behavior based on evaluations obtained from the students and the data are then fed back to the teacher.

Recent years, estimation methods for students' evaluations based on teaching behaviors were studied. Large repositories of presentation recordings often provide users with rating facilities. Pietro et al. explored nonverbal behavior (in particular arms movement and prosody) allows one to predict whether a video presentation is rated as low or high in terms of quality[3]. The experiments have focused on the nonverbal behaviors most important in an oral presentation, namely pose, gestures, movements and prosody. The results show that the mean pitch and position of arms allow one to predict whether a presentation is rated as high or low quality. However, this study didn't explore whether it is able to predict teaching behaviors based on students' evaluations.

Lessons can be improved by an improvement in course content and by an improvement in teaching behaviors. We previously proposed an instructor support method that aims to help instructors improve their own teaching behaviors [1]. We analyzed the relation between the average value of student evaluations of specific lessons and the number of times particular teaching behaviors occurred in the lesson. As a result, the relation between each lesson evaluation and teaching behavior was obtained, and it turned out that it is possible to estimate the number of times that specific teaching behaviors occurred by using lesson evaluations. Then, a model was built that shows the relation between the average value of each lesson evaluation and the number of times each teaching behavior occurred in the lesson. Additionally, a teaching behavior estimation function was proposed to estimate the number of times each teaching behavior had occurred. Figure 1 shows the teaching behavior estimation model built to evaluate the teaching behavior estimation function. The result of the evaluation experiment showed that university teachers would like to use the function and that the estimated teaching behaviors were effective in supporting lesson improvement. These results show that increasing the variety of teaching actions and refining the model leads to more effective lesson improvement support.

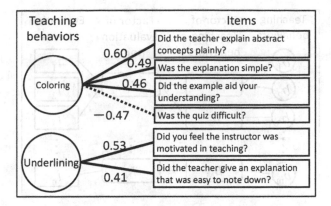

Fig. 1. Teaching behavior estimation model

3 Improvement of the Teaching Behavior Estimation Model

Among instructors who want to improve their lessons, the important teaching actions may differ by instructor. Moreover, according to the lesson form and course content, evaluation items may differ. In consideration of this, previous work built a model that assumed a one-to-one relation between lesson evaluation items and teaching behaviors (Fig. 1). Thus, the model in previous work assumes that teaching behaviors and student evaluation items are mostly uncorrelated. However, verification of this was not carried out in that work. If such correlations do in fact occur, then it is necessary to reinvestigate the correlation between the newly added teaching behaviors and the evaluation items and how the model is affected by the addition of new teaching behaviors. However, if a model is built that allows correlation between teaching behaviors or correlation between student evaluation items, it becomes possible to treat highly related mutual teaching behaviors equally. This allows minimal changes to the model with the addition of new teaching behaviors. Moreover, when estimating a certain teaching behavior, multi-correlation of student items can be prevented, which allows shorter evaluations. Therefore, when acquiring student evaluations, an advantage of this model type is that the burden on students is mitigated. For the above reasons, it is believed that an improved model should allow detailed analysis of the correlations among student evaluation items and among teaching behaviors.

This research aims at building an estimation model that is flexible on included teaching behaviors and student evaluation items. Figure 2 shows the model assumed by this research. The model comprises independent factors of teaching behavior and independent factors of student evaluation. Anything contained in a factor of an existing model can be incorporated into a factor into the revised model, but items not part of any existing factor require modification of the model to incorporation of the new factor.

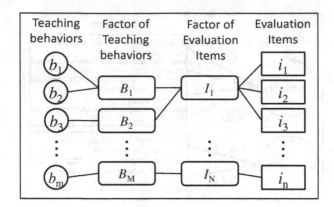

Fig. 2. The model incorporating factors

4   Methodology

In this research, the correlations between the independent factors of teaching behaviors and the independent factors of student evaluation are analyzed. First, data are collected in preparation. After determining the teaching behaviors to measure, collection of student evaluations and measurement of teaching actions are performed. Teaching actions in a lesson are measured by viewing and listening to video recordings of the lesson.

Then, the acquired data are analyzed. Factor analysis is applied to every teaching behavior and every student evaluation, which extracts the factors analytically. Canonical analysis is then performed on the factors of teaching actions and on the factors of student assessments, and correlations between factors are investigated.

4.1   Teaching Behaviors

We previously targeted two kinds of teaching actions, underlining and coloring [1]. However, to analyze the factors of teaching behaviors, it is necessary to measure many more kinds of teaching behaviors. We defined 27 concrete teaching behaviors to address this problem, on the basis of previous investigations into abstract teaching skill.

The behaviors defined in this research are blackboard writing behaviors, such as "uses an arrow or a line to connect two or more items written to the blackboard" and "draws a line on the blackboard and distinguishes the content when changing to a new topic"; oral behaviors, such as "orally checks whether there are any questions or comments from students" and "orally notes when changing to a new topic during the middle of a lesson"; and non-verbal behaviors, such as "folds arms when speaking" and "puts hand on waist when speaking."

4.2   Student Evaluations

The lesson is subject I at university T (a lesson about information mathematics). Student evaluations were acquired for 29 lessons (lessons 2–9, 11, 13 of the course in 2010, lessons 4–8, 10–13 in 2011, and lessons 3–9, 11–13 in 2012). The number of participants enrolled in the course varied from 80 to 110 students. To measure teaching behaviors, the lectures were videotaped. Table 1 shows some of the evaluation items. A 20-item questionnaire was used. A copy of the questionnaire was distributed at the end of each lesson. Participants answered each question item on a five-point Likert scale (from "1. Strongly disagree" to "5. Strongly agree"). The questionnaire required about 5 minutes to complete teach time. The questionnaire was completed in a machine-readable format, and students were informed in advance that the evaluation would not influence their course results. In addition, no feedback about the evaluation results was given to the instructor.

5   Results

The relations between the factors of teaching behaviors and the factors of student evaluations are analyzed. First, factor analysis is applied to student evaluations. The independent factors are extracted, and the features of each factor are considered. Next, factor analysis is applied to teaching behaviors, the independent factors are extracted, and the features of each factor are considered. Finally, canonical analysis is applied to the factors of student evaluations and the factors of teaching behaviors, and the relations among factors are clarified.

5.1   Measurement of the Frequency of Teaching Behaviors

The number of times that the instructor performed specified behaviors during each session was measured. Two fourth-year students viewed and listened to videos of lectures (about 2200 minutes) and measured the number of times that specific teaching behaviors occurred. To check the reliability of measurements, the two students' results were compared. Ten lecture videos and ten behaviors were randomly selected. When the two students were compared on number of recorded occurrences, the measurement results for 9 of 10 behaviors were in agreement. We treat this as sufficient reliability in measurement and decided to use the data for analysis. The measured teaching behaviors were totaled by lesson.

In 29 lessons of subject I, 23 kinds of teaching behaviors were observed. Among teaching behaviors, 6 were seen only once in 29 lessons. We therefore decided to use data on the remaining 17 kinds of teaching behaviors, excluding the teaching behaviors seen only once.

Table 1 shows the value of the number of times that the teaching behaviors were seen per session. The table shows that the number of times depends strongly on the kind of teaching behavior. Certain behaviors stand out as occurring particularly frequently, such as "underlines a word or a sentence…," "draws a frame…," "changes the color of chalk…," and "enumerates two or more items on blackboard." The instructor tends to frequently use blackboard actions for emphasis.

Table 1. The value of the number of times teaching behaviors occur per lesson

Teaching behaviors	2010 2nd	2010 3rd	…	2012 13th
Underlines a word or a sentence on the blackboard	6	16	…	7
Draws a frame around two or more pieces of information on the blackboard	6	15	…	10
Changes the color of chalk when writing a word or a sentence on the blackboard	7	4	…	19
Enumerates two or more items on the blackboard	6	7	…	5
Uses an arrow or a line to connect two or more items written on the blackboard	10	5	…	7
Draws a frame around one word or sentence on the blackboard	0	0	…	13
Asks whether students understood the content	3	7	…	3
Set the task for students during the session	2	3	…	0

5.2   Factor Analysis

Factor analysis was applied to each evaluation item. Factors were extracted for eigenvalues greater than 1. As a result of factor analysis, three factors were extracted whose cumulative contribution ratio was 80.67%. Factor loadings are shown in Table 2. It is thought that the f_{i1} is "an evaluation factor about the lesson content," because it has a large absolute value for the factor loadings "Did you understand the lesson content" "Did you master new knowledge?" and "Were you satisfied with the lesson?" It is thought that f_{i2} is "an evaluation factor about the method of methods of delivery" because it has a large absolute value for factor loadings "Was the writing on the blackboard legible?" and "Did the instructor give an explanation that was easy to note down?" It is thought that f_{i3} is "a factor of self-teaching" because it has a large absolute value for factor loadings "Did you prepare for the lesson?" and "Did you review the pre-lesson notes?"

After this, factor analysis was applied to teaching behaviors. Factors were extracted for eigenvalues more than 1. As a result of factor analysis, four factors were extracted whose cumulative contribution ratio was 39.42%. Table 3 shows the factor loadings. Factor f_{b1} is a "question-emphasis behavior factor" because it has a large absolute value for factor loadings "orally checks whether there are any questions or comments from students" and "orally notes when changing to a new topic during the middle of a lesson." Factor f_{b2} is a "blackboard writing behavior factor" because it has a large absolute value for factor loadings "changes the color of chalk when writing a word or a sentence on the blackboard" and "uses an arrow or a line to connect two or more items written on the blackboard." The factor f_{b3} is "planned explanation factor" because it has a large absolute value for factor loadings "enumerates two or more items on the blackboard" and "explains a certain concept orally according to the phenomenon which may happen actually." The factor f_{b4} is an "overbearing behavior factor," because it has a large absolute value for factor loadings "folds arms when speaking" and "puts hand on waist when speaking."

Table 2. Factor loadings (student evaluations)

Evaluation Items	f_{i1}	f_{i2}	f_{i3}
Did you understand the lesson content?	**0.94**	0.08	0.12
Did you master new knowledge?	**0.91**	0.24	-0.02
Did you grasp the importance concepts of the lesson?	**0.90**	0.14	0.30
Were you satisfied with the lesson?	**0.88**	0.38	0.16
Were the explanations simple?	**0.88**	0.36	0.16
Were you interested in the lesson?	**0.84**	0.20	0.26
Did the examples aid your understanding?	**0.80**	0.51	0.03
Did the instructor plainly explain abstract concepts?	**0.78**	0.46	0.16
Was your attitude to study positive?	**0.64**	0.14	-0.05
Was the volume of the instructor's voice suitable?	0.07	**0.89**	-0.01
Was the writing on the blackboard legible?	0.26	**0.86**	-0.02
Did you feel the instructor was motivated in teaching?	0.25	**0.83**	-0.03
Did the instructor give an explanation that was easy to note down?	0.50	**0.80**	0.11
Was the quantity of material in the lesson appropriate?	0.49	**0.60**	0.36
Did you prepare for the lesson?	0.13	-0.14	**0.98**
Did you review the pre-lesson notes?	0.12	0.12	**0.89**

Table 3. Factor loadings (teaching behaviors)

Teaching behaviors	f_{b1}	f_{b2}	f_{b3}	f_{b4}
Orally checks whether there are any questions or comments from students	**0.76**	0.15	0.52	0.07
Orally notes when changing to a new topic during the middle of a lesson	**0.60**	0.26	0.14	0.03
Uses an arrow or a line to connect two or more items written on the blackboard	0.06	**0.75**	0.41	-0.15
Changes the color of the chalk when writing a word or a sentence on the blackboard	-0.09	**0.54**	0.20	0.05
Draws a frame around two or more pieces of information on the blackboard	-0.07	**0.45**	-0.37	0.13
Enumerates two or more items on the blackboard	0.09	0.15	**0.52**	-0.06
Orally explains a concept by giving actual examples	-0.55	0.03	**0.48**	0.36
Set the task for students during the session	0.14	-0.25	**0.47**	0.15
Draws a line on the blackboard and distinguishes the content when changing to a new topic	-0.21	-0.02	**0.46**	-0.24
Folds arms when speaking	-0.15	0.39	-0.33	**0.67**
Puts hand on waist when speaking	-0.18	-0.27	-0.01	**0.41**

5.3   Canonical Correlation Analysis

Canonical analysis was applied to the teaching behavior factors and the student evaluation factors by using each factor score for 29 lectures of subject I. Three axes were extracted by canonical analysis. Table 4 shows the structural coefficients. The considerations of each axis of canonical analysis are shown below.

Axis 1
- The absolute values of the structural coefficients of the "Lesson content" and "Deliberate explanation" are large. If there is a lot of planned explanation, the evaluation of the lesson content is likely to be low. This indicates that there is excessively planned behavior and too much content in the lesson (rushing through many topics by using itemized statement items, etc.), which interrupts student understanding of the content.

Axis 2
- The absolute value of the structural coefficient of "the evaluation factor about the method of delivery" and "the behavior factor of blackboard writing" is large. If blackboard writing behavior occurs often, the evaluation of the method of delivery will be high.

Axis 3
- The absolute value of the structural coefficient of an "overbearing behavior factor" and "the factor of self-study" is large. Overbearing behaviors reduce the evaluation of "self-study."

Table 4. Structured coefficients

factors	Axis 1	Axis 2	Axis 3
free variables (teaching behavior)			
f_{b1}: Question and emphasis	0.33	-0.40	-0.47
f_{b2}: Blackboard writing	-0.47	**-0.86**	0.19
f_{b3}: Deliberate explanation	**0.80**	-0.26	0.35
f_{b4}: Overbearing behavior	0.01	-0.07	**-0.80**
bound variables (students' evaluation)			
f_{i1}: Lesson content	**-0.89**	0.36	-0.28
f_{i2}: Method of delivery	-0.46	**-0.82**	0.35
f_{i3}: Self-study	-0.07	0.39	**0.92**

Table 5. Correlation between factors

	fi1: Lesson content	fi2: Method of delivery	fi3: Self-study
f_{b1}: Question and emphasis	-0.21	-0.01	-0.19
f_{b2}: Blackboard writing	0.13	**0.42**	-0.06
f_{b3}: Deliberate explanation	**-0.51**	-0.12	0.01
f_{b4}: Overbearing behavior	0.05	-0.05	-0.20

The correlation coefficients between each factor pair are shown in Table 5. The following factor combinations were founded to be correlated:

— (a) "Deliberate explanation" and "Lesson content,"
— (b) "Blackboard writing" and "Method of delivery," and
— (c) "Overbearing behavior" and "Self-study."

For relations (a) and (b), a correlation of medium degree was found, and a weak correlation was found for relation (c). Thus, correlations can be observed between factors of teaching behaviors and factors of student evaluations. This result suggests that a model can be constructed that estimates the factors of teaching behavior from the factors of student evaluations.

The factors of teaching action and the factors of student evaluations can be clarified, and the following advantages accrue from building a model using the factors.

- A factor can be replaced without influencing other factors in the model.
  The correlation coefficient of a model will change if teaching behaviors or student evaluation items are exchanged in the model because of the one-to-one correlation between teaching behavior and student evaluation items. However in our proposed model between factors, instructors can exchange teaching behaviors and student evaluation items without affecting the correlation between factors. For example, if an instructor wants to evaluate the effect of chalk colors, the value of "the factor of blackboard writing" can be calculated from the number of times that color was used, and the results can be compared by means of the value of the average value of "the evaluation factor about the method of delivery." Thus, it is possible to include teaching behaviors in a model without changing the correlation model, such as here without having a student evaluation item on chalk color.

- It is possible to reduce the number of student evaluation items.
  The burden on students from evaluations can be reduced. For example, it is possible to reduce the number of items to 6 by using each 2 items for each of the 3 extracted factors.

6   Conclusions and Future Work

This research aimed at the improvement of the teaching behavior estimation model to support improvement in instructors' lessons. A model comprising teaching behavior factors and student evaluation factors was proposed. To verify whether such a model is feasible, canonical analysis was applied to the factors of teaching behaviors and the factors of student evaluations. As a result, the factors of teaching behaviors and the factors of student evaluations were correlated. This result showed that model construction is possible.

As a future subject, we plan to construct a more flexible model. For lessons in different academic years and on different subjects, measurement of teaching behaviors and acquisition of student evaluations will be performed, and the accuracy of the model will be estimated. Furthermore, it would be useful to show the relation between the factors of teaching behaviors and the factors of student evaluations to instructors. By knowing the teaching behavior factors, student evaluation factors, and their relations, it should be possible to identify teaching behavior groups that would affect student evaluations. We would like to investigate the effect on lesson improvement from sharing such information with instructors.

Acknowledgements. This research was partially supported by a Grant-in-Aid for Scientific Research (No. 24300291, 2012–2015) from the Japanese Ministry of Education, Culture, Sports, Science and Technology.

References

1. Kometani, Y., Tomoto, T., Furuta, T., Akakura, T.: Video feedback system for teaching improvement using students' sequential and overall teaching evaluations. In: Yamamoto, S. (ed.) HCI 2013, Part III. LNCS, vol. 8018, pp. 79–88. Springer, Heidelberg (2013)
2. Stalmeijer, R.E., Dolmans, D.H.J.M., Wolfhagen, I.H.A.P., Peters, W.G., van Coppenolle, L., Scherpbier, A.J.J.A.: Combined student ratings and self-assessment provide useful feedback for clinical teachers. Adv. in Health Sci. Educ. 15, 315–328 (2010)
3. Salvagnini, P., Salamin, H., Cristani, M., Vinciarelli, A., Murino, V.: Learning How to Teach from "Videolectures": Automatic Prediction of Lecture Ratings Based on Teacher's Nonverbal Behavior. In: 3rd IEEE International Conference on Cognitive Infocommunications, pp. 2–5 (2012)

A Study on Exploration of Relationships between Behaviors and Mental States of Learners for Value Co-creative Education and Learning Environment

Tatsunori Matsui[1], Yuki Horiguchi[1], Kazuaki Kojima[2], and Takako Akakura[3]

[1] Faculty of Human Sciences, Waseda University, Japan
matsui-t@waseda.jp
[2] Learning Technology Laboratory Teikyo University, Japan
kojima@lt-lab.teikyo-u.ac.jp
[3] Faculty of Engineering, Tokyo University of Science, Japan
akakura@ms.kagu.tus.ac.jp

Abstract. From the view point of value co-creation in education and learning environment, it is important to cultivate competency and literacy for learning for both learners and teachers. For realizing value co-creative education and learning environment, detection of learners' mental states during their learning activities plays very important role at this environment. In this context, it is an important task to implement an e-learning system that can automatically detect changes of learners' mental states by observing their behaviors in learning activities. In this study, we conducted an experiment to explore relationships between mental states and behaviors of a learner on our experimental tools designed along with an assumption of a learning environment with an e-learning system. We focused on mouse and face movement as the behaviors. The results of the experiment revealed some features about the behaviors and the mental states.

Keywords: e-leaning system, automatic estimation, mental states, value co-creation, education and learning environment.

1 Introduction

From the view point of value co-creation in education and learning environment, it is important to cultivate competency and literacy for learning for both learners and teachers. For realizing value co-creative education and learning environment, detection of learners' mental states during their learning activities plays very important role at this environment. In this context, it is an important task to implement an e-learning system that can automatically detect changes of learners' mental states by observing their behaviors in learning activities.

On the other hand, current e-learning systems are classified into two types: synchronous and asynchronous systems. In the former systems, learners can learn anytime and anywhere without under any time and spatial constraints. However, teachers cannot observe the learners' behaviors on the system to estimate their understanding. Although the latter systems allow teachers to observe learners, such systems imposes time

S. Yamamoto (Ed.): HIMI 2014, Part II, LNCS 8522, pp. 69–79, 2014.
© Springer International Publishing Switzerland 2014

constraint on the teachers and learners because they have to simultaneously work. Therefore, it is an important task to implement an asynchronous system that can automatically detect changes of learners' mental states by observing their behaviors. Here, we call such a system an estimation system.

Several studies have addressed implementation of the asynchronous e-learning systems that estimate learners' mental states, such as impasses in problem solving or impressions of problem difficulties perceived by learners. Ueno's estimation system has succeeded in detecting unusual states of learners by measuring response time required to solve each problem[1]. However, it cannot specify sources that causes the unusual responses in problem solving processes because it's based on the response time. An estimation system by Nakamura and his colleagues can detect sources of unusual behaviors based on learners' responses[2]. To detect the sources, it needs learning contents that embed particular materials, such as buttons to present hints. A system by [3] judges whether or not learners find problems difficult based on behavioral data: eye and face movements acquired through a stereo-camera, and interval time among input operations on the system. Because the specific device stereo-camera is required, it may be difficult to actually adapt the system to practical e-learning environments.

From a different perspective, an asynchronous e-learning system for students in full-time employment has been developed and used practically[5]. The system contains the class evaluation functions. Existing class evaluation is almost always carried out either 1) for an entire course delivered within a set time frame (for example, six months or a year), or 2) on an individual lecture basis. These methods, however, do not provide information on how a specific part of the course or lecture has been evaluated. This research has developed an e-Learning system where classroom lectures are videotaped and teaching evaluation data can be collected chronologically in line with replay time. Additionally, when teachers were provided with feedback on the relationship between class content and time-series data, time series course evaluation was found to be effective in helping teachers improve lecture delivery.

In order to adapt an estimation system into ordinary e-learning environments, it should require no specific devices. In our previous study[4], we have proposed an estimation system that detects unusual behaviors during problem solving based on velocity of mouse movements. Although the system can specify sources of unusual behaviors in problems to some extent, we consider it needs further study to refine its model of the behavioral detection. According to the concept "no specific devices" described above, we conducted an experiment that examined relationships between behaviors and mental states of a learner in order to expand the detection model for implementation of a system that possesses more accurate estimation.

2   Development of Experimental Tools to Observe a Learner's Behaviors

Due to our final goal of implementing an estimation system that is feasible in practical e-learning environments, we acquired all experimental data through a common PC and popular peripheral devices. Prior to the experiment, we had developed an experimental tools along with the assumption of a practical e-learning environment. The experimental tools were comprised of three components: a mouse data collector to record mouse movements, a face data collector to record face movements, a learning interface to present learning contents to a learner, and an analyzer to instantly process the data.

2.1 The Mouse and Face Data Collectors

[2] reported that it was effective in accurate estimation of learners' impressions of problem difficulties to evaluate terminal features such as intervals of mouse operation and facial features such as a behavior of inclining one's face. Based on their finding, we acquired data shown in Table 1, which could be obtained through a common laptop computer.

The mouse data collector recorded coordinates of a mouse cursor's position on a monitor {x, y} and states of a mouse button {stat(on, off)} with 60 Hz sampling rate as the mouse data. The face data collector obtained the face data with analysis of images input through a web camera embedded above a monitor panel in the laptop computer. The face data collector used OpenCV for the image analysis. A position of a learner's face {x, y} was represented as a central point of a face extracted from each input image. A face inclination was represented by roll inferred with an inverse trigonometric function computation based on a difference between central points of eyes. A distance between the face and a monitor {z} was inferred based on a distance between central points of eyes {w}. Using those methods described above, the face data collector could obtained the face data with 5-7 Hz sampling rate. Table 2 indicates ranges where the face data collector can obtain the face data.

Table 1. Behavioral data of learner

Mouse data	$\{x, y, stat\}$ (Sampling-rate: 60Hz)
Face data	$\{x, y, z, \theta\}$ (Sampling-rate: 5-7Hz)

Table 2. Ranges where face data can be obtained

Distance between face and monitor $\{z\}$	15.7 - 31.5 inch
Inclination of face within $\{\theta\}$	± 20 degree

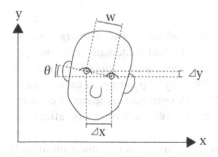

Fig. 1. Face data

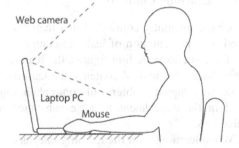

Fig. 2. Posture in using a laptop PC of experimental tools

2.2   The Learning Interface and Analyzer

The learning interface was constructed from a browser component that displayed learning contents in full screen mode. The interface was designed along with an assumption of a setting where a learner solved problems presented in a learning environment with an e-learning system. A screenshot of the interface is shown in Figure 3.

Furthermore, the analyzer for data obtained was used in this experiment. The analyzer had functions of data visualization and playback. It was used to instantly present a learner's behaviors to himself in the interview within the experiment.

Fig. 3. Screenshot of learning interface

3   The Experiment

Our aim in this experiment was to examine relationships between behaviors and mental states of a learner in a learning environment with an e-learning system. Data of the behaviors was gathered through the collectors mentioned in the previous section, and data indicating the mental states was obtained from the learner's protocol data.

3.1   Learning Contents

It is experimentally confirmed that features of tracks where mouse pointers pass depend on representation of learning contents, such as textual sentences or figures [4]. On the contents including figures, the features of the tracks are strongly influenced by their shapes. On textual contents, the features hardly vary depending on each content. Thus, we adopted problems of comprehending English sentences as learning contents used in the experiment because substance of each problem would not affect the behaviors.

When learning with the learning interface, a learner answered to a question in each problem by selecting one of five choices. The learner had only to operate mouse. That was intended to exclude keyboard operation on the learning interface. Scroll operation was also excluded by adjusting the size of fonts and the number of words in each problem so that all information included in the problem could be simultaneously displayed into a screen. Moreover, the number of words in each problem was cautiously set so that any problem could not be solved in a short time. The average time required to solve problems used in the experiment was about five minutes. In order to observe mental states such as impasses, we selected difficult problems from a workbook for civil service exams in Japan.

Table 3. Learning contents

Domain	Reading English sentences
Format	Multiple-choice
Time limit	Nothing

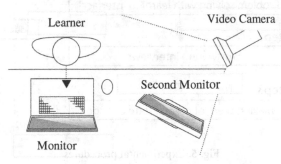

Fig. 4. Experimental setting

3.2   Experimental Setting

In the experiment, a learner worked with the experimental tools that had been installed in a laptop computer with a built-in web camera (Apple MacBook Pro with a 17inch monitor). As shown in Figure 4, the learner's behaviors were recorded with a video camera. The secondary monitor presented time codes and information sent from the collectors. Those were also recorded in the video data in order to synchronize the video data with data obtained through the collectors.

In this experiment, the input device the learner operated was limited to a mouse. The learner was instructed not to keep his right hand away from the mouse. That was intended to make the learner necessarily operate the mouse, or to prevent a behavior of touching a monitor to trace words.

3.3   Experimental Procedures

Figure 5 indicates experimental procedures. At first, a learner answered to a question of a problem presented by the learning interface (Step 1). He had been instructed to talk about what he was thinking as much as possible. His behaviors were recorded with the video camera. After the learner solved the problem, he was asked to watch the video and data from the analyzer, and then reported what he had been thinking by responding to questions from the experimenter (Step 2). In Step 2, the learner was allowed to operate the video playback (e.g., stop or play). To prevent the learner from forgetting his thought, he was asked to report immediately after every problem solving had finished. Each report was also recorded with the video camera. The learner was then asked to make a sheet like as shown in Figure 6 (Step 3). He described statements expressing changes of his mental states on the sheet. A battery of the three steps is called as a trial. Before experimental trials, the learner was engaged in some training trials.

In the experiment, protocol data of a learner was acquired with both of a think aloud method and a retrospective report method. The learner had been asked to talk about what he was thinking while problem solving in Step 1, and he was asked to

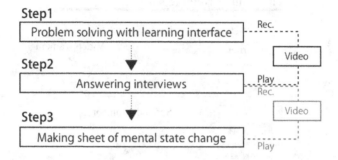

Fig. 5. Experimental procedures

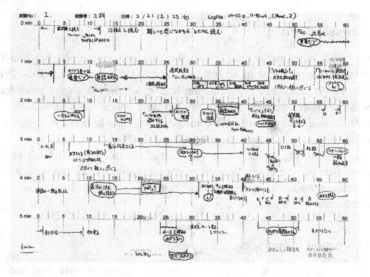

Fig. 6. Instance of sheet for mental state changes

report his thought in Step 2. The think aloud might inhibit the learner's thinking for the problem solving because it imposed mental load to talk. Thus, we didn't strictly force the learner to talk on problem solving, nor we said nothing to the learner until the problem solving finished. The retrospective report was used to interpolate the data from the think aloud.

4   Analysis of the Experimental Data

According to the procedures mentioned in the previous section, we preliminarily performed the experiment to verify our experimental tools. In the experiment, one undergraduate participated as a learner. The learner was engaged in three experimental trials after four training trials. We examined relationships between behaviors and mental states of the learner.

Behavioral data comprising mouse and face movements was acquired by the collectors and velocities of the movements were computed by the analyzer. And Data of the mental states was extracted from sheets made by the learner in Step 3.

4.1   Classifications of the Mental States

Several statements exposing mental states such as impasses or hesitations (e.g., "I don't know this word", "I have no idea what this sentences says", or "I can't decide which is the correct answer") were observed in the sheets in Step 3. Therefore, we defined a period of a impasse as moments when the learner had specified a statement as a don't know state. The learner's behavioral data in the periods of impasses was compared with that in whole periods. We also defined a period of hesitations as moments when the learner had specified a statement as a can't decide state.

Table 4. Time of periods of impasses

	Time required to problem solving	Total time of periods of impasses
Q.1	390 sec.	26.5 sec.
Q.2	234 sec.	14 sec.
Q.3	362 sec.	36 sec.

4.2   Computation of Velocities of Mouse and Face Movements

The collectors recorded coordinates of positions of a mouse cursor and the learner's face in each moment. Velocities of the mouse and face movements were computed by following formulas. A velocity of the mouse movement was computed from total moving distances within every 0.1 second. That of the face movement was computed from total distances among coordinates within one second period, because the sampling rate was not constant.

5   Results of the Experiment

5.1   Features of Mouse Tracking

In each of the three trials, the learner read sentences tracking them with the mouse cursor. In all 14 periods of impasses in problem solving processes of Step 1, words or sentences the cursor pointed were consistent with those the learner reported as sources of the impasses.

5.2   A Relationship between Velocities of Mouse Movements and Impasses

Velocities of mouse movements were different between in the periods of impasses and in other periods. Figure 8 indicates averages and standard deviations of the velocities. Each black bar indicates their averages and standard deviations in whole problem solving processes of Step 1, and each gray those in each of the 14 periods of impasses. As shown in the figure, there were definite differences between the periods and whole processes. This result confirmed that the impasses made the mouse movements slower.

Fig. 7. Instance of mouse tracking

5.3   A Relationship between Hesitations and Face Movements

The learner kept his face away from the monitor six times during problem solving of Step 1. Particularly in Problem 3, he did four times. The learner was asked to evaluate difficulties of problems by using five scales after the three trials had finished. Table 5 indicates the evaluations by the learner. He actually evaluated Problem 3 was most difficult. In the moments when the learner's face was away (found in the video data in

Step1) were corresponding to periods of hesitations. Graphs in Figure 9 show partial data of distances between the learner's face and monitor. In the graphs, vertical axis represents distances between the learner's face and monitor and horizontal time elapsed. Lower points in the graphs indicate that his face was more distant from the monitor. As the graphs represent, the learner had once kept his face away and then put it back along with each hesitation.

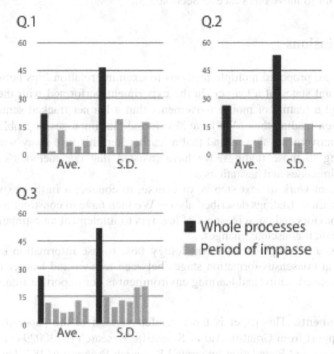

Fig. 8. Velocities of mouse movements

Table 5. Relationship between frequencies of behavior to keep learner's face away and difficulties of problems

	Behavior to keep learner's face away	Difficulties of problems
Q.1	1 time	3
Q.2	1 time	3
Q.3	4 times	5

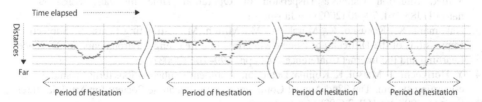

Fig. 9. Moments of behavior to keep learner's face away and his mental states

5.4   Discussion

The results above confirm that the experimental tools developed in the current study can grasp changes of a learner's mental states. Moreover, we believe that the tools can specify sources that cause impasses and hesitations by monitoring the behavior to track words described in Section 5.1, the velocity of mouse movements in Section 5.2, and the behavior to move one's face in Section 5.3.

6   Conclusions

In this paper, we proposed multiple methods to examine relationships between behaviors and mental states of a learner. In the experiment performed with the methods, we have found a feature of mouse movements that a learner tracked sentences with the mouse when reading them. We have also found that impasses in problem solving made mouse movements slower, and that a learner kept his face away when hesitating. According to those findings, we have insisted that our methods can specify source of the impasses and hesitations.

Our important work in next step is, of course, to conduct a further experiment in order to verify those findings described above. We then have to construct a model that associates behaviors and consciousness of learners to implement an estimation system that can sense their conscious changes.

In addition, a development of methodology how to use information on learners' mental states at consensus formation stages between teacher and learner for sharing more appropriate education and learning environment is our important future work.

Acknowledgements. This paper is the extended version of the paper [6]. This research got support from Grant-in-Aid of Scientific Research (22300294) and Service Science, Solution and Foundation Integrated Research Program of JST(Japan Science and Technology Agency)/RISTEX(Research Institute of Science and Technology for Society).

References

1. Ueno, M.: Online Outlier Detection for e-Learning Time Data. IEICE Journal(D) J90-D(1), 40–51 (2007) (in Japanese)
2. Nakamura, Y., Akamatsu, N., Kuwabara, T., Tamaki, M.: Method for Detecting a Learner's Stalled Situation Using a Dispersion of Operation Time Intervals. IEICE Journal(D-I) J85-D-I, 79–90 (2002) (in Japanese)
3. Nakamura, K., Kakusho, K., Murakami, M., Minoh, M.: Estimating Learners' Subjective Impressions of the Difficulty of Course Materials in e-Learning Environments. In: Distance Learning and the Internet Conference 2008, pp. 199–206 (2008)
4. Y. Horiguchi, T. Matsui, K. Kojima; Detection of student's subconscious turns on studying in e-learning system, The 22nd Annual Conference of the Japanese Society for Artificial Intelligence, 2008, pp.1C1-2 (2008) (in Japanese).

5. Tonomura, T., Kometani, Y., Furuta, T., Akakura, T.: Student Evaluation Feedback Functions of an Asynchronous e-Learning system for Enhancement of a Lecture Video. Journal of Japan Society for Educational Technology 35(Suppl.), 193–196 (2011) (in Japanese)
6. Horiguchi, Y., Kojima, K., Matsui, T.: A Study for Exploration of Relationships between Behaviors and Mental States of Learners for an Automatic Estimation System. In: Proceedings of 17th International Conference on Computers in Education, pp. 173–176 (2009)

A Music Search System for Expressive Music Performance Learning

Tomoya Mikami[1,*] and Kosuke Takano[2]

[1] Graduate School of Information and Computer Sciences,
Kanagawa Institute of Technology, Japan
`s1385009@cce.kanagawa-it.ac.jp`
[2] Department of Information and Computer Sciences,
Kanagawa Institute of Technology, Japan
`takano@ic.kanagawa-it.ac.jp`

Abstract. In this paper, we present a music search system that focuses on performance style to cultivate a pupil's expressive performance of music. The system allows pupils to learn the performance style to be mastered by obtaining both model and non-model content. By browsing non-model content that is similar to the quality of a pupil's performance, the pupil can quickly identify his/her areas that require improvement. In addition, the pupil can improve his/her performance skill by repeatedly imitating the models. We evaluate the capabilities of our music search system regarding the extraction of performance style from a classical music source and the precision of the music search results for performance style.

Keywords: music retrieval, performance expression, musical performance learning, MIDI.

1 Introduction

In elementary school music education, it is important to foster not only a basic ability of musical activities but also love, sensibility, and sentiment for music by appreciation and expression. For example, when teaching students to play instruments, teachers should encourage pupils to develop the ability to perform based on the musical elements and mood by listening to models as well as understanding the musical score.

In this study, we present a music search system that focuses on performance style to cultivate a pupil's expressive music performance [1, 2]. Our system consists of two main components: performance style extraction using a pre-defined set of rules and a music search that is based on the performance style. The first component extracts the performance style from MIDI data by analyzing the MIDI sequence of a performance. The music search component then retrieves music data based on the performance style extracted from the user's real-time performance with a MIDI instrument.

---

* Corresponding author.

S. Yamamoto (Ed.): HIMI 2014, Part II, LNCS 8522, pp. 80–89, 2014.
© Springer International Publishing Switzerland 2014

Our system provides two types of music content to pupils for their music performance learning. One is model music that matches the pupil's goal of expressive music performance, and the other is non-model music that is similar to the pupil's current performance. Using our system, pupils can learn the performance style to be mastered by repeatedly listening to the models and imitating them. Meanwhile, by browsing the non-model music, the pupil can quickly identify his/her areas that require improvement. Thus, our system fosters a rich expression of the pupil's music performance through the learning process using both the models and the non-models that are suggested by a search results.

In this study, we evaluate the capability of our system in extracting the performance style from a classical music source and the precision of the music search results of performance style.

2   Learning Scenario

Figure 1 shows an example of a learning scenario using our music search system. To suggest music content (audio and movie) to a student, the system returns both model music and non-model music content based on the student's performance style, which

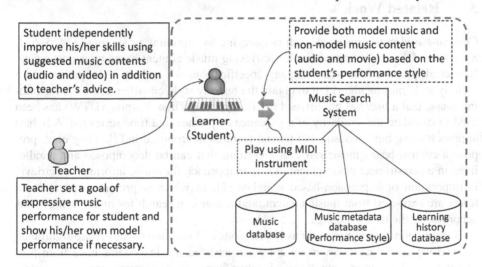

Fig. 1. Example of a learning scenario

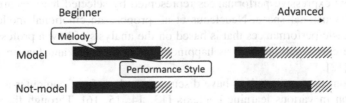

Fig. 2. Parameters of the music search

is extracted from an actual performance using a MIDI instrument. When a teacher indicates negative points about the student's performance, the teacher can make the student logically understand the point. In such a case, the teacher might suggest non-model music that is similar to the current quality of the student's performance so the student can quickly understand the areas that require improvement. Thus, our music search system allows the student to independently improve his/her skills using suggested music content in addition to the teacher's advice.

We incorporate two attributes in the music search: melody and performance style. If the melody attribute is determined to be important, our system retrieves similar music content based on the melody. In contrast, if a student is interested in the performance style, the system suggests similar music content based on the performance style. For example, when a beginner uses the system to browse relevant music content, he/she might be interested in obtaining model and non-model content based on the melody because it is easier for a beginner to improve his/her performance in the early stage of learning by studying music with the same melody. An advanced learner might put more weight on the performance style because he wants to compare his performance to several types of music (Figure 2).

3   Related Work

Content-based music retrieval, such as querying by humming or singing [3, 4, 5, 6, 7, 8], is one of the major approaches for retrieving music content based on acoustic data. Kuo et al. propose four types of query specifications for melody style queries and a melody style mining algorithm to obtain the melody style classification rules for finding music that a user has not listened to [4]. Dynamic Time Warping (DTW) has been used to calculate the similarity of a sequence of pitches in a time series [6]. A hybrid approach using both acoustic and textual features is proposed in [7]. Yang et al. propose a content-based music retrieval algorithm that can be decomposed and parallelized in a peer-to-peer environment. Another approach for music information retrieval is impression or expression-based searches [9], in which impression or emotional terms are extracted from music content, and a user can search for music using terms according to the user's feelings.

Because human feelings, such as impressions and emotion to music, are significant for various music activities, many computer-assisted music systems have been proposed to model a user's emotions, visualize impressions, create expressive performances, and other uses [10, 11, 12]. In [10], machine learning techniques are used to evaluate how expressive performances represented by selected features are clustered in a low-dimensional space. Neocleous et al. propose an emotional modeling technique for music performances that is based on the analysis of how a professional musician represents emotions such as happiness, sadness, anger and fear in violin performances [12].

In addition, many researchers have discussed the benefit of computer-assisted music education in various learning contexts [13, 14, 15, 16]. Through the interactive learning process of experiencing music impressions, students can increase their understanding of important factors that affect the mood of music, such as tonality, rhythm, tempo, pitch, melody, and harmony [13]. Morijiri discusses the feedback effect that listening to recordings of their own performances has on piano performers and states that performers can improve by listening to their recordings. Ng [15] proposes an interactive multimodal feedback system in which the playing gesture is visualized using 3D motion capture technology. Furthermore, Ogura discusses the benefit of providing a model piano performance for beginners, especially in terms of rhythm, taste of music, tempo, and fingering [16].

4   Proposed System

Figure 3 shows an overview of the proposed music search system. A pupil first inputs the performance information as a search query by playing a MIDI instrument. The music search system then provides both model music content and non-model music content.

In the following sections, we describe the main components of the system, which include a performance style extractor and a music search engine that focuses on the performance style.

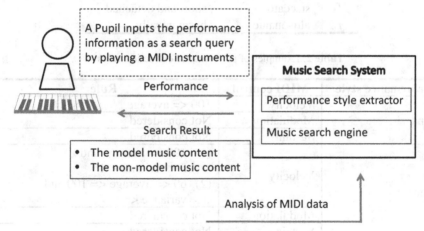

Fig. 3. Overview of our system

4.1   Performance Style Extraction

To retrieve music content to improve a pupil's expressive music performance, we extract the performance style from MIDI data.

Several music symbol types (tempo, dynamics, and style) are used to evaluate performance in musical expression. In particular, style is used to instruct emotional expression for music performance. We choose 38 performance styles from the music expression marks; several styles are shown in Table 1.

The performance styles are extracted based on a pre-defined set of rules that analyzes the values of expressive MIDI controls, such as velocity, modulation, and sustain. Velocity (0 to 127) is a MIDI control of loudness; higher values indicate louder sounds. Modulation (0 to 127) provides a sound fluctuation effect like *vibrato*. In addition, sustain (on or off) provides the sound duration. We design a rule set for performance style extraction using these MIDI controls. Examples of these rules are shown in Table 2. The extracted music performance style is used for the music search process.

Table 1. Examples of performance styles

ID	Style	Meaning
f_1	grandioso	with grandeur
f_2	doloroso	sorrowfully
f_3	cantabile	in a singing style
f_4	furioso	furious
f_5	espressivo	expressively
f_6	schwach	composed
f_7	placido	pacific
f_8	staccato	short and detached
f_9	altisonante	harmonically

Table 2. Examples of performance extraction rules

Performance style	MIDI control	Rule
Grand	Velocity	100 <= average
	Modulation	Not considered
	Sustain	Not considered
Estito	Velocity	(1) 100 <= average and 5 < variance < 10 (2) 60 <= average <= 100 and variance <= 5
	Modulation	Not considered
	Sustain	Not considered
Altisonante	Velocity	A few notes have average differences that are greater than 10
	Modulation	More than once
	Sustain	No considered
Piangendo	Velocity	A few notes have average differences that are greater than 20
	Modulation	More than once
	Sustain	Not considered

4.2 Music Search Based on Performance Style

In the music search process, the system calculates the similarity between input MIDI performance data $MIDI_q$ and each MIDI data file $MIDI_i$ in the music database. The similarity calculation is performed as follows:

Step 1: The MIDI data are vectorized to $\textbf{style}_q$ and $\textbf{style}_i$, respectively, by applying the performance rule shown in Table 2. The feature vectors $\textbf{style}_q$ and $\textbf{style}_i$ are 38 dimensional vectors that are featured using the 38 performance styles f_x. Examples of performance styles are shown in Table 1.

Step 2: The similarity of the performance style between $\textbf{style}_q$ and $\textbf{style}_i$ is calculated using a cosine measure.

$$SIM_{style}\left(\textbf{style}_q, \textbf{style}_i\right) = \left(\textbf{style}_q \cdot \textbf{style}_i\right) / \left\|\textbf{style}_q\right\| \left\|\textbf{style}_i\right\| \qquad (1)$$

Step 3: The similarity of the melody between $MIDI_q$ and $MIDI_i$ is calculated using a Dynamic Time Warping (DTW) algorithm [6, 17].

$$SIM_{melody}\left(\textbf{melody}_q, \textbf{melody}_i\right) = DTW\left(\textbf{melody}_q, \textbf{melody}_i\right) \qquad (2)$$

Step 4: Finally, the similarity between $MIDI_q$ and $MIDI_i$ is calculated as the summation of SIM_{style} and SIM_{melody}.

$$SIM\left(MIDI_q, MIDI_i\right) = \alpha \cdot SIM_{style}\left(\textbf{style}_q, \textbf{style}_i\right) + \frac{1-\alpha}{DTW\left(\textbf{melody}_q, \textbf{melody}_i\right)} \qquad (3)$$

$$(0 \le \alpha \le 1)$$

When we apply equation (3) in the music retrieval process, the parameter α should be set to a proper value according to the learning level and purpose. For example, when a pupil searches for the model music content in the early stages of learning, the search system should emphasize the melody factor because it is easier for the pupil to follow an example. After the learning is repeated, the pupil might want to listen to several pieces with similar performance expressions but different melodies; in this case, the search system should emphasize the performance style factor.

5   Experiment

We evaluated the performance of our system based on (i) the accuracy of the performance style extraction from a MIDI classical music source and (ii) the precision of the music search based on the extracted performance style.

5.1   Experiment 1

In experiment 1, a skilled musician created 75 MIDI files of famous classical music with different performance styles. To evaluate the accuracy of the performance style extraction, we used short music clips (average time: 12 seconds) with the same melodic parts from one classical music song (title: *Amazing Grace*) to create the 75 MIDI files. For the evaluation, the same musician defined the correct performance style of each MIDI file by listening to them. We calculate precision and recall as follows:

Recall = (Number of performance styles extracted by the proposed rule)
        / (Number of correct performance styles estimated by the musician)

Precision = (Number of performance styles)
          / (Number of performance styles extracted by the proposed rule)

Table 3. Examples of performance styles extracted by the pre-defined rules

Music ID	Extracted performance style	Correct performance style
Amazing 24	Expressively	Calm
Amazing 44	With grandeur, expressively, harmonically	With grandeur, expressively
Amazing 63	Calm, extinguished	Calm, extinguished

Table 4. Average accuracy of performance style extraction

Average Recall	Average Precision
0.68	0.49

Table 3 shows examples of the performance style extraction results using the rules defined in Table 2. The proper performance styles are extracted for Amazing Grace 44 and 63. However, for Amazing Grace 24, the performance style "Expressively" is extracted instead of "Calm". The reason for this result is that the person who defined the correct performance style could not perceive the expressivity by ear because Amazing Grace 24 is too calm, although it is rich in variation.

Table 4 shows the average accuracy of the performance style extraction. The average recall is high, but the average precision is slightly lower; this is because our system cumulatively extracts the proper performance styles that match the extraction rule as shown in "Amazing Grace 44" in Table 3.

5.2   Experiment 2

In this experiment, we used 60 MIDI files to evaluate the precision of the music search based on the extracted performance style. The 60 MIDI files are short music segments (average time: 9.34 seconds) from three classical music songs (*Amazing Grace*, *Hungarian Dances No.5*, and *Fauré by Pelléas et Mélisande*) that include 20 different performance styles. For the evaluation, we input each MIDI file as a query and ranked the MIDI files based on a similarity score, which was calculated as described in Section 4.2. We set the parameter α in equation (3) to 1, so we can evaluate only the music search based on the performance style. In addition, we define the correct music content of each query MIDI file as follows:

1. The same musician from Experiment 1 defined the correct performance style for each MIDI file.
2. Each MIDI file was vectorized based on the performance styles, and their similarity scores were calculated as described in Section 4.2.
3. We defined the correct MIDI file m_c for a query MIDI file m_q, where the similarity score between m_c and m_q is greater than 0.8.

Tables 5 and 6 show the ranking results for music queries Amazing 13 and Faure 10, respectively. The performance styles of Amazing 13 extracted by our rule are expressively, calm, and short and detached. Table 5 shows that our method can identify the proper music content based on the performance style of Amazing 13 and not by the melodic similarity. Similarly, Table 6 shows that our method can obtain proper music content for the query music file Faure 10, whose performance styles are calm, raging, and short and detached.

In addition, Figure 4 shows the average recall precision rate of the search results using all 60 MIDI files as queries. These results confirm that our system can retrieve appropriate music content based on the performance style that a user plays on a MIDI device.

Table 5. Top 5 results (Query music: Amazing 13)

Rank	Music ID	Score	Extracted performance style	Correct performance style
1	Hungarian 16	0.816	Expressively, short and detached	Expressively, calm
2	Hungarian 17	0.707	Raging, short and detached, pacific	Expressively, pacific, short and detached
3	Amazing 1	0.707	With grandeur, short and detached	Expressively, such as tempo, short and detached
4	Amazing 6	0.707	Expressively, short and detached, such as tempo, mournful	Expressively, such as tempo, short and detached
5	Faure 14	0.632	Expressively, such as tempo, short and detached	Short and detached, quick and lively

Table 6. Top 5 results (Query music: Faure 10)

Rank	Music ID	Score	Extracted performance style	Correct performance style
1	Amazing 16	0.816	Calm, expressively, mournful	Expressively, such as tempo, with grandeur, short and detached
2	Faure 2	0.730	Calm, expressively	Mournful, heavily, spread
3	Faure 9	0.730	Calm, raging, short and detached	Mournful, expressively, spread
4	Amazing 17	0.730	Calm, expressively, spread	Extinguished, such as tempo, with grandeur, short and detached
5	Faure 3	0.707	Calm, expressively	Expressively, spread

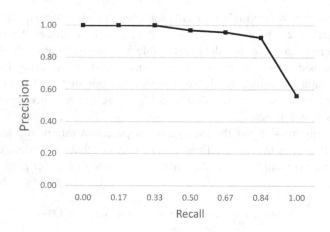

Fig. 4. Average recall precision rate of the search results

6　Conclusion

We presented a music search system that focuses on performance style, in which the performance styles are extracted based on a pre-defined set of rules, and the music contents are retrieved based on the performance style. Our music search system allows a pupil to obtain both model and non-model music content by inputting a performance as a search query by playing a MIDI instrument. Experiments were used to evaluate the accuracy of our system for performance style extraction and music search.

In the future, we will perform experiments using our system at an elementary school. We will validate the effectiveness of the proposed music system and improve the system based on feedback from teachers and pupils.

References

1. Chika, O., Kazushi, N., Yohei, M., Takashi, S.: A Facilitating System for Composing MIDI Sequence Data by Separate Input of Expressive Elements and Pitch Data. IPSJ Journal 44(7), 1778–1790 (2003) (in Japanese)
2. Suzuki, T., Tokunaga, T., Tanaka, H.: A Case-based Approach to the Generation of Musical Expression. IPSJ Journal 44(7), 1778–1790 (2003) (in Japanese)
3. Ghias, A., Logan, J., Chamberlin, D., et al.: Query By Humming – Musical Information Retrieval in an Audio Database. Proceedings of ACM Multimedia 95 (1995)
4. Kuo, F.-F., Shan, M.-K.: Looking for new, not known music only. In: IEEE-CS Joint Conference on Digital Libraries, pp. 243–251 (2004)
5. Zhu, Y., Kankanhalli, M.: Music scale modeling for melody matching. In: Proceedings of the Eleventh ACM International Conference on Multimedia (MULTIMEDIA 2003), pp. 359–362 (2003)
6. Jang, J.-S.R., Lee, H.-R.: Hierarchical Filtering Method for Content-based Music Retrieval via Acoustic Input. In: Proceedings of the Ninth ACM International Conference on Multimedia (MULTIMEDIA 2001), pp. 401–410 (2001)
7. Cui, B., Liu, L., Pu, C., Shen, J., Tan, K.-L.: QueST: querying music databases by acoustic and textual features. In: Proceedings of the 15th International Conference on Multimedia (MULTIMEDIA 2007), pp. 1055–1064 (2007)
8. Yang, C.: Peer-to-peer architecture for content-based music retrieval on acoustic data. In: Proceedings of the 12th International Conference on World Wide Web (WWW 2003), pp. 376–383 (2003)
9. Kitagawa, T., Kiyoki, Y.: Fundamental Framework for Media Data Retrieval Systems Using Media-lexico Transformation Operator. In: The Case of Musical MIDI Data, Information Modeling and Knowledge Bases, vol. 12, pp. 316–326. IOS Press (2001)
10. Mion, L., De Poli, G., Rapana, E.: Perceptual organization of affective and sensorial expressive intentions in music performance. ACM Transactions on Applied Perception 14, 1–21 (2010)
11. Yang, Y.-H., Homer, H.: Machine Recognition of Music Emotion. ACM Transactions on Intelligent Systems and Technology, Article No. 40 (2012)
12. Neocleous, A., Ramirez, R., Perez, A., Maestre, E.: Modeling emotions in violin audio recordings. In: Proceedings of 3rd International Workshop on Machine Learning and Music, vol. 147, pp. 17–20 (2010)
13. Kirke, A., Miranda, E.R.: Survey of Computer Systems for Expressive Music Performance. Survey of Computer Systems for Expressive Music Performance 42(1) (2009)
14. Morijiri, Y.: The effect of self-evaluation on piano performers: using feedback by listening to a recording after performance. Journal of the Graduate School of Humanities and Sciences 12, 111–119 (2009) (in Japanese)
15. Ng, K.: Interactive feedbacks with visualisation and sonification for technology-enhanced learning for music performance. In: Proceedings of the 26th Annual ACM International Conference on Design of Communication, pp. 281–282 (2008)
16. Ryuichiro, O.: A Trial to Utilize a Performance Model for ML Learning: Give the Singing and Playing Video of the Song of the Child to the Learner. Annual Report of the Faculty of Education, Bunkyo University 46, 77–84 (2013) (in Japanese)
17. Myers, C.S., Rabiner, L.R.: A comparative study of several dynamic time-warping algorithms for connected word recognition. The Bell System Technical Journal 60(7), 1389–1409 (1981)

The Value Improvement in Education Service by Grasping the Value Acceptance State with ICT Utilized Education Environment

Yoshiki Sakurai

NEC Learning, Ltd., Learning Scientist, Japan
sakurai.y.ab@m.titech.ac.jp

Abstract. Value co-creation in education service with an ICT utilized environment is argued. Service provider (teacher) does data collection and analysis on learning behavior of each service receiver (students), proposes the improved service content successively based on the result of analysis, and gradually improves his competency. This paper describes some methodologies of learning behavior data collection and analysis.

Keywords: service engineering, value co-creation, learning analytics, formative evaluation, xAPI, LRS.

1 Introduction

Recently, value co-creation has become an important issue in the service research field. Shimomura et al showed the basic definition of service, from the viewpoint of service engineering, as "the act in which a service provider causes the service receiver's desired change of state in exchange for consideration" [1]. We expand this definition to the ecosystem of service stakeholders considering service provider's change of state, and discuss service value co-creation in this paper. Many studies related to the change of a service receiver's state, in other words the perception of the service value, have been performed in the past. But there have been relatively few studies about changes to the service provider.

Simultaneousness is generally known as one of the typical characteristics of service. For example, a hotel employee will observe the state of guests and will make minute adjustment of his service on site in order to improve customer satisfaction, as well as increasing the service value. Consequently, the employee himself will achieve the change of his state through the reactions of the customers, acquiring the ability of better service provision. Improvement of his ability (competency) is the most important of all possible desirable changes of state for a service provider. In this paper, we consider the learning at the time of a service encounter as the most important factor which influences competency improvement. First, we make a premise that a service provider can learn at the time of a service encounter because of the simultaneousness of service. As can be easily imagined, we also think this on-site learning will be the most effective and efficient means of learning.

S. Yamamoto (Ed.): HIMI 2014, Part II, LNCS 8522, pp. 90–98, 2014.
© Springer International Publishing Switzerland 2014

Although once difficult, grasping the state of a service receiver can be achieved easily thanks to the recent developments in ICT. Therefore, a service provider can grasp the value acceptance state of the service receiver in real time, and can correct the service contents accurately by collection and analysis of this information in a service encounter. As a result, it's possible to cause a desirable change of state for both of the service provider and service receiver, including learning for the service provider. Picking up the education service, we will discuss the effect of the utilization of information systems for the collection and analysis of real time state of the service receiver in this paper.

2   Model for Value Co-creation in the Education Service within an Environment Utilizing ICT

Arai, Shimomura, and Murakami have proposed "S3FIRE1306" as a model of value co-creation in service. Based on this model, we propose the modification corresponding to the education service in Figure 1, adding the competency and information channel in the context of classroom lectures, which are the most general type of education service.

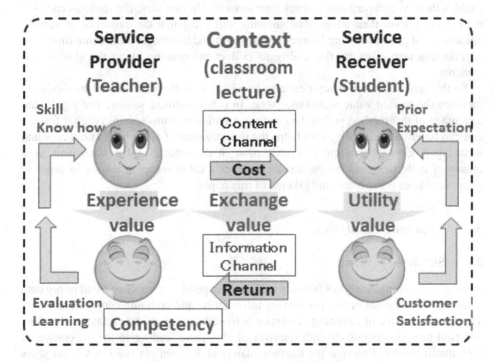

Fig. 1. Value co-creation model of the education service

A service provider (namely, a teacher) gives his service (namely, classroom lectures) to service receivers (namely students). A skilled teacher may manage the lecture contents which weren't incorporating into syllabus planning, according to the information about the state of students, such as whether students understood the contents sufficiently or not at this time, what concepts best held the attention of the students, etc. The teacher will accumulate experience and gradually improve his teaching skills, which are his competency. It's very important for teachers to change such know-how from tacit knowledge to explicit knowledge in order to share this information among many teachers. Such activities have long been carried out as "lesson research." But in many cases, only the data of class observation and questionnaires were used as information for investigation. Until now, collecting data on the state of students in real time has been virtually impossible.

The educational environment has seen remarkable changes in these past 5 to 10 years, made possible through the introduction of equipment that utilizes ICT. One major example of this is the introduction of electronic blackboards and tablet PCs in primary and secondary education. This introduction of equipment is a revolution in the methods and tools used to provide service. In other words, it is an actuator. It is dramatically transforming the traditional lesson to a learner-centered environment. For example, if students write the answer to a quiz incorporated in their electronic textbook, and then the answers of every student are lined up on the electronic blackboard, this enables them to compare and discuss their answers. In this way, the students can find the correct answer themselves. The students will recognize the existence of various opinions, and get the learning literacy of self-regulated learning. At the same time, ICT introduction also gives us the ability to collect information about the state of the students.

So this introduction of equipment also provides us with the tools and methods to measure the service value acceptance state. In other words, a sensor. The significant advantage of this method is that data and information is collected in a digital format, and can be visualized easily. This helps the investigation of a teacher's know-how and lecturing process. Expanding ICT utilization in the educational environment as a means of collecting data on the service receiver's value acceptance state in order to improve classes is the main study theme of this paper.

3 Learning Analytics

3.1 SCORM

Interest in Learning Analytics is rising rapidly. It depends on the same trend of big data analysis as a hot issue in the research for information and communication technology. The aim or purpose of Learning Analytics is to collect various data related to learning and find new viewpoints through analysis of this data, leading to the generation of high-quality learning service and learning materials. It is only in the last several years that the word itself has attracted attention, but similar studies and measures were precedent already in the field of e-learning, or ICT-enhanced education. The creation of SCORM (Sharable Content Object Reference Model) is largely thought to have lead to the spread of e-learning. SCORM was an e-learning platform and a content standardization specification. The main purpose of SCORM was the assurance of e-learning content portability. When providing an education through e-Learning, besides the e-Learning courseware itself, an LMS (Learning Management System) is needed to deliver content and to manage and register the learning historical data. SCORM, having been created as an international standard to allow easy cross-LMS transferability of content, has made a great contribution to the spread of e-Learning. But while it has provided for the portability of content, at the same time it has also limited the scope of standardization for information on students' learning histories (beginning and ending of learning, test scores, etc).

3.2   xAPI

Efforts to create the next generation SCORM standard had started in ADL (Advanced Distributed Learning) [2], and its first version (V1.0.0) was published in 2013 under the name xAPI. It doesn't limit the collection of data to that of just e-learning activities, but also data collection from the classroom learning activities. We have to consider the concept of LRS (Learning Record Storage) in this standard carefully. It aims to collect data related to the various kinds of learning experiences and unify the database management. LRS may be appropriate to realize the concept of Learning Analytics and apply it in the improvement of classroom learning.

3.3   IMS Caliper

IMS GLOBAL, which is an international standardization organization, announced the Learning Measurement Framework IMS Caliper in 2013[3][4]. This framework consists of the following three concepts.

(a) IMS Learning Metric Profile
(b) IMS Learning Sensor API and Learning Events
(c) IMS LTI/LIS/QTI

(b) and (c) are almost the same concept as that of xAPI. But it should be noted that (a) further aims to standardize the metrics of learning activities. While it's still under consideration, it may possibly become a foundation of big data analysis in the learning field in the future.

4   Study of Learning History Data Analysis

4.1   Preceding Study-1

Practical Learning Analytics study in the field of education is also being advanced concurrently with the worldwide standardization activities described in the previous chapter. The analysis of the learning history data recorded on LMS by Gohda et al (2013) [5] is the latest study on Learning Analytics in e-learning in Japan. The transition of learning dates for every partial unit of the e-learning program is analyzed for about 3 months. According to the analysis of this data, the authors had classified learner's learning behavior into 7 patterns; "deadline focus," "periodical learning" "getting ahead," "random," "declining motivation," "mountain shaped," and "middle stage catching up"

4.2   Preceding Study -2

Katase et al tried to analyze the learning behavior in the classroom lecture through the page view history data of each student using a simulated e-textbook [6]. They investigated the correlation between the synchronous rate and personality factors of each student. Synchronous rate was calculated by the time rate of the situation that the target student had been viewing the same page of what teacher showed in the front screen. Personality factors was classified by the Big Five. As a result of analysis, they've found that it seems that the students with high levels of "Extroversion" or "Openness to Experience" on the Big Five tended to have low synchronous rates. It can be presumed that both of them are likely to learn with self-regulated style rather than follow the teacher faithfully.

5   Visualization of Learning Behavior

5.1   Experiment

We assume that it'll be useful and effective for a teacher, as a service provider, to recognize the value acceptance state of the students as service receivers. So we tried to verify the effect of the visualization of learning behavior. We created an experimental environment using the same environment of the preceding study introduced in 4.2.

Subjects of this experiment were the 62 first-year students of a vocational school. PCs and simulated e-textbook data were provided to all of the students, so they could see any page of the text on the PC display. Experiment had been held in the lecture of communication skill. The lecture consisted of two 50-minute lessons with a 10-minute break between lessons. In the first lesson, the teacher explained the operation of simulated e-textbook but he didn't mention it any more. In the second lesson, teacher announced to students to use the function of page turning on the simulated e-textbook freely. 30 minutes into the lecture, the teacher instructed the students to perform an exercise. The exercise was easy to answer if students had seen the previous pages of the simulated e-textbook.

A data server collected "page view data" for every time the student changed the page they were browsing. This data consisted of student ID, new page number, and the time. The teacher's "page view data" was also collected in the same way based on their use of the PC. Data was only collected for the second 50-minute lesson.

5.2   Result

There are 5 graphs of typical leaning behavior patterns observed in this experiment. The browsing page transition graphs of the teacher is shown here superimposed with those of the target student. The red line with circle dots is the data of the teacher, while the undotted blue line with is the data of the target student. Horizontal axis shows the time. The start time of the operation explanation was 73, the start time of second lesson was 103, and the start time of exercise in the second lesson was 128. The vertical axis shows the page number of e-textbook from 1 to 16. Each graph of the 5 students is shown in Figure 2-6 with our estimation below.

Student 12001 didn't perform page turning in the first 15 minutes of the second lesson, but at Time 118 he suddenly performed page turn backward to almost the start page (page 4) and then followed the teacher's page. However, during the exercise, he also performed backward page turning. The synchronous rate was 27%.

It seems that student 12001 wasn't interested in the lesson initially, but in the latter part of the lesson he studied eagerly with the learning activity of looking back on the textbook.

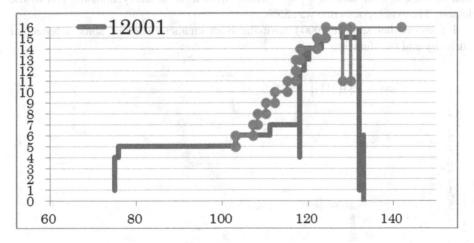

Fig. 2. Visualizing the transition of browsing page (teacher vs. student 12001)

Student 12015 followed the teacher's page turning in the first 15 minutes of second lesson, but stopped page turning on Time 117 until the end of the lesson. The synchronous rate was 52%, and the synchronous pattern was almost inverted with that of student 12001(described above).

It seems that student 12015 had the willing to learn in the first half of the lesson, but he got tired of the lesson or the e-textbook.

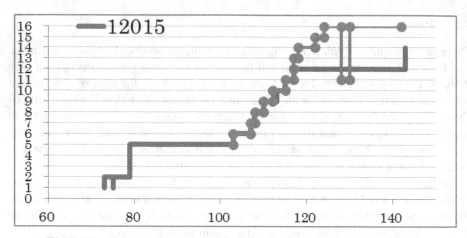

Fig. 3. Visualizing the transition of browsing page (teacher v.s student 12015)

Student 19004 took a specific activity at the start of lesson. He read through to the end of the textbook (page 16) on Time 106, when the teacher showed the page 6. After that he followed the teacher's page turning with a slight delay until the end of the lesson. The synchronous rate was 55%.

I t seems that student 19004 have the both characteristics of some intellectual curiosity and faithfulness.

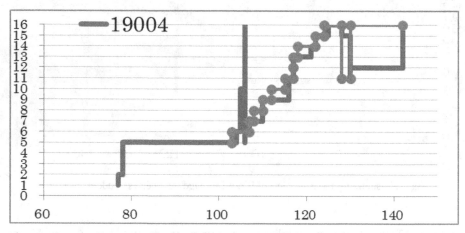

Fig. 4. Visualizing the transition of browsing page (teacher vs. student 19004)

Student 16001 actively read through the textbook during the period of operation explanation in the first lesson. In the period of the second lesson, he followed the teacher's page turning faithfully. Only on Time 112 did he perform page turning backward to the first page of the lesson (page 5). The synchronous rate was 71%.

It seems that student 16001 have the characteristics of slightly strong faithfulness because the synchronous rate was fairly high.

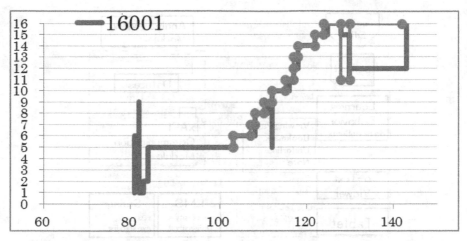

Fig. 5. Visualizing the transition of browsing page (teacher vs. student 16001)

Student 12019 took the page turning activity to the end of the textbook twice during the period of operation explanation in the first lesson. In the period of the second lesson, he almost followed the teacher's page turning, but there was a unique activity of page turning backward 6 times. The synchronous rate was 53%.

It seems that student 12019 has the characteristics of a steady learning style.

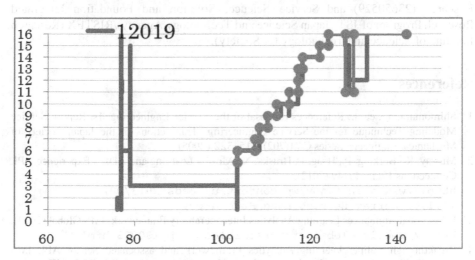

Fig. 6. Visualizing the transition of browsing page (teacher vs. student 12019)

6   Conclusion and Future Issue

In this paper, the effectiveness of collecting and analyzing the value acceptance state of service receivers was investigated. The usefulness of learning behavior data is suggested in education service. In the following research, We will develop the prototype

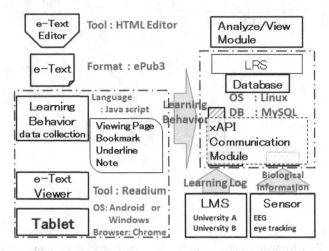

Fig. 7. Learning experience data collecting and analyzing system

LRS(Learning Record Store) and experiment system shown in Figure 7 taking account of typical global standards mentioned in chapter 3.

Acknowledgement. This research received support from Grant-in-Aid of Scientific Research (23650529) and Service Science, Solution and Foundation Integrated Research Program of JST (Japan Science and Technology Agency)/RISTEX (Research Institute of Science and Technology for Society).

References

1. Shimomura, Y., et al.: References Proposal of the Service Engineering: 1st Report, Service Modeling Technique for the Service Engineering. Transactions of the Japan Society of Mechanical Engineers, Series C 71(702), 315–322 (2005)
2. Murray, K., Berking, P., Haag, J., Hruska, N.: Mobile Learning and ADL's Experience API. Connections 12(1), 45–49 (2012),
   http://www.adlnet.gov/wp-content/uploads/2013/08/
   12.1.05_Murray_Berking_Haag_Hruska.pdf
3. IMS Global Announces Learning Analytics Interoperability Framework. IMS Global (2013), http://www.imsglobal.org/pressreleases/pr130923.html
4. Breakthrough Caliper Learning Analytics Framework and associated Sensor API. IMS Global (2013), http://www.imsglobal.org/IMSLearningAnalyticsWP.pdf
5. Gohda, Y., Yamada, M., Matsuda, T., Kato, H., Sato, Y., Miyagawa, H.: Categorization of Learning Behavior in e-Leaning. In: Proceedings of the 38th Annual Conference of JSiSE (2013)
6. Katase, T., Sakurai, Y., Yamamoto, H.: Influence of the character factor on using the digital textbook and notebook. In: Proceedings of the 28th Annual Conference of JSET (2012)

Developing an Education Material
for Robot Literacy

Hidetsugu Suto[1] and Makiba Sakamoto[2]

[1] Muroran Institute of Technology, Muroran, Japan
[2] Gifu City Women's College, Gifu, Japan
info@sdlabo.net

Abstract. An education material for training regarding robot literacy
has been developed. Robot literacy means an ability to have appropriate
relationships with intelligent robots. It can be considered as a kind of
media literacy because robots can transmit the designers' intentions to
the users. People who were born on and after the Internet appearance
called "digital natives." They have novel moral values and behave different way from old generation people in the Internet societies. These facts
cause several troubles between the two generations. Thus, the necessity
for media literacy education has increased. These days, as same as the
Internet technologies, robotics technologies are also advancing rapidly. It
is forecasted that the people who is growing on and after home robots
have become popular, "robot native," will appear. As same as media literacy education, robot literacy education for robot native also ought to
become important in the future. In this paper, a card game as a robot literacy education material for elementary/junior hi schoolers' is proposed.
The players can learn critical thinking for home appliance robots during
enjoying the game.

1 Introduction

Several practical home appliance robots, such as nursing-care robots, living assistance robots, etc. have been developed, and a life with home robots has got
a grip on reality. It is easy to assume that our life will change significantly by
introducing such new technology home robots. However, actual effects of such
robots on our life are still unclear. Stories of "life with robots" always have been
told from developers' viewpoints. The stories were created based on the developers' assumptions and wishful thinkings. However, the actual stories of our life
after introducing such home appliance robots have not been known yet. Hence,
we have to discuss about the change of our life from the viewpoint of potential
users in order to get ready for facing unprecedented situation, living with home
robots.

Looking back at history, dissociation of consciousness between different generations was accelerated by appearing new technology media. One of the reason is
that they understand a medium with different ways. In other words, people who
belongs to one generation understands mechanisms of a medium through experience of the evolution process, and the people who belongs another generation

S. Yamamoto (Ed.): HIMI 2014, Part II, LNCS 8522, pp. 99–108, 2014.
© Springer International Publishing Switzerland 2014

accepts the medium as a black-box system because they faced with the medium as a mature system when they were in childhood. Because of the difference, their behaviors with a medium are also different. The differences could be a reason of dissociation of consciousness between different the generations.

Current practical home robots, e.g. Sony AIBO and iRobot Roomba, can be distinguished as machines at a single glance. In addition, their functions and purposes can be estimated easily from their appearances. So the users can operate them appropriate ways which are supposed by the designers. Natural communication ability with human is also studied [1] as well as their mechanisms and functions. Unfortunately, the attempts have not achieved yet. Thus, when we show a robots, we never think that it is a human being. However in a station in which there are super real humanoid which cannot be distinguished as a robot easily. They can communicate with us naturally like a human. Does a person who is living with such a robot from an early age can consider it as just a machine?

The authors have proposed an educational concept of "robot literacy" for such generation students [2]. Robot literacy means an ability which required when we live with home robots. In this paper, a card game as a robot literacy education material is proposed. The card game has been developed by using a method which is developed for creating training games for office workers. The players can improve their critical thinking for home appliance robots during enjoying the game.

2   Robot Literacy

2.1   What Is Robot Literacy?

People who is immersed in digital communication technologies, e.g. cellular phone and the Internet in their childhood called digital native [3, 4]. They was born after the end of the 20th century, and nowadays they are advancing into the society. Meanwhile, the people who was born before the end of the 20th century are called digital immigrates. While digital immigrate considers the new technology media as extension of traditional media such as telephone, television and newspaper, digital native considers them as quit novel tools because they did not experience the evolutional process.

Digital natives use the Internet naturally as if using water and air. They are living in the new societies generated by the new technology media, and they have new sense of values for the relationships in the societies. They easily make connection with others by using relationships in the Internet and create new business and organization [5]. It has been pointed out that they think information always exists in the Internet and it is free, they do not distinguish their relationship in the Internet from the relationship in real-societies, they are not interested in the age and title of others. These characteristics very often cause the trouble with digital immigrate people.

Similarly, it is expected to appear "robot native" in the near future because symbiosis with home robots has became more likely. Figure 1 shows the relationships between time line and conceptual model of digital immigrate, digital

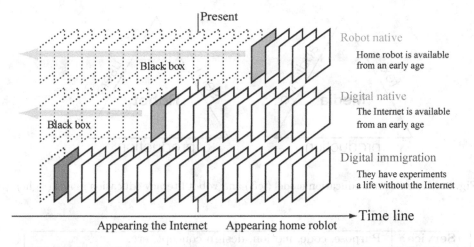

Fig. 1. Relationship between appearance of new technology media and the users' conceptual models

native and robot native. The square boxes in the figure show a conceptual model of a technology. As shown in this figure, new concept models are created always based on old conceptual models. Thus we cannot understand the mechanism of a new coming technology without learning. Otherwise, we only can accept the technology as just a black-box system.

Unlike information media on the Internet, robot has physical structure and physical interface. Thus same effects on the users are bigger than the Internet cases. In addition, if it is used improper ways, it should cause serious damages on the operator. Thats are why that the literacy education for the home appliance robot users is important.

2.2 Robot Literacy Education Model

Figure 2 (left) illustrates idea of media literacy education model developed by Suzuki [6]. In this model, the domains of media which should be learned are represented. This model consists of three domains, text, audience and production, and each domain includes several elements. For instance, text domain includes story, genre, concept etc., audience domain includes culture, gender, education, etc., and production domain includes technology, law, management, etc.

The authors have proposed a robot literacy education model based on the media literacy education model as shown in Fig. 2 (right). This model also consists three domains corresponding the three domains in the media literacy education model, service, user and production. Each domain has several elements as shown in the following table.

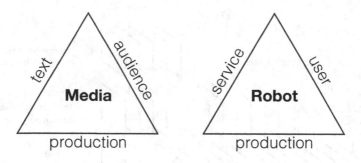

Fig. 2. Media literacy education model (left) and robot literacy education model (right)

Service	Purpose, code, motion, design concept, etc.
User	Culture, gender, generation, education, experience, etc.
Production	Technology, management, distribution, regulation, law, etc.

The authoers have developed a game for learning production domain because it is the most difficult domain to image for higher-grade elementary schoolers and junior high-schoolers.

3   Developing an Education Material

3.1   Transformation Modeling Protocol

Transformation modeling protocol [7] is a method for developing education game which is used in in-house training programs. The process of developing a game with this method is shown in following list:

1. The stories which should be taught for the leaners are described.
2. Subjects, variables, actions are extracted from the stories. If an action is stochastic, the probability is also defined.
3. The structures of subjects, variables, and actions are described as a class diagram, a state machine diagram, a sequence diagram, and a flow chart.
4. The structures of subjects are translated into a card game model.
5. Rules of the card game are generated in accordance with the above card game model.

3.2   Game Desgin

A card game as an education material for robot literacy has been developed by using transformation modeling protocol method. The basic design of the game is shown in the this section.

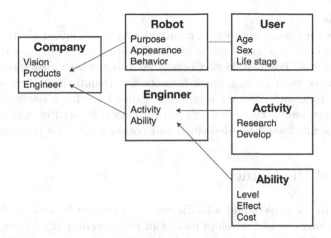

Fig. 3. Class diagram of an example story

Story

In this game, each player roles a designer of home appliance robots. They belong to a robot manufacturing company. Their motivation is developing robots which make profits for their own company. If they success to develop a useful robot for the targets, they can obtain big benefit. Meanwhile, if their products cause any trouble, they may be gotten losses.

Items

The following items have been extracted from the above story. The class diagram which represents a relationship between each item shown in Fig. 3 as a class diagram.

Subject. 'Engineer,' 'company,' and 'user' are included in the game as subjects.

Variable. A robot character is represented with three variables, 'appearance,' 'purpose,' and 'behavior.'

'Appearance' can take an adjective such like cute, cool, casual, formal, etc.

'Purpose' can take a noun which represents a purpose of the robot, such as pet, cleaning, house work, caring, etc.

In 'behavior', characteristics of the robot are described. For example, the following sentences are described in this variable for cooking robot: "Considering nutritive valve," "Taking priority to taste," and "Obey just the user's request."

'Technical capability' represents a designer's ability. Players can improve their ability to choice "develop" as an action.

'Vision' represents the company's policy for developing products. This parameter reflect potential users of the company and affects on the relationship between a type of developed robot and the profits.

Action. Engineers can choice their action from 'technical research' or 'product development.' If the engineer choice technical research, ability of the designer is improved.

Point Table

Point table shows gains and loses of companies by distributing a robot. A gain or lose is determined by a combination of vision, appearance, purpose and behavior mentioned above. For instance, a concierge robot which promotes their own product usually should bring much benefits for a company which has internet shopping system, and cute pet robot may cause loses for a company which do not have many family customers. Such production structures which should be tough to students have been described and translated to the point table.

4   Rule of the Game

From three to six players and a facilitator are involved in a game. Each player roles a robot engineer and develops robots for his/her company. Developed robots are distributed and used in a users' house. If the robot work effectively, the company gains rewards, beside the robot occurs a trouble, the company takes losses. The gains and losses of the company become points of a player who developed the robots. Thus each player has to consider the suitable design of the robot in accordance with their main users.

Four types of cards, robot, technology, development and event cards, are used for the game. The usage of the cards are followings:

Robot card. Each player get a one robot card from the facilitator at the start of the game. A company name to which the player belongs is described on a side of the card. A vision of the company also described on same side of the card. Another side of the card is divided into three area, purpose, appearance and behavior. A development card, which is described below, is attached on each area. Examples of robot cards are shown in Fig. 4.

Technology card. Technology card represents the player's ability to create new robots. An ability point is shown on the cards. Each player can hold five development cards, and the summation of the points which indicated on each card represents the player's ability. If a player choice "research" for his/her action, the player can exchange a technology card with another one in the stack. If the player draw a card with higher point than discarded one, the player's ability is improved. Fig.5 shows examples of the technology cards.

Development card. Development cards are used for developing robots. These cards are divided into three types, purpose, appearance and behavior. A card can be attached on the correspond area of robot card. The three elements are completed, the robot get ready for distribution. The required ability point to use the element is shown on the cards.

The commodity value of the robot depends on the combination of these three cards.

Event card. Event cards show the uncertain incidents for the company. It causes any benefits or losses for the player. The effect of each event depends on the types of dispatched robots.

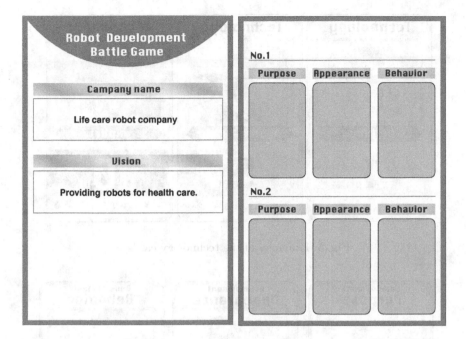

Fig. 4. Examples of the robot cards

In the begging of the game, each player get a robot card and five technology cards, and some development cards from the facilitator. Each player puts them on the table with face up.

The first player have to decide the action, technical research or product development. When the player selects technical research, the player can discard a technology card, which is not enough for the player, and can draw another one from the stack. If the player success to draw a card which is better than the discarded one, the player's development ability is improved.

Beside, the player selects product development, he/she must show one development card in his/her hand and attache it on the his/her robot card. Here, the player's ability must be larger then required ability point indicated on the development card. When the three elements are completed, the robot is distributed. When a robot is distributed, the player draw one event card, and obey the instructions.

Then, the player draw a development card from the stack. The next player do the same way. The first phase finished when all players done above steps, and it moves to the next phase. After each phase the facilitator calculates gains and loses of each player in accordance with the point table. After 10 phases, the player who got the most points is declared as the winner.

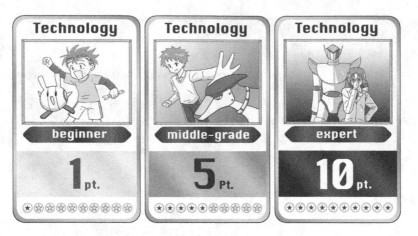

Fig. 5. Examples of the technology cards

Fig. 6. Examples of the development cards

Fig. 7. Examples of the event cards

5   Conclusion

Robot literacy is a new educational concept for home appliance robot ages. In robot literacy education, thinking home robot critically is requested.

In this paper, a card game as a robot literacy education material has been proposed. This game have been developed by using transformation modeling protocol method. The players can learn production system of home appliance robot and can improve their critical thinking abilities effectively during enjoying the game.

The education of robot literacy is very difficult because the actual situations with home appliance robots have not been revealed yet. Game material such as the proposed one is one of the possible solutions for the situation, because the players can consider several possibilities of that.

The game has developed for learning the production domain of robot literacy education model. Of course, games for the other domains also can be developed with the same method.

Acknowledgement. This work was supported by Grants-in-Aid for Scientific Research from the JPSP (No. 23653260 and No. 23611025).

References

[1] Taniguchi, T. : Constructive approach towards symbol emergence system. NTT Publishing Inc. (2010) (Japanese)
[2] Suto, H.: Robot Literacy – An Approach for Society with Intelligent Robots. Internet Studies (to Publish)
[3] John, G.: Born digital: understanding the first generation of digital natives. Basic-Books, New York (2008)
[4] Michael, T.: Deconstructing Digital Natives: Young People, Technology, and the New Literacies. Routledge (2011)

[5] Mimura, T.: Digital native. NHK Publishing Inc. (2009) (Japanese)
[6] Suzuki, M.: Study Guide Media Literacy –beginning guide. Liberta Publishing (2009) (Japanese)
[7] Goto, Y., Takizawa, Y., Takahashi, S.: Hybrid Approach of Agent-based and Gaming Simulations for Stakeholder Accreditation. In: The 4th World Congress on Social Simulation, in CD-ROM, Taipei, Taiwan (2012)

Development of Teaching Material Volume Calculations Using a Wooden Puzzle

Takamitsu Tanaka[1], Masao Tachibana[1], and Ichiro Hirata[2]

[1] Iwate University, Japan
[2] Hyogo Prefectural Institute of Technology, Japan
{taktak,tatimasa}@iwate-u.ac.jp, ichiro@hyogo-kg.jp

Abstract. This paper explains the development of a wooden puzzle containing wooden joints designed to teach elementary school students how to calculate volume. An experiment was performed with the puzzle, which is a cube with wooden joints, targeting 1st-grade students. The shape of the puzzle is known to be difficult for children to work with. Next, we introduce the results of a test of volume calculation designed for children and describe the methods used to teach volume calculation in Japan. Finally, we compare the concepts of volume calculation and how to create a three-dimensional object in 3 D–CAD to reveal that the ideas are almost identical.

Keywords: Wooden Joint, Wooden Puzzle, Volume Calculation, Design.

1 Introduction

In 2008, the authors carried out a study of a toy with a wooden joint. There are more than 200 different wooden joints used in furniture and architecture in Japan. This research represents the first time a wooden joint has been applied to a toy. As we experimented making toys, we were contacted by an elementary school mathematics teacher who expressed interest in using the toy to teach students how to calculate volume. With this background, the current investigation began in 2013.Children were recruited to participate in the experiment. We used 3D-CAD to design puzzles with five different types of cornerstones and then created a three-dimensional (3D) object using a 3D printer. The concept of volume calculation learned in elementary school and the design process of the 3D-CAD puzzles are similar. Therefore, this study describes the basic idea for studying volume calculation using digital learning materials and calculating volume through stereolithography.

2 Experiments Puzzle

The toys can be easily assembled due to the simplicity of the joints and learning to calculate the volume of a solid cube or rectangle can be done by 5th or 6th grade pupils in Japan. The first step is to learn the theory of volume and assembling a solid

S. Yamamoto (Ed.): HIMI 2014, Part II, LNCS 8522, pp. 109–117, 2014.
© Springer International Publishing Switzerland 2014

cube or rectangle can help. Then, the calculation of the volume of a rectangular parallelepiped several associated therewith to be learned how to calculate the volume of basic. There are a number of ways elementary school teachers can teach volume calculation in math classes. In current textbooks, figures are only shown in two dimensions making complex volume calculations difficult. Therefore, elementary school teachers must either teach volume calculation in the classroom, or develop a model of teaching materials for children to learn on their own. Currently, few wooden toys are available for this area of teaching. Of the types that are available, some are color-coded and can be built to show volume from $1 cm^3$ up to $1000 cm^3$. These teaching materials are sufficient when dealing with simple volume calculations but inadequate in slightly more complex computational problems. Because of this problem, using a blackboard illustration to explain a complicated shape does not provide the necessary information. Teachers can instruct students on how to calculate a line as depicted in Fig. 1.

Fig. 1. Materials volume calculations are currently used

Fig. 2. Experimental observation of students

The process of this calculation method is considered similar to the process of assembling a wooden puzzle. The research was conducted in the hope that students may be able to learn volume calculation. The first puzzle discussed is a wooden cube. This type of puzzle is freely available in many countries and is a popular game. When assembling the components, the user can understand how the cube goes together. This type of product is easy to manufacture and looks attractive. As the shape of the prototype of the three-dimensional object is easy to understand, the production of a wooden cube puzzle was examined. In addition, an observation and experiment model for the experimental observation is described. When designing the puzzle for this study, 3D-CAD was used in order to save time. The puzzle was designed with 7 parts, each side measuring 6 cm after assembly. The design was based on the knowledge of how children play and it was decided to use only a small number of parts so that volume calculation would be easier. Elementary schools' create a modeling many kinds of component count is large, but it is expected that variations of modeling is extremely reduced component count is less. On the other hand, it can be inferred that assembling the cube and is easy number of parts is small. The students observed in this study were from 2nd grade and 5th grade and given 15 minutes to complete the puzzle. The results from this observation were as follows: no students from 2nd grade were able to complete the puzzle. However, one 5th grade student was able to complete the puzzle without any help and a further two students finished when given some instructions.

3   Current Status of Teaching Methods of Volume Calculation in Japan

3.1   Teaching System Volume Calculation

Japanese education on system volume calculation presents two calculation methods: "Measure the volume using an instrument" and "Use other ways to determine the volume." The strategy "Use other ways to determine the volume" consists of two sub-strategies: learning formulas for the volume of shapes such as cuboids, cubes, pillars, cones, spheres, etc., and calculating the volume of complex figures that represent a combination of cubes or rectangular solids. This study addresses volume calculation for complex figures.

3.2   Teaching about Volume

This section describes the methods used to teach about volume and volume calculation in Japanese schools, which starts in first grade.

As with length or area, students are taught to measure volume in four stages:

(A)   Direct comparison
(B)   Non-direct comparison
(C)   Measurement in non-standard units
(D)   Measurement in standard units

1st-grade students study (A) to (C), and 2nd-grade students study (D). Specifically, 1st-grade students participate in activities such as comparing volume and receive guidance from the teacher to enrich their learning experience, which forms the basis of their understanding of measurement and volume. 1st-grade students also engage in learning activities to compare methods (A) to (C).In 2nd grade, instead of using method (C) to measure volume, students learn method (D). That is, they learn how to take accurate measurements using a standard unit. Further, the volume of the water in the handle can be obtained by using subtraction or addition to calculate the sum or difference of the volume of water entering the two containers. The main purpose of this lesson is that the amount of storage stability holds for volume. Then, students will also understand that addition and subtraction may be applied. This learning forms a basis for determining the area and volume of a complex figure. Thus, in 1st and 2nd grade, students learn primarily through direct experience and activities, for example, by measuring and comparing in detail the amount of liquid in containers. Finally, they learn what represents the standard unit of measurement for liquid volume.

Next, I will describe how students learn to measure volume. In 3rd and 4th grade, students are taught to measure volume using fractions. Beginning in 3rd grade and continuing in 4th grade, they learn to use one and then two decimal places. In 4th grade, they also practice using liters (L) and deciliters (dL) as the standard units for measuring volume. They use a measurement instrument and express their measurements in a standard way. However, instead of measuring volume in 5th grade, students are taught to obtain the volume using calculation. Prior to this, in 4th grade, they learn about calculating the size of rectangles and squares. They also study the standard units used to represent area. In 5th grade, the students learn the concepts of unit volume. At this point, they study how to quantify the volume of many cubes (e.g., 1 cm3) and then progress to learning the formulas for calculating the volume of a cube or rectangle. Thus, in 5th grade, students clearly understand the idea of volume, volume measurement, and the use of standard measurement units. This allows them to capture the ideas used in integrated learning and volume calculation. Then, to learn how to quantify volume using an activity to investigate the volume of a cube or rectangular solid, the students are shown building blocks that are each a 1 cm cube and asked to consider how many sides there are. Through this study, students learn the formulas "volume = side × side × side of the cube" and "volume = length × width × height." Further, in the 6th grade, students are taught to determine the volume of cylindrical or prismatic shapes. In this case, they apply their knowledge of the formula "volume = base area × pillar of the body. "The volume of a cone is one-third that of a pillar with the same height and bottom area. This I learned for the first time in a middle school mathematics department. The volume of a sphere is two-thirds of the volume of the cylinder. In junior high school, as confirmed by this experiment, students learn the formula for the volume of a sphere and cone. To teach students how to calculate the volume of a cuboid, cube, pillar, cone, or sphere, teachers guide them in advanced thinking with the goal of enabling the students to "create a formula for the volume of their own shape." However, in the current way of teaching about volume, there is no formula for the volume of an original figure. Therefore, students need to learn how to determine the volume of complex figures. The most important method for obtaining the volume of a complex figure involves utilizing previously learned methods.

3.3   The Basic Complex Figure

As shown above, by 5th grade, students should learn about rectangles and cubes and know how to find the volume of a complex figure. However, our investigation of students' actual performance shows a tendency in regard to the only complex figure given. According to the survey results, the children have difficulty finding the volume of basic shapes. In 2013, the Iwate Prefectural Board of Education conducted a survey of 5th grade students. In the survey, the students were asked about how they could determine the area of a complex figure.

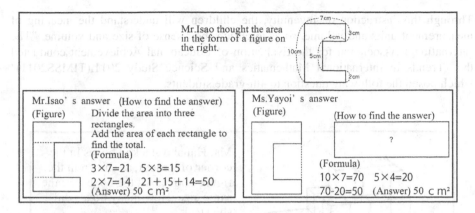

Fig. 3. Iwate Prefectural Board of Education conducted a survey of 5th grade

Ms. Yayoi determined the same area using a different method from Mr. Isao's.

Please write out Ms. Yayoi's method of solving the problem.

The children should answer, "Consider the large rectangle. Subtract the missing area."

The percentage of correct answers was 71.4%, meaning that about 30% of the students answered incorrectly. In 2001, the National Institute for Education Policy Research surveyed 6th grade students. The students were asked to write an equation for the volume of a stereo. The question is as follows. The percentage of correct answers for this question was 79.5%.

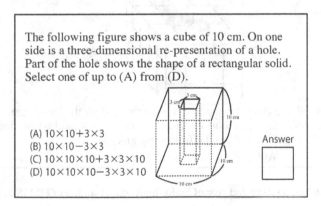

Fig. 4. National Institute for Education Policy Research surveyed

The results of these two questions, which are about a basic figure and complex figure, respectively, show that the children have weak performance in this area.

According to a research report on the curriculum, "Children will consider various rectangular cubes, and it is expected that you [the teacher] will provide a 3D shape composed of these units, and practice with it repeatedly. In addition, the children will actively incorporate the concepts of arithmetic into their calculation of volume.

Through this instruction on ingenuity, the children will understand the meaning of measurement units and volume, so as to enrich their sense of size and volume. "The International Association for the Evaluation of Educational Achievement conducted the "Trends in International Mathematics and Science Study 2011,(TIMSS2011)" which posed the following question to 4th-grade students.

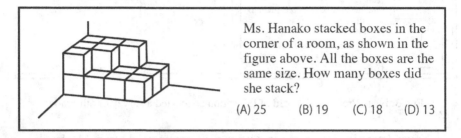

Ms. Hanako stacked boxes in the corner of a room, as shown in the figure above. All the boxes are the same size. How many boxes did she stack?

(A) 25   (B) 19   (C) 18   (D) 13

Fig. 5. Surveyed to 4th-grade students (TIMSS2011)

Among the 4th -grade students, 83.7% answered the question correctly (this number is 62.7% for international students).

In addition, the test administrators gave the following question to students in their 2nd year of junior high school.

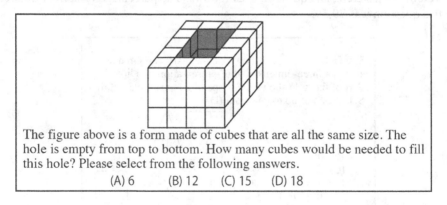

The figure above is a form made of cubes that are all the same size. The hole is empty from top to bottom. How many cubes would be needed to fill this hole? Please select from the following answers.

(A) 6   (B) 12   (C) 15   (D) 18

Fig. 6. Surveyed to 2nd year of junior high school students (TIMSS2011)

The correct answer rate for the Japanese students was 80.1% (46.8% for international students).As these results show, in learning about volume calculation, it is important that the children touch the molded products that are actually complex figures. Also, teachers should point out that the figure is a combination of a basic figure and complex figure to show the children how volume is important.

4   Relationship of Volume Calculation and 3D-CAD

Chapter 3 described the method of teaching volume calculation. By manipulating 3D objects in education on volume calculation, children can form hypotheses about how to calculate volume. In this chapter, we describe the common points shared by the design process of 3D-CAD and the concept of volume calculation.3D-CAD is a software program that allows the user to create a 3D shape on the computer. It recognizes two types of shape: a "solid type" and "surface type. "The design process for a "solid type" shape is similar to the process of creating a graphic in volume calculation. A solid 3D shape is created by combining the following two methods:

(1) Creating the shape using one-to-one geometry
(2) Cutting unwanted parts from a single mass

Fig. 7 is a diagram of a 3D shape that is used in a math textbook in Japan. We describe the design process of 3D-CAD using this shape as an example.

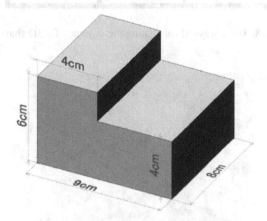

Fig. 7. Diagram of a 3D shape that is used in a math textbook in Japan

The design process of the shape shown in Fig. 8 may be any of the following three methods:

1) After creating a 4 cm x 6 cm x 8 cm cube, we add a 5 cm x 4 cm x 8 cm cube (Fig. 8a).
2) After creating a 9 cm x 4 cm x 8 cm cube, we add a 4 cm x 2 cm x 8 cm cube (Fig. 8b).
3) After creating a 9 cm x 6 cm x 8 cm cube, we delete the 5 cm x 2 cm x 8 cm cube (Fig.8c).

Even for the volume calculations for Fig. 7, the process is similar to the one described above. Based on the above description, we can say that the design process of

3D-CAD is effective as a method of volume calculation. Next, we will consider a complex 3D shape such as the one shown in Fig. 9 and discuss whether the same process applies.

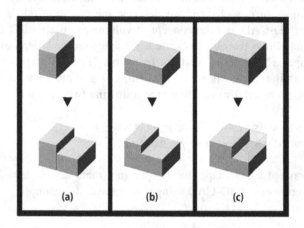

Fig. 8. Three ways of calculating the volume of a 3D shape

Fig. 9. 3D-Printer's model

Fig. 9 shows examples of complex 3D models created by a professional engineer using cubes in 3D-CAD. He used the methods "Creating the shape using to one-to-one geometry" and "Cutting unwanted parts from a single mass" as described above.

Therefore, it seems that the concept of volume calculation learned in elementary school is the same process used in 3D-CAD.This demonstrates that the process of creating complex 3D shapes in 3D-CAD (Fig. 10) can be applied to issues such as volume calculation in the near future.

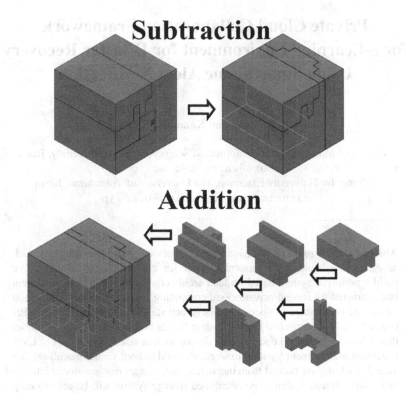

Fig. 10. Process of creating a complex 3D shape in 3D-CAD

5   Conclusion and Future Plan

This paper described the toy with wooden joints that we designed and discussed its application to educational materials on volume calculation.In considering the problems and teaching methods of volume calculation in Japan, we hypothesized the importance of children learning to handle 3D models.The investigation showed the concept of volume calculation can be applied in 3D-CAD.This indicates the possibility of teaching the concept of volume calculation using 3D-CAD.We also believe it may be possible in the future to teach materials on volume calculation using tablet PCs.

References

1. Tanaka, T.: The trial of the woodwork toy development for the small children using a wood joint. Society of Art Educa-tion in Univercity (45), 215–222 (2013)
2. Takagi, S.: Play Puzzle. Heibon. Ltd. (1981)
3. Fuji, T., Iitaka, S. (40 auteurs other), Atarashi Sansuu 5-I. Tokyo Shoseki Co., Ltd. (2011)

Private Cloud Collaboration Framework
for e-Learning Environment for Disaster Recovery
Using Smartphone Alert Notification

Satoshi Togawa[1] and Kazuhide Kanenishi[2]

[1] Faculty of Management and Information Science, Shikoku Univeristy, Japan
doors@shikoku-u.ac.jp
[2] Center for University Extention, The University of Tokushima, Japan
marukin@cue.tokushima-u.ac.jp

Abstract. In this research, we have built a framework of disaster recovery such as against earthquake and tsunami disaster for e-Learning environment. We build a prototype system based on IaaS architecture, and this prototype system is constructed by several private cloud computing fabrics. These private cloud fabrics are constructed to operate one large private cloud fabric under the VPN connection. The distributed storage system builds on each private cloud fabric; that is handled almost like same block device such as one file system. For LMS (Learning Management System) to work, we need to boot virtual machines. The virtual machines are booted from the virtual disk images that are stored into the distributed storage system. The distributed storage system will be able to keep running as one large file system when some private cloud fabric does not work by any disasters. The disaster alert such as Earthquake Early Warning can be caught by usual smartphone. And we control virtual machines status and virtual machines positioning on the private cloud fabrics by caught disaster alert notifications. We think that our private cloud collaboration framework can continue working for e-Learning environment under the post-disaster situation. In this paper, we show our private cloud collaboration framework and the experimental results on the prototype configuration.

Keywords: private cloud collaboration, disaster recovery, smartphone application, disaster alert notification.

1 Introduction

On March 11, 2011, a major earthquake attacked to Eastern Japan. Especially, the east coast of Eastern Japan was severely damaged by the tsunami attacking. In Shikoku area including our universities in Western Japan, it is predicted that Nankai earthquake will happen in the near future. There is an interval theory that Nankai earthquake occurs every 100 to 150 years on the Pacific side in Western Japan. It is expected to have Nankai earthquake in the next 30 years, and its occurrence rate is between 70 percent and 80 percent. We have to prepare the disaster for the major earthquake. It will be like Eastern Japan Great Earthquake that the damage caused by

S. Yamamoto (Ed.): HIMI 2014, Part II, LNCS 8522, pp. 118–126, 2014.
© Springer International Publishing Switzerland 2014

earthquake and tsunami was heavy. It is very important disaster recovery, and it is same situation for the information system's field.

On the other hand, the informatization of education environment on universities is rapidly progressed by evolutional information technology. Current education environment cannot be realized without education assistance system, such as LMS (Learning Management System), learning ePortfolio, teaching ePortfolio and so on. The learning history of students is stored by these education assistance system. The fact is that awareness of the importance of learning data such as learning histories and teaching histories. The assistance systems are important same as learning data. Today's education environment on universities depends on education assistance system with information technology infrastructure. If the education assistance system with students learning history is lost by natural disasters, we think it become equivalent to lost sustainability for educational activity.

In addition, an integrated authentication framework of inter-organization is used to share the course materials. For example, Shibboleth Federations is used to authenticate other organization's user for sharing the course materials within consortium of universities. Today's universities educational activity cannot continue smoothly without those learning data and assistance system.

We can find applications for constructing information system infrastructure by the private cloud technology for universities. Generally, those application examples are based on a server machine virtualization technology such as IaaS (Infrastructure as a Service).

For example, we can find Hokkaido University Academic Cloud [1]. One of the aims of this system is to provide a lot of Virtual Machines (VMs) which are kitted out with the processing ability of huge multiple requests by VMs administrator. The VMs administrator can get a constructed Virtual Machine (VM) with an administrator authority. It is server hosting service with adaptive configuration for VM's administrator. Other case is to provide huge resources for distributed data processing infrastructure such as Hadoop framework [2]. The target of these systems is to do the massively parallel computing. Their aims are to provide effective use of computer hardware resources, and providing a centralized control of computer hardware resources. It is different purpose for disaster prevention and the reduction of damage in earthquake situation.

Nishimura's study provides a remote data backup technology for distributed data keeping on multiple organizations such as universities [3]. This study is considered migration transparency of distributed backup data using a storage virtualization technology. This system guarantees a security of the backup data, and transparency by Secret Sharing Scheme. We think that the backed up data and its architecture are found to useful for disaster recovery. However, the main target of this architecture is to make the backed up data and keeping its transparency. Therefore, it is not designed to continue users request handling with user data.

In this research, we have built a framework of reducing earthquake and tsunami disaster for e-Learning environment. We build private cloud computing environment based on IaaS technology, especially our target is to build the private cloud collaboration framework. This private cloud environment and private cloud collaboration framework are constructed from any private cloud fabric with the distributed storage system into several organizations. The Learning Management Systems such as Moodle build on several private cloud fabrics. Each VM has a LMS and the related data. General IaaS platform such as Kernel-based Virtual Machine (KVM) [4], Xen [5] and VMware vSphere [6] has a live-migration function with network shared storage. General network shared storage is constructed by iSCSI, NFS and usual network attached storage (NAS) system. Unfortunately, these network shared storage systems are bound to any physical storages on the each organizations. As a result, it is difficult to do the live-migration of VMs between inter-organizations such as universities.

Our prototype platform is built with distributed storage system and KVM based IaaS architecture on a lot of usual server hardware with network interfaces. It is able to handle many VMs including LMS and the data with enough redundancy. And, this prototype platform will operate on the inter-organizations. As a result, our prototype platform will be able to integrative operate each organization's private cloud fabric. If one organization's e-Learning environment is lost by some disaster, it will be able to keep running same environment on other organizations environment. When the re-build an infrastructure on the damaged organization, lost environment will be able to reconstruct by other organizations environment. Therefore, we think that the damaged organization does not lose data such as learning history.

In addition, our prototype platform can get emergency earthquake alert by smart-phone via cell-phone carrier. Any cell-phone carrier will send emergency alert message when major earthquake happened. Our prototype platform can get these messages by installed our application program on the on-lined smartphone, and the private cloud collaboration controller of organized our prototype platform makes live-migration task for each VMs. As a result, we think that the damaged organization can keep running e-Learning environment automatically.

In this paper, we propose the inter-cloud cooperation framework between private cloud fabrics on several organizations, and we show a configuration of the prototype system. Next, we show the results of experimental use and examine these results. Finally, we describe future study, and we show conclusions.

2 Assisting the Disaster Recovery for e-Learning Environment

In this section, we describe the private cloud collaboration framework of e-Learning environment. Especially, the purpose of this framework is a disaster recovery for LMS such as Moodle, and to keep running LMS and related data.

Fig.1 shows a framework of disaster recovery assistance for the e-Learning environment. Each organization such as university has each private cloud fabric. Each private cloud fabric has several server hardware at least four machines to get enough fabric's redundancy, and network connections between several server hardware. Each server hardware does not independent other server hardware on the private cloud fabric. They provide computing resources and data store resources via VMs, their resources are changed adaptively by the request from the administrators. Each VM which exists on the private cloud fabric is generated from the resources in the private

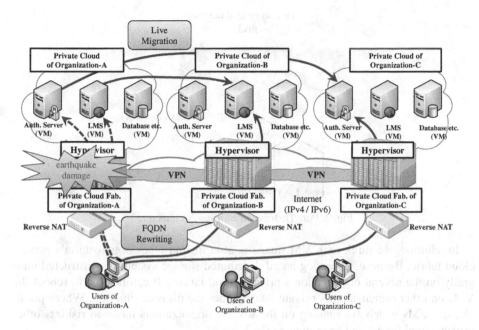

Fig. 1. Framework of Disaster Recovery Assistance

cloud fabric, it is able to process any function such as authentication, and LMS function on the VM. In addition, Each VM can migrate between other private cloud fabrics, and it is able to continue to keep processing.

A live migration function needs a shared file system to do the VM's migration. The product of Sheepdog Project [7] is applied to our framework. Sheepdog system is a distributed storage application optimized to QEMU and KVM hypervisor. Our proposed framework builds by KVM hypervisor, and Sheepdog distributed storage system provides highly available block level storage volumes. It can be attached to QEMU based VMs, it can be used to boot disk image for the VMs. Sheepdog distributed storage cluster does not have controller or meta-data servers such as any Storage Area Network (SAN) based storage system or other distributed storage system.

Fig.2 shows an architecture of pure distributed storage. The pure distributed storage system does not have metadata on the organized nodes. When the VM wants to get some data from distributed storage system, the consistent hashing method is used for searching target data from stored nodes of distributed storage system. The distributed storage system which is based on Sheepdog product does not have the single point of failure. Because, Sheepdog has a fully symmetric architecture. This architecture does not have central node such as a meta-data server. If some server hardware which compose Sheepdog cluster, it has small risk to lost the VM image file and history data.

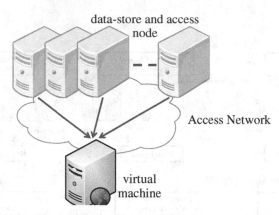

Fig. 2. Pure Distributed Storage Architecture

In addition, we think each VM image is able to find other organization's private cloud fabric. Because, Sheepdog based distributed storage system is constructed integrally on the several organization's private cloud fabrics. It can be able to reboot the VMs on other organization's private fabric under the disaster situation. Where possible, the VMs which are running on the several organizations move to riskless other private cloud fabric, and keep running the VMs.

Each private cloud fabric of several organizations has private cloud collaboration controller. A private cloud collaboration controller is constructed from customized smartphone and Libvirt Virtualization Toolkit [8]. Today's general smartphone has a function which catch the disaster alert notification. The disaster alert notification is delivered by mobile phone network using ETWS (Earthquake and Tsunami Warning System) message [9]. Our customized smartphone passes alert notification to the private cloud controller when the smartphone received ETWS messages. The private cloud controller which received alert notification makes live-migration command for controlled VMs.

However, if VMs migrate between several private cloud fabrics in working condition, it is not true that each organization's users can use several services. The hostname which is used to access the services, it must be rewrite to the previous organization's FQDN (Fully Qualified Domain Name). Generally, the users of organization-A want to access own LMS, they use the FQDN of organization-A. When the VM of organization-A is under controlled by the private cloud fabric of organization-B, that VM's FQDN has to provide the hostname related to organization-A. This function must operate at the same time as the live migration function.

We applied a reverse network address translation technology (reverse NAT) to keep users connectivity. The VMs which are providing LMS services migrate between several private cloud fabrics. These private cloud fabrics are deployed to inside of reverse NAT, and these are deployed same Layer2 segment under the L2VPN technology. When the VM migrate from one private cloud fabric to other private cloud fabric, the reverse NAT gets the migration status. The reverse NAT which is accepted the migration status can to rebuild DNS host entry.

As a result, we think we can assist to provide this inter-cloud framework against the disasters for e-Learning environment.

3   System Configuration

We show the configuration of proposed prototype system in Fig.3. This is a prototype system configuration of proposed framework.

This system has four components and two internal networks. The first one of the components is the node cluster. This is a core component of our prototype system. They are constructed by eight node hardware as shown by node1 to node8. The cluster which is constructed from node1 to node4 is placed same private cloud fabric. And the other cluster which is constructed from node5 to node8 is placed same private cloud fabric. These private cloud fabrics are placed different organization physically. These private cloud fabrics are connected with L2VPN such as EtherIP technology. And the IPsec technology is used to make a secure tunnel connection for L2VPN. As a result, both private cloud fabrics are organized same cluster logically.

This node hardware which is organized for private cloud fabric is based on Intel architecture with three network interfaces. Each node has the function of KVM hypervisor, virtualization API and Sheepdog distributed storage API. Each node can be used for the VM execution infrastructure, and it is also to use the composing element

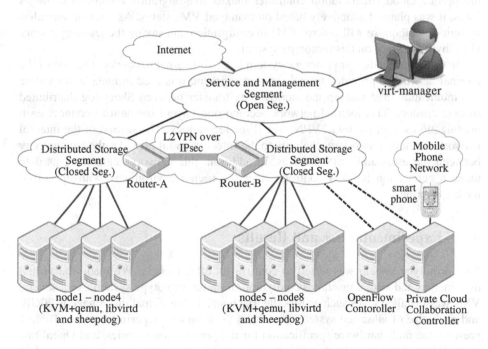

Fig. 3. Prototype System Configuration

of Sheepdog distributed storage system. As a result, it is realized sharing the hardware to use VM executing infrastructure, and it is implemented a reliability and a scalability of the storage.

The second one of the components is a Software Defined Network (SDN) controller based on OpenFlow [10] architecture. These servers which compose the VM execution infrastructure have the function of OpenFlow switch based on Open vSwitch [11]. This function is used for making optimum path dynamically, and it is also used for integrating several distributed storage.

The third one of the components is the Virtual Machine Manager [12]. An administration interface for VM's administrator is provided by virt-manager. This function is used for management several VMs by VM's administrator on this prototype system. The virt-manager uses Libvirt Virtualization Toolkit to make VM's management functions. Libvirt Virtualization Toolkit supports any hypervisor such as KVM/QEMU, Xen, VMware ESX and so on. Any hypervisor functions are abstracted by Libvirt functions, VM's management application is able to make control the VM's status.

The fourth one of the components is the private cloud collaboration controller. This cloud controller has functions, there are catching earthquake alert notification via smartphone, and making live-migration command for target node machines. And the private cloud collaboration controller has each VMs status on private cloud fabrics, it was caught from Libvirt Virtualization Toolkit and Virtual Machine Manager. When the private cloud collaboration controller makes live-migration command to target VMs, it was planned adaptively based on managed VMs status. As a result, any alert system of earthquake will control VMs live-migration and saving the learning history via Libvirt interface on this prototype system.

On the other hands, our prototype system has two internal networks. The one of the internal network is provided to make closed segment, it is used to make a keep-alive communication, and making the storage data transfer between Sheepdog distributed storage clusters. This internal network become one Layer2 segment to connect each organization's segment by L2VPN over IPsec technology. The second of the internal network provides network reachability to the Internet, and it provides the connectivity between the users and LMS services. In addition, this network segment is used to make a connection for VM controls under the secure environment with optimized packet filtering.

4   Experimental Use and Results

This prototype system was tested to confirm its effectiveness. We made the virtual disk images and virtual machines configuration on our prototype system. And, several VMs was installed LMS such as Moodle. Each size of the virtual disk image is 20GB, and each size of allocated system memory is 2GB on this experimental use. Table 1 presents the node hardware specification for the private cloud fabrics, and OpenFlow controller and private cloud collaboration controller specification are presented in Table 2.

Table 1. Specification of the Private Cloud Nodes

CPU Specification	AMD Opteron 3250 HE (Quad Core)
System Memory Capacity	16.0Gbytes
HDD Capacity	250Gbytes with SATA600 interface
Operating System	Ubuntu Server 12.04 LTS 64bit ed.

Table 2. Specification of OpenFlow Controller and Private Cloud Collaboration Controller

CPU Specification	Intel Xeon E3-1230 3.2GHz (Quad Core)
System Memory Capacity	16.0Gbytes
HDD Capacity	250Gbytes with SATA600 interface
Operating System	Ubuntu Server 12.04 LTS 64bit ed.

The prototype of the private cloud fabrics are constructed by eight node machines, and each node has 250Gbytes capacity HDD. The total amount of physical HDD capacity is about 2.0Tbytes. Each clustered node uses about 4Gbytes capacities for the hypervisor function with an operating system. We think this amount is ignorable small capacity. However, the distributed storage system has triple redundancy for this test. As a result, we can use about 700Mbytes storage capacity with enough redundancy. The total capacity of the distributed storage system can extend to add other node servers, exchange to larger HDDs, and taking both solutions. We can take enough scalability and redundancy by this distributed storage system.

We tried to do a live-migration in our prototype system. We make the test with two cases. One of the cases is to do live-migration in the same private cloud fabric. This case is targeted making live-migration in an organization. Other case is to do live-migration between private cloud fabrics. This case is targeted making live-migration inter-organization.

Table 3. Time of Live Migration

From node1 to node2 (same private cloud)	25.1 sec
From node1 to node5 (inter private cloud)	26.2 sec

Table 3 shows the time of live-migration for experimental trial. We used the operate VM's live-migration by the interface of Virtual Machine Manager. The time of live-migration for same private cloud fabric is needed 25.1 seconds. The time of live-migration for inter-private cloud fabrics is needed 26.2 seconds. We think that both experimental times is enough live-migration time for a disaster reduction of provided VMs. And, we could get a complete successful result with active condition.

In addition, the live-migration of these experimental use is operated by private cloud collaboration controller. We made simulated earthquake alert notification based on ETWS message, it was send to customized Android platform smartphone. The live-migration command was triggered by customized smartphone, and the live-migration process was success completely.

In the real situation, we think we will use an emergency notification of the disaster from any mobile communication carrier such as NTT DoCoMo, KDDI and Softbank via their smart phones. The custom application program is installed to any smartphone such as Android platform and iPhone platform. If we can get the information of emergency notifications via smartphone with near field communication method such as USB interface, Bluetooth communication method and so on, we will be able to make a trigger of VMs live-migration with more precision.

The results of this experimental use are pretty good. The time requirement for VMs migrating was a short period. However, the results were getting under the initial conditions. The VMs which are installed Moodle system were quite new condition. Generally, when the VMs are operated to continue long period, each VM has large history data. Therefore, the time of live-migration will need more than initial condition. We think we have to make the experimental use under the actual conditions.

5   Conclusion

In this paper, we proposed a framework of disaster recovery for e-Learning environment. Especially, we described an assistance to use our proposed framework, and we show the importance of an against the earthquake and tsunami disaster for e-Learning environment. We built the prototype system based on our proposed framework, and we described a system configuration of the prototype system. And, we shown the results of experimental use and examine.For the future, we have a plan to implement the function of getting earthquake notification from other smartphone such as iOS based smartphone. And we will try to test the cloud computing orchestration framework such as OpenStack and CloudStack. And, we will try to experiment confirming its effectiveness under the inter-organization environment with multipoint organizations.

References

1. Hokkaido University Academic Cloud Web Site,
   http://www.hucc.hokudai.ac.jp/hosting_server.html
2. Apache Hadoop Web Site, http://hadoop.apache.org/
3. Nishimura, K.: Studies on Offsite Backup Techniques for Manual Data Storing by Universities. In: 4th Symposium of Japan High Performance Computing and Networking Plus Large-Scale Data Analyzing and Information Systems (2012)
4. Kernel Virtual Machine Web Site, http://www.linux-kvm.org/
5. Xen Hypervisor Web Site, http://xen.org/
6. VMware vSphere Web Site, http://www.vmware.com/
7. Sheepdog Project Web Site, http://www.orsg.net/sheepdog/
8. Libvirt Virtualization Toolkit Web Site, http://libvirt.org/
9. 3GPP Specification detail: Earthquake and Tsunami Warning System (ETWS),
   http://www.3gpp.org/DynaReport/23828.htm
10. OpenFlow Web Site, http://www.openflow.org/
11. Open vSwitch Web Site, http://openvswitch.org/
12. Virtual Machine Manager Web Site, http://virt-manager.org/

Report on Practice of Note-Rebuilding Support System

Takahito Tomoto[1,*] and Tsukasa Hirashima[2]

[1] Faculty of Engineering, Tokyo University of Science,
1-3 Kagurazaka, Shinjuku-ku, Tokyo 162-8601 Japan
[2] Graduate School of Engineering, Hiroshima University,
1-4-1 Kagamiyama, Higashi Hiroshima City, Hiroshima 739-8527, Japan
tomoto@ms.kagu.tus.ac.jp

Abstract. Lectures in recent years have increasingly incorporated presentation software. Such lectures are problematic in that effective note taking is precluded because lecture slides present content in a preformed structure, reducing the need for thought during the note taking process. In presentation-type lectures, it is therefore necessary to propose tasks that confirm student understanding. Here we propose a "note-rebuilding" method, an adaptation of a kit-build method. We also report the results of constructing a learning support system with note-rebuilding and its experimental evaluation.

Keywords: Learning of structure, presentation software, lecture, learning support system.

1 Introduction

Lectures in recent years have increasingly incorporated presentation software. Such lectures are problematic in that effective note taking is precluded because lecture slides present content in a preformed structure, reducing the need for thought during the note taking process [1-3]. There are various learning support system for note-taking[4-7]. Especially, it is effective to reflect and rearrange the note. The reflection is called note-reflection[8-11]. In presentation-type lectures, it is therefore necessary to propose tasks that confirm student understanding as note-reflection. Here we propose a "note-rebuilding" method expanding note-reflection, an adaptation of a kit-build method[12-14].

In kit-build method, teachers divide prepared learning materials into parts, which learners reconstruct. This allows teachers to easily check learners' work by comparison with the original material. Here we propose a note-rebuilding method as follows. First, the teacher uses presentation software to create structured slides as he/she always does for his/her class . Second, the slide is divided into several parts. Third, learners are require to reconstruct the original slide based on the parts   The third step is designed on the assumption that the lecture is complete. This method promotes learner understanding of the lecture structure. We present the details of our note-rebuilding method. We also report the results of constructing a learning support system with note-rebuilding and its experimental evaluation.

---

* Corresponding author.

S. Yamamoto (Ed.): HIMI 2014, Part II, LNCS 8522, pp. 127–136, 2014.
© Springer International Publishing Switzerland 2014

2   Design of Learning Support System with Note-Rebuilding

2.1   Note-Rebuilding Method

Lectures present a variety of information. When confirming understanding of the lecture structure, it is inappropriate to make students summarize all the data present-ed; understanding the information and its structure is sufficient. We refer to structures in lecture data as "structure notes." In our note-rebuilding method, students construct structure notes, examples of which are shown in Figs. 1, 2, and 3.

Structure notes include important informational elements and the important infor-mational structures. In the proposed note-rebuilding method, pieces of information (mainly words and phrases) included in a structure note are called elements, and the informational framework of the structure without elements is called a skeleton. The two together are called parts. A skeleton and an element are given to a student, who assembles them appropriately, thus promoting understanding of the lecture. Figure 4 shows an example of structure note parts with a layered structure for the skeleton and its elements.

	Teacher	Learner
Task	Make slide	Rebuild notes
Aim	Improving lecture	Understanding lecture

Fig. 1. Tabular form

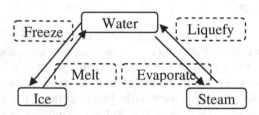

Fig. 2. Concept map form

1	Background
2	Development
	2.1 Model
	2.2 Structure
	2.3 Functions
3	Practice
	3.1 School A
	3.2 School B

Fig. 3. Layered structure form

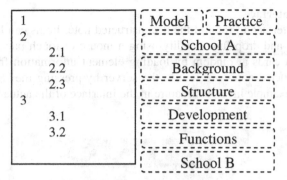

Fig. 4. Skeleton and elements

2.2   Learning Support System with Note-Rebuilding

We next described the design of a learning support system with note-rebuilding method. The system is composed of an interface that learners use to construct elements and a skeleton, and a comparison function to show the differences between notes built by different learners.   We developed this system as a web application using JavaScript on the client side and PHP on the server side. The developed system supports PC mouse operations and tablet PC touch operations.

Data of Structure Note

Structure note data contain information on correct answers about the structure notebook prepared by the teacher and reconstructed by students. These data include the kind of structure (tabular, concept map, layered, etc.), and their elements. Figure 5 shows an example of structure note information about a layered structure. In this example, the data describe a figure (number) and a figure-free (dot) itemized statement, and each phrase and the depth (level) of a class. The present system uses JSON forms, allowing compact descriptions. In future research we will develop an authoring function that can be used like presentation software.

```
{"ClassStructure":[
{"level":1,
"sentence":"Start MySQL ",
"type":"number"},
   {"level":2,
   "sentence":"mysql -u j**** -p -tee='filename.txt'",
   "type":"dot"},
{"level":1,
"sentence":"Confirm Database",
"type":"number"},
   {"level":2,
   "sentence":"SHOW DATABASES;",
   "type":"dot"},
```

Fig. 5. Example structure note about a layered structure

Note-Rebuilding Interface

Learners use this interface to rebuild the deconstructed note. Items can be easily manipulated with drag-and-drop functionality using a mouse or touch panel. This interface shows element cards at random by loading element information from structure note data. Reconstructed notes are sent to the server by pressing the "Send" button. Figure 6 shows an example layered structure in the interface of the actually developed system.

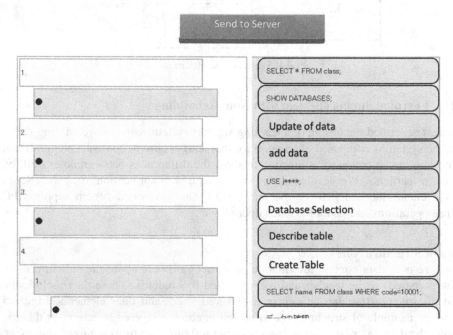

Fig. 6. A layered structure in the developed interface

Comparison Function

Learner answers are sent to and collected at a server. The result of having superimposed two or more student notes and the answer as prepared by the teacher are accumulated and displayed. Learners can then reflect on their own answers by comparison with other answers and the correct answer. In addition, teachers can reflect on their lecture to improve teaching. Moreover, teachers can immediately respond to inadequate learner understanding immediately following a lecture by providing supplementary explanation. Figure 7 shows an example of collected student answers in the layered structure.

Advantage of Note-Rebuilding Method

In this section, we refer to advantage of note-rebuilding method based on comparisons with multi-choice question method and fill-in-the-blank question method. Note-rebuilding method requires teachers to create structured slides as he/she always does

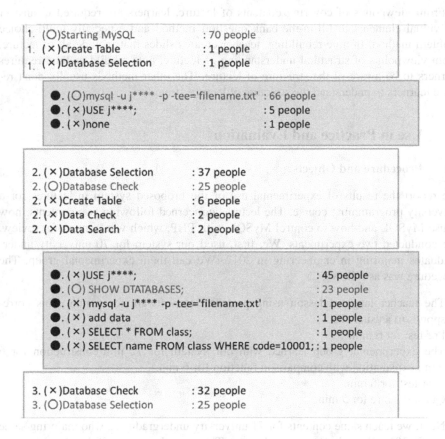

Fig. 7. Collected answers

for his/her class. And then, the slide is divided into several parts. Finally, learners reconstruct the original slide based on the parts. In contrast, multi-choice question method requires teachers to prepare problems that confirm student understanding and feasible wrong choices. Learners are required to select adequate choice. Fill-in-the-bank question method requires teachers to consider where they should make blank in various sentences. Learners are required to fill a blank by selection or description.

From viewpoints of simplicity of preparation, note-rebuilding method doesn't require teachers to do additional task if they prepared well-structured teaching slide. And it is easy to check whether learners' answers are right or not by comparison their answers to the original slide. In multi-choice question method, teachers are required to consider various adequate problems and feasible wrong choice. These are uneasy additional tasks. In fill-in-the blank question method, they are required to consider adequate sentences and blank. In addition, diagnosis function is necessary in free description.

From viewpoints of covering contents of lecture, learners are required to answer individual elements in fill-in-the-bank question method and especially multi-choice problem method. In note-rebuilding, teacher creates slides that include all of lecture. From viewpoints of structural understanding of lecture, note-rebuild method requires learners to be aware of the structure of lecture. The other methods usually don't require learners to understand the structure of lecture strongly.

3   Use in Practice and Evaluation

3.1   Procedure and Objects

We report the results of experimental use of the proposed system in lectures for a university programming course. The lectures concerned following two contents: how to use MySQL and how to control MySQL with PHP, which was content for review. We conducted two experiments. We, first, used our system for 70 university undergraduates majoring in engineering in 2012. We call them experimental group. The procedure was as follows:

1. The teacher taught a lesson using presentation software for 6 min. This corresponds to a usual class.
2. Pre-test for 6 min.
3. The experimental group learned with our system for 12 min(construction for 6 min., explanation with comparison function for 6 min.).
4. Post-test for 6 min.
5. Questionnaire for 5 min.

Next, we teach same contents for 71 university undergraduates who majoring same course in 2013. We call them control group. The procedure was as follows:

1. The teacher taught a lesson using presentation software for 6 min. This corresponds to a usual class.
2. Pre-test for 6 min.
3. The teacher taught for the control group using presentation software in detail for 12 min.
4. Post-test for 6 min.
5. And then, control group also use our system as experimental group for 12 min.
6. Second Post-test in control group for 6 min.
7. Questionnaire for 5 min.

The items on both pre-, post- and second post-tests were the same: subjects freely described the process of manipulating MySQL alone and manipulating MySQL using PHP. Adequate description of the procedure was scored as a right answer. We call the problem order problem. In addition, subjects are required to describe command corresponding to the procedure. Adequate description of the command was scored as a right answer. We call the problem command problem.

From the result of two experiment, we will consider the effect of our system. In the difference between pre-test and post-test in both experiment is our system and normal class with presentation software. So the result of them will reveal the effect of our system. Furthermore, in the second experiment, control group is required to learn using our system after post-test and to answer second post-test and questionnaire. It means that they learned two ways of normal lecture and using our system. The difference between post-test and second post-test in control group also reveal the effect of our system.

3.2   Result and Consideration

The table 1 and table 2 show the result of our two experiments.

First, we report the difference between experimental group and control group in order problems. We ran an analysis of variance (ANOVA) with group (Experimental group (a1), control group (a2)) as a between-subject factor A, and Timing (pre-test (b1), post-test (b2)) as a within-subject factor B. ANOVA results that an interaction were significant, with $p < .001$. The simple main effects within this interaction indicated that the effect of group was significant in post-test, but was no significant in pre-test. Scores in the experimental group were higher than the scores in the control group for the post-test, even though pre-test scores are same in pre-test. The same results are produced in both area about MySQL alone and PHP + MySQL. The result shows our system is effective for learning of order structure.

Secondly, we report the difference between experimental group and control group in command problems. We ran ANOVA with same conditions. In MySQL area, ANOVA results that an interaction were significant, with $p < .05$. In MySQL + PHP area, an interaction were no significant, with $p > .1$. The results shows our system may not be effective for memorizing of command.

Next, we report the difference between post-test and second post-test which is conducted after using our system in control group in order problems. We ran ANOVA with Timing (pre-test, post-test, second post-test) as a within-subject. ANOVA results indicate that all main effects were significant, with $p < .001$. In addition, multiple comparisons for Timing by Ryan's Q test indicated significant differences between three pairs of (post-test, pre-test), (second post-test, pre-test) and (post-test, second post-test) ($p < .001$). The same results are produced in both area about MySQL alone and PHP + MySQL. The result also shows our system is effective for learning of order structure.

Finally, we report the difference between post-test and second post-test in command problems. We ran ANOVA with same conditions. ANOVA results indicate that all main effects were significant, with $p < .001$. In addition, multiple comparisons for Timing by Ryan's Q test indicated significant differences between three pairs of (post-test, pre-test), (second post-test, pre-test) and (post-test, second post-test) ($p < .01$). The same results are produced in both area about MySQL alone and PHP + MySQL. The result shows our system is effective for learning of order structure.

Table 1. The average of order problems

	MySQL(Max:8)			PHP+MySQL(Max:7)		
	pre	post	2nd. post	pre	post	2nd. post
Experimental Group	1.97	5.36		0.40	3.39	
Control Group	2.22	4.15	5.41	0.49	1.18	3.70

Table 2. The average of command problems

	MySQL(Max:24)			PHP+MySQL(Max:21)		
	pre	post	2nd. post	pre	post	2nd. post
Experimental Group	4.61	8.10		0.36	1.33	
Control Group	4.43	9.82	11.3	0.75	1.85	2.97

Two results of order problems indicate that our system is useful for learning the order structure of information. Two results of command problems, however, indicate that our system is not always useful for memorizing of command. We guess that result is produced by the reason that learners are only required to consider the structure of information by reconstruction using cards. They are not required to memorize the contents of the card alone. They may memorize correspondence relation between command and procedure, but they could not memorize the command sentence.

Subjects were asked whether they could use our system effectively, and responded using a four-point Likert scale. Table 3 showed the questionnaire results.

Table 3. Questionnaire results

	Experimental Group	Control Group
Lecture content is easier to understand when using the system than when not.	3.3	3.2
It is easier to see what parts of the lecture I understand well when using the system than when not.	3.2	3.0
It is easier to see the point of the lecture when using the system than when not.	3.1	3.2
It is easier to understand the structure of the lecture when using the system than when not.	3.2	2.8

Table 3 shows that almost all subjects found the system useful for understanding lecture content, confirming well-understood parts, understanding the point of the lecture, and understanding the structure of the lecture. The results were that scores increased in both post-tests. Positive results were obtained despite adding time to use our system for 3 min and to explain to explain its comparison function.

4   Conclusion

We focused on lectures that use presentation software. In such lectures learners are not required to conduct tasks for understanding the lesson structure. We therefore proposed a note-rebuilding method and developed a learning support system for implementing the method. We focus on slides that many teacher make usually in lectures using presentation software. In note-rebuilding method, the slide is divided into several parts. Learners are require to reconstruct the original slide based on the parts. Actual implementation revealed that the method promotes the learner understanding of lecture structure.

Acknowledgements. This study was supported by a Grant-in-Aid for Scientific Research (B) No. 24300285 from the Japan Society for the Promotion of Science.

References

1. Kiewra, K.A.: Aids to Lecture Learning. Educational Psychologist 26(1), 37–53 (1991)
2. Armbruster, B.B.: Handbook of College Reading and Study Strategy Research, pp. 175–199. LEA (2000)
3. Kobayashi, K.: Combined Effects of Note-Taking/-Reviewing on Learning and the Enhancement through Interventions. Educational Psychology 26(3), 459–477 (2006)
4. Brandl, P., Richter, C., Haller, M.: Nicebook: supporting natural note taking. In: Proc. CHI 2010, pp. 59–60 (2010)
5. Chang, W.-C., Liao, C., Ku, Y.-M.: Designing Issues of Instructional Online Note-taking Systems in Practical Approach. In: Proc. of ICCE 2009, pp. 910–914 (2009)
6. Berque, D.: An evaluation of a broad deployment of DyKnow software to support note taking and interaction using pen-based computers. Journal of Computing Sciences in Colleges Archive 21(6), 204–216 (2006)
7. Moriyama, T., Mitsuhara, H., Yano, Y.: Prototyping Paper-Top Interface as Note-taking Support. In: Int. Conf. on Computers in Education 2010 (2010)
8. Carrier, C.A., Titus, A.: The effects of notetaking: A review of studies. Contep. Educat. Psychol. 4, 299–314 (1979)
9. Hartley, J., Davies, I.K.: Notetaking: A critical review. PLET 15, 207–224
10. Kewra, K.A.: A review of note-taking: The encoding-strage paradigm and beyond. Educat. Psycho. Rev. 1, 147–172 (1985)
11. Van Meter, P., Yokoi, L., Pressley, M.: College students' theory of note-taking derived from their perceptions of note-taking. J. Educ. Psychol. 86, 323–338 (1994)

12. Sugihara, K., Nino, Y., Moriyama, S., Moriyama, R., Ishida, K., Osada, T., Mizuta, Y., Hirashima, T., Funaoi, H.: Implementation of Kit-Build Concept Map with Media Table. Wireless, Mobile, and Ubiquitous Technology in Education, 325–327 (2012)
13. Yamasaki, K., Fukuda, H., Hirashima, T., Funaoi, H.: Kit-Build Concept Map and Its Preliminary Evaluation. In: Proc. of ICCE 2010 (2010)
14. Sugihara, K., Osada, T., Nakata, S., Funaoi, H., Hirashima, T.: Experimental Evaluation of Kit-Build Concept Map for Science Classes in an Elementary School. In: Proc. of ICCE2012,155F, pp. 17–24 (2012)

Visualizing Mental Learning Processes
with Invisible Mazes for Continuous Learning

Tomohiro Yamaguchi[1], Kouki Takemori[1], and Keiki Takadama[2]

[1] Nara National College of Technology
Nara, Japan
{yamaguch,takemori}@info.nara-k.ac.jp
[2] The University of Electro-Communications
Tokyo, Japan
keiki@inf.uec.ac.jp

Abstract. This paper presents the way to design the continuous learning process model based on general reinforcement learning framework for both a human and a learning agent. The objective of this research is to bring the learning ability of the learning agent close to that of a human. We focus on both the *reinforcement learning* framework for the learning agent and the *continuous learning* model of a human. However, there are two kinds of questions. First question is how to bridge an enormous gap between them. To fill in the missing piece of reinforcement learning whose learning process is mainly behavior change, we add two mental learning processes, *awareness* as pre-learning process and *reflection* as post-learning process. Second question is how to observe mental learning processes of a human. Previous methods of human learning researches mostly depend on observable behaviors or activities. On the other hand, a *learning process* of a human has a major difficulty in observing since it is a mental process. Then a human learning process is yet-to-be-defined. So it is necessary to add a new twist to observe the learning process of a human. To solve this, we propose a new method for *visualizing* mental learning processes with *invisible* mazes consisting of *invisible* walls which are perceived as a *sign* that is the number of walls in the neighborhood. Besides, we add *meta-actions* for expressing and summarizing something to be *aware* of learning from mistake or to be *reflected* on learning from experience. A learner can mark up his/her *sign*-action traces by *meta-actions* for future success. It turns out to *visualize* his/her mental *learning processes*. This paper reports our learning support system for a human learner to visualize his/her mental *learning processes* with *invisible* mazes for *continuous learning*.

Keywords: reinforcement learning, continuous learning, learning process, awareness, self-reflection, visualizing, invisible, sign, meta-action, learning goals.

1   Introduction

Researches on learning process are divided into two fields. One is a learning agent in Artificial Intelligence [12-13], the other is learning of a human in psychology [9].

S. Yamamoto (Ed.): HIMI 2014, Part II, LNCS 8522, pp. 137–148, 2014.
© Springer International Publishing Switzerland 2014

For the learning agent, reinforcement learning is the major framework since it auto-matically learns after a learning goal is set in the learning environment. The main feature of reinforcement learning is that the learning goal is given by the human de-signer. On the other hand, researches on human learning ability have been performed in various research fields such as psychology, education, business, and so on. One of the main features of human learning ability is that it covers a vast territory of learning ability including discovery of learning goals, *awareness*, *reflection*, self-regulated learning [16], or *continuous learning*.

The objective of this research is to bring the learning ability of the learning agent close to that of a human. We focus on both reinforcement learning framework for the learning agent and continuous learning model of a human. However, there are two kinds of questions. First question is how to bridge an enormous gap between them. Second question is how to observe mental learning processes of a human. Previous methods of human learning researches mostly depend on observable behaviors or activities. On the other hand, a learning process of a human has a major difficulty in observing since it is a mental process. Then a human learning process is yet-to-be-defined. So it is necessary to add a new twist to observe the human learning process.

To solve these problems, we propose a new method for *visualizing* mental learning processes with *invisible* mazes. We focus on *continuous learning* [17-18], and aim for modeling the unified continuous learning process model based on reinforcement learning framework for both a human and the learning agent. Our new approaches are following;

1. To fill in the missing piece of reinforcement learning whose learning process is be-havior change, we add two mental learning processes, *awareness* as pre-learning process and *reflection* as post-learning process.
2. The learning environment is the *invisible* maze consisting of *invisible* walls which are perceived as a *sign* that is the number of walls in the neighborhood.
3. We add *meta-actions* for expressing and summarizing something to be *aware* of learning from mistake or to be *reflected* on learning from experience. A learner can mark up his/her *sign*-action traces by *meta-actions* for future success. It turns out to *visualize* his/her mental *learning processes*.
4. For *continuous learning*, we design the sequence of *invisible learning goals* which allows the learner to discover them according to the learning ability.

This paper reports our learning support system for a human learner to visualize his/her mental *learning processes* with *invisible* mazes for *continuous learning*. The re-mainder of the paper is structured as follows: Section 2 gives a theoretical background on *continuous learning* and Section 3 presents the continuous learning process model with *invisible* mazes. Section 4 discusses several issues and Section 5 concludes the paper, addressing future work.

2   Background

This section describes a theoretical background of this research, *continuous learning*, *awareness* and *reflection*. The concepts awareness and reflection are viewed differently across the disciplines among Computer-supported cooperative work (CSCW), Computer-supported collaborative learning (CSCL), psychology, business, educational sciences, computer science, and so on. First we summarize an overview of *continuous learning* and its learning process which is compared with that of reinforcement learning, then current usage of *awareness* and *reflection* in the Workshops on ARTEL is introduced.

2.1   An Overview of Continuous Learning

The concept of continuous learning comes from Industrial and organizational psychology. Smita[15] reviews research on continuous learning. There are three levels, individual, group, and organizational level. At the individual level it is self-directed; at the group level it is collaborative. One of conceptual definitions of continuous learning is follows; "Continuous learning at the individual level is regularly changing behavior based on a deepening and broadening of one's skills, knowledge, and worldview" [14].

2.2   Learning Process Model to Achieve Continuous Learning [2]

A learning process model to achieve continuous improvement has been proposed [2]. Learning process is defined as a process that results in changed behavior. Learning process consists of six mental processes with the role of leadership. This model assumes a learner and the leader. The role of this leader is mentor or coacher rather than teacher [3].

2.3   Comparison of Continuous Learning with Reinforcement Learning

Figure 1 compares learning process between continuous learning and reinforcement learning. Figure 1(a) shows the learning process of continuous learning[2]. The major feature of it is that it circles each process and it has no end. The reason is that continuous learning is designed for an adult learner who is expected to spiral up along the endless learning cycle toward mastery of some professional skill. Thus it has commitment process to commit a *learning goal*. However, each process is mental process.

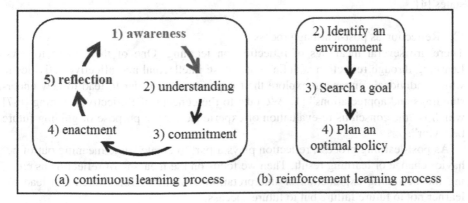

Fig. 1. A comparison of learning process

In contrast with it, Figure 1(b) shows the learning process of reinforcement learning. Its distinction is that its process has a start and an end. Since the objective of existing reinforcement learning is to find an optimal solution for the learning goal given by a human designer. Next section reviews *Awareness* and *Reflection* as important processes of continuous learning process.

2.4   Awareness and Reflection on Learning Processes

In the research field of Technology-Enhanced Learning (TEL) for human learners, *Awareness* and *Reflection* (AR) is one of the active research issues [10] [5]. 2013 year's theme for Workshop on this field, AR-TEL 2013 is: "How can awareness and reflection support learning in different settings (work, education, continuing professional development, lifelong learning, etc.). What are the roles that technology can play to support awareness and reflection in these contexts?" [5]. We refer our meanings of *Awareness* and *Reflection* from these workshops papers.

The common feature of Awareness and Reflection is focusing experience of a learner on some information for future improvement. The main differences between them are that Awareness relates to the perception, Reflection mainly relates to the action or the behavior consisting of perception and action.

(1) Awareness as pre-learning process

There are several meanings of awareness on learning.   Closely related meanings to our research are follows;

1.   Individual situational awareness is defined as "the perception of the elements in the environment within a volume of time and space, the comprehension of their meaning, and the projection of their status in the near future" [8].
2.   Awareness is increasingly related to finding appropriate learning objects, peers and experts or the 'right' learning path [11].

As pre-learning process, awareness plays an important part to trigger behavior change. Then we focus on the meaning of awareness as the need for distinction of indistinguishable perceptions or experience between future success and future failure. We assume that these indistinguishable perceptions occur by partially observable states [4].

(2) Reflection as post-learning process

There are several meanings of reflection on learning. One of them is as follows; Learning through reflection is defined as "those intellectual and affective activities in which individuals engage to explore their experiences in order to lead to new understandings and appreciations" [1]. We take to the concept of Reflective learning [6-7] which is "the conscious re-evaluation of experience for the purpose of guiding future behavior".

As post-learning process, reflection plays a part to create some meaning out of behavior change or learning result. Then we focus on the meaning of reflection as creating the becoming explanation or interpretation toward the rule which can lead the learner not to future failure but to future success.

3   Designing the Continuous Learning Process with a Maze Model

This chapter summarizes the design concepts for the learning environment and the continuous learning task. For modeling the continuous learning process as shown in figure 1, this paper formalizes them by a maze model with invisible walls and an invisible goal and designs the maze sweeping task which requires discovering and mastering invisible various learning goals of a learner. First we describe the flow of the continuous learning process, second, designing the learning environment as an invisible maze model is illustrated. After designing the continuous learning task by the maze sweeping,   we describe designing the sequence of learning goals.

3.1   The Flow of the Continuous Learning Process

Figure 2 shows the flow of the continuous learning process. This process consists of triple cycle. Innermost cycle is called a *trial*. A *trial* is defined as an transition sequence from start state to encountering either a goal state or a wall. In this cycle, a learner repeats an action and hie/her mental process including awareness until he/she results in either sucess or fail of the task.

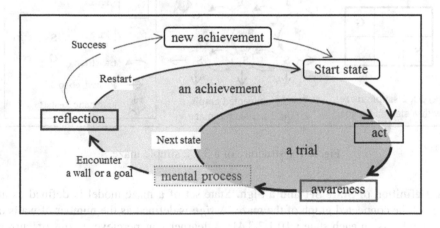

Fig. 2. The flow of the continuous learning process

Second cycle is called an *achievement*. A *achievement* is defined as the learning of a maze sweeping task with a fixed start and goal. In this cycle, the learner reflects the trial when the trial terminates by the encounter with a wall or a goal. After that, if current trial is not accomplished, he/she restarts the trial from start state. Outmost cycle is the   *continuous learning* cyle. When the learner accomplished current *achievement,* he/she can challenge next new achievement as he/she wants.

3.2   Designing the Learning Environment by an Invisible Maze Model

Designing a learning environment for a human learner, we adopt a grid maze model from start to goal since it is a familiar example to find the path through a trial and error process. A maze model is defined by five elements, state set, a *sign* of walls, transitions and walls, action set, and *meta-actions*, each of five elements is defined.

The Structure of a 2D Grid Maze. The n x m grid maze with four neighbors which is surrounded by walls in a rectangle shape consists of the n x m number of 1 x 1 squares. It is called a *simple maze*. Figure 3 shows the structure of a 2D grid maze. Figure 3 (a) shows a 3 x 2 simple maze with a start and a goal.

In a grid maze, every square that touches one of their edges except a wall is connected. Each square in a maze model is called a state. Each state is distinguished by the location. S is the start state of the maze, and G is the goal state of the maze. A maze model is described as a connected and directed graph in which a node is a state and a link is a transition between states. Figure 3 (b) shows the connected graph of the 3 x 2 simple maze. Note that a trial is an transition sequence from start state to encountering either a goal state or a wall.

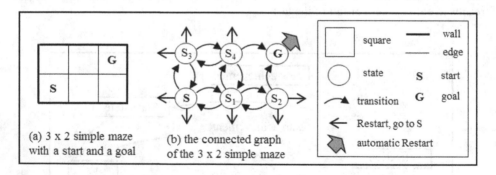

(a) 3 x 2 simple maze with a start and a goal

(b) the connected graph of the 3 x 2 simple maze

Fig. 3. The structure of a 3 x 2 simple maze

The Definition of State Set and a Sign. State set of a maze model is defined as all states of the connected graph of the maze. A *sign* is defined as the number of walls of four neighbors in each state ; {0,1,2,3,4}. A learner can percieve a sign of current state as the presence of invisivle/visible walls. Each state has several state variables as follows ;

1. Constant : Location(x, y) , Role(start ?, goal ?, Is-goal-invisible ?), *Sign*
2. Local (in a trial) : flag(visited ?)
3. Global (during trials) : state of attached markers, frequency of visit

Figure 4 shows an illustrated example of a simple maze with invisible walls. Figure 4 (a) shows the 4x4 invisible maze. Dashed lines are invisible walls which are invisible for a learner during trials. Figure 4 (b) shows an example of transition sequence.

In each state, whether visited or not is distinguished by its background color of the square either white (visited) or gray (not visited). Figure 4 (c) shows the distribution of signs among visited states in the maze. In each visited state, a number is displayed as a sign of surrounding walls.

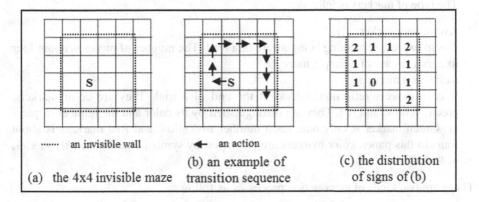

(a) the 4x4 invisible maze   (b) an example of
transition sequence

(c) the distribution
of signs of (b)

Fig. 4. An example of a simple maze with invisible walls

The Definition of Transitions, Walls and Action Set. Transitions between states in a maze model is defined whether corresponding square with four neighbors, {up, down, left, right} which is connected or not connected by a wall. They are represented as the labeled directed graph as shown in Figure 3 (b). Action set is defined as a set of labels to distinguish the possible transitions of a state. In a 2D grid maze model with four neighbors, a learner can execute four kinds of actions: {up, right, left, down} or relative actions: {forward, turn-right, turn-left, reverse}. Note that the action toward a wall results in the transition to start state to restart the trial.   Transition to a goal state results in automatic restart with the judgment whether the maze sweeping task is accomplished or not.

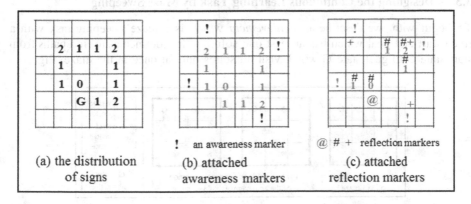

(a) the distribution
of signs

(b) attached
awareness markers

(c) attached
reflection markers

Fig. 5. An example of *meta actions* on an invisible maze

The Definition of Meta-actions. We introduce *meta-actions* to *visualize* his/her mental *learning processes*. *Meta-action* is defined to attach a marker on a state in the maze map for expressing and summarizing a learner's mental *learning processes*. Figure 5 shows an example of *meta-actions* on an invisible maze. Figure 5 (a) shows an example of the signs of a trial which results in the encounter with a goal state G.

The type of markers is follows;

1. Awareness marker: {!}
   It is to express something being aware in a trial. The number of pieces is about four in a trial in case of a simple maze.
2. Reflection markers:
   It is to express reflection process at the end of a trial. They are color markers, green, yellow, and red. They are distinguished by its color and the number of pieces. Green marker is only one. Each number of Yellow and Red markers is about four. In this paper, color markers are displayed by symbol characters; {@, +, +, +, +, #, #, #,#}.

There are two kinds of *meta-action* processes as follows;

1. Awareness process in a trial:
   In any time in a trial, an awareness marker can be attached in any state. Figure 5 (b) shows an example of attached awareness markers where the encounter with an invisible wall is previsioned. The typical usage is to attach it to the state when the learner becomes aware of something different or new.
2. Reflection process at the end of a trial:
   At the end of a trial, reflection markers can be attached in any state. Figure 5 (c) shows an example of attached reflection markers. In this case, @ marks a goal state, + marks a corner state of this maze, and ## marks feature points to prevision an invisible wall. The typical usage of them is to memorize the special event such as the encounter with an invisible wall or a goal, or to summarize the sign distribution in the searched maze. Reflection markers are remained during a train of trials.

3.3   Designing the Continuous Learning Task by Maze Sweeping

To begin with, we describe an *achievement* which is a maze sweeping task with a fixed start and goal which has at least one solution. It is defined as to find paths from start state S to goal state G which visit all states only at once in the maze. Figure 6

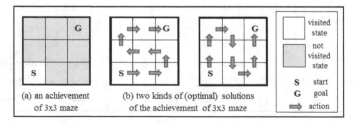

(a) an achievement of 3x3 maze
(b) two kinds of (optimal) solutions of the achievement of 3x3 maze

visited state
not visited state
S   start
G   goal
⇒   action

Fig. 6. An example of an achievement of 3x3 maze sweeping task

shows an illustrated example of an achievement of the 3x3 maze sweeping task. Figure 6 (a) shows an initial situation of an achievement of the 3x3 maze. Figure 6 (b) shows all solutions of the achievement as shown in figure 6 (a).

3.4   Designing the Sequence of Learning Goals

Designing the learning goals, the case of invisible simple mazes results in the difficulty of a partially observable state, it can be worked out by slightly broadening a learner's perceptual states to distinguish whether an invisible wall exists or not. The case of non-simple mazes results in more difficulty of partially observable states since they have various non- distinguishable states or situations. This paper describes the sequence of learning goals for the simple maze with a partially observable state.

Under simple and invisible mazes, the standard steps to master them are follows;

1. Find a goal state if it is invisible.
2. If walls are invisible, estimate the borders of the current maze such like wall-following behaviors as shown in figure 5.
3. Search all maze sweeping paths from start state to the goal state.

We focus on learning goals for the second step to estimate the invisible borders of a simple maze. Figure 7 shows an illustrated example of estimating an invisible wall for a partially observable state under simple mazes. First, under simple mazes, possible signs of any state are {0, 1, 2} as shown in figure 5. Since sign 0 means there is no wall, a state with sign 1 or 2 is a partially observable state where wall layout is nondeterministic. Figure 7 (a) shows the case which starts from sign 1 state.

To solve this, the learner should try to perceive a sign of neighbor state. If the learner encounters either a wall as shown in Figure 7 (b), or a sign 0 state, he/she can decide the direction of walls. In this case, an important learning goal to prevision an invisible wall is being aware of a sign sequence of 0 and 1 neighbor states. Figure 7 (c) shows that the sequence of "01!" suggests the direction of an invisible wall as !. It is derived from the sign pattern 01 as shown in figure 5(c). Note that this pattern for provisioning an invisible wall holds good only under simple mazes.

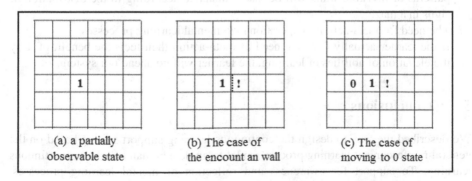

(a) a partially   (b) The case of   (c) The case of
  observable state   the encount an wall   moving to 0 state

Fig. 7. Estimating an invisible wall under a partially observable state

4   Discussions

Now we discuss several points for designing the learning environment for continuous learning support system.

1. easy to monitor the learning process of a learner
   The maze model can visualize the learner's learning process as the trace of his/her action sequence in the maze including trial and error. There are two kinds of advantages. For the learner, self-monitoring the learning process assists being conscious of his/her awareness and reflection stages. For the system, observing the learner's learning process enables to support it and to evaluate the effect of the learning support system.
2. capture the essential features of continuous learning task
   To evaluate a continuous learning task with invisible learning goals by the experiment with subjects within minutes, it is important to be easy to pass on meaning of the experimental task to a human learner
3. Adequate difficulty enough to keep the learner being conscious of thinking
   Too easy task may prevent the learner from his/her conscious thinking. The maze model with invisible walls provides the learner with various unexpected results or failures which signs consistent with and a sign of them.
4. Unexpected results or failures which can be experienced by the learner
   The learner feels awareness toward behavior change by facing such an unexpected failure.
5. Signs of failures which can be perceived by the learner
   Becoming aware of unexpected failures such as encounter an invisible wall, a sign of invisible walls in the neighborhood is designed. Thinking the meaning of the perceived sign, the learner will be able to estimate the position of the invisible wall as the ability of awareness.
6. Illusion or confusion leading to new failures as the temporal difficulty
   Early learning results obtained by a few experiences may result in such a difficulty because of partially observable state problem [4]. It also leads to the driving force for continuous learning. After gaining a wide variety of experiences, various patterns of invisible walls will be distinguishable according to the distribution of signs in a maze.
7. The need for meta-action to operationalize mental learning processes
   If the learner actually feels the need of meta-action then feels the benefit of it by the elevation of abilities of learning, the learner will go ahead our system.

5   Conclusions

We described the way to design the continuous learning support system based on the general reinforcement learning process model to guide a human to achieve continuous learning. To support for awareness and reflection of mental learning processes, we proposed visualizing these processes with invisible mazes in the learning environments, and meta-actions for expressing and summarizing something to be aware of learning by mistake or to be reflected on the learning experience.

As one of the future works, we are planning to design the collaborative continuous learning system between a human learner and the learning agent which is based on the general reinforcement learning framework.

Acknowledgements. The authors would like to thank Prof. Habib and Prof. Shimohara for offering a good opportunity to present this research. This work was supported by JSPS KAKENHI (Grant-in-Aid for Scientific Research (C)) Grant Number 23500197.

References

1. Boud, D., Keogh, R., Walker, D.: Reflection: Turning Experience into Learning. Routledge (1985)
2. Buckler, B.: A learning process model to achieve continuous improvement. The Learning Organization 3(3), 31–39 (1996)
3. Dorval, K.B., et al.: Leadership for Learning: Tips for Effective Mentoring and Coaching. In: McCluskey, K.W. (ed.) Mentoring for Talent Development Unknown Binding. Reclaiming Youth International (2003)
4. Kaelbling, L.P., Littman, M.L., Cassandra, A.R.: Planning and acting in partially observable stochastic domains. J. Artificial Intelligence 101, 99–134 (1998)
5. Kravcik, M., et al. (eds.): ARTEL2013: 3rd Workshop on Awareness and Reflection in Technology Enhanced Learning (2013), http://ceur-ws.org/Vol-1103/
6. Krogstie, B., Prilla, M.: Tool support for reflection in the workplace in the context of reflective learning cycles. In: 2nd Workshop on Awareness and Reflection in Technology-Enhanced Learning (ARTEL 2012), pp. 57–72 (2012), http://ceur-ws.org/Vol-931/
7. Krogstie, B.R., Prilla, M., Pammer, V.: Understanding and Supporting Reflective Learning Processes in the Workplace: The CSRL Model. In: Hernández-Leo, D., Ley, T., Klamma, R., Harrer, A. (eds.) EC-TEL 2013. LNCS, vol. 8095, pp. 151–164. Springer, Heidelberg (2013)
8. Kurapati, S., et al.: A Theoretical Framework for Shared Situational Awareness in Sociotechnical Systems. In: 2nd Workshop on Awareness and Reflection in Technology-Enhanced Learning (ARTEL 2012), pp. 47–53 (2012), http://ceur-ws.org/Vol-931/
9. Marton, F., Booth, S.: Learning and Awareness. Routledge (1997)
10. Moore, A., et al. (eds.): ARTEL 2012: 2nd Workshop on Awareness and Reflection in Technology Enhanced Learning (2012), http://ceur-ws.org/Vol-931/
11. Reinhardt, W., Christian, M.: Awareness in Learning Networks. In: 1st Workshop on Awareness and Reflection in Personal Learning Environments (ARTEL 2011), pp. 12–20 (2011), http://journal.webscience.org/703/1/editorial.pdf
12. Russell, S., Norvig, P.: Artificial Intelligence: A Modern Approach, 1st edn. Prentice Hall (1995)
13. Russell, S., Norvig, P.: Artificial Intelligence: A Modern Approach, 3rd edn. Prentice Hall (2009)

14. Sessa, V.I., London, M.: Continuous Learning in Organizations: Individual, Group, and Organizational Perspectives. Psychology Press (2006)
15. Smita, J., Trey, M.: Facilitating continuous learning: review of research on individual learning capabilities and organizational learning environments. In: The Annual Meeting of the AECT International Convention, Louisville (2012)
16. Schunk, D.H., Zimmerman, B.J.: Motivation and Self-Regulated Learning: Theory, Research, and Applications. Routledge (2007)
17. Takemori, K., Yamaguchi, T., Sasaji, K., Takadama, K.: Modeling a Human's Learning Processes to Support Continuous Learning on Human Computer Interaction. In: Yamamoto, S. (ed.) HCI 2013, Part I. LNCS, vol. 8016, pp. 555–564. Springer, Heidelberg (2013)
18. Yamaguchi, T., Takemori, K., Takadama, K.: Modeling a human's learning processes toward continuous learning support system. In: Habib, M.K., Paulo Davim, J. (eds.) Interdisciplinary Mechatronics, pp. 69–94. Wiley-ISTE (2013)

Decision Support

Association of CCR and BCC Efficiencies to Market Variables in a Retrospective Two Stage Data Envelope Analysis

Denis A. Coelho

Human Technology Group, Department of Electromechanical Engineering,
Universidade da Beira Interior, Calçada da Fonte do Lameiro, 6201-001 Covilhã, Portugal
denis@ubi.pt, denis.a.coelho@gmail.com

Abstract. The analysis compares constant returns to scale (CRS) and varying returns to scale (VRS) measures, by modeling the performance of internet companies using a two-stage DEA process. In the DEA literature, process efficiency is widely measured by a CRS measure, CCR, and a VRS measure, BCC, which were proposed by Charnes et al. (1978) and Banker et al. (1984), respectively. Measuring the performance of Internet companies using two-stage DEA was also presented by Cao and Yang (2011). The results of the analysis reported in this paper suggest that both forms of DEA efficiency scores are relevant to measure the performance of Internet companies.

Keywords: Decision support systems, E-commerce, Evaluating information, Internet companies, Investment analysis.

1 Introduction

Previous work on the study of association between company specific indicators has been made considering national aggregate data (e.g. concerning manufacturing strategy, see Coelho, 2011). In evaluating Internet companies, the common approach is to focus primarily on a single variable or a small collection of financial ratios such as return on investment (ROI), return on equity (ROE) while ignoring the non-financial information in Internet industry (Cao and Yang, 2011). Although the ratio analysis provides useful information, it only portrays one facet of performance. Without the help of supporting non-financial information, financial information might be insufficient for judging an online business. Moreover, there are many factors related to an Internet company's performance such as assets, expense, number of employees and visitors, etc. Therefore, it is necessary to assess the performance of Internet companies in a multidimensional systems perspective. A small number of studies (Barua et al. 2004, Serrano-Cinca et al. 2005, Ho et al. 2011, Cao and Yang, 2011) have been conducted to evaluate Internet companies using data envelopment analysis (DEA).

Data envelopment analysis (DEA) is a nonparametric method in operations research and economics for the estimation of production frontiers (empirical heuristics standing for impractical or unattainable analytical optimization). It is used to

S. Yamamoto (Ed.): HIMI 2014, Part II, LNCS 8522, pp. 151–159, 2014.
© Springer International Publishing Switzerland 2014

empirically measure productive efficiency of decision making units (or DMUs). Non-parametric approaches have the benefit of not assuming a particular functional form or shape for the frontier, but do not provide a general relationship (equation) relating output and input. DEA is a linear programming technique used to evaluate the efficiency of decision making units (DMUs) on the basis of their multiple inputs and outputs (Charnes, Cooper and Rhodes, 1978; Banker, Charnes and Cooper, 1984; Butler and Li, 2005).

In the DEA methodology, formally developed by Charnes, Cooper and Rhodes (1978), efficiency is defined as a ratio of weighted sum of outputs to a weighted sum of inputs, where the weights structure is calculated by means of mathematical programming and constant returns to scale (CRS) are assumed. In 1984, Banker, Charnes and Cooper developed a model with variable returns to scale (VRS). Tone (1995) proposed a simple method for deciding the local returns-to-scale characteristics of DMUs (Decision Making Units) in Data Envelopment Analysis. This method proceeds as follows: first, the BCC (Banker-Charnes-Cooper) model is solved to find the returns-to-scale of BCC-efficient DMUs and a reference set for each BCC-inefficient DMU. Then the local returns-to-scale characteristics of each BCC-inefficient DMU is apprehended by observing only the returns-to-scale characteristics of DMUs in their respective reference sets.

An important decision in DEA modelling is the selection of inputs and outputs that are included in the specification, as different inputs/outputs combinations will produce different efficiency rankings of firms. A particular DMU may or may not be efficient depending on the selection of inputs and outputs. Decision makers may be reluctant to use a technique that is so sensitive to decisions taken at the modelling stage. Serrano-Cinca et al. (2005) suggest a new approach to the problem of deciding which inputs and outputs the model should contain. A series of DEA specifications are contemplated, and the resulting efficiency scores are analyzed using multivariate statistical techniques. There is a further problem with DEA: efficiency is a mere score between 0 and 1 (or between 0% and 100%). Two different DMUs may achieve the same DEA score while, at the same time, being very different: they just take a different route to the achievement of efficiency (Serrano-Cinca et al., 2005). By considering the series relationship of sub-processes within an entire production process, a relational two-stage DEA can overcome the disadvantages of a traditional DEA model (Cao and Yang, 2011). This is achieved by segmenting internal DMU processes and obtaining efficiency scores in two steps.

The aim of this study is to explore the effect on relational dual-stage DEA efficiency scores and extrapolative power of the latter of alternative modalities for returns to scale. To this end, data was used in hindsight, to apprehend which modality of relational dual-stage DEA measure of efficiency of DMUs (CCR or BCC) yielded efficiency measures with better predictive power.

2   Data

Data was obtained by matching the sample of Internet companies used by Serrano-Cinca (2005), which originated from the end of 2000 and comprised 40 companies, with the sample used by Ho et al. (2011), comprising 52 companies and dated from the end of 2005. The complete data set used is shown in Appendix, comprising 9 companies that resulted from the matching of the two afore-mentioned data sets.

The inputs and outputs considered by Serrano-Cinca et al. (2005) were:

- Input A: Number of employees
- Input B: Total operating expenses ($000)
- Input C: Total assets ($000)
- Output 1: Unique visitors
- Output 2: Revenues ($000).

A requirement of the DEA model is homogeneity. For this reason, all financial data in the Serrano-Cinca sample relates to end of 2000 year accounts. "Unique visitors" was taken at the end of March 2000 in order to avoid any distortion that might be introduced by the Christmas period.

On the other hand, the inputs and outputs considered by Ho et al. (2011) were:

- Input A: Total assets ($000)
- Input B: Operating expenses ($000)
- Output 1: Reach (average)
- Output 2: Page views (average)
- Output 3: Gross margin ($000)
- Output 4: Accumulative cash flow ($000)

All input and output data of the companies in Ho et al.'s sample is from 2005. The fiscal year of all financial data ends on 31 December 2005.

Total assets and operating expenses are featured in the two datasets, while number of employees is only featured in the first. Outputs are somewhat similar between both datasets, unique visitors from the first data set finds correspondence in reach and page views of the second dataset. Revenues, featured in the first data set, finds a correspondence in gross margin and accumulative cash flow in the second data set. In this way the dual-stage DEA modelling for the two times (2000 and 2005) is fairly similar, enabling a comparison of efficiency measures obtained for each point in time.

Additionally, end of 2000 fiscal year market capital and market price as well as 2012 data for end of 2012 year stock price, assets and equity was sought for the 9 companies. This was only successfully obtained for 5 companies, as four out of nine had been acquired by other companies and as hence were no longer publicly traded (details in the appendix). The models compared in this study were the input-oriented, constant returns to scale (CRS), envelopment form of the DEA (Charnes et al., 1978; Cooper et al., 2000) and the input-oriented, varying returns to scale (VRS), envelopment form of DEA (Banker et al., 1984).

3   DMU Process Modelling

With the data obtained as described in the previous section of this paper, the next step was to apply the models to analyse the data. One decision had to be made whether the analysis aimed to minimise inputs or maximise outputs for the processes under consideration. Both constant and variable returns to scale were used for comparison. The data from all decision making units (DMUs) in this study were subject to the calculation of the Frontier Analyst software based on the input minimizing-oriented CCR and BCC models, in order to obtain the dual-stage DEA efficiency values. According to Hussain and Jones (2010), Frontier Analyst uses the most tried and tested models in DEA, which, in academic literature, have proven to be the most robust. The two models used were the BCC model for variable returns to scale and the CCR model for constant returns to scale. Statistical analysis was developed with the support of STATA IC 12 software.

3.1   DEA Efficiency Model Choice

In DEA, the efficiency model can address one of two questions:

1. Given the level of outputs that a unit produces, by how much might the inputs be reduced while maintaining the current level of outputs? This is input minimisation, seeking to minimize inputs to produce the same outputs.
2. Given the current level of inputs used by a unit, what level of outputs should it be possible to achieve? This is output maximisation, seeking to maximize outputs given the current inputs.

Under the assumption of constant returns to scale (CRS), the efficiency results obtained from both the input minimisation and output maximisation options are identical. Hence, for the VRS modality the use of input minimisation or output maximisation depends on the situation being analysed (Hussain and Jones, 2010). In the case of the output maximisation model, an appreciation of whether it is actually possible to achieve the target outputs generated by the analysis is needed, e.g. if the output targets are considered to be unattainable because of external factors then this model is likely to be inappropriate. Alternatively, it may be that the inputs a unit uses are relatively inflexible in which case the output maximisation project might be best. Given the competitive nature of the domain of the sample data (Internet companies) in rather closely contained sectors (e-tailers, content, search), input minimization was chosen for the efficiency models of the BCC runs of the study.

3.2   Returns to Scale Alternatives

Data Envelope Analysis allows assessing the relative efficiency of units under a system of either constant or variable returns to scale. The efficiency results obtained from using the different scale assumptions are likely to be different. In the constant returns modality (CCR mode) outputs directly reflect input levels (i.e. doubling input produces exactly double outputs). In the varying returns modality (BCC mode) outputs fall off as input levels rise (i.e. doubling input produces less than double outputs). Using the variable returns to scale option allows the analysis more room to find optimal solutions (Hussain and Jones, 2010). The choice of model, constant (CCR) or variable (BCC), depends on the process being analysed. If any increase in input (resources) used yields a proportionate increase in outputs (results), then this indicates there is a linear relationship between inputs and outputs, so a constant returns to scale model should be used. If however, an increase in inputs does not yield the same increase in outputs, then the variable returns to scale model ought to be used, as a non-linear relationship between results and resources would have been identified. This is the fundamental issue this study tackles, with both alternatives tested on the data. The hypothesis is that variable returns to scale are more adequate to Internet companies than constant returns to scale.

3.3   Dual-stage DEA Process Modelling

The DEA model for the 2000 data retrieved from Serrano-Cinca (2005) was established in a dual-stage process. Controlled inputs for stage 1 (marketability) were number of employees, total operating expenses and total assets, with output of stage 1 modelled as unique visitors. For stage 2 (profitability), and the same data, unique visitors were modelled as controlled inputs, with revenues modelled as output (additionally stage 1controlled inputs were considered as uncontrolled inputs for stage 2). The efficiency scores obtained for the two stages of each DMU were multiplied resulting in the overall dual-stage efficiency score. This process was developed twice, considering for the minimising input DEA efficiency approach, both the CCR modality and the BCC modality.

For the 2005 data retrieved from Ho et al. (2011), controlled inputs considered for stage 1 (marketability) of the dual-stage process modelling were total assets and operating expenses. For stage 1 process modelling, outputs considered were reach and page views. The latter stage 1 outputs became stage 2 controlled inputs, with outputs modelled as accumulative cash flow and gross margin, while for stage 2 (profitability) operating expenses and total assets were modelled as uncontrolled inputs. For this data, both the CCR modality and the BCC modality were implemented, based on a minimising input DEA efficiency approach.

4   Analysis of Results

As expected, no unit received a lower efficiency score using variable returns to scale, than they did with the constant returns to scale model. Any units which were operating with minimum input or maximum output levels were also found to be efficient using variable returns to scale (BCC), and so the total number of 100% efficient units is higher in this modality than in the CCR modality. Table 1 presents the dual-stage efficiency scores for the 2000 data obtained from Serrano-Cinca et al. (2005). Table 2 presents the same kind of scores for the same Internet companies, but considering 2005 data obtained from Ho et al. (2011). In both cases the dual-stage efficiency scores are obtained from the Data Analysis Envelope (DEA) approach described by Cao and Yang (2011), where stage 1 refers to marketability and stage 2 refers to profitability of Internet companies. For both time periods, there are more efficient DMUs in the BCC modality than in the CCR modality.

Table 1. Relational dual-stage efficiency scores (Cao and Yang, 2011) for 2000 data, obtained for both CCR and BCC modalities, considering input minimisation

Unit name	2000 data						ratio
	CCR			BCC			BCC Ek / CCR Ek
	Ek1	Ek2	Ek	Ek1	Ek2	Ek	
ADBL	17,4%	7,9%	1,37%	95,20%	91,5%	87,11%	63,4
AMZN	19,3%	100,0%	19,3%	19,50%	100,0%	19,5%	1,0
CNET	93,7%	9,6%	9,0%	97,20%	10,8%	10,5%	1,2
EBAY	91,6%	14,5%	13,28%	94,00%	15,3%	14,38%	1,1
EDGR	24,8%	23,5%	5,83%	100,0%	100,0%	100,0%	17,2
INSW	44,8%	9,1%	4,08%	57,10%	15,4%	8,79%	2,2
LOOK	100,0%	5,2%	5,2%	100,0%	6,8%	6,8%	1,3
TSCM	24,9%	13,4%	3,34%	39,60%	27,8%	11,01%	3,3
YHOO	100,0%	100,0%	100,0%	100,0%	100,0%	100,0%	1,0

Table 2. Relational dual-stage efficiency scores (Cao and Yang, 2011) for 2005 data, obtained for both CCR and BCC modalities, considering input minimisation

Unit name	2005 data						ratio BCC Ek / CCR Ek
	CCR			BCC			
	Ek1	Ek2	Ek	Ek1	Ek2	Ek	
ADBL	23,8%	36,3%	8,64%	45,7%	41,5%	18,97%	2,2
AMZN	36,1%	100,0%	36,1%	36,3%	100,0%	36,3%	1,0
CNET	41,9%	9,6%	4,02%	43,7%	100,0%	43,7%	10,9
EBAY	12,3%	100,0%	12,3%	12,6%	100,0%	12,6%	1,0
EDGR	21,3%	35,6%	7,58%	100,0%	100,0%	100,0%	13,2
INSW	17,1%	100,0%	17,1%	100,0%	100,0%	100,0%	5,8
LOOK	19,9%	100,0%	19,9%	48,5%	100,0%	48,5%	2,4
TSCM	81,1%	100,0%	81,1%	100,0%	100,0%	100,0%	1,2
YHOO	100%	13,2%	13,2%	100,0%	100,0%	100,0%	7,6

Moreover, for 2005 CRS (or CCR) efficiency scores compared to the 2000 ones, Yahoo kept its marketability maximum efficiency, loosing its profitability maximum efficiency, resulting in the loss of its maximum relational dual-stage efficiency. Amazon improved marketability efficiency while keeping its maximum profitability efficiency. Four other DMUs attained maximum profitability efficiencies, with improvement in dual-stage efficiency over the 5 year period for all, except for Ebay, which dropped in marketability over the period.

In what concerns the evolution of VRS or BCC efficiency scores over the same 5 year time period, the number of DMUs with maximum relational dual-stage efficiency doubled. Audible.com suffered a very steep drop in both marketability and profitability efficiency, while CNet lost marketability efficiency while improving profitability efficiency, quadrupling overall dual-stage efficiency.

The last column in both Tables 1 and 2 shows the ratio of BCC over CCR relational dual-stage efficiency. The biggest decrease in the ratios for the 5 year time period concerns Audible.com as its BCC overall efficiency dropped steeply with a slight increase in its CCR overall efficiency.

Table 3 presents the results of analysis of market capital increase and stock price increase over the period 2000-2005, and up to 2012 for market price only. Differences between market price and capital changes in the 2000 to 2005 period indicate that either public-offerings occurred in the meantime with capital increase, or stock options were exercised, or insider stock acquisition took place.

Table 3. Market capital and market price change

Unit Name	2000-2005 Market Capital increase	2000-2005 Market Price change	2005-2012 Market Price change	2000-2012 Market Price change
ADBL	1180%	1429%	-	-
AMZN	119%	240%	463%	1813%
CNET	201%	82%	-	-
EBAY	1136%	472%	30%	641%
EDGR	306%	96%	-	-
INSW	18%	175%	-	-
LOOK	82%	-70%	-76%	-93%
TSCM	404%	229%	-77%	-26%
YHOO	431%	178%	-50%	39%

Analysis of association was carried out over the whole data set, including original data and the results presented in Tables 1, 2 and 3. Statistically significant Pearson correlation coefficients are shown in Table 4. Moreover, a linear regression analysis was carried out for market price change over the period 2000 to 2005 based on the beginning of period data and the relational dual-stage efficiency analysis results for the same time (Table 5). Due to very small numbers (n=5) of surviving independent companies by the end of 2012, regression analysis was not possible for market price change over the period 2005 to 2012.

The results of analysis of association shown in Table 4 reveal the importance of the constant returns to scale dual-stage efficiency in predicting market capital in 2005. These results also shed light on the high strength of association between market price change in the period from 2000 to 2005 and ratio between VRS and CCR dual-stage DEA efficiency based on 2000 data. The Linear regression analysis results performed on the former, shown in Table 5, obtained a very high determination of 94,70%, significant at $p<0.05$. Significance of regression coefficients and standardized coefficient values corroborate the importance of the aforementioned ratio.

Table 4. Pearson correlation coefficients attaining statistical significance

	(1)	(2)	(3)	(4)	(5)	(6)	(7)	(8)	(9)	(10)	(11)
(1)	1			0,683*							
(2)		1							0,897◊		
(3)			1			0,747*	0,886◊	0,754◊		0,741*	
(4)	0,683*			1			0,832◊				
(5)					1				0,807◊		
(6)			0,747*			1					
(7)			0,886◊	0,832◊			1				
(8)			0,754◊					1		1,000	0,983◊
(9)		0,897◊			0,807◊				1		
(10)			0,741*					1,000◊		1	0,982◊
(11)								0,983◊		0,982◊	1

* - p<0.05, ◊ - p<0.01, r – ratio, incr. – increase, ch. – change, n=9 for 2000 and 2005 data, n= 5 for 2012 data; (1) - 2000 Ek CCR; (2) - 2000 r. Ek BCC / CCR; (3) - 2000 market capital; (4) - 2005 market capital; (5) - 2000-2005 market capital incr.; (6) - 2000 market price ; (7) - 2005 market price ; (8) - 2012 market price; (9) - 2000-2005 market price change; (10) - 2005-2012 market price change; (11) - 2000-2012 market price change.

Table 5. Linear regression analysis of Market price change over the period from 2000 to 2005, based on CRS and VRS relational dual-stage DEA measures of efficiency and market data

Variable	Coefficient	Std. Error	t	P>|t|	[95% Conf. Interval]		Std. Coeff.s
2000 Ek CRS	6.275	3.946	1.59	0.21	-6.28	18.83	0.444
2000 Ek VRS	-6.670	2.798	-2.38	0.09	-15.58	2.23	-0.637
2000 r .Ek	0.276	0.047	5.84	0.01	0.12	0.42	1.284
2000 mark. pr.	-0.269	0.190	-1.42	0.25	-0.87	0.33	-0.347
Regr. Const.	2.745	1.397	1.96	0.14	-1.70	7.19	-

r. – ratio BCC / CCR, Ek – relational dual-stage efficiency of DMU, n=9.

5   Discussion

The question whether variable returns to scale are more adequate to dual-stage DEA efficiency measures of Internet companies than constant returns to scale, remains to be answered. The results, from hindsight of the period from 2000 to 2005, suggest that both CRS and VRS modalities should be considered in DMU efficiency assessment of Internet companies, considering a relational dual-stage DEA analysis.

The CCR efficiency and the ratio of BCC efficiency over CCR, were found in the sample considered to be moderately to strongly associated with end of period market capital (r=0.683, p<0.05) and stock price increase in the period (r=0.897, p<0.01), respectively.

While the Dual-Stage efficiency obtained from the CCR modality of DEA showed predictive power (considering the correlation between this efficiency score obtained from 2000 data and the market capital of the units in 2005), it was the ratio between the dual-stage efficiencies (BCC over CCR) that exhibited the highest correlation with market price increase of the units in the five year period. The small sample and the particular characteristics of the 5 year period encompassed (dot com bubble burst in the collapse of the Internet sector in the year 2000) do not enable generalising the results. This notwithstanding, the results suggest that both forms of dual-stage DEA efficiency score modality may be relevant for judging investment alternatives for Internet companies. Future research, on a wider empirical basis is needed to confirm these findings.

References

1. Banker, R.D., Charnes, A., Cooper, W.W.: Some models for estimating technical and scale inefficiency in data envelopment analysis. Management Science 30(9), 1078–1092 (1984)
2. Barua, A., et al.: DEA evaluations of long-and short-run efficiencies of digital vs. physical product 'dot com' companies. Socio Economic Planning Sciences 38(4), 233–254 (2004)
3. Butler, T.W., Li, L.: The utility of returns to scale in DEA programming: an analysis of Michigan rural hospitals. European Journal of Operational Research 161(2), 469–477 (2005)
4. Charnes, A., Cooper, W.W., Rhodes, E.: Measuring the efficiency of decision making units. European Journal of Operational Research 2, 429–444 (1978)
5. Cao, X., Yang, F.: Measuring the performance of Internet companies using a two-stage data envelopment analysis model. Enterprise Information Systems 5(2), 207–217 (2011)
6. Coelho, D.A.: A study on the relation between manufacturing strategy, company size, country culture and product and process innovation in Europe. International Journal of Business and Globalisation 7(2), 152–165 (2011)
7. Cooper, W.W., Seiford, L.M., Tone, K.: Data Envelopment Analysis—A Comprehensive Text Models, Applications References and DEA-Solver Software. Kluwer, Boston (2000)
8. Ho, C.T.B., Liao, C.K., Kim, H.T.: Valuing Internet Companies: A DEA-Based Multiple Valuation Approach. Journal of the Operational Research Society 62(12), 2097–2106 (2011)
9. Hussain, A., Jones, M.: An Introduction to Frontier Analyst® 4, Version 4.0. Banxia Software Ltd. (March 2010), for Frontier Analyst version 4
10. Serrano-Cinca, C., Fuertes-Callén, Y., Mar-Molinero, C.: Measuring DEA efficiency in Internet companies. Decision Support Systems 38(4), 557–573 (2005)
11. Tone, K.: A Simple Characterization of Returns to Scale in DEA. Journal of the Operational Research Society of Japan 39, 604–613 (1996)

Exploring Similarity

Improving Product Search with Parallel Coordinates

Mandy Keck[1], Martin Herrmann[1], Andreas Both[2], Dana Henkens[3], and Rainer Groh[1]

[1] Technische Universität Dresden, 01062 Dresden, Germany
{mandy.keck,martin.herrmann,rainer.groh}@tu-dresden.de
[2] Unister GmbH, Barfußgäßchen 11, 04109 Leipzig, Germany
andreas.both@unister-gmbh.de
[3] queo GmbH, Tharandter Str. 13, 01159 Dresden, Germany
d.henkens@queo-group.com

Abstract. Faceted browsing is an established and well-known paradigm for product search. However, if the user is unfamiliar with the topic and the provided facets, he may not be able to sufficiently reduce the amount of results. In order to increase the understanding of the bidirectional relation between facets and result set, we present an interface concept that allows manifold approaches for product search, analysis and comparison starting with a single product or a summarizing visualization of the entire data set. Moreover, various product features can be analyzed in order to support decision-making. Even without detailed knowledge of a specific topic, the user is able to estimate the range and distribution of characteristics in relation to known or desired features. Conventional list-based search forms do not provide such a quick overview. Our concept is based on two visualization techniques that allow the representation of multi-dimensional data across a set of parallel axes: parallel coordinates and parallel sets.

Keywords: Visual Search Interfaces, Information Visualization, Parallel Coordinates, Motive-based Search, Big Data, E–commerce.

1 Introduction

Although sophisticated algorithms and semantic search approaches exist, product search in large data sets is still a major challenge for web users. Deciding on a product is based on the analysis and comparison of multi-dimensional product data. However, typical web interfaces with simple search masks and result lists do not support the user sufficiently for these tasks. Particularly in the context of financial data, where complex search masks often overstrain non-experts, alternative entry points are required. Fuzzy filters or query-by-example approaches can increase the understanding of the various attributes of product data and can help to improve the precision of the individual search query. To address this challenge, we developed an interface concept based on the visualization technique of parallel coordinates that allows the analysis of various attributes at a glance. Our concept enables the comparison and exploration of

S. Yamamoto (Ed.): HIMI 2014, Part II, LNCS 8522, pp. 160–171, 2014.
© Springer International Publishing Switzerland 2014

similar products to support the evaluation of products and to improve decision-making [1]. The concept combines the search paradigm of faceted browsing and query-by-example to facilitate the search in a bidirectional way. Thus, huge result sets can be quickly narrowed down to smaller subsets or single products and the analysis of products with similar properties can be improved. Furthermore, the distribution of product data is shown to allow the modification of search criteria.

The interactive parallel axis approach that we present in section 3, covers two interface concepts: the first is based on parallel coordinates (see section 2.2) and the second is based on parallel sets (see section 2.3). Both concepts provide insights into patterns and dependencies of multi-dimensional data. To evaluate the suitability for different search tasks, we provide a preliminary user study in section 4.

2   Related Work

This section covers different search and visualization techniques to explore and analyze multi-dimensional data sets.

2.1   Faceted Browsing

A popular interface paradigm to explore a product database is the principle of Faceted Browsing, which many e-commerce sites use (e.g. amazon.com, ebay.com). Faceted Browsing allows multiple access points for the search and the iterative refinement of the result set. Therefore, the products have to be structured using a Faceted Classification [2]. This classification method describes items through a combination of facets, where each facet addresses a different property. In the context of product search, a product can have the facets "product type", "customer rating", and "price". Each facet contains different facet values (e.g. the facet "product type" contains the facet values "books", "movies", "music", etc.) and usually one value per facet describes an item. Additionally, a hierarchy can be used to organize the facets in several subcategories (e.g. hierarchical structuring of the product type in "book", "textbook", and "computer science") [3]. A Faceted Browser allows the navigation in this data structure and the construction of complex search queries by selecting facet values [4]. The user can explore the data collection by restricting or increasing the result set iteratively.

2.2   Parallel Coordinates

The visualization technique of parallel coordinates (PC) allows the two-dimensional representation of multi-dimensional data across a set of parallel axes [5]. Each parallel axis represents one attribute of the multi-dimensional data set, whereas all axes are arranged side by side. A polyline represents a single data item and intersects each axis at the appropriate value (see Figure 1 left).

First implementations of parallel coordinates introduced by Inselberg [5] used straight lines to connect each intersection point of a data item. Since multiple items often share the same intersection points, it becomes difficult to trace the path of a single item. Different approaches have been developed to overcome this "crossing problem". Graham et al. [14] propose adding curvature using continuous gradients, and spreading of close intersection points depending on their positions in the proceeding and following axis to a larger region on the axis.

Another important challenge is to reduce visual clutter. Data mining tasks usually require analysing a large amount of datasets. Due to the overlapping of hundreds of lines, it becomes impossible to identify meaningful patterns. In order to overcome this problem and reveal hidden information, several strategies like colour coding or frequency and density calculations [15] can be applied on the tangle of lines. Bundling of similar multidimensional items is another approach to spatially separate and unravel lines and therefore maintain the user's ability to recognize correlations between the data attributes [13].

Typically, parallel coordinates show their strength in analysing continuous data types, but some fields of application also require analysing categorical data. Rosario et al. [12] propose mapping a class to a single point on an axis and indicate the degree of similarity by the spacing between the points. Teoh et al. [11] and Riehmann et al. [7] extend the point to a vertical area indicating the number of items included in the corresponding category. Riehmann et al. also use this approach to reduce the crossing problem by distributing the lines on this constructed interval [7].

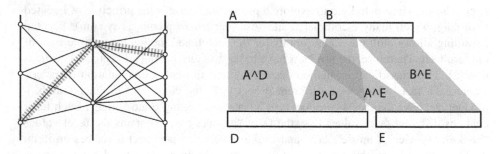

Fig. 1. Parallel coordinates (left), parallel sets (right)

2.3   Parallel Sets

The visualization technique parallel sets (PS) is mostly used for categorical data attributes and is well suited for the visual analysis of large, complex data sets. The basic layout is derived from parallel coordinates, with the axes being replaced by containers representing categories. These containers are scaled according to the frequency of the corresponding category [10]. Instead of single lines, the containers are connected by polygonal streams representing the logical conjunction of the adjacent containers. The size of these streams give an impression of the frequency of items included in the conjunction (see Figure 1 right). Since the complexity of this visualization is independent from the number of regarded items, it is well suited to obtain a fast overview over large-scale data sets.

3   Visual Interface for Product Search

While Faceted Browsing became a common paradigm for product search in the last years, parallel coordinates and parallel sets are mostly restricted to scientific data-mining tasks. With our concept, we try to introduce and evaluate these two concepts in the area of financial data exploration. We propose that users can strongly benefit from the possibility of discovering patterns and interpreting correlations of the manifold characteristics of financial products. Even without detailed knowledge of the topic, the user can get an impression of the range and distribution of characteristics in relation to known or desired features, which cannot be accomplished with conventional list based search forms.

3.1   Data Preparation

To test our visualisation concepts, we use a set of financial products including certificates, leveraged products, and warrants. From the great variety of features, we chose eight of the most meaningful characteristics to describe a single financial product. These features include categorical data (e.g. *underlying value*) as well as continuous data (e.g. *performance*) and ordinal data (e.g. *investment term*). Since parallel sets require categorical data, continuous data needs to be classified. This can be achieved by defining ranges either automatically (with equidistant or logarithmic intervals or by using natural breaks) or by defining meaningful intervals manually.

An advantage of categorical data representation is that a category can be either generalized or specialized and can be organized into a hierarchy. Therefore, an attribute can be viewed on different levels of abstraction. To allow this semantic zoom ability, we added meta-information about the underlying hierarchy for each axis. For categorical attributes, we identified all possible entities of a feature and added the parent items manually. For continuous attributes, only the top hierarchy levels were defined manually, while lower levels were identified by automatic methods.

3.2   Interface Concept

The interface is divided into a parallel axis view and a list view containing item title and description (see Figure 2). This allows the exploration of the database in a bidirectional way. Starting with the left side the user can get an overview of the underlying data structure and the distribution of product data. The presented result list on the right side can be reduced by various filters. Selecting items in the result list highlights the corresponding elements in the axis view and supports the identification of similar products.

The visual representation of the axis is composed of spatially separated container elements representing the facet values. The height of each container, in reference to the overall height of the axis, shows the distribution of data items within the facets and allows the analysis of predominant values. Additionally, it reduces the over-plotting situation at crowded points for the PC view and simplifies the explicit selection and tracing of a single curve or stream [7].

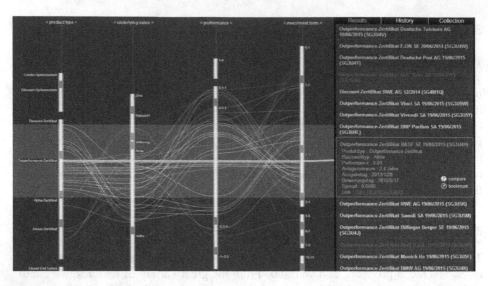

Fig. 2. Interface concept with parallel coordinates (left) and result list (right): the comparing feature centers the selected product; the fuzzy filter (light grey) reduces the amount of polylines

Interaction with Axes. The parallel axes are the main control elements of the visualization and offer a range of interactions for manipulation. Mouse scrolling zooms the selected axis (see Figure 3 left). This semantic zooming allows the user to explore the underlying hierarchy of a facet and thus to generalize or specify his current selection. Connected containers indicate the same parent in the hierarchy. Apart from zooming, each axis can be dragged vertically and horizontally, granting the user full control of the position, ordering, and spacing of axes. The rearrangement of axes allows a better comparison of two axes of interest. To adjust the complexity of the provided facets, axes can be added or deleted.

Facet Filter. Selecting a container activates a filter, leaving only items matching the facet value (see Figure 3 middle & right). Multiple filters can be activated on one or different axes to create complex filters as known from Faceted Browsers (logical disjunction within an axis, logical conjunction on different axes). Showing facet values and products in one representation holds the advantage that the user can immediately see which filters have a strong influence on his current selection and how much he has to alter his query to get better results. It also allows a quick comparison of different products and an in-depth analysis of the database. For instance, the user can determine the best product types depending on the lowest risk and the highest performance.

Result List. The right side of the interface provides the result list. The result view is constructed based on the selections made in the visualization on the left side. Brushing visually links a product on the left side to the associated list item. Clicking one item in the list provides detailed product information (see Figure 2).

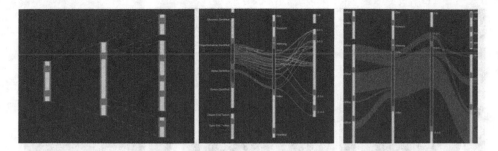

Fig. 3. Zoomable axis to support hierarchical facets (left), facet filter with parallel coordinates (middle) and parallel sets (right)

History. Each explored item is added to the history list for subsequent analysis or comparison. If an item was added to the history, it is highlighted in both views to distinguish them from unexplored or new products. If an item seems particularly interesting, it can be bookmarked and stored in a separate collection. When the user switches to the history or collection, the axes view is synchronized, allowing a direct comparison of the previously selected items.

The visualization of product data is based on two different visualization techniques that are described in section 3.3 and 3.4.

3.3   Parallel Coordinates

As described in section 2.2, the parallel coordinate concept uses lines to display the attributes of each item in the dataset. Intersections points with the axes define the property of each characteristic. Using categorical instead of continuous axes allows the distribution of intersections along the whole container equally and lead to an individual intersection point for each line. Adding curvature to the polylines (see Figure 4) further reduces the crossing problem described in section 2.2 and simplifies the tracking of individual lines.

Apart from the representation of product items, the concept of parallel coordinates supports two other features depending on the particular visualization technique:

Fuzzy Filter. The visual complexity of parallel coordinates increases with the number of displayed items. To address this problem, we introduce a fuzzy filter, represented by a scalable rectangular zone around the median line of the visualization. This filter adjusts the opacity of the lines depending on a calculated relevance value. The value represents the average distance of all intersection points of a line to the median line of the visualization. If the relevance is above a threshold, controlled by the size of the filter zone, a line becomes visible. The opacity further indicates the relevance of the visible lines. In contrast to the facet filter mechanism, the fuzzy filter is implemented to explore subsets with similar properties. Both filters can be combined to address concrete information needs (facet filter) as well as vague ideas (fuzzy filter).

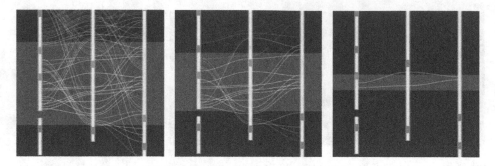

Fig. 4. Fuzzy Filter for data exploration

Filter operations can be executed either by dragging the desired facet values onto the filter zone or by scaling the filter zone to broaden or narrow the scope. The first method allows quick "scanning" of one dimension of the data set with regard to other selected attributes. The second option supports focusing on a range of interest and reduces visual clutter (see Figure 4). The visual attribute "opacity" indicates the relevance of items and is mapped to each polyline in the visualization and to every item in the result list.

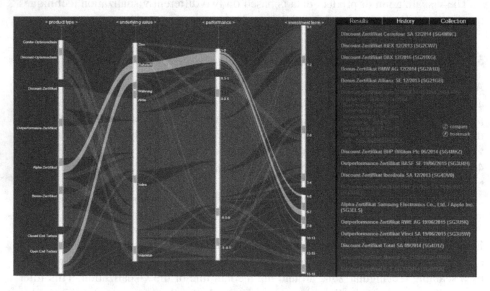

Fig. 5. Interface concept with parallel sets: selecting a product in the result list highlights the corresponding streams between the parallel axes

Comparing. When an interesting item is found in the result list, the comparing feature can be used to identify products with similar properties. This function automatically centers all interpolation points (intersections) to the median line of the visualization (see Figure 2). Furthermore the result list is rearranged to match the order of displayed lines and to put similar objects next to the centered list object. The method is well suited for a search-by-example approach where the user starts his search by selecting an item of interest matching his expectations in one or more characteristics. Previously selected and examined products are indicated as red polylines which allows the visual separation of uninspected products in the focused area and supports a feeling of finiteness.

3.4   Parallel Sets

Parallel Sets are well suited to visualize large sets of categorical data as described in section 2.3. Therefore, we adapted this technique to our flexible axes framework. The streams between the axes represent subsets of the whole dataset possessing the two properties of the connected facet values. Mouse-over highlights all subsets, which contain the same items of the current subset. Clicking on a particular subset present the contained products in the result list on the left side. The facet filter, presented in section 3.2, can be used to reduce the result set and to hide mismatched subsets as well. Using mouse-over in the result list highlights all subsets containing the focused item and allows the identification of its properties (see Fig. 5).

4   Evaluation

In a preliminary user study, we evaluate the suitability of both interface (see Fig. 2 & Fig. 5) concepts for three different tasks (analysis, comparison, and search tasks). We were interested in measurable values (solution time for different search tasks and error rate) as well as user feedback regarding to the acceptance of both interface concepts and the provided features. Therefore, we developed two prototypes implemented in JavaScript using D3.js[1] to create interactive SVG visualizations. Both prototypes visualize a subset of a real-world data set containing 120 financial products and use four axes to describe the following exemplary characteristics: *type of product* (categorical data divided into 3 high-level and 8 low-level categories), *underlying asset* (categorical data divided into 6 high-level and 50 low-level categories), *investment term* (continuous data classified into long-term, medium-term and short-term investment on first hierarchy level, and divided into sorted annual categories on second hierarchy level), and *performance* (continuous data divided into 5 sorted high-level and 20 low-level categories). Both interfaces offer the presented features in section 3: facet filter, zooming & panning of all axes, rearrangement of the axes, and result list with history and collection. Parallel coordinates additionally provide the introduced comparison feature and fuzzy filter.

4.1   Methodology

Thirteen users (7 females) in the age range of 23 – 60 years (M = 30.23, SD = 9.98) participated in the user study. According to their personal assessment (scale from 1 = extensive experience to 5 = no experience), most of them were not familiar with PC

---

[1] http://d3js.org/, Last accessed: 07.02.2014.

(M = 4.08, SD = 1.15) and PS (M = 4.53, SD = 0.88). Before they started with the experiment, we shortly introduced both visualization techniques, the underlying data set, and the range of features offered by both prototypes. Afterwards, they had some minutes to familiarize themselves with both interfaces. We switched the interface (PC or PS) during the experiment and the order was counterbalanced between participants. The participants had to solve 9 tasks per interface, divided into 3 task types with 3 tasks per type: analysis of the financial data (e.g. "Which product group contains the most products with an investment term between 1 and 2 years?"), comparison of two products (e.g. "Find a similar product with the same type of product and a performance as close as possible") and search for a financial product (e.g. "Find a product with currency as underlying asset and an investment term of approximately 3 years").

A task was solved when the user identified one result that matched his given task. He or she was free to decide when this was the case. This could be a particular facet value (analysis task) or a particular product (comparison and search tasks). During the experiment, we measured completion time (start and end of each task were indicated by the user) and error rates (results were classified in "0 = incorrect", "1 = partial match" and "2 = perfect match"). After each experiment, the participants had to complete a questionnaire to evaluate each interface concept regarding effectiveness, learnability, satisfaction, joy of use, efficiency, and range of functions. Finally, they had to complete a questionnaire which evaluated individual features (facet filter, zooming & panning of all axes, rearrangement of the axes and result list, comparing, and fuzzy filter) offered by PC and PS regarding usefulness and usability. Both questionnaires used a 5-point Likert scale (0 = Strongly Disagree, 4 = Strongly Agree) to point out their personal opinion to the given features.

4.2   Results

Time and errors were subjected to 2 (*system: PC, PS*) x 3 (*task: analysis, comparison, search*) repeated measures ANOVAs. Subjective ratings were compared between both systems with t-tests.

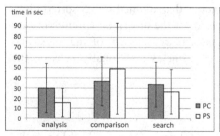 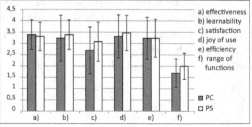

Fig. 6. Solution time for all tasks (left), results of the questionnaire for PC and PS (right) (Error bars represent standard deviations)

In terms of solution time, there was no significant difference between PC and PS, $F(1,12) = 1.71, p = .215$ (PC: M = 33.34s, SD = 19.73; PS: M = 30.36s, SD = 23.99). But there was an interaction between *system* and *task*, $F=(2,24) = 10.21, p < .001$. The difference between both systems were significant with regard to the tasks: PS was faster than PC for analytical tasks, $p = .017$, and for search tasks, $p = .023$. PC was faster than PS for comparing tasks, $p = .015$ (see Figure 6, left).

We analysed errors to evaluate the precision of each system. With both systems, most tasks have been solved correctly (PC: perfect match = 88.9%, partial match = 7.7%, incorrect = 3.4%; PS: perfect match = 94.9%, partial match = 3.4%, incorrect = 1.7%). But there was no main effect of *system*, $F(1,12) = 2.28, p = .157$, and no interaction between *system* and *task*, $F(2,24) = 0.62, p = .548$.

The evaluation of the questionnaire revealed no significant differences between both systems referring to perceived effectiveness (PC: M = 3.38, PS: M = 3.31), learnability (PC: M = 3.23, PS: M = 3.38), satisfaction (PC: M = 2.69, PS: 3.07), joy of use (PC: M = 3.31, PS: 3.46), efficiency (PC: M = 3.23, PS: M = 3.23) and range of functions (in this case means "0 = too little" and "4 = too much": PC: M = 1.69, PS: M= 2), all |t| < 2.5, all $p > .05$ (see Figure 6, right).

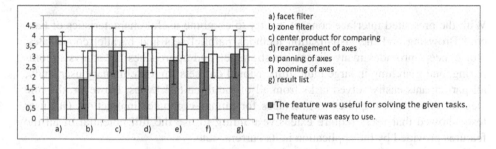

a) facet filter
b) zone filter
c) center product for comparing
d) rearrangement of axes
e) panning of axes
f) zooming of axes
g) result list

■ The feature was useful for solving the given tasks.
□ The feature was easy to use.

Fig. 7. Evaluation of the features offered by both systems

In the second questionnaire, we evaluated the individual opinion regarding usefulness and usability of the individual features. The facet filter was one feature that was used most frequently to reduce the result set, whereas the fuzzy filter was used less often. All features were easy to use (all mean values between "agree" and "strongly agree") (see Fig. 7). We observed different opinions regarding the fuzzy filter. For some participants it was helpful to reduce the visual clutter and to extend the facet filter (fuzzy filter for vague information need, facet filter for concrete information need). However, during some tasks (especially the analysis task), the fuzzy filter was disturbing because it hides some values in its initial state.

4.3   Discussion

As results have shown, both approaches match the needs of a user while performing a search for financial products. Although the participants of the study were no experts considering financial products, PS as well as the PC enable them to solve the given tasks (perfect match: 88.9% - 94.9%) in a time that is considered as adequate.

Eventually, the positive objective results were underpinned by the subjective feedback by the users considering learnability (M = 3.23 - 3.38) and joy of use (M = 3.31 – 3.46). During the experiments we observed that PC was leading to a faster solution time as soon as a bidirectional interaction was required and a detailed product view and comparison were needed (see Figure 6, left). On the other hand, PS has shown a tendency to provide a higher satisfaction (see Figure 6, right). However, the data was not significant.

Because of a lack of experienced users it is not possible to provide a comparison to the needs of expert users. As there was also no actual real-world search-driven application for financial products available for evaluation it is also not possible to estimate the superiority of PS and PC above current industrial applications. However, experts of the cooperating company have given the feedback that such existing applications are difficult to understand and create no joy of use for unexperienced users. Hence, we can assume that PC and PS are capable of providing a better interface at least for this user group.

5   Conclusion and Future Work

With the presented interface concept, we try to combine useful characteristics of Faceted Browsing and the visualization methods parallel sets and parallel coordinates. Our concept provides many distinctive strategies and approaches for analysis, comparing, and searching in large multi-dimensional datasets. In a preliminary user study, all participants easily solved tasks from all of the three task types. However, the rule "less is more" often applies to interfaces for human-computer interaction. Our user tests showed that users require extensive training to use the full potential of all the features provided by the application in its current state.

Focusing not only on experts but also on casual users, further advancements of the application could include a step-by-step introduction of features or a wizard proposing different approaches depending on the current task.

Especially when dealing with large amounts of data, the sequence of executed tasks plays a significant role for the success of a decision process. Starting with the full view on all features might not be the best choice. With the help of parallel sets applied to a few chosen attribute features, the user could be encouraged to make a preselection before investigating the subset in detail.

Our concept for fuzzy filtering proved to be convenient in solving comparison task but also confused some users who were trying to solve a search task. While both filters influence the displayed result set, it was often not evident to the user why there are only few displayed results. Additional interface elements can indicate the amount of excluded results for each activated filter.

Further improvements are necessary for the spreading of intersections on each axis. A class-internal reordering of these positions depending on zoom level, filters, attribute value and neighbouring axis could help to reduce visual clutter and enhance the accuracy of the fuzzy filter.

Acknowledgments. This work has been supported by the European Union and the Free State Saxony through the European Regional Development Fund (ERDF). The research presented in this article has been conducted in cooperation of the Chair of Media Design -Technische Universität in Dresden, Unister GmbH from Leipzig and queo GmbH from Dresden, Germany. Thanks are due to Severin Taranko, Viet Nguyen, Marcus Kirsch and Romy Müller for their invaluable feedback and support in this research.

References

1. Keck, M., Herrmann, M., Both, A., Gaertner, R., Groh, R.: Improving Motive-Based Search. In: Streitz, N., Stephanidis, C. (eds.) DAPI 2013. LNCS, vol. 8028, pp. 439–448. Springer, Heidelberg (2013)
2. Ranganathan, S.R.: Elements of Library Classification. Asian Publishing House, Bombay (1962)
3. Hearst, M.: Design recommendations for hierarchical faceted search interfaces. In: ACM SIGIR Workshop on Faceted Search (2006)
4. Polowinski, J.: Widgets for Faceted Browsing. In: Smith, M.J., Salvendy, G. (eds.) HCI International 2009, Part I. LNCS, vol. 5617, pp. 601–610. Springer, Heidelberg (2009)
5. Inselberg, A., Dimsdale, B.: Parallel coordinates: A tool for visualizing multi-dimensional geometry. In: Proc. of IEEE Visualization, pp. 361–378 (1990)
6. Graham, M., Kennedy, J.: Using curves to enhance parallel coordinate visualizations. In: Proc. of the Seventh International Conference on Information Visualization, pp. 10–16 (2003)
7. Riehmann, P., Opolka, J., Froehlich, B.: The Product Explorer: Decision Making with Ease. In: Proceedings of the International Working Conference on Advanced Visual Interfaces (AVI), Capri, Italia, pp. 423–432 (2012)
8. Stefaner, M., Müller, B.: Elastic lists for facet browsers. In: 18th International Conference on Database and Expert Systems Applications (DEXA 2007), pp. 217–221. Regensburg (2007)
9. Ware, C.: Information Visualization. Perception for Design. Elsevier Ltd., Oxford (2004)
10. Bendix, F., Kosara, R., Hauser, H.: Parallel Sets: Interactive Exploration and Visual Analysis of Categorical Data. Transactions on Visualisation and Computer Graphics 1 (2006)
11. Teoh, S., Ma, K.: PaintingClass: Interactive construction, visualization and exploration of decision trees. In: Proceedings Knowledge Discovery and Data Mining. ACM Press (2003)
12. Rosario, G.E., Rundensteiner, E.A., Brown, D.C., Ward, M.O., Huang, S.: Mapping nominal values to numbers for effective visualization. In: Proceedings IEEE Information Visualization, pp. 80–95. IEEE CS Press (2003)
13. Heinrich, J., Luo, Y., Kirkpatrick, A.E., Zhang, H., Weiskopf, D.: Evaluation of a Bundling Technique for Parallel Coordinates. In: GRAPP/IVAPP 2012, pp. 594–602 (2011)
14. Graham, M., Kennedy, J.: Using Curves to Enhance Parallel Coordinate Visualizations. In: Proceedings of the Seventh International Conference on Information Visualization, IV (2003)
15. Artero, A.O., Oliveira, M.C.F., Levkowitz, H.: Uncovering Clusters in Crowded Parallel Coordinates Visualizations, Information Visualization. In: IEEE Symposium on INFOVIS 2004 (2004)

ChoiceLog: Life Log System Based on Choices for Supporting Decision-Making

Junpei Koyama, Keiko Yamamoto, Itaru Kuramoto, and Yoshihiro Tsujino

Kyoto Institute of Technology, Matsugasaki, Sakyo-ku, Kyoto 606-8585 Japan
`lifelog@hit.is.kit.ac.jp`

Abstract. When we are faced with choices, we often make decisions based on past experiences where we faced similar choices. If we could refer these choices, we would be able to make better decisions. In this paper, we propose a new life log system called "ChoiceLog". ChoiceLog can record the options that user choose and the options that they reject. Further, it can display recorded data via searches and notifications in order to support decision-making. We implemented ChoiceLog as an iOS application and conducted two evaluations to estimate its usefulness. From the results of the evaluations, we found that ChoiceLog could support decision-making processes in cases where there were a large number of choice selection logs. Moreover, for long-term use, we are planning to make it possible to filter notification from ChoiceLog based on date, time, and preset or user-customizable tags.

Keywords: life log, decision-making, watershed events, choice, mobile, location-base, ChoiceLog.

1 Introduction

There are two types of watershed events in our lives. First, incidental events (e.g., a disaster or winning a lottery). Second, events with choices (e.g., what to eat for lunch, or which car to buy) that are referred to below as "choice events". When we face the latter type, we want to make the best possible decision based on past experiences where we faced similar choices. If we could recall those choices, we would be able to make better decisions.

In this paper, we focus on life log systems for dealing with such choices. Life log systems are used widely for archiving activities, analyzing trends, and sharing information [1]. In terms of decision-making, these systems should enable the user to find logs that are suited to the current choice event. However, it is difficult for users to recall past situations using log data (i.e., pictures, movies, text and geo-tags) that are recorded in conventional life log systems. The reason for this is that conventional systems do not include capabilities for recording information about options that were selected, options that were rejected, and the results from these choices.

Some decision-making systems are currently available for supporting decision-making processes. However, it is difficult for users to perform efficient

S. Yamamoto (Ed.): HIMI 2014, Part II, LNCS 8522, pp. 172–183, 2014.
© Springer International Publishing Switzerland 2014

decision-making with these systems because they do not record log data about the options that the users rejected.

In order to solve these problems, we propose a new life log system called "ChoiceLog" for supporting decision-making.

2   Related Works

2.1   Life Log System

A life log is collected in order to allow users to recall past experience and to support decisions about future behaviors based on those experiences [2].

In this paper, Kanzaki et al. [3] proposed a life log system for healthy life based on pictures of food. the phrase "life log" refers to an archive of personal experiences that includes video, audio, location data, and other types of data. The phrase "life log system" refers to a system that can be used to record and search data in a "life log." We also use these words.

Logs can be collected in manually or automatically. In the former case, a user inputs text, captures images, and records movies, location data, and other types of data. This means that the user can determine the type of contents that are included and the volume of logs that are recorded. However, it is difficult for users to record the logs and determine how to search them. Foursquare [4] is a life log system that is specifically designed for recording location data. It allows users to recall activities based on location data. In this system, the user must perform "check-in" operation at each location. However, this system is unable to record logs about locations that the user does not visit. Therefore, the user cannot search for logs about locations, where the user has planned but not visited, because such logs do not exist in the system.

If the logs are collected automatically, users are freed from the trouble of manually recording the logs. Life Log Video [5] is a life log system that uses various sensors to collect data automatically. However, the users' subjective responses, such as "delicious" and "funny," cannot be included in the logs. Therefore, it is difficult for users to find logs because there are no tags or keywords that reflect their subjective viewpoints. Moreover, users cannot record detailed logs about their choices because it is difficult to extract information about choices from sensor data.

There are many researches that have attempted to make it easier for user to collect logs and search for them. For example, FoodLog [6] records photos of meals in log entries and calculates nutritional balance data automatically. However, it is impossible for the user to record information about dishes and restaurants that has not been selected because this system is narrowly focused on managing information about the nutritional balance properties of food.

2.2   Decision-Making Support System

There are existing researches and systems that have been designed in order to support decision-making processes. Kuramoto et al. [7] proposed a support system for choices about restaurants. Their system draws out the user's preferences and needs as the user interacts with a variety of agents with different opinions. However, this system does not record histories of interactions with agents or the restaurants that users have chosen. Further, it does not use previous logs for future recommendations. Therefore, users are required going through the same process with agents every time they use this system. It is considerably inefficient for users to be unable to make decisions based on past decisions and experiences.

3   ChoiceLog: Life Log System Based on Choices

In order to solve these problems, we propose a new life log system that is referred to as "ChoiceLog." ChoiceLog records the options that users actually select and the options that they reject. It also displays recorded logs via searches and notifications in order to support decision-making.

ChoiceLog supports decision-making when a user faces similar choice events. It allows the user to reflect on past choices and other options that were rejected so that decisions can be made efficiently. ChoiceLog records logs that include the options that were available during a choice event. We refer to this log unit as a "choice selection" (e.g., "lunch," "color of cardigan") and refer to the selectable options in the log unit as "choices" (e.g., "hamburger," "chicken burger," or "cheese burger").

When a user wants to record a choice selection, the user inputs details about the choice in the ChoiceLog using text and/or photos. Then, the user enters checkmarks the options that were actually selected. ChoiceLog records the location data that is associated with this choice automatically. These features enable the user to search for data about past choices using text or location data. In addition, ChoiceLog sends automatic notifications to users about certain types of past choice selections that were recorded at locations that are near the user's current location. This type of notification does not require the user to input any text or actively search for data. As a result, ChoiceLog can reduce the burden on the user and prevent the user from missing a chance to benefit from the information in the ChoiceLog.

The following example shows how ChoiceLog can be used to enable effective decisions. One day, a man orders curry at a restaurant. A few days later, he visits the same restaurant and orders curry again. However, ChoiceLog displays a notification on his smart-phone about the past choices that he made at this location. When he sees the notification, he recalls that he wavered between selecting curry and beef steak and chose curry. Further, he remembers that he did not enjoy the curry. As a result, he decides to change his order and selects beef steak instead. In this situation, the user was able to make an appropriate decision because of the ChoiceLog and was able to avoid repeating the same mistake.

4   Implementation

4.1   Overview

ChoiceLog is implemented as an iOS application and uses the camera and GPS functions so that users can easily record data and store photos related to choice selections and perform searches based on location data.

When a user faces a choice event, the user launches ChoiceLog and records a choice selection using the following five steps:

1. The user enters a title for the choice selection in order to identify it.
2. The user enters details for each choice with text and/or photos.
3. The user enters checkmarks for the choice(s) that are selected.
4. The user decides whether location data is attached to the choice selection.
5. After the user enters the data that are mentioned above, ChoiceLog records them as a choice selection.

The user can delete a choice selection itself or change the name of a choice selection at any time. ChoiceLog includes a function for searching choice selection based on the entered keywords. Further, the user can search for choice selections that were previously recorded in the vicinity of the current location. These logs for previous choice selections are indicated by pins on a map. The user can also obtain information about previous choice selections in the current vicinity via automatic notifications from ChoiceLog.

4.2   Interface

Figures 1, 2, 3, and 4 show screenshots from ChoiceLog.

Figure 1 shows the "Top view" that a user sees first when launching ChoiceLog. In this view , the user can obtain a list of recorded logs that is ordered from newest to oldest.

If the user wants to record a new log, the user navigates to the "Add choice selection view" (Fig. 2) by clicking the top-right button. In this view, the user can enter the name of the choice selection and the choices that are available. When the user clicks the "add a choice" button, a new field is added in order to allow the user to enter the name of choice. The user can also capture a photo and attach it to a certain choice by clicking on the photo frame to the left of the choice. When the user clicks on the right edge of a text input field, the user can attach a checkmark to this field. Checkmarks are used to indicate the choices that the user actually selected. If the user wants to attach location data to a choice selection, the user turns the "Location" switch on. When the data have been recorded for the choice selection, the user clicks the "Done" button in the top-right corner of this view. This action returns the user to the top view.

The "Detail view" (Fig. 3) is displayed when the user clicks a choice selection in the top view. This view shows the name, time, and location for the previously recorded choice selection. It also displays the names, photos, and checkmarks for the choices that are related to the choice selection. In this view, the user can

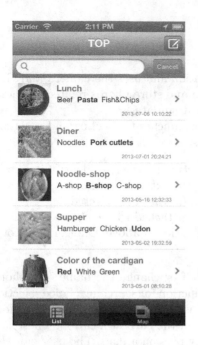

Fig. 1. Top view   **Fig. 2.** Add choice selection view

edit or update the data by clicking the "refresh" button in the top-right corner. The user can return to the top view by clicking the top-left button.

The "Location search view" (Fig. 4) is displayed when the user clicks the "Map" button in the lower-right corner of the top view or the detail view. The map and pins are displayed for the log that is associated with the location that is close to the user's current location. When the user clicks a pin, the name of the choice selection is displayed. When the current location in the view is incorrect, the user can update current location by clicking the "refresh" button in the top-right corner.

4.3   Notification

ChoiceLog uses the iOS Local Notification functionality to send notifications to the user about the choice selection whose location data is close to the user's current location. Figure 5 shows a notification for the choice selection for the "Noodle-shop." When the user clicks on this notification, ChoiceLog is launched and the detail view is displayed for the choice selection. ChoiceLog sends notifications about choice selections that are located close to the user's current location each time the user moves 50 [m].

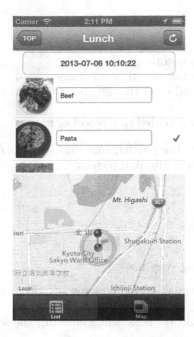

Fig. 3. Detail view   **Fig. 4.** Location search view

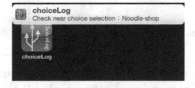

Fig. 5. Notification

5   Short-Term Evaluation

We performed an empirical evaluation in order to evaluate the usefulness, advantages, and disadvantages of the system based on the opinions of participants. We asked participants to use ChoiceLog in their daily lives during this evaluation. We used a prototype of ChoiceLog during this evaluation. The prototype included all the functions that are described in Section 3, except for the photo attachment function.

5.1   Procedure

We asked one teacher and four students who were majoring in information science to participate in the evaluation. We interviewed each of them in private after they had used the prototype for one week. We asked the following questions during the interview:

1. Describe situations where ChoiceLog was useful.
2. Describe situations where ChoiceLog was not useful or a nuisance.
3. Were there items that you could not record even though you wanted to do so?
4. What new function(s) would you like to see added to ChoiceLog?

At the beginning of the evaluation, we told the participants that the experimenter could browse the participants' logs for evaluation purposes.

5.2   Results

The results from the interview were as follows:

(1) Describe situations where ChoiceLog was useful

- I felt that ChoiceLog was useful when I was wavering between several menu choices at the school cafeteria.
- I used ChoiceLog to decide what I should do next while entering the log data.
- I used ChoiceLog for reminders by entering information about tasks that I needed to complete at home or for school.

(2) Describe situations where ChoiceLog was not useful or a nuisance

- I felt the notification was not appropriate for my situation at that time.
- I had trouble when composing sentences about choice selections and/or choices.
- I had trouble while entering the name of choices.
- I would like to be able to attach comments to logs (e.g., This restaurant is not good.).
- I would like to be able to combine the logs for choice selections that are recorded at the same location.
- The current location on the map was occasionally incorrect.

(3) Were there items that you could not record even though you wanted to do so?

- I did not record logs because I was tired of entering text.
- I did not want to record some logs because of concerns about my privacy.

The answers for this question were similar to the answers for question (2). The participants pointed out that entering text was cumbersome. For the former question, we also asked what type of situations caused them to feel tired. The answers were as follows:

1) Entering text was simply dull.
2) There was insufficient time to enter text for logs. For example, one participant was with a friend and another wanted to enter a log, but the train had just arrived.

(4) What new function(s) would you like to see added to ChoiceLog?

- I would like to receive notifications about choice selections related to the current time of day.
- I would like to be able to search logs based on the type of choice selection such as "drink," "restaurant menus," "foods," and other relevant categories.
- I would like to be able to use templates for entering text about a choice selection and choices.
- I would like to be able to record logs using voice input.
- I would like to be able to check other people's data for the current location.
- I would like to be able to access logs from other people that are similar to my logs.

5.3   Discussion

From the results for question (1), we concluded that ChoiceLog is useful for decision-making for choice events that occur frequently, such as making menu selections in a school cafeteria. However, the experiment did not highlight any other situations where ChoiceLog was useful. This was probably due to the short, one-week length of the experiment. Because of this short time period, the participants could not record log data a sufficient number of choice selections and they did not have adequate opportunities to be reminded about previous choice events. Therefore, there were insufficient choice selection logs to support decision-making. A long-term experiment is needed in order to confirm the usefulness of ChoiceLog as a decision-making support system.

However, there were some cases where the participants used ChoiceLog for other purposes. For example, some of the participants used the ChoiceLog to record to-do lists and reminders. We plan to consider other uses for ChoiceLog in a future work.

In addition, there are some improvements that are needed for the long-term use of ChoiceLog. From the result for questions (2) and (3), it can be seen that users felt that entering text for logs was tedious and difficult. It is important to make the text entry process simple and easy. If it is not easy, the users might stop entering choice selections. This could lead to failures during decision-making owing to the lack of valuable logs. We expect that the addition of a photo capturing function will improve the usability of ChoiceLog.

The results from questions (2) and (4) suggest that it is essential to send notifications that are suited to the user's current situation, based on time and location.

6   Long-Term Evaluation

We performed an empirical evaluation in order to evaluate the usefulness of ChoiceLog as a decision-making support system. This evaluation was based on actual cases where the system was used. During this evaluation, we asked participants to use ChoiceLog in their daily lives. In order to solve the problem with small numbers of logs that is described in 5.3, we conducted the evaluation over a long-term period of about 6 months.

The participants used a version of ChoiceLog that included some of the improvements that are mentioned in 5.3. These included

1. the implementation of a photo attachment function in order to make ChoiceLog less reliant on text input,
2. the implementation of an editing function for changing the names of choices,
3. the optimization of the timings of notifications, and
4. fixes for bugs.

6.1   Procedure

Six subjects participated in this evaluation, including one teacher and five students who were majoring in information science. They used ChoiceLog for six months and were interviewed every two weeks. During the interviews, the participants were asked to describe situations where ChoiceLog was helpful or unhelpful. We asked the participants to capture screenshots of ChoiceLog so that they could remember the situations where they felt that the information or notifications in ChoiceLog were helpful or unhelpful.

6.2   Results

There are five cases that were obtained during the interviews:

Case 1 (HELPFUL)

One day, a participant was wondering whether to purchase her usual item or the seasonal special at a confectionery shop. Because she was considering the choices, she launched ChoiceLog and searched for a log from the list. She remembered that the seasonal special at this shop had been delicious when she had visited before. Therefore, she decided to purchase the seasonal special.

Case 2 (HELPFUL)

Before lunch time, one of the participants wondered whether to order lunch from shop A or shop B. When he considered the possibilities, he recalled that he had recorded logs about these shops in ChoiceLog and he had not liked the lunch he ordered at shop A. Therefore, he decided to order lunch from shop B.

Case 3 (UNHELPFUL)

At about noon, one of the participants received a notification from ChoiceLog as she was walking near a station. The notification was about a beer that she had purchased at a restaurant near that station. She felt uneasy about this notification because she did not want to receive such notifications during the daytime.

Case 4 (HELPFUL)

When one of the participants started to cook dinner using items in the refrigerator, he recalled that he had recorded a log about the dinner that he had cooked two days ago. He searched for the log for that dinner in a list in ChoiceLog and found the dinner menu for that day and others as well. Therefore, he could cook dinner using the other menu.

Case 5 (HELPFUL)

When one of the participants walked by a shop, she received a notification from ChoiceLog. The notification was about an item. She had been confused about which of the two items to purchase. She had bought the former item. The log was recorded ten days prior. Because of this notification, she was able to recall that she needed to purchase the item and that it had been out of stock previously. In this case, she did not purchase the item immediately because she did have adequate time. However, she purchased it the next day. Because of ChoiceLog, she was able to remember that she had to buy an important item.

6.3 Discussion

ChoiceLog was useful for decision-making in cases 1, 2, 4, and 5. Based on cases 1 and 5, we found that ChoiceLog can support the decision making process when there is a large number of choice selection logs, as mentioned in 5.3.

In cases 1, 2, and 4, the participants recalled the contents of previously recorded logs when they searched for or referred to the logs for decision-making purposes. This suggests that the mere act of recording choice selections makes it easier for participants to recall previous situations where they faced similar choices. However, it can be difficult to perform efficient searches for logs for choice events from the distant past.

This is because the user may forget the data that are recorded in ChoiceLog or the volume of the log data may become large. The results from case 5 suggest that the notification function in ChoiceLog may serve as an effective of as a solution against this problem. If the period of evaluation was longer and the number of logs was larger, we might be able to determine the effectiveness of the notifications for decision-making.

Based on the results from the long-term evaluation, we found additional areas where ChoiceLog can be improved. In case 3, the user wants to suppress certain notifications because they are not appropriate for her current situation. This result indicates that ChoiceLog should allow users to control notifications using filters that are based on dates and times.

In addition, some participants wanted to receive notifications based on their current location. For example, some users do not wish to receive any notifications when they are at their office or home, but want to receive notifications when they are shopping. Therefore, ChoiceLog should allow users to determine the locations where they want to receive notifications.

Some often, participants wanted to be able to select preset tags or user-customizable tags when they are entering titles of choice selections instead of being required to enter text for the title. Implementing this change would make ChoiceLog effective. It would make it easier for users to record and search for logs and it would make the titles of notifications more meaningful as well.

7   Conclusion

We proposed a new life log system called "ChoiceLog" for supporting decision-making processes. ChoiceLog can record the choices that users actually select and the choices that they reject. It can also display recorded data via searches and notifications in order to support decision-making when users are faced with similar choice events. ChoiceLog includes three main functions. It records choice selections with text and/or photos. It displays choice selections based on searches by keywords or locations and it notifies users about certain choice selections that were recorded at locations that are close to the user's current location.

We implemented ChoiceLog as an iOS application and evaluated its usefulness. During the short-term evaluation, we found that ChoiceLog was useful for decision-making for choice events that occurred frequently. However, we found that, owing to the short-term nature of the experiment (i.e., one week), the only place where the participants found that the ChoiceLog was useful was in the school cafeteria. During the short-term evaluation, we received input regarding potential improvements. Therefore, we improved the process for entering choice selections.

Further, we conducted a long-term experiment in order to confirm the usefulness of ChoiceLog as a decision-making support system. We found cases where ChoiceLog can be useful for decision-making during choice events. We found that ChoiceLog could support user decisions in cases where there are a large number of choice selection logs. However, it can be difficult to perform efficient searches when there is a large volume of log data. In order to solve this problem, we are planning to make it possible to filter notifications from ChoiceLog based on the date, time, and preset or user-customizable tags.

We are planning to include further evaluations of the usefulness of ChoiceLog in a future work after the introduction of these improvements.

References

1. Tokyo University Ambient Social Infrastructure Study Group: Real World Log. PHP publishing, Tokyo (2012) (Japanese)
2. Kidawara, Y., Zettsu, K., Kawai, Y., Minakuchi, M., Miyamori, H., Kashioka, H.: Utilization of digital content based on life log in the real-world. Journal of Information Processing 50(7), 613–623 (2009) (Japanese)
3. Kanzaki, Y.: Analytical Method of Based on Background of Food Image for FoodLog System. Kouchi University of Technology (2012) (Japanese)
4. Foursquare Labs INC.: Foursquare, https://www.foursquare.com (last access date January 26, 2014)
5. Tancharoen, D., Yamasaki, T., Aizawa, K.: Practical experience recording and indexing of life log video. In: Proceedings of the 2nd ACM Workshop on Continuous Archival and Retrieval of Personal Experiences, pp. 61–66 (2003)
6. Aizawa, K.: Life log for practical use. Institute of Image Information and Television Engineers Journal 63(4), 445–448 (2009) (Japanese)
7. Kuramoto, I., Yasuda, A., Minakuchi, M., Tsujino, Y.: Recommendation System Based on Interaction with Multiple Agents for Users with Vague Intention. In: Jacko, J.A. (ed.) Human-Computer Interaction, Part II, HCII 2011. LNCS, vol. 6762, pp. 351–357. Springer, Heidelberg (2011)

Research on User Involvement in Automobile Design Development

Focusing on the Problems of Design Evaluation

Noboru Koyama[1], Mikio Yamashita[2], and Mizuki Nakajima[1]

[1] Higashiooi, Shinagawa, Tokyo, Japan
{n-koyama,nakajima-mizuki}@aiit.ac.jp
[2] Tsutsujigaoka, Hanayashiki, Takarazuka, Hyogo, Japan
mikio-yamashita@takara-univ.ac.jp

Abstract. The problems of design evaluation and decision-making have been ongoing challenges since design has held a position in industry. The large amounts of development investment in the automotive industry, and the importance of design in ultimate product value, have made the development of systems for evaluation and decision-making urgent topics. However, they have yet to achieve perfection, and are still beset by many problems. In our research on these topics, we have focused our research on user-participatory product design, especially the problems of evaluation and decision-making in the midst of the design development process. This paper discusses the current state of one aspect of these, the panel evaluation system, and looks at the challenges it faces.

Keywords: User involvement, panel evaluation, and design management.

1 Research Background and Process

Automobiles are hardware packed with the most advanced technologies, but they are also products that users use with all of their senses — it would be fair to call them emotional products, with an impact on people's feelings. It is therefore no exaggeration to say that the purpose of automotive design development is all about using the senses to create designs that will attract consumers. By "design" here, we are not referring merely to exterior aesthetic design (styling design). Because users use all of their senses when using automobiles, every contact point involved in their usage must create customer satisfaction. On the other hand, from the standpoint of corporate management, since new vehicle development requires huge investment, there is no room for errors that would prevent companies from recovering their investments. Therefore, top management expects designers to utilize their capabilities to the fullest extent and push them to develop innovative, original designs that are unlike, or even slightly better than, those of their competitors. The challenges in design management are how to retain talented designers and how to create systems and structures that elicit designers' full potentials. However, even if companies could succeed in retaining and utilizing talented designers, this does not guarantee that original designs will

S. Yamamoto (Ed.): HIMI 2014, Part II, LNCS 8522, pp. 184–192, 2014.
© Springer International Publishing Switzerland 2014

be realized. The reason is that regardless of the quality of the ideas the designers create, if those ideas are not picked up and commoditized in a timely and appropriate manner, the ideas that the designers worked so hard to create will remain unseen by the public. The key to eliminating this problem lies in the method of design decision-making during the development process. Major manufacturers have been making efforts to improve the method and process of design evaluation and decision-making to minimize decision-making errors. One of these methods is called the "clinic." This consists of soliciting the thoughts of actual car users, or people representing them, as reference information during the stage of developing designs. Specifically, a third party not involved with the development evaluates the product development concepts and results, or completed products, verifies the design's merits and points out potential and actual negative points, with the goal of increasing the product's ultimate marketability and enhancing customer product satisfaction. When this evaluation is performed by potential customers outside the company (target-users), it is said that there was "direct user involvement in design evaluation", and when it is performed, for confidentiality reasons, by people inside the company who are not directly involved in development, serving as customers, that there was "indirect (provisional) user involvement in design evaluation."

The automobile development process has been largely standardized around the world. An overview is presented below.

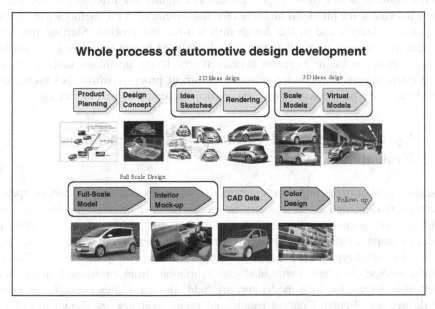

Fig. 1. Automotive Design Development Process

Looking at the current situation of user involvement in the process of vehicle development, as broadly described in the figure 1 above, there are several points to note in the process stages from upstream to downstream. First, one point we can mention in the upstream part of the process is market and consumer surveys to obtain information required for the development of new models or updates to current models. The first checkpoint in avoiding failures in new car development is verifying facts such as whether the market exists for the model to be introduced, and what kind of current car users are going to want next. Therefore, market and user surveys are a must at the product planning stage, and the first step in user involvement is early-stage contact with potential and current users by staff involved in vehicle development.

Second, a typical example of user involvement in the midstream is the so-called "panel evaluation system", in which intermediate design results are evaluated by selected people ("panelists") who are not involved in product development. This system is widely used in the automotive industry. The panelists described here are sometimes employees from inside the company, though they are sometimes from outside the company. When in-house members perform evaluations, it is called "provisional user involvement in the evaluation process", and when outside participants perform evaluations, it is called "user involvement in the evaluation process." Finally, a typical example of user involvement in the downstream is the activity of asking actual users to evaluate a product after the product's launch. The primary objective in this case is to reflect the opinions and requests of users in related models or next-generation models. Another major objective is to verify if there is any difference between the results of the panel evaluation conducted during that particular model's development stage and the evaluations of customers post-launch. If a significant difference is discovered, it may indicate some problems and room for improvement in the methods used during the panel evaluation and in the design decision-making process. Starting from this problem awareness vantage, we studied and analyzed recent trends in user involvement, focusing on major Japanese manufacturers, in the upstream, midstream, and downstream stages of the automotive development process, while also taking into consideration the perspective of user experience, including human interfaces.

2   Upstream User Involvement in Design Development Evaluation

Assessing market needs and trends is essential when developing new cars or updates to current models, and is the first step in successful development. In-house research divisions have accumulated many years of survey data, which serve as a base for product planning, but they also perform surveys of target users for the vehicles they are developing. A typical method used is the FGI (Focus Group Interview). FGIs use specific methods to select, invite, and gather opinions from envisioned target users. Lively discussions, led by a moderator, are held, and users' awareness, latent needs, and desires are elicited. Concept panels and image sketches are shown in order to better express the vehicle concepts being developed, and determine trends in the design images users desire. What developers want to know is what future users desire, but, generally speaking, users are very familiar with the present situation, but cannot clearly express themselves regarding the future. For example, when discussing keywords such as "advanced design," "originality," "sporty," or "luxury," users have a wide range of impressions and images, which are difficult to understand, both in terms of content and intensity. Therefore, actual photographs and images of automobiles or other products are used, to estimate content and intensity. The human interface method of evaluation can be used for this. Data can be obtained from a statistically significant number of study subjects, and threshold values and trends can be analyzed, the results being used in decision-making.

3 Midstream User Involvement in Design Development Evaluation

The midstream area is the most important part of "user involvement." A typical method used is the "panel evaluation" which this research has looked at. "Panel evaluation" is defined as below.[1]

It is a frequently used evaluation method in the automotive industry. The people selected to take part in these evaluations are called "panelists." Panelists may come from within or outside the company. To distinguish between these, an evaluation process using panelists from outside the company is often called a "clinic" or a "product clinic." From here onward, "panel evaluation" will be used as a general term that includes "clinics"

3.1 The Panel Evaluation and Clinic Systems of Japanese Automobile Manufacturers

The Toyota Motor Corporation, a major manufacturer using panel evaluations, has at all times over 100 registered potential panelists in various departments within the company. Multiple evaluations are performed during the model design phase, linked to the project development process. These evaluation results are used as reference materials by the design decision meeting to select which models to commoditize.

The panelists come primarily from planning divisions such as the product planning, domestic planning, and overseas planning divisions. They have sufficient knowledge and capabilities to understand new car concepts, and, notably, are able to perform not only evaluations of present conditions, but also forward-looking evaluations. These panel evaluations are considered as reference information only, and the highest evaluated designs are not necessarily the ones that are ultimately selected.

On the other hand, the Nissan Motor Company used to have its own external, independent evaluation company, which it had perform evaluations. Evaluations were held by outside panelists from the general public, with a high degree of similarity to

---

[1] Panel evaluation" is a method which consists of obtaining evaluations of designs during the product design development phase from the standpoints of third parties who are not directly involved in development, verification of design value, and identification of latent and manifest negative points, in order ultimately to improve product value and customer satisfaction.

target users, but they tended to evaluate designs for cars to be released several years in the future based on their current knowledge and sensibilities. A great deal of money was spent on these evaluations, and a great deal of importance was placed on the results. However, in recent years, especially after the partnership with Renault, it is said that the panel evaluation system itself has almost fallen out of use.

Japanese manufacturers show a major tendency to position the results of panel evaluations and clinics as reference information only, and it is not uncommon for the ideas and models given the highest evaluations to be passed over in actual design decision-making. In particular, Toyota considers evaluation results (especially from outside clinics) to be nothing more than current user evaluations, and the company looks at evaluation trends, not clinging to the model with the most positive evaluations, but discussing the trends in a design committee looking two or three years into the future when making decisions. Decisions are not made by a small number of members, but through a greater consensus.

3.2   Problems with Current Panel Evaluations and Clinics

Prior research has discovered the following problems and challenges faced by the current panel evaluation and external clinic system. When looking at the results of panel evaluations, people are swayed by the scores assigned by panelists, and, depending on the composition of the discussion members, it may be impossible to freely express opinions. Many cases have been observed in which designs that were selected based on the results of panel evaluations and ultimately made into products were not properly verified for how they would be evaluated in the actual marketplace. That is, evaluations, selection processes, and judgments are not given proper verification. For some time, many companies used external clinics, but recently there have been many results which point to a lack of potential effectiveness in this approach, so we have heard that in recent years, Toyota has completely abandoned external clinics.

3.3   New Efforts by the Toyota Motor Corporation

The panel evaluation system has become an essential part of Toyota's decision-making process, with the system being repeatedly improved, but this has also had negative effects. One, for example, is that the company has shown a tendency to aim for the average. One aspect that has been pointed out is that there is a tacit panel evaluation 'pass' score for approval, and committee members (executives) participating in the design decision-making discussions are influenced by these scores.

This is why a new evaluation method was used for the "86" project, the first sports car design in some time for Toyota, and one which held a special place in the heart of the new president.

As Japan's automotive industry has matured and diversified, one sports car model after another has been discontinued. Toyota is no exception. Lagging sales resulted in models no longer being profitable, and, spurred by the prolonged recession, production was discontinued. For a time, Toyota had no sports car models. However, sports cars have ardent fans, and popularity remained high for rare used sports cars and foreign cars. Young people are losing their interest in automobiles, and Toyota, in order to restore the allure and dream of cars, believed that it was important to propose new styles, which would pursue the "fun to drive" attraction of automobiles to its ultimate extreme, while at the same time responding to environmental and other demands of the day. They also believed that the key to the success of the sports car would be in creating new added value, such as by creating environments and opportunities that would provide greater joy to users. Toyota also had a history of famous FR sports cars that even today maintain an overwhelming level of popularity, such as the S800, the 2000GT, and the 86 (previous original model), and it heard the voices of those calling for these cars to be rolled out again.

In particular, since the launch of the original 86, users and various parts manufacturers have developed tuning parts and kept the 86 alive. Their efforts helped make the model a classic, and one of the few sports cars that is truly user-centric. The chief engineer decided to bestow the name of "86" on the newly developed sports car model, carrying on the spirit and history of the sports car.

The chief engineer decided to go back to basics and change the automotive design process from the ground up. His goals were twofold. "Creation of a car based not on numbers, but on pursuing the ultimate in fun," and "a level of individuality that creates strong opinions, both pro and con, instead of an automobile project based on internal consensus."

In particular, since the launch of the original 86, users and various parts manufacturers have developed tuning parts and kept the 86 alive. Their efforts helped make the model a classic, and one of the few sports cars that is truly user-centric. The chief engineer decided to bestow the name of "86" on the newly developed sports car model, carrying on the spirit and history of the sports car.

The chief engineer decided to go back to basics and change the automotive dsign process from the ground up. His goals were twofold. "Creation of an automobile based not on numbers, but on pursuing the ultimate in fun," and "a level of individuality that creates strong opinions, both pro and con, instead of an automobile project based on internal consensus."

Fig. 2. Previous Model 86

Fig. 3. New Model 86

The design department followed the chief engineer's lead, deciding to greatly overhaul their own design decision-making process. They were led by a belief that when developing a sports car, the standard consensus-driven decision-making process, in which the tastes and opinions of many people are reflected, would prevent the creation of individualistic designs, the achievement of the designers' ideals, and the production of a sports car that would enthrall fans. They decided to select "sports car panelists" for their internal panel evaluation, get feedback that closely reflected the opinions and tastes of customers, and make design decisions with a small number of people. They created a list of sports car drivers inside the company, had them give their evaluations of and comments regarding sketches and trial models, added them to the standard panelist evaluation results, and reported the results to the design deliberation committee. The model positively evaluated by this special panel differed completely from that selected by the standard panelist evaluation, and the scores of the two groups clearly diverged. In the end, the model (design) which was positively evaluated by the sports car panelists was selected as the production model, and, as hoped for, the car received a lot of buzz for its unique design.

The design decision-making processes used by Japanese automotive manufacturers such as Toyota was to present the results of panel evaluations using a seven point scale to executives at the design evaluation committee meetings, using them as reference data for decision making. Interviews with Toyota showed that although these evaluations were called 'references', in reality, depending on the model and type, there were implicit required threshold scores which had to be met for the vehicles to be approved.

Our latest interviews found that scores have not been reported in design evaluation committee meetings in the past few years (especially since the head of the design division changed), and that panel evaluation results are no longer reported as scores in official design evaluation committee meetings, instead, only opinions and comments from the evaluations are presented. Also, with the conversion of Lexus brand into an internal company (as Lexus International), deliberatios are held independently, and decisions are made by small groups, with 10 or fewer executives in attendance. Compared to the past, when almost 50 related executives would attend, as well as the respective managers, and consensus would be sought within this large group, its current decision-making style has clearly shifted from the traditional Japanese model to a more Western model. Time has yet to tell whether this approach is appropriate, but looking at the distinctive Toyota designs shown at recent motor shows, it is clear that tremendous changes are taking place.

4   Downstream User Involvement in Design Development Evaluation

Finally, an example of downstream user involvement is, as discussed earlier, asking users to evaluate a product after the product's launch. Generally speaking, this is performed between 6 months and a year after the product roll-out. The primary objective is to reflect the opinions and requests of users in related models or next-generation models, but, more importantly for design development, to verify if there is any difference between the results of the midstream panel evaluation for that model and the evaluations of customers post-launch. This type of evaluation is not being performed sufficiently, and there is a lack of objective verification of the effectiveness of the panel evaluation system, casting its reliability into question. There is therefore a need to create and use tools to achieve sufficient communication with users and as criteria for decision-making.

5   The Future

The panel evaluation system has a long historical accumulation of use in the automotive industry, but its effectiveness is beginning to be disputed. However, this does not mean that new, effective measures have been developed to replace the panel evaluation system in order to tackle the eternal challenge of error-free design decision-making. Nor could it be said that the current system has been perfected, with no room for improvement. Automotive design has traditionally focused on exterior design development, but user evaluations now encompass the entire user's experience, and it may be time to recognize the need for the implementation of more multidimensional perspectives in design evaluation itself. This is a new challenge for design management.

References

1. Koyama, N., Yamashita, M., Fujito, M., Kawarabayashi, K., Morinaga, Y., Kitani, Y.: Differences of Design Decision on Product Design Development through Comparative Research on Japanese, European and American Automobile Industries. The Journal of Kansei Engineering International 8(2), 160–174 (2009)
2. Koyama, N., Yamashita, M., Kawarabayashi, K., Yoshida, S., Fujito, M., Morinaga, Y., Chen, J.: A Comparison Study on the Use of Review Panel Evaluations for Decision-Making in Vehicle Design by Japanese, European and U.S. In: The Proceedings of the International Conference of Kansei Engineering and Emotion Research, KEER 2010, pp. 1798–1809 (2010)

3. Kawarabayashi, K., Yamashita, M., Fujito, M., Sakamoto, K., Kitani, Y., Koyama, N., Morinaga, Y.: Study on User Involvement in Hardware, Software and Service Integrated Type Design Development. In: The Proceedings of the International Conference of Kansei Engineering and Emotion Research, KEER 2010, pp. 2394–2404 (2010)
4. Nakajima, M., Igarashi, H.: A Relationship Between the Process of Light Changing and the Human Emotion Variation. In: The Proceedings of the Kansei Engineering and Emotion Research International Conference, KEER 2010, p. 37 (2010)
5. Koyama, N., Yamashita, M., Yoshida, S.: A Practical Case Study of Panel Evaluations for Vehicle Design Development. International Journal of Affective Engineering 12(2), 349–354 (2013)
6. Kawarabayashi, K., Fujito, M., Sakamoto, K., Kitani, Y., Yamashita, M., Koyama, N., Morinaga, Y.: Strategic Design Management Methods in Major Japanese Electronics Companies. International Journal of Affective Engineering 12(2), 325–335 (2013)

Human-Centered Interfaces for Situation Awareness in Maintenance

Allan Oliveira[1], Regina Araujo[1], and Andrew Jardine[2]

[1] Federal University of São Carlos, São Carlos, São Paulo, Brazil
{allan_oliveira,regina}@dc.ufscar.br
[2] University of Toronto, Toronto, Ontario, Canada
jardine@mie.utoronto.ca

Abstract. In Maintenance, a vital activity in industry, ineffective Situation Awareness (SAW) is responsible for 13-17% of accidents. Therefore, a successful SAW has the potential of leveraging safety and efficiency, especially in field work. Bibliographic revision shows that the main gap to develop this idea is the conflict between the structure of Maintenance (procedural) and that of SAW (dynamic). Using a holistic study to elaborate a conclusive definition of SAW in the field, our work was able to solve this dichotomy of structures by developing a conceptual framework which maintains the task-oriented nature of field operation while clustering SAW inputs into entities to outline their potential effects. This Conceptual Framework of Situation Awareness in Maintenance (CFSAM) acknowledges the link between SAW and UIs, and creates a definitive list of multiple factors/entities that supports responsiveness and improves reliability and resilience. The seven entities identified are: task, equipment, system, environment, team, enterprise and personal. To each of these entities, CFSAM assigns a role in the UI design, and analyses challenges and solutions. This new approach of considering SAW-oriented design is a multidisciplinary effort and so far the results are promising: it facilitates an efficient design of SAW in maintenance field work, increases the focus on safety and efficiency and leverages the potential of developing a coherent system with high level of adherence.

Keywords: Situation Awareness, Human Centered Computing, User Interface Design, Maintenance.

1 Introduction

60-80% of errors in industry are attributed to humans [1] and 15-20% of these errors involve maintenance [2]. A widespread practice in all industries, the processes of Maintenance is developed in order to keep the physical assets suitable for fulfilling their function.

This routine, has an impressive impact in overall finances, personnel safety and the product quality. Because of its importance, it has received a big focus from industry and academia and has evolved with technologies such as Condition Based

S. Yamamoto (Ed.): HIMI 2014, Part II, LNCS 8522, pp. 193–204, 2014.
© Springer International Publishing Switzerland 2014

Maintenance, Prognostics and Health Management, E-Maintenance and Internet of Things. Nevertheless, this area still lacks further studies in User Interfaces (UI) for field personnel.

A UI designed for maintenance field operators could prevent part of the human errors involving maintenance, by presenting information in a goal-driven mode, while filtering data and adapting their presentation layout according to the user situation, mental model and hardware (the device in use). The goal-driven information UI is developed based on the understanding of the work process, thus being able to select from a range of information and display only what is necessary, when it is necessary. By doing this, the UI supports the user Situation Awareness (SAW). To be adaptable to the real world, this UI must be also integrated with the E-maintenance system (to provide coherent and updated solutions) and it must provide request-driven access to information, becoming a part of the industrial workflow.

This breakthrough approach differs from most studies for field personnel developed nowadays, because they focus on Augmented Reality [3], applied in laboratories with ideal conditions, disregarding the user Situation Awareness in real work contexts. This approach is misleading, because it ignores the fact that 88% of human error is due to problems in Situation Awareness [1], giving a roughly 13-17% of errors in industry caused by lack of Situation Awareness in maintenance.

Situation Awareness (SAW) is one of the cornerstones of human-centered systems. Currently applied in many industries, such as aviation [4][5], mining [6], oil/gas [7], rails [8] and others [9], it involves the perception of elements in the environment, the comprehension of these elements and the situation and the projection of future consequences and elements' status [1]. SAW enhances the decision making capacity of users by providing a framework to assist displaying the right information in the right time. By doing so, it prevents errors and improves the levels of efficiency and safety.

New display technologies (e.g. Augmented Reality Head Mounted Displays) are expected to provide access to the desired information more easily whenever requested. However, safety and reliability are not improved through more exposure to data and technology [9] and the optimal use of SAW is influenced by the way information is presented [1]. Therefore, the best process for UIs to work when selecting data are the SAW guidelines. Ignoring these rules would cause the UIs to backfire, increasing the occurrence of human errors and ultimately causing a rejection of such displays in industry. Consequently, maintenance, as well as others field work areas, demand studies specifically in SAW, anticipating solutions to reduce the large amount of errors this area faces and developing feasible ways to use the new visualization technologies available.

Maintenance was selected as the basis for this study because it encompasses the three traits below, whereas other industrial processes do not comprehend them entirely:

- Complexity: the need to comprehend equipments, identify a problem and fix it, while having a procedural (manuals) and non procedural (diagnosis) aspects;

- Safety: the importance of safety for the worker (human life), for the equipment (may cost millions of dollars) and for people interacting with the equipment afterward (an airplane defect may risk several people lives);
- Efficiency: the response time to reduce downtime of equipments.

This paper introduces a conceptual framework to SAW that can be applied in UI systems for maintenance field personnel. The framework defines the entities of importance of Situation Awareness in maintenance field work and how they affect SAW. The objective is to fill the gap of current studies in the area and assist designers to create human-centered User Interfaces that provide SAW to their users. This framework can be futurely replicated to other less complex procedures (such as Operation and Production).

The paper is structured as follows: Section 2 is a review of Situation Awareness, mostly applied to maintenance; Section 3 explains the Conceptual Framework for Situation Awareness in Maintenance; Section 4 discusses the entities of SAW in maintenance and some problems and solutions; Section 5 is discussions and conclusion.

2   Situation Awareness in the Maintenance Process

Situation Awareness in maintenance field work has not been extensively explored, compared to Command & Control, because of the strong procedural element in this scenario, which contrast to the situational nature of SAW. However, whenever reliability and resilience are important, such as it is in maintenance, there must be a focus on being responsive to situations [8]. Also, poor SAW is an acknowledged source of errors in maintenance [2]. Finally, SAW is directly correlated to the UI [1].

Coherently to these assertions, in order to improve SAW through User Interfaces, static information/context must be considered a part of a user SAW, regardless of their non-situational nature, because of their effect on users' perception of their situation. For instance, even though the risks of maintaining and testing the speed regulator in a power generator unity are always the same (electric shock, height fall, high pressure, oil leaking), keeping them in the user working memory through UIs may reinforce the mindset to assure a safe and effective work. Moreover, such information will also assist the user's decision-making process by providing comprehensive context for an analysis of the situation.

Besides the implications of displaying static and non-static information, a comprehensive study of SAW in maintenance must consider that a system/domain [8] may contain multiple types of Situation Awareness, as stated by Golightly et. al, and, furthermore, awareness itself could be composed of several factors, as identified by Carrol et al. [10].

Three areas of application of SAW were identified as important for maintenance: field maintenance, industrial field operation and UIs. The works of Endsley and Robertson [4] and Golightly et. al [8] identified four elements as the basis of SAW in maintenance field work: understanding the equipment, to identify problems (diagnosis) and predict failures (prognosis); maintaining team synchrony, to collaborate and coordinate tasks to achieve a common goal; comprehending the environment and their risks, to avoid accidents; having a good corporate environment, to have a standardized work routine and terminology and good communications with other areas for shift scheduling and provisioning of assets.

Considering SAW in industrial field operations, Nazir et al. listed several factors influencing an operator's SAW, mainly environmental, team work and personal factors [11]. Sneddon et al. exposed that the most significant impact in SAW is caused by stress, and not fatigue/workload and sleep disruption [7]. They also proved that Situation Awareness is associated with safety indicators, such as unsafe behavior, near misses and accident history. Likewise, Bullemer analyzed major incidents from industry, discovering that 50% involved failures associated with SAW [9]. According to him, team work and awareness could be improved with better communication, supervision, pre-job briefing and User Interfaces.

Chinoy and Fischer also appointed the need to improve UIs in SAW [5]. They listed several design and system guidelines, such as "Show radar coverage especially in light" and "Information tailored to user need", with a focus on a net-centric approach that integrates several databases.

An essential requisite to improve UI and maintain SAW over interruptions is defining design guidelines. John and Smallman created four design principles to this situation [12]. They are: 1) UIs should provide an indicative of changes automatically; 2) UIs must use unobtrusive notifications; 3) UIs should provide summary descriptions of each change, allowing users to choose priorities; 4) For busy displays, UIs should make information about changes be accessed only on demand, to avoid clutter.

Also concerned with SAW in UIs, Endsley and Jones developed fifty design guidelines [1], going from how to organize and present information, to dealing with alarms, automation and multiple and distributed operators.

Finally, Carrol et al. devised design strategies focused on notifications, to support Activity Awareness, a concept similar to SAW, but with an emphasis on project work that supports groups in complex tasks [10]. They structured Activity Awareness around four entities, situation, group, task and tool. Then, they evaluated the information requirements for each factor and created design strategies to support their awareness.

Improving upon literature for SAW in maintenance and operations field work, combined with at-work analysis, this paper uses the strategy of structuring Situation Awareness around seven entities, each one of those with its respective requirements and design strategies. These entities compose the Conceptual Framework for Awareness in Maintenance, presented in the next section.

3   Conceptual Framework for Situation Awareness in Maintenance (CFSAM)

The first of its kind, CFSAM was defined based on a holistic study of the maintenance process, which included mapping of the different types of information essential to the field operator of maintenance and their categorization into seven entities. To each of these entities it was attributed its own "awareness", a set of information that should ensure the best service-level possible. To respond to a broad range of contexts, these entities are combined to generate the user Situation Awareness in maintenance. This approach by CFSAM demands a different definition of SAW in maintenance field work, because it recognizes the need for understanding and knowledge of the ongoing procedure (and other static information connected to the surrounding context) to form a user Situation Awareness. Thus, it differs from Command & Control, in which SAW is based only in dynamic information.

The goal of CFSAM is to better define SAW in industrial field work, particularly maintenance, providing an up-to-date framework that can be used to identify the main SAW problems and point potential solutions related to each entity. The framework will help understand the entities in the maintenance work and assist UI designers knowing at any time, what information is useful to users. It will also leverage users' adherence level by providing a dependable source of information with optimized display according to the surrounding environment.

To establish the set of entities that compose CFSAM, the initial step was mapping the information typically required by operators to ensure an effective maintenance in the field. This material was used to understand the maintenance activity and the main inputs for the decision-making process. The flowchart generated, together with the works of [2,4,5,6,7,8,9,10,11], was the basis for devising an initial structure of SAW in maintenance. To proof-read this method, this proposal was revised according to interviews with specialists.

As a result of the mapping, the inputs of CFSAM were clustered into seven entities, named after the focus of their assessment, as demonstrated in figure 1: personal, task, equipment, system, environment, team and enterprise. Each entity is composed by singular elements which influence the perception of awareness to them, further explained later in this paper.

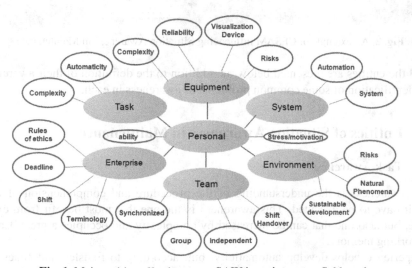

Fig. 1. Main entities affecting users SAW in maintenance field work

Furthermore, figure 2 demonstrates how different kinds of information can be combined with CFSAM to form an UI. In the figure, the information pool is on the left side, structured with the entities from CFSAM and with examples and a visual abstraction. On the middle part, information is being filtered according to CFSAM, which considers the seven defined entities and their Situation Awareness. Finally, in the right side, both users, red and blue, have information displayed to them to assist in their work. Even if both users are performing the same procedure, different information could be displayed to them, to improve their current SAW.

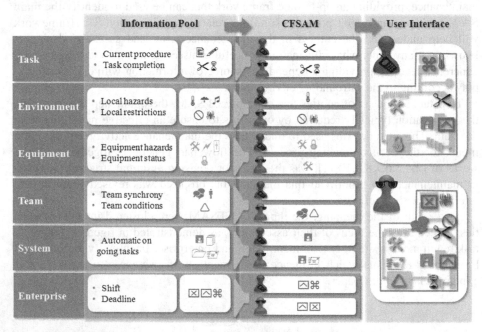

Fig. 2. An example of CFSAM influencing Situation Awareness in Maintenance

All the entities are presented below, in addition to the definition of their awareness and identification of some common problems of awareness in each.

4   Entities of Situation Awareness in Maintenance

4.1   Task Awareness

Task Awareness is the understanding of the procedure and comprehension of how does it have to be executed. This awareness is the one that most benefit from experience, but also one that can be increased by complexity and occupies a great deal of the working memory.

Experience helps develop automaticity, but, according to Endsley and Jones [1], human working memory is a big limitation in SAW and systems need to consider it in their design, or else errors are possible to occur.

A solution to maintain Task Awareness is using Interactive Electronic Technical Manuals augmented by Augmented Reality, so that it is possible to view projected in the equipment instructions and CAD/CAE data.

Some of the common problems to SAW related to Task Awareness are:

- The task tends to take all the focus from situation assessment [8];
- In the end of a task, the focus is even more reduced in situation assessment [8];
- Repetitive task results in complacency [7];
- Not understanding the work/task proposed [8];
- Distraction/lack of focus during work [8].

4.2 Equipment Awareness

Equipment Awareness is the understanding of the equipment and its behavior. It is generally considered the most important Awareness in maintenance, even defined as the concept of SAW in maintenance [4] and is particularly useful to assist in diagnosis of problems. Two important aspects of this awareness are risks and reliability.

Risks should ideally be treated as an event with: association, duration, area-of-effect and priority.

- Association: useful to determine the entity responsible for this risk, so that an UI for a risk can be designed once and used for every procedure related to the entity;
- Duration: important for the process of maintaining awareness during a task;
- Area-of-effect: specified so that coworkers can be aware of the range of a risk;
- Priority: mostly used to avoid information overload, since higher priority risks should have better salience (such as the color red or a flashing light).

Besides, whenever possible, Augmented Reality is the best media to display risks, because it can lessen the cognitive processing by displaying a risk on top of its source.

Reliability is how close the equipment is to a breakdown, verified through age (Reliability-Centered Maintenance), prognostics and reading of sensors (Condition-Based Maintenance). If the status of the equipment being worked points to an imminent or close breakdown, UIs should inform users and display risks associated with it.

To keep Equipment Awareness, besides using risks and reliability, UIs should allow users to view on demand information about equipment and they should focus on assisting diagnosis of problems, with a list of general problems and their visual cues.

Finally, another particular aspect of Equipment Awareness is the visualization device. Comprehension and ability to use this device can influence a user Situation Awareness, thus users need to be trained in the device before engaging any activity.

Some of the common problems to SAW related to Equipment Awareness are:

- Confusing translation of documentation of imported equipments;
- Specialists failing to understand the functional relationships of equipment when problem solving [5], normally by use of incorrect mental model [16];
- No documentation update [5][8];
- Equipment too complex and risks not known to user.

4.3   System Awareness

System Awareness in maintenance is being aware of the computational, electrical, mechanical and hydraulic systems and how they control the process, in simpler terms, the automation in the system. Automation is the smart management of a system using technology, so that it operates without human direct control [6], and there is a high potential in automations to distract, overcharge and confuse operators, instead of supporting them. Therefore this awareness is centered on users understanding systems controlled actions and how they influence his/her work.

With the growth of automation, a new set of human factors have arisen, such as: how is information displayed in automated systems, how is the system controlled, do the operators accept the system, what happens when the system fails, boredom associated to a change in work from execution to monitoring, how does the system deal with SAW, disqualification and behavioral changes in operators depending on the level of automation and how this impact in risks.

UIs should focus on keeping user aware of automation by informing actions of the systems, as if the system was a coworker, and supporting direct system control.

Some of the common problems to SAW related to system awareness are:

- User "out-of-the-loop" with automations [1];

4.4   Environment Awareness

Environment Awareness is being aware of the surrounding considering the risks and consequences of the work and it is essential for keeping a high level of SAW. This awareness is considered by Nazir et al. as the Situation Awareness in industrial field work [11] and defined as the perception of changes in the physical parameters, the comprehension of the changes and anticipation of consequences.

In some domains, barriers are an important tool for safety, because they can prevent dangers in the workplace. Therefore UIs should take advantage of Barriers and inform users when they are present, to assist maintaining Environment Awareness.

UIs should also be designed to with the following principles:

- Avoid risks: in an industrial ambient, dangers caused by high temperatures, electricity, radioactivity, etc, are common and human-centered interfaces should focus on keeping users aware of them when they are present;
- Adapt to visibility issues: in case of diminished visibility (fog) Augmented Reality is a good technology for path guidance, being able to display the factory layout;
- Noise limiting UIs: workplaces with heavy machinery have loud sounds or noises that make it impossible to use sound/speech based interfaces. Therefore, they must not be used in this scenario, even with the increase in processing capabilities;
- Provide sustainable development: correct and ecological procedures of waste disposal should be ensured by a human-centered interface.

Also, some of the common problems to SAW related to environment awareness are:

- Unexpected leaking;
- Lack of organization and cleanliness and unclear procedure of waste disposal;
- Mistakes on understanding the factory layout (access to the wrong equipment) [11];
- Lack of visibility, because of darkness (night) or weather (fog) [8][11];
- Risks not known to user.

4.5   Team Awareness

Team Awareness is an essential element in a maintenance process, important for coordinating and maintaining a collective awareness as a group with the same goals and because 40% of accidents in industry are caused by lack of Team Situation Awareness [9]. As stated by Endsley and Robertson [4], errors frequently occur in team work because information is not shared or passed between teams. Therefore, individuals need not only to comprehend the task they are doing, but also what the team is doing, because this will influence their decision making and performance.

In this paper, considering SAW and HCI in maintenance, team work was structured in three types:

- Synchronous: procedures with actions performed in a fixed order;
- Group: unrelated procedures with the same goal on the same set of equipments;
- Independent: unrelated procedures with different goals but on the same equipment/location.

In case of Synchronous work, the order of tasks, and dependencies among tasks, could be mapped and UIs should display accomplished tasks of coworkers and their current task. In case of Group work, UIs should display beginning and end of tasks of coworkers. Notifications are a possible UI solution, and they could be integrated to the UI in case of Synchronous work or unobtrusive in case of Group work.

Considering only the guidelines above, in cases of teams with 5 or more members, information overload will be inevitable in synchronized and group work. Therefore a guideline was introduced for this case. In Synchronous teams, only tasks blocking the user should be displayed, and the current task of coworkers should be hidden, but possible to access when desired. In case of Grouped teams, only one message about coworkers should be displayed at a time (others messages could enter a queue and be displayed in order).

Another important aspect considered in team awareness is shifts handover during a task. Logs are generally used for this, informing events that happened during the last user turn. However, the new user should also be informed of: current progress of the task, current step to execute, current state of teammates.

Some of the common problems to SAW related to Team Awareness are:

- Poor communication with the team [4], especially of critical information [5];
- Poorly prepared planning and last minute changes [8];
- Shift handover trades a user with developed SAW for another with low initial awareness [9];
- Number of stakeholders too high for a manageable communication [5].

4.6   Enterprise Awareness

Enterprise Awareness is being aware of company controlled factors that influences the work, such as shift scheduling, workload/deadlines, assets, standards/terminologies and ethics rules of the work place.

Shifts, deadlines and workload can influence a person awareness ratio. Small deadlines or big workloads can cause stress, night shifts changes the circadian cycle and both can diminish cognitive capacity, impairing SAW. Also close to the end of a shift, users tend to focus only on the task and forget their surroundings, therefore UIs should further highlight events in this period (such as risks).

Additionally, because of the importance of the social component in the interface, studying the ethics and behavior rules of the work place are essential for guiding the design of a behavioral awareness interface. For instance, in some work places silence is mandatory, thus speech interfaces are not a good choice.

Finally, another cause of problems in Enterprise Awareness is the lack of use of standards and the different terminologies among stakeholders. Both can be ensured by an UI designed to standardize processes and nomenclature in a corporate environment.

Some of the common problems to SAW related to enterprise awareness are:

- Smaller attention to details and situations when close to the end of shift [8];
- Inconsistent documentation and terminology among stakeholders [5];
- Pressure to solve problems in short periods of time [7];
- Constant disruption of the circadian cycle due to 7days-7nights shifts schemes [7];
- Unavailability of spare parts [4].

4.7   Personal

Personal Awareness is related to the user and his/her characteristics and should be taken into account to create UIs that are compatibles to each user mental model. Factors such as ability (experience, training and skill), general cognitive level, motivation and stress should be considered to interfaces adaptations.

A simple manner to use these and others personal factors is to create profiles (similar to Personas) and adapt UIs to them, instead of each factor. Thus, a stressed experienced user could be fitted in the same profile of a novice user.

Some of the common problems to SAW related to Personal Awareness are:

- Lack of experience, preparation and training in the work and evaluating risks [1][5][7];
- Lack of motivation [2];
- Long work shifts with no rest [7].

5   Conclusion

This paper presents a conceptual framework to structure effective User Interfaces for maintenance field operators using Situation Awareness. In this sense, SAW is structured around seven entities, each requiring specific information to ensure awareness. The combination of these entities creates a context to analyze and perform operational maintenance processes, improving their efficiency and efficacy (leading to a higher level of safety), and also decreasing the number of errors and their criticality.

This method allows the framework proposed to streamline UI design by: 1) categorizing entities of interest in maintenance; 2) identifying important information in each entity; 3) presenting the common problems of SAW and possible solutions to them. The conceptual nature of this framework grants it flexibility to be used in any domain. Additionally, this method can be easily combined with other design solutions, which increases the value it adds in scenarios with high equipment costs or great risks.

However, the conceptual nature of this framework implies in leaving problems of SAW in UI design for maintenance unsolved and they will be addressed in a future work. For instance, it does not assist in determining priority of information, or defining a fixed criteria to select which information should be displayed to avoid information overload. Moreover, this conceptual framework does not specify how to display each type of information (according to their entity category), nor the ideal method to design UI for maintenance.

These shortcomings will be addressed by defining a methodology to design and develop User Interfaces for maintenance field work considering the Situation Awareness guidelines presented in this study. We also intend to propose a solution to increase Motivation in maintenance, because this is a lever to increase the level of awareness [7].

Concluding, today insufficient SAW is one of the main causes of errors in industries. Therefore, this cognitive model should be the basis of any system design process, especially if it involves complexity, safety and efficiency (such as maintenance field work). However, the present SAW-oriented design methodologies ignores the necessity of combining the principles of Physical, Social and Applied sciences, such as psychology, ergonomics, information management and HCI. This problem is addressed by this study by developing the foundation for SAW in industrial field work: the CFSAM, based on a theoretical and practical analysis of maintenance and a holistic study of SAW in maintenance. This innovation accelerates the UI design process, ensures that it provides adequate SAW to users, makes certain that developers/designers consider every area of knowledge relevant for maintenance and provides guidelines to increase the level of coherency and adherence of the system developed.

Acknowledgments. The authors wish to thank CNPq and FAPESP for the support to the INCT-SEC Project, processes 573963/2008-8 and 08/57870-9.

References

1. Endsley, M., Jones, D.: Designing for Situation Awareness: An Approach to User-Centered Design, 2nd edn. CRC Press (2011)
2. Dhillon, B., Liu, Y.: Human error in maintenance: a review. Journal of Quality in Maintenance Engineering 12(1), 21–36 (2006)

3. Henderson, S., Feiner, S.: Exploring the Benefits of Augmented Reality Documentation for Maintenance and Repair. IEEE Transactions on Visualization and Computer Graphics 16(1), 4–16 (2010)
4. Endsley, M., Robertson, M.: Situation Awareness in aircraft maintenance teams. International Journal of Industrial Ergonomics 26(2), 301–325 (2000)
5. Chinoy, S., Fischer, D.: Advancing Situational Awareness for Technical Operations. In: Annual Air Traffic Control Association Conference Proceedings, pp. 16–27 (2011)
6. Lynas, D., Horberry, T.: Human factor issues with automated mining equipment. The Ergonomics Open Journal 4(S2-M3), 74–80 (2011)
7. Sneddon, A., Mearns, K., Flin, R.: Stress, fatigue, situation awareness and safety in offshore drilling crews. Safety Science 56, 80–88 (2013)
8. Golightly, D., Ryan, B., Dadashi, N., Pickup, L., Wilson, J.R.: Use of scenarios and function analyses to understand the impact of situation awareness on safe and effective work on rail tracks. Safety Science 56, 52–62 (2013)
9. Bullemer, P., Reising, D.: Improving the Operations Team Situation Awareness: Lessons Learned from Major Process Industry Incidents. In: American Fuel & Petrochemical Manufacturers Annual Meeting, pp. 1–12 (2013)
10. Carroll, J.M., Neale, D.C., Isenhour, P.L., Rosson, M.B., ScottMcCrickard, D.: Notification and awareness: synchronizing task-oriented collaborative activity. International Journal of Human-Computer Studies 58(5), 605–632 (2003)
11. Nazir, S., Colombo, S., Manca, D.: The role of Situation Awareness for the Operators of Process Industry. Chemical Engineering Transactions 26, 303–308 (2012)
12. John, M., Smallman, H.: Staying Up to Speed: Four Design Principles for Maintaining and Recovering Situation Awareness. Journal of Cognitive Engineering and Decision Making 2, 118–139 (2008)

Data Driven Enterprise UX: A Case Study of Enterprise Management Systems

Sumit Pandey and Swati Srivastava

Clarice Technologies, Baner, Pune, India
{sumit.pandey,swati.srivastava}@claricetechnologies.com

Abstract. This paper describes and makes a case for a data driven user experience design process for Enterprise IT. The method described employs an approach that focuses on defining the key modules (objects) in an enterprise IT software and the data sets used by these modules very early in the design process. We discuss how mapping parent child relationships between key entities in the software and the linked data helps create a holistic view of the product ecosystem which in turn allows the designer to create an uncluttered information architecture and user journey that maps closely to mental construct of the system in the user's mind. We further argue that in the present age of big data, working with well-defined data sets and visible data relationships creates a valuable information repository for the designer to take decisions regarding task optimization and building business intelligence in the system itself. We also discuss the urgent need, advantages and methods of 'consumerizing' the Enterprise UI to increase users productivity and reduce the learning curve. Lastly, these ideas are exemplified through a real life case study for an enterprise server management system.

Keywords: User Experience Design, Consumerization, Design Process, Enterprise IT, User Centered Design, Data Driven Design, Design Patterns, Case Study.

1 Introduction

Enterprise IT refers to hardware and software that helps power business processes which often form the backbone of many consumer-facing services. Traditionally, these IT systems dealt primarily with structured data, (i.e. data stored in an organized fashion in databases or other forms of record storage) and were deployed as standalone data processing systems for record keeping, accounting and data storage [1][2]. These systems have always played a pivotal role in enabling services involving complex interactions between users, applications, services and devices and have evolved to become distributed systems characterized by very high levels of complexity. [3]

With an unprecedented amount of mobile and internet access coupled with cloud computing and social media, there has been an explosion in the amount of unstructured user generated data being created in the form of emails, multimedia, webpages, photos etc. This is in contrast to the structured data that traditional IT systems worked

S. Yamamoto (Ed.): HIMI 2014, Part II, LNCS 8522, pp. 205–216, 2014.
© Springer International Publishing Switzerland 2014

with which was easier to analyze and customize. The abundance of unstructured data [4] presents a wealth of new forms of information, which could lead to newer systems of business intelligence and analytics. Consequently, decision makers at all levels [5] across organizations expect ready access to relevant and actionable information to make better and smarter decisions faster. This can be clearly seen with the increasing demand for big data systems and intelligent analytics across business domains. These advances had a huge impact on the way that large-scale enterprise systems think about data and how the data becomes actionable information. Their role is no longer limited to being data storage/data entry and configuration silos but organizations are increasingly relying on them to be scalable decision making support systems.

There has also been a growing trend of "dual use" devices, networks and services, used both by consumers and businesses like tablet and smartphone devices along with workplace policies like "Bring Your Own Device" [6]. This trend is referred to as "consumerization" [7]. With millennials [8] comprising almost 40% of the enterprise IT workforce, consumerization is a trend the industry cannot afford to ignore [9][10] since the mental models and interface expectations of the present day enterprise workforce stems from the easy to use and refined interfaces of consumer applications rather than legacy CLI interfaces. [11]

Both of these factors have led to a change in the landscape and focus of enterprise IT. The current wave of enterprise IT is based on an industry wide demand for real-time/intelligent analytics systems coupled with improved and adaptive UX [3]. This paper presents a structure for a design process to work with enterprise management systems referred to as the Data Driven Enterprise UX process. This process is outlined using a real life case study of a project completed during our practice as UX consultants at Clarice Technologies. The project was located in the enterprise server and device management space and helps underline the efficacy of the design method in the design of complex enterprise IT software. Further, the paper argues how the process helped us align user goals with the high scalability, feature focused and legacy constraint driven requirements of the enterprise. We then summarize the process and present lessons learned from the case study presented followed by concluding remarks.

2   Enterprise IT and User Experience

Although consumerization of IT systems was initially seen as a trend chiefly linked to dual use devices and a way where consumers brought devices of personal use to their workplace, it has since lead to a fundamental shift in the way enterprise users expect software to behave and perform. On the other hand, rapid technological advances have changed the way that large-scale enterprise systems think about data and how this data becomes actionable [12].

This makes the design of enterprise IT software a challenging and compelling space for user experience designers to work in.

Enterprise IT presents an interesting premise where the designers have to effectively combine the understanding of human behavior, technology and processes to create a system that adheres to workflows and expectations of the target user, works within the technological constraints of legacy systems as well as one which analyses and provides quick and easy access to data that leads to intelligent business decisions. But while technologies like virtualization, cloud computing and storage and software defined networking have been developed rapidly to meet the evolving requirements of enterprise IT, UX has continued to play the role of a retrofitted solution applied on top of fundamentally disconnected feature driven system modules. User insight evaluation and research methods continue to have a micro-level focus on specific modules and tasks rather than taking a top-down, macro-level view of the entire product ecosystem. Hence, current enterprise UX processes tend to overlook opportunities of information flow between system modules along with opportunities for data interoperability and building a consistent product language and may look aesthetically pleasing at the outset but are fundamentally broken from an experience standpoint. As mentioned earlier, in the face of the changing role of IT systems and evolving expectations from the workforce, UX processes need to identify, mold and juxtapose disparate data sets and present them according to user context and role. UX can be a way to increase employee retention and concentration, decrease training time and a way to create a better consumer experience [11].

The process of creating Enterprise IT software can be split into three principal components [3]:

1. Gathering relevant data and information.
2. Transforming data into insightful and targeted performance indicators and operational parameters.
3. Mapping indicators and functions to business objectives and operational constraints leading to the execution of appropriate actions.

Consequently, the requisite goals for an effective design process for enterprise IT can be listed as the following:

1. Restructuring the data sets and modules with an emphasis on highlighting logical relationships, hierarchy and dependencies.
2. Using the uncovered relationships and their priority to optimize tasks and make data more actionable and insightful. Explore possibilities of creating deeper customized analytics and offering insights helping the large scale enterprise evolve, improve and adapt.
3. Create a user interface that maps to the user's mental model and aids the users in performing tasks on the system more efficiently and with fewer errors.

3   Data Driven Enterprise UX

We recognize that the nature of data plays a very important role in crafting the interactions for any enterprise system. To design the user experience of systems, which serve as a reference for important business decisions along with being task-performing tools, it is imperative to view data not just as the content going into different screens and system modules but as a cluster of interlinked information sets. Further, this approach helps in identifying logical object-data links that can be further classified by user context. Interactions, navigation systems and screens designed keeping these information sets in mind result in interfaces which are tailored to the tasks as well as the content being presented. These ideas serve as the building blocks for a data driven model for enterprise UX that we present in this paper. This model is aimed at aiding the creation of a scalable and adaptive strategy suited to the needs of the new generation of IT systems. We outline the steps of the proposed design process in the following sections (Fig. 1).

Fig. 1. The Data Driven Enterprise UX Process

3.1 Understand

The understanding phase of the design process should be driven by subject matter experts and end user (if possible) workshops and interviews. These workshops are aimed at creating a specialized product ecosystem model that we refer to as the 'Data-Object-User' model. The focus of this model is to collaboratively map the various user roles and usage contexts, the primary objects that the product is going to be built around and the detailed information and datasets (and their subsets) that the product deals with. Akin to object oriented programming [13] principles of creating parent-child relationships through inheritance and encapsulating key data sets into objects and classes, this model maps user roles and data access relationships along with data dependencies and relationships at a very early stage. During the course of discussions and participatory workshops, parent child relationships between objects along with logical object-data links and possibilities of data and information flow within and outside the product are also identified.

3.2 Define

Jon Kolko, in his paper on Abductive Thinking and Sensemaking describes the process of synthesis as (a process where) "designers attempt "to organize, manipulate, prune, and filter gathered data into a cohesive structure for information building." [14] During the process of synthesis, we try and identify information clusters and reorganize the dataset discovered during the 'understanding' process into object centric, task centric or task-object hybrid modules. This is done by aligning the objects and actions identified into a consumable hierarchy that maps to the users mental model in the closest possible fashion. For instance, a generic data consumption and visualization system is prone to dealing with a large variety of data-objects and in such a scenario the user's journey typically starts with a task that needs to be completed. In such a scenario, the designer might be inclined to assign the highest priority to the tasks/actions the system exposes and consequently group the objects based on the requirements of the tasks. In contrast, for a system where the objects are limited, the user's journey would typically start by identifying the object he/she is most interested in followed by contextually identifying the tasks that need to be performed. Such a system might be better served by creating a object centric or a hybrid hierarchy. Subsequently, detailed screen flows are created. Each screen in the screen flow outlines high-level information sets that need to be presented on it as well. The identification and placement of information sets is in accordance to the user roles and requirements and it maps the data relationships identified in the Data-Object-User model to screen level information that is presented to the end user. It also allows for examining the relevance of the information presented at a micro, i.e. screen level as well as the flow of information presented at a macro, i.e. task level. While these flows are being fleshed out, possibilities of automation, optimization and anomaly prediction need to be considered and accommodated as well.

3.3   Create

The screen-data flows identified during synthesis should be converted to detailed wireframe mockups built with interaction models focused on surfacing, presenting and manipulating data in a meaningful and easy to consume manner. Fresh interaction and visual paradigms should be developed to present the identified information set. Design has emerged as a clear differentiator in the consumer application space because the availability of multiple, often free, options, users rarely choose an application with a badly conceived experience. Users tend to prefer uncluttered and focused interfaces with fewer but more relevant options. The designer could potentially look at interaction models being used in the consumer product domain [15] to build concepts with increased familiarity and reduced cognitive load for the end user. Specialized views and sub views, popularly referred to as microinteractions [16], based on different combinations and juxtapositions of the same dataset could be created to the specialized needs of a specific user role/context. In the case of mobile contexts, an adaptive/responsive strategy could be developed using a mobile first framework.

4   Case Study 1: Server and Device Management System

This web based management and monitoring console was a part of a broad set of offerings from a large unified service delivery management company providing end-to-end network and application-based solutions. The brief was to redesign the existing user interface considering some legacy constraints and adding some new feature sets. The software was successful in the market but was receiving a lot of usability complaints that made the company consider a ground up redesign exercise. The software consisted of several interconnected modules catering to various customer requirements. Although the software modules were functionally very well thought out, it relied on extremely data rich screens laid out with a feature centric navigation. This resulted in a very complicated system for the end user who had to rely very heavily on their training to navigate through the software and to interpret the data as well, since the data connections were not well represented in the system. Furthermore, as users performed action that affected these data sets directly, the system needed a forgiving and feedback oriented UI, to reduce the user's overall cognitive load. The following sections outline the redesign process using the Data Driven Enterprise UX process.

4.1 Understand

As discussed, the first step of the re-design exercise was gaining an in depth understanding of the service ecosystem. The project was conducted in a four month sprint, which left little time for gaining access to end users. The design team had access to the product and sales managers to conduct interviews and workshops. The two initial sessions involved the managers giving a detailed walkthrough of the software ecosystem. On the basis of these workshops, the design team outlined the as-is ecosystem in the form of a mind map in collaboration with the client's team, validating it as we moved forth. This mind map was a mix of data-object and modules. The next sessions involved exhaustive discussions with the client executives regarding the user types and the actions performed by them along with modules (objects) and data accessed by them to perform these actions. These sessions provided two important insights. First, the relations and interdependence of data as designed in the system; secondly users' actual navigation pattern to perform the required actions. Subsequently, the design team did a comparative study of these two mind maps to identify the following main components:

- Data Sets (e.g.: User lists/Upgrade files/Login time).
- Objects accessing the data sets. Modules like Activity logs accessing data sets like login/log out times from the event log and data sets from the other modules.
- User Roles and logical navigation between the modules to suit the users' workflow, habits and needs. During the understanding phase, logically related data sets and key objects began to surface, even though they were scattered around in the whole system in the original design.

After involved discussions with the client team the design team started re-architecting the system's ecosystem and subsequently re-organizing the granular details within the modules. This step was one of the most intense and important steps.

The design team analyzed the existing product ecosystem and based on the user goals and the data-object relationships uncovered, created the Data-Object-User model. To create this model, the design team re-thought the clustering of the uncovered the data sets and then re-organized the data-object relationships (Fig. 2) to align them to workflows and key user tasks. E.g. the deployment data set in the current system had hardware (infrastructure specifications) as a part of the configuration module. This data set had no immediate relation with the configuration of the system itself. Hence, this data set was pulled out of the configuration module and a separate module created for it. For an end user working in the configuration module the task became a lot more uncluttered and focused and hence he/she could perform it faster.

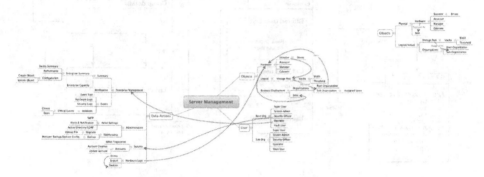

Fig. 2. Data-Object-User Model

4.2   Define

Although design synthesis strictly focuses on the end user needs and habits, in enterprise software, legacy business is an important constraint that cannot be overlooked. The re-arrangement of the components in the eco-system also takes into consideration the business logic. Designers are always end user advocates in this process but there are certain points in legacy systems where a hard bargain has to be struck and an appropriate design has to be created around these legacy constraints. These constraints play an important role when the screen flows and subsequently the information architecture are being designed. Considering these legacy constraints and the finalized Data-Object-User model, the key user tasks were arranged into a descriptive screen flow as described earlier. These flows (Fig. 3) show the user journey through the new eco-system for accomplishing various tasks. These screen flows gave an in-depth representation of the relationship between data sets and objects. For e.g. one of the primary task of monitoring the network was detailed till user viewing an anomaly, doing root cause analysis and taking action to remedy or report the same, is shown in one complete flow. In addition, screen flows also started outlining the high level actions on the data sets. This formed the foundation for next steps of creating detailed wireframes.

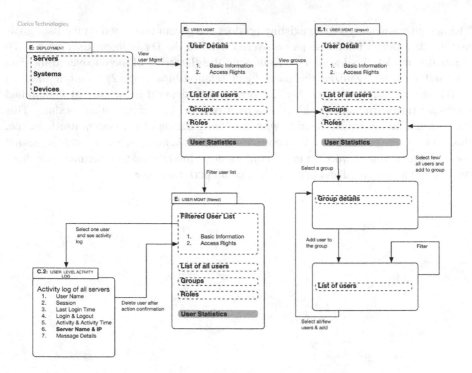

Fig. 3. Information/Screen Flows

4.3   Create

Enterprise UIs rampantly follow a common UI pattern of showing all the data and all the related actions at once at the top panel creating a very busy interface. This UI was no different. The screens included a couple of dashboards along with more detailed data screens. Design team followed a consistent approach of showing summarized high-level information before displaying the detailed data set. Borrowing from the consumer application pattern that makes use of contextual actions to de-clutter the interface, the design team refrained from displaying the whole set at once. Each module had a set of global actions and subsequently based on the selected data set, the contextual actions were displayed.

We realized that we could take a page out of the consumer application design patterns to enhance the overall experience of the server management application as well. Hence, we adopted a layered information dissemination approach by pushing the less frequently accessed information and actions further and deeper into the UI and by indicating the most relevant information bits on the top level overlaid with clear drill-down indicators.

While crafting the detailed design for the system the design team consciously worked towards creating a user interface which has the ease of use and clarity as that of a consumer application. Although enterprise applications encompass far more complex data sets of very high scale, the interactions when broken down on a per use case basis, often have a similar nature to consumer applications. e.g. Add/Delete/Configure actions. Furthermore, it should be understood that in this scenario, human nature and behavior is a common factor. Although the users of enterprise application are generally trained but when they perform similar actions in a more complex manner in the context of enterprise software than while using a consumer application, it results in frustration. Additionally, they are not able to leverage their mental model that evolves from using consumer applications on a day-to-day basis and even in their work, while multitasking on the same system as the enterprise software. A word of caution while following this process: the security and integrity of data and business logic should not be compromised while attempting to create a simpler interface.

We outline the process of designing consumerised microinteractions [16] through some examples below:

— The existing UI of this system displayed all the user information related data fields at all times in most of the forms even though in more than half the use cases the fields were not even needed till they were actually needed for a specialized use case. To reduce the complexity of the forms which the user was expected to fill, the design team took the "Progressive Disclosure" approach by using radio buttons on the table itself to convey only one column of the table was to be filled to complete the form. The whole UI was designed such that it showed a minimum number of fields when only one user was to be added but UI expanded itself dynamically for batch additions of the user. (Fig. 4)

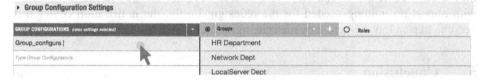

Fig. 4. Progressive Disclosure

— A popular consumer application – Gmail [17] provides a very interesting microinteraction that lets the user quickly view any sent email right after it has been sent. This caters to the often-practiced habit of users to confirm if they sent the correct content and to the correct people. In order to create an interface that provides ample reassurance to the user performing critical actions in complex enterprise systems, this pattern was borrowed and used in this system. Whenever the user performed an activity such as adding a user, or configuring a device etc., a view details link was provided to the user in case he/she wanted to see the results of his/her activity and wanted to revert or make any further changes (Fig. 5).

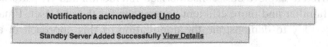

Fig. 5. Contextual links for validating actions

— Not only do clear data-object relationships help in identifying areas for task optimization and creating optimal data clustering, they also potentially help identify possible areas of adding an automation or business intelligence. One such example was the deployment module that was initially used to display static counters and reports but was identified as a module that had the potential to transform into a fully dynamic and customizable reporting tool. For instance, the user could select different types of device specifications in a multitude of different combinations to create a comparative report as required (Fig. 6).

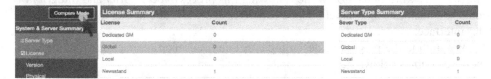

Fig. 6. Comparative reporting module

4.4   User Validation

The final UI created as a part of this redesign exercise was converted into HTML prototypes and the screens were tested with actual end users. The users mentioned that they felt a sense of cognitive relief as the system was aiding them with intelligent suggestions and the improved action clustering helped them move almost in a guided path through the system. Additionally, the interface paradigms were similar the ones they usually came across and they were able to decipher the way to use them easily with almost no training needed for the redesign. Lastly, the notification center had become like an inbox where they manage, monitor, archive and take actions.

5   Conclusion

The Data Driven Enterprise UX process is designed as data centric process that targets task optimization as well as putting important data usage patterns collected through system logs and expert interviews, to work as a reference for taking important business decision. This process follows the core tenets of the user centered design process and juxtaposes it with an early and deep understanding of the data models upon which enterprise IT systems are built. Time-tested tools of the design process are put to use to uncover these data relationships and object hierarchies and their correlation to the end user's journey. This helps create possibilities for the creation of interfaces that provide access to data in a contextual relevant manner and helps optimize user tasks as well as exposes opportunities for adding business intelligence. In addition, we tried to explore how consumerised interaction and UI patterns could help in creating a familiar and more efficient experience for the end user. Finally, we presented a case study to demonstrate the application of this approach in a real world scenario.

During the requirement gathering phase, mind maps were created to reflect the existing ecosystem and in the internal relationships of the between the modules and data sets utilized by these data sets. Key archetypes were identified followed by crucial tasks performed by them. With enough domain knowledge and understanding, the existing system was re-architected. As discussed in section 4.1, existing modules (objects) were analyzed to create the Data-Object-User model that helped in an in-depth understanding of data-object relationships. This analysis included exploring the purpose, dependencies, hierarchy and actions present in the modules. As can be seen in in section 4.2, this provided better guidance to the design team and helped create more efficient workflows for the user by optimizing and automating certain aspects of tasks. This also resulted in the identification and reduction of redundant data display and actions in the UI.

Another direct and important contribution of the Data-Object-User model was the vocalization of ideas from the high-level decision makers, relating to further ways of employing the data for gaining better insights. This is clearly demonstrated in the redesign of the server and device management system's deployment module as discussed in section 4.3.

As mentioned in section 3.3, with the advent of cheaper technology, smartphones and tablets, incorporating consumer driven interaction patterns has become imperative in the design of enterprise UI. It also aligns with the goals of a design team to create a user-friendly interface with low learning curve and can potentially lead to great insights and fresh approaches during the 'create' (section 3.3) phase. One of the approaches to accomplish this is to understand the intention of the user's task and compare it to similar tasks in the consumer product domain. However, the design team must always be wary of oversimplifying the UI to the extent that it starts compromising data security and integrity. Experts at the client side must always verify this while the wireframes are being designed and shared.

Acknowledgements. We thank Milind Sonavane for agreeing to be a perpetual sounding board for our ideas and insights and the UCD team at Clarice Technologies for their constant help and support.

References

1. Moore, G.: Systems of Engagement and the Future of Enterprise IT: A Sea Change in Enterprise IT. AIIM White Paper (2010)
2. Lara, Z.: Enterprise Software History, Part 2: Minicomputers to the PC,
   http://blog.softwareadvice.com/articles/enterprise/
   software-history-part-2109062011/
3. Delic, K.A., Dayal, U.: Adaptation in Large Scale Enterprise Systems. ACM Ubiquity 2004, p. 1 (August 2004)
4. Structure, Models and Meaning: Is "unstructured" data merely unmodeled?, Intelligent Enterprise,
   http://www.informationweek.com/software/information-management/structure-models-and-meaning/d/d-id/1030187

5. Fisher, D., DeLine, R., Czerwinski, M., Drucker, S.: Interactions with Big Data Analytics. ACM Interactions 19(3), 50–59 (2012)
6. Gartner Predicts by 2017, Half of Employers will Require Employees to Supply Their Own Device for Work Purposes, Gartner, http://www.gartner.com/newsroom/id/2466615
7. Moschella, D., Neal, D., Opperman, P., Taylor, J.: The 'Consumerization' of Information Technology. CSC Research White Paper, El Segundo (2004)
8. Generation, Y.: They've arrived at work with a new attitude. USA Today, http://usatoday30.usatoday.com/money/workplace/2005-11-06-gen-y_x.htm
9. The consumerization of IT: The next-generation CIO. PwC Center for Technology and Innovation Report, 3-6 (2011)
10. Gillett, F.: Forrester, Employees Use Multiple Gadgets For Work — And Choose Much Of The Tech Themselves, http://blogs.forrester.com/frank_gillett/12-02-22-employees_use_multiple_gadgets_for_work_and_choose_much_of_the_tech_themselves
11. Mcree, J.: UX for Enterprise: Part I. Universal Mind, http://blog.universalmind.com/ux-for-enterprise-part-i/
12. Krieger, M.: Revolution or Evolution: What is Big Data's impact on enterprise information systems? Enterprise CIO Forum, http://www.enterprisecioforum.com/en/blogs/mrkrieger/revolution-or-evolution-what-big-datas-i
13. Pierce, B.: What is Object-Oriented Programming? Types and Programming Languages. MIT Press (2002)
14. Kolko, J.: Abductive Thinking and Sensemaking: The Drivers of Design Synthesis. MIT's Design Issues 26(1) (Winter 2010)
15. Nazarian, S.: Enterprise UX - How can we transform enterprise user experience to be more mobile, flexible, and responsive? Design Mind, http://designmind.frogdesign.com/articles/enterprise-ux.html
16. Saffer, D.: Designing Microinteractions, Microinteractions. O'Reilly, 2 (2013)
17. Gmail, http://www.gmail.com

Decision Support Based on Time-Series Analytics:
A Cluster Methodology

Wanli Xing[1], Rui Guo[2], Nathan Lowrance[1], and Thomas Kochtanek[1]

[1] School of Information Science and Learning Technologies, University of Missouri,
Columbia, MO 65211, USA
{wxdg5,njl1352}@mail.missouri.edu, KochtanekT@missouri.edu
[2] Department of Civil and Environmental Engineering, University of South Florida,
Tampa, Columbia, FL 33620, USA
rui@mail.usf.edu

Abstract. Web analytic techniques have become increasingly popular, particularly Google Analytics time-series dashboards. But interpretations of a website's visits traffic data may be oversimplified and limited by Google Analytics existing functionalities. This means website mangers have to make estimations rather than mathematically informed decisions. In order to gain a more precise view of longitudinal website visits traffic data, the researchers mathematically transformed the existing Goggle Analytics' log data allowing the vectors of website visits per each year to be considered simultaneously. The methodology groups the data of an example website gathered over an 'x' year period into 'y' clusters of data. The results show that the transformed data is richer, more accurate and informative, potentially allowing website managers to make more informed decisions concerning promoting, developing, and maintaining their websites rather than relying on estimations.

Keywords: Temporal analytics, Google analytics, cluster analysis, decision support, website management.

1   Introduction

Web analytics are equally valuable for profit and nonprofit and many website mangers have turned to web analytics techniques to help them make more informed decisions about adverting, site development, and site maintenance [1]. Google Analytics (GA) has become a leading tool in this context and can provide quick access to metrics to ascertain traffic levels and visitor distribution [2]. There are some limitations to these metrics. One is Spider visits are indistinguishable from true visitors. Spiders are computer programs that access sites to update databases [3]. Also visits alone can lead to an overestimation of a site's visitor traffic because some visitors will leave if a page is having trouble loading or stay for too brief an amount of time to matter [4,5]. Second, when analyzing web metrics, it is important to remember that no firm inferences regarding user's intentions can be made solely from web metrics [6, 7]. These limitations aside, GA temporal metrics can still be informative.

S. Yamamoto (Ed.): HIMI 2014, Part II, LNCS 8522, pp. 217–225, 2014.
© Springer International Publishing Switzerland 2014

Temporal fluctuations of when visits are occurring have had noticeable effects on the interpretation of web traffic [8]. Categories of certain queries trend differently over varying periods of time, supporting the importance of temporal analysis [9]. Temporal factors also relate to the quality of web searches, name search effectiveness and efficiency [10]. Temporal analysis has also been applied to study the dynamics of blogger's posting behaviors [11]. Search engine transactional logs and time series analysis has been established as a viable means of anticipating future web traffic on sites [12]. Because of these benefits the GA time series dashboard is a frequently used tool to provide a rough estimate of overall trends of visits to web sites [13-16].

Current time series analysis of GA data is following two thematic paths. One of these is based on website managers observing the GA time traffic dashboard and using the visits chart to roughly estimate the overall trend of the visits to the website. These estimations do have their uses. In one study a website experienced a decline in usage and these GA visits data were used to help interpret the reasons behind the decline [16]. Another study made uses of two years' worth of GA visits data for a health professional education website to inform findings, allowing a trend to predict that this particular site would further expand to be a global source on genetics-genomics education [14]. The drawback is that these conclusions about their websites evaluated over time depended on observation and estimation of the GA dashboard rather than accurate computation. Because of this, interpretations of visitor's traffic data may be oversimplified [17] and subject to limitations endemic to Google Analytics' existing functionalities

The second theme of use for time series analysis of GA data is based on using regression analysis of the website visits traffic data over a certain period of time and comparing its relationship with other website metrics. Plaza [18, 19] tested the relationship examining the effectiveness of entries (visit behavior and length of sessions) depending on their traffic source: direct visit, in-link entries over an approximately two-year period. Wang et al. [20] studied over a one-year period whether users behave differently during weekdays and weekends, finding a number of significant relationships between several key traffic variables and web metrics.

Many website managers are not likely to run regression analysis on their page traffic, so a more precise quantitative method could be helpful in comparison with the current estimations. None-the-less website users' behaviors are very important information to understand the market demand and to make strategic plans for a web system. Their visiting patterns can vary significantly over a long period of time. In order for the web managers to make decisions effectively, marketing and maintenance plans should be created in suitable intervals that are in line with the visiting patterns. For example, the webmaster should promote any products or services when they have the highest visits to their website, but schedule maintenance for the website when there are the fewest visitors. How can we more precisely identify users' visiting patterns over a longitudinal period rather than using a rough estimation through GA Dashboard?

To answer this question, we investigated a data mining method to provide a longitudinal and accurate view for web managers to use so that they can make decisions more effectively. By capturing temporal features of a website users' behavior with a mathematical method and analyzing each year simultaneously, clustered results should provide a more accurate grouping of high, low, and median traffic levels and their corresponding dates. This study utilizes the Truman library website (http://www.trumanlibrary.org/) to illustrate a proposed methodology, but the application of this methodology is not limited to this type of website, as any website evaluated with GA should be able to use this method. This approach transforms GA log data from a somewhat limited interpretive state to something that is richer, more accurate, and informative.

2   Methodology

2.1   Method

Cluster analysis is classified as data set into groups that are relatively homogeneous within themselves and heterogeneous between each other on the basis of a chosen set of variables [21]. Therefore, it served our purpose for identifying groups of time slots which the website master can depend on to make informed decisions for their web systems. A cluster methodology for pattern identification of the website is shown in the following figure (Fig 1). GA provides a rather solid basis to accomplish the cluster analysis because it automatically collects all the visits data and their associated visits time for us.

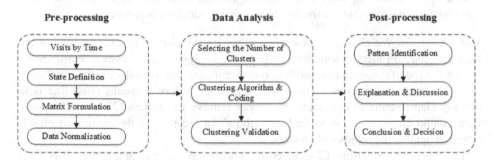

Fig. 1. Time-Series Analytics Framework

Pre-processing. In terms of gathering the visits by time, the first step is to access GA, which enables one to export data in different granularity such as hourly, daily, weekly, monthly and yearly based on the needs of the analysis.

The system state is an abstract representation of the condition of a system at some point in time [11]. Based on the different granularity of the data (e.g. week, month) collected by GA, we could capture the temporal feature of the website user's behavior with a mathematical method. The state definition used here is a vector of website visits in a certain time window (visits/day, visits/week etc.) and the time feature (a dimension of the time that website visits occurs) for each year. Since this research aims to look at analysis over a longitudinal period of time, for instance, identifying user visiting patterns in one-year period. The data samples are thus multidimensional because the vectors of website for each year are considered simultaneously.

Therefore, the system states in our study are defined as follows, assuming there are M representative years in the log datasets and yearly visits are recorded into T time intervals. Then the data A, a K (M+1) × K (T) matrix, will have the format as following (1).

$$
A = \begin{bmatrix}
a_{11} & a_{12} & \cdots & a_{1M} & a_{1(M+1)} \\
a_{21} & a_{22} & \cdots & a_{2M} & a_{2(M+1)} \\
\vdots & \vdots & \ddots & \vdots & \vdots \\
a_{(T-1)1} & a_{(T-1)2} & \cdots & a_{(T-1)M} & a_{(T-1)(M+1)} \\
a_{T1} & a_{T2} & \cdots & a_{TM} & a_{T(M+1)}
\end{bmatrix}
\tag{1}
$$

In order to smooth the different data visits to scale among different years, the elements in this matrix should be properly normalized, which following equation is carried out prior to the cluster analysis so that make the data dimensionless (2).

$$atm' = atm - a m s m \qquad (t=1,2,\cdots, T; \quad m=1,2,\cdots, M+1) \tag{2}$$

Where a_{tm}, $\bar{a}_m$ and s_m represents original, average, and standard deviation of website visits or time variables, respectively, for any particular observation.

Data Analysis. We choose K-means algorithm for the clustering analysis, one of the most popular non-hierarchical methods to do the analysis [25]. However, before moving on the specific K-means algorithm, one significant step is to decide the number of clusters we are going to use. The common practice before K-means clustering is to employ Gap-statistic to determine the proper number of clusters [22, 23]. The basic idea behind Gap-statistic is to find an "elbow" in the plot of the optimized cluster criterion against the number of clusters, K.

For this purpose, letting E_N^* denote the expectation under a sample size of N from the reference distribution, the optimal value for the number of clusters is then the value K for which the "Gap" is the largest. K is the number of clusters, N is sample size, and W_K denotes an overall average within the cluster sum-of-squares (3).

$$\text{Gap}_N(K) = E_N^* \{\log(W_K)\} - \log(W_K) \tag{3}$$

Those interested in the theoretical details of this method can refer to the Tibshirani, Walther, and Hastie's original paper [23]. In terms of the cluster algorithm details, in general, elements are grouped according to their similarities, and in K-Means cluster, the distance between them. In this study, squared Euclidean distance is employed to calculate the distance between clusters, where d_{ij}^2 is the squared Euclidean distance between state elements i, and j; x_{im} is the mth element in state i; and $x_{jm}x_{ik}$ is the mth element in state j (4).

$$d_{ij}^2 = \sum_{m=1}^{M+1} (a_{im} - a_{jm})^2 \qquad (i, j = 1, 2, \cdots, T; \quad m = 1, 2, \cdots, M+1) \qquad (4)$$

Vilifying the optimal number of clusters is also a critical step in cluster analysis. In our study, we implemented the Silhouette measure to vilify the efficiency of the selected number of clusters. For more Specific information on the Silhouette Coefficient refer to Rousseeuw's work [24].

Post Processing. After cluster analysis, post processing is conducted to determine the intervals and identify the visits' patterns. Another important step in our procedure is to explain the patterns. This requires the webmaster in conjunction with the context to infer meaning out of the pattern and make the informed decision.

2.2   Research Context

To demonstrate this approach, we chose a library website – Truman Presidential Library http://www.trumanlibrary.org/libhist.htm.

2.3   Dataset

Google Analytics was used to gather data over five years from August first, 2008 to July thirty-first, 2013. To better serve the purpose of the study, clickstream data pertaining to time was collected. We downloaded the CSV files containing weekly visits of website as shown bellow (Fig 2).

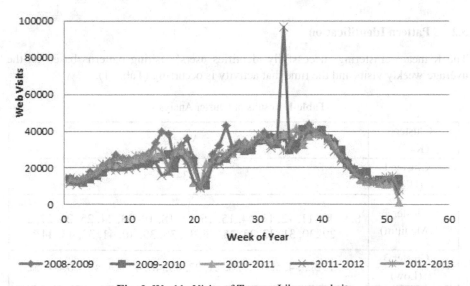

Fig. 2. Weekly Visits of Truman Library website

3   Results

3.1   Cluster Numbers

To choose the optimal number of clusters, the Gap statistic measure was conducted by coding in R. Below, we first show the observed and expected log (Wk) and compare the Gap values against the number of clusters in our case study (Fig. 3). Second, we show the Gap values against the number of clusters in our case study(Fig. 3). Due to these results we chose three as the number of clusters for K-Means algorithm in the next step.

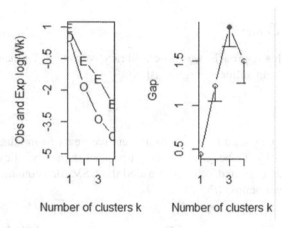

Fig. 3. Gap Function

3.2   Pattern Identification

The K-means clustering successfully identifies users' visiting patterns based on the average weekly visits and the time that activity is occurring (Table 1).

Table 1. Results of Cluster Analysis

Cluster (K=3)	Week
Cluster 1 (High)	34
Cluster 2 (Medium)	8, 9, 10, 11, 12, 13, 14, 15, 16, 17, 18, 19, 23, 24, 25, 26, 27, 28, 29 ,30, 31, 32, 33, 35, 36, 37, 38, 39, 40, 41, 32, 43, 44
Cluster 3 (Low)	1, 2, 3, 4, 5, 6, 7, 20, 21, 22, 45, 46, 47, 48, 49, 50, 51, 52

3.3   Cluster Validation

In order to validate the number of the selected clusters a Silhouette Coefficient was calculated. The "elbow" occurs when the number of clusters is three, which indicates the efficiency of our three cluster analysis.

3.4   Explanation

These results better inform the web manager of their peak traffic week, which would be week 34. Any important updating should be done before this high traffic week, it also informs the site manager of an optimal week for advertising or promoting if necessary. Cluster 3 indicates ideal times for site maintenance.

4   Discussion

Our methodology groups 52 weeks into different clusters based on the five years of click streaming data. These different clusters can help managers to develop plans for allocating resources in a more efficient fashion than making estimations based on looking at line graph data for individual years. For example, plans might be made for website maintenance, for adjusting time/task efforts and for the allocation of human resources better suited for expected website visiting conditions for particular dates or times. Therefore, managers, instead of basing decisions on a simple observation and estimation, obtain reliable quantified results that can be used to improve the quality of their decision-making. Keep in mind GA time series traffic dashboard only show a line graph of visit information chronologically (Fig. 4). While one could create an overlapping graph, like what was done for this paper (Fig. 2) and see major peeks and dips, it is still not precise. It is clear that some years have outliers, but our method clarifies grey areas, showing what are the true peaks across five years and what qualifies as the cut off points for high visit peaks and low visit dips. Ultimately this adds more mathematical confidence in the accuracy of high and low traffic times. This method offers a more precisely quantified and longitudinal point of view, and thus has the potential to be applied in different contexts and for different usages. They can simply redefine the abstraction state and time granularity. The next logical step would be to develop a tool to enhance GA allowing this mathematical clustering method to use GA visit data and be calculated for GA users, rather than hoping the site managers would be able and willing to use this procedure.

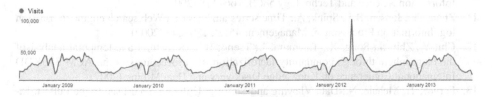

Fig. 4. GA view of visits to Truman Library website

5   Conclusion

As an exploratory study, this research presented an application of mathematical modeling using time series distributed click steaming data that GA collected for a library website to provide a more accurate account of past visits site traffic patterns. This new methodological framework based on advanced analytical techniques was developed to more accurately examine the visitors' behavior patterns over time, allowing for more confident web site management decisions to be made by site managers. In the future, we recommend the investigation of visitors' behavior patterns from different traffic sources (direct, reference or search engine) as well as return visitors' navigation in comparison with that of new visitors. This would help to identify the loyal users of a website, and other behavior characteristics could be further explored in an extended study as well.

References

1. Marek, K.: Getting to Know Web Analytics. Using web analytics in the library, pp. 11–16. ALA Store (2011)
2. Clifton, B.: Advanced web metrics with Google Analytics. John Wiley and Sons, Inc., Indianapolis (2012)
3. Phippen, A., Sheppard, L., Furnell, S.: A practical evaluation of Web analytics. Internet Research 14(4), 284–293 (2004)
4. Mullarkey, G.W.: Internet measurement data - practical and technical issues. Marketing Intelligence & Planning 22(1), 42–58 (2004)
5. Dreze, X., Zufryden, F.: Is Internet Advertising Ready for Prime Time? Journal of Advertising Research 38(3), 7–18 (1998)
6. Grimes, C., Tang, D., Russell, D.: Query Logs Are Not Enough. In: Workshop on Query Logs Analysis: Social and Technological Challenges, Banff, Canada (2007)
7. Weischedel, B., Huizingh, E.: Web Site Optimization With Web Metrics: A Case Study. In: International Conference on Electronic Commerce (ICEC 2006), pp. 463–470 (2006)
8. Khoo, M., Pagano, J., Washington, A.L., Recker, M., Palmer, B., Donahue, R.A.: Using web metrics to analyze digital libraries. In: Proceedings of the 8th ACM/IEEE-CS Joint Conference on Digital Libraries, pp. 375–384. ACM (2008)
9. Jansen, B.J., Spink, A.: How are we searching the World Wide Web? A comparison of nine search engine transaction logs. Information Processing & Management 42(1), 248–263 (2005)
10. Beitzel, S.M., Jensen, E.C., Chowdhury, A., Frieder, O., Grossman, D.: Temporalanalysis of a very large topically categorized web query log. Journal of the American Society for Information Science and Technology 58(2), 166–178 (2007)
11. Zhang, Y., Jansen, B.J., Spink, A.: Time series analysis of a Web search engine transaction log. Information Processing & Management 45(2), 230–245 (2009)
12. Chi, Y., Zhu, S., Song, X., Tatemura, J., Tseng, B.L.: Structural and temporal analysisof the blogosphere through community factorization. In: Proceedings of the ACM SIGKDD International Conference on Knowledge Discovery and Data Mining (2007)
13. Farney, T., Mchale, N.: Data Viewing and Sharing: Utilizing Your Data to the Fullest. Library Technology Reports 49(4), 39–42 (2013)

14. Kirk, M., Morgan, R., Tonkin, E., McDonald, K., Skirton, H.: An objective approach to evaluating an internet-delivered genetics education resource developed for nurses: using Google Analytics™ to monitor global visitor engagement. Journal of Research in Nursing 17(6), 557–579 (2012)
15. Pakkala, H., Presser, K., Christensen, T.: Using Google Analytics to measure visitor statistics: The case of food composition websites. International Journal of Information Management 32(6), 504–512 (2012)
16. Kent, M.L., Carr, B.J., Husted, R.A., Pop, R.A.: Learning web analytics: A tool for strategic communication. Public Relations Review 37(5), 536–543 (2011)
17. Kumar, C., Norris, J.B., Sun, Y.: Location and time do matter: A long tail study of website requests. Decision Support Systems 47(4), 500–507 (2009)
18. Plaza, B.: Monitoring web traffic source effectiveness with Google Analytics: An experiment with time series. Aslib Proceedings 61(5), 474–482 (2009)
19. Plaza, B.: Google Analytics for measuring website performance. Tourism Management 32(3), 477–481 (2011)
20. Wang, X., Shen, D., Chen, H.L., Wedman, L.: Applying web analytics in a K-12 resource inventory. The Electronic Library 29(1), 20–35 (2011)
21. Guo, R., Zhang, Y.: Identifying Time-of-Day Breakpoints Based on Nonintrusive Data Collection Platforms. Journal of Intelligent Transportation Systems (2013)
22. Everitt, B.S., Landau, S., Leese, M.: Cluster Analysis, 5th edn. John Wiley & Sons, Ltd. (2011)
23. Tibshirani, R., Walther, G., Hastie, T.: Estimating the Number of Clusters in a Data Set via the Gap Statistic. Journal of Royal Statistical Society, B63, Part 2, 411–423 (2001)
24. Rousseeuw, P.J.: Silhouettes: A Graphical Aid to the Interpretation and Validation of Cluster Analysis. Journal of Computational and Applied Mathematic 20(1), 53–65 (1987)
25. Xu, C., Liu, P., Wang, W., Li, Z.: Evaluation of the impacts of traffic states on crash risks on freeways. Accident Analysis & Prevention 47, 162–171 (2012)

Information and Interaction
in Aviation and Transport

"A Careful Driver is One Who Looks in Both Directions When He Passes a Red Light" – Increased Demands in Urban Traffic

Martin Götze[1], Florian Bißbort[1], Ina Petermann-Stock[2], and Klaus Bengler[1]

[1] Institute of Ergonomics, Technische Universität München Boltzmannstraße
15, 85747 Garching, Germany
goetze@lfe.mw.tum.de, florian@bissbort-altdorf.de,
bengler@tum.de
[2] Volkswagen AG, Konzernforschung K-EFFB/A, Brieffach 1777, D-38436 Wolfsburg
ina.petermann-stock@volkswagen.de

Abstract. This paper summarizes the requirements of an HMI concept for urban areas including the vehicle components: Head-Up Display, the Instrument Cluster, and the Acceleration Force Feedback Pedal. The research addresses all qualitative and quantitative requirements of the aforementioned HMI components as well as urban areas and scenarios itself and warnings in general. The results contain almost 150 confirmed requirements by different sources and lay the foundation for future experiments in this field.

Keywords: HMI, HCI, urban, driving, cockpit, hud, fpk, instrument, cluster, force, feedback, pedal, affp, warnings, adas, assistance.

1 Introduction

The witty quote in the title of this paper comes from the late Ralph Marterie and resonates familiarly with urban driving. Although the driver is obviously very careful passing the crossroads, he at the same time ignores or overlooks the red light and proceeds to cross the road. The mental and visual workload seems to be too high and the human-machine-interface (HMI) did not support the driver well enough to avoid a potentially dangerous situation. This can happen because of several reasons, especially in urban areas, like higher complexity of the situation (Schröder, 2012), multiple road users or obstructions of road signs or parked cars (Schartner, 2013). Nevertheless, driving has become much safer the last years (Reif, 2010). This increase of safety is partly due to the increase of security systems and legal provisions (Hütter, 2013). However, accidents still do occur. According to Hütter (2013) in 2011, left/right turns, U-turns, entrances and exits, right of way, speed violations and short distances, were associated with the majority of auto accidents with personal injuries. Most of these complex situations and use cases can be assisted by advanced driving assistance systems (ADAS). Additionally, it is necessary to avoid overloading the driver with unhelpful visual, acoustic or haptic information. For this reason, the information

S. Yamamoto (Ed.): HMI 2014, Part II, LNCS 8522, pp. 229–240, 2014.
© Springer International Publishing Switzerland 2014

presented in the HMI needs to be limited and presented carefully in order to not further increase the already demanding scenario of urban driving (Gevatter, 2006). Existing HMI concepts are characterized in particular by one-off solutions that would overload the driver considering the growing variety of functions with competing and uncoordinated information (Lange, 2008).

In order to keep the workload in urban driving low, we propose a generic and integrative HMI concept with warnings and information presented on specific components in the car; namely, the Head-Up Display (HUD), the instrument cluster (IC), and the Accelerator Force Feedback Pedal (AFFP). These components are able to give a detailed visual and haptic feedback to the driver without causing too many gazes away from the road. The HUD is especially suitable for warnings (Reif, 2010) while the IC can present detailed information without distracting the driver. Additionally, the AFFP presents information haptically (Lange et al., 2010), with the advantage that such signals are processed faster relative to visual feedback (Merat et al., 2008) and do not interfere with other information channels (Wickens, 2002).

The first step to a new and improved HMI concept for urban areas is to first review the previous literature on the three HMI components mentioned, evaluate how to apply these in urban traffic, and to understand the specific characteristics of urban traffic itself (Popiv et al., 2010).

The development of this new generic and integrative HMI concept is part of the collaborative research project UR:BAN (Urbaner Raum: Benutzergerechte Assistenzsysteme und Netzmanagement - Urban Space: User oriented assistance systems and network management) which started in 2012 (UR:BAN, 2013). Thirty partners including automobile and electronics manufacturers, suppliers, communication technology and software companies, as well as research institutes from different cities, have joined in this cooperative project to develop advanced driver assistance and traffic management systems for cities. The focus is on the human element in all aspects of mobility and traffic. The research objectives will be pursued in three main thematic target areas: Cognitive Assistance, Networked Traffic System, and Human Factors in Traffic.

2   Qualitative and Quantitative Requirements

2.1   Urban Areas and Scenarios

In 2010 about 68% of all accidents with personal injury occurred in urban areas. Those accidents resulted from several reasons wherefore a holistic approach of the driver, vehicle, and environment seems to be reasonable (Ehmanns et al., 2003). The urban area is characterized by high density traffic with different kinds of road users (ex. bicycles, motorcycles, trains, pedestrians, and cars). Additionally, the scenarios are more complex because of the shorter time window, increased decision making, and the fast sequence of road signs and other notifications (see Fig. 1). Consequentially, the probability of warnings or information by the ADAS is much higher. Table 1 shows the research results found for urban areas and scenarios.

Table 1. Relevant urban area and scenario considerations according to different literature sources. The table describes key concepts that need to be considered when developing a novel HMI concept.

HMI concept requirements and or considerations	Source
Complexity of the traffic situation and their elements	(Schröder, 2012)
High vigilance performance at intersections	(Schröder, 2012)
Demand of information acquisition and vehicle operation while changing direction	(Schröder, 2012)
Distinction of urban intersections (traffic light vs. Driveway)	(Schröder, 2012)
No permanent warnings or intervention in self-controlled situations	(Reif, 2010)
Compliance of difficulties for the elderly with the required fast responses in complex and novel situations	(Winner, 2012)
Driving experience, driving style and driver type	(Winner, 2012)
Intuitive comprehensibility of the information	(EN ISO 15005, 2002)
High priority information with appropriate representation	(EN ISO 15005, 2002)
High traffic density in urban areas	(Schartner, 2013)
Diversity of road users	(Schartner, 2013)
High frequency of traffic signs in urban areas	(Schartner, 2013)
High frequency of necessary maneuvers in urban areas	(Schartner, 2013)
Faster decision making need in urban areas	(Schartner, 2013)

2.2   Warnings in General

Warnings can be categorized in terms of presentation timing and content. The "warning dilemma" describes the reliability of a presented warning dependent on the time to collision (TTC). While reliability increases with a shorter TTC left, the effectiveness increases when the driver is given more time to react. Moreover, if the system produces too many false warnings, it might be rated as less accepted and users might even turn it off (Winner et al., 2012). Usually, the information or warning presentation time can be categorized as four points of time: urgent warnings, warnings, early warnings or information, and continuous information (Petermann-Stock & Rhede, 2013). Tab. 2 shows the four points in time when the information or warnings are presented in the HMI concept.

Table 2. Categorization of the point in time when information or warnings are presented

Category	Presentation time
Urgent warning	0.9s – 1.5s TTC
Warning	1.5s – 2.5s TTC
Early warning / Information	>2.5s TTC
Continuous information	-

The content of information can be separated into the categories: action directives/request, situational information, attention control, conditional information, and detailed information. A distinction is made between the range and the complexity of the shown information. As can be seen in Table 3, all categories are aimed at triggering a different driver reactions.

Table 3. Categorization of the content of information given with a warning or information

Category	Description
Action directives/request	Concrete presentation of the required reaction e.g. demand to brake, navigation instructions
Situational information	Specific warning with indication of the type or location e.g. lane change warning
Attention control	General increase of attention or non-specific reference to risky situations e.g. warning tone
Conditional information	Representation of the vehicle state e.g. display of availability or indication
Detailed information	Numerical values or text content e.g. speedometer

Action directives place a high demand on presentation capability, as the action for the driver must be clearly described. This, however, depends on how the driver perceives and consequentially understands this information. In contrast, the situational information leaves the decision of how to appropriately respond to a given situation, up to the driver. It offers him more support than warnings for attention control, because the nature of the critical situation and the location of a potential threat are shown. The presentation of conditional information is important because of the existing technical limitations of current ADAS, as the driver must be referred to the lack of functional readiness of such a system.

In addition to the different presentation times in Table 2, the following three quantitative requirements were found in the literature for warnings in general.

Table 4. Quantitative requirements found for warnings in general

Quantitative warning requirements	Source
Area around the line of sight for peripheral information (most precise discovery for peripheral information in this area): 25° vertical / 35° horizontal	(Liu, 2003)
Time interval of two warnings: ≥ 3 seconds	(Thoma, 2010)
Point in time for most effective information of the driver (time to last possible warning): ≥ 1s / optimal 2-3s	(Naujoks, Grattenthaler & Neukum, 2012)

While only a few quantitative requirements were found for warnings, Table 5 shows the qualitative requirements.

Table 5. Qualitative requirements found for warnings signals and information presented

Qualitative warning and information requirements	Source
Linking the position where the warning is shown with the content of information	(Schartner, 2013)
Consideration of the "warning dilemma" and appropriate implementation of the warning	(Winner, 2012)
Avoidance of false reports	(Winner, 2012)
Display the warning near the center field of view for slight deflection and rapid perception	(Commission of the European Communities, 2008)
Avoid the exclusion of the driver from the "loop" for driving task	(Ehmanns, Zahn, Spannheimer & …)
Binding of most of the attention to the driving task	(EN ISO 15005, 2002)
Application of the laws of ergonomic design	(Bengler, 2012)
Chronological and content-based coordination of each successive warning	(Reif, 2010)
Warning includes one of the following: directives for action, situational information, attention control, conditional information or detailed information	(Reif, 2010) (Naujoks, Grattenthaler & Neukum, 2012) (Winner, 2012)
Predictability of situation danger by warning	(Thoma, 2010)
Driver information as late as possible and as early as necessary	(Naujoks, Grattenthaler & Neukum, 2012)
Avoidance of warning tones when presenting driver information	(Naujoks, Grattenthaler & Neukum, 2012)
No detailed information in the peripheral field of view	(Liu, 2003) (Petermann-Stock & Rhede, 2013)
Avoidance of information in critical situations (except warnings)	(Muigg, Meurle & Rigoll, 2008)
Avoid the driver's exposure by warnings	(Winner, 2012)
Conformity with user expectations	(VDI/VDE 3850-3, 2004)
Easy and fast learnability (Place, Design, and link to concrete actions)	(Petermann-Stock & Rhede, 2013)
Clearly located, correlate with need for action, and same quality at the same position	(Petermann-Stock & Rhede, 2013)
Low visual workload – discrete levels in warning situations with a reduced color range (yellow, red)	(Petermann-Stock & Rhede, 2013)
High consistency (clear cascades of strategy, avoidance of multiple assignments of the HMI components, avoid redundancies)	(Petermann-Stock & Rhede, 2013)
Tend to use haptic signals later and visual signals ealier	(Petermann-Stock & Rhede, 2013)
Avoid cognitive capture	(Burghardt, 2009)

Table 5. (*continued*)

Information presented on different HMI components regarding the same issue needs to be associated in some way	(Burghardt, 2009)
Faster visual fixation of dynamic objects	(Burghardt, 2009)
Consistent use of the colors red, yellow and green according to their meaning	(ISO 2575, 2010)
Use existing and standardized graphics designing new symbols	(ISO 2575, 2010)
Shape of symbols according to their importance and meaning	(VDI/VDE 3850-1, 2000)
Representation of visual information as long as necessary	(EN ISO 15005, 2002)
No coverage of warning messages	(VDI/VDE 3850-1, 2000)
Represent the right information at the right time	(Commission of the European Communities, 2008)

HMI Components. Every component of the HMI concept has specific advantages and disadvantages (Ablassmeier et al., 2007) regarding presenting warnings or information in urban areas. The aim of the current article is to provide the ground work to develop a generic HMI concept that incorporates as many advantages as possible and eliminates, when feasible, as many disadvantages as possible. For this reason, the characteristics and requirements of those components have been specified from earlier studies and publications.

2.3   Head-Up Display (HUD)

The Head-Up Display is a relatively new visual HMI component which projects information in the driver's windshield. In this case, a virtual image is produced by mirror systems with a perceived optical distance of about two meters in front of the vehicle hood. Originally HUDs were developed as monochrome, but newer versions are developed with polychromatic capability (Schneid, 2008).

The biggest advantage of a HUD is that relevant information is given central in the visual field, meaning that distraction and diversion of the gaze are reduced to a minimum. This of course involves the danger that too much and unimportant information will be shown which unnecessarily increases workload. Table 6 summarizes the qualitative requirements and Table 7 the quantitative requirements found for the HMI component HUD.

Table 6. Qualitative requirements for the HMI component Head-Up Display

Qualitative requirements of the HUD	Source
Usable for Pop-ups, icons, and control information	(Petermann-Stock & Rhede, 2013)
Level of detail: HUD < IC	(Petermann-Stock & Rhede, 2013)
No overlap of the driving scene	(Winner et al., 2012)
The HUD is not a substitute for the IC (additionally)	(Reif, 2010)
Avoid the overload with content	(Reif, 2010)
Restricted to time-critical, situational, and dynamic information	(Weber, 2005)
Presentation of safety relevant information	(Winner et al., 2012)
Presentation of driving related content & prioritized content	(Abel et al., 2005)
Continuous adaption of the brightness to the background	(Abel et al., 2005)
Targeted use of the HUD for binding of attention to the road	(Abel et al., 2005)
Use the advantage of faster RT of the HUD compared to the IC	(Raubitschek, 2008) (Liu, 2003)
For presentation, consider the "shrink effect", "cognitive capture", "novelty effect", and the "information clutter"	(Liu & Wen, 2004)
Consider the "perceptual tunneling effect"	(Raubitschek, 2008)
Use the advantage of a more constant maintaining of the speed	(Liu & Wen, 2004)
Use the advantage of a stricter observance of road signs	(Liu & Wen, 2004)
Use the better awareness of speed with a HUD	(Liu & Wen, 2004)
Clearly structured representation (consistent allocation)	(Weber, 2005)
Lower complexity of information and design	(EN ISO 15005, 2002)
No representation of important information at the corners of the displayed area	(Weber, 2005)
No static indicator lamps in the HUD	(Weber, 2005)
Avoid warnings right before take-over requests	(Weber, 2005)
Avoid using the colors red and blue (at night time)	(Raubitschek, 2008)
Use the "fading effect" for changing information	(Milicic, 2010)
Avoid animations (grabbing attention) for information, it should be reserved for warnings	(Raubitschek, 2008)
Useful use of scaling for prioritization of messages	(Milicic, 2010)
Useful use of dimming for selective attention control	(Milicic, 2010)
Avoid overlap of content	(Milicic, 2010)
Specific fade-out of irrelevant content	(Milicic, 2010)
The amount of textual content should be limited to a minimum	(Milicic, 2010)
Avoid straight lines due to distortion in the displayed area	(Milicic, 2010)

Table 7. Quantitative requirements for the HMI component Head-Up Display

Quantitative requirements of the HUD	Source
Minimum character height (at a distance of 3 m): 10.47 mm (= 12")	(DIN EN ISO 15008, 2009)
Optimal character height (at a distance of 3 m): 17.45 mm (= 20")	(DIN EN ISO 15008, 2009)
Display duration of road signs shown: ≥ 5 seconds	(Liu, 2003)
Maximum time of glances of the road to the HUD: < 2 s	(Liu & Wen, 2004)
Structuring the viewing areas according to the line of sight: 2°	(Weber, 2005)
Maximum number of colors: 4	(Raubitschek, 2008)
Luminance of the HUD: ≥ 17'000 cd/m²	(Raubitschek, 2008)

2.4   Instrument Cluster (IC)

The traditional version of the instrument cluster shows warning and indicator lights with fixed symbols or small graphics for predetermined information. In addition, in a physical display, the speed and RPM are shown. A more variable representation is provided with graphic modules in the middle of the IC, which are able to display dynamic and changeable graphics and text content in addition to the control lights and analog displays (Winner et al., 2012).

The most versatile concept that is now used mainly in premium vehicles is the freely programmable instrument cluster (FPIC). With this type of cluster, all information is combined on to a large graphics screen, which enables the virtual simulation of an analog speedometer and RPM, and additionally detailed graphical content such as navigation maps, night vision systems, or other ADAS (Eckstein et al., 2008).

Tables 8 and 9 summarize the qualitative and quantitative requirements found in the literature for the HMI component instrument cluster.

Table 8. Qualitative requirements for the HMI component instrument cluster

Qualitative requirements for the instrument cluster	Source
Suitability for driving relevant information, early warnings, and warnings in general	(Petermann-Stock & Rhede, 2013)
Link warnings with audible alerts and suitable colors	(Petermann-Stock & Rhede, 2013)
Suitable communication of detailed information in a generic way	(Petermann-Stock & Rhede, 2013)
Intuitive design of the content	(Burghardt, 2009)
Use the IC for monitoring / dynamic information	(Reif, 2010)
Taking longer glance aversion into account	(Abel et al., 2005)
Taking possible fatigue caused by accommodation into account	(Abel et al., 2005)
Presentation of driving related content & prioritized content	(Winner, 2012)
Higher RT with the use of colors	(Winner, 2012)

Table 8. (*continued*)

Display the same type of information in the same area of the display	(EN ISO 15005, 2002)
Taking the lack of a missing local context into account	(Burghardt, 2009)
Use the advantage of analog displays with round panels	(Burghardt, 2009)
Taking higher distraction of digital displays compared to analog displays into account	(Burghardt, 2009)
Display IC content in coordination with the HUD content	(Burghardt, 2009)
Restrict the amount of information displayed to an optimum	(Belotti et al., 2004)
Smaller font size needs a better contrast to be read	(Belotti et al., 2004)
Taking a higher luminance level for elderly into account	(Belotti et al., 2004)
Choose colors according to day or night time	(Götze et al., 2013)
Strategic use of "color fading"	(Belotti et al., 2004)
Differentiation of information and warning content	(Belotti et al., 2004)
Positioning of the content according to priority / frequency	(Belotti et al., 2004)
Limited and fixed number of familiar symbols	(Belotti et al., 2004)
Taking the size of the IC into account	(Belotti et al., 2004)

Table 9. Quantitative requirements for the HMI component instrument cluster

Quantitative requirements of the instrument cluster	Source
Minimum character height (at a distance of 1.2 m): 4.19 mm (= 12")	(DIN EN ISO 15008, 2009)
Optimal character height (at a distance of 1.2 m): 6.98 mm (=20")	(DIN EN ISO 15008, 2009)
Compliance of the process of accommodation: 0.3 – 0.5 s	(Reif, 2010)
Representation adapted to the used size of the FPIC: 10" – 14"	(Winner, 2012)
Consideration of the best visual acuity: radius 9 cm	(Burghardt, 2009)
Percentage of the usable display area: 1/3	(Burghardt, 2009)
Luminance contrast between symbols and background: day time: $\geq$ 3:1, night time: $\geq$ 5:1, sunshine: $\geq$ 2:1	(DIN EN ISO 15008, 2009)
Luminance ratio between the display and environment: $\leq$ 10:1	(Belotti et al., 2004)
Minimum spacing between words: width of the letter "o"	(DIN EN ISO 15008, 2009)
Minimum pixel matrix for symbols: 32 px × 32 px	(DIN EN ISO 15008, 2009)

2.5 Acceleration Force Feedback Pedal (AFFP)

The acceleration force feedback pedal is characterized by two functions additionally to the already known feature to accelerate the vehicle in longitudinal direction. On the one hand, it is possible to continuously transmit information like the maximum allowed speed (Lange et al., 2008) and, on the other hand, the driver can get situational warnings like upcoming collisions (Thierfelder, 2007).

The AFFP enables the possibility to add the haptic channel to a new, innovative, and integrative HMI concept with advantages for directives for action in particular. Other benefits are that the driver's visual attention is kept on the road scene and the action indicated by the component is executed with the component itself (Zell et al., 2010).

Tables 10 and 11 summarize the qualitative and quantitative requirements found.

Table 10. Qualitative requirements for the HMI component acceleration force feedback pedal

Qualitative requirements of the AFFP	Source
Avoid vibration of the AFFP for transmit information	-
Use "double ticking" to implement a gear switching point	(Lange et al., 2010)
Use the haptic channel for directives for action	(Lange et al., 2008)
Use adjustable action point to indicate "maintain speed"	(Lange et al., 2008)
Use action point to support distance control to vehicle ahead	(Lange et al., 2008)
Driver can overrule the action point at any time	(Lange et al., 2008)
Some information do not require additional visual notifications (e.g. maintaining the right speed)	(Lange et al., 2008)
Use the potential of transmitting information without gaze movement	(Lange et al., 2008)
Increased sense of security when using visual and haptic elements	(Lange et al., 2008)
Discreet information for the driver (driver not exposed)	(Zell et al., 2010)

Table 11. Quantitative requirements for the HMI component acceleration force feedback pedal

Quantitative requirements of the AFFP
Maximum number of signals: 2 (counter-pressure, action point)
Maximum number of escalating signals: 1

3   Conclusion

The aims of this study were to collect qualitative and quantitative requirements for a generic HMI concept, and to evaluate the urban settings itself, warnings in general, the Head-Up Display, the instrument cluster, and the Acceleration Force Feedback Pedal. The results contain almost 150 confirmed requirements by different sources and lay the foundation for future experiments in this field. The next step will be to build a first version of the generic and integrative HMI concept and evaluate it in the simulator.

References

1. Abel, H.-B., Adamietz, H., Leuchtenberg, B., Schmidt, N.: Integration von Night-Vision und Head-Up-Display im Kraftfahrzeug. ATZ 107(11), S.984–S.989 (2005)

2. Ablassmeier, M., Poitschke, T., Wallhoff, F., Bengler, K., Rigoll, G.: Eye Gaze Studies Comparing Head-Up and Head-Down Displays in Vehicles. In: Proc. ICME 2007, Beijing, China, July 2-5, pp. 2250–2252 (2007)
3. Bellotti, F., Gloria, A., de Poggi, A., Andreone, L., Damiani, S., Knoll, P.: Designing configurable automotive dashboards on liquid crystal displays. Cognition, Technology & Work 6(4), 247–265 (2004)
4. Bengler, K.: Produktergonomie. Lecturenotes. TU München (2012)
5. Burghardt, S.: Anzeigekonzepte für ein frei programmierbares Kombinationsinstrument. Diplomarbeit, Universität Koblenz Landau, Koblenz (2009)
6. Commission of the European Communities. Update of the European Statement of Principles on Human-Machine-Interface, Brüssel (2008)
7. DIN EN ISO 15005. Straßenfahrzeuge - Ergonomische Aspekte von Fahrerinformations- und -assistenzsystemen - Grundsätze und Prüfverfahren des Dialogmanagements. DIN Deutsches Institutfür Normung e. V., Berlin (2002)
8. DIN EN ISO 15008. Straßenfahrzeuge – Ergonomische Aspekte von Fahrerinformations- und Assistenzsystemen – Anforderungen und Bewertungsmethoden der visuellen Informationsdarstellung im Fahrzeug. DIN Deutsches Institut für Normung e. V., Berlin (2009)
9. Eckstein, L., Knoll, C., Künzner, H., Niedermaier, B., Schumann, J.: Interaktion mit Fahrerassistenz- und Fahrerinformationssystemen im neuen 7er BMW. In: Integrierte Sicherheit und Fahrerassistenzsysteme, vol. 24, VDI/VW-Gemeinschaftstagung, Wolfsburg, 29. und 30 (2008), VDIBerichte2048. Düsseldorf: VDI
10. Ehmanns, D., Zahn, P., Spannheimer, H., Freymann, R.: Integrierte Längs- und Querführung: Ein neues Konzept für Fahrerassistenzsysteme. ATZ 105, 346–352 (2003)
11. Gevatter, H.-J.: Handbuch der Mess- und Automatisierungstechnik in der Produktion. 2. Aufl. Springer, Berlin (2006)
12. Götze, M., Conti, A.S., Keinath, A., Said, T., Bengler, K.: Evaluation of a New Cockpit Color Concept under Mesopic Lighting for Urban Driving. In: Marcus, A. (ed.) DUXU 2013, Part IV. LNCS, vol. 8015, pp. 359–366. Springer, Heidelberg (2013)
13. Hütter, A.: Verkehr auf einen Blick. Statistisches Bundesamt, Wiesbaden (2013)
14. ISO 2575. Road vehicles - Symbols for controls, indicators and tell-tables. International Organization for Standardization, Genf (2010)
15. Lange, C., Bubb, H., Tönnis, M., Klinker, G.: Sicherheitspotential und Verbrauchsreduzierung durch ein intelligent geregeltes aktives Gaspedal. In: Tagungsband der 3. Tagung Aktive Sicherheit durch Fahrerassistenz, Garching, April 7-8 (2008)
16. Lange, C., Arcati, A., Bubb, H., Bengler, K.: Haptic Gear Shifting Indication: Natrualistic Driving Study for Parametrization, Selection of Variants and to Determine the Potential for Fuel Consumption Reduction. In: Proceedings 3rd Applied Human Factors and Ergonomics (AHFE) International Conference, Miami, U.S. (July 2010)
17. Liu, Y.-C.: Effects of using head-up display in automobile context on attention demand and driving performance. Displays 24(4-5), 157–165 (2003)
18. Liu, Y.-C., Wen, M.-H.: Comparison of headup display (HUD) vs. head-down display (HDD): driving performance of commercial vehicle operators in Taiwan. International Journal of Human-Computer Studies 61(5), 679–697 (2004)
19. Merat, N., Jamson, A.H.: The Effect of Stimulus Modality on Signal Detection: Implications for Assessing the Safety of In-Vehicle Technology. Human Factors: The Journal of the Human Factors and Ergonomics Society 50, 145–158 (2008)
20. Miličić, N.: Sichere und ergonomische Nutzung von Head-Up-Displays im Fahrzeug. Dissertation, TUMünchen. München (2010)

21. Muigg, A., Meurle, J., Rigoll, G.: Negative Auswirkungen von situativ ungünstigen Meldungen.3. Tagung Aktive Sicherheit durch Fahrerassistenz. TU München, München (2008), http://mediatum.ub.tum.de/node?id=1145120

22. Naujoks, F., Grattenthaler, H., Neukum, A.: Zeitliche Gestaltung effektiver Fahrerinformationen zur Kollisionsvermeidung auf der Basis kooperativer Perzeption. In: 8. Workshop Fahrerassistenzsysteme, FAS 2012. IZVW, Darmstadt (2012)

23. Petermann-Stock, I., Rhede, J.: Intelligente Strategien für nutzerzentrierte MMI Konzepte im urbanen Raum. In: VDI Gesellschaft Fahrzeug- und Verkehrstechnik (Hrsg.), Der Fahrer im 21. Jahrhundert (VDI-Berichte, Nr. 2205, pp. S.263–S286) (2013)

24. Popiv, D., Rommerskirchen, C., Rakic, M., Duschl, M., Bengler, K.: Effects of assistance of anticipatory driving on driver's behaviour during deceleration situations. In: 2nd European Conference on Human Centred Design of Intelligent Transport Systems (HUMANIST), Berlin, Germany (2010)

25. Raubitschek, C.: Prioritätenorientierte Implementierung einer Menüinteraktion im Head-up Display für den Automobilbereich. Diplomarbeit, TU München, München (2008)

26. Reif, K.: Fahrstabilisierungssysteme und Fahrerassistenzsysteme. Vieweg+Teubner Verlag / GWV Fachverlage, Wiesbaden (2010)

27. Schartner, A.: Evaluation von MMI-Anzeige-Konzepten für Fahrerassistenzsysteme in urbanen Verkehrssituationen. Semesterarbeit, TU München, München (2013)

28. Schröder, T.: Analytische Betrachtung der Auswirkungen komplexer Verkehrssituationen. Diplomarbeit, TU München, München (2012)

29. Schneid, M.: Entwicklung und Erprobung eines kontaktanalogen Headup-Displays im Fahrzeug. Dissertation, Technische Universität München, München (2008)

30. Thoma, S.: Mensch-Maschine-Interaktionskonzepte für Fahrerassistenzsysteme im Kreuzungsbereich. Dissertation, TU München, München (2010)

31. Thierfelder, S.: Konstruktion eines aktiven Gaspedals. Semesterarbeit, TU München, München (2007)

32. UR:BAN. UR:BAN - Benutzergerechte Assistenzsysteme und Netzmanagement. urban-online.org (2013), http://urban-online.org/en/urban.html (retrieved January 28, 2014)

33. VDI/VDE 3850-1. Nutzergerechte Gestaltung von Bediensystemen für Maschinen. Verein Deutscher Ingenieure/Verband Der ElektrotechnikElektronikInformationstechnik, Düsseldorf (2000)

34. VDI/VDE 3850-3. Nutzergerechte Gestaltung von Bediensystemen für Maschinen – Dialoggestaltung für Touchscreens. Verein Deutscher Ingenieure/Verband Der ElektrotechnikElektronikInformationstechnik, Düsseldorf (2004)

35. Weber, J.: Anzeigekonzepte für Head-up Displays.Diplomarbeit, TU München, München (2005)

36. Wickens, C.D.: Multiple resources and performance prediction. Theoretical Issues in Ergonomics Science 3, 159–177 (2002)

37. Winner, H., Hakuli, S., Wolf, G.: Handbuch Fahrerassistenzsysteme: Grundlagen, Komponenten und Systeme für aktive Sicherheit und Komfort. 2. Aufl. Vieweg + Teubner, Wiesbaden (2012)

38. Zell, A., Leone, C., Arcati, A., Schmitt, G.: Aktives Fahrpedal als Schnittstelle zum Fahrer. ATZ 112(4), S.276–S.279 (2010)

Neural Networks for Identifying Civil Pilot's Operation Sequences

Zhuoyuan Jiang[1], Qin Lu[1], Yuandong Liang[1], and Bin Chen[2]

[1] Flight Test Center, COMAC, Shanghai
[2] Shanghai Aircraft Design and Research Institute,
COMAC, Shanghai
moreaction111@163.com

Abstract. "Human Error", as we all know, is inevitable during the flight process of civil aircraft. It is one of the most significant reasons for civil aircraft accidents and incidents. Therefore, to identify and avoid "Human Error" is becoming more and more urgent.

In order to restrict the influence of "Human Error", the wrong sequence of civil pilot's operation must be detected and a warning should be provided for pilot or intelligent action to correct the wrong sequence of operations.

A set of effective behavior coding system is developed for expressing the pilot's operations. Pilot's operation behaviors can be quantized and operation sequences can be coded. And the set of effective pilot's behavior coding system plays an important role in reducing the probability of flight accidents caused by "Human Error".

For identifying whether the pilot's operation sequence is right, a database of codes of pilot's operation sequences should be built. By comparing with the codes in the database, a wrong operation sequence can be detected. Generally speaking, the database containing codes of all possible correct and wrong operation sequences is difficult to set up. As a matter of fact, the database we can develop is just a part of all possible codes of operation sequences. Therefore, those naturally correct operation sequences but not in the database may be detected as wrong ones by comparing with the correct codes in the database. This paper adopts neural networks to identify any codes of operation sequences (in database and not in database) accurately. The incomplete database is trained by neural networks to find the rule for identifying whether a specific operation sequence is correct. If the specific pilot's operation sequence disobeys the rule, a warning will be provided for pilot to rectify the operation, which reduces the probability of accidents caused by "Human Error" and realizes the intelligent identifying function.

Keywords: Human Error, Operation Behavior, Coding system, Neural Networks.

S. Yamamoto (Ed.): HIMI 2014, Part II, LNCS 8522, pp. 241–252, 2014.
© Springer International Publishing Switzerland 2014

1   Introduction

Civil plane pilot assumes tasks of piloting and airplane management in the flight profile from taking off to landing. It may lead to serious incidents or even huge aeronautical disasters once there exist human errors in the operational processes of airplane equipment that requires high safety or well functions.

In recent years, with the development of automation of civil airplane, civil aviation incidents that caused by mechanical equipment and automation system decreased, meanwhile, proportion of human errors increased by years. Statistical analysis shows that the proportion of incidents caused by human errors is very high. Generally speaking, the proportion of incidents caused by human errors is more than 70%.

Therefore, to enhance the safe level of civil airplane heavily, inappropriate operational actions of civil airplane pilots should be in control and incline.

It is known to all that everyone makes mistakes. The thought that flight safety can be guaranteed by expecting no human errors is unreal. We can only hope that mistake avoidance of the plane itself and function of fault-tolerance can lower the rate of incidents that caused by human errors.

In this paper, BP neural network is adopted to find the rule for identifying whether a specific operation sequence is correct. If civil pilots perform the wrong operation sequence, the operation will be detected as human error by BP (Back-Propagation) neural network. Then such operations will not be carried out, which prevent the accidents caused by human error.

The prerequisite of the training of BP neural network is the quantitative description of civil aviation pilot's fundamental operational actions, i. e., to build code rules of civil aviation pilot's basic operational actions. For this reason, this project introduce the coding system for civil aviation pilot's basic operational actions, realizing standard expression and quantitative description, providing a new settle thought for computer auto detection and identification of human errors, enriching present functions of warning and alarming, lowering the difficulty of finding mistakes, providing references for error prevention and risk aversion, improving flight safety level in essence.

2   Basic Operational Actions and Definition of Characteristic Actions

Although operations of pilots in flight process vary, they were built by several basic movements. Our code object is civil planes' basic operation action of pilot. We fixed 19 basic movements, which is called 19 therbligs, see table 1.

Table 1. Therbligs

Category	Name	Symbol	Definition
1	Reach	Re	Movement that approaches object
2	Grasp	G	Movement that holds object
3	Whirl	W	Movement that makes object pivot
4	Press	Ps	Movement that makes object move in the direction of force
5	Pull Out	PO	Movement that makes object move in the direction of source force
6	Tread	T	Movement that controls movement of object by foot
7	Release	Rl	Movement that departs object
8	Inspect	I	Movement that compares to standard
9	Report	Rp	Movement that expresses current situation of object
10	Search	Sh	Movement that fix the position of object
11	Select	St	Movement that select object
12	Plan	Pn	Movement that delays for planning operational program
13	Hold	H	Movement that keeps the statement of object
14	Position	P	Movement that adjusts the position of object
15	Pro-Position	PP	Movement that places object to avoid 'position' movement when object is used
16	Rest	Rt	Movement for rest
17	Unavoidable Delay	UD	Inevitably halt
18	Avoidable Delay	AD	Evitable halt
19	Find	F	Movement that finds object

3 Design of Code of Basic Operational Actions

3.1 Dimensions of Code

Code is the only mark of code object, except for the functions that it can precisely define main part, movement, operation object and time, provide information on code object, distinctly reflect categories, attributes, features, etc. of code object, code of measures that are used to reduce human errors and redundancy code that is used to avoid miss of code in transmission are included. Six kinds of code structures are adopted now: hierarchy code, abbreviation code, sequence code, condition code, check code and compound code. We apply following code structure according to requirement of code content and every code structure's feature under code principles. Fig 1 Code Structure of Pilot's Basic Operational Actions.

Abbreviate code + Sequence code + Condition code + Position Code + Time code + Check code

Fig. 1. Code Structure of Pilot's Basic Operational Actions

Abbreviate Code. Operational main part that involved in the process of pilot's actual operation-human's body regions are few, and there are only 19 pilot's basic operational therbligs, then we can use the way of mnemonic code, easily to grasp. Mnemonic code belongs to abbreviate code and is commonly used. It selects several critical letters from name and specification of code object to be code or part of code, with way of association to help memorize, easy to understand.

Fig 2 are the expressions of operational main part and abbreviate code of basic action, two letters for body regions, 1~2 letters for basic action. See operational main part and abbreviate code of basic action in table 2.

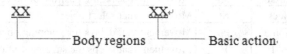

Fig. 2. Structure of Abbreviate Code

Table 2. Body Regions and Abbreviate Code of Basic Action

Body Regions						
Hand (H)		Foot (F)		Head (H)		Else(Es)
Left hand (LH)	Right hand (RH)	Left foot (LF)	Right foot (RF)	Eye (HE)	Mouth (HM)	Else(Es)
Basic Actions						
Reach (Re)	Grasp (G)	Whirl (W)	Press (Ps)	Pull Out (PO)	Tread (T)	Release (Rl)
Inspect (I)	Report (Rp)	Search (Sh)	Select (St)	Plan (Pn)	Hold (H)	Position (P)
Pre-position (PP)	Rest (Rt)	Unavoidable-delay (UD)	Avoidable-delay (AD)	Find (F)		

Sequence Code. In a certain phase of flight, it may involve operating a same object several times or repeating a basic action in the process of operating an object, thus, we should position the action by sequence code to describe the difference in the process. Sequence code is simple and commonly used. It put positive integers or alphabets to code objects. Simple to code, well to use, convenient to manage, easy to add, have no limits for the order of code object. However, it is hard to memory for the code itself does not provide any information about code object.

Fig 3 is the expression of sequence code.

Fig. 3. Structure of Sequence Code

Among above, order number A-the M times operation for a same operational object in a certain flight phase, the span is 1~99;

Order number B-repeat a basic action N times in M times operation of operational object, the span is 1~99.

Condition Code. In order to keep the continuity of action, in case of action omission in the process of pilot's operation and reduction or avoidance of human errors, we classify the attributes of basic actions into 3 groups, which are denoted by condition code. To select the right code to satisfy the demand and combine them in a predefine order in use.

Condition code (condition combination code) is commonly used in the system of surface classification, entry in each surface is coded by its principle. Combining code in each surface as needed and order predefined in use. Code structure is flexible; it can be single or combination. It is convenient to change and expand for it is classified by surface. A condition code can reflect the whole recorded information features, as well as part features when it is partly used. It is elastic and specially suitable for dynamic compound quick inquiry, summing and other operations. Condition code has much more values in the design of information management system. However, the volume use rate of condition code is low.

The expression mode of condition code is shown as figure 4. Overlapping attribute of pilot's basic operational actions, the way of classification and concrete meaning of connect attribute are shown as table 3. If pilot's operational actions do not comply with the request of condition code, alarm can be used to draw pilot's attention.

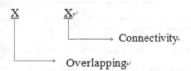

Fig. 4. Condition Code Structure

Table 3. Action attribute classification

	code	meaning
Overlapping	A	This action cannot overlap with other actions (except independent actions).
	B	This action can overlap with other actions.
	C	Totally independent, can overlap with any actions
Connectivity	1	Connect with AB category actions in required time
	2	Connect with any other overlapping actions in required time.

Position Code. As operational object is the object used in a specific flight phase, we should consider two aspects on operational object: flight phase and use object. Flight phases of Airbus are detailed and there is a lot of equipment in cockpit. The way of coding of all phases and equipment just start from 1 may increase the complexity of coding procedure. Therefore, we can apply layer code, breaking down from whole to part, to help code.

Layer code belongs to the kind that is commonly used for linear taxonomic hierarchies. It is a code that ordering by the relation of subordinate of object of classification and hierarchies. The code is cracked into several hierarchies, which is in accordance with the classification of code object. The code can definitely express categories of the classification objects, have strict subjection relations, and each hierarchy is meaningful. It is easy for computer to sum and summary as it has easy structure and high capacity. We should do some classifications before design, then to code and establish instruction of classification.

In addition, to indicate the shape features of equipment of cockpit from code and restrict action type, we can define the shape attribute by condition code; as a result, the position code of cockpit equipment consists of hierarchy code and condition code, which named compound code. Compound code includes two or more independent codes, flexible, easy to expand and mark part can be nimble used.

Therefore, we have a clear expression of the position of used operational object in the process of flight operation of pilot. The full expression is showed as Fig. 5. Hierarchy code and operational equipment's condition code are expressed as table 4;

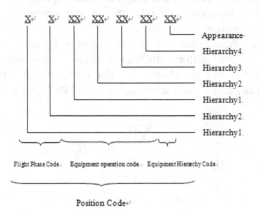

Fig. 5. Position Code Expression

If to adjust impulse force by using throttle lever in phase of climbing, throttle lever's position can be denoted as 4103100011. 8,9-bit code for 0 is the same with other classification median plus, no special significance. If transfer display mode in the phase of take-off taxi, then navigation mode button classification code is 3202031007.

Table 4. Flight Phase Layer Code

Flight phase							
Start up (1)	Taxi (2)	Take off (3)	Climb (4)	Cruise (5)	Descent (6)	Approach (7)	Landing (8)
Start up	Taxi	Take off	Climb	Cruise	Descent	Approach	Landing

Start up (1)	
Engine auto starts up (1)	Engine manual starts up (2)

Taxi (2)				
Propulsion push out (1)	Taxi and steering (2)	Brake check (3)	light control inspection (4)	Take-off fragmentary verification (5)

Take off (3)				
Propulsion set (1)	Taxi (2)	Rotation (3)	Minus propulsion altitude (4)	Acceleration altitude (5)

Climb (4)				
Climb monitor (1)	Speed change (2)	Acceleration climb (3)	Set barometer reference (4)	Terminate landing light (5)
Terminate seat belt indicator light (06)	EFIS options (07)	Check radio navigation page (08)	Transfer second flight plan (09)	Check best/highest altitude (10)

Cruise (5)			
Use of Flight Management System (1)	Gradient climb	Fuel monitor (3)	Approach preparation (4)

Descent (6)	
Guide and monitor (1)	Mode transfer (2)

Approach (7)				
ILS approach (1)	Imprecise approach (2)	Rotation approach (3)	Visual approach (4)	Precise approach (5)

Landing (8)				
Trim (1)	Call (2)	Dive (3)	Taxi (4)	Brake (5)

Table 5. Appearance Attribute Condition Code

Appearance Attribute				
Button (01)	Swtich(no cover) (02)	Cover switch (03)	Electirc switch (no cover) (04)	Electric switch（with cover） (05)
Electric switch(Spring attachment) (06)	Screw (07)	Select button (08)	selector (09)	keystoke (10)
Stick (11)	Wheel (12)	Handle (13)	Treadle (14)	Light (15)
Indicator light (16)	Monitor (17)	Indicator (18)	Hub (19)	Storage (20)
Pack (21)	Mask (22)			

Time Code. Generally speaking, the proportion of incidents that caused by human error in civil aviation incidents is more than 70%. Once a motion absent happened in the operational process, the consequence will be very serious, even huge aviation disastrous incidents. In case of omission of pilots' operational actions, the condition code requires pilot should complete a certain action at a regulatory time which may avoid action omission. The times involved in this process are the last time of action itself and time between this action and next action. We can use time code to denote time, that is, to add time property to code. The format of time code is: xxHxxMxxS, of which xx stands for number. Time code can be expressed as figure 6.

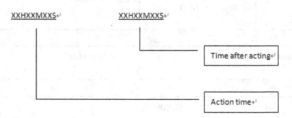

Fig. 6. Time Code Structure

Check Code. Generally, Check bit in the coding structure is the token of check code. In the process of structure designation of primary code, computing check bit attached to primary code with prescriptive mathematical method in advance, then the computer would calculate check bit in the same way when use the check code, it is definitely clear to see whether the input is right by comparing these two check bits. Cyclic redundancy code (CRC) is one of the most common used check bits. Cyclic redundancy code produced at sending terminal is sent to receive terminal by adding to the back of information bit. To check the received information with the same algorithm that produces cyclic redundancy code, if there is a mistake, then receive terminal makes a resend notice. CRC is good at error detection, low cost, and easily coded, while it is hard to detect errors made by 2 bits or more.

4   Standard Operation Sequence

In this paper, the operations of Airbus 320 in the stage of climb are taken as an example for explaining the coding system. In order to be familiar with the pilots' operations and guarantee the safety of flight, the codes of operation in the stage of climb are shown as table 6.

Table 6. Operations of Airbus 320 in the Stage of Climb

Operation Step	Operation code
1.Monitor Climb	RHRh0101B1N04010301100100H00M01S00H00M01S29111
	RHPs0101B1N04010301100100H00M01S00H00M01S29111
	HEIt0101B1N04010301100100H00M01S00H00M03S29111
	RHRl0101B1N04010301100100H00M02S00H00M02S29111
	LHRh0101B1N04010302130100H00M02S00H00M02S29111
	LHPs0101B1N04010302130100H00M03S00H00M01S29111
	HEIt0101B1N04010302130100H00M01S00H00M01S29111
	LHLl0101B1N04010302130100H00M01S00H00M01S29111
2.Change Velocity	HMRp0101C1N04020000000000H00M02S00H00M01S29111
	EHRh0101B1N04020201021000H00M01S00H00M01S29111
	EHGp0101B1N04020201021000H00M01S00H00M01S29111
	EHWl0101B1Y04020201021000H01M00S00H00M01S29111
	EHPO0101B1N04020201021000H00M01S00H00M01S27012
	EHRl0101B2N04020201021000H00M01S00H00M01S29111
3.Accelerate Climb	HMRp0101C1N04030000000000H00M03S00H00M01S29111
	EHRh0201B1N04030201120100H00M01S00H00M01S29111
	EHPs0201B1Y04030201120100H00M01S00H00M01S29111
	EHRl0201B1N04030201120100H00M01S00H00M01S29111
	EHRh0201B1N04030201051000H00M01S00H00M01S29111
	EHPs0101B1Y04030201051000H00M01S00H00M01S29111
	EHRl0101B1N04030201051000H00M01S00H00M01S29111
	HEIt0101B2N04030101001700H00M02S00H00M01S29111
4.Adjust GasPressure Meter	RHRh0101B1N04040202020700H00M01S00H00M01S29111
	RHGp0101B1N04040202020700H00M01S00H00M01S29111
	RHWl0101B1Y04040202020700H01M00S00H00M01S29111
	RHRl0101B1N04040202020700H00M01S00H00M01S29111
	HEIt0101B2N04040101001700H00M02S00H00M01S29111

Table 6. (*continued*)

5.Adjust Cruise Altitude	HMRp0101C1N04050000000000H00M03S00H00M01S29111
	RHRh0101B1N04050301090100H00M01S00H00M01S29111
	RHPs0101B1Y04050301090100H00M01S00H00M01S29111
	RHRl0101B1N04050301090100H00M01S00H00M01S29111
	RHRh0101B1N04050301010100H00M01S00H00M01S29111
	RHPs0101B1Y04050301010100H00M01S00H00M01S29111
	RHRl0101B1N04050301010100H00M01S00H00M01S29111
	RHPs0101B1N04050301210100H00M01S00H00M01S29111
	RHRl0101B1Y04050301210100H00M03S00H00M01S29111
	RHPs0102B1Y04050301210100H00M03S00H00M01S29111
	RHPs0103B1Y04050301210100H00M03S00H00M01S29111
	RHRl0101B2N04050301210100H00M01S00H00M01S29111
6.Engine's Anti-icing	EHRh0101C1N04060419020400H00M01S00H00M01S29111
	EHPs0101B1Y04060419020400H00M01S00H00M01S29111
	EHPs0101B1Y04060419030400H00M01S00H00M01S29111
	EHRl0101B2N04060419030400H00M01S00H00M01S29111
7.Tilting Radar	EHRh0101B1N04070307040700H00M01S00H00M01S29111
	EHGp0101B1N04070307040700H00M01S00H00M01S29111
	EHWl0101B1N04070307040700H01M00S00H00M01S29111
	EHRl0101B1N04070307040700H00M01S00H00M01S29111
8.Turnoff Landing Light	EHRh0101B1N04080422060200H00M01S00H00M01S29111
	EHPs0101B1N04080422060200H00M01S00H00M01S29111
	EHPs0101B1N04080422070200H00M01S00H00M01S29111
	EHRl0101B1N04080422070200H00M01S00H00M01S29111
9.Turnoff Seatbelt Light	EHRh0101B1N04090425010200H00M01S00H00M01S29111
	EHPs0101B1N04090425010200H00M01S00H00M01S29111
	EHRl0101B1N04090425010200H00M01S00H00M01S29111
10.EFIS Option	RHRh0101B1N04100202090100H00M01S00H00M01S29111
	RHPs0101B1N04100202090100H00M01S00H00M01S29111
	RHRl0101B1N04100202090100H00M01S00H00M01S29111
	HEIt0101B1N04100301071700H00M02S00H00M01S29111
11.Check Radio Navigation	RHRh0101B1N04110301140100H00M01S00H00M01S29111
	RHPs0101B1Y04110301140100H00M01S00H00M01S29111
	RHRl0101B1N04110301140100H00M01S00H00M01S29111
	HEIt0101B1N04110301071700H00M02S00H00M01S29111
12.Call Second Flignt Plan	RHRh0101C1N04120301160100H00M01S00H00M01S29111
	RHPs0101B1Y04120301160100H00M03S00H00M01S29111
	RHRl0101B2N04120301160100H00M01S00H00M01S29111
13.Check Ideal/High Altitude	RHRh0101B1N04130301090100H00M01S00H00M01S29111
	RHPs0101B1Y04130301090100H00M03S00H00M01S29111
	RHRl0101B1N04130301090100H00M01S00H00M01S29111
	HEIt0101B1N04130301071700H00M02S00H00M01S29111

5   BP Neural Network for Identifying Operation Sequence

Rumelhart, McClelland and their colleagues realize the importance of neural networks in dealing with the information. They developed the learning algorithm of BP network in 1985, which makes the assumption of multi-layer network come true.

BP network can deal with any nonlinear mapping problems. It is mainly used in four aspects: approximation of function, mode recognition, classification, and data compression.

Basically, two pilot's actions can be linked as one operation sequence. For example, (RHRh0101B1N04010301100100H00M01S00H00M01S29111,   RHPs0101B1N040-10301100100H00M01S00H00M01S29111) is an operation sequence. Therefore, the number of input channel of BP network is chosen as two. The second code is executed after the first code. And the code need to be transferred into binary system, for example, RHRh0101B1N040103011001-00H00M01S00H00M01S29111 is transferred as 01010010 01001000 01010010 01101000 0000 0001 0000 0001 01000010 0001 01001110 0000 0100 0000 0001 0000 0011 0000 0001 0001 0000 0000 0001 0000 0000 01001000 0000 0000 01001101 0000 0001 01010011 0000 0000 01001000 0000 0000 01001101 0000 0001 01010011 0010 0111 0001 0001 0001(This process is simple, and will not be introduced in this paper). The BP neural network is illustrated as Fig. 7. The network has two neurons and single hidden layer. The output result of right operation sequence is defined as 1, while the output result of wrong operation sequence is defined as 0. For example, the output of input (RHRh0101B1N04010301100100H00M01S00H00M01S29111,   RHPs0101B1N040-10301100100H00M01S00H00M01S29111) is 1, however, 0 for (RHPs0101B1N040-10301100100H00M01S00H00M01S29111,   RHRh0101B1N04010301100100H00M-01S00H00M01S29111).

The operation sequences of Airbus 320 in the stage of climb are chosen as database to train the BP neural network.

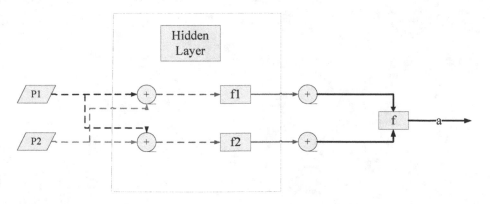

Fig. 7. BP Neural Network

After training, the BP neural network will deal with the operation sequences as table 7 (5 random demonstration examples).

Table 7. BP Neural Network Training Rseult

Input	Output	Result
(RHPs0101B1N04010301100100H00M01S00H00M01S29111, HEIt0101B1N04010301100100H00M01S00H00M03S29111)	1	√
(LHPs0101B1N04010302130100H00M03S00H00M01S29111, LHRh0101B1N04010302130100H00M02S00H00M02S29111)	0	√
(EHRh0201B1N04030201120100H00M01S00H00M01S29111, EHPs0201B1Y04030201120100H00M01S00H00M01S29111)	1	√
(EHRh0101C1N04060419020400H00M01S00H00M01S29111, EHPs0101B1Y04060419020400H00M01S00H00M01S29111)	1	√
(RHRh0101C1N04120301160100H00M01S00H00M01S29111, RHRl0101B1N04110301140100H00M01S00H00M01S29111)	1	×

6   Conclusion

In this paper, Basic operation code method is introduced, which providing a new thought for computer automatic detection and distinguishment of human error, enriching existing warn and remind functions and offering references for error prevention and risk avoidance. From the examples in table 7 in part 5, the accuracy of BP neural network is 4/5(80%), which means BP network does work but not ideal enough. Still some wrong operation sequences are not detected. Further work is focused on increasing the accuracy of network.

A Study of Drivers' Blind Spot in Used of Eye Tracking

Yen-Yu Kang[1,*], Yuh-Chuan Shih[2], Chih-Chan Cheng[2], and Chi-Long Lin[3]

[1] National Kaohsiung Normal University, Kaohsiung City 824, Taiwan (R.O.C.)
yenyu@nknucc.nknu.edu.tw
[2] National Defense University, Taipei City 112, Taiwan (R.O.C.)
[3] National Taiwan University of Arts, New Taipei City 220, Taiwan (R.O.C.)

Abstract. This study employed driving simulation and eye tracking to explore the situational perception of drivers under various weather and road conditions. This study sampled 16 subjects, all of whom were required to hold a valid driver's license. Experimentation was based on factorial design; the independent variables were weather (sunny, foggy) and road conditions (road work, pedestrians crossing the road, and balls appearing suddenly). The dependent variables included Time to First Fixation (TFF)(sec), First Fixation Duration (FFD) (sec), Total Fixation Duration (TFD) (sec), Fixation Count (FC) (frequency). Results showed that under good weather conditions, drivers are more aware of road conditions, resulting in shorter TFF with resulting higher FC and longer TFD. The influence of road conditions on TFF, FFD, TFD and FC varied according to the situation. Overall, our results demonstrated the feasibility of using eye trackers to explore the situational perception of drivers.

Keywords: situational perception, eye tracker, gaze, weather.

1 Introduction

Poor driving is the cause of many types of traffic incident, and as a result, many countries are actively developing electronic alert systems to reduce the risk of accidents. However, few studies have examined how drivers visually track objects in their line of sight. The results of such an investigation could help the developers of road safety systems to enhance the alertness of drivers and overcome the problem of blind spots.

Actual vehicle testing can be difficult and dangerous; therefore, this study used a driving simulator and eye tracker to explore the situational perception of drivers under various weather and road conditions. Our aim was to understand how drivers visually react to road conditions and traffic incidents, and identify the strategies they employ in response, in order to elucidate the relationship between visual response and road safety.

Previous studies on driving simulators have discussed the mental workload (Cantin, Lavallière, Simoneau, & Teasdale, 2009), the function of road signs (Horberry, Anderson, & Regan, 2006), the impact of visual position on driving (Wittmann, Kiss, Gugg, Steffen, Fink, Pöppel, & Kamiya, 2006), collision warning time, driving distractions, and reactions to rear-ending incidents (Lee, McGehee, Brown, & Reyes, 2002).

---

* Corresponding author.

S. Yamamoto (Ed.): HIMI 2014, Part II, LNCS 8522, pp. 253–260, 2014.
© Springer International Publishing Switzerland 2014

Perception is the endless cycle of interaction between people and their surroundings. Endsley (1988) proposed that a pilot's perception can be defined as an inner awareness of his/her surroundings, including control panel signals, the field of vision, and personal factors, such as emotions, personal capacity, training, experience, goals, and workload management. Situational perception is extremely important in environments that require staff to be highly aware of their surroundings, such as aviation, nuclear power plants, medical facilities management, military maneuvers, and driving.

Increasingly sophisticated simulation methods are being developed in many fields, and this is particularly true in the case of driving simulators. These methods eliminate many of the dangers posed by the actual operation of vehicles and helps to reduce experimentation costs. Simulation also enables researchers to carefully set and then repeatedly test the parameters they are examining, such as climate, terrain, and the environment, thereby enhancing the efficiency of experimentation. The movement of the eyes is a direct reflection of human cognitive processes. For the purposes of this study, the key indicators of eye movement were Fixation Duration and Number of fixations.

2   Methodology

2.1   Subjects

The subjects in this study were 16 undergraduate and graduate students, all of whom possessed a driver's license and had corrected visual acuity of at least 1.0. The subjects were required to provide basic information such as age, height, weight, birthdate and driving experience. The average subject was 22 years of age with two years of driving experience over distance of 1,500 km.

2.2   Experimentation

Driving Simulator. This study simulated true-to-life road conditions, based on a simulator comprising a host computer (including control screen), projector (including projection screen) and adjustable seat (as shown in Fig. 1).

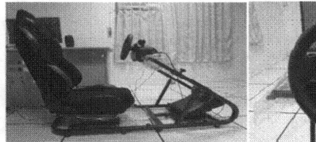

Fig. 1. Driving simulator

Eye Tracker. This study used the Tobii X2-60 eye tracking system, which includes a camera and infrared sensor. Infrared light is shone onto the eyes, such that the position of the pupil is determined by differentiating between the low reflectivity of the pupil and the high reflectivity of the iris.

Experimental Environment. The lab was 2.5m long and 2.5m wide, with the temperature set at 26±2 °C, allowing subjects to complete the exercises in a comfortable environment.

Simulated Scenario. The objective of this experiment was to test the reactions of drivers under various weather and road conditions. The weather in the simulations was sunny or foggy (Fig. 2.4) and road conditions included road work, pedestrians crossing, or a ball bouncing into the street (Fig. 2).

Fig. 2. Weather: Sunny or foggy

Fig. 3. Road work, pedestrians crossing, and a ball bouncing into the street

2.3   Experiment Design

Our analysis was based on a factorial design, including the independent variables of weather (sunny, foggy) and road conditions (road works, pedestrians, or a ball appearing). To prevent subjects from being influenced by their familiarity with routes, we designed two different routes of similar length and number of turns, to match the weather simulation (sunny, foggy). Each driving scenario occurred twice. To prevent learning effects from influencing experiment parameters, the weather conditions were randomly selected.The dependent variables were Time to First Fixation (TFF)(sec), First Fixation Duration (FFD) (sec), Total Fixation Duration (TFD) (sec), Fixation Count (FC) (frequency).

2.4   Experimental Process

The experiment was divided into two phases: Preparation and Formal Experimentation.

1. Preparation:
   (a) Room temperature was set at 26±2 °C
   (b) Adjustment and testing of driving simulator
   (c) Calibration of eye tracker
   (d) Explanation of experiment guidelines
   (e) Teaching subjects how to operate the driving simulator

2. Formal Experimentation
   The experiment was meant to test the reactions of drivers to unexpected road conditions in two types of weather. The 16 subjects were randomly categorized into two groups:
   (a) Sunny – Route 1; Foggy – Route 2
   (b) Foggy – Route 1; Sunny – Route 2. Each subject completed two rounds of simulation driving.

3   Results

We first conducted ANOVA of TFF, FFD, TFD and FC, the results of which are presented in Table 1:

Table 1. ANOVA results

Factor \ Dependent variables	TFF	FFD	TFD	FC
Climate			*	*
Road conditions	**	**	***	**
Climate*road conditions			*	

*:p<0.05 ;   **p<0.01; ***p<0.001

Different road conditions, as well as the combined effect of weather with road conditions, significantly affected TFF. However, weather conditions alone did not have a significant influence. As illustrated in Fig. 4, TFF increased in foggy weather, particularly when road work was being performed, mainly because road work can be seen from much further than one can see pedestrians or bouncing balls, such that subjects became aware of road work more gradually as they approach. Foggy weather conditions lengthened TFF. Compared to road work, pedestrians and bouncing were more unexpected, attention-grabbing events, and therefore the effects of weather conditions were less pronounced.

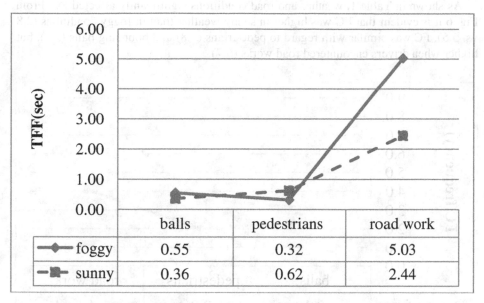

Fig. 4. Influence of weather – road conditions on TFF

Table 1 shows that only road conditions affected FFD. According to Fig. 5, FFD was longest in the case of road works (0.23 sec), with no significant difference in other scenarios (0.09 sec vs 0.11 sec). In addition, FFD was largely unaffected by weather (0.96 sec in sunny conditions and 0.82 sec in foggy conditions).

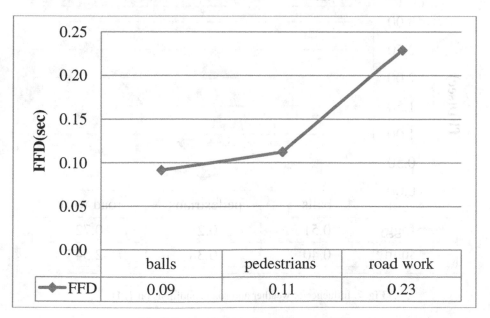

Fig. 5. Influence of road conditions on FFD

As shown in Table 1, weather and road conditions significantly affected FC. From Fig. 6 it is evident that FC was higher in sunny weather than in foggy conditions (2.8 vs. 5.5). FC was similar with regard to pedestrians (2.8) and bouncing balls (2.7), but higher when drivers encountered road works (6.7).

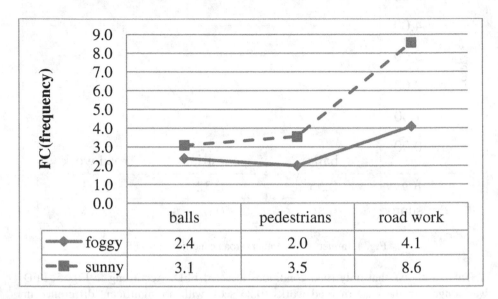

Fig. 6. Influence of weather and road conditions on FC

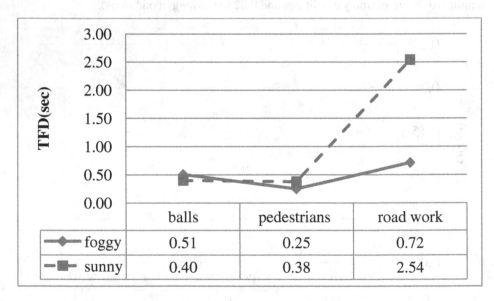

Fig. 7. Influence of weather and road conditions on TFD

Finally, TFD was significantly influenced by all major factors and their combined effects. Figure 7 illustrates the combined influence of weather and road conditions on TFD. Regardless of weather conditions, TFD did not vary considerably when pedestrians or bouncing balls appeared but was extended when road work was encountered. In sunny weather, the TFD for road work was longer.

Time to First Fixation (TFF) was shorter under sunny conditions than under foggy conditions, indicating that in good weather drivers are quicker to spot objects, resulting in higher FC and longer TFD, which in turn reduces the chance of accidents. Weather conditions did not significantly affect FFD. This means that once an object has been spotted by the driver, weather conditions are not a significant factor in FFD (sunny- 0.96 sec; foggy – 0.82 sec).

Road work tends to be static in nature, compared to dynamic subjects such as pedestrians and bouncing balls. Subjects were shown to glance at road work more frequently and for longer periods, perhaps because these distractions were is in the drivers' line of sight for a longer period of time, prompting drivers to pay more attention and thereby avoid collisions.

4   Conclusions and Recommendations

This study employed driving simulation and eye tracking to explore the situational perception of drivers under various weather and road conditions. Our objective was to understand how eye trackers could be applied to improve road safety.

Results show that under good weather conditions, drivers tend to be more aware of road conditions, resulting in shorter TFF, which leads to higher FC and longer TFD, thereby reducing the risk of accident. The influence of road conditions on TFF, FFD, TFD and FC varied according to the situation.

The three scenarios simulated in this study included road work observable from a distance, pedestrians crossing well ahead of the vehicle, and balls suddenly bouncing into the street at a very close range. Drivers took note of construction barriers from a distance and made sure that the width of the road was sufficient to allow them to pass. Drivers noticed pedestrians as they appeared and noted speed limit markers. Balls bouncing into the street meant that drivers concentrated on dodging these objects and were attentive to their driving speed. A schematic trajectory is presented below:

Fig. 8. Eye tracking for different road conditions

This study demonstrated the efficacy of eye trackers in exploring the situational perception of drivers. Our results a valuable reference for the development of systems used to monitor drivers and/or alert them of dangers. Nonetheless, eye trackers must be used carefully because many factors, such as wearing glasses, blinking, or external lighting, can interfere with their use. Simulated driving environments could also be designed to include more diverse scenarios and parameters to facilitate more in-depth study.

References

1. Cantin, V., Lavallière, M., Simoneau, M., Teasdale, N.: Mental workload when driving in a simulator: Effects of age and driving complexity. Accident Analysis and Prevention 41, 763–771 (2009)
2. Endsley, M.R.: Design and evaluation for situation awareness enhancement. In: Proceedings of the Human Factors and Ergonomics Society Annual Meeting, vol. 32(2), pp. 97–101. SAGE Publications (1988)
3. Goldberg, J.H., Kotval, X.P.: Eye movement-based evaluation of the computer interface. Advances in Occupational Ergonomics and Safety, 529–532 (1998)
4. Gugerty, L.J., Tirre, W.C.: Individual differences in situation awareness. Situation Awareness Analysis and Measurement, 249–276 (2000)
5. Harter, S.: The construction of the self: A developmental perspective. Guilford Press (1999)
6. Horberry, T., Anderson, J., Regan, M.A.: The possible safety benefits of enhanced road markings: a driving simulator evaluation. Transportation Research Part F 9, 77–87 (2006)
7. Lee, J.D., McGehee, D.V., Brown, T.L., Reyes, M.L.: Collision Waring Timing, Driver Distraction, and Driver Response to Imminent Rear- End Collisions in a High- Fidelity Driving Simulator. The Journal of the Human Factors and Ergonomics Society 44, 314–334 (2002)
8. Solso, R.L.: Cognition and the Visual Arts. The MIT Press, Cambridge (1994)
9. Vidulich, M., Dominquez, C., Vogel, E., McMillan, G.: Situation awareness: Papers and annotated bibliography (AL/CF-TR-1994-0085). Wright-Patterson Air Force Base. Air Force Material Command, OH (1994)
10. Wittmann, M., Kiss, M., Gugg, P., Steffen, A., Fink, M., Pöppel, E., Kamiya, H.: Effects of display position of a visual in-vehicle task on simulated driving. Applied Ergonomics 37, 187–199 (2006)

A Study on the Interface Design of a Functional Menu and Icons for In-Vehicle Navigation Systems

Ming-Chyuan Lin[*], Yi-Hsien Lin, Chun-Chun Lin, and Jenn-Yang Lin

Department of Creative Product Design and Management, Far East University, Tainan, Taiwan
{minglin,jylin}@mail.ncku.edu.tw, yisam0915@yahoo.com.tw,
purelin@ms17.hinet.net

Abstract. The progress in computer technology and information communication for consumer electronics and related intelligent products has greatly enhanced the usability of the global positioning system (GPS) of in-vehicle navigation systems (IVNSs). However, too many functions and information can be a burden to users while driving, which could include unsuitable icons, inappropriate framework configuration, redundant functional items and an unsuitable hierarchical configuration. The objective of this study is to develop a systematic platform to design the framework of functional menu layers and the corresponding functional icons based on analyzing user requirements. This research performed a three-stage assessment and an analysis on the graphical user interface, hierarchical layers of the functional menu such that the IVNS could be re-constructed based on the data collection and the analyzed marketed IVNS. IT is expected to provide reference information and a research process for designers to help create a more humanized, intelligent human-computer interaction.

Keywords: In-Vehicle Navigation System (IVNS), Menu Layer Configuration, Icon Design, Fuzzy Analytic Hierarchy Process (FAHP), Graphical User Interface.

1 Introduction

Due to the rapid progress in vehicle technology, many newly marketed products with intelligent functions are installed in vehicles to provide a more comfortable and convenient user environment for drivers. The global positioning system (GPS) of in-vehicle navigation systems (IVNSs) is one of the most common functions in a vehicle and is now considered essential equipment. With the assistance of an IVNS, the user can efficiently drive the vehicle to their desired destination without traditional guidebooks or maps. In general, there are two IVNS modes: (1) before driving and (2) while driving. The before-driving mode allows the user to set up the IVNS for the upcoming journey, whereas driving mode allows the user to readjust or modify the route while driving. The IVNS can also involve related communication, daily

---

[*] Corresponding author.

S. Yamamoto (Ed.): HIMI 2014, Part II, LNCS 8522, pp. 261–272, 2014.
© Springer International Publishing Switzerland 2014

information, leisure activity and entertainment guidance. Because an IVNS can integrate various functions into an intelligent system for driving, vehicle manufactures have tried to increase the number of functions in their IVNS to enhance the competition in global markets and satisfy user requirements. Several manufacturers have even designed particular functions or operational interfaces for their IVNSs to strengthen their respective technology. The functions and operational interfaces of an IVNS vary greatly and are based on the manufacturer' specifications and technological support. Most of the differences in the visual designs and functional segmentations appear in the menu functions and interface operation of the IVNS, which allow the user to operate the product based on their preferences and requirements. Despite these differences being the reasons why users choose a particular IVNS based on his or her preferences and use requirements, using intelligent products while driving will affect the quality and safety of driving. For example, inadequate interface information might make it difficult for the user to operate their IVNS, unsuitable icons and inappropriate configuration will confuse users, redundant functional items and an illogical hierarchical configuration will waste drivers' time when searching for functional items and increase the driver's mental workload. Furthermore, different IVNS brands have their own operational procedure and characteristics that will make the choice difficult. Green [1] suggested that an IVNS with redundant functions or an inappropriate icon design, interface framework and layer arrangement would confuse users during operation and cause users to spend more time searching for their desired function. PreiBner [2] recommended that the information interface design criteria of a vehicle should include the (1) use of a hierarchical structure in the multi-functional menu selection, (2) consider consistency and organization of related functions, (3) use simple images for functions and (4) consider the visual habits of users using the interface display. Amditis et al. [3] noted that a well-designed navigation system can enhance driving efficiency and reduce operational errors and accidents. Jung [4] introduced a context-sensitive visualization (CSV) method to incorporate users' internal contexts in the interactive product design by mapping out information onto the context models. Lin, et al. [5] considered that design a sub-window system in the IVNS to help reduce navigation errors. Cui, et al. [6] observed that the IVNS users tend to favor two-level hierarchies in grouping segments and use the similarity in content objects and applications. Cui, et al. also stressed that navigation history has to design in a content-centric way to organize and prioritize mobile interaction events and allow large individual differences. However, the usability of an IVNS based on the number of functional items, layer arrangement of the menu interface and visual icons may not satisfy users' requirements and still require further study and improvement. Therefore, the human-computer interaction interface in the IVNS should be designed and developed based on users' cognitive behavior to allow the contents to be displayed in the most comprehensible way. The objective of this research is to propose an appropriate interface design model for IVNSs; the analysis is followed by a validation experiment to recommend an optimum operation interface of an IVNS including a recommendation for a hierarchical layer configuration of functional items and icons that would help designers establish users' awareness on the graphical user interface and the information transmission mode of the electronic guide map.

2   Development Procedure

According to the research objective, there are three development stages for the proposed interface design model of an IVNS, which are the following: (1) identification and clustering analysis of functional items, (2) construction of an IVNS interface system and (3) system interface experiment.   Stage 1 includes (1) identification of the functional items and the (2) clustering analysis of the functional items.   In Stage 2, the construction procedure includes (1) determining the interface for the functional menu framework, (2) designing the icons for functional items and (3) constructing an interactive user interface.   For Stage 3, the procedure includes (1) experimental planning of the proposed system interface, (2) performing the system interface experiment and (3) analyzing the experimental results.   Note that the approach for the study (1) uses factor analysis [7] to obtain a clustering relation matrix of the functional items based on the usability scenario when using an in-vehicle navigation system, (2) conducts a hierarchical clustering analysis (HCA) [8] to categorize the functional items of an in-vehicle navigation system based on the clustering relation matrix, (3) applies a fuzzy analytic hierarchy process (FAHP) [9-10] to determine the optimum combination of functional items for the system interface design, (4) constructs a computer-aided system interface based on the identified functional items, layer arrangement and graphic icons and (5) uses a general human-machine interface measurement criteria to evaluate the usability of the developed system interface.

3   Identification and Clustering Analysis of Functional Items

The IVNS guides the user to the desired destination and prearranges routes for upcoming trips.   Different manufacturers will have different support techniques that make functional items of IVNSs differ significantly.   Note that different users (male or female) will also have different requirements for the functional items of an IVNS.   Current interface operation of an IVNS includes external type and built-in type, and types of manual operation include push button plus touch-panel type and full touch-panel type.   Most functional icons of a system interface of an IVNS appear in colors with a text explanation beneath the icons.   The existing IVNS products have the following design factors: screen size, display aspect ratio, interface background, main-interface, sub-interface, main-interface icon size, information of main-interface icons, number of icons in the sub-interface, number of interface layers, display switch mode, icon frames and font, which are shown in Table 1.   Based on the identified design factors for the interface design of IVNSs illustrated in Table 1, it is expected that this type of study would require customer opinions and preferences during the development process to ensure that the proposed model can satisfy a wide range of customer requirements.   As such, identifying functional items will be the first step of this study followed by classifying the identified functional items to determine the number of interface layers.

Table 1. Interface design factors for IVNSs

	Spec 1	Spec 2	Spec 3	Spec 4	Spec 5
Screen size	3.5 inch	4.3 inch	4.7 inch	5.2 inch	7 inch
Display aspect ratio	4 : 3	16 : 9			
Interface background	1 type	2 types	3 more types		
Main interface	single frame	upside: select area downside: search buttons	upside: power downside: select area	upside: power center: select area downside: search buttons	
Sub-interface	single frame	upside: select area downside: search buttons	upside: power downside: select area	upside: power center: select area downside: search buttons	
Main-interface icon size	same size	different sizes			
Information of main-interface icons	image	image and text	animation		
Number of icons in sub-interface	6	8			
Number of interface layers	2	3	4		
Display switch mode	click icon	click icon and switch the screen	click icon and confirm		
Icon frame	without borders	with borders			
Font	Times new roman	Arial	Arial bold		

3.1   Identification of Functional Items

Because the currently marketed IVNS products have a variety of operating systems, display types, number of functional items, representation icons and interface layers, this study begins with a market survey that includes all the functional items and the design of a functional requirement questionnaire to help identify user requirements for functional IVNS items.   The collection of functional items includes products from five brands: Garmin, Mio, Panasonic, TomTom and HOLUX.   A total of 61 functional items, which includes 39 common functions and 22 special functions, was collected.   These functions were then incorporated in a user experience questionnaire and forwarded to experienced users for evaluation.   The questionnaire included (1) basic information of the test subjects (2) IVNS use experience and (3) a scale of 5 points (1, 2, 3, 4 and 5 points) to evaluate the functional items.   Table 2 illustrates the collected 61 functional items and the identified 44 functional items based on 32 effective questionnaire results.   Note that in Table 2, the number without "*" refers to the identified functional items and will be used in the classification and interface layer analysis.

Table 2. List of collected and identified functional items

Common functions		Special functions	
Title	Description	Title	Description
1 Road	Search a road	40 Picture	Search by coordinates of a picture
2 Intersection	Search an intersection	41 Color	Set colors of the map
3 Address	Search an address	42 Simulate	Route simulation
4 Parking lot	Parking lot nearby	43 Museum	Search a museum nearby
5 Highway ramp	Search a highway ramp nearby	44* Pre-crash system	An automobile safety system
6 Gas station	Search a gas station nearby	45 Plan a route	Plan a route next days
7 Detour	Made a detour	46* Brightness	Day or night brightness
8 Organization	Search an organization	47* Auto Parking	An auto parking system
9 Attraction	Search an attraction	48* Phone	Connect to your phone
10 Volume	Adjust the volume	49* Current location	Show your current location
11 Restaurant	Search a restaurant	50* Voice	Introduce an attraction
12* Home	Navigate to my home	51* Voice setting	Set the voice function
13 Hypermarket	Search a hypermarket nearby	52* Voice command	Controlled by means of voice
14 My routes	Saving a route	53 119	Call 119
15 Public transport	Search a public transport nearby	54* Game	Play a game
16 Roadside assistance	Roadside assistance information	55* Plug-in	A plug-in software
17 Language	Language setting	56* Calculator	A calculator
18 Screen Calibration	Calibrate the position of screen	57* E-book	Read an e-book
19 Planning a route	Planning a route	58* Layout	Set the layout of frames
20 Hospital	Search a hospital nearby	59* Following	Follow the car
21 Map view	Change the map view	60* Diary	Keep a diary
22 Types of route	Set the route type	61* Poetry	Play the poetry
23 Bank	Search a bank nearby		
24 Help	Help you get going with your device		
25 Entertainment	Search a public entertainment		
26 Brightness	Adjust the screen brightness		
27 History	Search Records		
28 Reset	Perform a full reset		
29 Phone number	Search by phone number		
30 Quick search	Set a quick search icon		
31 Time/Date	Set the time/date format		
32 Accommodation	Search for accommodations nearby		
33 Bluetooth	Connect to Bluetooth devices		
34 Coordinate	Planning a route using coordinates		
35 Radio	Listen to the radio		
36 Movie	Play video		
37 Photo	Photo browsing		
38 Music	Play music		
39 Save mode	Go to save mode		

3.2 Clustering Analysis of the Functional Items

To classify the identified 44 functional items, a usability scenario questionnaire was designed and distributed to the testers. The usability scenario questionnaire used AIO- (activities, interests and opinions) [11] type questions to perform a factor analysis and analyze how the operation performance is affected by the key factors that transmit information during the process of human-computer interaction when using an IVNS. The research designed 25 AIO-type questions, which included 10 types of activities, 7 types of interests and 8 types of opinions. There were 106 effective questionnaire results. These results were forwarded to the statistical software SPSS for a factor analysis. This study defined 9 usability scenarios: (1) GPS system setup, (2) use of GPS while travelling, (3) travelling from one place to another place, (4) daily use of the GPS on duty, (5) change in the destination while driving, (6) use of GPS for none-GPS activities, (7) use of GPS before driving, (8) personal preference with the GPS setup and (9) use of GPS for an emergency. A relational evaluation between the identified functional items and the usability scenarios was then conducted with an interaction matrix. Points 0 and 1 were used to assess the relationships between the functional items and usability scenarios. These points correspond to no relation and with relation, respectively. 10 GPS-experienced subjects were asked to judge the items. The evaluation results were then used with Ward's method [7] in the SPSS software to generate a hierarchical structure for clustering groups. Table 3 illustrates one of the hierarchical clusters of the system interfaces. In Table 3, the main interface has 6 functional items; the sub-interface has a maximum of 10 functional items in the first layer.

Table 3. Example showing an alternative cluster of an IVNS system interface

Main interface menu		Sub-interface menu		Main interface menu		Sub-interface menu	
		Layer 1	Layer 2			Layer 1	Layer 2
Cluster 1	Category Search	Attraction	Gas station	Cluster 4	Amusement	Movie	
		Accommodation	Public transport			Photo	
		Entertainment	My routes			Radio	
		Restaurant				Music	
		Hypermarket		Cluster 5	Planning a route	Simulate	
		Picture				Plan a route	
		Organization				Planning a route	
		Museum				Detour	
		Bank		Cluster 6	Setup	Help	Quick setup
		Parking lot				Reset	Volume
Cluster 2	Quick Search	Intersection				Save mode	
		Address				Time/Date	
		Road				Screen Calibration	
		Map view				Brightness	
		Phone number				Color	
		Highway ramp				Types of route	
		History				Bluetooth	
		Coordinate				Language	
Cluster 3	Emergency	Roadside assistance					
		119					
		Hospital					

4   Construction of an IVNS Interface System

In constructing an IVNS interface system, there are two essential parts: (1) the functional menu framework evaluation and (2) functional icon design. The evaluation of the menu framework system is based on all the currently marketed IVNS interfaces and the result of the functional item clusters of the main interface and sub-interface. Determining the system interfaces is helpful in developing an IVNS interface system that will meet customer requirements. The framework specifications of the functional menu are considered as important parameters and will be evaluated with the FAHP approach. With regards to the functional icon design, this research uses a market survey, product catalogue collection and a questionnaire to identify higher cognition icons for design reference.

4.1   Determination of the Interface for the Functional Menu Framework

According to all the currently marketed IVNS interfaces, the functional menu framework consists of a main interface and a sub-interface. There are three types of main interfaces and three types of sub-interfaces based on the number of functional items in an individual display. Table 4 shows the parameters and levels of the functional menu framework. To select the most suitable system interface of the functional menu framework, the FAHP approach was applied in the evaluation process [9-10]. The evaluation criteria are based on human-machine interface measurement standards proposed by the International Standard Organization (ISO). Five measurement standards, which include fascination, tolerance, performance, efficiency, and ease of operation, were used. The five measurement standards were evaluated with fuzzy linguistic scales. The numbers, 1, 3, 5, 7 and 9, denote the least, less, medium, extremely and most important, respectively.

Table 4. Parameters and levels of the functional menu framework

Parameter		Level		
Main interface	Single frame	Top: selection area Bottom: browse area	Top: power area Bottom: selection area	Top: power area Center: selection area Bottom: browse area
Sub-interface	Single frame	Top: selection area Bottom: browse area	Top: power area Bottom: selection area	Top: power area Center: selection area Bottom: browse area
Maximum number of functional items	Main interface	4	5	6
	Sub-interface	6	8	10
Font		Times New Roman	Arial	Arial bold

The parameters and levels incorporated with the five measurement standards form a matrix with parameters and levels assigned in rows and five measurement standards assigned in columns. A questionnaire was also designed and distributed to test subjects via the internet.   30 test subjects evaluated each parameter level based on the five measurement standards on a fuzzy linguistic scale.   The collected data were then pooled by the geometric average method.   An alternative recommendation from the candidate system interfaces of the functional menu framework was selected to improve the system interface design.   The characteristics of the recommended parameter levels are the following: main interface with power area at the top and selection area at the bottom, sub-interface with power area at the top, selection area at the center and browse area at the bottom, 6 functional items in the main interface, 10 functional items in the sub-interface and font with bold.

4.2   Icon Design for Functional Items

In designing icons for functional items, this study first collected graphic icons from the currently marketed functional items and identified semantic image nouns so the questionnaire could be distributed to determine a suitable connection between user requirements and functional icons.   A total of 50 graphic icons, which included the main interface and sub-interface, was collected and redrawn [12].   The functional icons were designed using the computer software Adobe Flash CS3.   The candidate icons for the functional items were designed as a questionnaire and distributed to the test subjects.   The results indicated that users tended to accept daily or customary image graphics as icons.   It appears that icon graphics with embodied characteristics are more recognized by users.   Additionally, a simplified icon graphic will also provide a higher recognition.   These suggestions lead directly to helping identify five icon graphics design criteria:

1. Limit the size of an IVNS icon to 48x48 pixels with an area greater than 64 mm^2.
2. Use a single color as a background to obtain better tapping effect.
3. Simplify the graphic image, color and shape to make it easy for the users to understand.
4. Unify the style of icons to be a family image.
5. Allocate supplementary texts of functional items under the icons to enhance recognition.

Based on the aforementioned graphics design criteria for icons, the research developed 50 graphic icons for the corresponding functional items.   Table 5 shows the partial icons designed for specific functional items.   An integrated system interface design criteria, which includes the functional menu framework, layers of functional items and functional icons, was then determined.

4.3   Construction of an Interactive User Interface

An IVNS was developed based on the high-demand functional items and clustering rules, the design factors of the interface and the features of the functional icons. Constructing a system interface includes the following: (1) determination of the system panel, (2) arrangement of the functional menu framework, (3) retrieval and editorial process of the functional icon graphics and (4) development of an interactive

Table 5. Partial icon designs for specific functions

Item	Category Search	Entertainment	Gas station	Search	Restaurant	Public transport
Icon	Category	ENTMT	Gas	Search	Restaurant	PT
Item	Roadside assistance	Hypermarket	My routes	Amusement	Picture	Intersection
Icon	ERA	HYM	My routes	Amusement	Picture	Intersection
Item	Planning a route	Organization	Address	System settings	Museum	Road
Icon	Route	Org	Address	Settings	Museum	Road
Item	Attraction	Bank	Map view			
Icon	Attraction	Bank	Map view			

connection of the interface.   To construct the system interface for this study, an HP iPAQ 212 Enterprise hand held display was used, as shown in Figure 1.   The framework of the system interface, which includes 6 functional categories and 44 functional items, is illustrated in Figure 2.   An interactive interface of the operational framework from this study is shown in Figure 3.

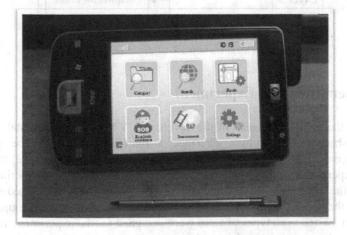

Fig. 1. Simulation of the IVNS system interface

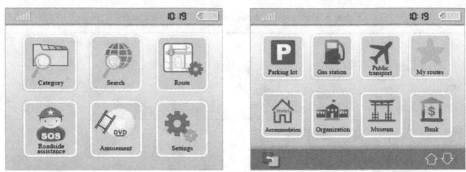

(a) Representation of the main interface (b) Representation of the partial sub-interface

Fig. 2. Representation of the proposed IVNS system interface

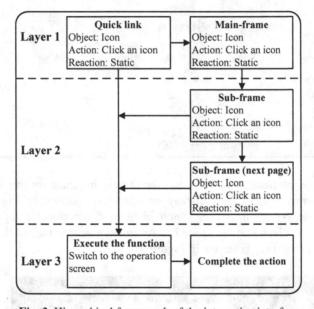

Fig. 3. Hierarchical framework of the interactive interface

5   System Interface Experiment

To evaluate the merits and faults of the developed IVNS, an experimental procedure was established for the system interface usability evaluation.   The procedure included (1) experimental planning of the proposed system interface, (2) the system interface experiment and (3) analysis of the system interface experiment.   In conducting the experiment, a comparison of two groups was conducted, with one group using the developed in-vehicle navigation system and the other group using the Garmin Nuvi 1370T.   10 types of tasks were designed for the experiment, and 20 test subjects who have design backgrounds were selected.   Note that 13 of the test subjects had experience using a GPS, whereas 7 test subjects did not have experience. The 10 types of tasks were (1) search for a gas station, (2) search for a roadside assistance, (3) adjust the screen brightness, (4) search for an address, (5) search for a culture center, (6) search for a crossroad, (7) search for a shopping center, (8) run the photo viewer, (9) search for a hospital and (10) search for an interchange.   During the experiment, the completion time (in seconds), number of times the user went back and forth between the layers, and number of mission errors were recorded and analyzed.

After the experiment, the 20 test subjects were asked to fill out a questionnaire regarding the user interface evaluation criteria.   The research defined 9 interface criteria for the evaluation, which are the following: (1) appropriate layout, (2) appropriate color, (3) easy to click, (4) easy to understand functional icons, (5) easy to understand texts, (6) avoid inappropriate touch, (7) easy to find functional items, (8) easy to learn the interface and (9) overall satisfaction.   The evaluation is based on a 1-5 scale judgment with 1, 2, 3, 4 and 5 representing extremely low, low, medium, high and extremely high satisfaction, respectively.   The results showed that the developed IVNS had a higher satisfaction than that of the comparison system.   However, the developed in-vehicle navigation system still has several individual tasks that require further improvement.

6   Conclusions

IVNS products have become extremely popular, and many intelligent mobiles are even equipped with a built-in IVNS.   The number of functional items in current IVNSs has increased gradually.   Their differences have also become more apparent, which makes it difficult for the user to choose.   Therefore, the designer is responsible for developing a friendly IVNS to meet user requirements.   The research proposed a procedure to construct an IVNS interface that integrated several approaches, such as a usability scenario model, AIO scale, factor analysis, hierarchical clustering analysis, fuzzy analytic hierarchy process and graphics design. The hierarchical cluster analysis was used in the first stage to classify the hierarchical configuration of the functional items.   Note that the fuzzy analytic hierarchy process was also used to evaluate the design factors of the framework configuration.   In the second stage, the specifications of the system menu framework were determined using a fuzzy judgment matrix, and a design process of the functional icons was used. A system simulation for the experimental evaluation was also conducted in the third stage for further improvement.   It was expected that through this research, the following results would be obtained: (1) a convenient connection between the graphical user interface in an IVNS and user cognition, (2) a friendly interface structure of the menu and digital content to enhance the operation performance, and (3) an appropriate mode of electronic information display on the vehicle windshield. In addition, this research provides reference information and a research process for designers to help establish users' awareness on the graphical user interface and the information transmission mode of an IVNS to make human-computer interaction more humanized and intelligent.

Acknowledgements. The authors are grateful to the National Science Council, Taiwan for supporting this research under the grant number NSC 102-2221-E-269-023.

References

1. Green, P.: In-Vehicle Information: Design of Driver Interfaces for Route Guidance. Transportation Research Board Meeting, Washington, D.C. Session 258B (1996)
2. PreiBner, O.: Design of Graphic Displays for Driver Information and Communication Systems. Computer Aided Animation. GmbH. AAAI Technical Report, SS-00-04 (2000)
3. Amditis, A., Pagle, K., Joshi, S., Bekiaris, E.: Driver–Vehicle–Environment Monitoring for On-board Driver Support Systems: Lessons Learned from Design and Implementation. Applied Ergonomics 41(2), 225–235 (2009)
4. Jung, E.C.: Methodology for Context-Sensitive System Design by Mapping Internal Contexts into Visualization Mechanisms. Design Studies 31, 26–45 (2010)
5. Lin, C.-T., Wu, H.-C., Chien, T.-Y.: Effects of E-Map Format and Sub-Windows on Driving Performance and Glance Behavior When Using an In-Vehicle Navigation System. I. J. Industrial Ergonomics 40, 330–336 (2010)
6. Cui, Y., Oulasvirta, A., Ma, L.: Event Perception in Mobile Interaction: Toward Better Navigation History Design on Mobile Devices. I. J. Human-Computer Interaction 27(5), 413–435 (2011)
7. Sharma, S.: Applied Multivariate Techniques. John Wiley & Sons, Inc., New York (1996)
8. Chen, M.-S., Lin, C.-C., Tai, Y.-Y., Lin, M.-C.: A Grey Relation Approach to the Integrated Process of QFD and QE. I. J. Concurrent Engineering: Research and Applications 19(1), 35–53 (2011)
9. Lee, W.B., Lau, H., Liu, Z.Z., Tam, S.: A Fuzzy Analytic Hierarchy Process Approach in Modular Product Design. Expert Systems 18(1), 32–42 (2001)
10. Li, T.S., Huang, H.H.: Applying TRIZ and Fuzzy AHP to Develop Innovative Design for Automated Manufacturing Systems. Expert Systems with Applications 36(4), 8302–8312 (2009)
11. Solomon, M.R.: Consumer Behavior: Buying, Having, and Being, 6th edn. Prentice-Hall, New Jersey (2004)
12. Lauer, D.A., Pentak, S.: Design Basics, 7th edn. The Cengage Learning Asia Pte, Ltd., Wadsworth (2008)

Advancement and Application of Unmanned Aerial System Human-Machine-Interface (HMI) Technology

Brent A. Terwilliger[1], David C. Ison[1], Dennis A. Vincenzi[1], and Dahai Liu[2]

[1] Embry-Riddle Aeronautical University – Worldwide, Daytona Beach, FL, United States
{brent.terwilliger,david.ison,dennis.vincenzi}@erau.edu
[2] Embry-Riddle Aeronautical University – Daytona Beach, FL, United States
Dahai.liu@erau.edu

Abstract. Interface designs native to handheld control and feedback devices (e.g., smartphones and tablets) are becoming more accessible within the small unmanned aerial system (sUAS) community due to increased usage in remote control (R/C) model aircraft platforms [33], improved processing to cost [4], and increased interoperability supporting custom development and programming [2], [33]. These smaller, power efficient control systems have the potential to change the paradigm of sUAS control to be more aligned with semi-autonomous operations based on their innate ability to provide intuitive user interactions [44], low cost, reduction of latency effects on control, and improved real-time configuration and data measurement [33]. The objective of this study is to identify common themes in the advancement and application of human-machine-interface technologies in UAS control. This paper proposes to review available literature, associated technology designs, and identify how the UAS community can best leverage this technology and interaction concepts to support safe and efficient operations of UAS.

Keywords: Human-Machine Interface, HMI, Unmanned Aerial System, UAS, sUAS, UAV, Intelligent, Intuitive, and Innovative (I^3) design.

1 Introduction

1.1 Current State of UAS HMI

The unmanned systems industry, specifically the UAS market, has been experiencing significant growth in the last three years due to maturation and advances in related technology, increased application opportunities, and availability of key components and materials [18], [48], [49]. Historically, this market has been supported by military/DoD needs [1], [6], [48]. However, with the Congressional mandates identified in the *FAA Modernization and Reform Act of 2012*, opportunities for civil and commercial use have begun to increase [6], [14], [48]. The domestic economic impact of integration of UAS into the National Airspace System (NAS), as mandated by Congress, is expected to exceed $13.6B between 2015 to 2017, reaching more than $82.1B by 2025 [5]. While government customers are anticipated to continue providing the largest source of economic support and growth in the near term, the

S. Yamamoto (Ed.): HIMI 2014, Part II, LNCS 8522, pp. 273–283, 2014.
© Springer International Publishing Switzerland 2014

commercial applications are expected to support the continued growth of this industry and market [5], [48].

The majority of commercial applications are projected to use micro to small UAS (sUAS), featuring low-cost designs that will be dedicated to specific uses [1], [48]. The designs and technology for these smaller systems are expected to initially come from the remote control or model aviation market [48]. This market already exhibits equipment featuring a high degree of complexity, capability, and support at a low price point [23], [26], [36]. Achieving the projected industry growth will require the confluence of three critical factors, the availability of enabling technologies, a need for use, and a viable economic climate [48]. While the current economic market appears ready for the availability of commercial sUAS, the regulatory framework is not. The FAA is not currently allowing commercial UAS operations in the NAS, but they are working to address this limitation for sUAS in the near term [15].

Unlike existing GCS interfaces, current interface technology has the potential to integrate a number of innovative developments in interface design, thus creating the potential to alleviate many of the existing interface issues currently of concern. Interfaces integrating intuitive design, touch screen capability and other innovative technologies currently existing in smartphones and tablets today (e.g., global positioning system [GPS], accelerometers, and gyroscopes) can be designed to feed the interface and control the sUAS in a much more intuitive manner than before. Dependency on legacy controls and software interfaces, lack of intuitive interfaces and sensory cues, low resolution interface fidelity, and high latency due to poor data link capabilities all contribute to poor information transfer, resulting in poor performance and reduced situational awareness.

1.2   UAS HMI Issues

Despite the great potential UASs provide, there are still a number of challenges facing the UAS community. For the past decade, much effort has been focused on developing new automation technology and interoperability, however, there has not been much investment focusing on the HMI for UAS systems. Despite the name given to these "unmanned" systems implying that the human is not involved, it is essential to remember that human operators are still involved in the control loop and operation of the vehicle, as well as interpretation of video and sensor data being collected and transmitted by the vehicle. It is not uncommon to find a single UAS to be monitored and controlled by a number of human operators. A well designed HMI is indeed critical for coordinating among UASs and multiple human operators.

The current state of HMI technology and design in UASs in use today contain many issues and challenges. Four major issues and challenges related to HMI deficiencies and design inadequacies are as follows:

1. There is no well-established standard for UAS HMI. The HMI among different UAS designers and manufacturers varies a great deal in terms of the information presentation and layout. Due to the high level of complexity involved in UAS HMI functionality, this often requires extensive amount of time for training to be able to use the HMI, and this lack of standardization leads to poor transfer of training between different systems.

2. The information presented in the HMI is often not optimized. There are large amounts of information involved in UAS operations, especially for multi-mission systems, where there are multiple teams of UASs and human operators are involved. When handling high stake, time pressured tasks under environmental uncertainty, it is essential that the HMI be intelligent enough to aid the human decision-making process in order to perform the tasks with accuracy and efficiency. The current HMIs lack this capability and level of functionality.

3. Related to HMI Issue 2, adaptability and flexibility are essential for effective HMI design. HMIs need to be adaptive to be able to adjust the level of automation to suit human operators' workload and increase their situational awareness, to minimize automation bias and build trust between human operators and UASs.

4. Finally, an examination of UAS literature reveals that one of the most prominent HMI issues is that of the sensory isolation of the operators (and other crew) due to their physical separation from the aircraft. Pilots and crew in manned aircraft have access to an abundance of multisensory information, aiding their understanding of the status of their aircraft in the environment [12]. Such information includes ambient visual input, and kinesthetic, vestibular, and auditory information, which can provide pilots with cues to the speed of travel, orientation, other elements in the vicinity, weather conditions, and aircraft health and status [22]. Currently, no such HMI exists that incorporates this type of information.

With the major sensory disconnects and lack of environmental cues found in UAS today, it is more important than ever to design control interfaces that project to the operator information that is necessary and vital to produce superior situational awareness outside the cockpit and away from the vehicle itself. With the new capabilities present in current interface technology and software, it is now possible to design functional, intuitive interfaces that take advantage of the available cues and impart the necessary information to maintain high levels of situational awareness needed for safe, efficient, and effective control of unmanned vehicles.

2   Regulation and Certification

Although there are few regulatory measures in place governing the development and certification of unmanned systems and their control systems, with the recent release of the FAA's UAS Roadmap document, some insight into what may be forthcoming has come to light. Currently, the primary regulatory guidance stems from FAA Order 8130.34 Airworthiness Certification of Unmanned Aircraft Systems and Optionally Piloted Aircraft. This guides users to 14 CFR Part 21 certification procedures for products and parts which allows for certification procedures similar to those for restricted category manned aircraft [16]. Other evidence appears that the FAA will use manned standards to guide the UAS certification process while at the same time trying to flexible with the unique needs for unmanned systems [46]. The FAA has also stated that UAS manufacturers should follow RTCA Operational and Functional Requirements and Safety Objectives (OFRSO) for UAS, Volume 1 which provides recommendations for UAS system level operational and functional requirements and safety objectives for UAS flown in the United States NAS under the rules and guidelines for civil aviation. This document provides a framework to support the development of future UAS performance standards and will prove useful to designers, manufacturers, installers, service providers and users in the development of future standards [17].

Various manned standards are likely to apply for UAS interfaces. These will likely include 14 CFR Part 23.1311 which lays forth requirements for electronic display systems providing for standardized information display and color codings. The FAA has also shown an affinity for applying existing software and hardware standards across airborne platforms. Thus applying standards outlined in DO-178B and ARINC 653, both of which govern the design and standards for complex avionics systems for use in airborne systems, is likely to be part of the future adoption of certification requirements for UASs. These dictate that systems operate at an acceptable level of safety through the design and verification of the viability and durability of both hardware and software and have been the accepted norms in manned aircraft for quite some time. Considering the concerns that the FAA has voiced over command, control, and communication, as well as sense and avoid, processes outlined by RTCA are the most relevant for moving forward with any UAS interface systems in development [19]. Moreover, the support of cross-application of hardware and software among numerous types of flight platforms through the standards of the Future Airborne Capability Environment (FACE) by the Department of Defense is likely to influence the potential adoption of tested and validated hardware and software protocols when using manned aircraft components in unmanned systems [11].

3 Applicable Technology

3.1 UAS Specific

The HMI for manned aircraft has been evolving with the incorporation of touch sensitive components, simultaneously able to depict information and accept user input, and voice recognition (e.g., multifunction displays for Lockheed Martin F-35 Joint Strike Fighter, Beechcraft King Air, custom General Aviation cockpits) [28], [38]. The use of such intuitive user interfaces provides the user with a wider variety of options for interacting with the system, while retaining situational awareness of the state and orientation of the aircraft given sufficient sizing of the display [28], [42]. For this research, applicable technology and associated research relating to HMI and user interfaces were examined and categorized as they relate to handheld controls, touch sensitive portable devices, autonomous control, commercially available user interface solutions, and customizable open source and proprietary user interfaces. Each of these categories is presented in the following subsections.

Handheld Controls. A common control configuration for sUAS requires the coordination of two-operators using a handheld input device and a laptop to affect aircraft control and obtain feedback in manual and autonomous/semi-autonomous operational modes [41]. In this arrangement, the first operator provides manual control of the aircraft using the handheld input device and live video from the aircraft, while the second monitors the position and inputs appropriate autonomous control parameters [41]. While singular operator control is possible with such a configuration there are several disadvantages, including reduced situational awareness, hardware limitations, and poor UI design [41].   Researchers at the Space and Naval Warfare Systems Center Pacific (SSCPAC) are performing research and development for a unified system, the Multi-robot Operator Control Unit (MOCU), to address improved usability, limitations of existing control systems, and increased interoperability to support control of a larger range of unmanned or robotic systems across multiple domains (e.g., land, air, sea, and underwater) [39], [41]. The design of the MOCU was made to be modular, flexible, and intuitive to support future expansion and development [41]. Researchers Stroumtsos et al [41] used the MOCO framework to develop a control and display interface to improve usability and system safety for a single sUAS operator [41]. Their custom configuration of the MOCO featured a simplified control interface (i.e., X-box controller), smaller hardware footprint (single laptop and radio), and a unified graphics-based user interface to improve situational awareness [41].

Touch Sensitive Portable Devices. One of the most critical considerations of implementing user interfaces for touch sensitive portable devices such as phones or tablets is determining how to present the data in the limited visible space (i.e. footprint), while retaining the ability to interact [3]. Arhippainen et al [3] hypothesized that three dimensional (3D) user interfaces could provide benefit given the ability to enhance a user's task. In support of their research, they developed a series of conceptual 3D UIs to perform iterative design and evaluation to gain a better understanding of user experience [3]. Their findings indicated that providing context-aware service multitasking provides positive results for users by simplifying and reducing the speed for interaction [3]. Such findings have merit in relation to the user interface needs of sUAS controls, such as reduced reaction timing and ability to obtain and maintain situational awareness through monitoring of map location and telemetry data in addition to the real-time video visualization.

Autonomous Control. Implementing autonomous control for sUAS requires incorporation of an autopilot with trajectory planning and path following (i.e., waypoint tracking) capabilities [8], [9]. Achieving trajectory planning and path following requires a user to input operational parameters (i.e., predefined constraints), such as waypoint locations, minimum and maximum airspeed, minimum and maximum altitude, and identification of specific areas to avoid [43]. The control parameters are entered using a graphical user interface (GUI), which also depicts the state of the aircraft using telemetry (i.e., state observations) during live flight [8], [43]. Researchers Tozicka et al [43], have identified an issue inherent to autonomous planning systems where the system is unable to account for conditions outside the predefined parameters (i.e., system is unaware of specific conditions). Such an issue can lead to scenarios where the calculated trajectory does not align with the needs or requirements of the operator [43], reducing the end usability of the system. Tozicka et al [43] developed a planning system that features improved conveyance of the planning processes to the user and inclusion of human-in-the-loop control to present multiple trajectory path options (i.e., diverse planning), which are used to select the final trajectory of the aircraft. This improved user interface incorporates touch control to reduce the reaction time and present alternative options (diversity) to increase system effectiveness and user trust in system autonomy [43].

Commercially Available User Interface Solutions. Several companies have begun to release small, portable, handheld control systems and associated software packages to address the growing need for a unified, intuitive, solution that support singular operator control of a variety of unmanned systems [7], [24], [25], [27], [32], [45], [47]. These handheld controls provide a myriad of features and capabilities, including intuitive interfaces, full motion video (live and playback), touchscreens, multiple-views, color-coded warning, caution, and advisory, real-time information display, vehicle state (e.g., fuel and battery remaining), and video overlays (text and graphics) [7], [24], [25], [27], [32], [45], [47]. The common feature of note among the various options is the ability to be customized for a specific platform and application, while retaining interoperability for use with multiple systems [21], [24], [25], [27], [32], [45], [47]. The U.S. DoD has identified a requirement for interoperability in future systems and that those companies with products featuring closed-architecture will need to adjust their strategies or lose market share [49]. The incorporation of interoperability in unmanned systems is anticipated to provide the DoD with up to $86 million in savings [21].

Customizable Open Source and Proprietary User Interfaces. The ability to improved interoperability and customization of interfaces has also been a core feature of open source projects for COTS autopilot systems (e.g., ArduPilot) and customizable propriety systems (e.g., WiRC) using software development kits (SDKs) [2], [50]. The PixHawk GCS, an open source software package developed for the PixHawk micro air vehicle (MAV) platform, features support for multiple aircraft (rotary and fixed-wing), deployment on multiple OS (Windows, Linux, MacOs, and Maemo) and hardware (PC, Mac, iPad, iPhone, and Nokia N900), and customization of the GUI [2], [35]. The user interface for PixHawk GCS provides the user with several views, including an engineer view, a parameters/setting/MAVLink view, and a pilot view [2]. The PixHawk design was recently updated to serve as an open-hardware autopilot solution for the open-source autopilot domain, providing new features such a direct programming scripting of autopilot operations, incorporation of peripheral sensors (digital airspeed and magnetometer), and data logging [34].

3.2   Non UAS User Interfaces

The non-UAS, aviation user interface has undergone a significant transformation since the World War II era. Allied and Axis aircraft laid the foundation for civilian aviation with the primary interfaces being based on analog gauges, switches, dials, buttons, and levers [40]. As jet aircraft were introduced, it became readily apparent that pilots and other crewmembers were being saturated with instruments as noted by the fact that the average 1970's era airline cockpit had more than 100 instruments to monitor and even more interfaces with aircraft systems and avionics [30]. A shift to simpler displays and interfaces occurred gradually with the introduction of glass cockpits, first with military aircraft, then migrating into civilian use. Originally only a repetition of common flight instruments on cathode ray tube (CRT) displays, glass cockpits have morphed into intelligent systems providing pilots with critical data and suppressing less necessary data. These "new multi-function interfaces [present] designers with the challenge to optimize the pilot's interaction with controls and tasks whilst maintaining the familiarity and functionality of the existing system" [30], thus a variety of novel human interfaces have surfaced.

The primary type of output interface has remained fairly constant, typically a CRT or liquid crystal display (LCD) screen showing intuitive instruments, colors, or symbols, to convey flight critical data. Other outputs include warning lights and other captions to draw attention to system status. Additionally, head's up displays (HUDs) have become relatively common in civilian aircraft so that pilots can monitor flight instruments and condition without having to look down at more conventional displays. More variety in input interfaces have surfaced with the growing complexity of output presentations. Two primary types of input interfaces exist: indirect and direct. Indirect (relative) require hand movements or other interactions to bring forth actions. Examples include QWERT or unconventional keyboards, rotary, trackball, and touchpad interfaces. Direct (absolute) types allow the user to directly access input features through touching desired outcomes, the most typical being a touchscreen [37]. Generally, indirect interfaces require a higher cognitive loading of the user whilst they were found better for repetitive and precision tasks [20]. Direct controls were found to be superior for selection actions and menu driven systems [37].

Stanton et al. [40] compared performance in two menu selection tasks among trackball, rotary controller, touch pad, and touch screen interfaces. They found that the touch screen performed best in drop down menu tasks as well as in action based menu tasks in terms of response times. In terms of performance of errors, touch screens showed only a slight advantage over other interfaces in drop down tasks while the rotary controller surpassed touch options for action based tasks. The highest level of interface usability was determined to be the touch screen, with the trackball being found to be second best. Touch screens provided the least amount of hand discomfort but had the highest level of body discomfort [37].

3.3   New HMI Technology

Little research has been performed toward collection of data to support the needs of the UAS community to determine requirements for new and innovative HMIs for UAS. The DoD has published "roadmaps" on a regular basis that provide high level overviews of desired technological functionality, but very little specific information about what that technology should include. As mentioned previously, the U.S. DoD has identified a requirement for interoperability in future systems and that those companies with products featuring closed-architecture will need to adjust their strategies or lose market share [49]. They also include verbiage that outlines the need for greater use of analytical automation that will enhance the UASs "cognitive behavior" but these documents say nothing about designing an interface that enhances the human operator's capability to operate these units efficiently and safely [49].

Consideration must be provided to the design and implementation of highly intelligent and intuitive interfaces if UASs are to be accepted by the public and safely operated over civilian airspace. These technologies should be designed to provide information to the human operator that compliments and enhances their abilities to operate the UAS. Recent research has identified six design improvements based on a cognitive work analysis performed using a limited pool of UAS operators and subject matter experts (SMEs). The six HMI design improvement needs identified were the need for: 1) better communication of system status and environment, 2) reduced demand on memory, 3) support for attention management, 4) more robust feedback-control loop, 5) improved error avoidance, detection, and recovery, and 6) support for information synthesis [31].

New HMIs must provide the human operator with the information needed to safely and efficiently operate the UAS while maintaining a delicate balance to ensure the human operator is not inundated with non-essential information. New interfaces should optimize the use of all sensory modalities and information processing channels available to the operator including visual, auditory, and tactile modalities. Interfaces that are innovative, intelligent, and intuitive (I^3) must dominate the market is humans are to remain an effective component of the UAS.

4   Conclusions

When new technologies are designed and developed, the HMI design needs listed must be recognized and addressed. The existing DoD roadmaps seem to address only the support for information synthesis aspect, but all of the needs identified are important from a human factors design perspective. With the obvious desire on the part of the military to develop more advanced and sophisticated automation for incorporation into UAS platforms, it is reasonable to assume that the same issues that plague manned aviation platforms will also manifest themselves in unmanned platforms (i.e. more automation, increased workload, increased potential for human error, decreased situational awareness, etc.) Using interface design principles and innovations from other domains may be helpful (i.e. intuitive design, touch screens, mobile device innovations, solid human factors information processing principles and guidelines), but real advances will only appear when new innovations designed to complement and enhance human capabilities are introduced and implemented.

References

1. American Institute of Aeronautics and Astronautics. UAV Roundup 2013. Aerospace America, July-August (2013),
   http://www.aerospaceamerica.org/Documents/
   AerospaceAmerica-PDFs-2013/July-August-2013/
   UAVRoundup2013t-AA-Jul-Aug2013.pdf (retrieved)
2. Anderson, C.: Introduction to PixHawk ground control station (including source code) (Web log post) (April 4, 2010),
   http://diydrones.com/profiles/blogs/introduction-to-
   pixhawk-ground?xg_source=activity (retrieved)
3. Arhippainen, L., Pakanen, M., Hickey, S.: Towards a 3D user interface in a touch screen device context: An iterative and evaluation process. In: ACHI 2013: The Sixth International Conference on Advances in Computer-Human Interactions, 47–52 (2013),
   http://www.thinkmind.org/download.php?articleid=achi_2013_
   3_10_20352

4. Aroca, R.V., Péricles, A., de Oliveira, B.S., Marcos, L., Gonçalves, G.: Towards smarter robots with smartphones. In: 5th Workshop in Applied Robotics and Automation, Robocontrol 2012 (2012),
   http://www.natalnet.br/~aroca/RoboControl.pdf (retrieved)
5. Association for Unmanned Vehicle Systems International. The economic impact of unmanned aircraft systems integration in the United States (2013),
   http://higherlogicdownload.s3.amazonaws.com/AUVSI/
   958c920a-7f9b-4ad2-9807-f9a4e95d1ef1/UploadedImages/
   New_Economic%20Report%202013%20Full.pdf (retrieved)
6. Association for Unmanned Vehicle Systems International. Unmanned aircraft system integration into the United States National Airspace System: An assessment of the impact on job creation in the U.S. aerospace industry (2010),
   http://uas.usgs.gov/pdf/AUVSI/0510JobsReport.pdf (retrieved)
7. Black Swift Technologies LLC. Products,
   http://www.blackswifttech.com/products.html (2013) (retrieved)
8. Chao, H., Cao, Y., Chen, Y.: Autopilots for small unmanned aerial vehicles: A survey. International Journal of Control, Automation, and Systems 8(1), 36–44 (2010), doi:10.1007/s12555-010-0105-z
9. Cowling, I.D., Yakimenko, O.A., Whidborne, J.F., Cooke, A.K.: A prototype of an autonomous controller for a quadrotor UAV. In: Proceedings of ECC (2007), Retrieved from the University of Arizona website,
   http://www2.engr.arizona.edu/~sprinkjm/research/c2wt/
   uploads/Main/paper1.pdf
10. Dension (n.d.). WiRC users manual v2.0 (Report no. WRC-9201-1),
    http://wirc.dension.com/sites/default/files/downloads/
    wirc_manual_v2_rel_mod11.pdf
11. Dion, B.: FACE, ARINC, DO-187C avionics standards help U.S. DoD's vision of reusing technology to take off. Military Embedded Systems (2013), http://mil-embedded.com/articles/face-vision-reusable-technology-take-off/ (retrieved)
12. Draper, M.H., Ruff, H.A., Repperger, D.W., Lu, L.G.: Multi-sensory interface concepts supporting turbulence detection by UAV controllers. In: Proceedings of the First Human Performance, Situational Awareness and Automation Conference, pp. 107–112 (2000)
13. Endurance R/C (n.d.). Guide to PWM and PPM, http://www.endurance-rc.com/ppmtut.php (retrieved)
14. Federal Aviation Administration (FAA). Integration of civil unmanned aircraft systems (UAS) in the National Airspace System (NAS) roadmap. Author, Washington, DC (2013a)
15. Federal Aviation Administration (FAA). Unmanned aircraft (UAS): Question and answers (2013b), http://www.faa.gov/about/initiatives/uas/uas_faq/ (retrieved)
16. Federal Aviation Administration. Airworthiness Certification of Unmanned Aircraft Systems and Optionally Piloted Aircraft (2013c),
    http://www.faa.gov/documentLibrary/media/Order/8130.34C.pdf
    (retrieved)
17. Federal Aviation Administration. Integration of civil unmanned aircraft systems (UAS) in the National Airspace System (NAS) roadmap (2013d),
    http://www.faa.gov/about/initiatives/uas/media/
    uas_roadmap_2013.pdf (retrieved)
18. Hayward, K.: Unmanned aerial vehicles: A new industrial system? Retrieved from Royal Aeronautical Society (2013),
    http://aerosociety.com/Assets/Docs/Publications/
    DiscussionPapers/UASDiscussionPaper.pdf

19. Federal Aviation Administration. Advisory circular 20-152 (2005),
    http://www.faa.gov/documentLibrary/media/Advisory_Circular/
    AC_20-152.pdf (retrieved)
20. Harvey, C., Stanton, N., Pickering, C., McDonald, M., Zheng, P.: To twist or poke? A method for identifying usability issues with the rotary controller and touch screen control of in-vehicle information systems. Ergonomics 54(7), 609–625 (2011)
21. Hoskinson, C.: Simplifying control of unmanned systems. Defense Systems (April 26, 2013), http://defensesystems.com/articles/2013/04/26/
    uas-command-and-control.aspx (retrieved)
22. Hopcroft, R., Burchat, E., Vince, J.: Unmanned Aerial Vehicles for Maritime Patrol: Human Factors Issues. DSTO-GD-0463. Department of Defense, Defence Science and Technology Organisation, Commonwealth of Australia (2006)
23. Huanh, Y., Thomson, S.J., Hoffmann, W.C., Lan, Y., Fritz, B.K.: Development and prospect of unmanned aerial vehicle technologies for agricultural production management. International Journal of Agricultural and Biological Engineering 6(3), 1–10 (2013)
24. Humanistic Robotics, Inc. (n.d.). Safe Remote Control System,
    http://humanisticrobotics.com/wp-content/uploads/2013/08/
    HRI_Safe_Remote_Control_System.pdf (retrieved)
25. Kutta Technologies (n.d.). Unified ground control station- UGCS,
    http://www.kuttatech.com/UGCS.html (retrieved)
26. Lacher, A., Maroney, D.: A new paradigm for small UAS. (2012), Retrieved from MITRE Corporation website
    http://www.mitre.org/sites/default/files/pdf/12_2840.pdf
27. Martin, L.: mGCS capabilities guide: Mini and small UAV ground control operator software (2013),
    http://www.lockheedmartin.com/content/dam/lockheed/data/ms2/
    documents/cdl-systems/mGCSCapabilitiesGuide-2013.pdf (retrieved)
28. McKenna, E.: Product focus: Cockpit switches. Avionics Today (January 1, 2013),
    http://www.aviationtoday.com/av/business-and-general-
    aviation/Product-Focus-Cockpit-Switches_78093.html (retrieved)
29. Mostafa, G.: FlyPad-fly your RC plane with your iPhone. The Tech Journal (June 6, 2010),
    http://thetechjournal.com/electronics/iphone/flypad-fly-
    your-rc-plane-with-your-iphone.xhtml (retrieved)
30. NASA. The glass cockpit (2000),
    http://www.nasa.gov/centers/langley/news/factsheets/Glasscoc
    kpit.html (retrieved)
31. Neville, K., Blickensderfer, B., Archer, J., Kaste, K., Luxion, S.: A cognitive work analysis to identify human-machine interface design challenges unique to uninhabited aircraft systems. In: Procedings of the Human Factors and Ergonomics Society 56th Annual Meeting (2012), doi:10.1177/1071813125611094
32. Northrup Grumman Corp. New release: Northrop Grumman, U.S. Navy demonstrate precision, wireless ground handling of X-47B unmanned aircraft (2012),
    http://investor.northropgrumman.com/phoenix.zhtml?c=112386&p
    =irol-newsArticle_print&ID=1759076&highlight= (retrieved)
33. Ott, J.: Announcing Iris, a totally-ready-to-fly UAV quadcopter with our next-gen autopilot,
    http://3drobotics.com/2013/08/iris-press-release/ (2013a) (retrieved)
34. Ott, J.: PX4 and 3D Robotics announce PixHawk,
    http://3drobotics.com/2013/08/px4-and-3d-robotics-announce-
    pixhawk/ (2013b) (retrieved)
35. PixHawk: Computer Vision on Autonomous Aerial Robots. (n.d.). About,
    https://pixhawk.ethz.ch/overview (retrieved)

36. Pullen, S., Enge, P., Lee, J.: Local-area differential GNSS architectures optimized to support unmanned aerial vehicles (UAVs). Presented at the ION Institute of Navigation International Technical Meeting, San Diego, CA (2013), Retrieved from Stanford University GPS Lab website: http://gps.stanford.edu/papers/LADGNSSforUAVNetworksITM2013final.pdf
37. Rogers, W., Fisk, A., McLaughlin, A., Pak, R.: Touch a screen or turn a knob: Choosing the best device for the job. Human Factors 47(2), 271–288 (2005)
38. Skaff, M.: F-35 Lightning II computer vision. SAE International (2010), http://www.fujitsu.com/downloads/MICRO/fma/marcom/convergence/data/papers/2010-01-2330.pdf (retrieved)
39. Space and Naval Warfare Systems Center Pacific. (n.d.). Multi-robot Operator Control Unit (MOCU), http://www.public.navy.mil/spawar/Pacific/Robotics/Pages/MOCU.aspx (retrieved)
40. Stanton, N., Harvey, C., Plant, K., Bolton, L.: To twist, roll, stroke or poke? A study of input devices for menu navigation in the cockpit. Ergonomics 56(4), 590–611 (2013)
41. Stroumtsos, N., Gilbreth, G., Przybylski, S.: An intuitive graphical user interface for small UAS. In: SPIE Proceedings 8741: Unmanned Systems Technology XV (2013), Retrieved from Space and Naval Warfare Systems Center Pacific website: http://www.public.navy.mil/spawar/Pacific/Robotics/Documents/Publications/2013/SPIE2013-Raven.pdf
42. Tang, Z., Zhang, A.: Human-machine-cooperation design methodology for civil aircraft cockpit. In: 2nd International Symposium on Computer, Communication, Control and Automation (2013), Retrieved from Atlantic Press website, http://www.atlantis-press.com/php/download_paper.php?id=10144
43. Tozicka, J., Balata, J., Mikovec, Z.: Diverse trajectory planning for UAV control displays (demonstration). In: AAMAS 2013 Proceedings of the 2013 International Conference on Autonomous Agents and Multi-Agent Systems, pp. 1411–1412 (2013), http://www.ifaamas.org/Proceedings/aamas2013/docs/p1411.pdf (retrieved)
44. Walker, A.M., Miller, D.P., Ling, C.: Spatial orientation aware smartphones for tele-operated robot control in military environments: A usability experiment. Proceedings of the Human Factors and Ergonomics Society Meeting 57(1), 2027–2031 (2013)
45. UAS Europe. SkyView: Ground control station (2013), http://www.uas-europe.se/documents/SkyView%20GCS.pdf (retrieved)
46. UAS Vision. Unmanned community making progress on airspace access (2013), http://www.uasvision.com/2013/08/12/unmanned-community-making-progress-on-airspace-access/ (retrieved)
47. Unmanned Systems Group (n.d.). Ground control stations (GCS), http://www.unmannedgroup.com/index.php?page=2&subpage=6&data=9 (retrieved)
48. U.S. Department of Transportation, John A. Volpe National Transportation Systems Center. Unmanned aircraft system (UAS) service demand 2015-20135: Literature review and projections of future usage (Report no. DOT-VNTSC-DoD-13-01) (2013), http://ntl.bts.gov/lib/48000/48200/48226/UAS_Service_Demand.pdf (retrieved)
49. U.S. Department of Defense. Unmanned systems integrated roadmap FY2013-2038 (Report no. 14-S-0553) (2013), http://www.defense.gov/pubs/DOD-USRM-2013.pdf
50. WiRC (n.d.). WiRC WiFi RC receiver, http://wirc.dension.com/wirc (retrieved)

Roma Crash Map: An Open Data Visualization Tool for the Municipalities of Rome

Valentina Volpi[1], Andrea Ingrosso[2], Mariarosaria Pazzola[2],
Antonio Opromolla[1], and Carlo Maria Medaglia[3]

[1] ISIA Roma Design, Piazza della Maddalena 53, 00196 Rome, Italy
{valentina.volpi84,anto.opro}@gmail.com
[2] CORIS, Sapienza Università di Roma, via Salaria 113, 00198 Rome, Italy
andrea.ingrosso@uniroma1.it, m.pazzola14@gmail.com
[3] DIAG, Sapienza Università di Roma, Piazzale Aldo Moro 5, 00185 Rome, Italy
carlomaria.medaglia@uniroma1.it

Abstract. The open data availability, promoted by the open government approach, does not correspond to an effective and organized use of them with the detriment of both citizens and PAs. We assume that a data visualization tool could help the spread of information in an easy and accessible way, even for what concerns open data. In this paper we will focus on the map, as one of the most suitable tools for the interactive representation of spatial related data. So, we will present the Roma Crash Map platform, a web application that allows to visualize the road crashes open data related to the 19 Municipalities of the city of Rome. In details, we will report the considerations about the selection and design of the visualization tools, according to the purpose to familiarize the users with participating tools integrating maps or more complex geographical systems.

Keywords: Data Visualization, Information Visualization, Road Crashes.

1 Introduction

Nowadays the citizen life in cities and territories is increasingly based on the analysis of large set of data. Whether we consider the technological or the human or the institutional aspect of the *smart cities* [1], *data availability* is an enabling factor to achieve a better quality in the citizen life. In particular, the possibility to freely access to public data and information to use and republish them without any restriction is considered the key factor of a successful governance. The idea that public and available data could lead to *transparency*, *participation*, and *collaboration* among citizens and Public Administrations (hereafter PAs) is strongly sustained by the *open data* (and more generally by the *open government*) approach over an increasingly number of world countries, including Italy [2].

The problem is that the availability of open set of data online, even though consistent with the standardized and interoperable process for the production and the release

S. Yamamoto (Ed.): HIMI 2014, Part II, LNCS 8522, pp. 284–295, 2014.
© Springer International Publishing Switzerland 2014

of open data, is not sufficient to engage the citizen on the particular matter or information contained into the dataset.

As a result of this observation, we assume that from the raw data to a "usable" one there is an entire process to implement, which necessarily includes *data visualization* design. In fact, we also assume that the latter were a well-defined and experienced way to make data more user-friendly.

In this paper we will present Roma Crash Map (hereafter RCM), a web application for the visualization on a map of open data about road crashes occurred in Rome between 2012 and 2013 (June), in order to show a possible way to bring open data to citizens and PAs.

Moreover we will focus on the map as favorite visualization tool for the open data that require spatial distribution and for all citizens (not only experts) willing to be aware in order to participate in smart cities and territories issues. Regarding this, we observe that, despite of the great spread and talk about the open data and the geo-visualization tools, a deeper attention needs to be paid towards *usability* and *user experience*. In section II we will introduce the concepts of open government and open data, as wider framework from which the tool we designed originated. Then, in section III we will give an overview on the state of art about usability evaluation of geo-visualization tools. A detailed description of the RCM platform will be given in section IV, along with the reflections, in section V, about the constraints met and the choices occurred during the designing of the user interfaces. Findings and future work will be illustrated into the last section (Conclusions).

2   Open Government and Open Data

Open data is an extended concept crossing different fields and fostering the spread of knowledge [3]. In the government field, the term is connected with *transparency* and *accountability* [5]. This is the basis for a smarter government, where PAs collaborate with citizens, enterprises, and communities on a specific territory, in order to provide them with services and applications addressing public and private demands.

As a practical application of these principles derived from the *open government* doctrine, whose cornerstone is the Open Government Directive issued on December 2009, many institutions and governments have distributed online the open dataset they collected. In Italy the national catalogue of open data (dati.gov.it), stemmed from several government data stores, has been published on October the 18th, 2011 [2].

In details, a dataset is considered *open* when it is made available online in open and freely accessible formats, without copyright restrictions, patents or other forms of control that restrict its re-use, and redistributed by anyone. It is subject only, at most, to the requirement to *attribute* and *sharealike* [6-7]. In order to be consistent with the international standard for the open data, the information released should be: *complete*, *primary*, *timely*, *accessible*, *machine-readable*, *non-proprietary*, free from licenses restricting their use (*freely-usable*), *re-usable*, *discoverable*, and *permanent* [7-8]. In general they had to be published in an open platform independent format that can be retrieved, downloaded, indexed, and searched by commonly used web search applications [9].

There are different formats used for open data. In this regard, the W3C elaborated a cataloging model based on a scale of values from one to five stars, i.e. from raw data (unstructured and not reprocessable file) to linked open data (interoperable open format). Only formats from the third level can be considered "open" [10].

Anyway, the doctrine at the basis of the *open data* promotes the largest spread of data, even raw. As a consequence, with the increasing of the number of data shared, also *data visualization* tools and *info-graphics* had spread, due to their ability in communicating information in a clearer and more effective way.

3   Related Work

The academic literature offers many studies about the transformation of data and geo-data in a usable form. First of all, in [11], the authors argue that the simple operation of releasing open data does not entail the immediate understanding of data by users. In particular, the bigger the dataset is, the more likely the user is unable to extract useful information. This difficulty can be overcome thank to efficient visualization tools [12], which need to be studied through usability methods [13].

According to [14], "*data visualization is the graphical presentation of data that can help reveal important traits and relationship*". In [15], the author identifies five steps in order to make visual communication more effective and efficient: 1 - definition of the problem; 2 - choice of relevant data; 3 - adoption of a visual matrix for the treatment of data; 4 - conversion of data into graphical visualization; 5 - interpretation and decision. This method is similar to the EDA (Exploratory Data Analysis) approach [16], where the visual representation is used to encourage statisticians to better explore data, and possibly formulate hypotheses. In order to obtain from a dataset the requested information that he/she needs, user should be able to zoom and filter the data [17].

The map is one of the better tools through which represent patterns and relationships in data, especially when integrated with other representation methods to provide different perspectives of data in multiple linked views [13]. In most cases, digital maps are the representation of data contained within a GIS, a system of storage, manipulation, analysis and management of geo-referenced data. Since GIS are complex systems [32], in the academic literature the usability studies focused on the evaluation of the operational tools rather than on the maps [18]. For these tools, a specific evaluation methodology is needed [13]. One of the aims of these studies is to facilitate the interaction, also on the part of users without expertise in using GIS [33].

Moving beyond the geographical aspect, the maps are considered as tools of knowledge construction [19]. In fact, especially web-based online mapping allows users to explore, analyze and visualize spatial dataset to better understand patterns. Moreover the maps display many different data and information (spatial, social, political, etc.) in a very intelligible way [20] and are useful in supporting problem's exploration and decision making, mainly if united to other graphical presentations [21] or multiple criteria decisions models (MCDM) [14].

In this context, GIS and other web-based mapping software can also foster the citizen's engagement and collaboration [20-22-23]. With regard to this, we mention: participatory geographic information system (PGIS) [24], public participation geographic information system (PPGIS) [25-26], volunteered geographic information system (VGIS) [27], and other open map tools generally based on open source software and web 2.0 tools [28-29]. Besides being valuable communication means used to actively involve citizens, they can be used also as instruments for monitoring the quality of public service in all its stages of implementation [30-31].

Mobility data offers several challenges in data analysis and visualization. Their attributes are not only spatial [34], but also temporal [35]. In [12], a description of the most used techniques for spatio-temporal data visualization is provided. Anyway, the map is the most appropriate interface to represent mobility data [34], since they can provide users clear and accessible information, deliver services more efficiently, and support decisions. Transportation, parking places, and traffic are a few examples of fields of application that take benefit from mobility data visualization [20].

4   Roma Crash Map

Roma Crash Map platform is a web application that allows to visualize the data about road crashes occurred in the Municipalities of Rome between the 1st January 2012 and 18th June 2013. Data is provided by the Local Police Roma Capitale and released by the Municipality of Rome at the dedicated web site (http://dati.comune.Roma.it). It is distinguished into three different datasets on the basis of the period to which they relate. Through the interaction with the map of the city of Rome divided into 19 Municipalities and a set of filters, the user can browse and compare available data about road crashes. We consider as possible interested users the following categories: PAs, which can quickly "visualize" the extent of the road safety problem and decide to use the data in other monitoring and decision-making tools; citizens interested in retrieving and comparing information about road crashes for different reasons, e.g. dangerousness of the area where he/she lives; journalists seeking for data useful for their reports; businesses, which might be interested in such data within the preparation of their marketing strategies. To create different map and graphs, the user combines some default type of data extracted from the dataset:

1. *Time slot of the occurred crash.* The time slots have been divided into periods of four hours (all the time slots; 00.00-02.59; 03.00-05.59; 06.00-08.59; 09.00-11.59; 12.00-14.59; 15.00-17.59; 18.00-20.59; 21.00-23.59).
2. *Year* (all years; 2012; 2013).
3. *Period of the year* (all the time; the first quarter; the second quarter; the third quarter; the fourth quarter).
4. *Weather* (all conditions; clear; fog; cloudy; rain; high wind; hail; snow; grazing sun).
5. *Lighting* (all lights; daytime hours; enough; insufficient; not present).

By default the web application shows the number of road crashes occurred on the basis of all the possible variables (all the time slots; all years; all the time; all weather conditions; all lights) in all the 19 Municipalities of Rome. The user can set the parameters of his/her research by selecting some filters corresponding to the variables above mentioned (Fig. 1). Another type of query is to compare two Municipalities on the basis of these variables. In addition to the said filters, the user has to select the name of the two Municipalities to compare. Through the reset function, the web application set the filters on the initial state.

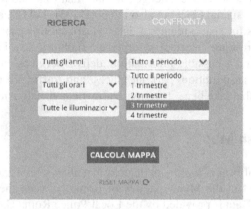

Fig. 1. Users can set the parameters of his/her research by selecting some filters

The results of the query are visualized on various tools, in respect of the benefits provided by each one in the information communication: interactive map (Fig. 2), graphs (Fig. 3) and tables (Fig. 4).

The user can select a specified Municipality by clicking the corresponding area on the map. The graphs and the table change, as a consequence, showing only the data about the selected Municipality.

The map provided in RCM (Fig. 2) is a thematic map obtained through a web mapping application, here OpenStreetMap. It represents the different Municipalities' areas on the basis of the numbers of crashes occurred according to the variation of different statistical variables. In details, the colors of the different areas vary proportionally according to the quantitative value of the data. Three different *hues* (Table 1) are used as a progression indicating the result of the comparison between the number of crashes occurred in the different geographic areas (Municipalities) in respect of three defined quantitative values (maximum, medium, and minimum number of crushes occurred). On the other hand, the *opacity progression*, from a dark to a light shade of the same hue, indicates the extent of the number of crashes occurred within a single zone in comparison to the maximum and minimum value in the dataset (according to the statistical variables set) (Fig. 5).

Below the map, four graphs, one for each type of information, visualize the comparison among the 19 Municipalities on the basis of the variation in the number of road crashes, deaths, injuries, and unharmed occurred in the specified conditions.

The graph chosen to visualize the results is the *polar area* chart, which gives an easy view of the value of each Municipality in respect to the others. Each Municipality occupies a portion of the chart characterized by a specific color (Fig. 3).

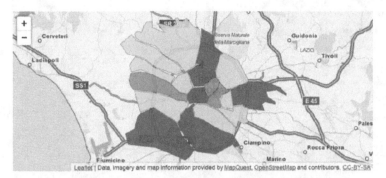

Fig. 2. Users can visualize on the map the results of the query

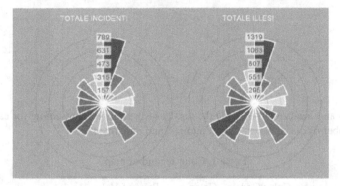

Fig. 3. Users can visualize on the graphs the results of the query. In particular, the above illustrated graphs represent for each Municipality the number of road crashes and of unharmed.

Another type of visualization is the table, which allows the user to better examine the numerical data value. The user can click the header of each column to sort (from the higher to the lower value) the list of Municipalities by number of the Municipality, road crashes, deaths, injuries, and unharmed. The table is hidden by default and can be shown or hidden by selecting the button, respectively, plus or minus.

As an additional reminder of the variables set for the query that is currently visualized, a legend with icons and tags is present below the map. In fact, despite the change of the filters' options, the results are not shown on the map until the user does not press the *calculate map* button. So a sort of visual reminder is needed.

Research and *Compare* are the main function of RCM that allow the query of the dataset, anyway there is also a function to download the data in the CSV format.

The user can interact with the map by scaling, zooming, panning, and shifting it, or selecting the colored area of Municipalities.

Municipio	Incidenti	Illesi	Feriti	Morti
Municipio I-Centro Storico	788	1281	536	2
Municipio II-Parioli	379	543	187	0
Municipio III-Nomentana-San Lorenzo	157	295	86	1
Municipio IV-Monte Sacro	370	686	190	3
Municipio V-Tiburtina	349	639	227	2
Municipio VI-Prenestino	234	394	163	3
Municipio VII-Centocelle	286	507	172	2
Municipio VIII-delle Torri	516	909	370	4
Municipio IX-San Giovanni	281	527	166	2
Municipio X-Cinecittà	350	720	234	0
Municipio XI-Appia Antica	343	670	198	3
Municipio XII-EUR	430	861	245	2
Municipio XIII-Ostia	524	1003	336	2
Municipio XV-Arvalia	312	625	197	0
Municipio XVI-Monteverde	289	527	135	2
Municipio XVII-Prati	312	585	153	0
Municipio XVIII-Aurelia	369	699	211	2
Municipio XIX-Monte Mario	293	481	156	0
Municipio XX-Cassia Flaminia	369	702	202	4
Totale #	6951	12664	4164	34

Fig. 4. Users can visualize on the table the results of the query, representing for each Municipality the number of road crashes, deaths, injuries, and unharmed

Table 1. Color legend of map

Color Code	Color	Type of Value
#bb3743	red	higher value
#e9ed5a	yellow	medium value
#6eacb6	blue	lower value

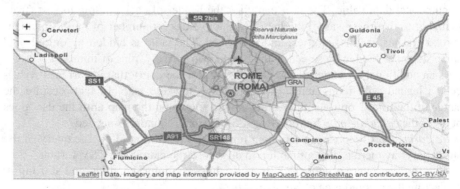

Fig. 5. Hue progression and opacity progression

The tools included within the platform make available for the user the following operation: locate, categorize, cluster, rank, compare (Table 2). These correspond to some of the basic visualizations operators that users might perform in a visual environment indicated by [13].

Table 2. Basic visualization operators and related RCM's tools

Visualization operator	Operational visualization task	Tools available
Locate	Indicate data items of a certain range of value	Graphs and table
Categorize	Define all the regions on the display, and draw boundaries. Indicate spatial positioning of elements of interest and spatial proximity among the different elements	Map divided into different colored areas corresponding to the 19 Municipalities of Rome
Cluster	Find differences in the data on the display	Filters, different colored map's areas, graphs, and table
Rank	Indicate the best and worst cases in the display for an attribute	Table with four type of information that can be sorted by clicking on the header of the relative column
Compare	Compare values at different spatial locations and the order of importance of objects (data items) accordingly	Compare filters, different colored map's areas, and graphs

5   Considerations about the Design of Roma Crash Map

Road safety is a sensitive issue, affecting both citizens and PAs. Consequently the need for information in respect of this issue is always high. We deem that, through RCM, the presentation of the information as derived from the dataset can be equally interesting and affordable both to professional actors and to inexpert users.

The larger part of the academic literature about the use of road crashes open data concerns the study of the determining causes of the crashes, along with possible solutions, and the use of related road crashes maps, often integrated with the GIS [36]. We found many examples of map disseminating open data about road crashes, especially in UK: CrashMap.co.uk, UK Casuality Map, Crash: Death on Britain's roads, Chicago Crash Browser, RoadSkillMap. In Italy two maps of road crashes were developed on the basis of data released by ISTAT (National Institute of Statistics), but no one focuses on the single Municipalities of Rome.

From an analysis of these maps, we found analogies and differences with RCM. In the former case, the use of different colors representing the crashes' numbers or seriousness, and the presence of filters (e.g. type of person involved, age, and seriousness) to set map and graphs.

In the second instance, the presence of a static map, the use of graphical elements to differentiate the type of information, the presence of a textual overview, and the representation of the exact location of crashes occurred.

In working with the data of the public datasets we faced different criticalities that influence the final aspect of the data visualization tool. Among the main problems observed there is the type of data contained into the released dataset. In fact, the datasets used in RCM were not a well-organized, consistent, and formatting error free set and were subjected to vary as a consequence of administrative changes[1]. Moreover they referred to three different time periods and had a different number of occurrences. So, before the development of the tool, it was necessary to operate on the data in order to make them usable within a single database created ad hoc.

We chose to use in the first place the variables that gave a panoramic of the road crashes in the city of Rome. Since the precise information on the location (address) of the single crashes was lacking, we chose to not focus on the information regarding the single event, such as the type of person involved in the accident with year of birth, gender, type of injury recorded, etc. This allows a simplification of the tool and the delivery of more consistent information to the users.

So, we tried to give the full set of data through the clearest and simplest user interface. The tools are shown on the basis of a hierarchical scale centered on the level of inference of the information at a first glance. In fact, the map and the graphs are immediately intelligible, while all the "numbers" included in the table (hidden by default) need a more careful reading. We maintained the assumption that using visual communication means is more useful and effective in getting involved the user, than showing at first "numbers". Moreover in showing too many elements at the first time risks to create confusion and disorientation in the user.

Lastly, in choosing the colors for the progressions, we considered the work of [37], but we adapted it to the need to simultaneously view two measurements about the numbers of road crashes occurred, i.e. the one related to the variation from one geographical area to another, and the other related to the extent of the phenomenon within a single zone. In addition, it was necessary to show the geographic information under the colored areas. So we mixed the full spectral progression, from which we select the two hues at the extremis (red and blue) and one at the medium (yellow), and the opacity progression, interpreted as a single-hue progressions, where the chosen color fade from a dark shade (the higher value in the dataset) to a very light or white shade (the lower value in the dataset) of relatively the same hue. In general, in choosing the colors to use we considered their visibility and their ease of identification, even at the lowest level of opacity. Moreover, in the selection of the three different hues we individuated a progression which was easy to distinguish and perceive even by a part of visual impaired users, although consistent as possible with the most common progressions used in cartography or *choropleth maps*. The colors were also used according to their cultural significance, as the red and yellow are warm colors generally indicating

---

[1] Via the Regional Law n. 25 of 6 March 1992, the XIV Municipality merged with the City of Fiumicino, causing an inconsistency of the Municipalities numeration. Moreover with the Capitoline Assembly Resolution no. 11/2013 the number of Municipalities has been reduced from 19 to 15. Anyway for the released dataset was still effective the division into 19 Municipalities.

an alarm or danger more or less intense, while the blue is a cool color conveying feelings of calm and relaxation. Another possible solution being considered for the visualization of the two measurements on a single map was the superposition of a texture to the colored area. However, because of the features of the web mapping tool used, it has not been possible to adopt this option [36].

6   Conclusions and Future Work

In designing the RCM we identified some features that can improve user experience when interacting with an open data visualization tool:

1. Use of updated and standardized datasets
2. Use of multiple methods of data visualization (map, graphs, tables, etc.)
3. Use of thematic maps as facilitators of "visual thinking" about spatially related data
4. Dynamicity and interactivity of data visualization tools
5. Hierarchical organization of the data visualization tools
6. Consistency of information
7. Use of visual reminders

Anyway, to verify if RCM effectively makes immediately usable the data and fosters the spread of the information contained into the open datasets, in future work we intend to evaluate the system through usability tests with the different categories of final users. In the intentions, RCM is an elemental tool to construct knowledge, allowing exploration at a basic level and fostering the adoption of more complex tools, e.g. integrating GIS. RCM offers some function to compare and filter data, which make clear to the user the content of the dataset. In fact RCM can be an example of how to show open data in a familiar way to the citizen, since maps can be used at different levels of the open government process, bringing different levels of benefits for citizens. In this regard, in the future, not only we will evaluate the tool, but we also will consider how it can be combined with monitoring ad decision making tools. In this context we will also study the utility and the mode of presentation of open data in mobility.

References

1. Nam, T., Pardo, T.A.: Conceptualizing smart city with dimensions of technology, people, and institutions. In: 12th Annual Int. Digital Government Research Conf.: Digital Government Innovation in Challenging Times, pp. 282–291. ACM, New York (2011)
2. Dati.gov, http://www.dati.gov.it/
3. Open definition, http://opendefinition.org/od/
4. May, P., Ehrlich, H.C., Steinke, T.: ZIB Structure Prediction Pipeline: Composing a Complex Biological Workflow through Web Services. In: Nagel, W.E., Walter, W.V., Lehner, W. (eds.) Euro-Par 2006. LNCS, vol. 4128, pp. 1148–1158. Springer, Heidelberg (2006)

5. Brito, J.: Hack, Mash, & Peer: Crowdsourcing Government Transparency. The Columbia Science and Technology Law Review IX, 119–157 (2008)
6. Open Knowledge Foundation: Open Data Handbook Documentation (2012), http://opendatahandbook.org/pdf/OpenDataHandbook.pdf
7. Cornero, A., Belisario, E., Epifani, S.: Vademecum Open Data: come rendere aperti i dati delle pubbliche amministrazioni. Formez PA, Dipartimento della Funzione Pubblica (2011), http://www.dati.gov.it/sites/default/files/VademecumOpenData.pdf
8. Transparency International Georgia: Ten Open Data Guidelines (2012), http://transparency.ge/en/ten-open-data-guidelines
9. White House, Open Government Directive (2009), http://www.whitehouse.gov/sites/default/files/omb/assets/memoranda_2010/m10-06.pdf
10. W3C, Linked Data - Design Issues (2006), http://www.w3c.org/DesignIssues/LinkedData.html
11. Vande Moere, A., Hill, D.: Designing for the Situated and Public Visualization of Urban Data. Journal of Urban Technology 19(2), 25–46 (2012)
12. Goncalves, T., Afonso, A.P., Martins, B.: Visual Analysis of Mobility Data. In: 14th IEEE International Conference on Mobile Data Management (MDM), vol. 2, pp. 7–10 (2013)
13. Koua, E.L., Maceachren, A., Kraak, M.-J.: Evaluating the usability of visualization methods in an exploratory geovisualization environment. International Journal of Geographical Information Science 20(4), 197–200 (2006)
14. Jankowski, P., Andrienko, N., Andrienko, G.: Map-centered exploratory approach to multiple criteria spatial decision-making. International Journal of Geographic Information Science 15(2), 101–127 (2001)
15. Bertin, J.: La graphique et le traitement graphique de l'information. Paris Flammarion (1977)
16. Tukey, J.W.: Exploratory Data Analysis. Addison-Wesley (1977)
17. Wongsuphasawat, K., Filippova, D., VanDaniker, M., Pack, M., Olea, A.: Visual Analytics for Transportation Incident Datasets. Transportation Research Record: Journal of the Transportation Research Board 2138, 135–145 (2009)
18. Andrienko, N., Andrienko, G., Voss, H., Bernardo, F., Hipolito, J., Kretchmer, U.: Testing the Usability of Interactive Maps in CommonGIS. Cartography and Geographic Information Science 29(4), 325–342 (2002)
19. Crampton, J.W.: Maps as social constructions: Power, communication and visualization. Progress in Human Geography 25(2), 235–252 (2001)
20. Daniel, S., Doran, M.A.: geoSmartCity: geomatics contribution to the smart city. In: 14th ACM Annual International Conference on Digital Government Research, pp. 65–71 (2013)
21. Casner, S.M.: A task-analytic approach to the automated design of graphic presentations. ACM Transactions on Graphics 10, 111–151 (1991)
22. Ganapati, S.: Using Geographic Information Systems to Increase Citizen Engagement. In: IBM Center for the Business of Government (2010)
23. Tao, W.: Interdisciplinary urban GIS for smart cities: advancements and opportunities. In: Geo-Spatial Information Science (2013)
24. Dunn, C.E.: Participatory GIS-a people's GIS? Progress in Human Geography 31(5), 616–637 (2007)
25. Kingston, R.: Public Participation in Local Policy Decision-making: The Role of Web-based Mapping. The Cartographic Journal 44(2), 138–144 (2007)

26. Sieber, R.: Public participation geographic information systems: a literature review and framework. Annals of the Association of American Geographers 96(3), 491–507 (2006)
27. Seeger, C.J.: The role of facilitated volunteered geographic information in the landscape planning and site design process. GeoJournal, Springer Netherlands 72(3-4), 199–213 (2008)
28. Hall, G.B., Chipeniuk, R., Feick, R., Leahy, M.G., Deparday, V.: Community-based production of geographic information using open source software and Web 2.0. International Journal of Geographical Information Science 24, 761–781 (2010)
29. Goodchild, M.F.: Citizens as sensors: the world of volunteered geography. GeoJournal 69(4), 211–221 (2007)
30. Elmorshidy, A.: The other side of the e-government coin: monitor from the people: building a new double-sided e-government conceptual model. International Journal of Business Strategy 12(1), 65–75 (2012)
31. Balena, P., Bonifazi, A., Mangialardi, G.: Smart Communities Meet Urban Management: Harnessing the Potential of Open Data and Public/Private Partnerships through Innovative E-Governance Applications. In: Murgante, B., et al. (eds.) ICCSA 2013, Part IV. LNCS, vol. 7974, pp. 528–540. Springer, Heidelberg (2013)
32. Komarkova, J., Jedlicka, M., Hub, M.: Usability user testing of selected web-based GIS applications. W. Trans. on Comp. 9(1), 21–30 (2010)
33. Nagel, T., Duval, E., Vande Moere, A.: Interactive Exploration of a Geospatial Network Visualization. In: 2012 ACM Annual Conference Extended Abstracts on Human Factors in Computing Systems Extended Abstracts, pp. 557–572 (2012)
34. Miaou, S.P., Song, J.J., Mallick, B.K.: Roadway Traffic Crash Mapping: A Space-Time Modeling Approach. Journal of Transportation and Statistics 6(1), 33–57 (2003)
35. Andrienko, G., Andrienko, N., Demsar, U., Dransch, D., Dykes, J., Fabrikant, S.I., Jern, M., Kraak, M.-J., Schumann, H., Tominski, C.: Space, time and visual analytics. Int.Journal of Geographical Information Science 24(10), 1577–1600 (2010)
36. Pazzola, M., Ingrosso, A., Opromolla, A., Volpi, V., Medaglia, C.M., Calabrìa, A.: Progettare con gli Open Data. Roma Crash Map: una piattaforma sugli incidenti stradali nel Comune di Roma. In: Forum PA, La Smart City al Servizio del cittadino. La Call for Papers di Smart Cities Exhibition 2013, vol. 1, pp. 91–103 (2013)
37. Robinson, A.H., Morrison, J.L., Muehrke, P.C., Kimmerling, A.J., Guptill, S.C.: Elements of Cartography, 6th edn. Wiley, New York (1995)

Predictive Probability Model of Pilot Error Based on CREAM

Xiaoyan Zhang[1], Hongjun Xue[1], Yingchun Chen[2], Lin Zhou[2], and Gaohong Lu[1]

[1] School of Aeronautics, Northwestern Polytechnical University, Shanxi Xi'an 710072, China
[2] Commercial Aircraft Corporation of China, Ltd. Shanghai 201210, China
zxyliuyan@sina.com, xuehj@nwpu.edu.cn

Abstract. Prediction of pilot error is key of human-machine interface design in the cockpit, and is also an effective way on the reduction of accident ratio caused by human error. CREAM (Cognitive Reliability and Error Analysis Method) has been chosen to build the predictive probability model of pilot error based on investigation of various methods. The pilot error model built can be used not only to analysis the reason of accident but predict the error probability in particular scene. The model is validated through the experiment that pilots read the altitude during flight in different visibilities and time limits. The CPC (common performance conditions) including cockpit design, crew communication and other environment such as weather condition is always analyzed and calculated during the whole task analysis and then the reason of pilot error can be discovered qualitatively. The results are important for cockpit design to improve the airplane safety.

Keywords: pilot error, CREAM, error probability prediction, human-machine interface, cockpit design.

1 Introduction

Human error during flight is an inaccuracy decision or action which influences system performance or efficiency even safety. The researcher and engineer always use the following models to analysis the human error such as SHEL[1], Reason[2, 3], HFACS[4, 5], CREAM[6,7,8,9,10] and MEDA[5]. The methods all have their advantages and disadvantages. CREAM as the typical second generation human reliability analysis method considers the error probability can be controlled by the ability of people controlling the situation. The model emphasizes the human performance is not a isolated random action but depends on the task condition or the environment. The task condition can determine the human response through influencing the human cognitive mode and the following effects in different cognitive situations. CREAM can not only analysis the reason of accident but predict the error probability in particular scene. The paper analysis the pilot error probability during approach and landing

S. Yamamoto (Ed.): HIMI 2014, Part II, LNCS 8522, pp. 296–304, 2014.
© Springer International Publishing Switzerland 2014

based on CREAM. The causation of error is also be analyzed. The method is validated by the experiment in the pilot simulator.

2   Error Probability Predictive Method Based on CREAM

The essence of CREAM is used to predict the error probability. for the purpose, First, analyze the people's task and the actual effect of the action, and then the basic CFP(cognitive failure probability) can be calculated, the final predictive error probability can be got by the analyzing the CPC(common performance condition) which can revise the basic CFP.

CREAM divide the cognitive action as observe, interpret, plan and execute, and every group has some failure modes. the cognitive action includes coordinate, communication, comparison, diagnose, evaluation, execution, maintain, monitor, observe, plan, record, adjustment, glance, inspection. And different cognitive action has its own cognitive performance. For CREAM the responding relation of the two is shown in table 1, and the basic CFP is shown in table 2.

Table 1. Cognitive activity and corresponding cognitive function

activity	cognitive function			
	observe	interpret	plan	execute
coordinate			√	√
communication				√
compare		√		
diagnose		√	√	
evaluate		√	√	
execute				√
identification		√		
maintain			√	√
monitor	√	√		
observe	√			
plan			√	
record		√		√
adjust	√			√
scan	√			
examine	√	√		

Table 2. Basic failure probability of cognitive failure mode

Cognitive function	failure mode	Basic value
observe	O1 Observable object error	0.001
	O2 wrong recognize	0.07
	O3 no observe action	0.07
interpret	I1 fail to diagnose	0.2
	I2 decision error	0.01
	I3 delay to interpret	0.01
plan	P1 wrong priority	0.01
	P2 inappropriate plan	0.01
execute	E1 wrong execution mode	0.003
	E2 wrong execution time	0.003
	E3 wrong execution object	0.005
	E4 wrong execution sequence	0.003
	E5 execution omission	0.03

CREAM has 9 CPC factors and everyone has its own three level, which affects the human performance as improving, inducing, and inapparent. Table 3 is the basic weight value of CFP.

$$P=1-\prod_{i=1}^{4}(1-CFP) \qquad (1)$$

Where, $CFP_{revised} = CFP_{basic} \times \sum weight$.

CFP_{basic} is the basic value of CFP in table 2, and $\sum weight$ is the product of all weight coefficient of CPC in table 3.

Table 3. CPC and its influence for reliability

No.	CPC	level	Impact of human reliability	Weight factor of cognitive function			
				observe	interpret	plan	execute
1	Perfectness of organization	Highly effective	improve	1.0	1.0	0.8	0.8
		effective	non- significant	1.0	1.0	1.0	1.0
		ineffective	lower	1.0	1.0	1.2	1.2
		Bad effect	lower	1.0	1.0	1.2	1.2
2	Working condition	superior	improve	0.8	0.8	1.0	0.8
		matching	non- significant	1.0	1.0	1.0	1.0
		mismatching	lower	2.0	2.0	1.0	2.0

Table 3. (*continued*)

3	Perfectness of HMI and operation support	support	improve	0.5	1.0	1.0	0.5
		general	non-significant	1.0	1.0	1.0	1.0
		tolerable	lower	1.0	1.0	1.0	1.0
		inadaptation	lower	5.0	1.0	1.0	5.0
4	Availability of plan/procedure	appropriate	improve	0.8	1.0	0.5	0.8
		accept	non-significant	1.0	1.0	1.0	1.0
		inappropriate	lower	2.0	1.0	5.0	2.0
5	The number of simultaneous objects	less than capability	improve	1.0	1.0	1.0	1.0
		Match with capability	non-significant	1.0	1.0	1.0	1.0
		more than capability	lower	2.0	1.0	5.0	2.0
6	Available time	enough	improve	0.5	0.5	0.5	0.5
		insufficient temporarily	non-significant	1.0	1.0	1.0	1.0
		insufficient always	lower	5.0	5.0	5.0	5.0
7	Working time	Daytime (adjust)	non-significant	1.0	1.0	1.0	1.0
		Nighttime (non-adjust)	lower	1.2	1.2	1.2	1.2
8	sufficient of training and experience	sufficient, experienced	improve	0.8	0.5	0.5	0.8
		sufficient, limited experience	non-significant	1.0	1.0	1.0	1.0
		insufficient	lower	2.0	5.0	5.0	2.0
9	Cooperation of the whole team	Highly effective	improve	0.5	0.5	0.5	0.5
		effective	non-significant	1.0	1.0	1.0	1.0
		ineffective	non-significant	1.0	1.0	1.0	1.0
		Bad effect	lower	2.0	2.0	2.0	5.0

3   Experiment

Experiment Settings. Experiment scene is assumed that an airplane of single engine landings under low visible condition and depends on the instrument to complete the task.

First group is a relative perfect CPC, and the altitude panel is digital, and the response time is not limited.

Second group models pilot has inadequate time to response, other conditions are the same as the first group.

Third group models pilot has inadequate time to response, and the interface is not so matching for pilot, which is the same as the first group.

The response time and the accuracy of the objects are both recorded.

The experiment is executed in man-machine-environment lab and the lighting, humidity, temperature and so on are all as usual.

The testees are all students who have sufficient train for the task; everyone will be tested 20 times.

Experiment Results. The experiment results are recorded as shown in table 4.

Table 4. The record data of experiment

No.	Altimeter (m)	Correct axtion	action by testee	accuracy	Reaction time(ms)
	810	g	g	1	3338
	430	g	g	1	979
			......		
Group one	190	e	e	1	1172
	830	g	e	0	3806
	Error probability 0.0278		RT 1435.628ms		Over time 0
	810	g	g	1	3338
	430	g	g	1	979
			......		
Group two	190	e	e	1	1172
	830	g	e	0	3806
	Error probability 0.0367		RT 1053.306ms		Over time 2
	810	g	g	1	3338
	430	g	g	1	979
			......		
Group three	190	e	e	1	1172
	830	g	e	0	3806
	Error probability 0.0778		RT 1159.611ms		Over time 3

The predictive error probability based on CREAM. For the CREAM method, the cognitive process of testee is simplified as four actions that are shown in figure 1.

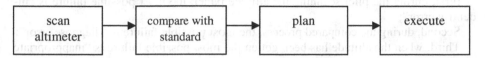

Fig. 1. The procedure of pilot reading altimeter

As mentioned before, there are four steps to calculate the predictive probability.
1. the CPC level and the weight coefficient
For the first experiment group, the conditions are all effective. The CPC level and the weight coefficients are shown in table 5.

Table 5. CPC and weight factor of first group

CPC	level	Impact for human reliability	Weight factor			
			observe	interpret	Plan	execute
Perfectness of organization	Highly effective	improve	1.0	1.0	0.8	0.8
Working condition	superior	improve	0.8	0.8	1.0	0.8
Perfectness of HMI and operation support	support	improve	0.5	1.0	1.0	0.5
Availability of plan/procedure	appropriate	improve	0.8	1.0	0.5	0.8
The number of simultaneous objects	less than capability	improve	1.0	1.0	1.0	1.0
Available time	enough	improve	0.5	0.5	0.5	0.5
Working time	daytime (adjust)	Non-significant	1.0	1.0	1.0	1.0
sufficient of training and experience	sufficient, limited experience	Non-significant	1.0	1.0	1.0	1.0
Cooperation of the whole team	Highly effective	improve	0.5	0.5	0.5	0.5

The second group has almost the same CPC as the first group except the time limit; the third group has also not so good man-machine matching comparing with the second group. The weight coefficients should be revised accordingly.

2. identify the most possible cognitive failure mode

To find the most possible cognitive failure, we should analyze the cognitive sequence.

First, during the pilot scanning the altitude panel, the most possible failure is "indentify error";

Second, during the compared process, the most possible failure is "diagnose error";

Third, when the altitude has been gotten the most possible failure is "inappropriate plan";

The last one is the testee does the action as he planned, so the most possible failure is "motion error".

3. the predictive failure probability

For the three groups the $CFP_{revised}$ are shown in table 6 to table 8.

Table 6. The calculated result of group one

Sequence	Cognitive activity	Cognitive function	Failure mode	Basic value	Weight	CFP
scan	scan	observe	O2	0.07	0.08	0.0056
compare	compare	interpret	I1	0.02	0.2	0.004
plan	plan	plan	P2	0.01	0.1	0.001
execute	execute	execute	E1	0.003	0.064	0.000192

Table 7. The calculated result of group two

Sequence	Cognitive activity	Cognitive function	Failure mode	Basic value	Weight	CFP
scan	scan	observe	O2	0.07	0.16	0.0112
compare	compare	interpret	I1	0.02	0.4	0.008
plan	plan	plan	P2	0.01	0.2	0.002
execute	execute	execute	E1	0.003	0.128	0.000384

Table 8. The calculated result of group three

Sequence	Cognitive activity	Cognitive function	Failure mode	Basic value	Weight	CFP
scan	scan	observe	O2	0.07	0.32	0.0224
compare	compare	interpret	I1	0.02	0.4	0.008
plan	plan	plan	P2	0.01	0.2	0.002
execute	execute	execute	E1	0.003	0.256	0.000768

We can use the equation (1) to calculate the error probability as follows:

$$P1 = 1 - \prod_{i=1}^{4}(1 - CFP) = 0.010758$$

$$P2 = 1 - \prod_{i=1}^{4} (1 - CFP) = 0.021448087$$

$$P3 = 1 - \prod_{i=1}^{4} (1 - CFP) = 0.032904$$

So the different error probability under three different CPC is 0.01, 0.02, and 0.03.

4   Discussion

The experiment results and the calculated data are both shown in table 9.

Table 9. Comparison result

group	Calculated	experiment
one	0.0108	0.0278
two	0.0214	0.0367
three	0.0329	0.0778

The calculation result is on the rise that is the same as the experiment result in the three different CPC. But the two also have differences. The exact value is not so accordant. The experiment data is greater than calculated value and the experiment data of group three increased sharply compared with group two. The two differences of result are analyzed as: 1) in the experiment the pilot manipulating the gear is substituted as key-press which may decrease the difficult of execution; 2) cognitive failure mode is discrete with CREAM, but in fact the condition which influences the human operation is not discrete. For example, for this experiment condition, in the "sufficient of training and experience" condition, the impact for the cognitive mode maybe is between "non-significant" and "lower" according to the testee level; 3) for the most possible cognitive failure mode choose, CREAM can only choose one, but sometimes there is definitely two choices. When subject chooses the different one there is a different result.

5   Optimized Suggestions

Although the CREAM has some shortages, the method is also meaningful for the purpose to decrease human error and keep security. The CREAM used in this research is not for the quantitive probability but to find the weakness of human-machine-environment during the analysis and evaluation procedure and improve the system reliability.

There are also some advices for the use of CREAM: 1) to find the most possible failure mode, the researcher should consider the capability of human itself. For different person there is a different performance; 2) the method which can make the

"Impact for human reliability" and "weight factor" consecutive should be researched and developed.

Acknowledgement. The paper is granted under National Basic Research Program of China (No.2010CB734101).

References

1. Civil Aviation Authority. Human Factors in Aircraft Maintenance and Inspection. Prebviously ICAO Digest No.12
2. Nongxin, C., Xin, T., Rui, L.: Application of REASON model to investigation of the aviation maintenance accident. Traffic Information and Security 2(30), 96–99 (2012)
3. Zengxian, G., Yifei, Z., Linghang, M., Yizhe, X.: Design of aircraft accidents analysis software based on reason model. Journal of Civil Aviation University of China 3(31), 6–9 (2013)
4. Wiegmann, D.A., Shappell, S.A.: Applying the Human Factors Analysisand Classification System (HFACS) to the analysis of commercial aviation accidentdata. In: The 11th International Symposium on Aviation Psychology. The Ohio State University, Columbus (2001)
5. Research team of human factors in aircraft maintenance of CAAC. Human factors' cases – maintenance error in civil aircraft, pp. 230–300. Civil aviation administration of China Press, Beijing (2003)
6. Yao, W., Zupei, S.: CREAM—A second generation human reliability analysis method. Industrial Engineering and Management 10(3), 17–21 (2005)
7. Bin, L., Qin, Y., Mao, L.: Study on prediction model of human factor failure probability based on CREAM. Journal of Safety Science and Technology 8(7), 57–49 (2012)
8. Ruishan, S., Yunxiao, C.: Application of failure probability of CREAM conflict solution by ATC. In: Proceedings of 2010 (Shenyang) International Colloquium on Safety Science and Technology. Northeastern University (May 2010)
9. Ruishan, S., Xin, W.: Application of failure probability of CREAM for judgment and decision-making in the cockpit. Journal of Safety Science and Technology 6(6), 40–45 (2010)
10. Yingjie, J., Zhiqiang, S., Erling, G., Hongwei, X.: The Method to Quantify Human Error Probability in Probabilistic Cognitive Control Mode. Journal of National University of Defense Technology 33(6), 175–178 (2011)

Safety, Security and Reliability

Management of On-Line Registries Information for Patient Safety in Long-Term Care

Fuad Abujarad[1], Sarah J. Swierenga[2], Toni A. Dennis[3], and Lori A. Post[1]

[1] Yale School of Medicine New Haven, CT, USA
{fuad.abujarad,lori.post}@yale.edu
[2] Usability/Accessibility Research and Consulting Michigan State University,
East Lansing, MI, USA
sswieren@msu.edu
[3] Department of Licensing and Regulatory Affairs State of Michigan, Lansing, MI, USA
dennist@michigan.gov

Abstract. The Michigan Workforce Background Check (MWBC) system combine data streams from various sources and online registries showing findings of abuse, neglect, misappropriation of property and health care fraud. Employers use MWBC to have an initial determination of the suitability of person for employment in Long-Term Care facility. In this paper, we demonstrate how *management of information* and the optimization of the human interface positively impact the patient safety and workflow, which is essential for effective public health management.

Keywords: Background Check, Registry Check, Long-Term Care, Health Information Technology, Usability, User-Centered Design, Patient Safety.

1 Introduction

Elderly persons in Long-Term Care (LTC) settings are exceptionally vulnerable to abuse, neglect, and exploitation necessitating special protective measures. Often, employers face critical staffing shortages that require immediate action [1,2]. The turnaround time for a comprehensive background check ranges from several days to several weeks. Prospective employers should have the opportunity to conduct a swift and efficient preliminary name-based background checks for potential employees. The public demand for information has resulted in registries and databases that contain information on criminal convictions, State Nurse Aide registries that list individuals with substantiated findings of abuse, neglect and misappropriation of property, and federal databases containing names of individuals and entities ineligible to receive Medicare and Medicaid funds because of program related crimes, abuse and/or neglect in a federally funded facility, felony controlled substance convictions and other related crimes.

From September 2004 through September 2007 the State of Michigan participated in a national pilot program to enhance background checks for workers in LTC, hospice and home health agencies. The U.S. Department of Health and Human

S. Yamamoto (Ed.): HIMI 2014, Part II, LNCS 8522, pp. 307–316, 2014.
© Springer International Publishing Switzerland 2014

Services provided $3.5 million through the Centers for Medicare and Medicaid Services to create an efficient and effective background check program, consisting of name-based registry checks and fingerprint-based criminal history checks to help prevent abuse and neglect of patients and residents and to reduce program fraud.

Prospective employees, independent contractors and individuals who are granted clinical privileges ("applicants") and who have direct access to a patient or resident, their personal property, treatment information or any other identifying information are required to undergo a background check that consists of a check of all available registries and a state and federal fingerprint-based criminal history check. The laws apply to applicants and employees in the following facilities or agencies ("covered facilities"):

- Nursing homes
- Homes for the aged
- Hospices
- Hospitals with swing beds
- Home health agencies
- Psychiatric facilities
- Intermediate care facilities for persons with mental retardation (ICF/MR)
- Adult foster care facilities

The background check program relies on the cooperation of many state and federal departments and agencies to provide and protect sensitive personal information and data. Michigan's program relies on a state of the art secure online system that centralizes the background check process by integrating registries and databases and by providing for secure communication.

The Michigan Workforce Background Check system (MWBC) combines data streams from several sources and online registries containing criminal history information as well as findings of abuse, neglect, misappropriation of property and health care fraud. LTC employers use registry check process of MWBC to make an initial determination of the suitability of person for employment in a LTC facility before committing resources to obtain fingerprint-based criminal records checks. In this paper, we demonstrate how management of information and the optimization of the human interface positively impact the patient safety and workflow, which is essential for effective public health management. Our research focuses on the use of user-centered design (UCD) methodologies to optimize the design and the implementation of an effective background check system in a complex organizational environment under challenging time constraints.

2   Background Checks

In this section, we describe two types of background checks. In Section 2.1 we describe the name-based background checks using registries. Then, in Section 2.2, we briefly describe the process of obtaining the biometric-based background check using fingerprints.

2.1   Registry-Based Background Check

Registries and online databases contain useful information for employers to evaluate the fitness of an applicant. Many employers in long-term care are required to check State registries and federal databases prior to hiring direct care staff and many take advantage of publicly available criminal history information. When conducting a name-based background check, employers access each online registry separately. Typically, the registry user interface requires the user to manually input the value of each search field. Each registry is a different data source and requires different search criteria. Once the search is complete, the user can then view result of that check. For example, the search of the Office of Inspector General (OIG) Exclusion list could return a person's name and other associated data indicating that they are on the exclusion list. The employer can make a determination whether or not to exclude an applicant upon the result of registry check. The manual process of checking each registry, individually, is time consuming, error-prone, and requires redundant data entry. We enhance this process by providing the employers with convenient, automated, and centralized access to a comprehensive set of online background registries.

2.2   Fingerprint-Based Criminal History Check

Upon successful completion of the registry checks, applicants must submit fingerprints to conduct a search of State and federal criminal records. A fingerprint vendor or police agency collects a set of ten rolled live scan images for each applicant and transmits the fingerprint images and applicant information to the State repository for a search through the Automated Fingerprint Identification System. The fingerprints are then forwarded to the Federal Integrated Automated Fingerprint Identification System for the federal search. When the responses are received, an electronic notification of a "hit" or "no hit" is sent to the background check system. If no record is found, the MWBC generates a letter notifying the employer that is sent by email, letting him or her know that results are available for review and that a final hiring decision is needed. The employer then indicates whether the applicant was hired or withdrew from the hiring process. If a criminal history record is found, a "hit" notice is sent to the system and the applicant record status indicates that the case is pending analysis. The Department of State Police sends a hard copy of the criminal history record to the requesting department, where an analyst reviews the record and makes an employability determination. At that point, the process mirrors the "no hit" process. An applicant or employee has the right to appeal the decision of the department.

3   The Registry Check Process

One of the components of the MWBC system is the registry check process, which combines data streams from various databases and online registries. Employers use this process to make an initial determination of the suitability of a person for employment in LTC facility before engaging in a lengthy and costly fingerprint based background check. In this section, we describe in detail the registry check process and how we optimize of the human interface to make it as intuitive as possible without disturbing the employer workflow.

3.1   Description of the Registries

Our system interfaces and integrates ancillary and external systems such as State and Federal systems, registries, and archives. During the development of the MWBC, we integrated the system with several of these registries and databases. Examples are included in Table 1.

Table 1. The list of the registries

No.	Registry Name	Link	Connection Type
1	U.S. HHS Medicare/Medicaid Exclusion List (OIG)	http://oig.hhs.gov/exclusions/	Downloadable File
2	Michigan Nurse Aid Registry (NAR)	https://registry.prometric.com/registry/publicMI	Downloadable File
3	Michigan Public Sex Offender Registry (PSOR)	http://www.mipsor.state.mi.us	Web service
4	Michigan Offender Tracking Information System (OTIS)	http://mdocweb.state.mi.us/OTIS2/otis2.html	Web service
5	Michigan Internet Criminal History Access Tool (ICHAT)	http://apps.michigan.gov/ICHAT/Home.aspx	Web service

The data were accessed by one of two methods. Some registries provide a real-time online access to the records of registry using web services. The second type provides a downloadable data file that contains the registry information. Once downloaded, the file can then be imported into database of the system to be used for subsequent searches. The download frequency depends on the frequency in which the data in the registry changes. If could be daily, weekly, monthly or as needed. We describe some of the registries in details below:

- **Office of Inspector General's (OIG) Exclusion Database** – The OIG maintains the List of Excluded Individuals/Entities for all state and federal health care programs under the authority of HIPPA and codified at 42USC 1320a-7. Bases for exclusion include convictions for program-related fraud and patient abuse, licensing board actions and default on Health Education Assistance Loans. Updated information is downloaded as it becomes available.
- **Michigan Nurse Aide Registry (MNAR)** – Prometric® provides testing and certification services for nurse aides in Michigan and maintains a public registry of certified nurse aides including findings of abuse, neglect or misappropriation of property. Updated database information is integrated as it becomes available.

- **Offender Tracking Information System (OTIS)** – This database contains conviction, parole and probation information for individuals who are or have been under the supervision of the Michigan Department of Corrections. The database and includes information about current and past prisoners and parolees. The system connection provides the most currently available information.
- **Public Sex Offender Registry (PSOR)** – This registry is developed and maintained by the Michigan State Police and includes conviction information for persons convicted of criminal sexual conduct or crimes against nature in Michigan or persons whose conviction occurred in another state and whose residence in Michigan and terms of probation requires them to register. The system connection provides the most currently available information.

As a consideration for the cost of preliminary checks, the registries and databases that do not charge a fee are placed at the top of the list and the fee-based registries are placed at the bottom of the list. Similarly, the registries that are easier to analyze and understand will be listed at the top. As shown in Fig. 2, we listed the registries based on these rules.

The Internet Criminal History Tool (ICHAT) registry was originally part of the registry check but was subsequently removed. The ICHAT contains Michigan criminal history information that meets criteria for public dissemination and is required for employers who want to conditionally employ workers while awaiting the results of a fingerprint-based check. The search is free for not-for-profit organizations; a fee of $10 per search is charged for all others. A link to the ICHAT is shown after the employer indicates an intent to conditionally employ the applicant.

3.2   Data Elements

When performing a name search, we primarily use the applicant's first and last name. Other demographic data can be used in the search only if the registry interface allows a search using additional fields. MWBC automatically maps search fields to the corresponding parameters of the registry interface to search for a possible match.

As is the case with any automated search operation, the search fields and the content of the registry database will determine the search result. For example, it is not required to capitalize the letters of the first and last name of the applicant. However, the correct spelling of the name is very critical. Special consideration is needed for names that contain punctuations. For example, if the search filed is hyphenated or if it contains an apostrophe. Specifically, some registries require that an individual with a hyphenated name should be checked under each of the last names in the hyphenated name (e.g., John Smith-Doe should be checked under John Smith and John Doe). Some of the most common data elements that are used to query the registries are listed in Table 2.

Table 2. The main data elementes for the registry check

Field Name	Data Type	Comments
First Name	Only alphabetic characters	No spaces, numbers, or special characters
Last Name	Only alphabetic characters	No spaces, numbers, or special characters
Date of Birth	MM/DD/YYYY	Either specific date or date range
License Number	Alphanumeric	Used for verification

3.3   System Architecture Overview

In this section we provide an overview of the registry check process design, and will delve into some details regarding each of the individual components. Throughout this section we provide justification for some of our design choices considering the requirements and constraints.

The flowchart in Fig. 1. gives an overview of the architecture of the registry check process. As shown in the flowchart, the high-level flow for the system is as follows. The system presents users with a page to input the applicant demographics, such as name (including: maiden name, nick name, alias), date of birth (DOB), address, and few other fields. Once users complete the data entry, they are presented with the *verify applicant information* page to check for errors. If all fields are correct, users can save the data and continue to the *"Registry Checks"* page. As shown in Fig. 2, users can access the results of a registry by clicking the registry name (e.g. Michigan Offender Tracking Information System (OTIS)). Based on the registry interface, a web services will be called to pass the search parameters to the registry search engine, eliminating the need for redundant re-entry of the applicant information.

3.4   Registry Results

Once the registry name is clicked, the results of the query are displayed in a separate window (or tab, depending on the Web browser of the user). The new window allows users to move between the results window and the MWBC easily as they review and record the results. The result of a registry search can be grouped in one of the following ways:

No Results Returned. The result window will show "*No results returned*" if the registry interface or web service indicates that no match can be found, which indicates that the registry does not include any findings that can be linked to the fields being searched.

Results Returned. The result window will show a list containing matching name(s) and users must verify that a similar or matching name does or does not belong to the applicant. For details users can click on the last name to find additional identifying information, such as date of birth, address or a physical description.

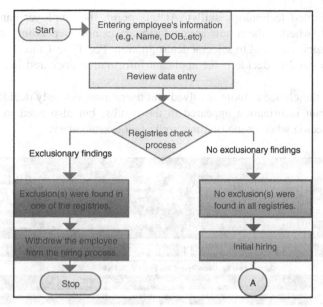

Fig. 1. A simple flowchart representing the registry check process

3.5   Reviewing Registry Results

The result review process will depend on the registry type and the registry database content. In this context, we identify two types of registries. Type1: users are checking the results of registries (e.g. OIG) that only require users to identify whether the applicant name is listed in the result of the inquiry, and Type2: users are checking the results of registries (e.g. OTIS) that require users to have a more in-depth analysis to the findings to decide whether the results are disqualifying or not. For more information on analyzing the results, we created a guide for each registry (\REF) to explain the content of the results. If verifying the information confirms that the employee appears in the results, users can then choose "Yes" to indicate that exclusionary findings exist in the result. Exclusionary findings in the results registry mean that the employee is ineligible for employment. If "Yes" is chosen, users will be unable to proceed with additional registry checks and will be directed toward the final employment determination.

3.6   Recording the Search Outcomes

Registry check outcomes are recorded as "Yes": Disqualified, "No": Not Disqualified. In some cases, we might need to add another outcome "Pending": Pending Review. The pending option is needed for the cases when users are unable to make determination or if the registry data are not available. As shown in Fig. 2., after each registry is checked, the employer is required to indicate a Yes or No outcome. This simple "red light, green light" approach is intuitive for employers (many of whom have limited technology skills). At this point, the employer can review the result to decide whether the results are exclusionary or not. Depending on the type of the registry, users will need to select a determination. For Type 1 the choice is simple and users only need to decide if the applicant information appeared in the results or not.

For Type 2 the choice is more involved and users must not only decide whether or not the applicant information appeared in the results, but also need to analyze the findings and decide whether the findings are in fact exclusionary.

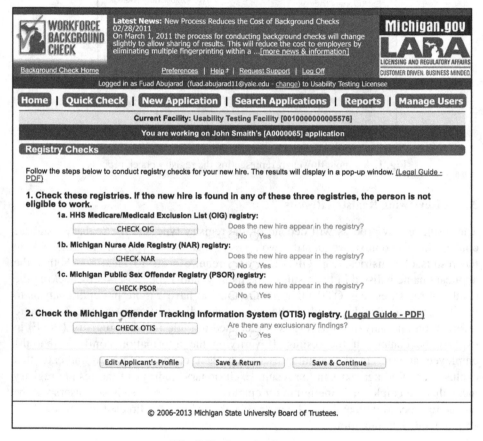

Fig. 2. Registry check screen

The employer reviews the results and determines whether to continue the registry search or not. Otherwise, the employer proceeds until all registries have been checked. For example, if the employer finds that the applicant is listed in the OIG results and choses *"Yes"*, when answering the question *"Does the new hire appear in the registry?"*, then the tool will give the employer the option to stop the search:

> You indicated that disqualifying information was found in one of the registries. Click 'Save & Continue' to continue.

However, if the results were not disqualifying then users will precede the search the next registry until all registries are checked. At this point, the system will display the following and complete the registry check

> You indicated that *no exclusions* were found in all registries. Click 'Save & Continue' to continue.

Once the search is completed the system will display the results back to users. At this point, users must review the results and determine if the findings are disqualifying or not. If the employer determines that there is no disqualifying information on the registries, a preliminary hiring decision is made. The employer may decide to conditionally hire the applicant, wait for the results of the background check, or withdraw the applicant from the hiring process.

4   User-Centered Design Approach to Registries Integration

During the design and development of the MWBC system we adopted UCD approach, which resulted in conducting multiple user experience evaluations throughout an iterative development process [3-5]. Usability-oriented focus groups were conducted with health care employers to identify their needs and expectations for checking the various online registries and managing the results. The feedback was used to create user interface requirements, produce user workflows and process diagrams for user interfaces, and create user interface prototypes. The prototypes were then evaluated in concept usability sessions, which measured the efficiency, effectiveness, and user satisfaction with the design approach.

The user evaluation uncovered valuable insights into how employers expected the system to function. For example, the study revealed that less technically-savvy employers had difficulty understanding how to go through the registry checking sequence. They tended to try to skip some of the registries (if there were too many names in the list), access them out of order, or incorrectly mark the findings as non-disqualifying, and then continue with the next registry check without checking all of the secondary windows containing the external registry results. Some users also did not understand how to make correct employability determinations based on the registry results that were displayed.

Armed with this critical information, our team was able to make adjustments to the screens and the process, requiring the users to check the registries in sequence and at least display the secondary registry results window. Additional on-screen help text was added, as well as on-screen messages indicating the status of the process. Refinements continued throughout the implementation phase, and then a formal usability evaluation and Section 508 accessibility compliance inspection were conducted on the final design before the Background Check system was released to production. User feedback has continued to be a key aspect of post-launch maintenance and enhancement activities [1]. By making the design of the MWBC user interface a high priority, the health care specialists within the LTC facilities assigned to conduct the background check on prospective employees found the system relatively easy to learn and use, which translated into program cost savings related to customer support and State analyst staffing levels.

5   Conclusion

Our development approach and the focus on applying UCD techniques resulted in a product that is usable, acceptable, comprehensive, efficient, and Intuitive. In this paper, demonstrated how management of information and the optimization of the human interface positively impact the patient safety and workflow, which is essential for effective public health management. More specifically, Since April 1, 2006, LTC healthcare employers have used registry checks to screen 798,773 candidates. Of these, 9,166 were immediately screened due to criminal convictions and numerous types of felony offenses from conditional employment in nursing homes, home health care and other long term care facilities.

References

1. Grant, G.: Safeguarding Vulnerable Adults over the Life Course. Adult Lives: A Life Course Perspective, 230–237 (2012)
2. Cooper, C., Selwood, A., Livingston, G.: The Prevalence of Elder Abuse and Neglect: ASystematic Review. Age and Ageing 37(2), 151–160 (2008)
3. Abujarad, F., Swierenga, S.J., Dennis, T.A., Post, L.A.: Rap Backs: Continuous Workforce Monitoring to Improve Patient Safety in Long-Term Care. In: Marcus, A. (ed.) DUXU 2013, Part III. LNCS, vol. 8014, pp. 3–9. Springer, Heidelberg (2013)
4. Swierenga, S.J., Abujarad, F., Dennis, T.A., Post, L.A.: Real-World User-Centered Design: The Michigan Workforce Background Check System. In: Salvendy, G., Smith, M.J. (eds.) HCII 2011, Part II. LNCS, vol. 6772, pp. 325–334. Springer, Heidelberg (2011)
5. Swierenga, S.J., Abujarad, F., Dennis, T.A., Post, L.A.: Improving Patient Safety through User-Centered Healthcare Background Check System Design. In: International Symposium of Human Factors and Ergonomics in Healthcare, vol. 2(1), pp. 21–28. Human Factors and Ergonomics Society (2013)

Improving Control Room State Awareness through Complex Sonification Interfaces

Barrett S. Caldwell and Jacob E. Viraldo

Purdue University, West Lafayette IN, USA
{bscaldwell,jviraldo}@purdue.edu

Abstract. Across a number of complex control room settings, there are concerns regarding operator information overload and alarm flooding. The evolution of control room technological capabilities has accelerated in recent years, due to drastic improvements in computer processing power, speed, and sensor integration. However, aging infrastructure and retiring senior operators in legacy control room systems such as chemical and power generation plants have begun to create opportunities for once-per-generation improvements in control room interface capabilities. Additional facilities, including power grid interconnection centers and computer network security monitoring centers, have created new generations of network operations control centers (NOCs). The authors' work is emphasizing the development and application of audification and parameter mapping techniques to generate engineering-based principles for presenting state-based auditory information to plant or NOC operators. There are no current systematic engineering-based principles used to apply sonification to control rooms or engineering system states in a clearly standardized way. Our current work in this domain examines the critical parameters that control room operators recognize and monitor in order to get a "sense of the plant" in nominal, degrading, or hazardous states. Principles and parameters for implementing these sonification techniques for power plant and NOC contexts are presented and discussed.

1   Introduction

Efforts to improve the design and implementation of human-machine interfaces for industrial control applications far predate the rise of the computer age. However, with the advent of digital computers, the scope and capability of control room information presentation to operators has increased substantially. The control and management of complex computer network operations themselves has now become an area of concern, especially due to issues of software network breakdowns, intentional attacks, and naturally occurring events that can threaten both physical and information infrastructure operations.

Distinct challenges face designers and operators of legacy control rooms (such as those for chemical processing, surface transportation, or power generation plants) and those of more modern systems (such as "cyber-operations" centers for civilian or military information networks). In the case of legacy control rooms, massive

S. Yamamoto (Ed.): HIMI 2014, Part II, LNCS 8522, pp. 317–323, 2014.
© Springer International Publishing Switzerland 2014

installed hardware systems and regulatory oversight requirements result in major technology and cost barriers associated with any new implementation of control room interface designs. As a result, many legacy systems are subject to very slow upgrade cycles, measured in years (if not decades) between generations of control room interface technologies. In the case of nuclear power plants in the US, for example, almost all plants currently operating are based on control room designs of the 1960s and 1970s. While some improvements have been made in display technologies, widespread implementations of new computer processing systems in such plants still greatly lag current capabilities of consumer-grade computer technologies. A particular gap exists in the use of complex sound signals to provide operators of infrastructure and network operations centers (NOCs) with information about the current state of critical plant parameters. For the remainder of this paper, we will use the term *sonification* to refer to the use of computer-generated audio signals to provide information to human operators about the state of a computer-monitored system or other dynamic process.

The goal of our present work is to investigate how to design and implement principle-based guidelines for sonification to provide improved information to control room operators to forestall, minimize, or even prevent adverse event outcomes in cyber-network or other high consequence infrastructure operations. By principle-based, we focus on combinations of systematic engineering, mathematical, music theory, and psychological processes that can be generalized across process dynamics and event progressions. Our initial focus is on the development of these guidelines in the context of a specific operational context: control and monitoring of a nuclear power generation facility.

2   Alarm Management vs. State Awareness

Alarms systems are intended to provide important support in the human operator's abilities to monitor and control an engineering infrastructure system. Audio alarms allow detection of whether a process or state is beyond acceptable limits (as defined by alarm thresholds). Reductions in costs for both sensor technologies and audio processing technologies have resulted in increase use of distributed alarms and audio alarm presentations in supervisory control environments. The management of audible (and visual) alarms in control room and other settings has become a major focus of human factors and process control management research (Sarter and Woods, 1995; Woods and Sarter, 2010).

One ongoing concern is that of "alarm flooding". Alarm floods occur when the number and timing of alarms presented to the operator interferes with (or, in some cases, actually prevents) the operator's ability to determine the current state of the engineering system and select / execute appropriate responses to return the system to a desirable state. Substantial advances have been made to the field of alarm management over several decades (Baldwin, 2012; Xiao and Seagull, 1999). However, research into human performance modeling has shown that the limit of operator abilities is approximately 10 alarms per 10 minute period (Reising, Downs, & Bayn,

2004). The Engineering Equipment and Materials User Association's (EEMUA) suggests an average alarm rate during normal operations of one alarm per 10 minutes (EEMUA, 1999), but rates of over three alarms per 10 minutes are common (Reising and Montgomery, 2005). This over-occurrence of alarms leads to operators using up limited resources, not only to both separate and manage these different alarms, but also to respond to the real conditions they represent.

When faced with alarm floods, operators are required to create and execute strategies to deal with limited and declining resources. They must detect, differentiate and manage the alarms themselves, and respond to the (uncertain) conditions represented by the alarms. Operators can become tentative or confused as they try to resolve individual alarms and their events. This confusion can also result from masking high-priority alarms with low-priority ones. Some operators may seek to manually bypass certain alarms and view them as "nuisance alarms" or those not critical to operations. As control room operators become exposed to ongoing levels of alarms that lose distinctive importance to identify adverse or emergency situations, they may even become conditioned to alarm floods, failing to give the alarms their due importance (see Koene & Vedam, 2000). Over time, alarm flooding can cause irritability, stress, confusion, or even panic among operators (Baldwin, 2012).

In order to provide improved state awareness using audio signals, there is first the question of recognizing and identifying how to present engineering system state information through computer-based audio signal processing technologies. Xiao and Seagull (1999) point out that there is a lack of general understanding of the actual information (meaning, not just signal detection) contained in an audio warning. In a variety of environments, humans and other animals use very complex audio signals to determine state, threat, and other dynamic conditions through localization and other techniques. Music is an apparently universal aspect of human experience, and the creation and appreciation of music has a number of complex features with both physiological and emotional meaning for behavior (Levitin, 2006). Rhythm, tonal quality, and other features of musical expression can be seen as a form of structural and temporal alignment in human cognitive processing (Bharucha, Curtis, and Paroo, 2012). Some authors even suggest that training paired with listening to music can increase attention and mindful awareness of flow (increased cognitive integration) (Diaz, 2013). These insights indicate that computer-based sonification interfaces, as well as an integration of engineering and music principles to tie system state to musical expression, can be used to improve operator awareness of engineering system state prior to the degraded conditions where alarm floods begin.

3   Forms of Sonification

Researchers in the area of sonification differentiate four distinct forms of providing system state or behavior information via audio signals (Hermann, Hunt, and Neuhoff, 2011). The first type, *auditory icons*, frequently use learned associations of sounds with particular artifacts (often legacy mechanical objects whose sounds were a necessary element of the prior system's operation). For instance, the electronically created sound of a camera shutter on a smartphone, or the sound of a clicking turn signal in a modern vehicle, are no longer due to the mechanical leaves or relays that created the original sound. However, because users now associate those sounds with the function of taking a picture or activating a turn signal, the auditory icon continues that association. In a similar fashion, *audification* represents the direct translation of a engineering or physical process into an audio trace. The click of a Geiger counter and the sound of static and tones in an analog radio represent characteristics of the physical world translated and processed in the audio spectrum.

By contrast, the *earcon* has been created distinctly to represent, as an audio symbol or trigger, a particular reference item. Tonal trademarks, such as the NBC or Intel logos, or theme representations associated with musical pieces (the opening notes of Beethoven's Fifth Symphony, the shark theme from *Jaws*) represent such audio symbols. The fourth type of sonification is described as *parameter mapping*, where naturally occurring engineering system parameters can be translated into sound notations or musical forms. For instance, imagine a power generation turbine rotating at 2000 rpm. A parameter mapping sonification of such a turbine in a control room could be represented by a flute playing at 2000 Hz. The sound of this turbine as perceived by an operator standing next to it may not hear a sound that directly represents a flute or other instrument at 2000 Hz. However, the mapping of 2000 rpm to 2000 Hz represents a straightforward parameter mapping.

Some sonification elements represent combinations of audification and parameter mapping. The musical compositions included in *IBM 1401: A User's Manual* (Johannsson, 2006) include tracks of the computer's magnetic memory causing interference with nearby radios (audification), but the orchestral representations of the rhythms and tones that comprise harmonies with the original memory tracks could be created as parameter mapping. (Such parameter mapping was not explicit, either contemporaneously or later: programmers could create "music" by writing computer programs to access memory in particular patterns, but there was no music created to indicate other aspects of computer memory usage or storage capacity.)

Timbre and rhythm are complex elements of a multidimensional perceptual process in human auditory behavior, a factor that has been researched in the psychological and human factors communities for decades (see Licklider, 1951 cited in Grey, 1977). However, as Grey (1977) has indicated, direct training on mapping timbre (sound profile) to specific instruments based on patterns of overtones and resonant frequencies is not easy for most human listeners. These types of findings suggest that parameter mapping or audification of very complex, fine grained distinctions between system parameters to specific instruments in a large orchestral representation may degrade, rather than enhance, the operator's ability to quickly discern subtle changes in system state. Context and expectation—the features that enable the listener's recognition of jazz syncopation or "hesitation" waltz forms—are additional elements of music and sound perception over time, which need to be studied with attention to serial correlation and sequences of musical phrases or movements (Schubert, 2002). Tempo and rhythm factors are important in expertise coordination context, especially when delays and information flow lags significantly affect expectations of the arrival of information or task updates (B. S. Caldwell, 2008).

The capacity to provide multi-dimensional and multi-function information to computer users in the audio domain has demonstrated considerable advances in recent years. Unlike designers and operators of NOC control rooms, computer and video game designers have quite actively exploited advances in computer-based audio processing to provide sonification and other audio information to game players. Immersive and realistic audio representations (thus incorporating auditory icon and audification techniques) as well as audio representation of game play status (representing parameter mapping) have been strong elements of maintaining player awareness and enjoyment in "first person shooter" video games (Grimshaw, 2008; Grimshaw and Schott, 2008). For these researchers, the characteristics of sound generated by objects in the game (as opposed to music soundtracks) are described as "diegetic" sound (Nacke, Grimshaw, and Lindley, 2010). (This description of diegetic sound seems to directly suggest at least auditory icon and audification elements of sonification, using either pre-recorded or computer-generated object representations. Game status (threat level, player health, etc.), while possibly musical in form, is more correctly described as parameter mapping diegetic sonification, rather than non-diegetic soundtrack music.) The process of generating diegetic sounds in computer games in order to enhance player state awareness and immersive gameplay experience appears to have a strong parallel to providing sonifications of engineering state for NOC and other control room operators.

4   Next Steps: Determining NOC Parameters and Principles

Digital signal processing and audio generation technologies are no longer the technological barrier to providing rich and robust audio interfaces to control room operators. Substantial work with users in computer game environments have demonstrated these users' immersion, performance, and usability effects both within game play and in task transfer settings (Chiappe, Conger, Liao, J. Caldwell, and Vu, 2013). In order to improve effectiveness and generalizability of control room design, however, systematic descriptions of engineering, mathematical (music form), and musicality (music perception) principles need to be applied to sonification efforts in audification and parameter mapping.

Our current work in this domain examines the critical parameters that control room operators recognize and monitor in order to get a "sense of the plant" in nominal, degrading, or hazardous states. Being able to transform these parameters into coherent auditory orchestrations to indicate current operational state is the near-term goal of this work. As parameters deviate in a continuous fashion from set points, mapping of those deviations in terms of rhythm, tone, and/or relative strength of instrumental mix can allow operators to monitor plant state in an omnidirectional, easily learned auditory format.

Statistical process control techniques can be used to increase volume of the sonification gradually and noticeably with increasing deviation from setpoint, rather than simply at threshold crossing past a control limit. Techniques for allowing human operators to determine and respond to control limit transitions as a performance enhancement and workload management strategy for improving state awareness and task effectiveness have been a goal for some time (B. S. Caldwell, 1997; Tulga and Sheridan, 1980).

Pilot interviews with nuclear and other power plant control operators have already begun, in order to identify the primary (quantitatively varying) plant state parameters of greatest importance to control room operators when monitoring plant health. Although detailed mapping of many parameters to specific instruments is problematic (Grey, 1977), relatively simple mappings of 3-6 critical plant parameters to instrument "families" in an orchestra (strings, brass, percussion) seems feasible. The specific mappings depend on the frequency and rhythmic nature of those parameters, but can be validated with cognitive walkthrough and perception-based usability evaluation techniques. In order to further increase the principle-based generalizability of this approach, the first author is also leading a study to conduct a similar research approach to identify critical cyberinfrastructure network parameters of importance to experienced NOC operators. There is still a strong need to determine the presentation of these parameters for NOC information *visualization*. However, the very high event rates of network flows or intrusion detections suggests that audification and parameter mapping techniques using similar parameter identification techniques have great promise for designs of NOC information *sonification*.

These techniques have substantial potential benefits over traditional alarm techniques, including proactive information presentation based on system state rather than sensor threshold crossing. The ultimate purpose of this research is not simply to improve alarm integration or reduce the sheer number of alarms impinging on operators during emergency situations. Proactive and forecast information highlighting sonification of NOC state trends can in fact forestall or even prevent some alarm state conditions from occurring. Increased sensemaking and critical parameter identification to operators can support more rapid determination and troubleshooting behaviors prior to the onset of emergency system conditions.

Acknowledgements. Portions of this research were funded by the Purdue University Faculty Scholar Program and Center for Education and Research in Information Assurance and Security (CERIAS) awards to the first author, and the US Department of Defense SMART Fellowship. The opinions and perspectives presented here are those of the authors, and not of any government or other agency.

References

1. Baldwin, C.L.: Auditory Cognition and Human Performance: Research and Applications. CRC Press (2012)
2. Bharucha, J., Curtis, M., Paroo, K.: Musical communication as alignment of brain states. In: Rebuschat, P., Rohrmeier, M., Hawkins, J.A., Cross, I. (eds.) Language and Music as Cognitive Systems, pp. 139–155. Oxford University Press, Oxford (2012)
3. Caldwell, B.S.: Components of information flow to support coordinated task performance. International Journal of Cognitive Ergonomics 1(1), 25–41 (1997)

4. Caldwell, B.S.: Knowledge sharing and expertise coordination of event response in organizations. Applied Ergonomics 39(4), 427–438 (2008)
5. Chiappe, D., Conger, M., Liao, J., Caldwell, J.L., Vu, K.P.L.: Improving-multi-tasking ability through action videogames. Applied Ergonomics 44, 278–284 (2013)
6. Diaz, F.M.: Mindfulness, attention, and flow during music listening: An empirical investigation. Psychology of Music 41(1), 42–58 (2013)
7. Grey, J.M.: Multidimensional perceptual scaling of musical timbres. The Journal of the Acoustical Society of America 61(5), 1270–1277 (1977)
8. Grimshaw, M.N.: Sound and immersion in the first-person shooter. International Journal of Intelligent Games & Simulation 5(1), 119–124 (2008)
9. Grimshaw, M., Schott, G.: A conceptual framework for the analysis of first-person shooter audio and its potential use for game engines. International Journal of Computer Games Technology 2008, 5–12 (2008)
10. Hermann, T., Hunt, A., Neuhoff, J.G.: The sonification handbook. Logos Verlag (2011)
11. Johannsson, J.: IBM 1401: A User's Manual (2006), http://ausersmanual.org (retrieved February 8, 2014)
12. Koene, K., Vedam, H.: Alarm management and rationalization. In: Third International Conference on Loss Prevention (2000)
13. Nacke, L.E., Grimshaw, M.N., Lindley, C.A.: More than a feeling: Measurement of sonic user experience and psychophysiology in a first-person shooter game. Interacting with Computers 22(5), 336–343 (2010)
14. Reising, D.V.C., Downs, J.L., Bayn, D.: Human Performance Models for Response to Alarm Notifications in the Process Industries: An Industrial Case Study. Proceedings of the Human Factors and Ergonomics Society Annual Meeting 48(10), 1189–1193 (2004), doi:10.1177/154193120404801009
15. Reising, D.V., Montgomery, T.: Achieving Effective Alarm System Performance: Results of ASM Consortium Benchmarking against the EEMUA Guide for Alarm Systems. In: Proceedings of the 20th Annual CCPS International Conference, Atlanta, GA, pp. 11–13 (2005)
16. Sarter, N.B., Woods, D.D.: How in the world did we ever get into that mode? Mode error and awareness in supervisory control. Human Factors: The Journal of the Human Factors and Ergonomics Society 37(1), 5–19 (1995)
17. Schubert, E.: Correlation analysis of continuous emotional response to music: Correcting for the effects of serial correlation. Musicae Scientiae 5(suppl. 1), 213–236 (2002)
18. Sloboda, J.A.: Music Structure and Emotional Response: Some Empirical Findings. Psychology of Music 19(2), 110–120 (1991), doi:10.1177/0305735691192002
19. Tulga, M.K., Sheridan, T.B.: Dynamic decisions and work load in multitask supervisory control. IEEE Transactions on Systems, Man and Cybernetics 10(5), 217–232 (1980)
20. Woods, D.D., Sarter, N.B.: Capturing the dynamics of attention control from individual to distributed systems: the shape of models to come. Theoretical Issues in Ergonomics Science 11(1-2), 7–28 (2010)
21. Xiao, Y., Seagull, F.J.: An Analysis of Problems with Auditory Alarms: Defining the Roles of Alarms in Process Monitoring Tasks. Proceedings of the Human Factors and Ergonomics Society Annual Meeting 43(3), 256–260 (1999), doi:10.1177/154193129904300327

Voice Activated Personal Assistant:
Acceptability of Use in the Public Space

Aarthi Easwara Moorthy and Kim-Phuong L. Vu

Department of Psychology, California State University Long Beach
1250 Bellflower Blvd, Long Beach, CA 90840 USA
aarthi.e.moorthy@gmail.com, Kim.Vu@csulb.edu

Abstract. Voice interface is becoming a common feature in mobile devices such as tablets and smartphones. Moreover, voice recognition technology is touted to mature and become the default method to control of a variety of interfaces, including mobile devices. Thus, it is critical to understand the factors that influence the use of voice activated applications in the public domain. The present study examined how the perceived acceptability of using the Voice-Activated Personal Assistant (VAPA) in smartphones influences its reported use. Participants were U.S. smartphone users recruited from Amazon Mechanical Turk. Results showed that participants preferred using the VAPA in a private location, such as their home, but even in that environment, they were hesitant about using it to input private or personally identifying information in comparison to more general, non-private information. Participants' perceived social acceptability of using the VAPA to transmit information in different contexts could explain these preferred usage patterns.

Keywords: Voice-Activated Personal Assistants, Voice Interface, Mobile Computing, Information Privacy.

1 Introduction

Voice recognition technology is developing rapidly, and it is anticipated to become not only the default input method in smartphones but also in automobiles and other home appliances such as the TV [1]. Because of the unique characteristics associated with voice input, including the overt verbalization of commands, privacy and acceptability concerns will influence the use and adoption of voice-based human-machine interfaces.

Traditional models from the technology adoption literature, such as the Technology Acceptance Model [2], the Unified Theory of Acceptance and Use of Technology [3], and Mobile Phone Technology Acceptance Model [4], identify factors that determine and moderate technology usage. However, the focus of these models has been on use of stationary desktop-based software or basic mobile phone voice services. These models have not fully explored social factors governing use of complex mobile

S. Yamamoto (Ed.): HIMI 2014, Part II, LNCS 8522, pp. 324–334, 2014.
© Springer International Publishing Switzerland 2014

phone applications enabling user interaction through novel methods such as voice activation.

Because the intelligent voice assistant application on smartphones is only a recent introduction, extensive research on Voice-Activated Personal Assistants (VAPA) user preferences has not been conducted. Siri, the voice-activated intelligent personal assistant that debuted with iPhone 4S in 2011 is thought to be the first implemented application, in which "voice recognition, information management, artificial intelligence, task fulfillment, and user interface cooperate in a way the general public finds usable and productive enough to adopt on a global scale of tens of millions devices" [5, p. 6]. However, there are also many concerns with using Siri and other VAPAs of its class. Notably, many users are concerned with the propriety of public use of the VAPA in front of strangers.

Given the recency of the technology, there is limited research on the topic of user concerns with the use of VAPA in public. Prior studies, in which participants evaluated intelligent assistive systems, have mainly focused on the efficiency and user preference of voice input when compared to other methods of information input such as text entry and direct manipulation. For example, Cox, Cairns, Walton, and Lee [6] found that user preference was higher and information input was faster with voice input method compared to multitap or predictive text-entry when composing a text message in "hands-busy" and "eyes-busy" situations. Zhou, Mohammed, and Zhang [7] found that users preferred a personal information management agent supporting natural language input through voice recognition, as these agents were perceived to be easier to use, more useful, and more efficient than traditional information management agents that did not support voice input. Users also reported that they were more likely to use personal information management agents supporting natural language than the ones that did not provide the voice input feature. While these studies using VAPA-like prototypes have analyzed efficiency and user preferences for information-entry in private, they have not explored user preferences with information entry into VAPAs in public.

However, findings from the social psychology domain suggest that presence of strangers might affect users' attitude towards the VAPA and their likelihood of using it in public locations because it might pose problems to users in social situations where their voice commands are audible to others. VAPA users might think that their actions are observed and assessed by others around them. This claim is supported by findings in social psychology, which have shown that the mere presence of observers might alter one's behavior, classically described as the Hawthorne effect [8, p. 232]. Therefore, the presence of others might make one shift more attention to the social situation and increase anxiety of evaluation. This theory about the attitudinal response to social settings was supported in a recent study on a popular VAPA, Siri. Siftar [9] surveyed Siri iPhone 4S users, and found that among regular users, who used Siri at least a few times per month, 32% feel uncomfortable and 11% feel embarrassed while using Siri in public. We can infer from this preliminary survey that there might be a social component influencing usage of mobile VAPA in public.

The new method of user interaction through voice that the VAPA has introduced in smartphones poses new challenges. The goal of the present study is to gain a basic understanding of the usage patterns of VAPA in public spaces. For the present paper, we report a subset of the data from the larger study. Specifically, this paper will report data that assessed users' likelihood of VAPA usage of two different smartphone tasks in a public (restaurant) versus private (home) location to enter private (Personally Identifiable Information) and non-private (general) information. We also examined users' reported acceptability ratings of using VAPA under the same contexts, and the correlation between users' likelihood of use and acceptability ratings.

2   Method

2.1   Participants

One hundred and twenty smartphone users completed an online survey about their VAPA usage preferences in various locations using Amazon Mechanical Turk (AMT). However, only "quality" responses from 76 participants were used for data analysis. "Quality" was defined as correctly selecting pre-specified answers for quality control questions. A little more than half of the participants were male (55%). Most participants were below 35 years (78%), had some college education (84%) and reported being Caucasian (84%).

2.2   Apparatus and Stimuli

An online survey titled "Smartphone Usage Preferences Survey" was designed using the survey development website SurveyMonkey. This generic title, which omitted mention of voice assistants, was intended to keep participants partially blind to the purpose of the study and thus prevent biased responses towards the voice assistant.

The main part of the survey consisted entirely of close-ended questions. For the purpose on the current paper, though, only the two relevant sections will be described. In the first section, the users reported their likelihood of using a voice assistant to perform two tasks in a public and a private location to enter private and non-private information on a scale from 1 to 7, with 1 standing for "not likely at all to use" and 7 standing for "extremely likely to use". In the second section, users rated the social acceptability of using the VAPA under the same contexts. This rating scale also ranged between 1 and 7, with 1 standing for "not acceptable at all" and 7 standing for "very acceptable to use".

The two tasks examined in this paper are texting and calling a contact. The location descriptions indicated the presence or absence of strangers to distinguish the public location (i.e., a relatively quiet, but crowded restaurant) from the private location (i.e., home alone). Private information was defined as Personally Identifiable Information such as last name and social security number that can be used to identify, track, or contact individuals. Non-private information was classified as non-unique and general details that U.S. residents are willing to discuss in front of strangers under normal circumstances such as one's first name or enquiries about one's day. For each type of information, example scenarios were included to illustrate when participants might need to input it. For example, for the task of calling a contact, the private information condition scenario was "Call John/Jane Carpenter" and the non-private condition scenario was "Call John/Jane".

2.3   Procedure

An invitation to participate in this survey was listed as a human intelligence task (HIT) on AMT. Using screening criteria incorporated into AMT, this HIT was made visible and accessible only to AMT workers who resided in the United States and had a task approval rating of 95% or above. It also indicated that survey participants were required to be smartphone users with prior experience of using a smartphone VAPA such as Siri, S Voice, or Google Now to be eligible to take the survey.

After reading the survey eligibility requirements and instructions, the AMT workers self-selected themselves as survey participants, if they wished to complete the HIT. To access the survey, they clicked on the provided survey hyperlink and navigated to the external website SurveyMonkey, in which the survey was administered. On the first page of the survey, participants were instructed to pay attention to all the questions as one of them contained a special code, which they had to correctly enter into the HIT verification text box in the AMT website to receive payment. Then, they indicated their electronic consent to the terms and conditions of the survey and their voluntary participation. Next, they completed the above-mentioned survey and obtained the special code. At the end of the survey, participants were thanked for their participation and again instructed to correctly enter the special code. Finally, they navigated back to the AMT website, entered the special code and submitted the HIT. The online survey took less than 30-minutes to complete and participants received a payment of $0.75 if their answers met the quality control requirements.

3   Results

The data reported in this paper is a subset of a larger study. The results section is divided into three sections. The first examines the VAPA likelihood of usage as a function of whether the task was being performed in a public or private location. The second section examines the social acceptability ratings of users performing the same tasks in a public or private location. Finally, the last section provides the correlational data between likelihood of VAPA usage and acceptability.

3.1   VAPA Usage Likelihood as a Function of Location and Content

Participants were asked to rate the likelihood of using their smartphone VAPA on a scale from 1 ("not likely at all to use") to 7 ("extremely likely to use") for the tasks of texting and calling a contact when entering private and non-private information in public and private locations. Then, they were analyzed using a 2 (task: texting and calling a contact) x 2 (type of content information: private and non-private information) x 2 (location: public restaurant and alone at home) within-subjects ANOVA.

All main effects were significant. The likelihood of using VAPA for calling a contact was greater than that for texting, $F(1, 75) = 34.328$, $p < 0.001$, see Fig. 1.

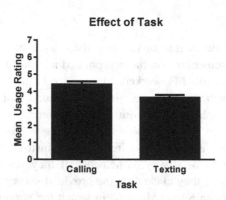

Fig. 1. Main Effect of Task for Likelihood to Use Voice as an Input Method

The likelihood of VAPA usage to enter non-private information was higher than that to enter private information, $F(1, 75) = 71.460$, $p < 0.001$, see Fig. 2.

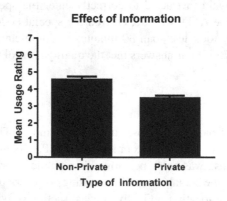

Fig. 2. Main Effect of Type of Information for Likelihood to Use Voice as an Input Method

Participants also gave a higher likelihood rating for using their VAPA to enter information at home than at a public restaurant, $F(1, 75) = 110.652$, $p < 0.001$, see Fig. 3.

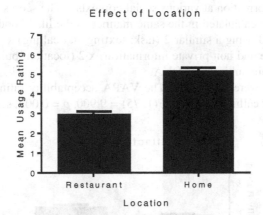

Fig. 3. Main Effect of Location for Likelihood to Use Voice as an Input Method

The two-way interaction between task and privacy of information was also significant, $F(1, 75) = 48.898$, $p < 0.001$, see Fig. 4. However, interaction between task and location, privacy of information and location, and the three-way interaction of all variables were not. Likelihood of VAPA usage for entering non-private information was comparable for the tasks of calling and texting. However, participants were more likely to use the VAPA to transmit private information while calling than while texting.

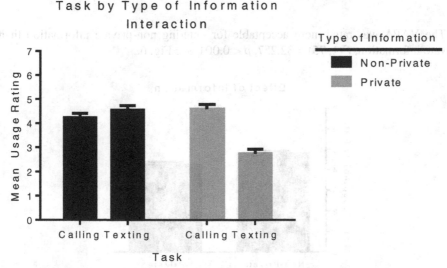

Fig. 4. Interaction of Type of Information by Task for Likelihood to Use Voice as an Input Method

3.2   VAPA Acceptability as a Function of Location and Content

Participants were asked to rate acceptability of using the VAPA to text or call a contact on a scale of 1 ("not acceptable at all") to 7 ("very acceptable") to enter private

and non-private information at various social contexts.   The scores for VAPA acceptability ratings were calculated in the same manner as the likelihood of usage ratings.
They were analyzed using a similar 2 (task: texting and calling) x 2 (type of content
information: private and non-private information) x 2 (location: public restaurant and
alone at home) within-subjects ANOVA.

All main effects were significant. The VAPA acceptability rating for texting was
greater than that for calling a contact, $F(1, 75) = 9.900$, $p = 0.002$, see Fig. 5.

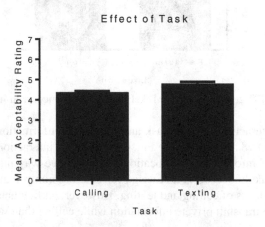

Fig. 5. Main Effect of Task for Acceptability to Use Voice as an Input Method

The VAPA was rated more acceptable for entering non-private information than
private information, $F(1, 75) = 32.257$, $p < 0.001$, see Fig. 6.

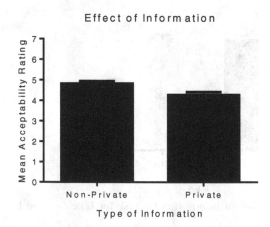

Fig. 6. Main Effect of Type of Information for Acceptability to Use Voice as an Input Method

Participants found it more acceptable to use their VAPA to enter information at
home than at a public restaurant, $F(1, 75) = 185.960$, $p < 0.001$, see Fig. 7.

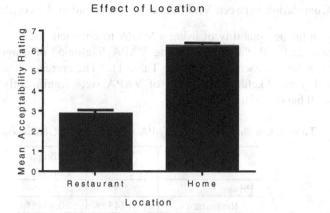

Fig. 7. Main Effect of Location for Acceptability to Use Voice as an Input Method

The two-way interaction between privacy of information and location was also significant, $F(1, 75) = 16.701$, $p < 0.001$. However, interaction between task and privacy of information, task and location, and the three-way interaction of all variables were not. The VAPA was more acceptable for transmitting non-private than private information; however, this difference in acceptability was more pronounced at the public restaurant than at home, see Fig. 8.

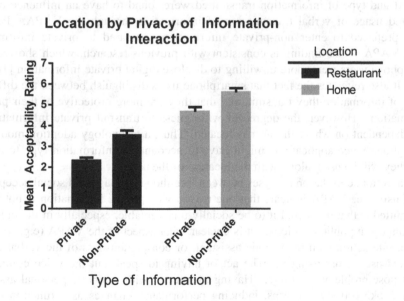

Fig. 8. Interaction of Location by Task for Acceptability to Use Voice as an Input Method

3.3   Correlation between VAPA Usage Likelihood and Acceptability

Ratings on the acceptability of using a VAPA to complete the two smartphone tasks were correlated with the corresponding VAPA likelihood of usage ratings for each information type at each location (see Table 1). The correlation analysis found that acceptability and likelihood of usage of VAPA were significantly positively correlated for all but one of the pairs.

Table 1. Correlation between VAPA acceptability and likelihood of usage

	Texting	Calling a Contact
Private Info		
Restaurant	0.345**	0.474**
Home	0.269*	0.342**
Non-Private Info		
Restaurant	0.267*	0.374**
Home	0.237*	0.220

Note: $* p < 0.05, ** p < 0.001$

4   Discussion

Results from the survey were consistent with findings from previous research: Social context and type of information transmitted were found to have an influence on the reported usage of verbal transmission of information through the VAPA. Participants preferred to enter non-private information compared to private information using VAPA. This finding is consistent with previous research, which showed that smartphone users were more unwilling to disclose digital private information [10, 11, 12]. It also reiterates the fact that smartphone users distinguish between the different types of information they transmit, and that they are more protective of their private information. However, the degree of willingness to transmit private information is also dependent on where the user is located. Thus, a technology adoption model for smartphone voice applications might have to account for information type to assess how they will be used, along with the location of the user.

In addition, correlation analyses between likelihood of usage and social acceptability of using the VAPA indicate that one reason why private information is not being transmitted is that users find it to be socially unacceptable, especially in the presence of strangers at public locations. It is unclear what aspect of the VAPA (e.g., verbalization, interaction with the robotic assistant, or conspicuousness of the verbal input) prevents users from using it. The act of having to speak out the voice commands might pose problems for users. Having to interact with a robotic personal assistant might evoke privacy concerns, inducing performance changes as a function of the user knowing that they are being observed, as in the Hawthorne effect [8, p. 232]. Users might also want to use discreet methods of information entry such as the keyboard more than conspicuous ones such as the VAPA. Any of the above reasons could justify the finding that participants were more likely to use the VAPA to enter non-private information than private information.

The findings on VAPA usage and acceptability by location also support previous research, which found that mobile phone users guarded their spoken conversations [13] and digital information [12, 14] from strangers. Presence of strangers in the co-located space of smartphone users and the resulting users' perception of attention to their conspicuous actions or information transmitted might deter them from using the VAPA in public spaces.

5   Limitations of Study

The survey method is based on the self-report of participant behavior, and may not reflect data patterns gathered by more realistic field studies. In addition, users may not be attending to all aspects of the survey when filling it out. We found that a large proportion (36.6%) of data collected from Amazon Turk to not meet the quality requirements of the survey. We limited this possibility in the present study by embedding quality control questions in the online surveys to ensure that the participants are paying attention to the survey questions.

The present survey also asked users to make various assumptions that eliminated technological and human errors related to the smartphone tasks when making their assessments about their likelihood of VAPA usage. Therefore, the participants' reports may reflect usage under the best case scenario, rather than actual usage.

References

1. Knight, W.: Where speech recognition is going | MIT Technology Review (2012), http://www.technologyreview.com/news/427793/where-speech-recognition-is-going/
2. Davis, F.D., Bagozzi, R.P., Warshaw, P.R.: User acceptance of computer technology: A comparison of two theoretical models. Management Science 35(8), 982–1003 (1989)
3. Venkatesh, V., Morris, M.G., Davis, G.B., Davis, F.D.: User acceptance of information technology: Toward a unified view. MIS Quarterly, 425–478 (2003)
4. Van Biljon, J., Kotzé, P.: Modelling the factors that influence mobile phone adoption. In: Proceedings of the 2007 Annual Research Conference of the South African Institute of Computer Scientists and Information Technologists on IT Research in Developing Countries, pp. 152–161. ACM Press, New York (2007)
5. Siftar, J.: The adoption and appropriation of Siri. Unpublished master's dissertation. University College London, University of London, UK (2012)
6. Cox, A.L., Cairns, P.A., Walton, A., Lee, S.: Tlk or txt? Using voice input for SMS composition. Personal and Ubiquitous Computing 12(8), 567–588 (2008)
7. Zhou, L., Mohammed, A.S., Zhang, D.: Mobile personal information management agent: Supporting natural language interface and application integration. Information Processing & Management 48(1), 23–31 (2012)
8. Sullivan, L. (ed.): The SAGE glossary of the social and behavioral sciences. SAGE, Thousand Oaks (2009)

9. Siftar, J.: Siri loves you, but do you love Siri? PowerPoint slides (2012), http://www.slideshare.net/JiriSiftar/siri-loves-you-but-do-you-love-siri

10. Karlson, A.K., Brush, A.J., Schechter, S.: Can I borrow your phone?: Understanding concerns when sharing mobile phones. In: Proceedings of the 27th International Conference on Human Factors in Computing Systems, pp. 1647–1650. ACM Press, New York (2009)

11. Khalil, A., Connelly, K.: Context-aware telephony: Privacy preferences and sharing patterns. Paper presentation, 20th Conference on Computer Supported Cooperative Work, Banff, Canada (2006)

12. Marques, D., Duarte, L., Carriço, L.: Privacy and secrecy in ubiquitous text messaging. In: Proceedings of the 14th International Conference on Mobile Human Computer Interaction, pp. 95–100. ACM Press, New York (2012)

13. Murtagh, G.M.: Seeing the "rules": Preliminary observations of action, interaction and mobile phone use. In: Brown, B., Green, N., Harper, R. (eds.) Wireless world: Social and International Aspects of the Mobile Age, pp. 81–91. Springer, London (2002)

14. Olson, J.S., Grudin, J., Horvitz, E.: A study of preferences for sharing and privacy. In: CHI 2005 Extended Abstracts on Human Factors in Computing Systems, pp. 1985–1988. ACM Press, New York (2005)

A Framework of Human Reliability Analysis Method Considering Soft Control in Digital Main Control Rooms

Inseok Jang[1], Ar Ryum Kim[1], Wondea Jung[2], and Poong Hyun Seong[1]

[1] Department of Nuclear and Quantum Engineering,
Korea Advanced Institute of Science and Technology,
373-1, Guseong-dong, Yuseong-gu, Daejeon 305-701, Republic of Korea
{nuclear82,arryum,phsoeng}@kaist.ac.kr
[2] Integrated Safety Assessment Division, Korea Atomic Energy Research Institute,
150-1, Dukjin-dong, Yuseong-gu, Daejeon 305-353, Republic of Korea
wdjung@kaeri.re.kr

Abstract. The operation environment of Main Control Rooms (MCRs) in Nuclear Power Plants has changed with the adoption of new human-system interfaces that are based on computer-based technologies. The MCRs that include these digital and computer technologies are called Advanced MCRs. Among the many features of Advanced MCRs, soft controls are a particularly important feature because the operation action in NPP Advanced MCRs is performed by soft control. Due to the different interfaces between soft control and hardwired conventional type control, different human error probabilities and a new Human Reliability Analysis (HRA) framework should be considered in the HRA for advanced MCRs. Although there are many HRA methods to assess human reliabilities, these methods do not sufficiently consider the features of advanced MCRs such as soft control execution human errors. In this paper, a framework of HRA method for evaluation of soft control execution human error in advanced MCRs is suggested.

Keywords: Advanced MCR, Soft control, Execution human error probability.

1 Introduction

The assessment of what can go wrong with large scale systems such as nuclear power plants is of considerable interest at present, given the past decade's record of accidents attributable to human error. Such assessments are formal and technically complex evaluations of the potential risks of systems, and are called probabilistic safety assessments (PSAs). Today, many PSAs consider not only hardware failures and environmental events that can impact upon risk but also human error contributions [1].

In addition, since the Three Mile Island (TMI)-2 accident, human error has been recognized as one of the main causes of nuclear power plant (NPP) accidents, and numerous studies related to human reliability analysis (HRA) have been carried out such as Technique for Human Error Rate Prediction (THERP) [2], Korean Human Reliability Analysis (K-HRA) [3], Human Error Assessment and Reduction

S. Yamamoto (Ed.): HIMI 2014, Part II, LNCS 8522, pp. 335–346, 2014.
© Springer International Publishing Switzerland 2014

Technique (HEART) [4], Success Likelihood Index Methodology (SLIM) [5], Human Cognitive Reliability(HCR) [6], A Technique for Human Event Analysis(ATHEANA) [7], Cognitive Reliability and Error Analysis Method(CREAM) [8], and Simplified Plant Analysis Risk Human Reliability Assessment(SPAR-H) [9] in relation to NPP maintenance and operation. Most of these methods were developed in consideration of the conventional type of Main Control Rooms (MCRs) and have been still used for HRA in advanced MCRs despite that the operation environment of advanced MCRs in NPPs has considerably changed with the adoption of new human-system interfaces such as soft controls that are based on computer-based technologies. In other words, these methods that have been applied to conventional MCRs do not consider the new features of advanced MCRs such as soft controls.

Due to the different interfaces between soft control and hardwired conventional type control, different human error probabilities and a new HRA framework should be considered in the HRA for advanced MCRs. Thus, given the absence of a HRA method that considers design features of soft control, the objective of this study is to develop a HRA method for evaluation of soft control execution human error by analyzing the characteristics of soft control in advanced MCRs.

2   Soft Control

2.1   Definition and General Characteristics of Soft Control

In NUREG-CR/6635, soft controls are defined as "devices having connections with control and display systems" that are mediated by software rather than physical connections [10]. This definition directly reflects the characteristics of advanced MCRs, including that the operator does not need to provide control input through hard-wired, spatially dedicated control devices that have fixed functions. Because of this characteristic, the functions of soft control may be variable and context dependent rather than statically defined. [10-11].

2.2   Task Analysis for Soft Control

A soft control task analysis is performed to identify human error modes and develop the framework of a new HRA method considering soft control.

Systematic Human Error Reduction and Prediction Approach (SHERPA) is useful when hierarchical tasks such as human involved tasks and procedures are analyzed [12]. As an example, Fig. 1 shows a task analysis using SHERPA.

The goal of the task is to reset the safety injection and auxiliary feedwater actuation signal. In order to achieve the goal, the operator selects "Reactivity system screen" from the operator console and resets the safety injection signal. For reset of the safety injection signal, there are other subtasks: "Press bypass button from the operator console", "Press the acknowledge button", and finally "Press bypass button using the input device for the safety component". Another subtask, "Reset the auxiliary feedwater actuation signal", performed to reset the safety injection signal, is then analyzed. The subtasks can be rearranged as shown in Fig. 2.

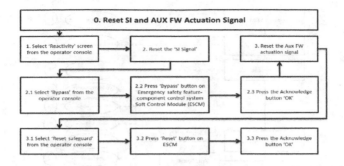

Fig. 1. Task analysis using SHERPA

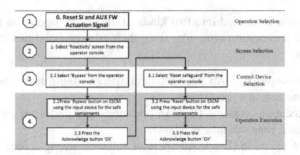

Fig. 2. Sequence analysis of a soft control task

Each subtask is included in one of four sub steps: operation selection, screen selection, control device selection, and operation execution. [11].

2.3   Soft Control Human Error Mode Classification

From the results of soft control task analysis, soft control human error modes already have been identified in several papers. [11, 13].

- Operation omission (E_1): An operator omits performing a sub task when performing a task. (one sub task in a task).
- Wrong object (E_2): An operator selects a wrong device when performing a task.
- Wrong operation (E_3): An operator performs a wrong operation, such as pressing the 'OPEN' button instead of the 'CLOSE' button.
- Mode confusion (E_4): An operator performs a right operation in a wrong mode.
- Inadequate operation (E_5): An operation is executed insufficiently, too early or for too long/short.
- Delayed operation (E_6): An operation is not performed at the right time.

However, soft control human error modes are modified to develop a new framework for the HRA method, as shown in Fig. 3.

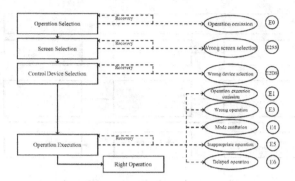

Fig. 3. Soft control human error modes

Operation omission is divided into two kinds of omissions, operation selection omission and operation execution omission, since their error probabilities should be considered separately.

- Operation omission (E_0): An operator omits performing a task when following a procedure (one task in a procedure).
- Operation execution omission (E_1): An operator omits performing a sub task when following a task. (one sub task in a task).
- Wrong screen selection (E_{2SS}): An operator selects a wrong screen when performing a task.
- Wrong device selection (E_{2DS}): An operator selects a wrong control device when performing a task.

Tasks	Possible human error modes							
1. Open PORV block valves	E0							
Press valve 'PV445' button			E2DS					
Press 'Manual' button				E1		E4		E6
Press the Acknowledge button 'OK'				E1				
Press valve 'HV6' button			E2DS					
Press 'Open' button				E1	E3			E6
Press the Acknowledge button 'OK'				E1				
2. Open Aux FW level control valves	E0							
Press 'Graphic' button		E2SS						
Select 'Feed Water System (FWS)'		E2SS						
Press valve 'HV313' button			E2DS					
Fully open the valve 'HV313'				E1			E5	E6
Press the Acknowledge button 'OK'				E1				
Press valve 'HV315' button			E2DS					
Fully open the valve 'HV315'				E1			E5	E6
Press the Acknowledge button 'OK'				E1				
3. Isolate letdown flow form ruptured S/G	E0							
Press set point control valve			E2DS					
Press 'Manual' button						E4		E6
Regulate controller setpoint of ruptured S/G PORV to 79.1 kg/cm²				E1			E5	E6
Press 'Auto' button						E4		E6
Press the Acknowledge button 'OK'				E1				
4. Close steam distribution valve which supplies flow to turbine driven	E0							
Press valve 'HV314' button			E2DS					
Fully close the valve 'HV314'				E1			E5	E6
Press the Acknowledge button 'OK'				E1				
5.Reset SI and AUX FW Actuation Signal	E0							
Press 'Graphic' button		E2SS						
Select 'reactivity system'		E2SS						
Press 'safety injection bypass' button			E2DS					
Press 'bypass' button				E1				E6
Press the Acknowledge button 'OK'				E1				
Press 'safety guard' button			E2DS					
Press 'reset' button				E1				E6
Press the Acknowledge button 'OK'				E1				

Fig. 4. Possible human error modes according to each soft control task

As a result of these modifications, the possible human errors during the process are classified into eight types by an additional analysis. Execution tasks in Emergency Operating Procedure (EOP) are then analyzed to verify which human error modes may occur for each soft control task, as shown in Fig. 4.

3 Development of a Framework for HRA Method in Consideration of Soft Control

3.1 Secondary Tasks

In the new operation environment of Advanced MCRs, the operation actions of operators are divided into primary tasks (e.g., providing control inputs to plant systems) and secondary tasks (e.g., manipulating the user interface to access information or controls or to change control modes). Interface management tasks are referred to as secondary tasks because they are concerned with controlling the interface rather than the plant [11].

3.2 Sequential Behavior for Unit Task Completion

As explained in the task analysis of soft control, each subtask is included in one of four sub steps: operation selection, screen selection, control device selection, and operation execution. In other words, the operator should follow the subtasks sequentially to complete one unit task according to four sub steps. If the operator fails to perform subtasks at any steps, the operator should recover the failure tasks and then continues to perform the next subtasks. For example, there is one unit task 'Control letdown flow of S/G to 20 liter/sec', as shown in Fig. 5.

In order to complete this unit task, the operator first should succeed in pressing the 'Graphic' button, which is one of the navigation tasks (secondary tasks). Next, the operator also should select 'Feedwater system' to find control device 'HV304' (secondary task). The operator then increases the letdown flow to 20 liter/sec and finally pushes the 'OK' button to send a signal to the control device. If the operator fails to perform any subtasks, failure subtasks should be recovered to continue performing the next subtask.

	Tasks	Possible human error modes					
121	13. Control letdown flow of S/G to 20 liter/sec	E0					
122	Press 'Graphic' button		E2SS				
123	Select 'Feed Water System (FWS)'		E2SS				
124	Press valve 'HV304' button			E2DS			
125	Increase letdown flow to 20 liter/sec	E1				E5	E6
126	Press the Acknowledge button 'OK'	E1					

Fig. 5. Example of task including sub tasks

3.3   Dependency among Subtasks

As shown in Fig. 4 and Fig. 5, given unit tasks contain different numbers of subtasks. Due to sequential behavior for unit task completion, failure or success of one subtask may affect failure or success of the next subtask if two subtasks are not mutually independent.

By adopting the dependency model from THERP [2], failure or success probabilities of unit tasks including subtasks can be estimated reasonably. However, determination of the level of dependency should be differently developed in our model by considering characteristics of new HSI and soft control.

Level of Dependence. The approach taken in the THERP handbook is to reduce the positive continuum of conditional probability to a small number of discrete points. THERP use five points: the two end points of zero dependence (ZD) and complete dependence (CD) plus three points in between. These intermediate points are called low dependence (LD), moderate dependence (MD), and high dependence (HD) [2].

Determination of Level of Dependence in Advanced MCRs. Determination of the level of dependency should be differently developed in our model by considering characteristics of new HSI and soft control.

The THERP approach to dependency assessment uses several parameters to determine the level of dependency between events, including same or different crew, time, location, and cues. Accompanying these parameters is a scale that rates dependency from zero (no dependency) to a value representing complete dependency [2].

However, several parameters defined in THERP should be modified considering the new features of advanced MCRs. Since soft controls are control devices having connections with control and display systems that are mediated by software rather than direct physical connections and their functions may be variable and context dependent rather than statically defined, location is not important when determining level of dependency.

NUREG/CR-6635 points out several causes of soft control human error that are possibly related to parameters for dependency level [10]:

- Description error: the similarity of an object, and the amount of separation between them, especially those presented via a graphical user interface.
- Misordering the component of an action sequence: reversed and repeated steps.
- Loss of activation errors: keyhole effect (the HSI may only have space for a few displays at one time).

From the survey conducted for NUREG/CR-6635, similarity of control devices and their tags in flat display panels and repetition tasks should be added as parameters to determine the level of dependency. Soft control has an additional unique characteristic known as group control. Group control refers to when the operator is able to control devices as a group.

After analysis of the feature of soft control, determination of the level of dependency for soft control is developed using a decision tree, as shown in Fig. 6. And conditional probabilities according to dependency levels are shown in Table 1.

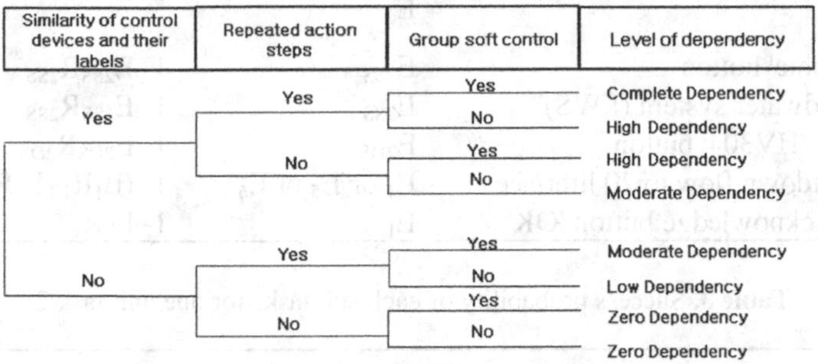

Similarity of control devices and their labels	Repeated action steps	Group soft control	Level of dependency
		Yes	Complete Dependency
	Yes	No	High Dependency
Yes		Yes	High Dependency
	No	No	Moderate Dependency
		Yes	Moderate Dependency
	Yes	No	Low Dependency
No		Yes	Zero Dependency
	No	No	Zero Dependency

Fig. 6. Decision tree for level of dependency

Table 1. Conditional probabilities acccording to dependency levels

Dependency level	Equation for P(B)
Complete	1.0
High	$[1+P(A)]/2$
Moderate	$[1+6P(A)]/7$
Low	$[1+19P(A)]/20$
Zero	$P(B)$

3.4   A Framework for HRA Method in Consideration of Soft Control

As explained in sections 3.1 to 3.3, a framework for a HRA method under consideration of soft control is developed using concepts of secondary tasks, sequential behavior for unit completion, and dependency among subtasks. In our model, a success path (a path where all subtasks succeed) is considered to calculate soft control execution human error probability (HEP) with consideration of dependency among tasks.

Concept of HEP Calculation. The success probability of each subtask depends on the human error probabilities according to human error modes classified in Fig. 4 and 5, and their recovery failure probabilities. Recovery failure probabilities according to human error modes are expressed as R_i. In other words, R_i equals the recovery failure probability of E_i (i=0, 1, 2SS, 2DS, 3, 4, 5, 6). The probability that the operator succeeds in each subtask for unit tasks 1 and 2 is then expressed in Tables 2 and 3, respectively.

Table 2. Success probability of each sub tasks for one unit task 1

Each task	Possible human error modes	Success probability
Control letdown flow of S/G to 20 liter/sec	E_0	1- E_0R_0
Press 'Graphic' button	E_{2SS}	1- $E_{2SS}R_{2SS}$
Select 'Feedwater system (FWS)'	E_{2SS}	1- $E_{2SS}R_{2SS}$
Press valve 'HV304' button	E_{2DS}	1- $E_{2DS}R_{2DS}$
Increase letdown flow to 20 liter/sec	E_1 or E_5 or E_6	1- $(E_1R_1+E_5R_5+E_6R_6)$
Press the Acknowledge button 'OK'	E_1	1- E_1R_1

Table 3. Success probability of each sub tasks for one unit task 2

Each task	Possible human error modes	Success probability
Open Aux FW level control valves	E_0	1- E_0R_0
Press 'Graphic' button	E_{2SS}	1- $E_{2SS}R_{2SS}$
Select 'Feed Water System (FWS)'	E_{2SS}	1- $E_{2SS}R_{2SS}$
Press valve 'HV313' button	E_{2DS}	1- $E_{2DS}R_{2DS}$
Fully open the valve 'HV313'	E_1 or E_5 or E_6	1- $(E_1R_1+E_5R_5+E_6R_6)$
Press the Acknowledge button 'OK'	E_1	1- E_1R_1
Press valve 'HV315' button	E_{2DS}	1- $E_{2DS}R_{2DS}$
Fully open the valve 'HV315'	E_1 or E_5 or E_6	1- $(E_1R_1+E_5R_5+E_6R_6)$
Press the Acknowledge button 'OK'	E_1	1- E_1R_1

If there is no dependency (zero dependency) among the subtasks, it is easy to calculate the HEP of two unit tasks (Human Error Probability of unit task 1, HEP_1 and Human Error Probability of unit task 2, HEP_2)

$$HEP_1 = 1 - \{(1 - R_0E_0) \times (1 - R_{2SS}E_{2SS}) \times (1 - R_{2SS}E_{2SS}) \times (1 - R_{2DS}E_{2DS}) \times (1 - (R_1E_1+R_5E_5+R_6E_6)) \times (1 - R_1E_1)\}$$

$$HEP_2 = 1 - \{(1 - R_0E_0) \times (1 - R_{2SS}E_{2SS}) \times (1 - R_{2SS}E_{2SS}) \times (1 - R_{2DS}E_{2DS}) \times (1 - (R_1E_1+R_5E_5+R_6E_6)) \times (1 - R_1E_1) \times (1 - R_{2DS}E_{2DS}) \times (1 - (R_1E_1+R_5E_5+R_6E_6)) \times (1 - R_1E_1)\}$$

where E_i=human error probabilities for each human error mode and R_i=recovery failure probabilities. However, if dependency among subtasks exits, the HEP calculation should be modified considering the level of dependency among subtasks using a decision tree for the dependency level.

The HEP of two unit tasks can then be calculated by applying the dependency level.

In the case of HEP_1, there is no dependency (ZD) among subtasks. Then,

$$HEP_1 = 1 - \{(1 - R_0E_0) \times (1 - R_{2SS}E_{2SS}) \times (1 - R_{2SS}E_{2SS}) \\ \times (1 - R_{2DS}E_{2DS}) \times (1 - (R_1E_1 + R_5E_5 + R_6E_6)) \times (1 - R_1E_1)\}$$

In the case of HEP_2, there is high dependency between subtasks 'Press valve 'HV313' button to Press the Acknowledge button 'OK'' and 'Press valve 'HV315' button to Press the Acknowledge button 'OK''.
Then,

$$HEP_2 = 1 - \{(1 - R_0E_0) \times (1 - R_{2SS}E_{2SS}) \times (1 - R_{2SS}E_{2SS}) \\ \times (1 - R_{2DS}E_{2DS}) \times (1 - (R_1E_1 + R_5E_5 + R_6E_6)) \times (1 - R_1E_1) \\ \times \frac{1 + (1 - R_{2DS}E_{2DS})}{2} \times \frac{1 + (1 - (R_1E_1 + R_5E_5 + R_6E_6))}{2} \times \frac{[1 + (1 - R_1E_1)]}{2}\}$$

Using the calculated HEP, the HEP calculation equation is generalized as follows.

$$HEP = 1 - \left\{(1 - R_0E_0) \prod \frac{1 + K(1 - \sum_{i \neq 0} R_iE_i)}{1 + K}\right\} \qquad (1)$$

where,
E_i = human error probabilities at human error mode i
R_i = recovery failure probabilities at human error mode i.
i = 1, 2SS, 2DS, 3, 4, 5, and 6 according to human error modes.
K=19, 6, 1, 0 depending on the dependency level

4   HEP Estimation Using Developed HRA Method

4.1   Nominal HEP Database According to Human Error Mode for Advanced MCRS Using Soft Control

Since the developed method is significantly dependent on nominal HEPs according to human error modes such as E_0, E_1, E_{2SS}, E_{2DS}, E_3, E_4, E_5, and E_6, a nominal HEP database such as a THERP table should be developed in advance. Although THERP tables are well organized, their nominal HEPs are not specific for advanced MCRs.

In a related study by the authors, nominal HEPs according to human error modes were developed by experiments using a mockup simulator for an advanced MCR [13].

Additional experiments performed by the same procedures as used in the previous experiments were performed to update the nominal HEP database. However, nominal HEPs according to human error modes should be modified for direct input of the developed HRA method. The results of this empirical study could not explain E_0 because no human error occurred. Moreover, E_{2SS} and E_{2DS} are derived as E_2. Nominal HEPs according to human error modes are modified by analyzing human error checklists for E_{2SS} and E_{2DS} and by using an assumption for E_0, as shown in Table 4.

Table 4. Modified nominal HEP according to human error modes

Human error modes	Nominal HEP	Human error modes	Modified nominal HEP
		E_0	5.00E-3 (Assumption)
E_1	4.63E-3	E_1	4.63E-3
E_2	7.85E-3	E_{2SS}	5.23E-3 (2/3 of E_2)
		E_{2DS}	2.62E-3 (1/3 of E_2)
E_3	7.25E-3	E_3	7.25E-3
E_4	6.52E-2	E_4	6.52E-2
E_5	2.35E-2	E_5	2.35E-2
E_6	7.25E-3	E_6	7.25E-3

4.2   Recovery Failure Probabilities

Recovery failure probabilities in this study are assumed using the recovery failure tree from K-HRA [3] and insight from performed experiments. In case of recovery failure probability of secondary tasks such as screen navigation tasks and control device selection tasks, it is assumed that the recovery failure probabilities are assigned as 0.01, since most screen navigation tasks are recovered in the performed experiments.

Three cases of recovery failure probabilities for HEP calculation are then selected, as shown in Table 5.

Table 5. Recovery failure probabilities

Case	R_0	R_1	R_{2SS}	R_{2DS}	R_5	R_6
Case 1	0.03	0.03	0.01	0.01	0.03	0.03
Case 2	0.05	0.05	0.01	0.01	0.05	0.05
Case 3	0.15	0.15	0.01	0.01	0.15	0.15

4.3   HEP Estimation

Based on the suggested HEP calculation method with the developed database including nominal HEPs in Table 4, recovery failure probabilities in Table 5 according to human error modes, and the dependency model, HEPs of two different unit tasks shown in Tables 2 and 3, respectively, are estimated.

Table 6. Result of HEP_1 and HEP_2 based on nominal HEPs, dependency level according to three cases recovery failure probabilities

Case	HEP_1	HEP_2
Case 1	1.48E-03	2.09E-03
Case 2	2.38E-03	3.39E-03
Case 3	6.87E-03	9.87E-03

In other words, once levels of dependency for each subtask are determined, input values from the database are inserted to the equation of HEP estimation. From the results of HEP_1 and HEP_2 based on nominal HEPs, dependency levels according to three cases of recovery failure probabilities are shown in Table 6.

5   Summary and Conclusion

This paper proposed a new framework for a HRA method for evaluation of soft control execution human error in advanced MCRs, because many HRA methods do not sufficiently consider the features of advanced MCRs such as soft control execution human errors due to the different interfaces between soft control and hardwired conventional type control.

In order to develop the new framework for the HRA method, a soft control task analysis was performed to identify human error modes. From the results of the soft control task analysis, the possible human errors during the process were classified into eight types. It was also identified that the operator should follow the subtasks sequentially to complete one unit task, and if the operator fails to perform subtasks, the operator should recover the failure tasks. Moreover, dependency among subtasks is considered by modifying the determination of levels of dependency in the THERP model. This modification is performed according to several causes of soft control human error pointed out in NUREG/CR-6635 that may be related to parameters for dependency level.

In our model, a success path is considered to calculate soft control execution HEP with consideration of dependency between two subtasks. By deriving two examples of HEP equations for representative soft control unit tasks in consideration of secondary tasks, sequential behavior, and dependency among subtasks, a HEP calculation equation is generalized. A database for inputs to the general HEP equation such as nominal HEPs and recovery failure probabilities is developed and applied to estimate HEPs. Finally, HEPs are estimated using the developed nominal HEPs by assuming three different cases of recovery failure probabilities.

Acknowledgement. This work was supported by Nuclear Research & Development Program of the National Research Foundation of Korea grant, funded by the Korean government, Ministry of Science, ICT & Future Planning (Grant Code: 2012M2A8A4025991) 2014M2A8A4025991).

References

1. Kirwan, B.: Human error identification in human reliability assessment. Part 1: Overview of approaches. Applied Ergonomics 23, 299–318 (1992)
2. Swain, A.D., Guttmann, H.E.: Handbook of Human-Reliability Analysis with Emphasis on Nuclear Power Plant Application. NUREG/CR-1278, U.S. Nuclear Regulatory Commission, Washington, DC (1983)

3. Jung, W.D., Kang, D.I., Kim, J.: Development of a Standard Method for Human Reliability Analysis (HRA) of Nuclear Power Plants. KAERI/TR-2961. Korea Atomic Energy Reaseach Institute, Deajeon (2005)
4. Williams, J.C.: HEART - A proposed method for achieving high reliability in process operation by means of human factors engineering technology. In: Proceedings of a Symposium on the Achievement of Reliability in Operating Plant, Safety and Reliability Society. NEC, Birmingham (1985)
5. Embrey, D.E., Humphreys, P., Rosa, E.A., Kirwan, B., Rea, K.: SLIM-MAUD: an approach to assessing human error probabilities using structured expert judgment. Overview of SLIM-MAUD. NUREG/CR-3518, U.S, vol. I. Nuclear Regulatory Commission, Washington, DC (1984)
6. Hannaman, G.W., Spurgin, A.J., Lukic, Y.D.: Human cognitive reliability model for PRA analysis. In: NUS-4531. Electric Power and Research Institute, San Diego (1984)
7. Forester, J.: Kolaczkowski. A., Cooper, S., Bley, D., Lois, E.: ATHEANA User's Guide. NUREG-1880, U.S. Nuclear Regulatory Commission, Washington, DC (2000)
8. Hollnagel, E.: Cognitive Reliability and Error Analysis Method - CREAM. Elsevier Science, Oxford (1998)
9. Gertman, D., Blackman, H., Marble, J., Byers, J.: Smith. C.: The SPAR-H Human Reliability Analysis Method. NUREG/CR-6883, U.S. Nuclear Regulatory Commission, Washington, DC (2005)
10. Stubler, W.F., O'Hara, J.M., Kramer, J.: Soft Control: Technical Basis and Human Factors Review Guidance. NUREG/CR-6635, U.S. Nuclear Regulatory Commission, Washington, DC (2000)
11. Lee, S.J., Kim, J., Jang, S.C.: Human Error Mode Identification for NPP Main Control Room Operation Using Soft Controls. Journal of Nuclear Science and Technology 48, 902–910 (2011)
12. Embrey, D.E.: SHERPA: A systematic human error reduction and prediction approach. In: International Topical Meeting on Advances in Human Factors in Nuclear Power Systems, Knoxville, Tennessee (1986)
13. Jang, I., Kim, A.R., Harbi, M., Lee, S.J., Kang, H.G., Seong, P.H.: An empirical study on the basic human error probabilities for NPP advanced main control room operation using soft control. Nuclear Engineering and Design 257, 79–87 (2013)

A Resilient Interaction Concept for Process Management on Tabletops for Cyber-Physical Systems

Ronny Seiger, Susann Struwe, Sandra Matthes, and Thomas Schlegel

Institute of Software and Multimedia-Technology, Technische Universität Dresden,
Dresden, D-01062, Germany,
{ronny.seiger,susann.struwe,thomas.schlegel}@tu-dresden.de,
sandra.matthes@mailbox.tu-dresden.de

Abstract. Using tabletop devices for controlling complex applications is rather uncommon as interaction on tabletops is still very error-prone. Especially in everyday life settings, there is a multitude of sources of distractions and input errors. The tabletop-based management of cyber-physical systems influencing both the virtual and the real world introduces new challenges with respect to reliability and fault tolerance of the user interface. In this paper, we present an interaction concept for complex management applications on tabletops introducing more resilient gestures for different stages of the interaction. The interaction concept provides more reliable interactions than the basic set of touch gestures does and proves suitable for more complex applications. A user study conducted as part of the work confirms the concept's increased accuracy without influencing the overall usability. As an example, we present a process management application for cyber-physical systems implementing the interaction concept.

Keywords: Process Management, Interaction Concept for Tabletops, Multimodal Interaction, Security and Reliability.

1 Introduction

In his visionary paper "The Computer for the 21st Century" Mark Weiser presented the idea of pervasive computing systems and devices being almost invisible to the users [1]. With the introduction of tabletop computers, these *ubiquitous systems* have reached a new level of seamless integration into the user's everyday life. A tabletop does not only play the role of an input device for digital applications but can also be treated like a piece of furniture positioned in central places within a house, offering space for interaction and for depositing physical objects [2]. However, with the development of applications for the interaction with large screen tabletop devices in everyday life new challenges arise: users might be inattentive; objects may lay on the input surface; clothing may touch the surface; multiple inputs may occur at once; environmental factors may distort the interaction. All of these factors could lead to input errors and thus

S. Yamamoto (Ed.): HIMI 2014, Part II, LNCS 8522, pp. 347–358, 2014.
© Springer International Publishing Switzerland 2014

to unintended behavior [3]. Hence, current applications usually provide only a limited set of functionality for controlling relatively simple digital objects and systems in order to prevent input errors [3].

Cyber-physical systems (CPS) are a further step towards ubiquitous systems. They combine digital (cyber) and real-world (physical) systems and objects to a new degree [4]. By integrating sensors and actuators with data processing units, embedded computers, and cloud services, a close connection between real objects and virtual objects is created. The emergence of *smart spaces* (smart homes, smart factories, smart offices) shows the increasing importance and spreading of CPS throughout all areas of everyday life. Controlling complex CPS involves not only manipulating virtual objects and processes but also influencing the real world. Therefore, control devices and user interfaces for CPS have to be designed with these new properties in mind. Particularly, input errors and unintended actions have to be avoided as they may have far-reaching consequences in both the cyber and the physical world. This is in contrast to the properties of tabletops, as they are very likely to produce input errors, especially when being used in interfering environments.

We therefore developed an interaction concept enabling more complex applications on tabletops, preventing unintended control actions and thereby allowing more critical operations. As an example, we picked a process management system comprising the visualization, management, and control of processes in a smart home environment. Processes allow the execution of services across application and device boundaries within complex systems in order to facilitate the automation of repeating sequences of activities. Therefore, they play an important role in adaptive and autonomous cyber-physical systems.

The paper is structured as follows: Section 2 discusses challenges that arise when using tabletops for managing CPS applications. Section 3 discusses related research. Section 4 presents our interaction concept for CPS applications on tabletops. Section 5 introduces our process management system. Section 6 evaluates and discusses our interaction concept and management application. Section 7 concludes the paper and shows starting points for future work.

2   Challenges

Tabletops are a new type of interaction device, which provides users with a large multi-touch screen usually mounted horizontally on a stand. A tabletop enables multiple users to interact with its user interface in parallel. Several researchers envision tabletops and tabletop-like devices to become more integrated into people's everyday lives in the near future [1,5]. In a smart home setting, an interactive tabletop could replace the classic coffee table and provide the residents with additional means for infotainment, communication, and control/management tasks.

However, when using a tabletop both as a piece of furniture and as a digital interaction device new challenges arise that have to be dealt with, especially in the context of cyber-physical systems:

- **N:1 Interaction:** In contrast to common touch-based input devices, e. g., tablets and smartphones, tabletops are usually not bound to and operated by only one user. Due to the large screen and interaction surface, several users are able to interact with the tabletop's user interface in parallel. This can lead to users influencing and interfering with each other [6].
- **Fixed Horizontal Screen:** Being mounted in a fixed position, the tabletop device provides no means for an adapting to the users current position. Therefore, users have to adjust their interaction habits to the properties of the tabletop. For example, the large screen makes it necessary to touch the UI elements holding the finger in a preferably steep angle in order to avoid additional contacts with the input surface by other fingers, the wrist, or a sleeve. Moreover, the interaction distances are likely to be increased compared to smaller screen devices.
- **Distracted Users:** Especially in everyday environments, users are not solely focussed on interacting with the input device. In addition to being in a hurry, a multitude of other sources can distract the user's attention from the tabletop's current user interface [7].
- **Environmental Distortions:** Depending on the technology implemented for input recognition on the tabletop, environmental and physical properties can have influence on the accuracy of the touch and gesture recognizers. For example, optical systems based on infrared light are very sensitive towards sunlight and are likely to mistake light beams for intended touch input. Physical objects lying on the tabletop's input surface may also trigger additional actions or distort the current interaction.

All of these factors have significant influence on the accuracy and usability of the applications developed for the tabletop. These issues can lead to unintended behavior triggered by imprecise or unintentional interactions [3]. This can be a major deal-breaker, especially when interacting with cyber-physical systems, as CPS also affect real world objects and processes [4]. Erroneous input, e. g., additional input events or wrong parameters, can trigger safety-critical actions or even cause damage to objects or people. The task of managing processes in cyber-physical systems increases the importance of correct and reliable user input as processes are intended to support the users by automating repeating activities. Tabletops do not seem to be suitable for the critical tasks of managing and controlling cyber-physical systems. As described in this section, there are several sources of input errors and issues that need to be dealt with when interacting with a tabletop in complex environments [7].

3   Related Work

Our intention is to develop a touch-based interaction concept providing reliable interactions for complex applications. Lambeck et al. [8] argue that traditional interaction and visualization concepts known from desktop applications (WIMP) can not be completely transferred to complex touch-based applications.

The authors present new interaction concepts and paradigms to enable the use of complex applications on tabletops.

In order to reduce frequent input errors and falsely triggered actions on tabletops as observed in [3,7], Lepinski et al. [9] and Moscovich [10] propose to apply marking menus and sliding gestures. From their observations, these interaction elements extend the basic touch gestures [11] and enable more reliable interactions. Providing visual feedback about the state of an interaction supports the user with preventing input errors. ShadowGuide [12] and Escape [13] are two systems employing techniques for the direct visualization of gestures and using advanced UI components for improving touch-based user interfaces.

In [14] Antle et al. developed an interaction prototype for a collaborative learning game on a tabletop device. User studies conducted with the help of this application showed that dragging and dropping gestures are suitable and accepted for collaboration scenarios. In [6] a comprehensive system for tabletop interaction is presented, which applies small sequences of interactions instead of single touch gestures. By using dragging and sliding actions as part of the interaction sequences, the authors achieve an observable reduction of input errors.

As the aforementioned concepts facilitate the design of a fault-tolerant interaction concept for tabletop devices, we will integrate the ideas of interaction sequences comprising sliding and dragging gestures, visual feedback, and customized UI components for touch-based applications into our interaction concept. In [8,15] management systems from the areas of production and disaster control are presented. We will base our process management system applying our interaction concept on these works.

When looking at current applications implemented on tabletop devices, we find that they often only provide relatively simple user interfaces in order to offer a good user experience. Showroom and game-like applications are the predominant use of tabletops nowadays. However, with the advance of tabletops and smart home technologies, we believe that tabletops will also be used for controlling more complex applications involving real-world objects and processes as parts of cyber-physical systems. Current tabletop interaction concepts and user interfaces are not designed with the properties of CPS in mind and are therefore not able to completely meet the requirements for secure and reliable interactions. Therefore, we developed a resilient interaction concept to be used for controlling complex CPS applications on tabletops.

4   An Interaction Concept for Management Applications

With respect to complex management applications, we find that menus and lists to select items and operations from are key elements for interacting with digital objects and information. These applications often provide a multitude of information and operations, which can be best represented in the form of lists and menus. However, the selection of list elements from a complex list is a very error-prone action on tabletops and often leads to an incorrect selection of an entry [9]. Performing an actual control operation in CPS could trigger critical real-world actions and processes. Hence, the interaction gestures used for selection and execution of an operation on a tabletop device have to be designed to tolerate possible input errors. We developed a multi-stage selection and confirmation procedure to be applied in management applications in order to reduce input errors.

4.1 Setup Stage (Non-critical Actions)

The *Setup* stage consists of non-critical actions for switching between views, configuring parameters, and browsing information. These actions do not manipulate data nor do they lead to an immediate change in a system's or an application's state. They can be reverted easily by simply returning to the previous state or reconfiguring the current selections using simple interactions. Therefore, unintended input does not lead to critical reactions nor does it increase the user's frustration level.

During the Setup stage, commonly known touch gestures can be used because input errors can be tolerated during this stage. In order to browse information and configure parameters, we apply basic touch gestures (e. g., tap, drag, spread, pinch, and slide [11]). As no immediate action is triggered, errors resulting from unintended input can be corrected easily by re-applying these basic gestures.

4.2 Selection Stage (Semi-critical Actions)

The *Selection* stage comprises the selection of menu items available with respect to a digital object. These items can be operations to be performed immediately on the object or additional information to be displayed (e. g., in a newly opened window). These semi-critical actions lead to a direct alteration of the digital (**cyber**) system's or object's state as well as to a change of the current information visualization. During this stage, input errors lead to the selection of a

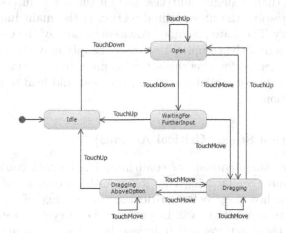

Fig. 1. State machine controlling the LinMark-Select gesture

wrong list item and thus to a wrong operation to be performed. Reverting the false selection usually is more complex and involves a combination of interactions, which raises the user's frustration level. Therefore, input errors should be avoided during this stage.

Using simple touch gestures (cf. Setup stage) for this activity can be very error-prone on tabletops as single touch events on the wrong area of the UI can trigger a false selection. Therefore, we introduce a sequence of composite gestures called "LinMark-Select" [9]. This sequence consists of a tap for initiating the selection process, a dragging action for the selection of an item, and a lifting movement for confirmation of the current selection (cf. Fig. 2a). An underlying state machine controls the states of this complex gesture (cf. Fig. 1) [6] and the user interface component provides visual feedback about the action's current state [12] and selected item (cf. Fig. 2a). The user can easily switch between available list items while holding the finger down as well as revert/cancel the selection procedure.

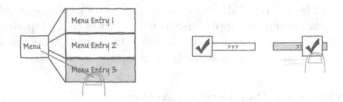

Fig. 2. LinMark-Select (a) and Safe-Select (b) gestures

With a state machine controlling the LinMark-Select procedure, erroneous input and incorrect touch events are ignored automatically. Only valid input events lead to a change and therefore to a progress of the selection sequence. Moving the finger in the direction of the desired list item is more intuitive and more robust [13] than a single imprecise tap on the list item [14], as with the LinMark-Select gesture the movement direction is the main indicator for the desired menu entry. The state machine allows corrections of the current selection and the cancellation of the complex gesture by simply moving the finger out of the active area. When performing this selection procedure, the user's attention is drawn towards the list of available options, which should lead to a more precise and correct selection.

4.3   Confirmation Stage (Critical Actions)

The *Confirmation* stage consists of confirming the current configuration of a selected action and thereby triggering its immediate execution. This stage is intended to be the last stage before critical actions having effects on real world (**physical**) objects and systems will be performed or a system's state is changed significantly. As these actions will influence both the cyber and the physical world, input errors have to be avoided in any case. Reverting wrong selections and false configurations usually means a considerable effort for the user to undo the triggered actions. Therefore, errors lead to a high level of frustration and may also cause damage to real-world objects.

Using simple touch gestures during this stage can be very error-prone as unintended touch events can lead to a false confirmation of an action to be performed. Therefore, we introduce the "Safe-Select" gesture for confirmation. This swipe gesture is often applied for unlocking a smartphone from the idle state. Performing this gesture involves sliding a finger along a control bar (cf. Fig. 2b). The user receives visual feedback about the current state of the action [12] and the operation will only be executed if the checkbox has been completely moved from left to right.

This confirmation gesture requires the user to pay attention to the active UI area and ignores every touch event outside the control bar. Only a complete slide of the checkbox along the control bar confirms the selected action to be triggered. This interaction is more robust than simple touch gestures for confirmation [10]. It can be canceled easily by moving the finger out of the control bar area or by sliding it back from right to left.

5 Process Management Application on Tabletops

Using our interaction concept, we developed a process management application for cyber-physical systems on a SUR40 tabletop with Microsoft®PixelSense™.

5.1 Process Information

In order to interact with processes in a smart home environment, the information related to available processes, running process instances, and the process execution engine's state first need to be visualized. In accordance with Shneiderman's Visual Information Seeking Mantra [16], we first present an overview of the complete process management system (cf. Fig. 3). Here, the user is able to zoom into and filter information concerning the *System State*, *Process Models*, and *Running Instances*. After selecting a specific view or process object, the application presents additional details regarding the selection.

System State Information. The *System State* view gives a concise overview of the process engine's current state including a log of recent events and errors that have occurred during process execution.

Process Model Information. The *Process Model* view presents a list of categorized processes (process models) available for execution. An additional property panel containing details can be opened for every process model. These details include general information (e. g., name, type, and input/output parameters), a log for process instances executed according to the particular model, and a graphical, scalable representation of the process model. Multiple property panels can be opened in parallel and moved freely on the UI by dragging gestures, allowing simultaneous and collaborative interaction among multiple users.

Process Instance Information. The *Running Instances* view displays an overview of current and recently executed processes (process instances). Similar to the process model view, a property panel can be opened with respect to every process instance. This panel presents general information including the current progress of an instance, data values, a log for this particular instance, and a graphical representation of the corresponding process model.

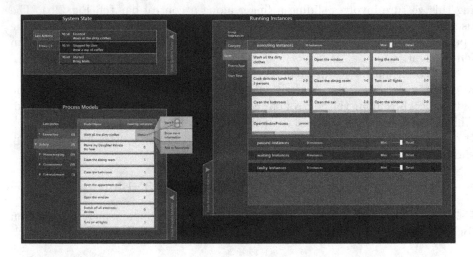

Fig. 3. Overview screen of the management application

5.2   Process Control

Setup Stage. In the context of our application, the *Setup Stage* applying only simple touch gestures comprises browsing through processes and process information, switching between different views, and setting parameters for the instantiation of processes. As these actions do not have immediate effects on the system or processes, simple touch gestures are sufficient for executing these setup actions.

Selection Stage. During the *Selection Stage*, an entry from a list of available menu entries is selected using the LinMark-Select gesture. We use this gesture for selecting operations to be performed on particular process models and instances. With every process, we provide a list of possible actions, e. g., opening a new window for starting an instance, changing its state, and opening a property panel (cf. Fig. 4a). These actions do have an immediate effect on the system's state and presentation of information and are therefore selected using the more resilient LinMark-Select gesture.

Confirmation Stage. The *Confirmation Stage* leads to the immediate execution of a real world process or a significant change in the system's state. Therefore, we apply the more robust Safe-Select gesture for confirming critical actions to be immediately triggered after the gesture. In our application, changing the state of a process instance (start, stop, pause, cancel) is confirmed using the Safe-Select gesture (cf. Fig. 4b) as well as the addition, deletion, and modification of process models. During the confirmation stage, only the current confirmation window can be interacted with allowing only one user to confirm or cancel the execution of the selected action.

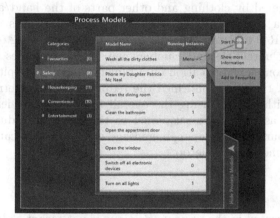

Fig. 4. The LinMark-(a) and Safe-(b) Select gestures used for process management

6   Evaluation and Discussion

An evaluation with respect to Nielsen's usability heuristics [17] shows good results regarding the usability of our interaction concept and management application. Nine out of ten of Nielsen's heuristics can be evaluated as "good" or even "very good". As managing processes in a smart home environment is yet not very common, users first have to get used to the terminology we applied in the process control system. The management system is currently in the stage of a prototype not including any help or documentation to support the user, which is the only major point of criticism with respect to the usability heuristics.

6.1   User Study

In order to evaluate our concept and application on a qualitative level, we conducted a small user study among ten computer science students and university employees in the age group from 20 to 39. All of the participants were already experienced in using touch devices and familiar with basic touch gestures. We chose this group of test subjects because they are open to interacting with new technologies and they are likely to understand the concepts behind the process management and CPS topics more quickly.

The user study was divided into two main tasks. First, the subjects had to use a file management software on the tabletop to open and copy some files using basic touch gestures, e. g., tap, long tap, double tap, and drag. Second, the subjects had to interact with our process management application to start and stop some processes as well as retrieve additional information regarding particular processes. The second task involved using our interaction concept including the LinMark-Select and Safe-Select gestures.

Using only basic touch gestures during task one, the participants struggled a lot with input errors triggered by clothing and other parts of the hand/arm when selecting items from a complex list as well as when opening files and the context menu on the SUR40 tabletop. The majority agreed that using only these basic gestures is very unreliable and cumbersome, which increases the effort of interacting with a complex application on a tabletop device. Despite a higher initial learning effort, the users confirmed the reduction of input errors and unintended behavior without decreasing the overall interaction efficiency for our interaction concept as they got accustomed to the newly introduced gestures quickly. All in all, our test subjects can envisage using our application for managing their smart homes on a tabletop.

6.2 Discussion

The interaction concept presented in the previous sections is not meant to be a complete set of interaction gestures necessary for a complex management application. It rather introduces new gestures/interaction sequences as well as user interface components that can be applied complementary to an existing interaction concept. Based on related work, existing concepts and gestures are put into a new context with respect to our application scenario: process management in CPS. The LinMark-Select and Safe-Select gestures should be considered when designing new interaction concepts for safety-critical applications as they reduce input errors and accidental actions. At the same time, acceptance and efficiency of the interactions are preserved as shown by our user study.

In order to further evaluate the management application for a broader target audience, the rather complex application has to be simplified with respect to its wording and its relatively high amount of text should be enhanced by graphics and icons. Elements from gamification can be used to introduce users to our interaction concept and to simplify access to the management application.

Although we started to design the interaction concept taking into account the high error rates of our optical tabletop device, several of the aforementioned sources for input errors also exist for other types of input recognition systems (e. g., capacitive touchscreens) and tabletops in general. When controlling critical actions in cyber-physical systems, there is a general need for failure tolerant user interfaces including multi-stage selection and confirmation procedures in order to prevent unwanted actions to be executed.

7   Conclusion and Future Work

In this work, we presented an interaction concept for selecting and executing safety-critical actions in cyber-physical systems (CPS). Tabletop devices will become more and more integrated into people's everyday lives as described by Mark Weiser's vision of ubiquitous systems. Due to a multitude of sources of input errors and distractions, there is a need for a fault-tolerant user interface especially for tabletops. We introduced a set of new gestures and UI elements dividing the interaction with complex management applications into three stages of different criticality for setup, selection, and execution actions. The new interaction concept can be applied to complex applications on touch-based devices in general preventing the user from adapting himself/herself to the properties of the device. With the newly introduced LinMark-Select and Safe-Select gestures we are able to reduce input errors without implementing additional error recognition and filter algorithms. User tests confirmed the reduction of input errors and the feasibility of our approach.

As part of our future work, we plan to test our interaction concept in a real-life smart home setting. Currently, the process management prototype is not connected to an actual process execution engine. The integration of both systems will be part of our cyber-physical systems research project. An extensive user study involving the execution of automated processes in a smart home and their control by a tabletop device will be conducted in the project's final stage in order to evaluate the overall usability and test the functionality of our integrated CPS infrastructure. We also plan to extend the management application to also comprise the management of smart home sensors, actuators, live camera streams, and service robots resulting in a comprehensive management application ready to be used in an actual smart home.

Acknowledgments. This research has been partially funded within the VICCI project under the grant number 100098171 by the European Social Fund (ESF) and the German Federal State of Saxony.

References

1. Weiser, M.: The computer for the 21st century. Scientific American 265(3), 66–75 (1991)
2. Shen, C., Ryall, K., Forlines, C., Esenther, A., Vernier, F.D., Everitt, K., Wu, M., Wigdor, D., Morris, M.R., Hancock, M., Tse, E.: Informing the design of direct-touch tabletops. IEEE Comput. Graph. Appl. 26(5), 36–46 (2006)
3. Ryall, K., Forlines, C., Shen, C., Morris, M.R., Everitt, K.: Experiences with and observations of direct-touch tabletops. In: Proceedings of the First IEEE International Workshop on Horizontal Interactive Human-Computer Systems, TABLE-TOP 2006, pp. 89–96. IEEE Computer Society, Washington, DC (2006)
4. Lee, E.: Cyber physical systems: Design challenges. In: 2008 11th IEEE International Symposium on Object Oriented Real-Time Distributed Computing (ISORC), pp. 363–369 (2008)

5. Milne, A.J.: Entering the interaction age: Implementing a future vision for campus learning spaces. Educause Review 42(1), 12–31 (2007)
6. Block, F., Wigdor, D., Phillips, B.C., Horn, M.S., Shen, C.: Flowblocks: A multi-touch ui for crowd interaction. In: Proceedings of the 25th Annual ACM Symposium on User Interface Software and Technology, UIST 2012, pp. 497–508. ACM, New York (2012)
7. Hornecker, E.: 'i don't understand it either, but it is cool' - visitor interactions with a multi-touch table in a museum. In: 3rd IEEE Intern. Workshop on Horizontal Interactive Human Computer Systems, TABLETOP, pp. 113–120 (October 2008)
8. Lambeck, C., Kammer, D., Weyprecht, P., Groh, R.: Bridging the gap: advances in interaction design for enterprise applications in production scenarios. In: Proceedings of the Conference on Advanced Visual Interfaces 2012, Capri Island, Italy (2012)
9. Lepinski, G.J., Grossman, T., Fitzmaurice, G.: The design and evaluation of multitouch marking menus. In: Proc. of the SIGCHI Conference on Human Factors in Computing Systems, CHI 2010, pp. 2233–2242. ACM, New York (2010)
10. Moscovich, T.: Contact area interaction with sliding widgets. In: Proceedings of the 22nd Annual ACM Symposium on User Interface Software and Technology, UIST 2009, pp. 13–22. ACM, New York (2009)
11. Wobbrock, J.O., Morris, M.R., Wilson, A.D.: User-defined gestures for surface computing. In: Proceedings of the SIGCHI Conference on Human Factors in Computing Systems, CHI 2009, pp. 1083–1092. ACM, New York (2009)
12. Freeman, D., Benko, H., Morris, M.R., Wigdor, D.: Shadowguides: Visualizations for in-situ learning of multi-touch and whole-hand gestures (2009)
13. Yatani, K., Partridge, K., Bern, M., Newman, M.W.: Escape: A target selection technique using visually-cued gestures. In: Proceedings of the SIGCHI Conference on Human Factors in Computing Systems, CHI 2008, pp. 285–294. ACM, New York (2008)
14. Antle, A.N., Bevans, A., Tanenbaum, J., Seaborn, K., Wang, S.: Futura: Design for collaborative learning and game play on a multi-touch digital tabletop. In: Proceedings of the Fifth International Conference on Tangible, Embedded, and Embodied Interaction, TEI 2011, pp. 93–100. ACM, New York (2011)
15. Nebe, K., Klompmaker, F., Jung, H., Fischer, H.: Exploiting new interaction techniques for disaster control management using multitouch-, tangible- and pen-based-interaction. In: Jacko, J.A. (ed.) Human-Computer Interaction, Part II, HCII 2011. LNCS, vol. 6762, pp. 100–109. Springer, Heidelberg (2011)
16. Shneiderman, B.: The eyes have it: a task by data type taxonomy for information visualizations. In: Proceedings of the IEEE Symposium on Visual Languages, pp. 336–343 (1996)
17. Nielsen, J.: Ten usability heuristics (2005)

From the Perspective of Service Engineering, The Development of Support Systems for Residents Affected by the Major Earthquake Disaster

Sakae Yamamoto[1], Kazuo Ichihara[2], Naoko Nojima[2], Yuichi Takahashi[1], Kosuke Ootomo[1], and KentaWatanabe[1]

[1] Faculty of Engineering, Tokyo University of Science, Japan
sakae@ms.kagu.tus.ac.jp
[2] Net & Logic Inc.
ichihara@nogic.net

Abstract. In a large Earthquake, the inhabitants need to protect themselves on their own. If that is difficult, residents need to help each other in between. However, there are very difficult to help each other at after the Earthquake. The supporting systems have been developed using the service engineering. This is, using ICT, an evacuate mechanism has been proposed. Moreover focusing on evacuation behavior in particular, a support system capable of safe haven has been developed. Especially a new method for measuring the quality of the evacuation has been developed too.

Keywords: Earthquake disaster, service engineering, quality of evacuation, ICT.

1 Introduction

The local government offers many kinds of public services for the inhabitants. In a disaster, this plays a very important role to the victims of the disaster. If a large disaster happens, and the service offering system is destroyed by the disaster, residents may be confused. This is very serious problem for the victim of the disaster, and very difficult problem, too. The reason is that a problem is constructed by many other problems, and these problems are complicatedly tangle. So it is very difficult to solve this problem. We must think about the correspondence method of the disaster creatively again carefully beforehand. We shall propose and discuss our new services of supporting the residents in the disaster at the time of a disaster. I considered services in particular about whether you make the offer method at the time of a disaster. We think in a situation called the ergonomics and service engineering in particular.

Discussions of disasters are not able to consider generally. The disaster is roughly divided into natural disaster and a human disaster. Furthermore, the natural disasters are classified in an earthquake, a flood, a typhoon, the volcano, etc. Recently, the Japanese people are paying attention to the disaster that will be caused by the major earthquake.

S. Yamamoto (Ed.): HIMI 2014, Part II, LNCS 8522, pp. 359–370, 2014.
© Springer International Publishing Switzerland 2014

The Japanese Government Institution announced that the major earthquake that is higher than magnitude 7 is generated with epicentral earthquake in a metropolitan area and its possibility is very high level. By this prediction of the scale of the damage is big, and a victim is expected with a majority. Therefore we need preparations in response to the disasters. Therefore, we decided to focus on when a large earthquake in the Tokyo metropolitan area has occurred.

We had four times of large earthquakes since 1995 and we suffered large damage. That is, we have experienced at the Great Hanshin-Awaji Earthquake (January 17, 1995 M7.3), Niigata Chuetsu earthquake (October 23, 2004 M6.8), Niigata Chuetsu offing earthquake (July 16, 2007 M6.8) and Great East Japan Earthquake (March 11, 2011 M9.0).

From these experiences, the policy of the government changed from the disaster prevention to the decrease of the disaster. We cannot prevent the earthquake disaster with a prior foresight for the moment. Therefore our government switched it to the conversion of reducing the scale of the disaster even if a large-scale earthquake was generated. Therefore our government requires for the people to perform. This period comes to need around ten days from 3days. It means that the local government restores during this period. That is, the residents firstly evacuate to the shelter, and to build and to manage the evacuation center and information of evacuee are accumulated, classified, and outgoing. In the disaster study, we need to consider events in time series. The requests of the victims of the disaster are changed, and the requests are associated with shortage things in the daily life, it means that the support methods in the disaster change in time series. So we focus on immediate after the large earthquake disaster in this study.

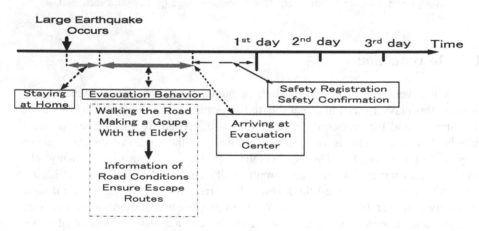

Fig. 1. The flow of the disaster research

1.1 Firstly Evacuation Is Important

In the Great East Japan Earthquake (2011.3.11), many of the victims were caused by delayed refuge. People shall be reconfirmed that the evacuation is important.

An evacuation is very important action for inhabitants in early phase of an earthquake. Therefore, we focused on the evacuating action of victims to evacuate to shelters in immediately after the disaster. Be carried out inhabitants have led to this evacuation is required. Then a new support refuge system is required, and we make adjust to be performed this system smoothly by using ICT.

In this paper, we assume that the victims of the disaster go to the evacuation center from their home after the large earthquake stopped, and we consider how to perform the victims of the disaster safely at the refuge action. The evacuation center has a hub function as the base of local inhabitants at the refuge. In other words, a refuge is an accumulation place of food, drinking water and necessary supplies. It is important to have the information of inhabitants to succeed in the distribution of the supplies to the victims of the disaster at this refuge. In addition, the local government and the exchanges of the information of the refuge are necessary. Our system becomes the premise to be provided with the mechanism mentioned above. Therefore the victims of the disaster go to the evacuation center, and it becomes necessary to convey safety information themselves.

We considered the safety of the information and we put the information at the time of the disaster to the remote outside server from the stricken area. In other words, we thought about the use of the cloud system. At first we thought about the refuge action support at the time of the disaster based on this information infrastructure system.

Refuge Support. Japanese government and the local government prepare the hazard maps. Based on the research of hazard areas in Japanese hazard research institutes, our government presents the dangerous area and illustrated to disaster areas as the hazard map. This purpose is that the inhabitants will prepare for a disaster while seeing this map. And our government expects that many people can search the evacuating route from the hazard map. However, the existing hazard map is not used.

The reasons seem to be as follows;

1. As for the hazard map contents are coarse.
2. The map is made from paper and people forget it put away.

Method to Support a Refuge Action. We put map information on a tablet terminal on the our based system and added support information more. We make the residents go to a evacuation center using the tablet terminal. Subsequent to evacuation, we make residents evaluate the usability of the tablet map. Furthermore, making the structure to evacuate to while helping an elderly person is necessary because the elderly person cannot evacuate alone.

Furthermore, making the structure to evacuate to while helping an elderly person is necessary because the elderly person cannot evacuate alone. In addition, we made hazard map and showed the effectiveness to raise quality of the refuge. we applied the service engineering about a disaster as above and showed the effectiveness of the aid package of the disaster action.

2   Purpose

We assume large earthquake has occurred in Tokyo metropolitan area, we will make a mechanism to help the victims at that time.   The information based system at the time of the disaster using the ICT is made. In addition, in order to raise quality of the refuge, the electronic hazard map is made and the effectiveness is evaluated.   Applying the service engineering about a disaster as above and the effectiveness of the aid package of the disaster action is shown. We assume earthquake has occurred; we will make a mechanism to help the victims at that time. As described above, by applying the engineering services related to disaster, we show the effectiveness of the support measures of behavior disaster.

3   Method

3.1   Creating a Scenario Immediately after the Earthquake

From 2007, at the Tansumachi Shinjuku area of Tokyo, We have made the investigation of residents' awareness about earthquake.   Inhabitants of this area is about 36000 people, the total number of survey respondents was 10%.   Is carried out evacuation drills further, we examined the evacuation of Inhabitants. We observed carefully their evacuation actions. We conduct evacuation drills along with the residents, I investigated the evacuation of residents. From this result, I made a proposal for evacuation scenarios below. Unlike the evacuation training until now, was the policy not to evacuate alone the elderly. We make a safe system to move along with the elderly and Inhabitants of the neighborhood. Of course, it uses ICT.

In addition, rather than a fixed route, made a scenario that gives the suspension of traffic in this evacuation drill.   It is not taught to the participants before training. This training is how to consider people to avoid traffic cutoff points, and to build the route of the destination to the evacuation. We were also observed behavior of Inhabitants at that time.   Participants of this training in the 250 total, we have created the evacuation scenario based on this. We investigated the quality of further evacuation.

General Rule. We show the general action of the victims of the disaster. This rule may vary according to an area. The victims of the disaster go to the refuge after the shaking of the earthquake is stopped. Therefore each resident informs his or her address where he or she is staying. Mainly it is the inhabitant's house, the parents' house, acquaintance's house or the evacuate center. The local government can grasp the personal safety of inhabitants at each refuge.   The local government can get grasp of a local refuge population and residents' situation from the enrollment of each refuge. When an elderly person evacuated, we found out many barriers to move elderly person from pre-conducted evacuation drills.   For example, in the evacuation streets, destruction of telephone poles, fences and walls will be blocking the road.   And also destruction of the road itself will be a factor of shut off further.   In practice our study, windowpane of the building facing the road will be destroyed and fallen on the road. This is very danger for walking people. And the collisions between cars at the intersection of many occur more often was expected. These are our results of research since 2006. Therefore we thought about a method to evacuate an elderly person safely first.

3.2   Our Proposing the Evacuation Support System

It will be described based on the schematic diagram shown in Figure 2 system. The numbers enclosed in parentheses shows the order of evacuation behavior from after the earthquake. We explained with the procedure and ICT system as follows;

(1) A Wi-Fi Mobile Terminals to the Elderly Person's House Beforehand are Distributed. In normal situation, the information about the disaster prevention is displayed on the screen. If the earthquake happen, screen changes immediately, and the instruction to touch the button on the screen directly is displayed (see figure 3). This mechanism is to be sent to automatically from the information center of the municipality when the earthquake occurs. If the earthquake happened, an earthquake early warning and an earthquake breaking news are displayed. This operation becomes the confirmation of an elderly person being in the home. And the safe information of elderly go to the evacuation center. The evacuation center direct the supporter to pick up the elderly with his information. If the earthquake happened, an earthquake early warning and an earthquake breaking news are displayed. This operation becomes the confirmation of an elderly person being in the home. And the safe information of elderly go to the evacuation center. The evacuation center direct the supporter to pick up the elderly with his information.

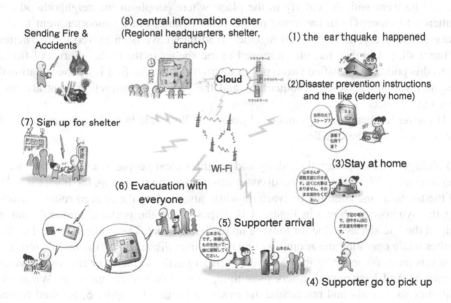

Fig. 2. Our Proposed the evacuation support system

(2) What is Displayed Next. Following two information are displayed repeatedly successively.

a) Fire off the stove in the room and turn off the stove in the kitchen.
b) Ready to bring out passbook, ancestral tablets, medicine, and other objects.

(3) Stay the Home Until Someone Will Pick Up You to Go to Evacuation Center.
A supporter is coming to you and you are waiting for a moment.

Fig. 3. When an earthquake occurs, the screen display is changed immediately as this

(4) Supporter Go to the Elderly Home. Supporter has a terminal toward the elderly person's house, and a supporter understands whether he should go to what elderly person's house at the terminal.

(5) Supporter Arrived at Elderly Home. Supporters went to the house of the elderly, and he went with the elderly to the place where people in the neighborhood are gathered together. Go to the home of the elderly other, other supporter went to the place where everyone is gathered together. And they have been moved to the shelter in them all.   And they have been moved to the shelter in them all.   Series of flows up to this point are classified two types of instructions.   The first is by the situational judgments of the regional headquarters, and the second is instructions that are prepared in advance.

However indication of regional headquarters will be able to replace the contents of the instruction by the situation.

(6) Refuge. The supporter, the elderly and neighborhood people evacuate to the evacuation center. While watching the disaster situation to the road map, the leader watched the terminal and continue to evacuate while also finding the desired route.   Moving the symbols as shown in Figure 4 is displayed on the portable terminal, and it helped the   leader as a clue for looking up the bypass line. The leader is moved to the shelter while operating the zoom function of the map displayed on the mobile terminal at this time. We made to artificially disasters of traffic accidents or fire, as shown in Figure 5. And happened disasters over time, was displayed on the map, We made experiments actually and researched the evacuated route. In Figure 5, resulted routes were shown.

(7) Register the Residents' Safety Information. The victims of the disaster went to the shelter for safety registration.   They have registered in writing the information of victims in registration form of paper. The IC-chip Card or the QR code printed on the card will be distributed to people who registered further.   Therefore it is necessary to convert to electronic information from the paper. It is necessary to input from the PC to do so.   We have proposed that the residents there are shelters to the input.   At that time, with a focus on the pull-down menu, I elaborated so as to reduce the keyboard as much as possible.   Data are thinking that you put in a server of shelter, and sends it to the server of the municipality it.   We thought that you save the data to an external server in this system for that. That is, a cloud.

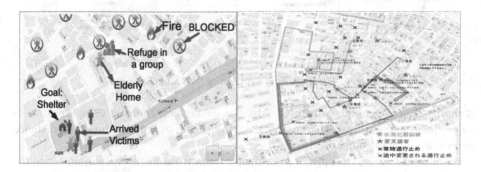

Fig. 4. The Screen of the group on the Tablet.   **Fig. 5.** The resulted routes on the leader's
The display in the evacuation center display   tablet
same screen image.

(8)The Central Information Center . This is put in the local government (branch office) or each refuge and, by the Wi-Fi function of the terminal which the leader of inhabitants group has, can grasp course information in the local governments.

3.3   Cloud System

Next figure 6 showed the disaster information system using the cloud and a diagrammatic view of the refugee support system.

3.4   Evaluation of Evacuation

We conducted evacuation drills in the region based on the proposed scenario. We have set the two regions. One is an elongated town in complex narrow road in the area with a complicated escape route.In the other area, there are factories and warehouses has simple road network, and their width of are not narrow.   The escape route

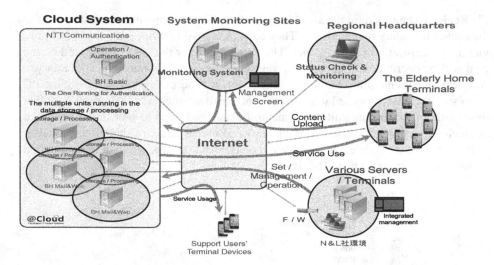

Fig. 6. The framework Concept of the Cloud System

is shorter than the complex town. Clearly, the evacuation route in complex town is longer than in small town.Therefore, measuring of the evacuation time and distance cannot be a correct comparison.

Participants were 21 people, and each participant is made an evacuation. Since assessing the quality of evacuation procedures in this experiment, on the assumption that the elderly could not escape alone, we did not experiment.

Observing the participants, we found that all people showed us the many types of evacuations between the start point and the goal point in some road closures according to the scenario.

We recorded the participant's utterances when each participant was moving, and analyzed them and we were able to find two factors. Those factors are composed of several elements.

That is as follows;

— State of grasped of the current position

> 1: State of grasping the location
> 2: State that does not grasp the current location
> 3: State of mistaken for a know the current location

— Strategy of route selection

> a: Trying to search exactly route for goal point
> b: Trying to go to the goal direction roughly
> c: Trying to grab clues to understand his place
> d: Trying to turn back to the middle

We were evaluated as a quality of refuge with a combination of twelve elements, this means, multiplying in 3 elements (in the State of bgrasped of the current position) and 4 elements(in the Strategy of route selection) . These combinations of the elements between assessing indicated the quality of evacuation.

Figures 7 and 8 were results of experiments.   Figure 7 was the result of easy to evacuate area (small town) indicated an high quality of evacuation,   and Figure 8 was shown   an worse the quality of evacuation.

These results reflected town phase, however, the better results subjects existed in both town.

So we should be research better subjects' action more.

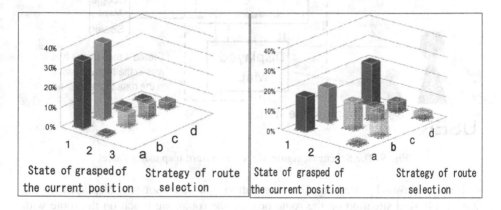

Fig. 7. The results of evacuation at small town   **Fig. 8.** The results of evacuation at complex town

We indicated one direction of the effectiveness for evaluation method for the evacuation.

3.5   e-Hazard Map

We researched other points. That is e-Hazard map. Residents are thinking that to survive a disaster while watching this map. Of course, municipalities   thought that residents to avoid a dangerous place by using the map, and perform evacuation. However, existing hazard map is made of paper. Therefore, it is difficult to determine the root and to make up-to-date information. The public institutions make, there is also complained that it is difficult to use coarsely content. Go and use it to display on the tablet this. Is shown in Figure 9 is the schematic.

We made a verification experiment using the e-hazard map was 21 people. The breakdown was 12 people using e-hazard map on the Tablet(iPad air), and 9 people using usual hazard maps have been published in the paper.

Method. It had been displayed hazard information in e-hazard map as same as on usual hazard map. This is in order to compare an e-hazard map and usual Hazard Map. We had registered in the information infrastructure of our system in existing hazard information. Using the e-hazard map on the tablet, we firstly tap the current and goal location.

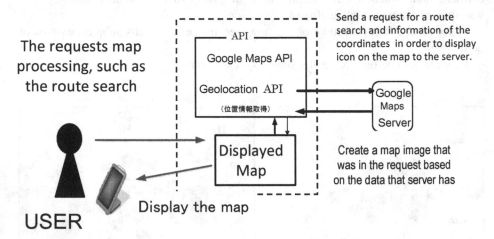

Fig. 9. The Schematic figure of the r e-Hazard map using Tablet

Route is shown by pressing the route button and then root was displayed. In the case of a hazard situation on the route or near the route, we touch on the route with the finger and shift to a safe direction. Then another route is shown. When you stop at the house of the elderly on the way, you shall tap the current location, the elderly home and the goal location. If so, then the root is shown on the order. We are shown in Figure 10 result.

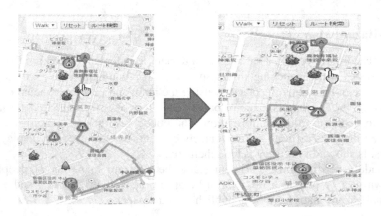

Fig. 10. The example of the route changing on the Tablet

Subjects of using e-Hazard map showed the higher quality of refuge than subjects with usual hazard map. Because e-hazard subjects highly grasped the situation of the current position as compared to the usual hazard map, the route selection policy is clear, evacuation high quality are made(see Figure 11and 12).

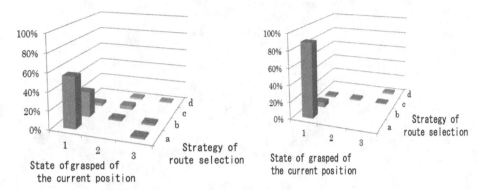

Fig. 11. The result of the using usual hazard map   **Fig. 12.** The result of the using e-hazard map

The e-hazard map can be seen that the evacuation of high quality are made, we have confirmed that this effectiveness.

4   Conclusion

We proposed a mechanism of evacuation of Earthquake. In order to perform the mechanism of this evacuation, we made a support system, that is, the foundation information system of disaster.   This system based on the ICT. We have experimentally verified the performance of this system. Focusing on the quality of evacuation, we built the new measurement of evacuation based on the introspection.   This idea was considered by perspective of service engineering. This was verified by evacuation practice its effectiveness and was verified at an e-hazard map further.

References

1. Asami, Y., Sakurai, M., Kobayashi, D., Ichihara, K., Nojima, N., Yamamoto, S.: Evaluation of the Map for the Evacuation in Disaster Using PDA Based on the Model of the Evacuation Behavior. In: Proceedings of 4th International Conference on Applied Human Factors and Ergonomics, pp. 6194–6921. CRC (2012)
2. Takahashi, Y., Kobayashi, D., Yamamoto, S.: Disaster Information Collecting/Providing Service for Local Residents. In: Salvendy, G., Smith, M.J. (eds.) HCII 2011, Part II. LNCS, vol. 6772, pp. 411–418. Springer, Heidelberg (2011)

3. Yamamoto, S., Ichihara, K., Nojima, N., Asami, Y., Fujioka, G., Iwasaki, A.: The Viewpoint of Ergonomics to Disaster Victim Support of Large Earthquake. Journal of the Japanese Ergonomics Society 48, 115–122 (2012)
4. Takahashi, Y., Yamamoto, S.: An Improvement of Disaster Information System for Local Residents. In: Yamamoto, S. (ed.) HCI 2013, Part II. LNCS, vol. 8017, pp. 217–222. Springer, Heidelberg (2013)

Communication, Expression
and Emotions

Investigating the Effective Factors of Communication for Family Members Living Apart

Nana Hamaguchi, Daisuke Asai, Masahiro Watanabe, and Yoko Asano

NTT Service Evolution Laboratories, 1-1 Hikari-no-oka
Yokosuka-shi Kanagawa 239-0847, Japan
{hamaguchi.nana,asai.daisuke,
watanabe.masahiro,asano.yoko}@lab.ntt.co.jp

Abstract. Parents have difficulty in communicating with their independent children that live separately. Much research has focused on this problem and most solutions provide parents' information to the children, despite the parents' desire to understand their children. To foster communication by the parent, our proposal takes the unique approach of providing the children's information to the parent. As an initial experiment, we conduct a 15 day field study with three households to investigate whether the information of the children prompts parent into communicating with their children, and if so, how and what information should be shared. The result show that little information can prompt communication by the parent and keep a favorable attitude toward the child. We also discuss the design requirements raised by our findings with the goal of improving communication between family members living apart.

Keywords: elderly people, family communication, field study.

1   Introduction

Communication between parents and their adult children is weakening due to the increase in the number of parents living apart from their independent children. In our country, the ratio of multigenerational households decreased from 29.7% in 1998 to 16.2% in 2010. Concurrently, there was a significant upswing in the percentage of households that contained only elderly people, either singles or couples, from 45.1% to 54.1% over the same period (Ministry of Health, Labor and Welfare, 2010). Furthermore, the ministry says that as the distance between the households of family members increase, the less they communicate with each other. Communication with family plays an important role in maintaining good health and an active mind, especially for the elderly. Gerontological studies say that the family provides the elderly with both physical support and motivation in life, both of which are necessary for living, and a lack of communication with the family degrades the subjective well-being of the elderly. Thus a key goal is to support communication between the children and their parents living apart.

The critical issue causing the drop in communication, the lack of opportunity to know the state of the partner, has been highlighted in several papers [1] [2] [3]. Most

S. Yamamoto (Ed.): HIMI 2014, Part II, LNCS 8522, pp. 373–382, 2014.
© Springer International Publishing Switzerland 2014

studies focus on providing the parent's information to trigger the adult child into initiating communication. However, some research suggests that parents desire to know their children's status more strongly than the reverse [4].

We hypothesize that information of the adult child should initiate communication. The information may give the parent a good opportunity to know their child's state and foster communication by the parent.

This study makes three contributions:

- We propose a unique communication support approach that uses information of the adult child
- We detail our 15 day field study involving three pairs of households
- We present two design requirements for communication support systems to link household members living apart

Section 2 introduces our research question and our new approach, and compares it to current alternatives. Sections 3, 4, and 5 demonstrate the effectiveness of our approach by discussing the field study results and the changes noted in the behavior of the parents and their attitude toward communication. Then, we identify some design requirements for communication between adult children and their parents based on our findings.

This study is the first step in designing a communication support system for parents and adult children living apart. The findings provide important perspectives and elucidate the design opportunities.

2   Related Work

As much previous research has suggested, when designing a system intended to foster communication between separated people we must carefully consider how to trigger the transfer the state of the partner.

The trigger most commonly adopted is informing the parent's status to the adult child. Digital Family Portrait is a picture frame which displays the parent's status as detected by sensors in the parent's home [2] [5]. The receiving terminal is located in the child's home and gives them some awareness of their parent. e-Home [6] is a communication system that includes home monitoring; it offers shared sticky notes and video-telephony for communication media while monitoring medication compliance. When the parent takes a medicine, a new sticky note indicating the event is automatically shared on both systems. Although those studies found that the parent's information could support the generation of connectedness or trigger communication, they limited communication initiation to just the child.

A few studies examined the equal provision of information to both parent and child. "Tsunagari-kan" communication [7] uses paired devices installed in the parent's and child's homes, each of which conveys presence information detected by motion sensors on the other side. It sounds when the user touches the unit. Shared Family Calendars [4] facilitates the sharing of calendar information between multigenerational family members. Although these studies reported that the parent perceived enhanced connection to their child by learning of their child's status, none of them examined the effect on communication or the ability to trigger communication.

To foster communication, the communication gap between the family members gave us a unique approach. Our approach is to pass to the parents their children's information to make the parents aware of their children's status. In the Shared Family Calendars' field study, all grandparents repeatedly reported enjoying seeing what their grandchildren were up to. On the other hand, the grandchildren did not look at the calendar of the grandparents [4]. This suggested that the parents were more interested in the younger generation than the reverse. Figure 1 shows the difference between our approach (right) and the others (left and middle). Past systems can be categorized into two types. One is shown on the left of Fig. 1. In this approach, the system makes the adult children aware of their parents' information and encourages adult children to initiate communication. eHome [6] and Digital Family Portrait [2] [5] are of this type. The other is shown on the middle of Fig. 1. In this approach, the system enables adult children and their parents to see each other's information and so encourages communication. Shared Family Calendars [4] is of this type. On the other hand, our approach is shown on the right side of Fig. 1. The system enables older adults to know about their children and encourages them to initiate communication.

We investigated what type of information should be shared with the parent. Technology has expanded the ability of people to share media and information with each other, such as photos [8] , video chat [9] [10], and schedules [4]. These media and information contain rich personal detail and help parents know the status of their separated children well. Although more informative media and more information are more helpful to the parent, the interaction between parent and child can become complicated. The Casablanca project [11] pointed out that simple, ephemeral as well as expressive interactions are surprisingly effective in homes. The information shared from child to parent needs to be less informative to simplify the interaction, while remaining keeping expressive.

In this paper, we investigate the following two questions.

- If the parents get to know about their children by receiving information, will they initiate communication with their children?
- How rich do the shared contents have to be for the parent to initiate communication?

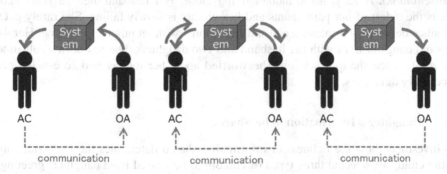

Fig. 1. Approaches for a communication support system linking an older adult (OA) and adult child (AC) living apart. (Left) The approach of eHome and Digital Family Portrait. (Middle) The approach of Shared Family Calendars. (Right) Our approach.

3   Method

We conducted a field study on three families from November 1st to November 21st of 2010. This section introduces the participants and describes how our study was designed.

3.1   Participants

Each of the three families had a parent living more than 120km from their child. All participants were female, i.e., mother and daughter, as it is said that females have a more positive attitude toward communication than males. In addition, all owned a mobile phone and were able to use the e-mail function.

The mothers satisfied two additional requirements. One was having no employment; a mother with a regular job would not have enough time to communicate with her daughter. The other was having no critical health problem; the daughter would contact her mother frequently if her mother had some health problems.

Household #1. A 57 year old mother living with her husband. Her 28 year old daughter is working as a clerical employee, and has lived apart from her parents since she got married three years ago. The mother wants to communicate with her daughter more frequently but she hesitates to call or e-mail her because she does not want to interfere with her daughter's independence.

Household #2. A 56 year old mother living with her husband and son. She is the busiest of the mothers. She belongs to a chorus and manages the group, has a part time job as a caregiver, and works on a little farm with neighbors. Her 22 year old daughter is a college student, and moved near her college one year ago because she wanted to concentrate on study. She works hard to complete her graduation thesis and pass a national examination to become a nurse. She also belongs to a chorus circle.

Household #3. A 75 year old mother living alone. Her husband died 28 years ago. She is the oldest of our participants and her vitality is slowly failing. She rarely goes out since developing a cataract, and she stays home without talking to anyone. Her 44 year old daughter lives with her husband and two daughters. She has been a full-time housewife since she quit her job. She worried about her mother and so e-mails her once every three days.

3.2   Daughter's Information to be Shared

To investigate how the richness of information shared determines the understanding of the child, we selected three types of content to be passed from daughter: greeting, photo, and today's news. They differ in degree of information richness.

Greetings. Greetings are the least information rich content of the three. There are several kinds of regular form according to time, such as "good morning" and "good night", they have no meaning other than as a greeting. Although greetings are less informative, they other expressiveness because they frequently open face-to-face communication in many situations. In particular, family members living together greet each other frequently.

Photos. Of the three contents, photos express the most personal information. Photos can capture a great scene directly. They are expressive as well as informative because of the power of visualization. As mentioned above, many previous studies use photos to support communication.

Today's News. Today's news lies intermediate between the first two. It is a text-based medium, the same as greetings, but can express more information than greetings. Today's news is also expressive content for family because it covers the topics found in the daily conversations of family members living together.

3.3   Procedure

We explored how our approach helps to prompt communication and how the richness of shared contents affects the parent by observing the behavior and attitude of the older adult toward communication when the above information is received or sent. The information was generated by adult children and sent via their own mobile phone to their parents' mobile phone in this field study. Mobile phones are a general information terminal in our country, and can transmit the above information easily. We separated the field study period into three phases. Each phase occupied five days including weekends as the participants had limited time to communicate during weekdays. In the first phase, participants were not given any instruction so we could observe their daily communication. In the second and third phases, the adult children were instructed to send their parents at least one e-mail that included targeted information everyday. The sets of phases and targeted information of each participant are shown in Table 1. Each participant undertook a one hour interview and questionnaires after each phase to assess the change in behavior and attitude toward communication and the partner.

Table 1. The three phases and targeted information of each participant

	Phase 1 11/1 – 11/5	Phase 2 11/9 – 11/13	Phase 3 11/16 – 11/20
Household #1	Daily communication	Greetings	Greetings
Household #2			Photos
Household #3			Today's news

3.4   Data Analysis

To elucidate how well children's information prompts parents to communicate with their children, we counted the number of times each parent initiated e-mail conversation voluntarily and compared the number in each phase. The questionnaires asked how many times each participant sent e-mail and who initiated the conversation. As we found that there were inconsistencies between mother and daughter in a few parts, we compared each response, and determined the correct number.

The interviews with the participants lasted a total of 15 hours and were audio-recorded and transcribed. The resulting data set was used when determining why the participants changed their behavior.

4   Result

Figure 2 shows the number of times each mother initiated e-mail conversation. The white, gray, and black bars show the number in phase 1, phase 2, and phase 3, respectively.

First, we explore how the greetings, the least informative contents of the three, changed behavior and attitude of mothers by comparing the number of phase 1 and 2. While mother #1 and #3 never initiated e-mail conversation in phase 1, they did once in phase2.

In the case of mother #1, the greeting e-mail from her daughter inspired voluntary contact by the mother on the last day of phase 2. She sent a greeting e-mail by herself by overcoming her sense of reservation, even though our instructions to her mentioned nothing about outgoing e-mail. According to the interview data, as she felt reassured by her daughter's greeting e-mail sent every morning, she just wanted to send a wonderful e-mail by herself.

> "I think we exchange energy with each other through the greeting e-mail. Especially if some emoticons are attached to the e-mail, I feel reassured strongly. I was encouraged when I received it, and I encouraged her by replying to it with a message full of emoticons. Then, the idea to send the wonderful e-mail from myself arose suddenly on the last day of this phase. I just wanted to do it. I thought I will be happy if I can sent it by myself." [Mother #1].

In case of mother #3, an incident that prevented her daughter from sending the greeting e-mail at the usual time caused her anxiety on the second day of phase 2. Her daughter usually sent e-mail, a greeting e-mail on the first day of phase 2 as well, around 9 p.m., but she did not because she had been out until late that day. Mother #3 was worried about her daughter and so texted her.

Although the graph shows that the number of communication sessions triggered by mother #2 decreased, the questionnaire data shows that the purpose of communicating changed in phase 2. She contacted her daughter because there was some kind of necessity to contact her daughter in phase 1. However, on the last day of phase 2, she sent an e-mail to share her feeling that she was relieved to have finished the second interview.

Second, we explore the impact of content richness by comparing the number of times mother #2 and #3 initiated e-mail conversation in phase 2 and phase 3. Both #2 and #3 showed an increase, but the cause was rather accidental. In the case of mother

#2, one of three times was to confirm her daughter's safety after an earthquake, but the others were same as phase 1. In the case of mother #3, some irregular events, e.g., her friend was operated on for cancer, and she would have an operation for her cataract soon, made her call to talk with her daughter.

Although the factors that initiated more communication in phase 3 than phase 2 were rather accidental, there were great differences in the number of replies to daughter's information and attitude toward it between phase 2 and phase 3. Figure 3 shows the number of replies sent by mother #2 and #3. The gray and black bars show the number in phase 2 and phase 3 respectively.

In the case of mother #2, the number of replies increase from three to twelve. In phase 2, the daughter sent greeting e-mail on three of five days. On one of the last two days, the daughter was too busy and forget to send the greeting, and another day, she almost forgot so her mother pushed her to send it. The mother replied once to each greeting e-mail. On one of the days in phase 3, mother #2's daughter sent a photo of stuff on her desk when she was studying, and the mother replied to encourage her daughter. The topic shifted naturally to those that were mostly related to the daughter's daily life. On another day in this phase, the daughter sent a photo of her new backpack, and the mother sent a positive response. They then talked about the daughter's schedule for the next day. Prior to the study, she tended to contact her daughter to achieve a specific goal rather than enjoying the companionship. In contrast, she sent e-mails about her daughter's daily life many times in phase 3. The mother's statement suggested that the photos of daughter's life were of interest to the mother and that they fostered communication about the daughter's life.

> *"Receiving the photo from her was a fresh experience for me. Unlike words, I could understand her more clearly because the photo appealed to my eye. And I saw something like a theme each in those photos rather than a sense of duty. As I could understand her life in detail, I naturally commented on it."*
> [Mother #2]

In the case of mother #3, the number of replies increased from two to nine. In phase 2, mother replied to her daughter's greeting e-mail on just one day (she sent e-mail twice to the greeting on that day). As only mother #3 seldom replied to greeting e-mails, we asked her to explain. She answered that it was because she did not get any instruction.

> *"Because you gave me no instruction last time. I understood I did not need to do anything so I did not reply to it. And whether I replied it to or not, the greeting e-mail would come again because you instructed he to do so. I thought there was no reason to reply to it. I was lazy about responding."*
> [Mother #3]

However, in contrast to phase 2, she responded to each e-mail with today's news in phase 3 even though the instruction to the mother was the same as in phase 2. Moreover, the daughter said in her questionnaire that she could see emoticons more frequently in her mother's e-mail. Surprisingly, the mother remembered all the news sent when we interviewed her at the end of phase 3, and she said she could understand her daughter's daily life specifically through the today's news.

"I do not think of replying to just a greeting email, but this time, she told me her daily life in detail. Indeed, she rarely discusses her story..." [Mother #3]

Although she was not aware she replied only to today's news, it was assumed that she enjoyed her daughter's news and responded to it without thinking. This change in the mother's behavior emphasizes the importance of the daughter providing more detailed information to foster communication by the mother.

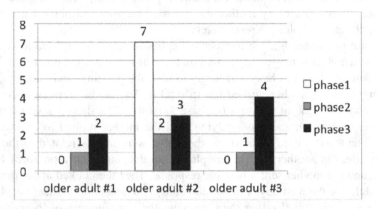

Fig. 2. The number of times each parent initiated e-mail conversation

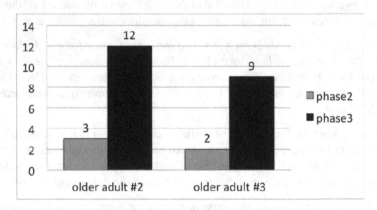

Fig. 3. The number of replies parent #2 and #3 sent

5   Discussion

We summarize the results as follows.

1. Child's information helps parent to initiate communication even if the information is as information-light as greetings.
2. The more informative the contents shared with parent are, the more parents are prompted to initiate communication.

However, according to mother #2, the reason why she responded more in phase 3 than phase 2 was not only because the shared contents were more informative but because she repeatedly received e-mails from her daughter. As we did not consider the impact of this repetitive transmission, further investigation with more participants is required to clarify the second item.

The interesting point we found in this field study is that even information-light contents can prompt communication by the parent and keep a favorable attitude toward the child; how much the child's information impacts the parent depends on whether the parent can find some value in sharing the contents. In phase 2, household #1 exhibited a unique event; the older adult sent a voluntary greeting e-mail even though she was never instructed to send it. This event was unique in that the child sent a greeting e-mail early in the morning when she was busy preparing to go to work. The parent knew her child was going to work at that time. In this situation, the parent found special value in exchanging energy through the greeting especially at the busy time of the morning. Her comment helped us to understand that she felt care from daughter through the greetings:

> "I felt happy when I received an greeting e-mail from her everyday. I understood that she remembered me and cared about me today as usual." [Mother #1]

To support communication between family members living apart, we should consider more carefully about how the support tool can maximize the value of communication. As our trial showed, value was created by the sense of care from the partner as well as by better understanding the child.

According to this finding, we find two design requirements for communication support systems. Both should be satisfied simultaneously by the same system.

1. Able to create a simple message in a simple way even when the sender is busy.
2. Able to convey rich personal information when the sender has enough time.

Designing a communication support system tends to be complicated with much information because the designer tries to supplement that channels that are not present with remote communication. However, the children, the sender side, are so busy generally that they sometimes have difficulty in communicating with their parents. To support the children in sending their information, the first requirement is essential. The communication support system should provide methods of different levels of complexity and enable users to freely select the method to suit their own circumstance.

6   Conclusion and Future Work

We showed the possibility that even information-light contents of child's life situation can trigger communication by the parent and keep a favorable attitude toward the child. A communication support system that gives users more pleasure must create short messages in a simple way while maximizing the richness of personal information. Our next step is to design a communication support system that offers the function of conveying adult child's information to assess whether our design requirements alter communication between family members.

References

1. Dey, A.K., De Guzman, E.S.: From Awareness to Connectedness: The Design and Deployment of Presence Displays. In: Proceedings of ACM CHI (2006)
2. Mynatt, E., Rowan, J., Jacobs, J., Craighill, S.: Digital family portraits: supporting peace of mind for extended family members. In: Proceedings of ACM CHI (2001)
3. Sunny, C., Peter, R., Brett, S.E.: The CareNet Display: Lessons Learned from an In Home Evaluation of an Ambient Display. In: Proceedings of Ubicomp (2004)
4. Plaisant, C., Clamage, A., Hutchinson, H.B., Bederson, B.B., Druin, A.: Shared Family Calendars: Promoting Symmetry and Accessibility. ACM Transactions on Computer-Human Interaction (2006)
5. Rowan, J., Mynatt, E.D.: Digital Family Portrait Field Trial: Support for Aging in Place. In: Proceedings of ACM CHI (2005)
6. Asai, D., Orszulak, J., Myrick, R., Lee, C., D'Ambrosio, L., Godfrey, K., Coughlin, J.F., de Weck, O.L.: Enhance Communication between Parents and Mature Children by Sharing Medication Information. Journal of Information Processing (2012)
7. Miyajima, A., Itoh, Y., Itoh, M., Watanabe, T.: Tsunagari-kan" Communication: Design of a New Telecommunication Environment and a Field Test with Family Members Living Apart. International Journal of Human-Computer Interaction (2010)
8. Romero, N., Markopoulos, P., van Baren, J., de Ruyter, B., IJsselsteijn, W., Farshchian, B.: Connecting the family with awareness systems. In: Ubi Comp (2007)
9. Judge, T.K., Neustaedter, C., Kurtz, A.F.: The Family Window: The Design and Evaluation of a Domestic Media Space. In: CHI (2010)
10. Ballagas, R., Dugan, T.E., Revelle, G., Mori, K., Sandberg, M., Go, J., Reardon, E., Spasojevic, M.: Electric Agents: Fostering Sibling Joint Media Engagement Through Interactive Television and Augmented Reality. In: ACM CSCW (2013)
11. Hindus, D., Mainwaring, S.D., Leduc, N., Hagström, A.E., Bayley, O.: Casablanca: Designing Social Communication Devices for the Home. In: Proceedings of ACM CHI (2001)

Learning Winespeak from Mind Map of Wine Blogs

Sachio Hirokawa[1], Brendan Flanagan[2], Takahiko Suzuki[1], and Chengjiu Yin[1]

[1] Research Institute for Information Technology, Kyushu University
{hirokawa,suzuki,yin}@cc.kyushu-u.ac.jp
[2] Graduate School of Information Science and Electrical Engineering,
Kyushu University
B.FLANAGAN.885@s.kyushu-u.ac.jp

Abstract. When faced with complex situations, it can often be hard to put into words and accurately express it appropriately. This becomes increasingly difficult when specialist expressions are required that are not used in everyday language. The problem is faced when trying to express in words to another person the wine that you just drank, or a wine that you want to drink to a waiter at a restaurant or shop assistant. It requires the expression in words of numerous senses including complex flavors, smells, colors, and personal emotion that is felt. These expressions are often subjective, with different people having using different expressions for the same wine. In this paper, we propose the use of wine related expressions collected from the internet and clustered to generate mind maps.

1 Introduction

It is the foundation of communication to express one's idea as language and to understand others' ideas from their message. Many years are required to master language. The course in which a child masters a native language is not necessarily the same as the course in which an adult masters a foreign language. Anyone who has lived in a foreign country for certain period would have experienced difficulties in expressing himself in the local language. At the same time, he would have experienced that he was able to make himself understood only by putting known words in order. The process of communication can be thought of as the transformation from those keywords in our brain into an actual sentence. The other side of the communication, i.e., those who listen to you talk, need to reproduce the feeling of the person who talked.

It would be natural to assume that we have something which represents words and relation of words in our brain. This idea is close to the notion of "interlanguage" by Selinker[16] who analysed how people learn and use foreign language. The present paper realises this "interlanguage" as a mind map to describe the relation of words.

There are mutually related words in a our mind. We express our thoughts using the words that we know and by constructing sentences that follow the

S. Yamamoto (Ed.): HIMI 2014, Part II, LNCS 8522, pp. 383–393, 2014.
© Springer International Publishing Switzerland 2014

grammatical pattern in our native language or in a foreign language we are learning. It is necessary to build an association chart or graph of such words in our head when we learn a language. The noun representing an object can be learned by seeing the concrete object. However, experience is required to master a linguistic expression that describes feelings or emotion. We need to learn the situation and context where such a feeling takes place. We need to learn with what kind of words are used.

Expressing one's own impression is a hard task even for expert. Emotional phrases would be the most difficult subject to learn for foreign language learner. Wine would be one of the best and most difficult material to learn sensory expressions. Indeed, wine experts and wine lovers write their tasting notes with cryptic comments and mysterious acronyms. Those phrases are called as wine-speak. They are wonderful objects to tease [15]. Quandt [12] complains and enjoys exaggerated and too personal expressions to describe wines. He listed 123 wine vocabularies then invented an algorithm to choose 10 or 15 words randomly. He applied his software to "Chateau La Merde, 1995", "Chateau Grand-Cul Coteneuve, 1998" and "Chateau L'Ordure Pomerol, 2004" to create tasting notes. Then he claimed that he was not be able to find the difference between the real wine tasting notes and the automatically generated wine tasting notes.

Writing a tasting note is not easy task. This paper proposes a system which helps the acquisition of expression showing feeling using wine blogs. Given a keyword, the system retrieves the documents that contain the word, extracts characteristic words of the search result and then constructs a mind map. The input keyword is shown as the root of the map. Typical sentences are shown by specifying a keyword in the map. This visualization and interaction helps users to learn sensory expression of wine tasting.

2 Related Work

2.1 Analysis of Wine Tasting Notes

There are many magazines and Web pages which cover wine tasting notes. Analysing those expressions is one of the research fields of experts. Caballero [2] analysed manner-of-motion verbs which are frequently used in wine tasting notes such as "earthy flavors run though this firm-textured red". She collected 6,000 tasting notes from the Wine Enthusiast, Wine Spectator and Wine Advocate. The tasting notes are very short text of 30 to 100 words, and selected 50 verbs and analysed the occurrences of verbs from the view points of intensity and persistence. She classified them with '+/− force', and collected 56 typical sentences that contain such verbs.

Paradis [9] carefully analysed how prime drinking time is expressed in 200 texts from 80,000 wine tasting notes of the Wine Advocate. 38 sentences are explained in detail. Paradis and Eeg-Olofsson [10] focused on the words representing sensory experiences of vision, smell, taste and touch in analysing 84,864 wine reviews of [6]. They examined the basic statistics such as, the frequency of the words and the combination of adjective seed and nouns, and gave 39 typical phrases of those sensory expressions.

2.2 Visual and Text Mining

Visualization for text analysis has been attracting many researchers. Hearst [5] spent one chapter on information visualization for text analysis. Alencar et. al. [1] classified visualization techniques based on input (single document or collection of documents) and purpose (content, relation, temporal analysis or interaction) of the analysis. The method we use in the present paper is classified in relation extraction from texts. They explained two techniques, i.e., WordNet and Phrase net, as relation analysis of keywords. In WordNet visualization, the set of keywords displayed varies according to the content. But the structure of the net is fixed and determined by the hierarchy of WordNet. The two words linked in a phrase net represents an adjacent occurrence of them in a sentence. The phrase net is useful to extract typical sample sentences. However, it does not give an overall structure of the documents obtained as search results. The analysis of adjacent relation requires dependency parsing and is not practically applicable to the large number of documents. The relation of words in a mind map, which we use in the present paper, represents a co-occurrence of the two words. This process is implemented by a standard inverted index of target documents, which is the same as ordinary search engines.

Kerren et. al. [6] constructed a visualization system for 84,864 tasting notes of the Wine Advocate. They implemented visualization for statistic analysis and used "word tree" to represent the relation of words in a sentence. There are two kinds of nodes – tags and words. The tags are the parts of speech such as JJ(adjectives) and NN(nouns). An edge from one word to another word represents an adjacent co-occurrence of the two words. In other words, it represents a context of a word. The word tree is useful to analyse each sentence one by one. However, the overall structure of sentences cannot be grasped from one figure. On the other hand, the mind map proposed in the present paper visualizes the whole documents obtained as the search result of a query.

2.3 Concept Map and Mind Map

Concept maps and mind maps are widely used for representing contents of documents and users' knowledge. Each node of a map represents a word and an edge represents relationship between two words.

Perez-Marin et.al. [11] proposes the use of concept maps to automatically generate students conceptual models from their free texts. The difference of concept map and mind map is in the meaning of edges. An edge of a concept map has meaning among a fixed set of semantic. On the other hand, an edge of a mind map is determined by users' intuition or by some algorithmic evaluation of the relation of the two words.

Lau et.al. [7] used concept maps automatically generated from e-learning environment messages to help teachers quickly understand their students learning progress and provide appropriate guided responses. They represent a word by the context vector and used the similarity of the words to construct the map. Zouaq and Nkambou [17] created ontology from 10-36 documents and evaluated them. The ontology they created is static and does not correspond to the context of the query. Egusa et. al. [3,8,13] visualized student knowledge as a mind map. Subjects are asked to draw their knowledge before and after exploratory search of particular topics. The mind maps are used to compare the effect of learning process.

The algorithm of map generation of the present paper is an extension of that in Flanagan et. al. [4], where they constructed mind maps automatically from user's twitter texts for helping communication between foreign language learners.

3 Mind Map Generation Algorithm

3.1 Wine Spectator Blogs

There are many magazines and Web sites which cover blogs and wine tasting notes. Bill Daley's "The Dalay Question" [1] is one of such Web sites where he writes on wines and food. There are research articles that analyse the wine tasting notes of Robert Parker's "Wine Advocate"[2]. "Wine Spectator" [3] is another famous magazine on wine which provides blogs as well as tasting notes. We chose blogs in "Wine Spectator" as an analysis corpus instead of tasting notes as other researches[2,9,10] did, because we thought that the vocabularies and phrase in tasting notes would be too specific compare to that in blog articles. Blog articles would be much better to learn words and phrases for ordinary people, particularly for English learners. Typical tasting notes are short sentences written in 30 to 100 words. Blogs are much longer than that. We collected 2,240 blogs from Wine Spectator. An average blog is written in 34 lines and contains 600 words. We constructed a search engine of the blogs using GETA[4] and realized a visualization system.

3.2 Mind Map vs. Co-occurrence Graph

We would like to visualize the contents of blogs that contain the query as a graph whose nodes are characteristic words and whose edges are relation of those words. Firstly, we have to determine how we choose the characteristic words from the search result. Secondly, we have to evaluate the importance of a relation of two words. Concerning to the choice of words, we adopt the Salton's measure [14] provided as a standard measure of GETA search engine. Naive choice of edges would be the co-occurring pairs of words. However, the graph obtained this way looks too complicated because of the numerous edges. Figure 1 compares the

---

[1] http://www.chicagotribune.com/features/food/
[2] http://www.erobertparker.com/info/wineadvocate.asp
[3] http://www.winespectator.com/
[4] http://geta.ex.nii.ac.jp/

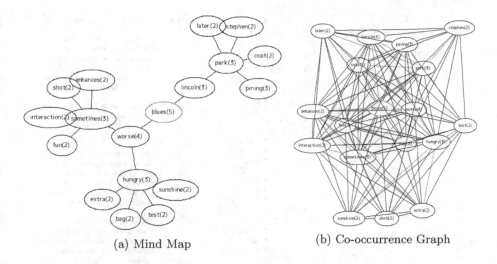

(a) Mind Map   (b) Co-occurrence Graph

Fig. 1. Comparison of Mind Map and Co-occurrence Graph

mind map obtained by our algorithm and the naive co-occurrence graph for the query "blue". Note that the red lines in the co-occurrence graph are the edges chosen in the mind map.

3.3 Depth First Spanning Tree

We construct a mind map of a given query based on depth first search of related words. Each word appears only once in a map, so that the map forms a tree with the query word as the root of the tree. Given a query word, the system retrieves the documents that contain the word. The top B characteristic words of the search result are determined according to the SMART measure. The top words are linked from the focused word unless the word does not appear in the tree already constructed. The expansion proceeds until the given depth D is reached.

```
input : w;
nextnodes = {w};
while(nextnodes is not empty){
  n = get-first-node(nextnodes);
  child = get-child(n);
  foreach c (child) {
    addedge(n,c);
    addnode(nextnode,c) unless appeared(c);
  }
  deletenode(nextnode,n);
}
```

Fig. 2. Mind Map Generation Algorithm

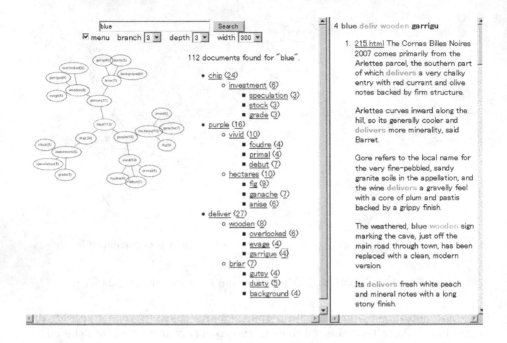

Fig. 3. Interactive System of Mind Map

Once a word is linked from a node, it never occurs as another node. Figure 2 shows the psuedo code of the algorithm.

4   Interactive System of Mind Map

Figure 3 displays the screen shot for a query "blue". Both of the breadth and the depth of tree expansion are set to 3. The input query is drawn in the red circle. Characteristic words are displayed as a tree as well as an indented list. A click on a word will generate another mind map of the word. The number following each word denotes the number of documents that contain the word. For example, the word "garrigue(4)" implies that there are four documents that contain all the keywords "blue", "deliver", "wooden" and "garrigue". The four documents are shown if we click the number attached to the word. In this case, the four documents are shown in the right frame. Note that only the sentences that contain one of the characteristic words are displayed. Thus, we can grasp the whole picture of the search result with a mind map, an indented list and with actual instances of the feature words.

5   Mind Maps of Sensory Expressions

Paradis and Eeg-Olofsson [10] analysed wine tasting notes based on sensory modalities (Table 1) and showed 39 typical sentences that contain sensory

Table 1. The sensory modalities [10]

modality	example
VISION	purple, ruby, straw, gold, light, dark
SMELL	fruity, floral, spicy, smoky, weak
TASTE & TOUCH	flabby, soft, heavy, thin, long, crisp

experience. In this section, we show 3 mind maps together with sample sentences that contain sensory expressions.

5.1   Mind Map of "Smoky"

Figure 4 shows the mind map for "smoky". The names of fruits such as peach, citrus, apricot, melon and orange, looked strange at first sight. We noticed that the map consists of an upper part and a lower part. In the upper part, we see kinds of grape – Marsanne and Rousanne. The names of fruits in the upper part are peach, citrus, appricot and melon. By clicking those words, we confirmed that those fruits and the grapes co-occured in sentences such as "Pay Les Sauvages (an appellation that is rapidly improving) is made from Marsanne with 10 percent Roussanne, and it shows candied citrus peel, lemon verbena and melon notes". Then we presumed some relationship between wines of Risling Kabinett and Auslese with orange mamalade and caramel. Indeed, it was confirmed by a sentence such as "The Kabinett 2007 ($19) expressed this beautifully, with its racy structure defining the mineral, orange and smoke flavors".

5.2   Mind Map of "Weak"

Figure 5 is an example of the mind map for the keyword "weak". The map displays three main branches off the root: dollar, hundred, and caressing. The related keyword "dollar" suggests an economic relation, which can be seen in the following example: "But the rapidly changing dynamics of the Australian wine industry and the weakness of the US dollar spell trouble". Most of the nodes of this branch are related to the effect that economic change has on the global trade of wine, and in particular the impact of changes in the US dollar and consumption of wine from certain regions. On investigation we found that the child node "Tyrrell" refers to the name of a family owned Australian winery that has commented on the recent hardships faced by Australian wineries because of the prolonged drought and the narrowing disparity between the US and Australian dollar that is driving up export prices of Australian wines.

The next related keyword "hundred" could suggest the numerous varieties or quantities of wines available. This is demonstrated in the following example that is taken from a single article: "They [the wines] shine brightest in the great years, but also transcend the weak vintages ⋯. Instead, a benchmark wine forme represents the emergence of an estate or terroir or even an entire region ⋯⋯ But there was just one potential classic among the several hundred that

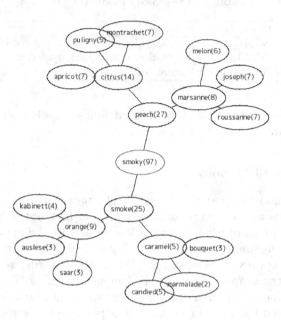

Fig. 4. Mind Map of "smoky"

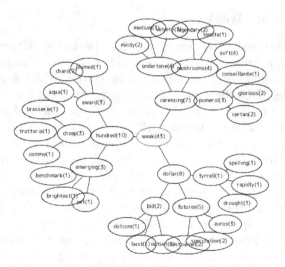

Fig. 5. Mind Map of "weak"

I tasted, and that was the 05 Columella from Eben Sadie". In this example the word hundred is used to describe the numerous wines that are available, from which the writer selects a single wine as a "potential classic". The words brightest and emergence are used to describe wines that standout among the hundreds of wines that are available.

The next related keyword "caressing" is usually associated with sensory touch. However, as seen from the results of the mind map, when used in the context of describing a wine it can be used to express how the wine feels. This can be seen in the following example which is an excerpt from an article that also uses the child nodes mushroom and soft: "The wine in my glass was good quality with currant bush, mushroom and chocolate aromas ⋯⋯ It was round, full bodied with soft and caressing tannins ⋯⋯ (I know it was a weak vintage for California!) But it reminded me of the early days of my career when I drank a lot of bottles of Clos Du Val from 1974 and 1975". In this context the word mushroom describes the smell, and soft and caressing describe the feel (in the mouth) of the tannins in the wine.

5.3   Mind Map of "Long"

Figure 6 is an example of the mind map for the keyword "long". As shown in the figure, the related words are divided into 2 main groups: "aromas" and "blackberry". The "aromas" group suggests a "taste and smell" relation, such

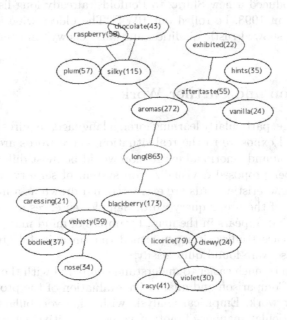

Fig. 6. Mind Map of "long"

as "after taste", "vanilla", "silky" and "chocolate". These related words can be found in the following example:

a) The Alsace Grand Cru Wintzenheim Hengst SGN, with about 240 grams RS, showed a strict nose of dried apricot and spice, followed by an intense, rich and elegant feel on the palate, with a long spicy "aftertaste" (95 points, non-blind).
b) Moving on to Pinot Gris, the Alsace Turckheim Herrenweg had the allure of candy, offering aromas and flavors of peach, quince and "vanilla" on an opulent, yet juicy and mouthwatering frame (90 points, non-blind).
c) It was drinking beautifully, with wonderful aromas of cherry, raspberry and milk "chocolate", and a palate that was full yet refined, "silky"-textured and long and refreshing.

The "blackberry" group suggests a "feeling" relation, such as "velvety", "caressing", "nose" , "bodied" and "chewy". These related words can be found in the following example:

a) Full-bodied, with "velvety" and rich tannins and loads of ripe fruit. Sweet tobacco, with fresh cep and hints of blueberries and blackberries. Raspberries and blackberries.
b) Hints of blackberry jam and fresh porcini. "Full-bodied", with super soft tannins and a round and "caressing" finish. Meaty and long.
c) The Roman-Conti was simply gorgeous from one barrel, exhibiting a "nose of rose" and violet, red fruits and spices.
d) He also introduced a new Shiraz to Penfolds' already long list of divergent styles when, in 1998, he rolled out RWT. The oldest wine in the tasting, Plexus 2003, showed rustic qualities, and was "chewy" in comparison to the other wines.

6   Conclusion and Further Work

Learning language, particularly learning foreign language, requires large amounts of experience and exposure to the real situation where words are used vividly. Sensory expression and emotional expression would be most difficult to master. The present paper proposed a visualization system of sensory words found in Wine blogs. Characteristic words are extracted and drawn as a mind map from the search result of the user's query word. Sample sentences are shown only by clicking a word that appears in the map. Examples of mind maps and sentences are analysed as case studies. It is confirmed that meaningful groups of words and typical phrase were found quite easily.

The mind map is much easier to understand compared with the co-occurrence graph of words. Comparison and qualitative evaluation of the proposed method will be a further work. Empirical analysis with wine vocabulary is necessary. Focusing on particular manner-of-motion verbs or positive/negative adjectives are an interesting application of the proposed method.

Acknowledgement. This work was partially supported by JSPS KAKENHI Grant Number 24500176.

References

1. Alencar, A.B., De Oliveira, M.C.F., Paulovich, F.V.: Seeing beyond reading: A survey on visual text analytics, Wiley Interdisciplinary Reviews. Data Mining and Knowledge Discovery 2(6), 476–492 (2012)
2. Caballero, R.: Manner-of-motion verbs in wine description. Journal of Pragmatics 39(12), 2095–2114 (2007)
3. Egusa, Y., Saito, H., Takaku, M., Terai, H., Miwa, M., Kando, N.: Using a concept map to evaluate exploratory search. In: Proceedings of 3rd Symposium on Information Interaction in Context, pp. 175–184 (2010)
4. Flanagan, B., Yin, C., Inokuchi, Y., Hirokawa, S.: Supporting Foreign Language Learning Using Mind-Maps. Journal of Information and Systems in Education 12(1), 13–18 (2013)
5. Hearst, M.A.: Search User Interfaces. Cambridge University Press (2009)
6. Kerren, A., Prangova, M., Paradis, C.: Visualization of sensory perception descriptions. In: Proceedings of the International Conference on Information Visualization, pp. 135–144 (2011)
7. Lau, R.Y., Song, D., Li, Y., Cheung, T.C., Hao, J.X.: Toward a fuzzy domain ontology extraction method for adaptive e-learning. IEEE Transactions on Knowledge and Data Engineering 21(6), 800–813 (2009)
8. Miwa, M., Egusa, Y., Saito, H., Takaku, M., Terai, H., Kando, N.: A method to capture information encountering embedded in exploratory Web searches. Information Research 16(3) (2011)
9. Paradis, C.: This beauty should drink well for 10-12 years A note on recommendations as semantic middles. Text and Talk 29(1), 53–73 (2009)
10. Paradis, C., Eeg-Olofsson, M.: Describing Sensory Experience: The Genre of Wine Reviews. Metaphor and Symbol 28(1), 22–40 (2013)
11. Pérez-Marín, D., Alfonseca, E., Rodríguez, P., Pascual-Nieto, I.: Automatic Generation of Students' Conceptual Models from Answers in Plain Text. In: Conati, C., McCoy, K., Paliouras, G. (eds.) UM 2007. LNCS (LNAI), vol. 4511, pp. 329–333. Springer, Heidelberg (2007)
12. Quandt, R.E.: On Wine Bullshit: Some New Software? Journal of Wine Economics 2(2), 127–135 (2007)
13. Saito, H., Egusa, Y., Takaku, M., Miwa, M., Kando, N.: Using Concept Map to Evaluate Learning by Searching. In: Proceedings of the 34th Annual Meeting of the Cognitive Science Society (2012)
14. Salton, G., McGill, M.J.: Introduction to Modern Information Retrieval. McGraw-Hill (1983)
15. Searle, R.: The Illustrated Winespeak: Ronald Searle's Wicked World of Winetasting. Souvenir Pr Ltd. (1983)
16. Selinker, L.: Interlanguage. IRAL-International Review of Applied Linguistics in Language Teaching 10(1-4), 209–232 (1972)
17. Zouaq, A., Nkambou, R.: Evaluating the generation of domain ontologies in the knowledge puzzle project. IEEE Transactions on Knowledge and Data Engineering 21(11), 1559–1572 (2009)

Age Difference in Recognition of Emoticons

Kun-An Hsiao and Pei-Ling Hsieh

Industrial Design Department,
National Kaohsiung Normal University
No.62, Shenjhong Rd., Yanchao, Kaohsiung, Taiwan
kahsiao@nknucc.nknu.edu.tw

Abstract. Emoticons are new visual or nonverbal communication cues used in digital interaction. Can elders recognize and discriminate emotional states from emoticons as well as young people can? This study uses emoticons to investigate recognizable emotional differences between thirty older and thirty younger adults. A total of 32 representative emoticons were used as stimuli, consisting of 24 realistic facial expressions, 8 abstract facial expressions, 11 positive emotions, 11 neutral emotions, and 10 negative emotions. Four questions, including "emotional state," "imitative level," "preference," and "understanding" of emoticons, were applied in the questionnaire. The results showed older adults to have a more positive response toward perceived emoticons than younger adults. The two age ranges have different cognition of the design appearances of realistic and abstract emoticons. Older adults showed less preference toward all emoticons than younger adults. The result also denotes older adults can analogize between realistic faces and emoticons.

Keywords: Age difference, Emoticon, Recognition.

1 Introduction

"Emoticon" is a portmanteau word formed from "emotion" and "icon." Initially, it was a textual face composed of punctuation-marks to convey one's mood or facial expression, first used on the Internet in 1982. Emoticons are commonly applied in e-mail messages, instant messaging or short messages as graphic representations of facial expressions. Walther and D'Addario [1] described that emoticons outweighed verbal content. Derks, Bos and Grumbkow [2] also indicated that using emoticons could inspire people's social meaning from messages. Huang, Yen and Zhang [3] pointed out that emoticons were not only enjoyable to use but also a helpful communication method. Their results showed that users could experience enjoyment, adding richness and utility to information, through emoticons.

In previous studies, handling different types of emotional information, elders presented a broader advantage in detecting these stimuli [4], and tended to experience or remember more positive emotions than young adults [5][6][7][8]. Older adults also easily memorized emotional goods, even slogans [9]. Appropriate strategies to manage decline of cognitive ability or neural deficits from aging become important for

S. Yamamoto (Ed.): HIMI 2014, Part II, LNCS 8522, pp. 394–403, 2014.
© Springer International Publishing Switzerland 2014

most elders. Mather and Carstensen [10] indicated that, compared with younger adults, strategic processes play a greater role in older adults' emotional attention and memory. Older adults showed more emotionally pleasant memory distortion for past choices and autobiographical information.

Socioemotional selectivity theory (SST) employs subjective studies of human emotion and behavior to propose an impressive and effective perspective interpreting cognition and changing behavior of older adults. Carstensen, Isaacowitz, & Charles [11] demonstrated the socio-emotional goal setting of individuals depends on perceived time left in life. One significant psychological goal in SST is the entire goal (like obtaining knowledge or a new social relationship); another is correlated with emotion (such as balancing emotions or feeling needed by others) [12]. Older adults realized that when future life is limited, they should prioritize social motives in an optimal goal setting to acquire more satisfying experience from social relationships and make more positive choices. People regulate their emotional states to optimize psychological well-being [13]. These studies demonstrated that elders tend to appear happy with a positive mental attitude in daily life. Would these emotional behaviors and responses of elders be similar when relating to natural or artificial objects?

Lee, Tang, Yu and Cheung [14] indicated that the emoticon was a simple, non-language-based, culturally neutral, non-verbal and easily-applied tool for investigation. They applied simple emoticons to assess patients' mood status and the results were comparable to Geriatric Depression Scale (GDS). For comparison with prior results, this study employs emoticons as experimental stimuli to explore differences of emotional cognition between older and young adults.

However, given the new visual cues of digital interaction, can elders recognize emoticons as well as young people do? Can they discriminate states of emotion from emoticons that convey facial expression and new social meanings? This study examines the following hypotheses: (H1) older adults can distinguish the emotion differences of emoticons such as normal emotional stimuli, (H2) realistic emoticons are more easily recognized than abstract emoticons and (H3) older adults will experience greater positive emotions toward emoticons than younger adults.

2   Methodology

2.1   Participants

Thirty younger adults (15 females, 15 males, mean age = 22.5 years, age range: 19-26 years) were recruited from the Chang Gung University. Thirty older adults (18 females, 12 males, mean age = 79.4 years, age range: 67-91 years) were recruited through two Senior Citizen Centers of Taiwan. They received a gift for their participation after the experiment. All participants had normal or corrected-to-normal visual acuity and no visual pathologies. There were eight additional participants: four younger adults (mean age = 26.5 years) and four older adults (mean age = 78 years), recruited in the same way as above to provide pilot test results for this study.

2.2   Material

This study applied familiar emoticons, commonly seen on MSN and interfaces of digital products collected from the Internet, as stimuli. Although emoticons range from facial or bodily expression in real photos to abstract punctuation-marks in the MSN application, this study emphasized design icons with facial expressions. Firstly, two hundred and fifty-two emoticons were widely collected from an iconic design website for instant messaging (IM) and text messaging (TM) software, representing facial expression or mood. After eliminating similar and blurred emoticons, a focus group comprising five designers (mean age = 27 years) with more than five years' design discipline and experience with emoticons were assigned to judge and categorize representative emoticons for further investigation. The features of representative emoticons will be taken as bases in related analyses of this study. The mode of presentation indicates whether emoticons are graphic icons or punctuation-mark icons. Therefore, the focus group needed to classify representative emoticons according to emotional expression and realistic design appearance.

The focus group was first asked to choose emoticons not only including the same design style, but also displaying different facial expressions. It then arranged the emoticons into "three emotional states:" positive emotion, neutral emotion and negative emotion. The next step was to sort emoticons into "two imitative levels," realistic and abstract facial expression, in each emoticon style. The experimental stimuli were controlled considering the elders' physiological and psychological capacity in judging emotional tests. Finally, the focus group extracted four emoticon styles including thirty-two emoticons as representative stimuli and basic categories in this study. Figure 1 shows the thirty-two emoticons consisting of twenty-four realistic facial expressions, eight abstract facial expressions, eleven positive emotions, eleven neutral emotions and ten negative emotions. There were four emoticon styles containing illustrated icons (Style a. from No. 1 to No. 6), three-dimensional facial icons (style b. from No. 7 to No. 15), two-dimensional facial icons (Style c. from No. 16 to No. 24) and punctuation-mark representation (Style d. from No. 25 to No. 32). To avoid color effects, including hue, value, chroma, and the interaction between colors and shapes, the experiment used grayscale emoticons.

Each sheet of the questionnaire included a first stage of personal information: age, gender, education, computer experience and emotional self-assessment on a 7-point Likert scale from sad to happy (1 = sad, 4 = neutral feeling and 7 = happy). The second stage randomly arranged each emoticon in a questionnaire booklet and each page included one representative emoticon and four questions: "emotional state", "imitative level," "preference," and "understanding." The judgment of "emotional state" evaluated the emotional expression of emoticons on a 7-point scale from negative to positive (1 = extremely negative, 4 = neutral and 7 = extremely positive). The judgment of "imitative levels" evaluated the degree of emotional realism on a 7-point scale from 1 (extremely abstract) to 7 (extremely realistic), to verify Hypothesis 2. The judgment of "preference" evaluated the degree of favor toward emoticons on a 7-point scale (1 = dislike very much, and 7 = like very much), allowing evaluation of the difference in preference toward different emoticons between two age subjects.

The additional question "understanding of this emoticon" clarified whether subjects realized what each emoticon represented. Subjects answered intuitively whether they could understand the emoticon (1 = yes, 2=no).

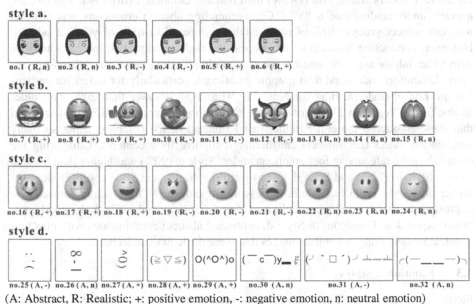

style a.

no.1 (R, n)   no.2 (R, n)   no.3 (R, -)   no.4 (R, -)   no.5 (R, +)   no.6 (R, +)

style b.

no.7 (R, +)   no.8 (R, +)   no.9 (R, +)   no.10 (R, -)   no.11 (R, -)   no.12 (R, -)   no.13 (R, n)   no.14 (R, n)   no.15 (R, n)

style c.

no.16 (R, +)   no.17 (R, +)   no.18 (R, +)   no.19 (R, -)   no.20 (R, -)   no.21 (R, -)   no.22 (R, n)   no.23 (R, n)   no.24 (R, n)

style d.

no.25 (A, -)   no.26 (A, n)   no.27 (A, +)   no.28 (A, +)   no.29 (A, +)   no.30 (A, n)   no.31 (A, -)   no.32 (A, n)

(A: Abstract, R: Realistic; +: positive emotion, -: negative emotion, n: neutral emotion)

Fig. 1. 32 representative emoticons

2.3   Procedures

Before answering the questionnaire, subjects had an introduction to the experiment's purpose and procedure, and then filled in personal data. Additionally, all subjects also needed to describe an example of an icon and to read a question aloud on the first test page to confirm their normal vision. The researchers accompanied each subject in whole process.

3   Results

3.1   Self-assessment of Emotion

Comparing the responses of emotional self-assessment between older and younger adults, this study applied an independent T test to analyze the judgments of the two age groups. The result showed a significant difference between older adults (M=5.77; S.D. =1.55) and younger adults (M=4.73; S.D. =1.17) (F=3.664; P =0.005<0.01): older adults reported more pleasure than younger adults under normal conditions.

3.2   Understanding of Emoticons

Older adults understood 70% of all emoticons, compared to 83% with younger adults. The understanding of abstract emoticons was obviously lower (from No. 25 to No. 32, the average understanding rate is 47%) than realistic emoticons (from No. 1 to No. 24, average understanding rate is 88%). Comprehending abstract emoticons was difficult for both subject groups (30% of older adults, compared to 63% of younger adults). However, eliminating the abstract emoticons, the understanding rate increases to 80% with older adults and 93% among younger adults. Textual emoticons, therefore, are more difficult to understand than graphic emoticons, particularly for elders. In particular, the rate of understanding for Nos. 27, 30 and 31 is lower than 20% with older adults; for no.26 and no.27 it is lower than 30% with younger adults. Researchers found that these emoticons are either unlike facial images, or too complex, using so many punctuation marks that subjects can hardly recognize their contents. Comparing the comprehension rate among four emoticon styles, Style c. (90%) was higher than Style a. (86%), Style b. (73%) and Style d. (30%) for older adults, and Style c. (96%) was also higher than Style a. (93%), Style b. (90%) and Style d. (63%) for younger adults. Style c. presented simple two-dimensional facial icons, and delivered easily-understood emotional expression. Emoticons of Style d. expressed abstract combinations with punctuation-marks, delivering unfamiliar images that were difficult to understand.

3.3   Emotional States

Firstly, researchers tested the correlation between categories by focus group and subjects' judgments of thirty-two emoticons expressing three emotional states. The results show positive correlation for both older adults (0.783, $P<0.01$) and younger adults (0.902, $P<0.01$), meaning the discrimination of emotional states was similar between the focus group and two subject groups. To examine the judgments of emotional state on all emoticons, this study applied an independent T test to analyze the judgments of two age groups. Older adults and younger adults differed significantly from each other ($F=6.115$; $P=0.002<0.01$). On average, the older adults ($M=4.24$; S.D. $=1.87$) feel more positive emotion for emoticons than younger adults ($M=3.98$; S.D. $=1.92$), whether they understand them or not. Removing abstract emoticons, the effect of emotional state on judgment of realistic emoticons is also significantly different between two different age groups ($F=1.619$; $P=0.001<0.01$). Older adults rated emoticons more than 4 ($M=4.29$; S.D. $=2.05$) more often than younger adults ($M=3.95$; S.D. $=1.98$), revealing a more positive reaction to emoticons. Figure 2 shows the dissimilar proportion of average scores in three emotional states between the two age groups. Further exploring average scores of three emotional states by two subject groups, the ANOVA test showed significant differences among positive, neutral and negative emotion states by older adults ($F(2, 957)=81.996$; $P=0.000<0.01$) and younger adults ($F(2, 957)=646.658$; $P=0.000<0.01$). The judgments of younger adults ranged broadly from 2.30 to 5.84 points, but those of older adults centered between 3.08 and 5.14 points. Older adults used more ambiguous and positive emotional criteria responding to these emoticons. These results verify H3: older adults will respond with greater positive emotion to emoticons than younger adults.

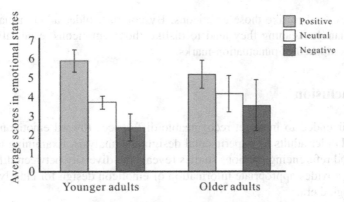

Fig. 2. Average scores of three emotional states by two age groups

3.4 Imitative Levels

On judgments of two imitative levels, older and younger adults differed significantly (F=7.572; P=0.019<0.05) on all emoticons, also differing significantly on realistic emoticons (F=111.144; P=0.000<0.01) and abstract emoticons (F=7.234; P=0.001<0.01) separately. The results show that the two age groups have different recognition of design appearances for realistic and abstract emoticons. For older adults, emoticons Nos. 10, 13 and 15 (realistic design) were evaluated as abstract (M=3.86< 4), while no emoticon belonging to abstract design was evaluated as realistic (M≦4). For younger adults, only emoticon No. 15 (M=3.90) (realistic design) was evaluated as abstract; and No. 28 (M=4.30), No. 29 (M=4.33) emoticons (abstract design), were evaluated as realistic. Both groups judged most emoticons composed of punctuation marks lower than 4, meaning both age groups considered this type of emoticon an abstract design. The responses of younger adults (from 1.50, highly abstract, to 6.23, highly realistic) appeared more extreme than older adults (from 3.13 to 6.17). The results demonstrate that H2, realistic emoticons are easier to understand than abstract emoticons, is tenable.

3.5 Preference

There were significant differences in preference judgments between older adults and younger adults (F=98.512; P=0.000<0.01) for the thirty-two emoticons. The average preference scores of older adults (M=3.79; S.D. =2.06) were lower than those of younger adults (M=4.21; S.D. =1.58), indicating that older adults had less preference toward all emoticons than did younger adults. Taking the two imitative levels separately, older adults and younger adults differed significantly on realistic emoticons (F=173.521; P=0.002<0.01) and abstract emoticons (F=1.787; P=0.000<0.01). Older adults (M=3.92; S.D. =2.18) gave lower preference scores than younger adults (M=4.22; S.D. =1.54) for both realistic and abstract emoticons, the same scores from older adults (M=3.43; S.D. =1.58) were also lower than younger adults (M=4.17; S.D. =1.70). Younger adults mainly gave scores greater than 4 on both imitative levels, meaning they tend to like those emoticons. By contrast, older adults usually scored them less than 4, meaning they tend to dislike those emoticons, especially abstract emoticons composed of punctuation-marks.

4   Conclusion

This study intended to interpret recognizable differences toward emoticons between younger and older adults by experimental design and analysis. Examining test data in this study and referencing previous studies reveals the diversity between different age groups and provides appropriate information of emoticon design for elderly people in the future digital era.

4.1   Design Effects of Emoticons

Based on the comprehension rate for all emoticons, researchers found that design effects strongly affected recognition of the emoticon. This included two aspects. First were the important features extracted from facial expression, and second was the quantity of information. Comparing facial organs or features among emoticon styles a., b. and c., Style c., mainly depicting only eyes and mouth, got the highest understanding rate. Emoticons such as Nos. 1, 2, 13 and 15, without or having unclear mouth features, elicit a lower understanding rate. This implies that eyes and mouth were key facial features delivering most emotional information. Other organs like eyebrows, teeth or nose, etc. had lower effect on emotional delivery. Regarding quantity of information, emoticons designed with too many unrelated features like hair, shadows or exaggerated expressions on eyes or mouth interfered with emotional recognition and caused the opposite effect. Although Style d. (using punctuation marks) generated the lowest understanding, especially for elder subjects (M=30%; S.D. =13%), No. 25 still acquired 57% understanding for elder subjects. Emoticon 25 applied a colon as eyes, and a bracket to simulate an unhappy mouth. This emoticon made of punctuation marks appropriately manipulated two design aspects portraying important facial features and a clear image to create a recognizable emotion. It proved designs must correlate with user's knowledge of the world [15].

4.2   Emotional Recognition of Elders

The results of emotional self-assessment and emoticon recognition of three emotional states showed significant differences between older and younger adults, where older adults feel more pleasure and positive emotion than younger adults. Older adults displayed more positive responses than younger adults to perceived artificial designs of emoticons. This confirmed similar results from past studies of emotional cognition when judging living objects such as human faces or natural objects   [4][16][10][17]. Therefore, researchers inferred that there was same judging valence of emotional cognition between living and non-living objects by elders. It also denotes older adults can analogize between realistic faces and varied emoticons by designs merging different emotional expressions. These results verify the tenability of H1, that older adults could distinguish the emotional differences of emoticons equally well as normal emotional stimuli. The results also could give evidences for further emoticon application and related designs on product interfaces or information communication for elders.

Why did elders feel more positive towards these emoticons? Socioemotional selectivity theory proposes that elders tend to shift towards emotionally meaningful goals and to satisfy or stabilize their emotional needs in social networks and objects in a limited time left to live [5]. Elders would therefore pay more attention to an important emotional target. Especially in attention and memory, elders would prefer positive and prevent negative information [10]. The activated brain states of elders also differ from young adults in processing and responding to different emotional stimuli [18] [19][20]. The emoticons represented the familiar human face and contained plentiful emotional expression, echoing arguments above. These could explain the cognitive differences of emoticons between two subject groups.

Judgment of emoticons' cognition differences had a broad range for younger adults but centralized for elder adults. Older adults kept more positive but ambiguous emotional criterion to response these emoticons. Charles, Mather and Carstensen [21] examined age differences in recall and recognition memory for emotional images also found younger adults show a wider portion of negative images than positive and neutral objects, but older and middle-age adults showed parallel emotional valence. Schaie [22] pointed out the cognitive ability of elders stayed high until around age 60, and then began to decline. The gradual decline of body and mind pushes elders to control moods and avoid extreme effects on both physiology and psychology. This caused older adults' recognition of emoticons to be more positive and centralized than younger adults.

4.3   Emoticon Preference of Elders

The preference scores of elders were smaller than the neutral score of 4, meaning they did not prefer many emoticons, especially those composed of punctuation marks. Young people commonly use these in online communicating tools such as bulletin boards, online chat, instant messaging and e-mail interfaces [23]. In this study, only two elders had experience with computers, meaning elders almost never used the emoticons. That is why older subjects showed lower understanding and unfamiliarity toward those emoticons. Why were the emotional judgments of elders toward emoticons higher and more positive than young adults, but their preference judgments significantly lower than those of younger subjects? For complex emotional cognition, Ross & Mirowsky [24] explained, elders possess both maturity and decline, which could be why older people report more positive emotions and more passive emotions simultaneously. The preferences are a process under many aspects of the decision environment and the judgment of preferences could be regarded the choice of objects [25][26]. Elders have the most common emotions like contentment, calm, and ease but of the elation and excitement [24]. These novel and unfamiliar emoticons obviously could not get the preferences by older people.

4.4   Limitations and Further Studies

Most elders had little experience using these interface elements. The using experiences to be an important factor influencing emotion and preference toward these emoticons. Though older adults may favor the familiar and dislike novel things, these emoticons seem to have innately new characteristics and also affect evaluative judgment. For young adults, these emoticon designs will be a common tool in their daily life when they become elders.

Although the artificial emoticon designs were the main subject in this study, it found age differences regarding emotional states and preference. Are there also existing age and recognition differences for comparing facial expressions between real human faces and emoticon? Can real human faces elicit more positive emotion and better preference than emoticons? Are these findings useful for elders on further application of digital communication? These questions merit further investigation.

Acknowledgment. This research was supported by the National Science Council of Taiwan under grant NSC98-2410-H-182-018.

References

1. Walther, J.B., D'Addario, K.P.: The Impacts of Emoticons on Message Interpretation in Computer-Mediated Communication. Social Science Computer Review 19(3), 324–347 (2001)
2. Derks, D., Bos, A.E.R., Grumbkow, J.V.: Emoticons and Social Interaction on theInternet: the Importance of Social Context. Computers in Human Behavior 23, 842–849 (2007)
3. Huang, A.H., Yen, D.C., Zhang, X.: Exploring the Potential Effects of Emoticons. Information & Management 45(7), 466–473 (2008)
4. Leclerc, C.M., Kensinger, E.A.: Effects of Age on Detection of EmotionalInformation. Psychology and Aging 23(1), 209–215 (2008)
5. Carstensen, L.L., Pasupathi, M., Mayr, U., Nesselroade, J.R.: Emotional Experience in Everyday Life across the Adult Life Span. Journal of Personality and Social Psychology 79(4), 644–655 (2000)
6. Charles, S.T., Reynolds, C.A., Gatz, M.: Age-Related Differences and Change in Positive and Negative Affect Over 23 Years. Personality and Social Psychology 80(1), 136–151 (2001)
7. Gross, J.J., Carstensen, L.L., Tsai, J., Skorpen, C.G., Hsu, A.Y.C.: Emotion and Aging: Experience, Expression, and Control. Psychology and Aging 12(4), 590–599 (1997)
8. Mather, M., Canli, T., English, T., Whitfield, S., Wais, P., Ochsner, K., Gabrieli, J.D.E., Carstensen, L.L.: Amygdala Responses to Emotionally Valenced Stimuli in Older and Younger Adults. Psychological Science 15(4), 259–263 (2004)
9. Carstensen, L.L., Mikels, J.A.: At the Intersection of Emotionand Cognition - Aging and the Positivity Effect. Current Directions in Psychological Science 14(3), 117–121 (2005)
10. Mather, M., Carstensen, L.L.: Aging and Motivated Cognition: the Positivity Effect in Attention and Memory. Trends in Cognitive Sciences 9(10), 496–502 (2005)
11. Carstensen, L.L., Isaacowitz, D.M., Charles, S.T.: Taking Time Seriously. A Theory of Socioemotional Selectivity. Am. Psychol. 54(3), 165–181 (1999)

12. Carstensen, L.L., Fung, H.H., Charles, T.S.: Socioemotional Selectivity Theory and the Regulation of Emotion in the Second Half of Life. Motivation and Emotion 27(2), 103–123 (2003)
13. Carstensen, L.L.: The Influence of a Sense of Time on Human Development. Science 312(5782), 1913–1915 (2006)
14. Lee, A.C.K., Tang, S.W., Yu, G.K.K., Cheung, R.T.F.: The smiley as a simple screening tool for depression after stroke: A preliminary study. International Journal of Nursing Studies 45(7), 1081–1089 (2008)
15. Norman, D.: The Design of Everyday Things. Doubleday, NewYork (1988)
16. Lee, T.M.C., Ng, E.H.H., Tang, S.W., Chan, C.C.H.: Effects of Sad Moodon Facial Emotion Recognition in Chinese People. Psychiatry Research 159, 37–43 (2008)
17. Mikels, J.A., Larkin, G.R., Reuter-Lorenz, P.A., Carstensen, L.L.: Divergent Trajectories in the Aging Mind: Changes in Working Memory for Affective Versus Visual Information with Age. Psychol Aging 20(4), 542–553 (2005)
18. Braver, T.S., Barch, D.M.: A Theory of Cognitive Control, AgingCognition, and Neuromodulation. Neuroscience and Biobehavioral Reviews 26, 809–817 (2002)
19. Gunning-Dixon, F.M., Gur, R.C., Perkins, A.C., Schroeder, L., Turner, T., Turetsky, B.I., Chan, R.M., Loughead, J.W., Alsop, D.C., Maldjian, J., Gur, R.E.: Age-related Differences in Brain Activation during EmotionalFace Processing. Neurobiology of Aging 24, 285–295 (2003)
20. Hedden, T., Gabrieli, J.D.E.: Insights into the Ageing Mind: A View fromCognitive Neuroscience. Nature Reviews Neuroscience 5, 87–96 (2004)
21. Charles, S.T., Mather, M., Carstensen, L.L.: Aging and Emotional Memory: The Forgettable Nature of Negative Images for Older Adults. Journal of Experimental Psychology: Genarl 132(2), 310–324 (2003)
22. Schaie, K.W.: Intellectual Development in Adulthood: The Seattle Longitudinal Study. Cambridge Univ. Press, Cambridge (1996)
23. Mock, K.: The Use of Internet Tools to Supplement Communication in The Classroom. Journal of Computing Sciences in Colleges 17(2), 14–21 (2001)
24. Ross, C.E., Mirowsky, J.: Age and The Balance of Emotions. Social Science & Medicine 66, 2391–2400 (2008)
25. Sharot, T., De Martino, B., Dolan, R.J.: How Choice Reveals and Shapes Expected Hedonic Outcome. Journal of Neuroscience 29, 3760–3765 (2009)
26. Lichtenstein, S., Slovic, P. (eds.): Construction of Preferences. Cambridge University Press, New York (2006)

Basic Study on Personal Space while Using Mobile Devices in Public

Shigeyoshi Iizuka[1] and Kentaro Go[2]

[1] Kanagawa University, Japan
shigeiizuka@gmail.com
[2] Interdisciplinary Graduate School of Medicine and Engineering,
University of Yamanashi, Japan
go@yamanashi.ac.jp

Abstract. In recent years, smart mobile devices have come to be widely used in our life spaces. This development has the potential to create major changes in the ways people communicate in public spaces. This paper presents two studies on a user's personal space while using a device in public: the first investigated mobile device use between three people; the second examined communicating private information on large, interactive displays in public spaces. Then, we introduced the basic concept for our future research on personal space while using mobile devices in public.

Keywords: personal space, public space, mobile devices, security.

1 Introduction

Today, information can be communicated regardless of time or place given the ubiquity of computers and the development of the Internet. Mobile devices in particular have come to be widely used in our life spaces in recent years, significantly influencing our activities. Therefore, it is thought that mobile devices will produce major changes to the ways we communicate in public spaces.

This paper presents two studies on personal space while using devices in public: the first investigated mobile device use between three people; the second examined the use of large public displays. Then, we introduce our basic concept on personal space research in the interactive display experience in public spaces; this will be the developed theme for our future research.

2 Observation of Mobile Device Use between Three People

To understand communication between two or more people while sharing a smart mobile device, we conducted an experiment consisting of three kinds of device-sharing methods (Iizuka et al., 2010). The purpose of this approach was to investigate

S. Yamamoto (Ed.): HIMI 2014, Part II, LNCS 8522, pp. 404–412, 2014.
© Springer International Publishing Switzerland 2014

the spatial relationships among the participants in each method of conversation using a smart mobile device.

Specifically, the following three methods were devised to share visual content on the display of a smart mobile device:

1. A device is passed mutually between the participants (mutually passed condition).
2. All participants look at content on a device that one person holds (device fixed to one person condition).
3. No one has a device during the experiment, but they talk about content seen beforehand (no device condition).

The participants were arranged into three-person groups; where possible, the group members were acquaintances. The experiment was conducted separately for each group.

Under each of the three above-mentioned conditions, each group used a small PC (VAIO type UX) (Figure 1) with a 4.5-inch display as a device shared between three people. Each group was directed to talk for two minutes about the picture displayed on the device (one picture was used for each condition; each picture was chosen at random from three images, as shown in Figure 2). The instructions given to the participants for each condition are shown in Table 1.

Fig. 1. Device for experiment

Fig. 2. Presentation images

Table 1. Instructions for the experiment

Condition	Instruction
Mutually passed	Please talk for about two minutes while looking at the picture on the device. Please pass the device around and show the image to each other.
Device fixed to one person	Please talk for about two minutes while looking at the picture on the device. Please have one person hold the device while the others look on.
No device	Please view the picture first and then talk about it for approximately two minutes.

The experimental environment was designed in a conference room at a university. A grid (60 cm spacing, three meters per side) was created on the floor using tape (Figure 3).

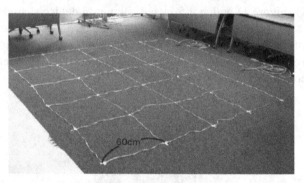

Fig. 3. Experimental grid

Before starting each trial, the three participants were gathered into one place to re-set their positions. During each experiment, all participants were allowed to move freely within the experimental grid. All experiments were recorded with a video camera. After the trials, we visually plotted the positions of each participant during each two-minute experiment using the grid in the video image. A sample result is shown in Figure 4.

Fig. 4. The situation under experiment

Here, we paid attention to the form of the triangle created by the positions of the three participants (Figure 5). The arrows in the figures indicate both the position and direction of each participant's step.

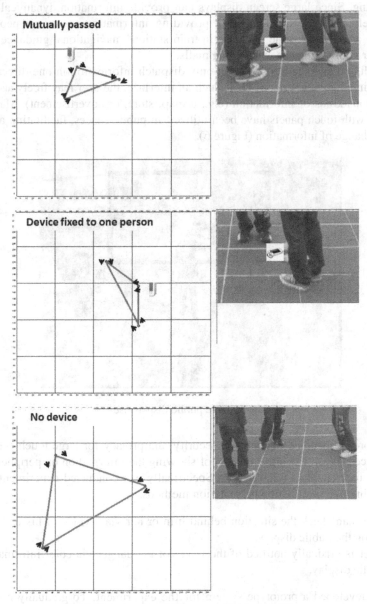

Fig. 5. Relationships between participant positions

In the "no device" and "mutually passed" conditions, the participants' positions formed equilateral triangles. The "device fixed to one person" condition, however, produced a number of obtuse isosceles triangles.

3   Examination of Large Public Display Use

In public spaces such stations and shopping malls, the practical use of large displays is increasing. Since large-screen displays can provide information dynamically, they are very effective for simultaneously providing information to several people. As such, they are used for time guidance in train stations, navigational guidance around stations, or goods guidance at shopping malls.

Some digital signage terminals not only dispatch information in one direction but also have interactive interfaces. With such an interface, the user may freely access via touch various kinds of information (e.g., a map, store, or advertisement). Many user interfaces with touch panels have been utilized in public spaces, facilitating an interactive exchange of information (Figure 6).

Fig. 6. Large public display use

Therefore, we studied information security and privacy for large touch screens in public spaces. We verified the validity of showing the information on peripheral danger to the user (Iizuka et al., 2014). Specifically, we conducted experiments using the following two information presentation methods:

- The user can check the situation behind him or her via a video of his or her back shown on the public display.
- The user is gradually notified of the grade of the danger via color information on the public display.

First, we developed a prototype system for the experiment. To gradually notify the user of danger, it was necessary to demarcate the space in front of the display according to distance. While a similar method has already been proposed by Vogel and others [1], in our model, the interaction of the user using the domain in front of the display does not change, and the divided domain is used as an index to notify the user of danger (Figure 7). Based on the distance (domain) from the display, the system gradually notifies the user of danger using color information (Figure 8):

- An arrow displays on the passing person in the image.
- A color frame displays on the outer frame of the user's workplace window.
- Both an arrow and a color frame are displayed.
- With no system

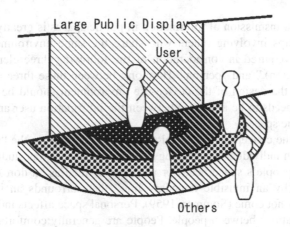

Fig. 7. The domain in front of the display

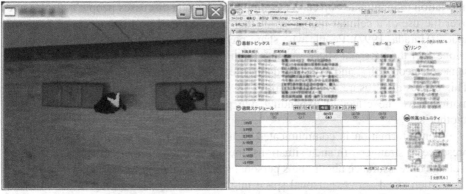

An arrow displays on the passing person in the image.

A color frame is displayed on the outer frame of the user's workplace window.

Fig. 8. Displaying information for users

The results found that notifying the user of "danger" did not necessarily reassure the user and could cause unease. It was suggested that displaying both an arrow indicating the position and direction of the passing person and a color frame based on the situation behind the user was more reassuring.

4   The Future of Personal Space within Public Spaces

The increasing ubiquity of services is expected to make computing all the more prevalent in public spaces. A great deal of digital signage has been installed in public areas, and displays that present information interactively are also increasing. Furthermore, people in public possess personal devices such as smart phones. People in public spaces communicate various information, and use their devices properly according to the situation.

However, the transmission of information in public spaces is greatly influenced by spatial relationships involving others who share the same environment. Therefore, new designs are required in consideration of the following three elements: "place," "device (information)," and "person." Harmony between these three elements is necessary—that is, the design of the device-use environment should be adapted to the place, and there needs to be a balance between the information user and others in the surrounding public space.

It is believed the concept of "personal space" originated from the "spacing" (leaving space between individuals) of ethology. "Personal space" was studied by Sommer as one index of people's space behavior and was defined as "a domain of a certain size demarcated by an invisible boundary line" that surrounds an individual, into which others may not come (Sommer, 1959). Personal space affects individual actions and regulates relations between people. People are generally comfortable when their personal space is maintained and uncomfortable when others invade it (Shibuya, 1985). Furthermore, personal space is elastic and rarely fixed. Elasticity is also seen in relation to inanimate objects (IT equipment). Harada discusses people's displeasure over the use of a cellular phone by another person based on the concept of personal space (Harada, 1997). People who share physical space with a person talking on the phone feel the personal space of the person on the phone has spread. This creates a sense of incongruity, and people suddenly feel the talker's "space" cannot be entered. This causes displeasure. In other words, IT equipment and the transmission of information have the effect of expanding one person's personal space and contracting another's.

When information is communicated in a public space, it usually happens in the presence of strangers. In such situations, the environment inevitably has an effect on feelings of reassurance about one's personal space in relation to others.

As mentioned above, personal space might also change according to the situation at a given time, the nature of the service, or the contents of the transmitted information (Knowles, 1976). We plan, therefore, to prepare two or more experimental scenarios, set up environments based on their respective features, and develop the idea of personal space through user evaluation (Figure 9).

Furthermore, following the basic experiment that explored the new style of information sharing and personal communication using a mobile device, we plan to conduct user evaluations that use similar scenarios supposing two or more use scenes (Figure 10) and introduce knowledge.

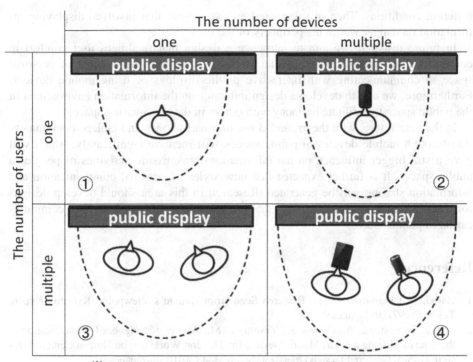

※Overhead view—the area inside the dotted line denotes personal space

Fig. 9. Use patterns of public display and mobile devices

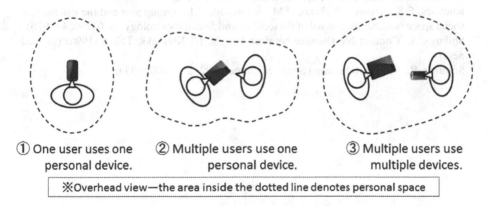

① One user uses one personal device.

② Multiple users use one personal device.

③ Multiple users use multiple devices.

※Overhead view—the area inside the dotted line denotes personal space

Fig. 10. Patterns specialized in mobile device use

5   Conclusion

We focused first on smart mobile devices, which are widely used in our life spaces and may greatly change how we communicate in public spaces. We presented the results of an experiment that observed communication between three people under different conditions. Then, we discussed an experiment that involved displaying information on danger within the periphery of the user.

In future research, we aim to introduce a design that facilitates user comfort in communicating information in public spaces by applying the concept of personal space to communicating with interactive public displays or using mobile devices. Furthermore, we aim to develop a design indicator on the information environment in the public space to facilitate harmony with others in the surrounding space.

In the near future, with the expanded use of smart phones and tablets, communication through mobile devices in public spaces will increase significantly, which will have a still bigger influence on the information-transmission activities of people in public spaces. It is further expected that new styles of personal communication and information sharing will be generated. Research in this area should develop designs for transmitting information in ways that are suitable for this new style of communication in public spaces.

References

1. Harada, E.: Inanimate Object Research Seen from Human's Viewpoint. KyorituShuppan, Tokyo (1997) (in Japanese)
2. Iizuka, S., Kodama, A., Ogawa, K., Yasumura, M.: Aspect of Neighbor Communication at the time of Sharing a Smart Mobile Device. In: The 2nd Workshop on Human Centered Design, Human Centered Design Organization, pp. 3–4 (2010) (in Japanese)
3. Iizuka, S., Naito, W., Go, K., Kinoshita, Y.: A Study for Presentation Method of Information about Circumference Situation for Personal Use of Interactive Large Public Display. IPSJ Journal, IPS Japan (to be appeared, 2014) (in Japanese)
4. Knowles, E.S., Kreuser, B., Haas, H.M., Schuchart, G.E.: Group size and the extension of social space boundaries. Journal of Personality and Social Psychology 33, 647–654 (1976)
5. Shibuya, S.: Comfortable Distance between People. NHK Books, Tokyo (1990) (in Japanese)
6. Sommer, R.: Studies in Personal Space. Sociometry 22, 247–260 (1959)

Soft Interface with the Ambiguity Creation of the Action by Avatar Controller Inducing the Embodiment

Shiroh Itai[1], Taketo Yasui[2], and Yoshiyuki Miwa[1]

[1] Faculty of Science and Engineering, Waseda University, Tokyo, Japan
itai@aoni.waseda.jp, miwa@waseda.jp
[2] Graduate School of Creative Science and Engineering, Waseda University, Tokyo, Japan
tyasui@ruri.waseda.jp

Abstract. To study about a creation of an action, we must study the mental and physical functions that create the action. Therefore, we focused on a rhythm controller that incorporated ambiguity in the relationship between the controller input and avatar motion, because determining this relationship requires the involvement of both mental and physical functions. In this study, we examined how controller manipulation methods changed when subjects performed similar avatar movements in different situations using the rhythm controller. From the results, we show that a regression plane by which the controller manipulation method (the relationship between the controller input and avatar motion) is approximated varies with the situation. Furthermore, we found that differences in intention could be expressed in the controller manipulation method. These show that the controller manipulation method of the rhythm controller flexibly changes depending on the situation, and is closely connected with the meaning of the action.

Keywords: Action, Embodiment, Ambiguity, Soft interface.

1 Introduction

Humans can improvise on taking an action that is appropriate to the situation in a complex environment. To study such action, it is not sufficient to consider the action as the motion expressed outside us. We must also study the mental and physical functions that create the action. However, it is generally difficult to elicit the mental and physical functions in a form that is observable outside us.

We believe that we have solved this problem by including mental and physical functions in the interface for operating an avatar in virtual space. Further, we have researched and developed a "rhythm controller" that creates avatar motion through rhythmic operation that precedes avatar motion [1-3]. This enables operators to treat their avatars like parts of their bodies. The result is not communicated through symbols, but through embodied communication in the virtual space. Furthermore, we developed a communication experiment system—the "Kendo" (Japanese fencing) match system—using this controller, and studied the creation of "Maai" and entrainment [4-6] generated by mental and physical functions. "Maai" in Japanese means the

S. Yamamoto (Ed.): HIMI 2014, Part II, LNCS 8522, pp. 413–422, 2014.
© Springer International Publishing Switzerland 2014

interspatial distance between individuals that can be determined by individual feelings, as suggested by E.T. Hall's theory of proxemics [7]. In-phase movement
emerges in a Kendo match using an avatar controlled by the rhythm controller. In this
movement, the distance between two avatars does not change much—when one avatar (subject) moves forward the opponent moved backward. Such avatar movement
corresponds to Maai. From the results, when Maai is improvisationally created between two avatars in a Kendo match, entrainment in multiple cycles is created. We
refer to entrainment in multiple cycles as "soft entrainment" [8] to differentiate it
from traditional entrainment explained by the theory of a normal coupled nonlinear
oscillator (phase model) [9-11]. We have also developed a method for enabling soft
entrainment in remote Kendo matches using the rhythm controller. We found that
many controller inputs can result in specific avatar motion in avatar operation using
the rhythm controller depending on the creation model of the soft entrainment.

Therefore, we consider that if focused on such an ambiguity of the rhythm controller, authors further advance the research of the mental and physical functions that
create the action. Because the relationship between controller input and avatar motion
is ambiguous due to the rhythm controller, operators can create avatar motion (action)
while freely deciding the controller manipulation method (the relationship between
controller input and avatar motion) through mental and physical functions. In fact,
determining this relationship requires the involvement of both mental and physical
functions (Fig. 1). Therefore, we consider that mental and physical functions are reflected in the relationship between controller input and avatar motion if the operator
creates the action (avatar motion) using the rhythm controller. For this reason, if the
avatar action is analyzed in relation to the controller manipulation method, we can
study the mental and physical functions that create the action. In contrast, for a normal controller in which avatar motion corresponds one-to-one with controller input,
the relationship between the controller input and avatar motion is unambiguous, and
the controller manipulation method is not changed (Fig. 2). Consequently, it is difficult to examine mental and physical functions from the controller manipulation method for a normal controller. Based on the concept above, in this study, we examined
how an operator's controller manipulation method changes when the operator
performs similar avatar motion in different situations using a rhythm controller.

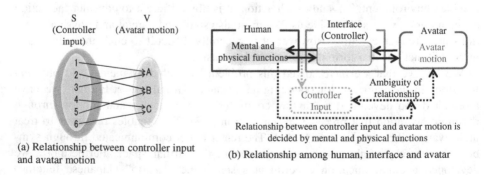

(a) Relationship between controller input
and avatar motion

(b) Relationship among human, interface and avatar

Fig. 1. Rhythm controller

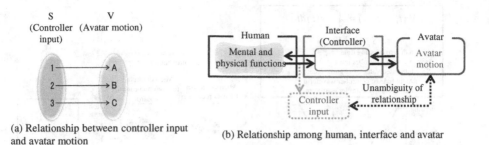

(a) Relationship between controller input and avatar motion

(b) Relationship among human, interface and avatar

Fig. 2. Normal Controller

2   Experiment System

We describe the method for examining the controller manipulation method (relationship between the controller input and avatar motion) when an operator creates avatar motion using the rhythm controller. First, we explain the transformation rule for creating the avatar motion using the rhythm controller. The operator must always create a rhythmic operation preceding the avatar motion for avatar operation with the rhythm controller. When the zero-cross was created on the controller waveform, as shown in Fig. 3, the controller waveform between zero-cross points up to two points prior to this incidence was integrated, and the thus the integrated value (ΔS) was used as a velocity output value for the next zero-cross point to operate the avatar. The transformation rule of the rhythm controller is a function in which the argument is the ΔS and the dependent variable is the avatar velocity (V). This ΔS, which is the area of a one-cycle waveform of the rhythm controller, is determined by the difference in the cycle (the interval between neighboring zero-cross points, ΔT) and the difference in the amplitude (ΔA). However, because the operator can independently change both the cycle and amplitude of the rhythm controller with freedom, the relationship between these variables (ΔT and ΔA) and ΔS is not unique. For example, the operator can create a specific size area using the methods below:

- Using this method, the operator creates ΔA with ΔT kept at almost zero.
- Using this method, the operator creates ΔT with ΔA kept at almost zero
- Using this method, the operator creates both ΔT and ΔA

Consequently, for the avatar operation with a rhythm controller for which the inputs are ΔT and ΔA, there are many controller inputs for realizing a specific avatar motion. Avatar velocity (V) can be expressed in the following form:

$$V = f (\Delta T, \Delta A) \qquad (1)$$

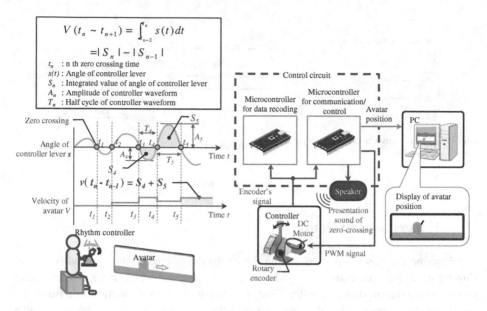

Fig. 3. Transformation rule of rhythm controller

Fig. 4. System Configuration

This function f expresses the relationship between controller input and avatar motion,—in other words, the controller manipulation method. As mentioned before, when the avatar is operated using the rhythm controller, the operator changes the method for creating the area of the controller waveform by adjusting its cycle and amplitude. Consequently, the operator can temporally (dynamically) change not only avatar velocity but also the controller manipulation method (function f). In this study, at the start of examining such a controller manipulation method, $(\Delta T, \Delta A, V)$ was plotted in a 3D scatter plot when the zero-cross was created on the controller waveform. Furthermore, we tried to estimate the function f by multiple regression analysis in which the explanatory variables are ΔT and ΔA, and the dependent variable is V.

Next, we describe the experiment system in which the operator moves the avatar with the rhythm controller. Fig. 4 shows the configuration of this system. This system requires the following three things: the real-time drawing of avatars on the display of a PC, the control of avatar motion, and the use of instrumentation for record purpose. We used two microcontrollers (mbed NXP LPC1768, clock frequency of 96 [MHz]). One controlled avatar motion and the communication of the avatar position data to the PC by 20 [ms] intervals. The other recorded the operation angle of the rhythm controller by 1 [ms] intervals. The operation angle of the controller was measured with a rotary encoder (NEMICON, resolution: 1600[P/R]) mounted on the operation lever of the controller.

3   Experimental Results

We observed how the controller manipulation method changed when the operator performed similar avatar motions in different situations. Specifically, we conducted three different experiments, as shown in Fig. 5 and listed here:

1. Forward and backward movement experiment: The subject freely moves the avatar backward and forward within given limits (Fig. 5(a)).
2. Chase up experiment: The subject moves the avatar backward and forward while avoiding running into an automatic avatar that drives the subject's avatar into a corner (Fig. 5(b)).
3. Kendo experiment: Two subjects use their avatars to play a simulated Kendo match (Fig. 5(c)).

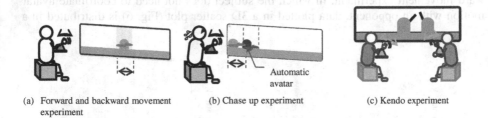

(a) Forward and backward movement   (b) Chase up experiment   (c) Kendo experiment
       experiment

Fig. 5. Experimental conditions

All subjects of these experiments were adept at operating the avatar using the rhythm controller. The chase up experiment required the creation of action that is complementary with the motion of the automatic avatar. However, there was no need for it in the forward and backward movement experiment. The Kendo experiment was similar to the chase up experiment in that action must be complementary with the motion of the opponent avatar. But for the Kendo experiment, the plot of the match is not decided ahead of time. Before the match, subjects cannot decide in what situations they will create and collapse Maai. Subjects needed to improvise creating the action with the opponent depending on the situation.

Table. 1 shows analysis results of the relationship between the controller input (ΔT, ΔA) and avatar motion (V) in the three experiments described above. From this table, we found that the avatar velocity (V) in all experiments was approximated by the regression plane determined from ΔT and ΔA, because the determination coefficient of the multiple regression analysis was near 1 in all experiments. Table. 1 shows that the partial regression coefficient of the forward and backward movement experiment, in which the subject does not need to coordinate avatar motion with the movement of an opponent, differs from the chase up and Kendo experiments, in which the subject needed to coordinate avatar motion with that of an opponent. These results show that the controller manipulation method (relationship between the controller input and avatar motion) varies with the situation.

Table 1. Results of the multiple regression analysis

		Partial regression coefficient		Standardized partial regression coefficient		Determination coefficient R^2
		ΔT	ΔA	ΔT	ΔA	
Forward and backward movement experiment (Subject Y)		73	71	0.5	0.54	0.97
Chase up experiment (Subject Y)		18	71	0.24	0.72	0.85
Kendo experiment	Subject Y :winner	17	94	0.10	0.90	0.95
	Subject K : loser	12	95	0.23	0.76	0.88

4   Discussion

In the previous section, we describe the change of the regression plane by which the function f is approximated due to experimental condition. In the forward and backward movement experiment, in which the subject does not need to coordinate avatar motion with an opponent, data plotted in a 3D scatter plot (Fig. 6) is distributed in a

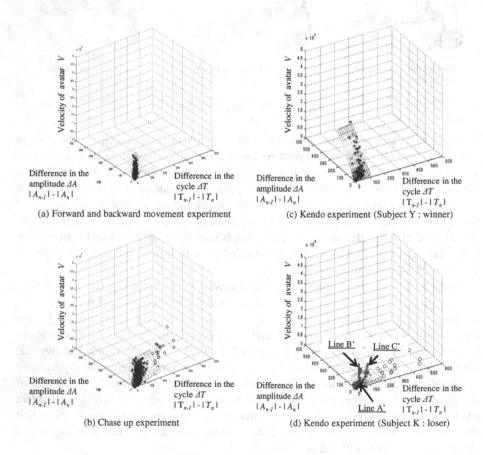

(a) Forward and backward movement experiment

(b) Chase up experiment

(c) Kendo experiment (Subject Y : winner)

(d) Kendo experiment (Subject K : loser)

Fig. 6. 3D scatter plot of (ΔT, ΔA, V)

line. In the chase up and Kendo experiments, it is distributed in a plane. In fact, in the forward and backward movement experiment, the correlation coefficient between explanatory variables (ΔT and ΔA) is 0.81—nearly 1. This indicates a high likelihood of reducing the number of explanatory variables in the multiple regression analysis. Therefore, we tried to approximate the result of the forward and backward movement experiment with a straight line using the analysis of the principal component as shown in Fig. 7. From the result, the determination coefficient of the regression line is 0.98—nearly 1. This result shows the validity of approximating the relationship between the controller input and avatar motion by simple linear regression analysis. Controller operation using the rhythm controller has two-degree-of-freedom (ΔT and ΔA). However, the subject (operator) creates avatar motion by virtually reducing the number of degrees of freedom in the forward and backward movement experiment, where the subject does not need to coordinate avatar motion with an opponent.

As shown in Fig. 8, in the Kendo experiment, data plotted in a 3D scatter plot is approximated by two regression lines in the regression plane given above. Fig. 8 shows the result for subject Y, who won the Kendo match. Line B in Fig. 8 is the controller manipulation method in which the operator fluctuates the ΔA, with the ΔT kept near to constant. Fig. 9(a) shows a time-series variation of two subject's avatar

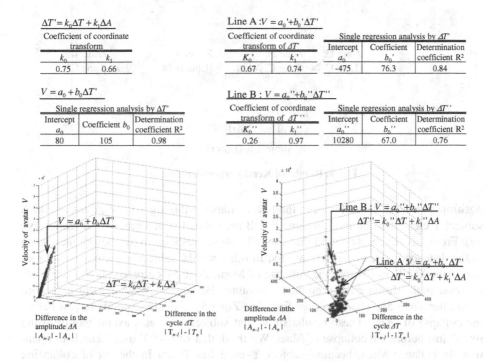

Fig. 7. Linear regression analysis in the move back and forth experiment

Fig. 8. Linear regression analysis in Kendo experiment

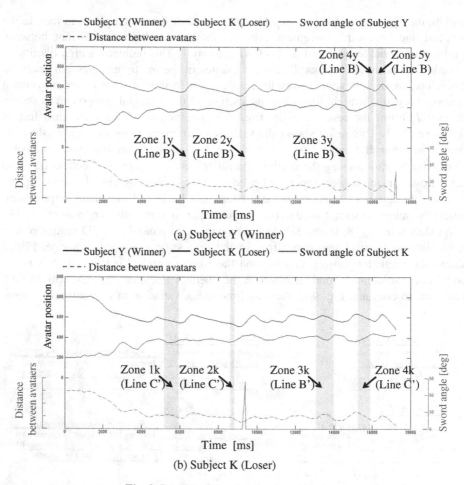

Fig. 9. Results of Kendo experimentAvatar

position and the distance between the two avatars. In this figure, the zones in which subject Y created avatar motion using line B are painted with a green band (zones 1y–5y). From this figure, we found that zones 1y–4y correspond to just before increasing in the distance between the two avatars. In other words, subject Y creates avatar motion using line B just before the collapse of Maai. Zone 5y corresponds to just before decrease in the distance between the two avatars. However, subject Y swings a sword soon after Zone 5y. Therefore, we find that Zone 5y also corresponds to just before the collapse of Maai. These results show that subject Y creates avatar motion using line B just before the collapse of Maai. We think that subject Y used Line B to intentionally collapse Maai, because subject Y used line B not in the act of collapsing Maai, but just before the collapse of Maai. Summarization of these results shows that the controller manipulation method is different when the intention is to create Maai and when the intention is to collapse it. Moreover, in this system, if subject Y creates avatar motion using the method in which the ΔT fluctuates, but ΔA is kept nearly constant, it's going to be more likely that the opponent (subject K) can anticipate the movement of subject Y's avatar because the operation rhythm of the controller is mutually transmitted as the sound. In this case, subject Y uses line B when intending to collapse Maai. Subject Y does not want the opponent to anticipate the motion of subject Y's avatar in this situation. Therefore, we found that subject Y creates avatar motion using the controller manipulation method that is appropriate for the situation. Further, the results of player K, who lost the Kendo match, show the same tendency (Fig. 6(d), Fig. 9(b)). From the result, we found that humans can improvise actions by changing the controller manipulation method depending on the situation.

In the Kendo match using this system, the forward motion of the avatar has two quite different meanings. One is to move forward to create Maai. The other is to move forward to collapse Maai. Results of this study show that by changing the controller manipulation method, subjects act in ways in which their movements are the same, but the meanings of the actions are quite different. This also shows that the controller manipulation method (the relationship between the controller input and avatar motion) flexibly changes depending on the situation, and is closely connected with the meaning of the action. Therefore, we consider this relationship (controller manipulation method) as the soft interface that is created by embodiment and has ambiguity.

Moreover, from the results of this study, we found that differences in intention, such as intending to create or collapse Maai, could be expressed in the controller manipulation method of the rhythm controller. This indicates that the rhythm controller can be useful for interfaces that estimate the internal states (feelings, intentions, and so on) of humans.

5   Summary

In this study, we examined how controller manipulation methods changed when subjects performed similar avatar movements in different situations using a rhythm controller that incorporated ambiguity in the relationship between the controller input and avatar motion. From the results, the controller manipulation method can be approximated by a regression plane in the chase up experiment and Kendo experiment, for which the subject needed to coordinate avatar motion with the motion of an opponent's avatar. For the forward and backward movement experiment, in which the subject did not need to coordinate avatar motion with that of an opponent's avatar, a regression line was enough to approximate the controller manipulation method. Furthermore, we observed that the controller manipulation method differed when a subject intended to create Maai and when the subject intended to collapse Maai in the Kendo match. Finally, we found that subjects could improvise action by changing the controller manipulation method depending on the situation.

Acknowledgment. This study is supported by Project Research "Principal of emergence for empathetic "Ba" and its applicability to communication technology" of RISE Waseda University, and Artifacts/Scenario/Human Institute of Waseda University.

References

1. Itai, S., Kudo, A., Miwa, Y., Aizawa, Y.: Creation and co-share of timing in an actual communication. In: Proc. of 2002 IEEE International Conference on Systems, Man and Cybernetics. CD-ROM (2002)
2. Itai, S., Miwa, Y.: Co-Existing Communication Using a Robot as Your Agent. In: Proceedings of the 2004 IEEE/RSJ International Conference on Intelligent Robots and Systems, pp. 1218–1225 (2004)
3. Itai, S., Miwa, Y.: Creation and co-share of "Maai" by the interface employing the embodiment. In: Proceedings of the 2004 IEEE International Workshop on Robot and Human Interactive Communication, pp. 193–198 (2004)
4. Condon, W.S., Sander, L.S.: Neonate movement issynchronized with adult speech. Science (183), 99–101 (1974)
5. Kendon, A.: Movement coordination in social interaction: Some examples described. ActaPsychologica 32, 101–125 (1970)
6. Webb, J.T.: Interview synchrony: An investigation of two speech rate measures in an automated standardized interview. In: Pope, B., Siegman, A.W. (eds.) Studies in Dyadic Communication, pp. 115–133. Pergamon, New York (1972)
7. Hall, E.T.: The Hidden Dimension. Garden City, N.Y (1966)
8. Itai, S., Miwa, Y.: Soft entrainment. Journal of the Society of Instrument and Control Engineers 51(11), 1059–1063 (2012) (in Japanese)
9. Winfree, A.T.: Biological rhythms and the behavior of populations ofcoupled oscillators. J. Theor. Biol. 16, 15–42 (1967)
10. Kuramoto, Y.: Chemical oscillations, waves, and turbulence. Springer, Berlin (1984)
11. Strogatz, S.: SYNC: The emerging science of spontaneous order. Hyperion Books, NewYork (2003)

Development and Application of Manga-Style Chat System Aiming to Communicate Nonverbal Expression

Junko Itou, Yuichi Motojin, and Jun Munemori

Faculty of Systems Engineering, Wakayama University,
930, Sakaedani, Wakayama 640-8510, Japan
{itou,munemori}@sys.wakayama-u.ac.jp

Abstract. In this research, we propose a chat system that makes it easy to convey nonverbal information by adopting the Japanese Manga style. Characters in the chat systems play roles as agents of users to express the users' emotional states. However, even if whatever the characters have faces and aspects, users are required to select the appropriate emotion of the character not to give an unexpected impression from the illustrations. It is very troublesome for users to choose manually various emotions at each message during their chat. So we focus on the the Japanese Manga style and make an attempt to reduce users' burdens.

1 Introduction

Online communication is widely spreading and tools of online communication become diverse, for example e-mail, chat system, remote meeting system, distance learning, and so on. There are also varieties of proposed tools on chat system from conventional text-based one to graphical one that agents in place of users talks in virtual space[1][2].

By using embodied character in chat system, the users obtain messages by watching embodied character's appearance as well as by reading plain texts. So these chat systems with visual components are expected to serve as a human interface to transmit nonverbal information more easily than conventional text-based systems.

Characters in the chat systems play roles as agents of users not only to express the users' emotional states or intentions which cannot be displayed by a chat message. As the result, it becomes clear what meaning the user implies for the chat messages. On the other hand, even if whatever the characters have faces and aspects, the system have to serve a same atmosphere to users who obtain information through the characters' chat. Therefore, users are required to select the appropriate emotion of the character not to give an unexpected impression from the illustrations. It is very troublesome for users to choose manually various emotions at each message during their chat. So we should reduce users' burdens.

In this article, we propose a chat system that makes it easy to convey nonverbal information by adopting the Japanese Manga style. A Japanese Manga has

S. Yamamoto (Ed.): HIMI 2014, Part II, LNCS 8522, pp. 423–434, 2014.
© Springer International Publishing Switzerland 2014

many methods to visualize and to transmit information such as directions of a character's eye gaze, signs placed in background and an arrangement of frames in the 2-dimensional plane.

This paper is organized as follows: in section 2, we will describe the problems about existing tools to output records by the comic style and related chat systems to support conveying nonverbal information. In section 3, we explain how our system supports emotional chat. We will show the experimental result on whether users can add nonverbal information to chat messages intuitively in section 4. Finally, we will discuss some conclusions and our future steps in section 5.

2   Related Works on Transmitting Nonverbal Information

The way to transmitting the nonverbal information includes emoticons, smileys, pictographs, and avatars. Emoticons and smileys are a combination of characters and the sign that can be employed to express a user's emotion. They are commonly used at the end of a sentence in e-mail, chat conversations, and even bulletin boards.

Pictographs and stamps are used as a picture on cellular phones and instant messengers[1]. Pictographs have various types, such as those expressing emotional states, or those depicting animals, plants, and buildings. Additionally, there are also varieties of proposed tools to support online communication including in chat, instant messengers and online games. Users can employ avatars as their agents in these systems. An avatar has a human-like body that can easily express the user's emotions as well as emoticons and pictographs can do.

These expression styles play an important role in expressing a user's emotions and intentions more accurately in text communication. Many expression styles have already incorporated communication systems. Instant messengers are applications that enable the members logged into chat with one another. Latest instant messengers allow users to exchange messages containing pictographs, animations and sounds.

Microsoft Comic Chat is a chat system that users can use various kinds of characters[2]. In this system, characters are drawn with various actions and a text balloon in the each frame according to user's selection. Users can choose a character and its emotion from the emotion wheel that is a circle with four axis expressing eight emotions. Users input a message in the text box and choose a particular expression, and then the character with the expression, the background image, and the message in a balloon are drawn in a square frame. A balloon is fixed at the upper area of a frame and the characters are drawn at the bottom area automatically.

ComicDiary is a system that creates a personal diary in comic style [3]. Users can exchange their individual memories to a comic automatically. ComicDiary adopts comic style as an expression form and focuses on the story constitution from introduction, development, turn, to conclusion, based on user's actions in visiting an exhibition hall. The system automatically chooses components including in words, characters and backgrounds from the component database and makes a twelve frames comic. On the other hand, users cannot touch plot development nor can users choose the component, e.g. the character's emotion.

Emoticons, smileys and pictographs can convey nonverbal information but users accordingly use particular expressions because there are too many kinds of options and it requires troublesome tasks to select a expression. There are the same problems in the Microsoft Comic Chat. The interface of the Microsoft Comic Chat is inconvenient for users to determine an expression appropriately and imposes the burden. Furthermore, the sequence of frames with characters is too simple, and the size and the shape of the frames are fixed, so it is difficult to understand the total direction of the conversation.

Thawonmas et al. proposed a system to summarize player experiences in online games as a comic style based on the player's game log [4]. This system divides the whole play into multiple intervals called scene based on game events and game characters' actions such as talk, change of viewpoint. Then the system determines the shape and the size of a frame based on bordering frames and the scenes automatically. The result comics have various shapes of frames so that users can obtain a feeling of rhythm and story line from the screen composition. However, this system uses capture images of the game inside a frame and automatically determines the rendering composition. Therefore users have no space to reflect their intentions and emotions in this system, too. Additionally, only balloons and capture image are just arranged in a frame. In contrast to this, Japanese Manga has many methods to visualize characters emotion or situation, and to transmit information using directions of a character's eye gaze, signs placed in background, shapes of balloons and an arrangement of frames in the 2-dimensional plane.

Based on the above discussions, we aim to develop a chat system that conveys emotional information intuitively and appropriately by applying the Japanese Manga style.

3   System Framework

3.1   Goal

Our goal is to realize the chat system incorporated with the Japanese style comic, "Manga", and to analyze how the system influence a chat. In the Manga, the layout of texts and pictures conveys variety of information as well as themselves convey. Manga has many rules to visualize and transmit information. The frame that is one of basic components of Manga consists of pictures of characters and backgrounds, balloons, signs like aggregate of lines, texts and so on. The combination of a heavy line is the frame and the sequences of the frames drawn in 2-dimensional plane are Manga. The arrangement of frames has temporal meanings to lead readers to the next frames according to the story. Fig.1 shows the typical sequence of frames. This is Japanese comic style. Readers start from the upper-right frame and read to left of the same row. Then, readers return to rightmost frame of one frame below. Authors can lead readers' gazes and can express emotions, inflections, atmospheres and times by arrangement of frames.

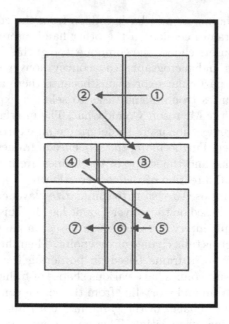

Fig. 1. The typical sequence of frames in Japanese comic

Authors draw a comic using the numerous onomatopoeic, the signs expressing emotions or feelings such as cold sweat or anger, the camerawork, the balance of black and white, and lines that give the feelings of stringency or brightness. These can also transmit a wide variety of information by size and the arrangement of the components in a frame. We adopt these methods to the chat system.

Our main target is the persons who can understand how to read Manga. Manga is popular throughout the world especially among young people. In Germany, Japanese comics has sold over 10 million copies in 2008 and the market is second to France in Europe[5]. On the last page of most of Manga sold in other countries such as America, France and Germany, that is the first page of books in these counties, an attention that a reader is starting at the wrong end of the comic and explanations how to read Manga are shown using an illustration like Fig.1 [6][7][8]. Many people in these countries become familiar with the culture, so this system can apply partially in other countries.

In the remainder of this section, we will propose the Manga style chat system that appends nonverbal information to the exchange messages.

3.2 System Overview

Let us consider a pair of persons A and B to explain our chat system. We denote user A's character by character A and user B's character by character B. The overview of the characters is shown in Fig.3. Users can choose which character

Fig. 2. The example of arranged frames

they use but they cannot use the same character at one time. These characters have four kinds of emotions that are 'the ordinary', 'the happiness', 'in trouble' and 'in thinking'.

3.3   System Structure

Our chat system is constructed of a server and a client connected to a network. Users start this system then the window comes up as shown in Fig.4.

The main space displays the frames with pictures and chat message. After user A inputs a message in the field of the message box and clicks the emotion button, the information is sent to the computer of user B. The emotion buttons are also the submit button. The clients of user A and B illustrate a frame which includes the character A's picture expressing the selected emotion and the balloon with the chat message in the main space of both clients. The example of inserted multiple frames is shown in Fig.5.

Fig. 3. Characters in Manga-style chat system

3.4   Emotions of Character

We performed a preliminary search to investigate which emotion users wanted to use. Experimental subjects are six Japanese college students. They ordinarily use a smiley in chat and they understand how to read Manga. At first we selected four kinds of emotions that were 'delight', 'anger', 'sadness' and 'pleasure'. These emotions are basic expressions in theater training. We indicated the subjects that they had a chat using the four emotions according to the chat message. As the result of this experiment, users answered they could not discriminate the 'delight' from 'pleasure', they rarely used the emotion of 'anger', and they wanted to use the emotion expressing calm atmosphere. From these comments, we determined the four emotions such as 'the ordinary', 'the happiness', 'in trouble' and 'in thinking'.

The frame expressing 'the ordinary' uses a basic round balloon and doesn't use special signs in the background so that this frame describes balanced situation.

The frame expressing 'the pleasure' uses a fluffy balloon to describe the atmosphere that the character gets lively. The character moves his/her hands to induce an uplifting feeling. There are signs of brightness in the background. Furthermore, we employ the composition to be looked up to express positive impression.

The shape of balloon in the frame expressing 'in trouble' is awkward circle to express a sense of anxiety. The character looks down with the sign describing cold sweat. There are many black spaces using aggregate of lines in the background.

Many small lines are arrangement around the face of the character in the frame of 'in thinking'. This method gives the atmosphere to readers that the character is shrouded in the cobweb feelings. Additionally, it is reported that persons maintain their eye contact when they are not interested in talking with

Fig. 4. The chat window

their partner [9][10]. We adopt this result to the character that is sunk in thought. The character takes his/her gaze from the partner's face.

These features are peculiar to Japanese comics.

3.5   Arrangement of Frames

Users input chat message and click the emotion button, then the system determines the position and the size of the new frames. The chat window shows two frames at each row. One row contains two size of frames whose width is different.

The system inserts a new frame at right area in a row when the row has no frame. When the row has one frame at right area, then a new frame is placed at the left side and a new row is inserted below the row. Same size frames are not placed at one row and column as shown in Fig.5. This arrangement is applied for effects in visual guidance and preventing monotonous compositions.

Fig. 5. The example of arranged frames

4   Experimental Results

4.1   Experimental Outline

We conducted a comparison experiment to investigate whether users can add nonverbal information to chat messages intuitively and whether our system can reduce users' burdens. Furthermore, we analyze the influence on users' behaviors that the agents' aspects make. The target system for comparison is the Microsoft Comic Chat.

Experimental subjects were 20 college students made up of 16 males and 4 females. They ordinarily used a smiley in text communication. They were divided into ten pairs. We instructed each pair to chat for ten minutes using each system. The five pair used our system in first and other five pair used the Microsoft Comic Chat in first considering the influence of order effects. In both system,

Table 1. The result of the questionnaire result on the proposed system

Questionnaire item	1	2	3	4	5	6	7	Ave.
(i) I could choose the emotions according to my messages.	0	0	3	2	7	6	2	5.1
(ii) I could add my emotions or intentions to my messages.	0	0	1	5	8	5	1	5.0
(iii) I could understand emotions or intentions from partner's messages.	0	0	0	3	7	7	3	5.5
(iv) It was easy to understand the emotions from the sequence of frames.	0	1	0	1	1	10	7	6.0
(v) There were many emotions I could choose.	1	4	8	6	1	0	0	3.1
(vi) The number of the emotions I could choose was enough.	1	1	8	5	3	0	2	3.8
(vii) I felt burdened to choose the emotions.	6	6	3	1	3	1	0	2.6
(viii) The pictures in frames brought excitement to the conversation.	0	0	1	1	6	8	4	5.7
(ix) The pictures in frames influence the conversation.	1	1	2	1	5	7	3	5.1
(x) It was easy to understand the directions of conversation in reading a log.	1	1	3	4	2	3	6	4.9

the subjects were imposed no restrictions in using these systems but we gave the chat topics such as a movie, memories of a travel and the things after they had been college students. We showed them the list of characters and emotions preliminarily then the subjects chose one character freely. We didn't control the combination between the character's gender and a participant's gender, so some participants play different gender character. In the end of the experiment, we asked the subjects to answer some questions.

4.2 Experimental Result

We denote the experiment using the proposal system by exp_p and the experiment using the comparison system by exp_c. The result of the questionnaire is described in Table 1 and Table 2. The numbers mean the participants who selected the point on a seven-point scale. Table 3 shows the average numbers that all subjects sent messages.

4.3 Discussion on Transmission of Nonverbal Information

The questionnaire item (i) and (ii) are the evaluations in sending messages and the item (iii) is the evaluation in receiving messages. As shown in Table 1 and Table 2, the evaluation values of each item for our system exceed the values for the comparison system, however the gap is small. From the result, it revealed that both the systems allow users to emotional chat in the same level.

Table 2. The result of the questionnaire result on the comparison system

Questionnaire item	1	2	3	4	5	6	7	Ave.
(i) I could choose the emotions according to my messages.	0	1	3	4	8	3	1	4.6
(ii) I could add my emotions or intentions to my messages.	1	1	2	3	8	2	3	4.7
(iii) I could understand emotions or intentions from partner's messages.	0	0	1	4	5	7	3	5.4
(iv) It was easy to understand the emotions from the sequence of frames.	3	5	5	4	1	2	0	3.1
(v) There were many emotions I could choose.	0	1	1	2	2	9	5	5.6
(vi) The number of the emotions I could choose was enough.	0	3	4	2	3	4	4	4.7
(vii) I felt burdened to choose the emotions.	0	1	0	2	6	5	6	5.6
(viii) The pictures in frames brought excitement to the conversation.	0	2	2	2	9	3	2	4.8
(ix) The pictures in frames influence the conversation.	5	4	2	5	3	0	1	3.1
(x) It was easy to understand the directions of conversation in reading a log.	2	0	6	6	4	1	1	3.9

Table 3. The average numbers that all subjects sent messages

Experiment	exp_p	exp_c
Average numbers	15.8	17.0

In this experiment, some participants played different gender character. We conducted hearings with the pairs including the participants about the influence. Most of them answered that they read the chat dialog with two characters as a story of third persons rather than their agents dialog. They didn't feel uncomfortable in the gender mismatch, further, part of them enjoyed the mismatch for instance he made the female character speak with slang and the partner could understand the intention and the situation properly.

In the free description field, participants answered it was more easy to understand the partner's emotions visually in exp_c because they could control intensity of emotions even if the same emotion was chosen and they enjoyed the over actions and the reactions. In exp_p, they felt a flow and progress of conversation and sometimes chose mismatched emotion purposely then enjoyed the mismatch between the facial expression and speaking. Totally they didn't have empathy for the characters but they enjoyed reading and making Manga story by the third persons in both system from the result of free descriptions and hearings.

4.4   Discussion on Ease of Interpretation of Nonverbal Information

The participants rated higher evaluation for our system on the item (iv) in Table 1 and Table 2. Additionally, users answered that it was difficult to understand the order of frames and messages in the comparison system, and that they could understand the character's helpless atmosphere easily. As the result, users can understand the nonverbal information from the chat window in our system.

4.5   Discussion on the Number of Emotions

By comparing the result of the values of the item (v) in Table 1 and Table 2, we obtained higher value in the comparison system than the proposed system. On the other hand, there was little difference on the result on the item (vi). The participants commented for our system that they had hardly any trouble in exchanging messages and that it was just number in choosing the emotions. So we conclude that our system satisfied users nearly as much as the comparison system in expressing emotions even if there are few of emotions. Furthermore, large number of emotions in the comparison system influenced the burden for users in choosing the appropriate emotion.

4.6   Discussion on Burdens in Using the System

It is cleared that the participants felt emotionally exhausted in choosing the emotions in exp_c from the values of the item (vii). They answered that choosing the emotion is burdensome task when they wanted speedy exchange of messages and that there were similar expressions so it was a hassle task to choose. This result is linked to the result in subsection 4.5.

4.7   Discussion on Influence to Conversation

Finally, we discuss the result that the systems influenced to conversations. As shown in Table 3, there are no differences on the average number that one participant sent messages at each system. On the other hand, the result of the item (ix) in Table 1 and Table 2 shows different value. The participants answered that all balloons were placed at the top of each frame so they could not pay attention to all area of frames, including in the characters illustraions in exp_c. In exp_p, they wrote in the field of free description that they felt a sense of movement from the camerawork and the composition.

As a result, we conclude that our system provided movement for the chat conversation and enlivened the conversation without reducing the number of exchange messages.

5   Conclusion

In this article, we propose a chat system incorporated Manga-style aiming to convey emotional information intuitively and appropriately. The proposed system displays input texts and pictures including in a balloon, a background and an emotional character that a user chooses. By the repetition of exchanging frames, users can understand the direction of the conversation. Furthermore, they can convey their intention to the partner and receive the partner's intention.

We performed an experiment for comparing the proposed system and the existing chat system. From the results of the questionnaire and analysis of log data, our system can minimize the burden on choosing the emotions but the ability of expression on nonverbal information is as well as the existing system.

For the next step, we should implement the feature that signs to announce that the partner is inputting are displayed. Secondly, the participants in the experiments were all Japanese. We should investigate how the difference of calture influent the result.

Acknowledgments. This work was supported by JSPS KAKENHI Grant Number 25330320.

References

1. LINE, http://line.naver.jp/ja/ (access on October 29, 2013)
2. Comic Chat - Resources,
   http://kurlander.net/DJ/Projects/ComicChat/resources.html
   (access on October 29, 2013)
3. Sumi, Y., Sakamoto, R., Nakao, K., Mase, K.: ComicDiary: Representing Individual Experiences in a Comics Style. In: Borriello, G., Holmquist, L.E. (eds.) UbiComp 2002. LNCS, vol. 2498, pp. 16–32. Springer, Heidelberg (2002)
4. Thawonmas, R., Shuda, T.: Comic Layout for Automatic Comic Generation from Game Log. In: Ciancarini, P., Nakatsu, R., Rauterberg, M., Roccetti, M. (eds.) New Frontiers for Entertainment Computing. IFIP, vol. 279, pp. 105–115. Springer, Boston (2008)
5. Japan External Trade Organization: Content market in Germany, pp. 26–45 (2009), http://www.jetro.go.jp/jfile/report/07000040/05001678.pdf (access on October 29, 2013) (in Japanese)
6. Toriyama, A.: Dragon Ball, vol. 3. Viz Media LLC (2003)
7. Tamura, Y.: Basara, vol. 3. Viz Media LLC (2003)
8. Ohba, T., Obata, T.: Death Note, Band 1. Tokyopop GmbH (2006) (in German)
9. Beattie, G.W.: Sequential patterns of speech and gaze in dialogue. Semiotica 23, 29–52 (1978)
10. Kendon, A.: Some functions of gaze direction in social interaction. Acta Psychologica 26, 22–63 (1967)

Concepts and Applications
of Human-Dependent Robots

Youssef Khaoula, Naoki Ohshima, P. Ravindra S. De Silva, and Michio Okada

Interactions and Communication Design Lab,
Toyohashi University of Technology, Toyohashi 441-8580, Japan
{youssef,ohshima}@icd.cs.tut.ac.jp, {ravi,okada}@tut.jp
http://www.icd.cs.tut.ac.jp/en/profile.html

Abstract. Relational artifacts (human-dependent) should have two aspects of subjective effects: Rorschach and evocative. During interaction, a robot has to anticipate the state (relationship) of the interactive person from the emotional to cognitive level to convey its Rorschach response. Consequently, the robot should behave as an evocative object to indicate the characteristic of animacy, which should accomplished using a potentially interactive architecture to coordinate the Rorschach and evocative effects. In this paper, we present two kinds of relational artifacts – a sociable trash box (STB) and a Talking-Ally.

Keywords: Relational artifacts, Rorschach and evocative effects, Hearership, Addressivity.

1 Introduction

As a newly emerging concept, previous studies have been concerned with developing a human-dependent robot [10][2]. Some research has defined a similar concept as either relational artifacts or a relatively operational robot. This concept can be defined as a robot being able to understand the situation of a human being (interactive user) in the relationship. The main attribute of the human-dependent robot (relational artifacts) is to convey its "attention" and "concern" of the interactive user by reading his/her state of mind to continue the interaction. A robot has to express attention and concern through stimulus interaction through its social cues (non-verbal behaviours, vocal interaction, etc.) by coordinating the cues of the interactive user [9].

Turkle [9] has discovered that relational artifacts (human-dependent robot) should have two aspects of subjective effects: Rorschach and evocative. During the interaction, if a robot can interpret/understand and express the user's relationship with the robot from an emotional to cognitive level then these can be defined as a Rorschach response. The second aspect addressed is that the robot should behave as an evocative object, which is concerned with how the robot reflects the aliveness (e.g., animacy), state of thought, and belief of defining status through its behaviours and interactions, while realizing the manners

S. Yamamoto (Ed.): HIMI 2014, Part II, LNCS 8522, pp. 435–444, 2014.
© Springer International Publishing Switzerland 2014

of the interactive person. This is due to the fact that a relational robot has to be proficient in behaving as an evocative object with the Rorschach effects.

Initially, few researchers were able to begin their work with relational artifacts (robots) from a different prospective. Okada [10][8] has been working on a child-dependent robot (relational artifacts) with a minimal designing concept to design a robotic platform to explore what are the essential factors in a child-dependent robot. Children are a better age group to explore the effectiveness of relational artifacts, because several studies have shown that children are able to naturally interact with robots as if they were interacting with their toys. Turkel [9] reported on a series of studies with a commercially available robotic (Paros, Furbys, etc.) platform by utilizing a group of the children to explore the essential factors in designing relational artifacts for medical and therapeutic vocations.

Fig. 1. Children interacting with the STB

Cynthia [3] developed an expressive anthropomorphic robot called Kismet that can engage with a natural facial expression, gaze direction, and vocal interactions. The study focused on developing a robot which is capable of engaging with human caregivers using natural social cues. The robot was capable of perceiving the state of human activities and appropriately responding to their social cues. Our focus here is on relational artifacts rather than on the frequencies and task outcome of human-robot interactions. In particular, we address the question of how to build up a novel active learning/interactive architecture to enhance the Rorschach and evocative capabilities of the robot. In addition, we explore how robots situated in a social relationship with the interactive user and how the interactive users are able to express their sense of relationship and their meaning through the interactions. In this paper, we introduce two kinds of relational artifacts (human dependent robot) called a social trash box (STB) robot and a Talking-Ally, with their concepts and applications.

2   Human-Dependent Robots

We used different perspectives in designing these two relational robots in a human-centric environment. A social trash box robot is a human-dependent robot that cannot collect the trash by itself, but conveys its intention to collect the trash from human assistance. Since the STB has to interpret/infer and express the user's relationship with the STB from at every stage of the interaction, it should demonstrate the characteristic of animacy to reflect aliveness in the interaction. In our second platform of Talking-Ally, we focus on developing the utterance generation mechanism to interact with the user in real time. Having the robot talk during the interaction is really challenging, as it strongly taps into the relational artifacts. By considering the aspects of Rorschach and evocative, we developed an utterance generation mechanism by considering hearership and addressivity.

3   Human-Dependent Sociable Trash Box (STB) Robot

Our main objective is to obtain child-assistance in collecting trash from a public space, while establishing a social interaction between the child and the robot (Figure 1). Our robot is capable of displaying manifold affiliation behaviors to build social rapport with the goal of collecting trash in and around an environment. In particular, the STB is a child-dependent robot that walks alone in a public space for the purpose of tracing humans and trash and collecting trash. In a crowded space, STBs move toward trash by engagement, using an attractive twisting motion (behaviors) and vocal interaction to convey its intentions to children. The robot is incapable of collecting trash by itself. In this sense, children have to infer the intentional stance of the robot or expectation for interaction with the STB. It is a novel concept to be able to collect trash while creating social rapport with children. The robot engages by using twisting and bowing motions as children place trash into an STB container. In order to collect the trash, each of the STBs communicates with one another to create a distance between one another to avoid collapsing.

3.1   Designing

We implemented the minimalism designing mechanism for STB robots (Figure 1). STB has two parts as its body (upper and lower), and the upper part contains three servomotors: one for twisting itself to the left and right, and the other two motors for bending forward and backward. The lower part has two servomotors for moving its entire body to the left and right directions. The STB contains three kinds of sensors and a single camera to obtain environmental informatics: a pyroelectric infrared sensor, an infrared ray sensor (IR sensor), and a distance sensor [10].

3.2   Experiment

To evaluate the effectiveness of the child-dependent robot (STB), we conducted an experiment using a natural setup of a child-centric environment (Developmental Center for Children) as a public space by using the five action scenarios; move toward trash (MT-I), communicate (electronically) with other STBs to move and create a distance with them (MT-G), move to a crowded space without communicating with other STBs (MC-WC), move to a crowded space to communicate with other STBs (MC-C), and STBs do not move and behave (NMB). When looking attentively at the videos, we categorized three main behaviors of the children: interest to the STB (Int-to-STB), indirect interaction (showing the interests far from the STB) with the STB (Ind-Int-STB), and state of collect the trash to the STB (St-Colt-Trash). The following Table 1 shows the behaviors of the children based on the STB action scenarios.

Table 1. Table depicted the child's behaviors are based on the STB's behaviors: PT (children place trash into the STB's container), and DPT (children have not placed trash into the container)

STB's Action Scenarios	Child's Behaviors		
	Int-to-STB	Ind-Int-STB	St-Colt-Trash
MT-I	PT=0, DPT= 9	PT=10, DPT= 0	PT=3, DPT=3
MT-G	PT=0, DPT= 6	PT=8, DPT= 5	PT=4, DPT=7
MC-WC	PT=0, DPT= 5	PT=3, DPT= 2	PT=6, DPT=8
MC-C	PT=0, DPT= 4	PT=2, DPT=13	PT=4, DPT=6
NMB	PT=0, DPT= 0	PT=1, DPT=3	PT=2, DPT=5

We attempt to link the trash box action scenarios with the children's behaviors (reactions or feedback) in the contexts of trash collection from the child assistance. In the present experiment, 108 children (between the ages of 4 and 11 years old) participated in naturally interacting with the STBs.

3.3   Moving vs. Immobile STBs

A chi-square test was employed to determine if either the STBs' movement or immobility (fixed as a typical trash box in the corner) was independent of the collection of trash. Each context was tested separately. The resulting p-value ($\chi^2=6.87$, d.f.=1, p=0.009) was less than the critical p-value of 0.05 for the STB movement scenario, while in the case of the STB immobile scenario, the p-value ($\chi^2=1.31$, df =1, p=0.252) was greater than the critical p-value of 0.05. The results therefore indicate that the null hypothesis can be rejected in the STB moving scenario and that a significant relationship exists between the two groups. However, in the STB immobile scenario, the null hypothesis cannot be rejected, indicating nonsignificant relationship between the two groups. The results of the above statistical method therefore reveal that the STB movement was essential in conveying its intentions toward collecting trash.

3.4   STBs Moving Direction toward to Trash vs. toward to People

In the former experiment, we discovered that the STBs' movements were most important in collecting the trash with child assistance. Accordingly, we have to reveal the direction of the STB, whether it is toward trash or toward people, in order to evoke its intentional stance in the children's minds. We therefore employed a chi-square method to evaluate the relationship between the trash (STB movement) and the trash collection from the children. The resulting p-value (χ^2=9.35, d.f.=1, p=0.002) was smaller than the critical p-value of 0.05. These results indicate that the null hypothesis can be rejected and that the two groups have a significant relationship. We applied a similar procedure for the context of STBs moving toward people, with a resulting p-value (χ^2=2.38, d.f.=1, p=0.123), which was greater than the critical p-value of 0.05, meaning the null hypothesis can't be rejected. This reveals that the STBs' movement toward the children did not correlate with the collection of the trash with child assistance.

3.5   STBs Moving (Interacting) as a Swarm vs. Individually

In this phase, we were interested in discovering whether the swarm behaviors (moving around public space as a group) or individual behaviors (moving around public space individually) were more effective in triggering the intentional stance of the STB in the children's minds. We considered the behaviors of the child subjects (Int-to-STB, Ind-Int-STB, and St-Colt-Trash) with the STB action scenarios of MT-I (individual behaviors) and MT-G (swarm behaviors). For this purpose, we employed a chi-square test to verify the relationship of the robot's demeanor (behavior as individual or group) and the trash collection via the child assistance. The results revealed that the p-value (χ^2=4.00, d.f.=1, p=0.046) was less than the critical p-value of 0.05, indicating the null hypothesis can be rejected and that the STBs' demeanor (individual or group) had a strong relationship with the trash collection. When carefully analyzing the contexts, we found that when the STBs moved in a group, many children (70%) interacted with the STBs compared with when the STBs moved individually (i.e., only 30% children participated to the interaction). In this sense, we believe that the group movement of the STBs more effectively helped to convey their intentions and to establish social rapport with the children than when the STBs moved around individually in the space.

4   Concept of Talking-Ally

The speaker refers to the hearer's behavioral information (nonverbal and vocal) to structure (organize) his/her utterance, and is also capable of dynamically aligning the structure of the utterances according to the resources (nonverbal and verbal) of the behavioral variation. Within a conversation in the interactions between hearer and speaker, the hearer is reacting to a speaker through nonverbal channels (e.g., attention coordinate, eye-gaze following etc) or a vocal response (e.g., back channel) toward prompting the interactions, which is defined as hearership in the conversation [4]. The concept of hearership is a resource (referring eye-gaze behaviors) for Talking-Ally to shape its utterance generation by considering the state of the hearership in dynamic interactions (Figure 2).

Bakthin [1] is suggested on the concept of addressivity, which can be defined as that through individual words can be directed toward someone, and then become completed utterances consisting "of one word or one sentence, and addressivity is inherent not in the unit of language, but in the utterance." The addressivity is a kind of never-ending communication that changes toward shaping the communication while adapting to the hearer's communication variations. The hearer influences the speaker's utterance generation mechanism, which is a prompt to adding/modifying sentences in order to coordinate a productive conversation [7]. Talking-Ally coordinates the addressee's eye-gaze behaviors (state of the hearership) to change the structure of the utterance generation (synchronized with bodily interactions) toward addressivity.

4.1   Design of Talking-Ally

We followed the minimal-designing concept to develop the Talking-Ally as depicted in Figure 2, which has three flexible points (head, neck, and torso) to generate bodily interactions with the user. All of its external appearance (body) is made with artificial wood, and its eyes and head are designed on the iPod visualizer. The face-lab is located on the table to track the user's eye gaze-behaviors in real-time. Talking-Ally has a voice synthesizer to generate an interactive conversation (in Japanese) by obtaining a news source (through RSS) in real-time while synchronizing it's bodily interaction (nodding, leaning it's body to the left and right, and eye-gaze is able to follow and look around the environment) through servo-motors [6].

The Utterance Generation. Talking-Ally is interactively disseminating the news from the web (through RSS) to the participant and simultaneously some exciting (sport-based) TV-program is broadcasted behind the robot to obtain attention variation from the addressees (participants). The manipulation of attention variation is utilized to obtain a variety of utterance generation patterns which can evaluate the performance of Talking-Ally. We employed a simple method to track the addressee's attention-region which is a primal reference to generate/adjust the robot's speech interactions. The robot decides the addressee's attention-region according the frequency scores of the eye-gaze behaviors in each region by considering them at every 60 frames as a segmentation point (states of the hearership). Parallel to the robot, the virtual-plane is constructed. The virtual plane is divided into six regions: two regions for Talking-Ally, two regions for room-environment (away from robot), and two regions for TV. The robot synchronizes the position of the eye-gaze coordinate with virtual-plane to determine the attention-region of the user.

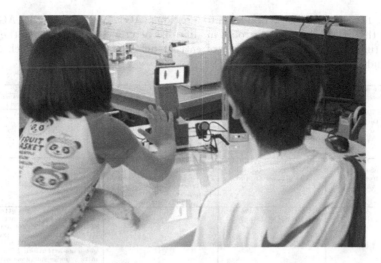

Fig. 2. Talking-Ally is interaction with children

Based on the addressee's attention-region, Talking-Ally decides the relevant news sources, turn-initial, and entrust behaviors to generate its utterances. Table 2 lists the relevant robot's behaviors (non-verbal and utterance) in each region and execute randomly (region-wise) for speech interaction while synchronizing the bodily-interaction (process of the addressivity). Any change (variation) of the addressee's behaviors has the influence of changing its bodily interactions, attention-coordination, and structure of utterance in the dynamic adaptation unit. The whole process continually concatenates toward getting-back/keeping the addressee's attention (influences) by changing the structure of utterances to enhance the degree of communicative persuasion of Talking-Ally.

This study mainly focuses on exploring the performance of an utterance generation mechanism in order to enhance the persuasive power of the robot's communication and the effectiveness of the communication (naturalism of robot's communication) while Talking-Ally interactively disseminates exciting news from the web. Our study is mainly concerned with the dynamic interactive history of the robot (utterance generation/adaptation and non-verbal communication) and addressee (attention behaviors/adaptation through eye gaze behaviors) to evaluate the above performance.

4.2 Experimental Protocol

A total of 14 participants (aged between 20 and 24 years) were involved in the experiment in four separate sessions in which the conditions of the robot (interactions) were changed as follows: A-(attention-coordination ($-$), turn-initial and entrust behavior ($-$)), B-(attention-coordination ($-$), turn-initial and entrust behavior ($+$, random)), C-(attention-coordination ($+$), turn-initial and entrust behavior ($+$, random)), and D-(attention-coordination ($+$), turn-initial and entrust behavior ($+$)). The ($-$) indicates that robot did not considered these

Table 2. The virtual plane is divided into 6 regions (AG1, AG2, AG3, AG4, AG5, and AG6); at that particular time the robot modifies its utterance by considering the eleven types of turn-initials (TI) or six types of entrust-behaviors (EB) while synchronizing its six kinds of bodily interactions (BHV)

Human behaviors (Attention regions)	Robot's bodily interaction	Resources for utterance generation	
		Turn-initials (indirect request)	Entrust behaviors (direct request)
AG1, AG2 (Space of Talking-Ally)	BHV1(Initial-position), BHV3(Nodding)	TI1: "a-a", TI2: "ano-", TI3: "anone", TI4: "anosa", TI5: "e-tto", TI6: "e-ttone", TI7: "etto", TI8: "etto-", TI9: "ne-ne", TI10: "ntto", TI11: "nttone"	–
AG3, AG4 (Looking around the environment)	BHV4(Trun left-side), BHV5(Trun right-side), BHV6(Look around)	TI1: "a-a", TI2: "ano-", TI3: "anone", TI4: "anosa", TI5: "e-tto", TI6: "e-ttone", TI7: "etto", TI8: "etto-", TI9: "ne-ne", TI10: "ntto", TI11: "nttone"	–
AG5, AG6 (Attention to the TV)	BHV2(Bending forward), BHV3(Nodding)	–	EB1: "kite ne"—get attention, EB2: "kite yo"—get attention, EB3: "kite yone"—get attention, EB4: "kotti mite ne"—get gaze-attention, EB5: "kotti mite yo"—get gaze-attention, EB6: "kotti-mite yone"—get gaze-attention

channels in the condition and the (+) sign indicates that the robot considered these channels in the interactions. All participants participated in four sessions (A, B, C, and D), and each of the sessions took approximately three minutes to complete.

4.3   Results

We might consider the experimental conditions of B and D because within condition B, the robot did not trace the addressee's attention (tracking the eye-gaze behaviors) but randomly executed the utterance generation (mixing with turn-initial and entrust-behaviors). The condition did plainly not consider the state of the hearership. But in condition D, the robot traced the addressee's attention (state of the hearership) to generate the utterances (mixing with turn-initial or entrust-behaviors) while synchronizing its bodily interaction (whole process of addressivity). By comparing B and D, we can extract the persuasiveness power of the robot when integrating both hearership and addressivity.

We have gathered the turn-initials or entrust-behavior of Talking-Ally and relevant addressee's attention behaviors during the interactions for all of the participants (number of times) for both conditions (Figure 3(left-side)). The robot used a turn-initial or entrust behavior which was quite higher than the number of times in condition B, and also proportionally increased the obtaining of the attention of the addressees with a percentage of 68%; but in condition D, the usage of filler or entrust-behavior was reduced and also started to increase the acquisition of attention of addressees with 73%.

The response time of the addressee was another worthwhile parameter to use in evaluating the power of the robot's communication, because a lower responsive-time significantly indicated the persuasiveness of the robot's communication – both the clearness of the communication and the degree of influence

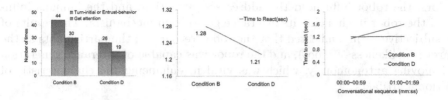

Fig. 3. Figure showed the selected addressee's responses (attention) within the selected segment for condition B and condition D. Here the addressees' attention-behaviors (red-color) when the robot utilized the turn-initial or entrust-behaviors (blue-color) during the interactive condition of B and D (left-side figure). The center figure shows the average responsive time within the segment and right-side of the figure depicted the responsive time within the selected segment according to the time interval.

of the communication, etc. [5]. Figure 3 (center and right-side) shows one of addressee's response (attention) times according to the robot's turn-initial or entrust-behaviors in the middle of the interaction (one of segmentations) that might be a perfect manifestation in comparing conditions B and D. The center figure shows the mean value of the responsive time within the selected segment. This indicates that the responsive time in D was lower than that of condition B, indicating that when we integrate hearership and addressivity, the addressee's response time begins to decrease. The right-side of Figure 3 shows an interesting pattern of responsive time. At some point in the segment, the addressee's response (attention) time in condition B suddenly increases, but the attention response time in interactive condition of D starts to decrease.

5   Conclusion

We have presented two relational artifacts which were developed using different perspectives. An STB is a human-dependent robot that collects the trash from a public space by conveying its intention. Movement is a main characteristic used in gaining the attention of people or animals. We believe from the above results that characteristic of attention-grabbing is gaining more consideration as an effective means to infer an object (e.g. robot) or people's behaviours. Another important aspect is the use of rich social cues (e.g., vocal interaction or twisting behaviours) based on the contexts, as these factors help to map various perceptions to infer someone's behaviours, e.g., intentional stance about an STB. We can examine similar perspectives by way of inferring a robot's behaviour in a child's mind. Accordingly, the results suggest that the STB movements and social cues directly correlated with the trash collection from the child assistance.

The results of the Talking-Ally showed that the resource of the hearer (state of hearership by tracing the addressee attention) was significant in generating/adjusting to the structure of the utterance generation mechanism (toward addressivity) to persuade the addressees. Additionally, the analysis of dynamic interaction showed that both the human and robot influenced each other's behaviors: the robot influenced the addressees' attention, and the humans influenced the robot in changing its utterance generation mechanism. The results of the subjective rating indicated that the robot recognized the participants as the hearer (life-likeness of robot), and the robot was capable of utterance generation and moving autonomously, which was vital in enhancing the characteristic of relational artifacts.

Acknowledgement. This research has been supported by both Grant-in-Aid for scientific research of KIBAN-B (21300083) and Grant-in-Aid for scientific research for HOUGA (24650053) from the Japan Society for the Promotion of Science (JSPS).

References

1. Bakhtin, M.: The problem of speech genres, pp. 60–102. University of Texas Press, Austin (1986)
2. Breazeal, C., Scassellati, B.: A context-dependent attention system for a social robot. In: IJCAI, pp. 1146–1153 (1999)
3. Brooks, R.A., Breazeal, C., Irie, R., Kemp, C.C., Marjanovic, M., Scassellati, B., Williamson, M.M.: Alternative essences of intelligence. In: AAAI/IAAI, pp. 961–968 (1998)
4. Goodwin, C.: Embodied hearers and speakers constructing talk and action in interaction. Belmont, CA: Wadsworth 16(1), 51–64 (2009)
5. Lutz, R., Swasy, J.L.: Integrating Cognitive Structure And Cognitive Response Approaches To Monitoring Communications Effects. Association for Consumer Research (1977)
6. Ohshima, N., Ohyama, Y., Odahara, Y., De Silva, P.R.S., Okada, M.: Talking-ally: Intended persuasiveness by utilizing hearership and addressivity. In: Ge, S.S., Khatib, O., Cabibihan, J.-J., Simmons, R., Williams, M.-A. (eds.) ICSR 2012. LNCS, vol. 7621, pp. 317–326. Springer, Heidelberg (2012)
7. Okada, M., Kurihara, S., Nakatsu, R.: Incremental elaboration in generating and interpreting spontaneous speech. In: Proc. of 3rd International Conference on Spoken Language Processing, pp. 103–106 (1994)
8. Okada, M., Sakamoto, S., Suzuki, N.: Muu: Artificial creatures as an embodied interface. In: 27th International Conference on Computer Graphics and Interactive Techniques (SIGGRAPH 2000), The Emerging Technologies: Point of Departure (2000)
9. Turkle, S., Taggart, W., Kidd, C.D., Dasté, O.: Relational artifacts with children and elders: the complexities of cybercompanionship. Connect. Sci. 18(4), 347–361 (2006)
10. Yamaji, Y., Miyake, T., Yoshiike, Y., Silva, P.R.S.D., Okada, M.: Stb: Child-dependent sociable trash box. I. J. Social Robotics 3(4), 359–370 (2011)

Co-creative Bodily Expression
through Remote Shadow Media System

Yoshiyuki Miwa[1], Atsushi Nishide[2], Naruhiro Hayashi[2],
Shiroh Itai[1], and Hiroko Nishi[3]

[1] Faculty of Science and Engineering, Waseda University, Tokyo, Japan
miwa@waseda.jp, itai@fuji.waseda.jp
[2] Graduate School of Creative Science and Engineering, Waseda University, Tokyo, Japan
atsushi-n@fuji.waseda.jp, 884naruhiro@toki.waseda.jp
[3] Faculty of Human Science, Toyo Eiwa University, Kanagawa, Japan
hiroko@toyoeiwa.ac.jp

Abstract. In this paper, we discuss media technology that enables the co-creation of bodily expressions between remote locations. To realize this, we designed a common background media space through bodily expressions, and by sharing this media between separate locations, we attempted to share the stages between these locations. The background media we developed was a large number of particles that flow in association with bodily movements. From our experimental results, we discovered that it is indeed possible to integrate different stages into a shared stage by enclosing the stage within background media.

Keywords: Communication, Background, Co-creation, Expression, Shadow media.

1 Introduction

A shadow is inseparable from its body. In previous studies, by focusing on the nature of this relationship, we developed a shadow media system that promotes the generation of awareness and images through the body, supporting the creation of bodily expressions by creating a gap between the body and the shadow through an artificially transformed shadow (i.e., shadow media) [1]. We also demonstrated that shadow media naturally co-creates connections between participants in group bodily expression [2].

Moreover, to continuously create and develop expressions, it is important to connect performers on stage (as well as the stage itself) to the audience and the environment surrounding them; however, conventional media spaces neglect the relationship between the performers, their audience, and the environment [3-5]. Thus, to incorporate the effects of the audience and the environment into the media space, we developed a shadow media system using a slit screen, which opened the media space to the outside of the physical stage itself [6].

In this study, on the basis of the previous study, we aim to integrate media spaces open to audiences that are geographically separated; this supports the co-creation of

S. Yamamoto (Ed.): HIMI 2014, Part II, LNCS 8522, pp. 445–454, 2014.
© Springer International Publishing Switzerland 2014

bodily expressions between remote locations. We developed a network to connect media spaces that are open to audiences and geographically separated. Furthermore, to integrate separate stages, we focused on the background of the shadow media space. By doing this, we created a common background media space through bodily expressions, and by sharing this media between the separate locations, we attempted to share the stages between remote locations. Specifically, we developed background media in which movement of the remote audience and performers are reflected as a flow of particles. We integrated this background media into the remote communication system described above; by doing so, we successfully support the co-creation of bodily expressions between remote locations.

2   Remote Shadow Media System

2.1   Design of the Shadow Media Space

Co-creation of bodily expressions with a remote partner requires the integration of remote stages. To address this requirement, we focused on the background of the shadow media space; we tried to integrate the remote stage by sharing the background media, as shown in Fig. 1. This background media must be associated with the body; therefore, we selected one's shadow as an interface to connect body and background, and we developed background media that has a strong connection with shadow. Furthermore, shadow media systems using slit screens were installed in two locations, and a network was developed to share the shadow media and background media of the people on stage in separate locations. The details of this setup and our experiments are described in the subsections that follow.

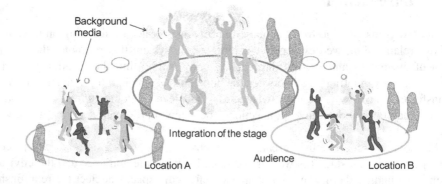

Fig. 1. Integration of remote stages using background media

2.2   Design and Development of the Background Media

To realize our design concept, we developed background media built on bodily shadow motion. Thus, we considered the following problems:

1) How do we design media that depict a performer's motions as background media?
2) How do we integrate the motions of remote performers as one background?

To address these problems, we designed a background media focused on flow. More specifically, by creating a flow based on each performer's every movement in different locations, we integrated individual movements as a whole stream. Furthermore, to promote the integration of the stage through bodily interactions with the background media, we decided to display a large number of small particles as the background media. Thus, we created background particle media in which a large number of particles moved on a fluid vector field F that vary due to time changes in human body images obtained through thermal cameras; this approach is illustrated in Fig. 2.

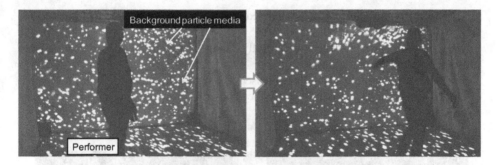

Fig. 2. Background media

We implemented these concepts into the background particle generation algorithm shown in Fig. 3.

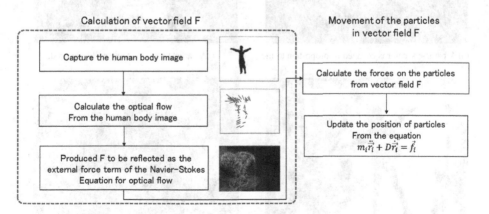

Fig. 3. Generation algorithm of background media

Vector field F is generated based on optical flows of human body images. The optical flow is calculated from the human body image obtained by a thermal camera—by binarizing its thermal distribution image. As a way to reflect body movements (i.e., optical flow) in F, we produced F to be reflected as the external force term of the Navier–Stokes equation for optical flow. The operation processing sequence described above was implemented using a fluid simulator [7]. More specifically, 5000 particles that make up the background media are moved from fluid vector field F. Particles are moved, depending on the vector field, by calculating and updating their positions and velocities in 25 fps.

With respect to projected particles, we developed a software that can change the number of particles, their colors, and their shapes via a graphical user interface. Furthermore, we can change the background media according to the variety of the stage; in particular, we describe this as follows:

(Fig. 4(a)) A particle's color is changed in proportion to the force from the vector field to create a sense of depth.

(Fig. 4(b)) A particle's size is temporally changed in random order to generate stereoscopic effects and naturalness.

(Fig. 4(c))   A particle's orbit is expressed as a residual image.

(Fig. 4(d)) Particles are pulled to the body (shadow media) using the Boids algorithm.

(a) A particle's color is changed in proportion to the force.

(b) A particle's size is temporally changed.

(c) A particle's orbit is expressed as a residual image.

(d) Particles are pulled to the body using the Boids algorithm.

Fig. 4. Bodily expression using several different types of background media

2.3   Development of Shadow Media Communication System

To open the media space to the audience and the surrounding environment, we pre-viously developed a slit screen composed of reed-shaped screens arranged in a line [6]. In this current study, we installed the media space using a slit screen across re-mote locations, and attempted to integrate each stage to share both the background and shadow media. To accomplish this, we developed the following systems:

(1) A communication system that enables the share of both the background and shadow media between remote locations

(2) Calibration software that adjusts the shadow's location, shape, and scale in ac-cordance with the respective spaces

Fig. 5 shows the communication system (1) we have developed. This system con-sisted of a server (i.e., the information management PC) and a client (i.e., the media-processing PC). The server managed client information and exchanged such information with each server in the remote locations. This provided the ability to share the information of shadow media between remote PCs. We used UDP with Winsock for our communication system. Furthermore, we selected run-length encod-ing as a compression method of the shadow media image sent to the remote PC, because the same data tended to align in the binarized shadow media image.

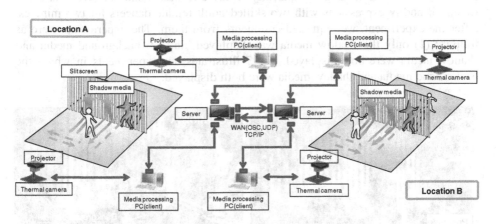

Fig. 5. Shadow media communication system

Next, the calibration software (2) was developed to change the angle, size, and po-sition of the received shadow image (Fig. 6). For this process, a received image of the remote person's shadow was combined with an image of the local person's shadow. Then, the combined image was transformed and projected on the local location. To simplify calibration, we transmitted the remote stage information, including the screen size and acquisition range of the thermal camera, between remote servers.

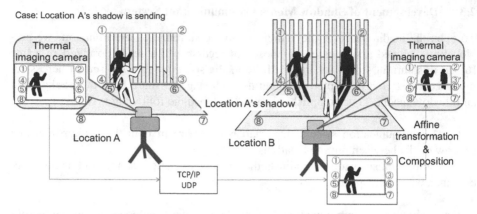

Fig. 6. Calibration of remote person's shadow position

3   Support for the Co-creation of Bodily Expressions between Remote Locations

Using our proposed system, we conducted an experiment in which bodily expressions were improvisatorially created by performers in separate locations. We installed slit screens (2.3 m × 6.5 m) at geographically separate locations and conducted an experiment of bodily expressions with two skilled adult female dancers for two minutes. After the experiment, we requested comments from them. The experiments were as follows: (1) only the shadow media was displayed; and (2) background media and shadow media were both displayed. Fig. 7 illustrates our experiments in which the background media and shadow media were both displayed.

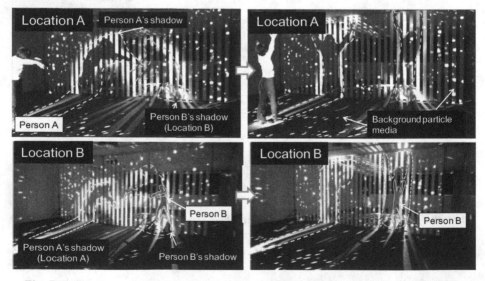

Fig. 7. Bodily expressions between remote locations with shadow and background media

Table 1. Comments about bodily expression by use of the shadow media and background media

Experiment Condition	Comments
Only shadow media was displayed	"I felt a warm connection." "I created images with slow movements." "I didn't feel like my partner was in a remote location." "I felt like creating something with the remote partner."
Background media and shadow media were both displayed	"I felt as if my partner was in the same location that I was. The background expanded my image." "Because of the background media, it felt easier to create expression. It felt like everything was coming together." "I felt that we shared the same atmosphere, and that we could create a world with depth." "As particles flowed with my actions, I felt my remote partner was on the same stage. I felt that we saw the same things, felt the same feelings, and were expressing in the same world."

Table 1 shows comments obtained from the experienced dancers. When both the background media and shadow media were displayed, compared with conditions that only the shadow media was displayed, we observed the performers making bodily expressions while passing through the slit screen and moving around the entirety of the stage, and using the background flow as a trigger to create expression. From the table, the performer commented that "The background expanded my image" and that with the background, "I felt that we shared the same atmosphere, and we could create a world with depth." These comments indicate that background media successfully produced a shared stage between remote locations and supported the creation of improvised expressions.

Miwa which is one of the authors has developed (WSCS) a system that sends shadows between remote locations, enabling communication with an accompanying feeling of co-existing between remote partners because of the shadow's inseparable relationship with the body [8]. Although this system enabled performers in remote locations to share this space, it was difficult for the performers to share emotions and to improvise co-creative bodily expression with the remote partner. From our results here, we expect to solve that problem by sharing background media that is associated with shadow media. In other words, we feel that background media that reflects bodily movement through shadow media can help remote performers share emotions.

Therefore, we conducted experimental discussions that investigate the effect of background media. In particular, a performer watched a remote performer's movements through only background media sent from a remote location. We received positive comments from the performer who was watching the background media, including "I felt like the atmosphere changed," "I felt a sign of the remote person, so I unconsciously avoided it," and "I felt something on my skin, my heart was moved." From these comments, we concluded that background media could convey images of a remote body's overall movements. We further concluded that this enables the sharing of emotion and an enhanced feeling of connection with the remote partner.

We therefore attempted to integrate the stages of a performance of bodily expression between Tokyo and Sendai which are 200 kilometers away (Fig. 8). The audience who watched the Sendai performance in Tokyo provided such comments as "I felt that the remote stage was close," "When the remote performer passed through the slit screen, it felt as though he was on the same stage," and "I felt like I was able to share images with the performer." These anecdotal results show that our system could support expressing conditions and the atmosphere of the stage to remote audiences, and could assist audience enter a remote stage and create bodily expressions with remote performers.

Fig. 8. Performance using background media between Tokyo and Sendai

4   Towards a Multipoint Communication System That Takes into Account the Audience

To incorporate the effects of audiences that exist in various locations, we require a communication system to connect to multipoint remote locations and integrate the data from each location; such a configuration is shown in Fig. 9.

The data sent from each location should be compressed; therefore, we have devised a communication system that uses a cloud server, as shown in Fig. 10. Instead of human body images, the differentiating characteristic of this system is the exchange of skeletal data from a Kinect device and shadow media information, such as types of shadow media and color, using the cloud. To achieve this, we decompressed skeletal data into a shadow image; more specifically, we have prepared a model of shadow image and skeletal data that associates the skeletal data with contour points of shadow. This enables us to move the shadow image based on the movements of the skeletal data. Compared to our previous system, we succeeded in significantly reducing

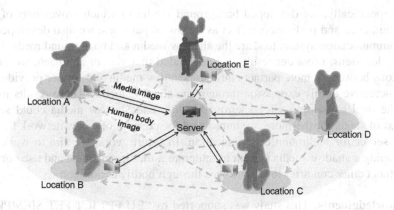

Fig. 9. Multipoint communication System

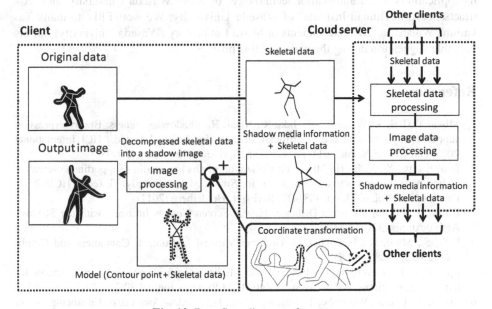

Fig. 10. Data flow diagram of system

the amount of communication data and realized high-speed multipoint communications. Furthermore, we plan to research the design of the media space, including audiences in multiple points using this system.

5   Conclusion

In this study, we developed a telecommunications system for integrating open media spaces separated by distance through shadow media and background media.

More specifically, we developed background media in which movements of the remote audience and performers reflect as a flow of particles; we also developed a media communication system to share the shadow media and background media between remote locations. From our results, we concluded that via our approach, we can share emotions between remote partners through shadow media and further provide a stage for co-creative bodily expression through the shadow media. These results indicated that the dual expression via background media and shadow media could share the context of stage. Furthermore, we introduced the concept of a new network that uses a cloud server for multipoint communication. In future work, we aim to work toward developing a shadow media system to integrate a multipoint stage and use our system to connect other countries to share stages through bodily expression.

Acknowledgments. This study was supported by "EU FP7 ICT FET SIEMPRE (Social Interaction and Entrainment using Music PeRformance Experimentation) Project" (No.250026), the Project Research "Principal of emergence for empathetic "Ba" and its applicability to communication technology" by RISE Waseda University, and "Artifacts/Scenario/Human Institute" of Waseda University. We would like to thank Takafumi Watanabe, graduate students at Miwa Laboratory (Waseda University), for his valuable suggestion during the course of this project.

References

1. Miwa, Y., Itai, S., Watanabe, T., Iida, K., Nishi, H.: Shadow awareness: Bodily expression supporting system with use of artificial shadow. In: Jacko, J.A. (ed.) HCI International 2009, Part II. LNCS, vol. 5611, pp. 226–235. Springer, Heidelberg (2009)
2. Iida, K., Itai, S., Nishi, H., Miwa, Y.: Utilization of shadow media - supporting co-creation of bodily expression activity in a group. In: Smith, M.J., Salvendy, G. (eds.) HCII 2011, Part I. LNCS, vol. 6771, pp. 408–417. Springer, Heidelberg (2011)
3. Bitton, J.: Flirting Across a Distance: How a Screen Creates Intimacy with the Shadow. Ambidextrous, 32–33 (2008)
4. Fels, S., Mase, K.: Iamascope: A GraphicalMusical Instrument. Computers and Graphics 2(23), 277–286 (1999)
5. Sparacino, F., Davenport, G., Pentland, A.: Media in performance: Interactive spaces for dance, theater, circus, and museum exhibits. IBM Systems Journal 39(3), 479–510 (2000)
6. Miwa, Y., Itai, S., Watanabe, T., Iida, K., Nishi, H.: Shadow Awareness: Enhancing theater space through the mutual projection of images on a connective slit-screen. Leonardo, the Journal of the International Society for the Arts, Sciences and Technology (SIGGRAPH 2011 Art paper) 44(4), 325–333 (2011)
7. Stam, J.: Real-Time Fluid Dynamics for Games. In: Proc. Game Developer Conf. (2003)
8. Miwa, Y., Ishibiki, C.: Shadow Communication: System for Embodied Interaction with Remote Partners. In: Herbsleb&, J., Olson, G. (eds.) Proceedings of 2004 ACM Conference on Computer Supported Cooperative Work (CSCW 2004), pp. 467–476. ACM Press (2004)

Favor Information Presentation and Its Effect for Collective-Adaptive Situation

Asami Mori, Tomohiro Harada, Yoshihiro Ichikawa, and Keiki Takadama

The University of Electro-Communications, Tokyo, Japan
{arthur,harada,yio}@cas.hc.uec.ac.jp, keiki@inf.uec.ac.jp

Abstract. This paper focuses on *favor information* among people as the factor to lead a group to "collective-adaptive situation" and explores its effect in "Barnga" as the cross-cultural game which aims at investigating how the players make an appropriate group decision. For this purpose, we propose the "favor marker" which appears as a favor for other players in Barnga system. The subjective experiment results with this system have been revealed that the players in both the system-based communication and face-to-face communication lead the collective-adaptive situation by using the favor markers, while being conscious on the difference of card rules which caused conflicts among players. In detail, the following implications have been found: (1) when the players meet their conflict at the first time, their intentions tend to be appear from their behaviors (e.g. gesture) without using the favor maker in the face-to-face communication, while their intentions are appeared by actively using the favor marker in the system-based communication; (2) after some conflicts, the favor marker in both types of communication showed the effect on making an aware of the difference of the card rules and facilitating behavior affected by such differences, which contributes to deriving a smooth group decision making.

Keywords: Human-agent interaction, group decision making, collective-adaptive situation, favor information, Barnga.

1   Introduction

In daily life, we often meet situations where we have to make a decision in a group when working together. Such group activities have a great potential of deriving larger results than the individual activities, but it's difficult to make a consensus of all opinions of members because the members have their own different mind even if they belong the same group. To investigate such a situation, Ushida et al. employed Barnga [1] as the cross-cultural game which aims at investigating the social group whose members have different mind. In their research, they designed the computer agent who tries to lead a group to collective-adaptive situation in the Barnga system [2]. Although Ushida's agents supported to lead a group to collective-adaptive situation by changing their opinions, the players in Barnga game respect other's opinion, arbitrate between their decisions, and change their behaviors, which indicates the difficulty of reaching the collective-adaptive situation.

S. Yamamoto (Ed.): HIMI 2014, Part II, LNCS 8522, pp. 455–466, 2014.
© Springer International Publishing Switzerland 2014

To overcome this problem, we focus on a *favor emotion* from other people as the one of the signals of human behaviors. According to Cialdini [3], such favor emotion becomes the factor of changing people's behaviors to adapt to others without causing large complaints. From such a feature, the purpose of this paper is to investigate an effect of the *favor information* in order to lead a group to collective-adaptive situation by introducing "favor marker," which is a function to express a sign of favor for other players in the Barnga system. Concretely, we analyze how the favor marker gives an influence on the players' behaviors and group's situation through the subject experiment on the Barnga system with the favor marker. For this purpose, we investigate whether the groups will reach the collective-adaptive situation or not by comparing the Barnga system with and without the favor marker.

This paper is organized as follows. The next section introduces Barnga game. The people's behavior is classified in Section 3, and the favor information is proposed in Section 4. Section 5 conducts the experiment and Section 6 discusses their results. Finally, our conclusion is given in Section 7.

2   Barnga Game

This section describes the features and specific rule of Barnga [1].

2.1   Features of Barnga

Barnga is studied in the context of the gaming simulation (GS) [4] as the cross-cultural experiences and its effectiveness in the cross-cultural understanding was reported from the viewpoint of the educational training [5]. Barnga is a trump game, where four or more players are allocated in the different tables and repeat to decide one winner in the table separately. The features of Barnga are summarized as follow:

(a) The card rules for the players are a slightly different from others depending on their first allocated table (See Section 2.2). For example, the diamond is the strongest suit in one table, while the heart is the strongest in the other table. What should be noted here is that the players are not told such a difference among the card rules. After a definite period in the game, a part of players move to the other table and then they begin to play the new game. Although the players in the same table nominate one winner at the same time according to their card rule, the different nominations for a winner occur in the new game because of the different rules in the same table.

(b) Since Barnga prohibits the verbal communications among the players in the game, it is difficult to communicate their intention even if their nominations are different.

From the above features, it is necessary for the players to decide one winner in a table by selecting a winner which does not follow their rules or decide no winner in order to proceed the game.

2.2   Card Rule

The card rule which defines the strength of cards is summarized as follows:

(a) There are the following two kinds of the strength order of card number from 1 (A) to 7.

    (i) (strong) 7, 6, 5, 4, 3, 2, A (weak)
    (ii) (strong) A, 7, 6, 5, 4, 3, 2 (weak)

(b) The strongest suit is defined as "trump."

For example, in a certain card rule, 7 is the strongest number and heart is the strongest suit. In Barnga game, the card which has the strongest number and same suit as the suit played first is strongest in a game basically. However if trump card is played, the card which have the strongest number and trump suit is the strongest. For instance, In Fig. 1(a) clover 5 is the strongest because it has the same suit as the first card and the highest number. In Fig. 1(b) heart 2 is the strongest because it has the trump suit. In Fig. 1(c) heart 4 is the strongest because it has the highest number in the trump suit.

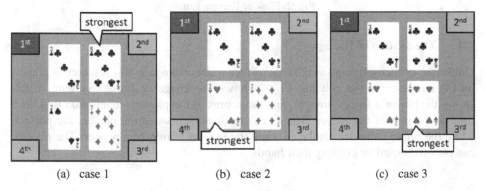

(a) case 1   (b) case 2   (c) case 3

Fig. 1. Winner decision

2.3   Game Flow

Fig. 2 shows the game flow in Barnga, which is summarized as follows.

1. Seven cards are dealt to each player.
2. Each player plays a card from their hands by turns.
3. Each player nominates a player as a winner according to their card rules. When these nominations are the same, one winner is determined. In the case of different nominations or no nomination, the players should continue to nominate the same or different player as the winner by returning to (3).
4. A winner gets a score and they return to (2) until a time limit is over.
5. 1 round is completed, and both players with the highest/lowest scores move to another table.
6. (1)~(5) is repeated during a predetermined time period.

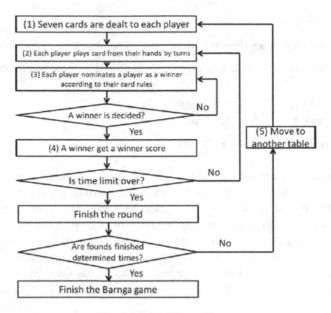

Fig. 2. Flow of Barnga game

2.4 The System of Barnga

Unlike the ordinary Barnga as the face-to-face game, Barnga in this research is played on the computer in the systems. Fig. 3 shows the image of Barnga system, which shows the player's names, images, and the scores of the players, in addition to a time limit and a turn of the player. The cards are displayed when the players are played, while the finger icons are displayed when the players nominate a winner. The players can play their card by clicking their hands.

Fig. 3. Barnga Client Display

3   Player's Behavior Characteristic Classification

This paper employs the player's behavior characteristics and group situation classified by Ushida et al. [2] using Fuzzy C-means Clustering [7].

3.1   Player's Behavior Characteristic

As shown in Table 1 and Fig. 4, the three types of the players are classified by θ_N and θ_O defined as the average of the following two indicators: (1) insistence N_{ind} (the degree of nominating a winner) and (2) cooperation O_{ind} (the degree of following an opponent rule). Both indicators are calculated as follows, where G_{T_i} is the number of the game times as a target time (1 round in this experiment) in a table T_i, N_{round} is the number of times that a player nominate a winner in a target time, and N_{other} is the number of times that a player nominate a winner according to the opponent rule.

$$N_{ind} = \frac{N_{round}}{G_{T_i}} \tag{1}$$

$$O_{ind} = \frac{N_{other}}{N_{round}} \tag{2}$$

Fig. 4 shows features of each type. (i) Claiming player nominates a winner following the rule he first taught, (ii) Supporting player nominates a winner following an opponent rule and (iii) Quiet player doesn't nominate a winner at the time to select a winner.

Table 1. Classification of player's behavior characteristics

Behavior Property	Feature
(i) Claiming player	Nominate a winner according to their own rule.
(ii) Supporting player	Agree with a winner nominated according to the opponent rule.
(iii) Quiet player	Does not nominate a winner.

3.2   Group Situation

Ushida et al. [2] divided the group situation into the following four types of situations.

(a) **Domination situation:** In this situation, the players who have the same rule only nominate a winner and others do not nominate, which contributes to proceeding the game because only one winner is nominated. In contrast, the players who have different rules cannot insist on their opinions in this situation.

(b) **Confusion situation:** In this situation, the game does not proceed because all players tend to not nominate a winner due to an unclear of who should be nominated.

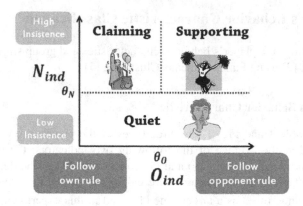

Fig. 4. Classification of Behavior Types

(c) **Insisting situation:** In this situation, the game does not proceed because the players who have different rules insist to nominate different winner, which causes the conflict.

(d) **Collective adaptive situation:** In this situation, the claiming players coexist with the supporting players who have a different rule but change their nomination according to the claiming player's opinion.

The four type of the group situation is classified by the three types of the players as shown in Table 2. In this table, "*1" means an existence of the players who have the same rule, "*2" means an existence of the players who have the different rules, and "*3" does not require an existence of the specific players. In (a) domination situation, there is no supporting player who has the different rule from claiming players. In (b) confusion situation, all players are quiet players. In (c) insisting situation, there are claiming players who have different rules. In (d) adaptive situation, there are supporting players who have different rules from claiming players.

Table 2. Behavior characteristics in group situations

Group Situation	Claiming player	Supporting player	Quiet player
(a) Domination	Y*1	N	Y
(b) Confusion	N	N	Y
(c) Insisting	Y*2	*3	*3
(d) Adaptive	Y*1	Y	*3

4   Favor Information Expression

4.1   Behavior Pattern Classification

As described in Section 2, the players first play a card according to their own rules without knowing differences among the rules. Such a situation may occur the situation where the players nominate the different winners according to their own rules. This is not good from the viewpoint of making a consensus of the opinions among all players, but the game cannot proceed if nobody compromises with opponent rules. To overcome this situation, the players have to change their behaviors from the negotiation perspective. From this perspective, Cialdini classified the following seven patterns of the people's behavior, one of which is the factor in leading others to recognize requests in the one to one negotiation [3].

(1) **Fixed-action patterns:** It is the character that people do not analyze every matter carefully and make decision but responds to the trigger feature automatically. For instance, people respond to the feature "expensive" with judging to be "high quality." This character has a possibility of drawing out the compliance by producing the trigger feature intentionally.

(2) **Reciprocation:** It is the character that people bring back when they are given, even if they do not want to be given. This character is required socially because they are criticized if they do not bring back when they are given.

(3) **Commitment and consistency:** It is the character that people tend to behave in consistency because of the public eye and to make easier the action selection. This character promotes people to take action on what they accept to do once.

(4) **Social proof:** It is the character that people tend to behave in mimicry of others, especially the people who is similar to their decision in the uncertain situation, for example, there is information which is not known whether it is true or not.

(5) **Liking:** It is the character that people are liable to accept the request from more favorable, attractive people or whom they contact with in better situation.

(6) **Authority:** It is a character that people follow the authority which is proven by title, clothes, or ornaments.

(7) **Scarcity:** It is the character that people assign more value to opportunities when they are less available. They have a psychological reactance when they lose freedom of accessibility.

Among the above characters, we focus on (5) *liking* in this research because (i) the favor is the basic element of emotion which can change someone's feeling in a short time negotiation; and (ii) various favorable emoting functions such as web clap or "Like" button are used frequently to encourage communication in SNS or web services.

4.2   Favor marker

As the function to show a favor for other players in Barnga game, we implement the "favor marker" on the Barnga system. Figs. 5 and 6 show the user interface of Barnga system and how to use the favor marker, respectively. There are buttons written "Like" (hereafter, we call it Like button) which is below of other player's avatar images as shown in Fig. 6 and the player can display the favor marker by clicking the Like button nearby the target's image you want to show your favor at any times in a game. The players can see and understand that every favor marker in the table means a favor from others. After the player show the favor marker as the right of Fig. 6, the

"Like" text on the button he clicked change to "cancel" and he can cancel the favor marker by clicking the button again. The favor marker does not affect the game rule, victory, or defeat.

In the previous Barnga system which does not have a favor maker, the manifestation of intention of the players are limited, for example, only by nominating a winner or not, or taking time in playing a card. In contrast, the players become to be possible to manifest their favor for others distinctly by using the favor marker on Barnga system, which supports to derive the agreement among the players.

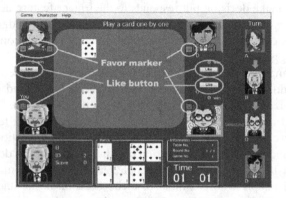

Fig. 5. Interface of Barnga system and favor marker

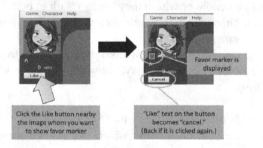

Fig. 6. How to use and display favor marker.

Table 3. Cases

	Case1	Case2
Communiaction	Face-to-face	System-based
Rule difference	Known	Known
Subjects	4	12 (4 players in each 3 tables)
Rounds	1	3
Time limit in a round	20 minutes	

5   Experiment

5.1   Cases

Table 3 shows the cases in our experiments. Subjects are 20-26 years old Japanese stundents of The University of Electro-Communications. There are 3 males and 1 female in case 1 and 10 males and 2 females in case 2. Case 1 conducts s Barnga game with the *face-to-face* communication employing the favor marker. In this case, the players have the favor marker *card* and they can express this card to other players during a game. The communication without the favor marker is prohibited. The players wear sunglasses and masks to hide their expression. We record this experiment on video and provide questionnaires after the game. Case 2, on the other hand, conducts Barnga game with the *system-based* communication (as shown in Fig. 5) employing the favor marker. The players are told that they can display or cancel the "favor marker" to others freely and they are not indicated to use the marker in the particular situation or for particular intention. We record this experiment by getting a data from logs of player's behavior in the game and provide questionnaires after the game.

The essential difference between cases 1 and 2 is to investigate the effect of the favor marker by comparing the results of the face-to-face communication and system-based communication (*i.e.*, the favor marker card vs. the favor marker in the computer). What is the same between cases 1 and 2 is that all player knows Barnga rule, *i.e.*, they understand clearly that others may have different rule as the first step towards our final goal.

5.2   Evaluation

The questionnaires ask the behavior and its intention, the frequency in use of the favor marker and its intention, the way to interpret the favor marker. Using these questionnaires, we evaluate quantitatively and qualitatively how to use the favor marker and whether the group reaches or not the collective-adaptive situation.

5.3   Results

Case 1: Face-to-Face Communication. The nominations mostly conflict at first and then some players change their nomination. Although the players told not to communicate verbally, they try to express their opinion by their behavior speed or small motions at the early step of the game when they are conflict. After they calm down, they begin to use the favor marker card mainly as a signal to inform that they have the same rule.

Case 2: System-Based Communication. When conflicting their nomination at first, they change their nomination similarly as case 1. They use favor marker to decide a winner in earlier than case 1. Although they cannot communicate without the favor marker, they smoothly reach at the collective adaptive situation. Fig. 7 shows the example of the transition of the behavior characteristics and Table 4 shows the result of the percentage of the group situation and use of the favor marker in case 2. In this figure, the behavior characteristics of four players in the same table are plotted in this graph. In detail, such characteristics in the first half and the last half of one round are plotted as points on the graph and arrows which connect these points means the transition of behavior characteristics from the first half to the last half of the round. The vertical axis indicates insistence (N_{ind}), the horizontal axis indicates cooperation (O_{ind}), the horizontal dotted line indicates average of N_{ind} (θ_N), and the vertical dotted line indicates average of O_{ind} (θ_O) as described in subsection 3.1. From, the quiet players become the supporting player (Fig.7 (a)) and then the domination situation changes to the collective adaptive situation (Fig.7 (a)). A quiet player also becomes a supporting player in adaptive situation (Fig. 7 (b)). From table 4, the groups in all tables reach at the adaptive situation, and 92% of the players use the favor marker.

In order to investigate the reason why we obtain such a result, the questionnaires are analyzed. This analysis suggests that all players expect to use the favor marker to show their sympathy or bond to the players who have the same rule. The analysis also clarify that the players firstly nominate a winner according to their own rule which causes the conflict of the nominations and then they change their nomination by using the favor marker to decide a winner.

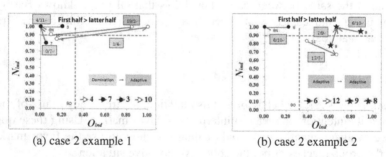

(a) case 2 example 1   (b) case 2 example 2

Fig. 7. Transition of the behavior properties in Case 2

Table 4. Percentage of group situation and use of favor marker

Group Situation				Use of favor
(a)Domination	(b)Confusion	(c)Persistence	(d)Adaptive	marker
0%	0%	0%	100%	92%

6   Discussion

6.1   Way to Use Favor Marker

The common role of the favor marker (including the favor marker card) in both the face-to-face communication and system-based communication in Barnga game is to express a sign of sympathy to others. The players show the favor marker for someone who have the same or similar rule, and guess their relation and intention. This indicates that the favor marker is used to smooth the communication.

The difference of using the favor marker in the face-to-face communication and system-based communication, on the other hand, is summarized as follows: (1) in the face-to-face communication, the players cannot stop to express their emotion from their gesture even though their communicating without the favor marker is prohibited. It can be said that gesture come out naturally and it is prior communication way to the favor marker. This is the reason why the players express their emotion with their behaviors in the case of confusion or confliction but they come to use the favor marker after becoming to be calm; and (2) in the system-based communication, the players could not show their emotion, intention and mind with gesture, meaning that the players can only express such emotional behaviors by the favor marker.

6.2   Comparing System-Based Communication under the Situation Where Players Knows Rule Difference or Not

Our previous research [8] conducted the Barnga game with the system-based communication employing the favor maker under the condition where the players do *not* know the rule difference. The research [8] reported that the half of groups reach at the domination situation while other half reach at the collective adaptive situation. Some players try to change their behaviors and lead a group to the collective adaptive situation by using the favor marker, which indicates that the favor marker can work for their agreement. However, some players use the favor marker to say unfavorable emotion. Due to such a different using of the favor marker, the players cannot understand each other by reading mind in showing the favor marker.

By comparing with the result in the research [8], the result in this paper suggests that favor marker is effective on leading the collective adaptive situation when players have a common purpose such as deciding a winner. Conversely, the intention in favor marker is not transmitted when they have different purpose such as deciding a winner or winning a game like in [8]. This indicates that we have to promote the players to have a common intention to collect a group.

7   Conclusion

This paper focused on the *favor information* among people as the factor to lead a group to "collective-adaptive situation" and explored its effect in "Barnga" as the cross-cultural game which aims at investigating how the players reach at the group decision making. For this purpose, we proposed the "favor marker" which appeared a favor for other players in Barnga system. The subjective experiment results with this system have been revealed that the players in both the system-based communication and face-to-face communication lead the collective-adaptive situation by using the favor markers, while being conscious the difference of card rules which caused conflicts among players. In detail, the following implications have been found: (1) when the players meet their conflict at the first time, their intentions tend to be appear from their behaviors (e.g. gesture) without using the favor maker in the face-to-face communication, while their intentions are appeared by actively using the favor marker in the system-based communication; (2) after some conflicts, the favor marker in both types of communication showed the effect on making an aware of the difference of the card rules and facilitating behavior affected by such differences, which contributes to deriving a smooth group decision making.

What should be noticed here is that these results have only been obtained from one example, Barnga. Therefore, the further careful qualifications and justification, such as an analysis of results by increasing the number of the players, are needed to generalize the effectiveness of the favor maker. The further effect of the favor information should be investigated in the case where the players could unify a meaning of showing their favor information. Such important directions must be pursued in the near future in addition to the following future research: (1) an exploration of the requirement for turning awareness to other players to agree their opinions in a whole group or awareness such as changing way to display the favor marker, and (2) an investigation of the effect of other emotional signals for group decision making.

References

1. Thiagarajan, S., Steinwachs, B.: Barnga: A simulation game on cultural clashes. Intercultural Press (June 1990)
2. Ushida, Y., Otani, M., Ichikawa, Y., Sato, K., Sato, H., Hattori, M., Takadama, K.: Modeling Collective Adaptive Agent and its Interaction through Cross-Cultural Game. In: 39th SICE Symposium on Intelligent Systems (March 2012)
3. Cialdini, R.B.: Influence: Science and practice, 4th edn. Allyn & Bacon (2012)
4. Greenblat, C.S.: Designing games and simulations: An illustrated handbook. Sage Publications, Inc. (1988)
5. Batten, J.D.: Teaching CulturalAdjustment Through a Simulation Game: A Preliminary Report on Proceduresand Findings of an Intercultural Group's BARNGAExperience. Ibaraki Christian Collage Bulletin 28, 239–257 (1994)
6. Fujihara, T.: Gaming Simulation of Human Relationship. Kitaohji Shobo Publishing (2007)
7. Bezdek, J.C.: Pattern Recognition with Fuzzy Objective Function Algorithms. Advanced Applications in Pattern Recognition, pp. 1–13. Plenum, New York (1981)
8. Mori, A., Harada, T., Kitagawa, H., Takadama, K.: Favor Information Presentation and its Effect for Collective Adaptive Situation. IEICE Transactions on Fundamentals of Electronics, Communications and Computer Sciences (2014) (submitted)

The Effectiveness of Assistance Dogs Mounting ICT Devices: A Case Study of a Healthy Woman and Her Dog

Chika Oshima[1,2], Chisato Harada[2], Kiyoshi Yasuda[3,4],
Kimie Machishima[2], and Koichi Nakayama[2]

[1] Japan Society for the Promotion of Science
[2] Saga University, Saga, Japan
[3] Chiba RosaiHospital, Chiba, Japan
[4] Kyoto Institute of Technology, Kyoto, Japan

Abstract. Recently, various information communication technologies (ICT) devices, such as smartphones, digital voice recorders, and miniature cameras, and various types of content are effective to cope with various symptoms of dementia. However, dementia patients often forget to take their ICT devices with them and forget where they put their devices. We considered the concept that ICT devices are delivered when individuals with dementia need to do tasks instructed by the devices. In general, dogs tend to run after their owners. Therefore, we came up with assistance dogs mounting ICT devices on their back. The dogs run to their owners when smartphones on their backs emitted alarms. In this paper, we conducted to examine the effectiveness of a smartphone mounted on a dog's back compared to a fixed device. A healthy female was asked to turn off the alarm and to perform a task on a voluntary basis when the smartphone emitted the alarm. The results of the case study suggested that individuals with dementia would be willing to perform daily the tasks when instructed to do so by a smartphone mounted on the backs of their dogs.

1 Introduction

Individuals with dementia often forget to execute daily tasks and have poor motivation to perform these tasks. There are many researches that aim to provide appropriate information to individuals with dementia by using information communication technologies (ICT) devices. Yasuda et al. [1] evaluated the use of a digital voice recorder as a voice output memory aid. Their results showed that the digital voice recorder assists patients with prospective memory impairment. "SenseCam [2]" is a wearable camera that continuously records a person's daily activities automatically. "Memory Glasses [3]" is a wearable, proactive, context-aware memory aid based on the "MIThril platform" and wearable sensors. This system has a function that delivers remembers to the wearer under appropriate circumstances. "MemoClip [4]" is a context-aware personal reminder and schedule device in the form of a badge. A person wears it on his/her chest. "Medical

S. Yamamoto (Ed.): HIMI 2014, Part II, LNCS 8522, pp. 467–478, 2014.
© Springer International Publishing Switzerland 2014

Mood Ring [5]" allows a caregiver to monitor the temperature, heart rate, and blood oxygen level of a patient in the form of a ring. This device is equipped with two light-emitting diodes. A detector measures the intensity of the transmitted light. Just how much light passes through depends on the oxygen levels and the volume of the blood in its path. However, some individuals with dementia often forget their ICT devices and where these items are located.

There are some band-aid sensor systems. "Lifetouch [6]" analyses every heart beat to provide continuous real-time heart rate, respiration rate and heart rate variability. A band-aid thermometer [7] is used "Bluetooth Low Energy LSI" that works by an electric current of 10mA. This system transfers a value of the thermometer to a smartphone via Bluetooth and tha smartphone records it. If a small display adds to band-aid sensor systems in the near future, such problems, forgetting devices, may be solved. However, some individuals with dementia will put a band-aid off. In addition, they often dislike these devices or refuse to wear them.

Furthermore, due to a lack of any psychological interaction with the devices, some individuals do not perform the daily tasks instructed by the devices [8]. Researches conducted on schedule prompter systems may help to address this problem. Examples of such systems are provided below: "InBad [9]" is a memory aid system for bathroom-related daily care. The system learns user behavior patterns and detects deviations from the learned pattern in order to notify the user of a forgotten task. Kuwahara et al. [10] developed system that remotely supports the daily lives of people with dementia at home using reminiscence video and a reminiscence conversation system with a schedule prompter to produce relaxation and prevent behavioural disturbances. The reminiscence video and the reminiscence conversation improve psychological stability. Yasuda et al. [11] developed "a navigational video" to prompt the patient to move to his/her personal computer. They then conducted an experiment to examine an effect of the navigational video. The results of the experiment showed the system significantly improved some patients' abilities to complete their household tasks. However, in some cases, the subjects did not hear the sound and voices on the video because they were not in the same room as the computer. Based on the aforementioned, we can identify two requirements of an ideal device for individuals with dementia to receive appropriate information:

1. The individual with dementia should not have to carry any device. The devices should be delivered when individuals with dementia need to do tasks instructed by the devices.
2. The device should be designed in such a way that the individual is willing to comply with its instructions for performing tasks

At present, some robots can alert the aged person that it is time to take medicine and can move to another space autonomously. They were developed in consideration of healing and therapeutic elements and are used at home and in nursing homes. "Paro [12]" is a therapeutic robot with five kinds of sensors: tactile, light, audition, temperature, and posture sensors. "PaPeRo petit [13]" is a robot with a camera, a microphone, and a sensor that detects people. It uses a cloud computing system. It detects the actions and utterances of an aged individual and submits this information automatically to a Social Networking Service. "Palro [14]" is an autonomous humanoid robot, which can have an intellectual conversation and walk on two legs. Once the user programs information into the computer, Palro alerts the person at the appropriate time.

Actually, some aged people like such a robot, and some aged people do not. It is still unclear how many aged people are willing to comply with instructions for performing tasks from the robots. Moreover, it is still difficult for such a robot to go upstairs quickly.

On the other hand, dogs tend to run after their owners even in the second floor of their house. Dogs also have often been used in therapy [15]. Research has shown that dogs can help to relieve stress. Individuals with dementia might have a more positive outlook on performing tasks if their dogs bring the ICT devices. Therefore, we came up with the concept of mounting an ICT device on dogs [16].

Dogs would be happy to accompany their owners (individuals with dementia) in their daily activities. With some training, the animal can be taught to rush to its owner when the smartphone mounted on the dog's back emits an alarm. The ICT device will complement the dog's ability to be useful.

In this study, we examined the effectiveness of a device mounted onto a dog compared to that of a fixed device. We built an application for smartphones where the user can set an alarm and display a message highlighting particular tasks that have to be performed at specific times. We conduct a case study with a healthy female. We examine the effectiveness of a smartphone mounted on a dog's back compared to a fixed device. She is asked to turn off alarms and perform a task on a voluntary basis when the smartphone emitted an alarm.

2 Development of the Application

We built an application for an android smartphone, FleaPhone CP-D02. It was developed by Java Version 7 Update 21 using a development kit, Android SDK 1.0. The display of the application consists of three parts: setting the time of the alarm, inputting a messageCand a completion button setting. A user (an individual with dementia or his/her caregiver) can set an alarm for an arbitrary time and input a message that the individual with dementia has to perform/complete a task.

3 Case Study

We examined whether an individual better performs tasks instructed by a smartphone mounted on a dog than tasks instructed by a fixed smartphone.

3.1 Subject

The subject in our case study is a healthy person (the mother of one of the authors) who is 50s. She has a five-year old female toy poodle that is kept indoors. Fig. 1 shows the dog with the smartphone on its back. It took one week for the dog to become accustomed to having the smartphone mounted on its back. The subject trained the dog to run to its owner when the smartphone emitted a specific sound. This training took only three days. The case study was conducted after one-month continuous training.

Fig. 1. The dog mounts the smartphone on its back

3.2 Method

The case study is conducted for five days over the course of one week. The subject is asked to turn off the alarm on the smartphone and to perform the allotted task on a voluntary basis.

Two same smartphones which are mounted the application are prepared. Both smartphones used in the study are the same. Fig. 2 shows the two conditions of the case study. One smartphone (named "Set-A") is mounted on the dog, and the other (named "Set-B") is placed in a predetermined location in the living room. The sound of the alarm is different for Set-A and Set-B. The volume of the alarm is the same in each case. The volume is such that someone sitting in the next room can not hear it. The smartphones record the length of time before the alarm is turned off.

An experimenter sets the time when each smartphone emitted the sound each day. The case study is performed from 9 a.m. to 9 p.m. The 12 hours are divided into four parts. In each part, each smartphone emits an alarm at a random time. The subject has a maximum of eight chances of hearing the alarms, and the subject does not know when the smartphones emit the alarms.

The experimenter instructs the subject to do these performances on a voluntary basis when the smartphones emit the alarms. We employ the Kraepelin test [17] as a task. This test requires the individual to perform calculations as fast and as accurately as possible. The test is a boring task and involves mental stress similar to that experienced by individuals with dementia who have to take medication. Each test takes 30 seconds to complete.

Fig. 2. Setup for the case study

The application can record the number of questions answered and the number of correct answers. After the case study, the subject was asked to fill out a questionnaire. The question items are as follows:

1. Did you experience any difficulties when you used the smartphone in the case study?
2. How did you feel about your dog before the case study?
3. How did you feel about your dog when it responded to the alarm and came to you?
4. How did you feel when the smartphone fixed in the living emitted the alarm? The answers are scored from 1 to 5, with 1 denoting "I did not think at all" and 5 denoting "I thought so very much."
   (a) I was happy.
   (b) I was nervous.
   (c) I wanted to turn off the alarm as soon as possible.
   (d) I felt that it was troublesome to turn off the alarm.
   (e) I considered leaving the emitting alarm.
5. Please state how you felt when the fixed smartphone emitted the alarm.
6. How did you feel when the smartphone mounted on the dog emitted the alarm? The answers are scored from 1 to 5, with 1 denoting "I did not think at all" and 5 denoting "I thought so very much."
   (a) I was happy.
   (b) I was nervous.
   (c) I wanted to turn off the alarm as soon as possible.
   (d) I felt that it was troublesome to turn off the alarm.
   (e) I considered leaving the emitting alarm.
7. Please state how you felt when the smartphone mounted on the dog emitted the alarm.
8. How did you feel when you performed the Kraepelin test on the smartphone fixed in the living room? The answers are scored from 1 to 5, with 1 denoting "I did not think at all" and 5 denoting "I thought so very much."
   (a) I enjoyed calculating.
   (b) I enjoyed manipulating the smartphone.

(c) I was nervous.

(d) I thought that I should calculate as quickly as possible.

(e) I thought that I should correctly answer as many questions as possible.

(f) I reluctantly performed the test.

9. If you had other feelings or an emotional shift when you were performing the test on the fixed smartphone, please write those down.

10. How did you feel when you performed the Kraepelin test using the smartphone that was mounted on the dog? The answers are scored from 1 to 5, with 1 denoting "I did not think at all" and 5 denoting "I thinked so very much."

(a) I enjoyed calculating.

(b) I enjoyed manipulating the smartphone.

(c) I was nervous.

(d) I thought that I should calculate as quickly as possible.

(e) I thought that I should correctly answer as many questions as possible.

(f) I reluctantly performed the test.

11. If you had other feelings or an emotional shift when you were performing the test on the smartphone mounted on the back of the dog, please write those down.

12. What was the dog doing while you performed the test using the smartphone mounted on its back?

13. What did the dog do after you completed the test?

4   Results

Table 1 shows the times that the smartphones emitted the sounds and the length of time until the subject turned off the alarm. A blank space means that the subject did not turn off the alarm in 60 seconds. The subject turned off the alarm in 22 - 54 seconds in Set-A and in 22 - 60 seconds in Set-B. The average time to turning off the alarm for Set-A and Set-B was 35.77 and 37.44 seconds, respectively ($SDs = 10.0, 13.8$, respectively).

Table 2 shows the number of times that the subject turned off the alarm. The subject turned off the alarm 13 times in Set-A and nine times in Set-B. The rate of turning off the alarm (success) was 76.47% and 52.94%, respectively ($z = 1.08$, no difference).

In Set-A, the number that the subject could not turn off the alarm was only four. In two of these, although the dog responded to the alarm, it could not find its owner (out of the house on one occasion and on the second floor on another occasion). The dog was unable to deliver the smartphone to the subject in 60 seconds. On the other two occasions when the alarm emitted, the dog did not run to the subject. In Set-B, the number that the subject could not turn off the alarm was eight. The subject did not hear the alarms because she was not in the living room.

Table 3 shows that the number that the subject calculated and the number of correct answers in the Kraepelin test. The number of calculations was 39 - 49 in

Table 1. The times that the smartphones emitted the sounds

Day	section	time	length of time (sec.)	time	length of time (sec.)
		Set-A (dog)		Set-B (fixed)	
1	1	15:28	25	16:15	–
2	2	9:42	39	9:39	40
	3	13:48	35	14:25	60
	4	16:00	22	17:41	–
	5	18:31	54	18:03	22
3	6	10:12	35	9:34	32
	7	12:37	22	14:53	–
	8	16:16	53	16:52	24
	9	18:44	–	19:42	–
4	10	11:52	46	11:34	60
	11	14:14	37	13:08	–
	12	17:25	–	16:57	37
	13	20:19	–	19:25	–
5	14	11:37	36	9:44	40
	15	12:13	31	13:32	–
	16	15:02	30	17:51	–
	17	18:08	–	19:43	22
M	–	35.77	–	37.44	
SD	–	10.0	–	13.8	

Table 2. The number of times that turned off the alarm by subject oneself

	Set-A (dog)	Set-B (fixed)
turn off	13	9
sum	17	17
rate (%)	76.47	52.94

Set-A and 36 - 46 in Set-B. The average number of questions answered in Set-A and Set-B was 44.15 and 41.78, respectively (SDs = 3.0, 3.3, respectively). In Set-A, the number of correct answers was 32 - 45, whereas it was 31 - 44 in Set-B. The average number of correct answers was 40.6 in Set-A and 37.7 in Set-B (SDs = 4.0, 4.5, respectively).

Table 3. The number that the subject calculated and the number of correct answers

day	section	Set-A (dog)				Set-B (fixed)			
		time	correct	sum	rate (%)	time	correct	sum	rate (%)
1	1	15:28	37	40	92.5	16:15	–	–	–
2	2	9:42	45	46	97.8	9:39	35	39	89.7
	3	13:48	42	42	100.0	14:25	40	43	93.0
	4	16:00	44	46	95.7	17:41	–	–	–
	5	18:31	41	42	97.6	18:03	34	38	89.5
3	6	10:12	43	46	93.5	9:34	39	43	90.7
	7	12:37	43	47	91.5	14:53	–	–	–
	8	16:16	32	39	82.1	16:52	42	45	93.3
	9	18:44	–	–	–	19:42	–	–	–
4	10	11:52	43	47	91.5	11:34	42	45	93.3
	11	14:14	34	41	82.9	13:08	–	–	–
	12	17:25	–	–	–	16:57	32	36	88.9
	13	20:19	–	–	–	19:25	–	–	–
5	14	11:37	38	44	86.4	9:44	31	41	75.6
	15	12:13	44	49	89.8	13:32	–	–	–
	16	15:02	42	45	93.3	17:51	–	–	–
	17	18:08	–	–	–	19:43	44	46	95.7
M	–	–	40.62	44.15	92.0	–	37.67	41.78	90.2
SD	–	–	4.0	3.0	–	–	4.5	3.3	–

We compared the results of Set-A and Set-B. In both, questions in some sections were not answered because the subject had not noticed the alarm and had not performed the test. Hence, we included only the results of the sections that the subject had completed in both Set-A and B: section 2, 3, 5, 6, 8, 10, and 14. We compared the medians of the number of all answers between Set-A and Set-B (signed-rank test). The results did not show a significant difference between the sets (two-sided test, $T = 7.0, P = 0.297$). In addition, we compared the medians of the number of the correct answers between Set-A and Set-B (signed rank test). The results revealed no significant difference between the sets (two-sided test, $T = 6.5, P = 0.297$).

Table 4 shows the responses of the subject to the questionnaire. The subject did not find it difficult to operate the smartphone. (see (1)). Before the case study, she expressed a mixture of anticipation, as well as anxiety about her dog (see (2)). In practice, when the dog responded to the alarm and came to her, she was impressed (see (3)). When the smartphone mounted on the dog emitted, she was a little happier than the fixed smartphone emitted (see (4) and (6)). She explained why she could not sometimes turn off the smartphones (see (5) and (7)). In the case of the fixed smartphone, when she was cooking, she did not notice the alarm. In the case of the smartphone mounted on the dog, the dog took a nap in the early evening and therefore did not take the smartphone to the subject when the alarm sounded.

She was happy to perform the Kraepelin test on either set (see (8),(9), and (10)). The Kraepelin test was meant to simulate the boredom/stress encountered in repetitive drug taking by dementia patients. We wanted to simulate the situation where an individual with dementia does not want to take medicine. We expected that the subject would be more willing to performs the tests instructed by the smartphone mounted on the dog than the tests instructed by the fixed smartphone. However, the results showed that there was no difference in the subject's willingness to perform the tests on the mounted and fixed smartphones (see (8) and (10)).

5 Discussion

There was no significant difference between Set-A and B with regard to the number of times that the subject turned off the alarm. Moreover, there was no significant difference between the sets in the number of questions answered or in the number of correct answers. If the same experiment was conducted with a large number of subjects, we would expect to observe significant differences between Set-A and B.

It is clear that the dog's owner was quicker to turn off the alarm on Set-A than on Set-B because the dog was trained to run to its owner when the alarm emitted. In contrast to what we expected, it took only three days to train the subject's dog. However, the term for the training may be different depending on the character of the dog and the relationship between the owner and his/her dog before starting the training.

We expect that an individual with dementia would be more willing to perform tasks if his/her dog brought the smartphone to the owner. In our case study, we considered that the Kraepelin test was boring. Unexpectedly, the subject (a healthy person) enjoyed the test using both Set-A and B, finding it a brain-training exercise. On the other hand, she answered that she was a little happier when the smartphone mounted on the dog emitted the alarm than when the fixed smartphone emitted the alarm. She was also impressed when her dog took the smartphone to her. Therefore, we consider that individuals with dementia will be willing to perform daily tasks through the influences of their dogs.

As the other agenda, we have to consider the viewability of the display. In reality, individuals with dementia will not have to perform tasks like the Kraepelin test on the display. However, they would need to be able to read a message, push a button, and input a message on the display. If they remove the smartphone from their dogs to read the message well, they will forget to re-mount it on their

Table 4. Questionnaire response

(1)	None.
(2)	I believed that my dog ran to me when the smartphone emitted an alarm because it was trained to do so. On the other hand, as the dog was unwilling to put the wear, I wondered if the dog runs.
(3)	As the dog is small, it might find the smartphone too heavy. I was impressed that the dog came to me when the alarm sounded. I was delighted that our daily training yielded results. I realized how important trust is between people and dogs.
(4)	(a) 3 (b) 2 (c) 2 (d) 1 (e) 1
(5)	I did not notice that the smartphone was emitting an alarm while cooking because the alarm was quiet.
(6)	(a) 4 (b) 2 (c) 2 (d) 1 (e) 1
(7)	The dog did not respond to the alarm in the early evening because it took a nap at that time.
(8)	(a) 5 (b) 3 (c) 2 (d) 5 (e) 4 (f) 1
(9)	I enjoyed the test because it was a brain-training exercise. Sometimes, I touched the different answer from what I considered because of hasty move. I was concerned about the accuracy of my answers.
(10)	(a) 5 (b) 3 (c) 2 (d) 5 (e) 4 (f) 1
(11)	None.
(12)	The dog sat quietly when I performed the test.
(13)	The dog made a point of shaking itself after it stood up.

dog's back. We should consider how best to adapt the smartphone, so that individuals with dementia can perform the required tasks without removing the phone from the dog's back.

6 Conclusion

In this paper, we examined whether a healthy female subject better performed a task instructed by a smartphone mounted on a dog's back than a task instructed by a fixed smartphone. First, we trained the dog to run to the subject when the smartphone mounted on its back emitted an alarm. The dog training took only three days. Then, we conducted a case study where the subject turned off the alarm and performed a Kraepelin test on the smartphone on a voluntary basis. We used two settings to determine the potential effect of the dog on the willingness of the subject to perform the test: In one, the dog ran to her owner when the smartphone mounted on its back emitted the alarm. In the other, the subject ran to the smartphone fixed in the living room when the smartphone emitted the alarm. After turning off the alarm, the subject had to perform the Kraepelin test on the smartphone in both settings.

Based on the results, there were no significant differences between the sets in the number of times that the subject turned off the alarm or in the number of correct answers. However, the subject was a little happier when the smartphone mounted on the dog emitted the alarm than when the alarm was emitted by the fixed smartphone. We consider that individuals with dementia will be willing to perform daily tasks through the influence of their dogs.

In the future, we will mount sensors on dogs and detect the current situation of individuals with dementia. The goal is to provide appropriate support to such patients using a smartphone mounted on the back of the patient's dog.

References

1. Yasuda, K., Misu, T., Beckman, B., Watanabe, O., Ozawa, Y., Nakamura, T.: Use of an IC Recorder as a Voice Output Memory Aid for Patients with Prospective Memory Impairment. Neuropsychol. Rehabil. 12(2), 155–166 (2002)
2. Hodges, S., Williams, L., Berry, E., Izadi, S., Srinivasan, J., Butler, A., Smyth, G., Kapur, N., Wood, K.: SenseCam: A Retrospective Memory Aid. In: Dourish, P., Friday, A. (eds.) UbiComp 2006. LNCS, vol. 4206, pp. 177–193. Springer, Heidelberg (2006)
3. DeVaul, R.W., Pentland, A.S., Corey, V.R.: The Memory Glasses: Subliminal vs.Overt Memory Support with Imperfect Information. In: Seventh IEEE ISWC, pp. 146–153 (2003)
4. Beigl, M.: MemoClip: A Location-Based Remembrance Appliance. Pers. Ubiquit. Comput. 4(4), 230–233 (2000)
5. Asada, H., Shaltis, P.: Medical Mood Ring. MIT Technology Review (April 2004)
6. Isansys: LifeTouch, http://www.isansys.com/en/products/sensors
7. Lapis semiconductor: Band-aid thermometer, http://www.kumikomi.net/archives/2013/12/in12lapi.php (in Japanese)
8. Yasuda, K.: Rehabilitation through Portable and Electronic Memory Aids at Different Stages of Alzheimer's Disease. Les Cahiers De La Fondation Me'de'ric Alzheimer 3, 97–107 (2007)
9. Bayen, U.J., Dogangün, A., Grundgeiger, T., Haese, A., Stockmanns, G., Ziegler, J.: Evaluating the Effectiveness of a Memory Aid System. Gerontology 59, 77–84 (2013)
10. Kuwahara, N., Yasuda, K., Tetsutani, N., Morimoto, K.: Remote Assistance for Individuals with Dementia at Home Using Reminiscence Systems and a Schedule Prompter. Int. J. Comput. Healthc. 1(2), 126–143 (2010)
11. Yasuda, K., Kuwahara, N., Kuwabara, K., Morimoto, K., Tetsutani, N.: Daily assistance for individuals with dementia via videophone. American J. Of Alzheimer's Dis. & Other Dementias 28(5), 508–516 (2013)
12. PARO Robots U.S., Inc.: Paro, http://www.parorobots.com/index.asp

13. NEC: PaPeRo petit, `http://www.nec.com/index.html`
14. Fujisoft Incorporated: Palro, `http://palro.jp/`
15. Dimitrijević, I.: Animal – assisted therapy: A new trend in the treatment of children and adults. Psychiatria Danubina 21, 236–241 (2009)
16. Yasuda, K., Kuwahara, N., Nakamura, M., Morimoto, K., Nakayama, K., Oshima, C., Aoe, J.: Assistance Dogs for Individuals with Dementia Using ICT Devices: Proposal of Human-Computer-Animal Interface. In: ICHS 2012. CD-ROM (2012), OS01_1010
17. Google Play: Kraepelin test for job junting and brain training, `https://play.google.com/store/apps/details?id=jp.lumireis.kraepelin` (in Japanese)

Effects of Peer Pressure on Laughter

Mamiko Sakata[1] and Noriko Suzuki[2]

[1] Faculty of Culture and Information Science, Doshisha University, Japan
msakata@mail.doshisha.ac.jp
[2] Faculty of Business Administration, Tezukayama University
1-3 Tatara Miyakodani, Kyotanabe City, 6100394, Japan
nsuzuki@tezukayama-u.ac.jp

Abstract. Our study was conducted to identify and analyze specific conforming behavior. We looked at how laughter is expressed and tried to examine if the decision "to laugh" or "not to laugh" is affected by conformity and peer pressure. Our study tried to show whether or not peer pressure influenced the study subjects in expressing laughter in experimental situations where they watched comedy videos with other people. Based on the assumption that the subjects' recognition of such comedy videos to be "funny" and their actual "laughing" behavior did not necessarily coincide, we examined how the viewers' judgment was influenced by the general atmosphere or other viewers' attitudes. The results of our study proved that the subjects' behavior was largely affected by the peer pressure exerted by the other viewers even though their subjective evaluations of the comedy videos were not.

Keywords: multimodal interaction, human behavior.

1 Introduction

Consciously or unconsciously, people tend to conform to the opinions and behavior of the majority when they are in a group. Conformity is an action in which one makes judgments or choices against his/her own wishes by agreeing with the majority of the people around them. Sometimes, an individual's tendency to conform to the majority leads to "peer pressure", which forces the majority's opinions or behaviors on dissenting individuals. Suppressing one's own wishes, opinions or emotions to conform to the majority can jeopardize individual characteristics and freedom in thought and behavior. Furthermore, social pressures demanding conformity from individuals can hinder both personal and social development. On the other hand, conformity is often necessary for social groups to function smoothly.

In this study, we investigated the factors that promote or hinder conformity by conducting well-designed specific experiments. Social interactions between different individuals are profound, complicated and greatly varied. When examining human-computer interactions, one also needs to pay attention to socially-induced actions such as conformity. For example, when designing robots, computers or agents equipped with human-like social characteristics, it is important to design an interface based on

S. Yamamoto (Ed.): HIMI 2014, Part II, LNCS 8522, pp. 479–488, 2014.
© Springer International Publishing Switzerland 2014

the algorithm of social interactions. This study makes observations from such a perspective and suggests further studies on the topic.

Many studies have been conducted to identify the factors that promote or prevent such behavior. One study (Ash, 1955), for example, revealed the following: If at least one individual, out of the majority who had been pre-instructed to give wrong answers, gave the correct answer, the experiment subject was not inclined to conform to the majority. However, if that one correctly-answering individual switched to the majority, the subject became more submissive, more readily conforming to the majority.

Deutsch & Gerard (1955) reported that conforming behavior decreased drastically when study subjects did not have to reveal their judgments to the colluding, pre-instructed experiment participants or the experimenter.

Muranaka et.al. (2004) proved with a psychological experiment that people conform to computer agents in manners similar to the way they conform to other humans. Ota et.al. (1996) suggested a decision-making model based on people's conforming tendencies and proved that it was possible to induce human-like conformity by changing the internal stability level. In this way, research in conformity is expected to contribute greatly to building human models or designing HCI.

Our study was conducted to identify and analyze specific conforming behavior. We looked at how laughter is expressed and tried to examine if the decision "to laugh" or "not to laugh" is affected by conformity and peer pressure. Our study tried to show whether or not peer pressure influenced the study subjects in expressing laughter in experimental situations where they watched comedy videos with other people. Based on the assumption that the subjects' recognition of such comedy videos to be "funny" and their actual "laughing" behavior did not necessarily coincide, we examined how the viewers' judgment was influenced by the general atmosphere or other viewers' attitudes.

2   Video Viewing Experiment

We conducted video viewing experiments using comedy videos as presented stimuli. In each experiment, one study subject viewed comedy videos with 15 fake viewers. The subject was not told that everybody else in the audience was a fake viewer. Altogether, 21 university students (nine males and 12 females) participated in our study as study subjects.

2.1   Laughter Suppression by Fake Audience

Our experiments were conducted under the following three situations: (1) All Laughing (all 15 fake viewers laughed during video viewing; (2) Five Laughing (five out of 15 fake viewers laughed); and (3) None Laughing (none of the fake viewers laughed). Seven study subjects were placed in the three different situations. The subjects' seating arrangements are shown in Fig. 1.

As shown in Fig. 1, the study subject sat in the second-from-the-left seat in the last row. The seating arrangements of the 15 laughing and non-laughing fake viewers in the three different situations, i.e., All Laughing, Five Laughing, None Laughing, are also shown in Fig. 1.

Fig. 1. Seating Arrangement for Different Situations

2.2   Experiment Scenario

Enlisting five university students, we conducted preliminary experiments to decide where the fake viewers should laugh. While viewing the comedy videos, the five students laughed spontaneously at 21 different scenes. Out of these, we selected six scenes and designated them to be "Never Laugh" scenes. The 15 remaining scenes were divided into two fake laughing groups – "Loud Laughs" and "Chuckle." Additionally, we designated three scenes as "Forced Laughing" scenes. These were the scenes where a laugh track (canned laughter) had been inserted in the videos, even though they were not the scenes which elicited spontaneous laughter from the preliminary viewers. We presented this experiment scenario to the fake viewers, who committed the protocol to memory. Then they all participated in a one-hour joint practice session.

2.3   Filming the Viewing Room

As shown in Fig. 2, the subjects' reactions/behaviors were filmed by two cameras. Two other cameras recorded the developments in the entire viewing room.

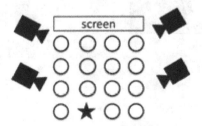

Fig. 2. Viewing Room

2.4   Procedure

In our study, the subjects and fake viewers were briefed on the general study procedure, followed by the showing of one-minute and three-minute comedy videos. After
the show, the study subjects were asked to fill out Questionnaire 1. Then, they were
told that all other people in the viewing room were fake viewers. They were then
debriefed. Next, the subjects were asked to fill out Questionnaire 2.

2.5   Questionnaires

After viewing the comedy videos, the study subjects filled in questionnaires about
their impressions in the following four categories: "Was the video enjoyable?", "Do
you want to see it again?", "Will you tell your friends about the video?" and "Do you
want to see a sequel to the video?" The subjects answered using a seven-point rating
scale (1. "Not at all."~7. "Yes, very much so."). After debriefing the subjects, they
were asked this question: "Was the viewing room conducive to laughter?" to be answered using the seven-point rating scale (1. "Not at all."~7. "Yes, very much so.").
Lastly, they were asked if they had sensed that all other people in the audience were
fake viewers (see Table 1).

Table 1. Question Items

Questionnaire 1	· Was the video enjoyable? · Do you want to see it again? · Will you tell your friends about the video? · Do you want to see a sequel to the video?	1. "Not at all."~ 7. "Yes, very much so."
Questionnaire 2	· Was the viewing room conducive to laugh- ter?	

3   Data Extraction

We used the annotation software ELAN (Fig. 3) to tag the study subjects' filmed behavior. By using this software, one can add the occurrences, frequency and durations
of tagged events and record them in chronological order.

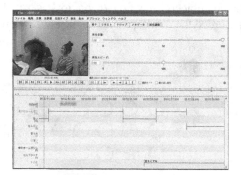

Fig. 3. Event -Tagging Example Using ELAN

Focusing on the expression of laughter in the subjects, we set up the following tag sets:

- Laugh: laughing with the mouth open.
- Chuckle: laughing with the mouth closed.
- Smile: smile retained after a laugh.
- Lip wetting: mouth-closing action.
- Glancing: casting a quick glance at the other people in the room.

We also tagged other characteristic actions.

4   Results

4.1   Questionnaire 1

Table 2 and Fig. 4 show how the study subjects evaluated the "fun" aspect of the comedy videos.

Table 2. Descriptive Statistics of Questionnaire 1

	All Laughing		Five Laughing		None Laughing		Sum	
	mean	SD	mean	SD	mean	SD	mean	SD
Was the video enjoyable?	5.29	1.38	5.29	1.60	5.86	0.69	5.48	1.25
Do you want to see it again?	4.43	2.37	4.14	1.77	5.29	2.14	4.62	2.06
Will you tell your friends about the video?	5.29	1.38	4.43	1.72	5.00	1.63	4.90	1.55
Do you want to see a sequel to the video?	5.71	1.11	5.29	2.21	6.00	1.83	5.67	1.71

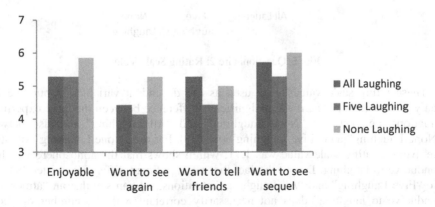

Fig. 4. Questionnaire 1: Rating Scale Values

These rating scale values were used as the dependent variables in our one-way analysis of variance. There was no significant difference between rating scale values. Under all experimental situations, the "Enjoyable" and "Want to see a sequel" categories scored highly. This showed that the subjective evaluation of the comedy videos was not affected by the viewing room atmosphere, i.e., All Laughing, None Laughing, etc.

4.2   Questionnaire 2

After completion of the study and the debriefing of the study subjects, we asked them if they were aware of the fake viewers in the audience (Questionnaire 2). The results of the seven-point rating scale answers regarding the "viewing room atmosphere" are shown in Table3 and Fig. 5 below.

Table 3. Descriptive Statistics of Questionnaire 2

	All Laughing		Five Laughing		None Laughing		Sum	
	mean	SD	mean	SD	mean	SD	mean	SD
Was the viewing room conducive to laughter?	4.00	2.16	5.29	1.11	1.71	0.76	3.67	2.06

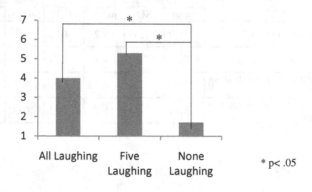

Fig. 5. Questionnaire 2: Rating Scale Values

These rating scale values were used as the dependent variables in our one-way analysis of variance. There was a significant difference between the three experiment situations, i.e., between "None Laughing" and "All Laughing" and also between "None Laughing" and "Five Laughing" ($p < .05$). For the "None Laughing" situation, the average rating scale value was 1.71, which shows that the atmosphere was least conducive to laughing. Due to the fact that no significant difference existed between the "Five Laughing" and "All Laughing" situations, we can say that an "atmosphere conducive to laughing" does not necessarily correlate with the number of people laughing.

Lastly, only one study subject out of 21 answered "I was vaguely aware" to the question, "Were you aware that all other people were fake viewers?" So this subject's data was deleted from evaluation before proceeding to further analysis of the recorded film.

4.3   Recorded Film Analysis

Table 4 lists the descriptive statistics of each analysis index (tag sets) shown in Chapter 3. We conducted one-way analysis of variance using these indices as dependent variables. We observed significant differences in the order of 5% for all of the indices.

Table 4. Descriptive Statistics of Expressed Behavior

	All Laughing		Five Laughing		None Laughing		Sum	
	mean	SD	mean	SD	mean	SD	mean	SD
Smile	42.66	34.47	23.02	28.98	1.22	3.22	22.26	30.27
Laugh	33.19	29.56	23.22	22.74	2.70	4.63	19.53	24.42
Chuckle	17.14	17.90	17.06	14.01	16.21	15.73	16.79	15.21
Lip-wetting	1.57	2.44	6.37	11.84	15.80	19.46	7.99	14.03
Glancing	.00	.00	.00	.00	2.78	3.60	.97	2.44

Fig. 6 shows the length of laughter under different study situations. The average length was 33 seconds for "All Laughing", 23 seconds for "Five Laughing" and only two seconds for "None Laughing." As "laugh" in this paper is defined as "laughing with the mouth open," the study suggests that the subjects felt uneasy about laughing with the mouth open in an atmosphere where all other people did not laugh.

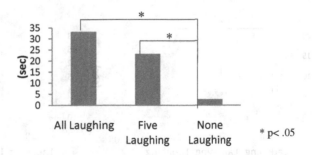

Fig. 6. Length of Laughter

Fig. 7 shows the length of "Smile", the state in which a person retains a smile after a bout of laughter. As shown, the average "Smile" time was 42 seconds for "All Laughing", 23 seconds for "Five Laughing" and only one second for "None Laughing." As described earlier, laughs are difficult to observe in the "None Laughing" environment, so it is only natural that a "Smile" was hardly observed in this situation. Contrarily, the "Smile" time was longest in the "All Laughing" situation. When the fake viewers create an atmosphere conducive to laughing, the study subjects showed "Smiles" and seemed ready to burst into laughter at any time.

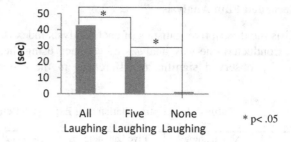

Fig. 7. Length of Smile

The results of our study showed that the subjects hardly laughed in an atmosphere non-conducive to laughing, i.e., when all the people around did not laugh. The results of Questionnaire 1 (Section 4.1) were interesting in that the subjects in the "None Laughing" situation evaluated the comedy videos to be "enjoyable" as much as in the "All Laughing" and "Five Laughing" situations. The subjects in the "None Laughing" atmosphere did not laugh, even though they felt the comedy videos were "enjoyable". The peer pressure from the "None Laughing" audience suppressed the laughter. Our study also showed that the subjects' evaluation of the comedy videos did not improve only because the audience was laughing more. In conclusion, whether or not the people around were laughing did not affect the evaluation of the comedy videos; however, it greatly affected the generation and expression of laughter by the subjects.

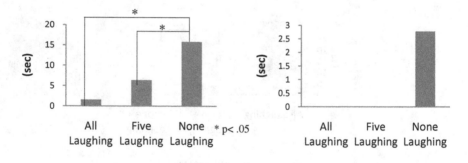

Fig. 8. Length of Lip Wetting   **Fig. 9.** Length of Glancing

Fig. 8 and Fig. 9 show the length of "Lip wetting" and "Glancing." As a result of the one-way analysis of the variance, both of these expressions appeared frequently in the "None Laughing" situation.

Lip wetting is considered to be a displacement behavior. The subject wants to laugh at a comical scene but suppresses it when nobody around is laughing. Displacement behavior is not a person's intended behavior but is generated when he/she is in a conflicting or stressful situation. A well-recognized displacement behavior is scratching the head when a person is embarrassed. In our study, frequent body posture shifting and neck and shoulder rotations were noted as displacement behaviors. Peer pressure suppressed laughter from the subjects in the "None Laughing" situations, which were obviously stressful situations.

Glancing was also frequently seen in the "None Laughing" situations. The subjects try to visually confirm the behavior of others around when no laughter is heard in comical developments in the video. Again, we observe insecurity in the subjects when they look around to check other people's reactions/behaviors to determine whether or not to go along with them.

Fig. 10. Lip Wetting   **Fig. 11.** Glancing

5   Discussion

The results of Questionnaire 1 revealed that the "fun" aspect was recognized regardless of the people around laughing or not laughing. Comedy shows often insert a laugh track, and studio audiences often include fake, pre-arranged cheering audience members. Such gimmicks, however, do not necessarily affect the "fun" aspect itself. As regards the viewing room atmosphere, the results of Questionnaire 2 revealed that when none were laughing, it was least conducive to laughter. However, "some people laughing" and "All Laughing" made no difference. As known from the experiments conducted by Ash (1955), the presence of at least one "like-minded" person was critical in our experiment. "Five laughing" and "Ten laughing" did not make much difference. It is necessary to determine where the threshold was in the none-to-five laughing situations.

While analyzing the results of the Questionnaires, the researchers also confirmed that the subjects' behaviors were greatly influenced by peer pressure: Under all experimental conditions, the decision to laugh or not to laugh was greatly affected by the attitude of the people around, regardless of the evaluation of the "fun" aspect. It is noteworthy that various displacement behaviors were observed in the "None Laughing" situation. Even when a subject finds the comedy video "fun", he or she was greatly stressed in a conflicting "None Laughing" situation.

The results of our experiment showed that "laughing" is quite a primitive behavior, but that it is also socially conditioned. A laugh is produced out of inter-human relationships. The knowledge gained from our experiment is expected to offer valuable insight into Relationality Design and Relationality-Oriented System Designs.

6   Conclusion and Future Work

This study aimed to examine the factors that encourage or discourage conformity. Specifically, the study examined the effects of peer pressure on laughter generation and expression by conducting experiments with comedy videos. The results of our study proved that the subjects' behavior was largely affected by the peer pressure exerted by the other viewers even though their subjective evaluations of the comedy videos were not.

The study presented herein is a basic inquiry into behaviors which are generated out of people-to-people interactions. The obtained knowledge is useful in designing man-computer and man-robot relationality. In order to induce any certain behavior, the atmosphere, interface design and agent behavior need to be examined closely.

References

1. Asch, S.E.: Opinions and Social pressure. Scientific American 193, 31–35 (1955)
2. Deutsch, M., Gerard, H.B.: A study of normative and informational social influences upon individual judgment. Journal of Abnormal and Social Psychology 51, 191–198 (1955)
3. Muranaka, A., Takeuchi, Y.: A User's alignment action in interaction with several agents. Technical report of IEICE, HCS2003-67, pp. 65–70 (2004) (in Japanese)
4. Ota, M., Iida, T., Kawaoka, T.: Decision Making Model Based on Conformity to Majority's Opinion. Transactions of the Japanese Society for Artificial Intelligence 11(6), 927–932 (1996) (in Japanese)

User Analysis and Questionnaire Survey

Misaki Tanikawa and Yumi Asahi

Department of Systems, Engineering, Shizuoka University
3-5-1 Johoku Naka-ku, Hamamatsu 432-8561, Japan
sleeplus0716@gmail.com
asahi@sys.eng.shizuoka.ac.jp

Abstract. The authors use the multivariate statistics. The authors study to clarify the type of game user. Order to clarify the user type. we conducted a survey about the game style to college students. Research method is the questionnaire. The authors was analyzed by SPSS and amos with it. As a result of using factor analysis, the user is divided into three types. Then performed a Structural Equation Modeling, it was confirmed the accuracy of the factor analysis model.

Keywords: Marketing, User Analysis, Questionnaire Survey, Japanese culture, SPSS, amos, Factor Analysis, Structural Equation Modeling.

1 Introduction

The authors use the multivariate statistics. The authors study to clarify the type of "Otome game" user. "Game" of this study means use the device for play.(Example: Play Station) Order to clarify the user type, we conducted a survey about the game style to college students.

1.1 About Otome Game

"Otome game" means love simulation game for women in Japanese. The word "Otome" means a young girl.

Fig. 1. Flow of the game

Otome game is a game genre like novel. Each one has own story. The player of the game handles a girl who is the heroine of the story. The player can change heroine's name. Of course, the player can change it into her name. And the heroine meets

S. Yamamoto (Ed.): HIMI 2014, Part II, LNCS 8522, pp. 489–497, 2014.
© Springer International Publishing Switzerland 2014

hand-some men of various characters in the game. She fall in love with one of them. As a result, the player who handles the heroine can enjoy virtual love with the man in the game. This story of the game branches when the heroine chooses one of the men. The number of the branches in a game is same as the number of the men in the game, so the player can fall in love with each man. This is like a romance novel which can choose heroine's partner.

Then, why Otome games are enjoyed in Japan? Japanese are generally slow in sexual development. And, Japanese tend to conceal own romance experiences. Japanese males are called "plant eating" in slang words. So, female wish for aggressive romance to the game.

1.2   Situation in Today's Japanese Market

Otome game is one of the game genres that is growing significantly in today's Ja-pan. Otome game market is forecasted to become about 15.6 billion yen in 2012. The market in 2011 is 14.6 billion yen. This is 30 percent extra compared with 2010. [1]

The history of Otome game goes back until 1994. But at that time, the game genre was not well known, that state continued for a while. However, a product had an explosive sales in 2002. Hereafter, Otome game has become to be known at once. After that, the products which became a big hit continued in 2006 and 2008. In 2010 Otome game came to be known more because famous product had been animated. More over, in 2011, an animated product did smash hit. To promote CD products related to the animation work, a lot of flags and the posters were located at JR Ikebukuro station. In 2013, promoting posters were posted at 13 JR stations nationwide. At first, Otome game was known by only a part of the game industry. However today, it is known by many people and was grown to very popular genre in Japan. In addition, if a product becomes big hit, a lot of related products are sold, such as CDs, Goods, or events. It has been also performed Popularity Index.[2]

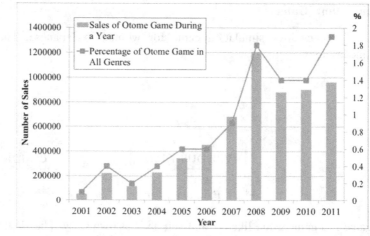

Fig. 2. The Total Sales Number of Otome Game During a Year and The Percentage of Otome Game Sales in Sales of All Game Genres[3]

These graphs show two kinds of numbers about sales of Otome game industry between 2001 and 2011. Green bar graph and left vertical line show the total sales number of Otome game during a year. Orange line graph and right vertical line show the per-centage of Otome game in all genres of game. These graphs also shows Otome game market is growing in Japan. Especially, because the percentage has been increase, it is clear that Otome game is known by people who did not play these games gradually.

1.3   Overseas Expansion

Recently, Otome game is also released in foreign countries. In 2012, Voltage Inc. began the service "A Prince's Proposal" for North America. The company already had purveyed the service "Pirates in Love", Otome game for North America. This took 21st place by the App store entertainment category of North America in August 2012. And in Asia, this took 1st place by the App store entertainment category of Singapore in same month. Moreover, another product of Voltage Inc. "My Forged Wedding" took 2nd place in same record. From above, it can be said that the acknowledgment level of Otome game in foreign countries is rising.[4]

1.4   Purpose of Research

As can be seen from above, the market of Otome game has expanded every year. However, today in Japan, Otome game industry do not enough analyze the user. Then, to search for "Needs requested from the otome game now", The authors decided to analyze the otome game user.

So, to search for the needs that are required for Otome game, the author decided to analyze the users.

2   Marketing Research of Otome Game

2.1   Questionnaire Survey

Before taking the questionnaire in a young girl gamers, authors have conducted a questionnaire about "game style" to college students first. In this questionnaire, The authors asked about the dating simulation game in particular. The authors went to 20 people a preliminary investigation before making the questionnaire. Question was improved on the basis of the preliminary investigation.As a result, The authors got the results of 333 people. The following is the content of the questionnaire.

- Sex
- Age
- Currently, Do you play a TV game by game machine?
- What kind of have a TV game machine?
- What kind of have a   mobile phone?
- Have you ever played the game in the mobile phone?

- What playing are you platform?
- Have you used the billing services?
- Have you ever played the download type's game?
- Which element is most important to you?
- Dou you know about Date-simulation game and Otome Game?
- Have you ever played Date-Simulation game?
- How many Date-simulation games have you ever played?
- How did you start Date-simulation game?
- Why do you continue dating simulation game?

2.2 Questionnaire Result

"Which element is most important to you?"

First, The authors questioned fourteen items about importance of the elements of games. The word "game" in this question include all genres besides Date simulation game.

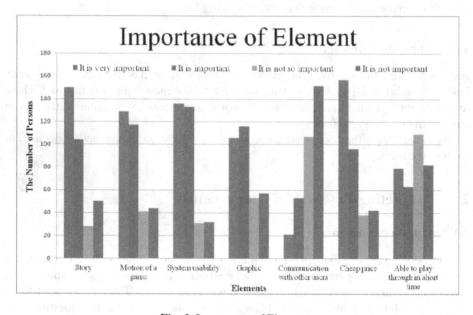

Fig. 3. Importance of Element

This is a graph about the questionnaire. The authors took out seven main items from the questions. These items are "the story", "the motion", "the system usability", "the graphic", "communication with other users", "the price", and "play through time". The most interesting information is that, the university student users think it is not important to communicate with another persons by a game. More than sixty percent of them play social games which has the function to share the world of the game with other players. But according to the comparison of importance of elements, these users do not think about importance of communication.

"Dou you know about Date-simulation game and Otome Game?"

This question about the awareness of Date simulation game made clear that more than half of men and women know about Date simulation game.

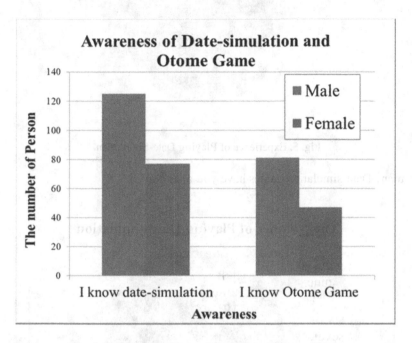

Fig. 4. Awareness of Date-simulation and Otome Game

The word "Date simulation game" mean not only Otome game, but also include Date simulation for men. More than half of the answerers know Date simulation game, but awareness of Otome game is relatively low.

"Have you ever played Date-Simulation game?"

The "Gal game" means Date simulation game for men that mentioned above. And in Japan, the word "Consumer" means the game consoles except mobile phone or smart phone. Play Station Portable and Nintendo DS are examples of Consumers. Many answerers play Gal games with Consumer consoles. But Otome games are played equally with both of the consoles, consumer and mobile phone hold similar number of percentage. Otome game in mobile phone have more users than Gal game in mobile phone. The reason The authors suggest is that the players of Otome game are mainly female, and they tend to hide the fact that they play Otome game, so they chose more private instrument, mobile phone, than Consumer console. On the other hand, the data of Gal game do not have difference between mobile and consumer. So men do not tend to mind to hide their fact.

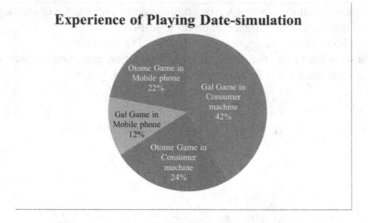

Fig. 5. Experience of Playing Date-Simulation

"How many Date-simulation games have you ever played?"

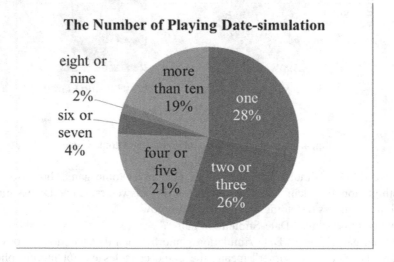

Fig. 6. Trigger to play Date-simulation

For this question, most of the answers shows that many users have played several numbers of Date-simulation game. But the users who play a lot of Date-simulation game also exist.

"How did you start Date-simulation game?"

The most numerous answers to this question are that the users friend recommended him or her to the game. The second highest answers are to see the web advertising. Ninety nine percent of Japanese university student use the mobile phone, so they tend to catch their information by the inter net with the phone.

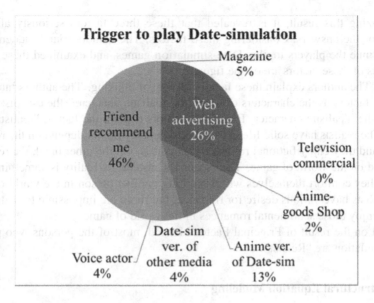

Fig. 7. Trigger to Play Date-simulation

2.3 Data Analysis

"Why do you continue playing Date-simulation game?"

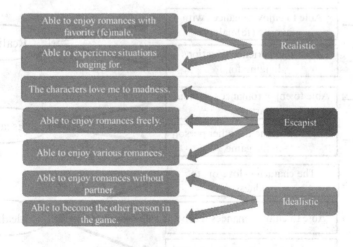

Fig. 8. Result of Factor Analysis

The answers for this question has dispersion. To understand more, The authors analyzed this results with factor analysis. The method in this study are "Principal Factor Method" and "Varimax Rotation." As a result, The authors could extract three factors.

Analyzing this result, it is revealed that these three factors seriously affect the choices of the answers. Considering these factors, The authors found hidden factors that continue the players to play Date-simulation games, and examined these factors. The kinds of these factors are on the figure.

Then, The authors explain these factors of way of thinking. The authors interpreted the three factors as the characters of users: the realistic character, the escapist character, and the idealistic character. First, The authors explain the factor, "realistic" character. The realists have solid life in real world, so they do not depend on the romantic fiction, and they enjoy fictional romance just as it is. On the other hand, the rests tend to depend on the world of game. The escapist's attitude for reality is something negative, so they comfort themselves with becoming another person in the world of game. The idealists have various desire for romance, but those are impossible to materialize, so they enjoy those sentimental romances in the world of game.

Based on the result of Principal Factor Method, most of the persons who play the Date-simulation are "Realist".

2.4   Structural Equation Modeling

The authors likened the results of the factor analysis in SEM.The authors was using the amos in the analysis. Corresponding item from each of the three factors are affected.We assumed the covariance between factors to all.The result, GFI became 0.925.AGFI became 0.809. Covariance of the latent variable is a good. It was a good result fit.

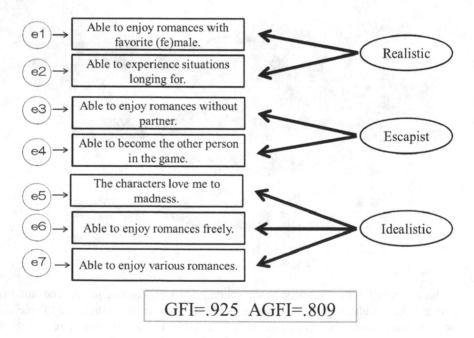

GFI=.925 AGFI=.809

Fig. 9. Structural Equation Modeling

2.5 Future Study Directions

Finally, The authors tell about the future direction of the study. This time, The authors could not collect sufficient answers, so The authors would like to study again with more plenty effective data. Hereafter, The authors would like to investigate more different user types with user study in different angle.

Also, I would like to improve the model for SEM.

References

1. Yano Econimic Research Institute. Investigation result 2012 concerning the Otaku market (2012)
2. Otome game of the year, `http://ogy.jp/contents/about.html` (last access July 2, 2014)
3. Enterbrain, Inc., Famitsu white book of Game 2012 (2012)
4. Voltage Inc. News Relese, `http://www.voltage.co.jp/news/p-release/2013/0523_01.html` (last access July 2, 2014)

Art, Culture and Creativity

To Relive a Valuable Experience of the World at the Digital Museum

Yasushi Ikei[1], Yujiro Okuya[1], Seiya Shimabukuro[1], Koji Abe[1],
Tomohiro Amemiya[2], and Koichi Hirota[3]

[1] Tokyo Metropolitan University, Tokyo 191-0065, Japan
ikei@computer.org
[2] NTT Communication Science Laboratories, Kanagawa 243-0198, Japan
amemiya.tomohiro@lab.ntt.co.jp
[3] The University of Tokyo, Tokyo 113-8656, Japan
uhirota@mail.ecc.u-tokyo.ac.jp

Abstract. This paper describes a new concept of bodily experience that
may be used in the future museum exhibit. An ordinary museum exhibits
objects to make themselves talk with their authenticity to visitors, however it does not provide an interaction and vivid context in which they
existed. A virtual experience system which creates multisensory stimuli
potentially presents the realistic state of valuable artificial objects in the
original environments. We think the *experience* of objects in a particular
space is another theme that a future museum needs to seek. A novel
rendering technique of a virtual body of a visitor is introduced where
multisensory displays impart the sensation of presence of an environment and objects of interest through a pseudo walking experience. This
digital museum device will add a new experience to relive a trip walking
around objects based on recorded data from a real tourist.

Keywords: bodily experience, virtual body, pseudo walking, experience
projection, ultra reality.

1 Introduction

A museum is the place where objects of certain value are presented and preserved
to hand the knowledge relating to and represented by the objects on to the next
generation. The knowledge coexists with the objects is transfered through the
instrumentation of museum exhibit by presenting at hand the real object worked
in the past. This method is an effective and only way to bring the real authentic
things over time to the present.

Although people can see and read about the exhibit of objects, usually they
can not *experience* actual use of them in real life. The real relation between
humans and artificial objects in a context is another crucial aspect that should
be passed to people in the future. Moreover, a very large object that spans over
an exhibit-room height or a historical architecture need to be presented by other
means than the current museum way of exhibit, that enable visitors to walk

S. Yamamoto (Ed.): HIMI 2014, Part II, LNCS 8522, pp. 501–510, 2014.
© Springer International Publishing Switzerland 2014

around and feel the environment that holds the objects. Our relation to a large artificial object is only grasped after we move around and see it from various angles and distances.

Thus, the experience to cognitively capture large objects distributed in a field requires a spatial motion of the visitor, specifically the walking through the field watching architectural structures as interested objects. This kind of experience has not been involved in an ordinary museum, and it is the experience usually possible at a real tourist spot where valuable structures stand. If a digital museum could present such tourist spots in the world, it can cover large objects distributed on the whole globe for guided experiences. These sight-seeing experiences of the world may be involved in a future digital (virtual) museum by accumulating the record of real experiences that tourists gained.

One of the key technologies of this virtual museum is an experience *projection* that the past experience of some tourist is shared by a visitor of the museum as if the visitor him-/herself has really walked and looked at the spot by own body. This *experience projection* is performed to a physical body of a visitor. In other words, it is a new presentation of a self-body to a visitor by an external stimulation that causes multisensory sensation of self motion. We investigate a novel methodology that creates first-person reliving sensation of a trip by a virtual self body representation based on a multisensory display.

As the first stage, we focused on representing a walking motion of a person, a kind of playback of prerecorded body motion. This opens a possibility to obtain experiences of other people who visited various sites with their own will at a future digital museum. It would provide the user with the opportunity of learning through the experience of other people, or in a sense, it might be considered as a kind of 'Total Recall [4]' movie where one could buy any experiences. This would provide a new style of exhibit for a digital museum using the virtual reality technology.

2   Representation of a Self Body

Experience has its base on a self body. The rendering of a self body is a long topic of the virtual reality technology. The three factors of the virtual reality were described by Tachi [14] as: a real-time interaction, a 3D space, and a self projection. The last factor, a self projection, is not very obvious issue, and it has not been sufficiently implemented and elucidated since it involves complicated cognitive and sensory aspect that is currently investigated in the light of neuropsychology.

Usually the self projection means that a projected self avatar is observable by both the current user of a VR space and other persons in the same VR space. It is an *objective projection* as it is apparently examined by anyone in the space—this is the first level of self projection. On the other hand in the light of a subjective view point—the second level of self projection, the self projection is considered that the user feels as if his/her body resides in the avatar, or in a weaker sense, his/her body coexist both at the avatar and the actual (real) self body (virtual coexistence).

In this *subjective projection*, the cognitive (conceptual) self body is virtualized and placed at the avatar [1] although the real body still exists in the real world and holds the control of the avatar. In this situation, it would be very interesting to think whether the avatar could control the cognitive self body. That is, the avatar that has a scenario of an experience drives the cognitive self body to provide a copy of the experience to the user. In reality, the scenario of the avatar is of special interest if it is of someone else who had a variety of valuable experience, e.g. world travels, physical presentations of top athletes, artistic skills of a living national treasure artist, or even a ride in a theme park and learning experience at the university.

The projection is from the avatar to the cognitive self body, which is a *back projection* (Figure 1) to usual self projection of the virtual reality. The external experience (of one person) is projected to the user through the self body. In this case, the self body itself is a medium to present the other person's body. It may also be written that the user dives into the other person's body. We call this *the virtual body technology by back projection* in which the user relives the experience of the other person. The *virtual body* is a rendered cognitive self body by the *back projection interface*.

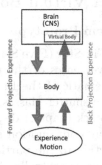

Fig. 1. Back projection in which a virtual body is rendered

3   Virtual Body

Cognition of a self-body and its rendering have been investigated in the context of a virtual body in a VR space [12,13]. A multisensory presentation is a crucial part of implementation by which a virtual body might be really considered as a self body as subjective projection. A high quality sense of presence is expected to be realized if we can properly integrate multisensory stimuli that produce the sensation of virtual self body as if it resided in the VR space, not in the actual state of the physical body. There are many evidences that a passive multisensory perception can easily create virtual body illusion [2] even if it was a whole body [1].

We consider here the method to create a dynamic virtual body illusion that is recognized in a different state from the real state of an actual body. For example, a virtual body of yourself is walking while the actual your body is sitting. This could also be said that your actual body is the medium that renders a virtual body in a different state in conjunction with the VR apparatus. As a part of VR rendering system the actual body displays a virtual body to the user's brain. In the course of this design, the actual body is physically moved appropriately by some haptic devices to evoke a virtual body sensation that creates a virtual experience. This is the ultimate goal, a kind of the ultra reality, of our multisensory display system introduced in the present paper.

To utilize the actual body to represent virtual body motion in a virtual world, multisensory input should be generated and integrated ingeniously. Among them, vestibular sensation is specifically crucial for the experience of spatial body motion and presence located in a relatively large space. A vestibular device such as a vehicle simulator is usually used to represent the movement of a transportation machine (e.g. automobile). It is not applicable to present the motion of the self body. For our purpose, a vestibular device needs to create a first-person sensation of own virtual body movement.

4   A Display System for Virtual Body Motion

4.1   Multisensory VR System Prototype

A multisensory display system, FiveStar (Five Senses Theater [7]) produces multiple modality stimuli to the five senses of the user, except for the gustatory sensation. Figure 2 shows a schematic of the FiveStar. The system consists of a stereoscopic visual display with shutter glasses, a 7.1 channel surround audio system, a tactile and force feedback (haptic) display system, a wind and scent delivery system, and a vestibular body motion system. These subsystems are integrated to provide an interaction to the participant along with a particular scenario of experience. Each device is controlled by a controller PC that is connected with each other by the 100 Mbps Ethernet on which an UDP message is broadcasted to synchronize each function.

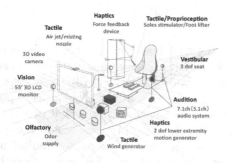

Fig. 2. Multisensory display (FiveStar)   **Fig. 3.** Motion seat (3-dof)

4.2   Vestibular and Haptic Display

Four types of display devices to create walking sensation were developed: a 3-dof motion seat and a lower limb stimulator consisting of a 2-dof horizontal motion plate, two vertical motion pedals, and tactile stimulators at soles and shinbones. These devices, in addition to a wind generator, are integrated to form a new type motion base system that evokes the sensation of walking.

Motion Seat. The motion seat, shown in Figure 3, is driven by three linear actuators that were implemented at the base of a FRP seat of an automobile. Three actuators are attached at the vertices of an isosceles triangle on a support plate. One actuator is placed at the front, and two are at the rear. The stroke of each actuator is 100 mm with a 0.01-mm resolution and the maximum velocity of 200 mm/s. The actuators are controlled by a pulse drive board in a control PC.

The motion of the seat has three degrees of freedom: a lift (vertical translation) with roll and pitch rotations. These are used to stimulate vestibular sensation while rendering of virtual walking motion. In addition, the seat is equipped with eight vibro-transducers at the back and bottom cushions. The vibration of transducers is used for small motion component that should be involved in the virtual motion rendering.

Lower Limb Stimulator. The lower limb stimulator (Figure 4) consists of a 2-dof horizontal motion plate, vertical motion pedals, and sole stimulators. These devices contribute to create sensation of a spatial bodily motion by making user's feet move in a two-dimensional plane, and by lifting lower extremities at the heel simultaneously. Synchronous motion of them evokes the sensation of a voluntary walking motion of the body in addition to the movement of the ground if needed.

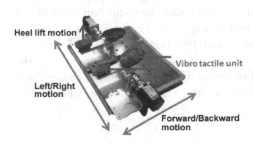

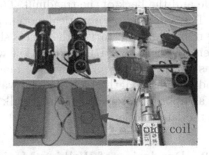

Fig. 4. Lower limb stimulator. A 2-dof horizontal motion plate (base), two vertical motion pedals, and toe/heel tactile stimulators at the soles.

Fig. 5. Tactile stimulators (voice coils). Six vibrator units in a pair of leg guards (top left), four vibrators in step boxes (bottom left), and four vibrators attached to the pedals.

Figure 5 shows tactile displays for lower limbs: shin stimulators in leg guards (top left), sole stimulators for toes and heels (bottom left and right). These present the tactile sensation that originated from the impact against the floor and consequent vibration during walking [15] in addition to a wind. These tactile displays were not used in the experiments written in the later section to investigate single stimulus independently, although the effects of them were especially crucial in displaying a virtual walking motion.

5 Rendering of Walking Motion

Walking is a full-body motion controlled dexterously by the spinal cord and the brain based on multisensory information that comes from the vestibular sensation, the kinesthesis and tactile sensation and the vision with an intention to walk that originated at the cortex [9,16]. It is clearly a voluntary motion in a sense, however not all of the motion is under conscious control. The cyclic rhythm of leg motion is mainly controlled by the CPG (central pattern generator [5]) in the spinal cord and the brain stem without direct intervention of subjective volition from the cortex. This allows that a passive body movement generated by an external device may be perceived as a part of voluntary walking motion. With this view, we investigated a passive stimulation method for a body that evoked the sensation of a voluntary walking. To determine the amount of stimulus to add to impart a walking sensation, a real walking motion was measured and referred to search an appropriate stimulus created by the display.

5.1 Spatial Trajectory of a Body during a Real Walk

The body trajectory during a real walk was measured by an optical spatial sensor (OptiTrak V100, NaturalPoint, Inc.) as a reference data for rendition of the motion seat and the pedals. A participant walked on a treadmill attaching markers at the head, the coxal bone, the toe and heals placing the sensor on the side and the back of the treadmill. The walking speed was 60 m/min.

The amplitude of a vertical motion at the head and the coxal bone was about 30 mm. The trajectory of the heel is shown in Figure 6. The horizontal displacement in the forward/back direction was about 600 mm, while the vertical lift was about 200 mm. Although the magnitude of a body motion depends on the body height (length of a leg) and a walking velocity, we will refer this amplitude as an approximate value of a real walk since a strict value is not crucial as shown in the later section.

5.2 Rendering of Walking Motion by Motion Seat

As a preliminary experiment, first we produced the same amplitude of a vertical motion as the real walking by the display system. The result was that the actual amplitude motion evoked an extremely larger sensation than the real sensation the subject received during the real walking. This might be ascribed to

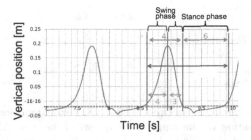

Fig. 6. Vertical motion of the heel

the difference in sensory processing in which sensory input could be attenuated when a voluntary motion was executed [3,8]. In the current condition without a voluntary actuation of a body, the added stimulus was felt as if the body was simply moved irrelevantly to a walking. In addition, the posture of sitting on a chair was different from walking of course, which would make the same amount of motion inappropriate for the equivalent perception of body motion.

An appropriate amplitude of a vertical motion (with roll and pitch motion) was experimentally searched by a participant based on the method of adjustment in a general psychophysical procedure. The adjustment involved three linear actuators so that the resultant motion had three degrees of freedom. In addition, to avoid the trajectory with the completely constant shape during steps of a walking motion, a 10 to 20 percent random fluctuation in amplitude was automatically introduced.

Figures 7 and 8 show the vertical motion that the participant adjusted, of the headrest and the left-hand support of the seat, respectively. Other parts, the right-hand support and the seating face, were also measured as well as some sites of the participant's body, although not discussed here. The amplitude of the headrest was about 1 to 2 mm, far smaller than the real walking motion, with some fluctuation included in the process of adjustment. The amplitude of the left-hand support was also about the same range (around 1 to 2 mm) that changed cyclically along with a walking phase. The amplitude of seat motion was about one fifteenth of the amplitude observed in the real walking.

5.3   Rendering of Walking Motion by the Pedals

Reciprocal lift motions were added to the participant's legs by two motion pedals shown in Figure 4 to evoke a sensation of walking while the participant sat on the seat with his shinbone set approximately vertical and the angle of the knee joint held to approximately 90 degrees. Based on the real trajectory of a heel (Figure 6), a similar trajectory was designed in the form as shown in Figure 9, and the trajectories around this form were displayed and rated by participants. The period ratio of the swing phase and the stance phase was 2:3 as observed in the real walking motion. Ascend/descend period ratio was also set after the real

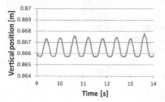

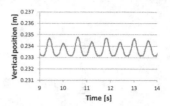

Fig. 7. Vertical motion at the headrest of the seat. Fluctuation of the amplitude is a part of the designated trajectory.

Fig. 8. Vertical motion at the left-hand support of the seat. Alternating amplitude indicates the roll motion involved in the motion rendering.

motion. This lifting motion was provided to two lower legs with a 180-degree phase difference. Ten stimuli of vertical lifting of {0.1, 1.0, 2.0, 5.0, 10, 20, 30, 40, 50, 60} mm at the heel were randomly presented to the participant for 10 times each. Seven male participants (the mean age of 22.4 years) rated the lifting stimulus in terms of the similarity to the sensation of a real walking, or the extent to which the walking sensation was evoked. A 5-scale rating (5 is most similar or evoking) was used. Before the session, participants walked on a level floor for 10 m at 1400 ms walking period paced by the sound of a metronome to memorize the sensation of walking. The participant wore headphones that provided a noise, and closed eyes during the rating session. During this evaluation session, the motion seat was fixed providing no motion cue.

The result is shown in Figure 10. The rating score of similarity to the sensation of the real walking was analyzed using a one-way analysis of variance (ANOVA) regarding the amplitude values of vertical lifting. The analysis revealed the significant effects of the vertical amplitude ($F(9, 54)=10.6$, $p<0.001$). In post-hoc comparisons (Fisher LSD test), amplitude values of 10 to 30 mm yielded a larger rating than others. This indicates that the optimal amount of lift was about 10 to 30 mm to evoke the sensation of walking in the case of the foot lifting motion. The value is around one tenth of the real lift motion. Regarding the motion shape, some participants commented that the motion direction change at the

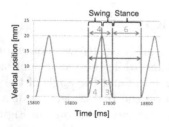

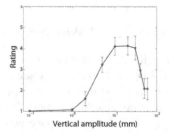

Fig. 9. Vertical motion pedal lift trajectory (heel motion)

Fig. 10. Pedal lift rating (heel motion rating, error bar denotes SE)

top position was too fast and it lessened the amount of similarity to the real walking.

6   Conclusion

We introduced a novel display system that will project the sensation of walking around a large object as an exhibit to a visitor of a future digital museum. The experience of a large object should involve multiple view points that are best provided by walking. Our working hypothesis is that a walking experience can be introduced through an externally actuated body motion that is perceived as if the participant walked by own feet voluntarily.

The display method was investigated after a body trajectory during a real walk was measured for a reference. Produced stimuli by display devices that projected a virtual walking was compared with the real walk. The equivalent amplitude of vertical motion on the display was as small as about one tenth to twentieth of the real motion. This small value is good for the implementation of the display since its mechanical structure can be much reduced to allow more places for use.

In this research, we set a hypothesis of a dynamic virtual body rendered by *the back projection*. Observed large difference between the real body motion and its equivalence on the display is considered to be related to the particular brain process of modulating sensory information based on the efference copy and the presynaptic inhibition [11] in addition to the conscious intention to walk [6]. The mechanism needs to be elucidated in conjunction with the field of neuropsychology.

Since the reality is perceived by the body interaction with the world, so that the body itself limits the reality. If we can assume the body as a medium of VR space media, then our experience will be augmented and expanded, since the body is the base of an experience. The direct consequence of this is that your experience can be that of the other person. The user can relive other's experience as if it occurred originally on the user. This may be said the user's body is replaced with the other's [10]. In other words, the user dives into the other's body and obtains his experience as depicted in [4]. If this technology is realized, the museum will obtain a new dynamic presentation method of human experience that is not provided by the current exhibit method of the museum. For this method the multisensory information is crucial in imparting the sensation of presence of an environment. In addition, a pseudo walking using recorded data from a real tourist will be the main part of experience of reliving a trip around objects.

Acknowledgements. The authors wish to thank Professor Michitaka Hirose at the University of Tokyo for his valuable advice on the present research. This research was supported by NICT (National Institute of Information and Communications Technologies).

References

1. Blanke, O.: Multisensory brain mechanisms of bodily self-consciousness. Nature Reviews. Neuroscience 13(8), 556–571 (2012)
2. Botvinick, M., Cohen, J.: Rubber hands 'feel' touch that eyes see. Nature 391, 756 (1998)
3. Cullen, K.E.: Sensory signals during active versus passive movement. Current Opinion in Neurobiology 14, 698–706 (2004)
4. Dick, P.K.: Total Recall. Gollancz (2012)
5. Dimitrijevic, M.R., Gerasimenko, Y., Pinter, M.M.: Evidence for a spinal central pattern generator in humans. Annals of The New York Academy Of Sciences 860(1), 360–376 (1998)
6. Haggard, P.: Conscious intention and motor cognition. Trends in cognitive sciences 9(6), 290–295 (2005)
7. Ikei, Y., Abe, K., Hirota, K., Amemiya, T.: A multisensory VR system exploring the ultra-reality. In: Proc. VSMM 2012, pp. 71–78 (2012)
8. Lambert, F.M., Combes, D., Simmers, J., Straka, H.: Gaze Stabilization by Efference Copy Signaling without Sensory Feedback during Vertebrate Locomotion. Current Biology, 1–10 (2012)
9. Perry, J.: Gait Analysis: Normal and Pathological Function 12 (1992)
10. Petkova, V.I., Ehrsson, H.H.: If I Were You: Perceptual Illusion of Body Swapping. PLoS ONE 3, 9 (2008)
11. Rossignol, S., Dubuc, R., Gossard, J.-P.: Dynamic sensorimotor interactions in locomotion. Physiol. Rev. 86, 89–154 (2006)
12. Slater, M., Marcos, D., Ehrsson, H., Sanchez-Vives, M.V.: Inducing illusory ownership of a virtual body. Frontiers in Neuroscience 3(2), 214–220 (2009)
13. Slater, M., McCarthy, J., Maringelli, F.: The influence of body movement on subjective presence in virtual environments. Human Factors: The Journal of the Human Factors and Ergonomics Society (1998)
14. Tachi, S., Sato, M., Hirose, M.: Virtual Reality. Corona Publishing Co., Ltd. (2010)
15. Terziman, L., Marchal, M., Multon, F., Arnaldi, B., Lecuyer, A.: King-Kong Effects: Improving Sensation of Walking in VR with Visual and Tactile Vibrations at each Step. In: IEEE International Symposium on 3D User Interfaces (IEEE 3DUI), pp. 19–26 (2012)
16. Whittle, M.W.: An Introduction to Gait Analysis (2007)

A Knowledge Distribution Model to Support an Author in Narrative Creation

Hochang Kwon[1], Sukhwan Jung[1], Hyuk Tae Kwon[2], and Wan Chul Yoon[1]

[1] Dept. of Knowledge Service Engineering, KAIST,
[2] Dept. of Industrial Systems Engineering, KAIST,
291 Daehak-ro, Yuseong-gu, Daejeon, 305-701, Korea
{hochang,raphael,htkwon,wcyoon}@kaist.ac.kr

Abstract. Adjusting the knowledge of characters and the reader is a critical task for an author in narrative creation. Throughout a narrative, both characters and the reader experience events according to their own timelines and perspectives. They interpret information accumulated through their experience and update knowledge to the narrative-world which the author constructed. In this paper, we present a *Knowledge Distribution Model* which supports an author in finely controlling the knowledge of characters and the reader. Within the model, the *Knowledge Structure* is constructed by connecting event, information, and knowledge. The *Knowledge State* is evaluated as the *degree of belief* under the knowledge structure. We adopted a probabilistic reasoning model to calculate the knowledge state. The change in knowledge state, defined as *Knowledge Flow*, is visually presented to the author. We designed a GUI prototype to implement the proposed modeling process, and demonstrated the knowledge flow with an actual cinematic narrative.

Keywords: knowledge distribution, knowledge structure, knowledge flow, narrative creation, authoring tool

1 Introduction

Narrative is an effective media to convey information and knowledge [1]. In a narrative, explained by a communication model [2], an author (sender) constructs a particular story-world composed of characters, background (space-time), and events to convey his/her message; the reader (recipient) understands this message by reconstructing it. Throughout this process, the author distributes various information/knowledge related to a message (theme) over the narrative, then the reader and characters (agents in narrative) comprehend them while they experience events. The author uses a variety of techniques and rhetorical devices to organize information/knowledge and control the knowledge of each agent in the narrative. This work is essential to attaining the completeness and a valuable narrative for several reasons:

First, the author's message is expressed by the information arrangement in the narrative. Adjusting the arrangement and the flow of the information is

S. Yamamoto (Ed.): HIMI 2014, Part II, LNCS 8522, pp. 511–522, 2014.
© Springer International Publishing Switzerland 2014

important to maintain the semantic consistency of the whole narrative. Second, it is also an important issue for the author to design coherent characters. The characters knowledge is closely related to their actions because they must have corresponding information/knowledge to act coherently. Third, the reader's knowledge is about when and to what extent the reader conceives the changes in information. This is directly connected with the reader's understanding of the narrative. Fourth, adjusting differences in knowledge between characters and the reader is a powerful narrative method to make the reader participate in the narrative and feel sympathy [3]. It is strongly related to reader's emotional responses, including suspense, surprise, and curiosity.

In spite of the importance of this process, it has been manually done in general practice, depending solely on the ability and knowledge of the author. In this paper, we propose a novel model to both represent the structure of information/knowledge and control the knowledge of the agents in a narrative. We designed this model to support the author's narrative creation.

2   Related Work

The literature on constructing a model for the knowledge of the agents in narrative writing can be divided into three categories.

The first group is about modeling the knowledge of characters in a story-world. Riedl et al. [4] constructed a knowledge structure of characters to maintain *character believability* using IPOCL algorithm. In their system, the knowledge of a character is regarded as constraints and guidelines for action. The Belief-Desire-Intention (BDI) model, which is well-known in the field of software agents, was applied to character's behavior [5]. The character designed by the BDI model updates knowledge, modifies goals, and executes plans in the process of narrative events. The next approach utilizes modeling a reader's inference in the narrative comprehension. The most representative research related to this topic is the work of Graesser et al. [6,7], which is based on the constructionist theory in psychology. They described how a reader constructs a knowledge-base and explain why actions, events, and states are mentioned in the narrative text. Based on former studies, an algorithm for generating discourse plans that prompt a reader's inference was suggested [8]. The last category is the research on the suspense model using the disparity of knowledge between character and the reader. Many studies on the suspense model are based on the Structural Affect Theory (SAT) suggested by Brewer et al. [9], in which a specific discourse structure is set up by manipulating the order of events. Based on the SAT, plan-based models that evoke a sense of suspense in readers are also suggested [10,11].

Many of the previous researches have paid attention to applying AI methods to the narrative generation system. The quality of automatically generated narratives, however, are still limited despite of computational advances. It is necessary to construct more flexible model that guarantees an author's participation in narrative creation. The desirable model has to provide the author with intuitive interaction for seamless creation work and to visualize the quantified changes of knowledge in narrative.

3   Narrative and Knowledge

3.1   Narrative Structure and Agents' Experience

The structuralism model pointed out that a narrative consists of story (content) and discourse (expression), and the basic unit of content is event [12]. The basic attributes of an event can be revealed by four-W questions: *Who does what? When and where?* At the early stage in the conception of a narrative, a number of loosely connected events are created in the author's mind. The author elaborates a set of events and composes a narrative by configuring those events with reference to causal and temporal relations. The events are ordered along two different time axes (timelines): a chronological *story-time* in a story-world along which characters experience the events, and a plotted *discourse-time* along which readers follow. The reader and characters jointly experience the events in a narrative; however, throughout the narrative, they accumulate experience according to their own timelines and perspectives. Each of them interprets the meaning of accumulated information based on successive experience and updates knowledge to the narrative-world which the author constructed. Fig. 1 shows how the author configures the events and makes the disparity of knowledge in a narrative.

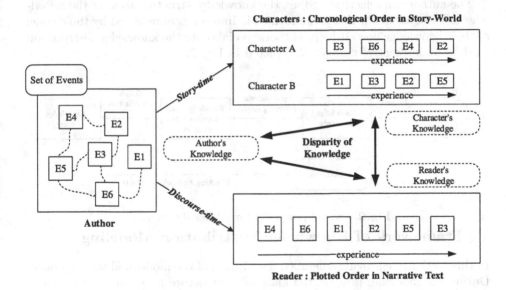

Fig. 1. Event configuration and the disparity of knowledge

3.2   Narrative Creation and Knowledge Distribution

In a narrative, only the author has all the information and knowledge. The author can adjust when, what and to what extent each agent gets to know by organizing events and information. We define this organizing process as *knowledge distribution* task, which must be carried out to create a valuable narrative. Simultaneously controlling a variety of knowledge of each agent, however, has fairly heavy cognitive workload, hence we devised a model to support the author's knowledge distribution work; the proposed model consists of three functional parts as follows.

The first part is the *knowledge structure*, where the events are arranged and the information and knowledge are set to reveal to each of agents. Under this structure, agents experience the events to acquire information and knowledge along their own perspectives and timelines. The second part is a reasoning model for computational agent modeling. At any particular time-point in a narrative, agents reason about the *author-settled* knowledge based on their accumulated information. The reasoning model performs this inference of agents using the computational methods. This model is independent of the knowledge structure, thus any kind of inference method can be applied. In this paper, we adopt a Bayesian method to demonstrate the probabilistic reasoning about the knowledge of agents. The last part is the *knowledge state* and the *knowledge flow*. The knowledge state is defined as the *degree of belief* about the knowledge specified by the author, which is calculated by the reasoning model. Sequentially experiencing the events, the knowledge state of agents is subject to change between *belief* and *disbelief*. The knowledge flow is defined by the trajectory of change in the knowledge state.

The author can selectively adjust the knowledge structure to alter the knowledge state of agents in this model, which is immediately reflected by the change of their knowledge flow. It helps authors to elaborate the knowledge distribution work in an interactive manner as depicted in Fig. 2.

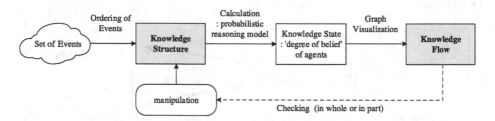

Fig. 2. Overall process of knowledge distribution

4   Framework of Knowledge Distribution Modeling

In this section, we provide a detailed description of the model and our approach. During the modeling process, the knowledge structure is constructed by relating the knowledge elements. The knowledge structure is the foundation of the knowledge state and flow calculated by a reasoning model on the assumption that a reader and characters are rational agents within a narrative.

4.1   Knowledge Structure

The proposed *knowledge structure* is modeled by connecting event, information, knowledge, and meta-knowledge. This structure is similar to the Data-Information-Knowledge-Wisdom (DIKW) hierarchy model [13] proposed in the field of information science. Fig. 3 shows the framework of knowledge structure and the author conducts the *knowledge distribution* on this workbench.

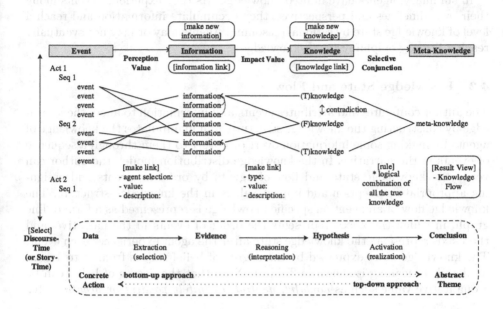

Fig. 3. Framework of knowledge structure and description

Event and Information. Events can be regarded as a set of data. Information that influences the knowledge state are extracted from a list of events. Agents obtain and accumulative the relevant information while experiencing the events. Each of agents has different perspective to events, hence information is obtained at a different level even for the same event. It is reflected by the *perception value* on the links between events and information. The author can finely express the difference between perspectives of agents in the narrative by assigning proper perception values for each agent.

Information and Knowledge. Information can be regarded as evidence of knowledge that the author set up within the narrative. The type and strength of the evidence are expressed by the *impact value* on the links connecting information and knowledge. Each item of information either concedes or rebuts the linked knowledge. Agents rationally reason about the knowledge based on the accumulated information in order to formulate and verify a hypothesis.

Knowledge and Meta-knowledge. Knowledge is expressed in a form of proposition, each with a value of *true* or *false*; the knowledge set up as false is a distractor that aims to confuse the agents. Meta-knowledge is the most important knowledge in the narrative because it is directly connected with the theme (message) that the author wants to convey. Meta-knowledge is a true proposition which can be deduced by logically combining all the true knowledge. Agents realize the meta-knowledge when all the true knowledge are known.

In summary, agents have limited knowledge. As they experience events along their own timelines and perspectives, they accumulate information and reach a level of knowledge state by rational reasoning. Agents may or may not eventually reach a literary epiphany (meta-knowledge).

4.2   Knowledge State and Flow

The author configures and attributes events and information to affect the knowledge by constructing the knowledge structure, and manipulates the knowledge of agents by making some information overt or covert to them through a sequence of events in the narrative. In the knowledge distribution model, the author can verify the knowledge state and flow of agents by ordering events and assigning appropriate perception and impact values in the knowledge structure. The knowledge flow of an agent on specific knowledge is represented as a form of line graph, in which the x-axis represents the order of events in the narrative, and the y-axis represents the knowledge state after the agent experiences each event. The knowledge state expressed by the degree of belief ranges from -1 to 1, and its detailed meaning is shown in Table 1. Note that the degree of belief can be a qualitative value such as *doubtful, neutral, definitely positive or negative*, etc.

Table 1. Detailed meaning of degree-of-belief values of knowledge state

Degree-of-Belief	1	0.5	0	-0.5	-1
Level of certainty	maximum	middle	minimum	middle	maximum
Interpretation	inevitable	probable		improbable	impossible
Dominance of information link	Information linked to the knowledge is positive		⋆	Information linked to the knowledge is negative	
On true knowledge	understanding			misunderstanding	
On false knowledge	misunderstanding			understanding	

⋆ Degree of belief = 0 can be interpreted in two ways:
1) Ignorance: No information is linked to the knowledge.
2) Uncertainty: Information linked to the knowledge contradicts, rendering it unjustifiable.

The knowledge flows of agents differ in most narratives as they experience events on different timelines with individual perspectives. This causes each agent to experience events in a different sequence and magnitude. Note that the proposed model assumes a rational agent and that the reasoning processes and capabilities of characters and the reader are identical.

4.3   Reasoning Model: Analytic Approach

In this paper, we took an analytic approach to calculate the knowledge flow from the knowledge structure. Among diverse methods that can be utilized, a probabilistic reasoning model based on Bayesian theory, one of the oldest and most traditional methods for dealing with uncertainty, was applied to calculate the inference process of narrative agents. For a hypothesis H, which is knowledge in our model, an agent's degree of belief in H is denoted as a *subject probability* of the agent, $P(H)$, that the agent believes H is true. Given a related event E to H, the degree of belief is denoted by $P(H|E)$.

The base model that we adopted was from the Abell's application of Bayesian probability to narrative inference [14]. It was initially intended to analyze narratives in social situations and can also be used to model the degree of belief in a narrative; only the agents are changed, from social individuals to characters and readers. The method uses the logarithm of the odds ratio of a hypothesis to show the degree of belief of an agent. With the use of odd ratio, the degree of belief changes more drastically as the magnitude of event increases. Applying the Bayes' rule, the agent's prior and posterior odds ratio are

$$Odds(H:\neg H) = \frac{P(H)}{P(\neg H)}, \ Odds(H:\neg H|E) = \frac{P(H|E)}{P(\neg H|E)} = \frac{P(E|H)P(H)}{P(\neg E|H)P(\neg H)}, \quad (1)$$

where the posterior odds ratio can also be shown as

$$Odds(H:\neg H|E) = L_E \times Odds(H:\neg H), \ \text{if} \ L_E = \frac{P(E|H)}{P(E|\neg H)} . \quad (2)$$

To measure how event E changes the odds of H against $\neg H$, a logarithmic function is used, where the sign of $\log L_E$ shows how E changes the degree of belief in H [15].

$$\log Odds(H:\neg H|E) = \log L_E + \log Odds(H:\neg H) . \quad (3)$$

Note that an appropriate clamping rule is needed since the logarithm cannot be evaluated in two extreme cases, $P(H) = 1$ and $P(H) = 0$.

There are two main differences between the assumptions of above Bayesian probability and our model. The one is that the values of the knowledge state varies from uncertainty to certainty with respect to two types of information (t): true or false, coded by 1 or -1, respectively. We adopted a linear mapping so that the closer $P(H)$ is to zero or one, the more certainly H is false or true, respectively, while the truth of H is uncertain where $P(H)$ is around 0.5. The other difference is that our model introduces the perception value as a measure of how much of the information is actually perceived by an agent. The *effective impact value* of information (v) can be defined as the product of the impact value and the perception value in the knowledge structure. Therefore, if each event carries single information, the equations must change as follows.

$$P(E|H) = \frac{1 + v \times t}{2}, \ P(\neg E|H) = \frac{1 - v \times t}{2}, \ \text{where} \ 0 \leq v \leq 1, t = \begin{cases} -1 & \text{fasle} \\ 1 & \text{true} \end{cases} \quad (4)$$

$$Odds(H:\neg H|E_{i+1}) = L_{E_i} \times Odds(H:\neg H|E_i) ,$$

$$\text{where} \ L_{E_i} = \frac{P(E_i|H)}{P(E_i|\neg H)} = \frac{1 + v_i \times t_i}{1 - v_i \times t_i}, \ Odds(H:\neg H|E_0) = 1.0 . \quad (5)$$

5   Case Study

In this section, the knowledge structure and flow of an actual cinematic narrative was analyzed using the proposed model. We chose a film *Incendies* (2010, Denis Villeneuve) as an example. In this film, the effect of war stained history on individuals is portrayed by a journey of twins following their mother's last will. This film would be suitable for validating the effectiveness of the proposed model for following reasons: First, it is a famous, multiple award-winning film with numerous reviews and critiques from which emotional responses for this film can be found. The dominant emotional responses of its viewers are found to be suspense and surprise by running keyword analysis on the reviews and critiques from *IMDB.com* and *Metacritic.com*. These emotional responses are closely related to the change in knowledge of agents as many researches on the SAT showed. Second, the main plot of the film is built around a certain secret created at the beginning of the film. The knowledge state of agents are constantly changing as the events are unfolded in narrative. This shows the importance of knowledge distribution task in narrative creation to elaborately adjust the knowledge flow of agents. Third, this film can be used as an example to show that the proposed knowledge distribution model is not only restricted to typical thriller or mystery narratives, but also can be applied to more generic drama narratives. Fourth, the knowledge flow of agents greatly varies with a notable difference between the story and discourse timeline, while the disparity of knowledge between the viewers and the characters are closely related to the theme of the narrative.

As a result of this analysis, thirty-seven events, seventeen information, six knowledge and one meta-knowledge were found from this film. Fig. 4 shows the knowledge structure of *Incendies* with the relevant list of events and information shown in Table 2. Based on the analyzed knowledge structure, Abell's Bayesian method for narrative inference model was applied to calculate the changes in the degree of belief for each agent. Fig. 5 shows different knowledge flows of the viewers and *Nawal* (the protagonist) in both story and discourse time.

Fig.5(a) and Fig. 5(b) represent how the viewer's knowledge changes over the different timelines. Fig. 5(b) shows the viewer's knowledge flow as he/she watches the film; it captures the viewer's realization of the fact that the twins (*Jeanne* and *Simon*) are siblings of *Nihad* (K4) in a late scene. A brief misunderstanding about the nature of *Abu Tarek*'s child (K2) and the gradual realization of *Nihad*'s fate is also captured. Such knowledge flows of the viewers are consistent with their emotional responses while watching the film. Viewers reinterpret the meanings of accumulated information when a sudden change is occurred in knowledge state, evoking suspense or surprise. Authors typically try to create such a change at the narrative's climax scene. Fig. 5(a), which depicts a potential knowledge flow of the viewers if the narrative is unfolded without flashbacks, shows a different knowledge flow; the viewers know about the identity of the twins' sibling much sooner and starts to have doubts about *Abu Tarek*'s child after learning the truth. Comparison between two timelines clearly shows that the knowledge flow of the viewers can be changed by reordering the events. This is a frequent activity in narrative creation, which grants the responsive controllability to the author.

Table 2. List of events (a) and information (b) for *Incendies*

Discourse order	Story order	(a) Event	ID	(b) Information
D7	S2	Nihad is born.	I1	Nawal is a mother of Nihad.
D13	S7	Orphanage is destroyed.	I2	Nawal is a mother of Jeanne and
D14	S8	Bus attacked by Christian terrorists.		Simon.
D17	S9	Nawal joins Islamic extremists.	I3	Abu Tarek raped Nawal.
D1	S10	Nihad is trained to become a soldier.	I4	Nawal gave birth to Abu Tarek's
D28	S11	Nihad becomes crazed with war.		children.
D19	S13	Nawal is sent to Kfar Ryat prison.	I5	Abu Tarek's children are twins.
D22	S14	Nawal becomes *the woman who sings*.	I6	Nihad has a tattoo on his heel.
D25	S15	Nawal is raped by Abu Tarek.	I7	Abu Tarek has a tattoo on his heel.
D26	S16	Nawal gives birth to Jeanne and Simon.	I8	Nihad is sent to an orphanage.
D31	I17	Nawal meets Chamseddine after release.	I9	National Party bombs the orphanage.
D34	S18	Nawal meets Nihad at the pool.	I10	National(N.) Party kills refugees.
D2	S22	Jeanne and Simon hears Nawal's will.	I11	Refugee camp becomes a ruin.
D21	S28	Jeanne meets former guard of Kfar Pyat.	I12	Nihad is sent to the refugee camp.
D27	S30	Jeanne and Simon meets former nurse of Kfar Ryat.	I13	Nihad became a soldier of Islamic resistance.
D29	S31	Simon searches for Nihad.	I14	Nihad is captured by N.Party.
D32	S33	Simon meets Chamseddine.	I15	Nihad became an executioner for
D33	S34	Janne and Simon get overwhelmed.		N.Party.
D36	S36	Nihad reads letters given by Jeanne and Simon.	I16	Executioner for N.Party is Abu Tarek.
			I17	Abu Tarek exiled to Canada.

(Unnecessary events are omitted.)

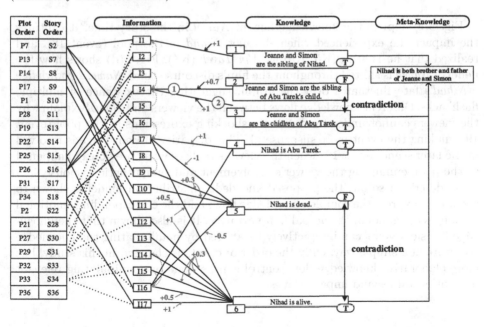

Fig. 4. Knowledge structure for *Incendies*. Event-information connection is show for *Nawal* (solid line) and *Jeanne Simon* (dotted line).

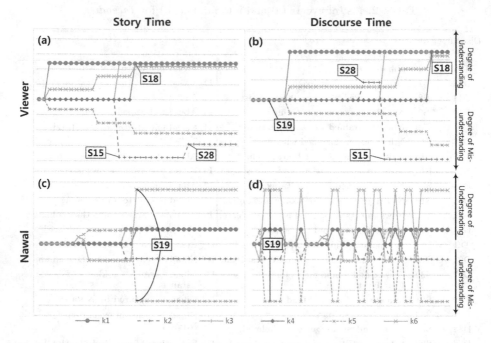

Fig. 5. Knowledge flow for viewer and *Nawal* with ordered event list as x-axis and degree of belief as y-axis, in story-time and in discourse-time

Fig. 5(c) depicts the knowledge flow of *Nawal* in the story-time. It captures the impact she experienced when she met *Nihad* in the pool (event 18), and realized that he is alive (K5, K6) as *Abu Tarek* (K4). Fig. 5(d) shows how the belief of *Nawal* is shifted throughout the film's discourse-time. *Nawal*'s knowledge of *Nihad*'s fate fluctuates over the graph, suggesting the existence of multiple flashbacks. Different knowledge flows between the viewers and *Nawal* explain why the viewers cannot understand *Nawal*'s shocking expressions at the pool (event 19), making the event more suspenseful. This disparity of knowledge is resolved in the later scene (event 18) when the viewers realizes what previously happened at the pool, enhancing the viewer's involvement and sympathetic response.

As described so far, the proposed knowledge distribution model is shown to accurately express the complex knowledge flows and the corresponding emotional responses of agents in the actual film narrative. It is also shown that the knowledge flows of agents can interactively be altered by manipulating the knowledge structure in a simple way. Only the order of events is changed in this study, but more elaborative knowledge flow control can be done by manipulating relevant perception values and impact values.

6   Conclusion

We proposed a knowledge distribution model that quantifies information/knowledge in a narrative and simulated the knowledge changes according to the development of events. We designed the model to practically support an author to create narratives. In this modeling framework, we first constructed the *knowledge structure* by connecting event, information, knowledge, and meta-knowledge, then calculated the *knowledge state* and plotted the *knowledge flow* using a probabilistic reasoning model. We also conducted a concrete case study with an actual cinematic narrative to show that our model clearly expresses the complicated aspects related to the knowledge flow.

The model we proposed in this paper has three advantages as follows.

First, with this model, it is possible to quantitatively analyze a narrative. The knowledge state of agents is formalized as the degree of belief, thus, it can be calculated by a proper computational method such as probabilistic reasoning model. A graph that expresses the knowledge flow quantitatively shows when and to what extent an agent's knowledge state changes. Second, this model allows better control of the knowledge flow by the author in an interactive manner. During the creating process, an author frequently revises the configuration of events and the attributes of information within the knowledge structure. Events and knowledge within the knowledge structure can frequently be added, altered, rearranged or deleted to modify knowledge flows, helping the author to more effectively create narratives. Third, our model can be extended by combining it with other narrative system. The model we proposed is flexible in that it can be combined with the AI planning method or the suspense model mentioned above. It is also possible to be used as an analytic tool, analyzing and categorizing famous narratives according to the pattern of knowledge flow. This work can contribute to narrative studies on theme and genre.

Our current model has several limitations. We are planning to address these limitations in future studies.

The first limitation is ignoring the fact that characters should act differently according to their roles and personalities. Because we assume the rational agent in our model, the difference among characters cannot be reflected in the reasoning process. It also cannot reflect how bias or errors influence the reader's reasoning. Secondly, for practical purpose, automation is needed to relieve author's cognitive load in building a knowledge structure. Two functions can be considered: automatic extraction of important information from events and link generation between information and knowledge. NLP studies have to be combined with a knowledge flow model for those functionalities. Finally, the studies on the internal relationships of information are needed. Based on the prior information, the meaning of newly obtained information can be altered. In many cases, the meaning of information is clearly revealed only if multiple pieces of supporting information are assembled. The variation of meaning using the internal relationships of information makes a pattern of knowledge flow found in many narratives. It should be investigated by analyzing various narratives.

References

1. Oatley, K., Green, M.C., Strange, J.J., Brock, T.C.: Narrative impact: Social and cognitive foundations. Narrative Impact: Social and Cognitive Foundations (2002)
2. Baxter, L.A., Braithwaite, D.O.: Engaging theories in interpersonal communication: Multiple perspectives. SAGE Publications, Incorporated (2008)
3. Howard, D.: How to Build a Great Screenplay: A Master Class in Storytelling for Film, 1st edn. St. Martin's Press, New York (2004)
4. Riedl, M.O., Young, R.M.: Narrative planning: balancing plot and character. Journal of Artificial Intelligence Research 39(1), 217–268 (2010)
5. Peinado, F., Cavazza, M., Pizzi, D.: Revisiting character-based affective storytelling under a narrative BDI framework. In: Spierling, U., Szilas, N. (eds.) ICIDS 2008. LNCS, vol. 5334, pp. 83–88. Springer, Heidelberg (2008)
6. Graesser, A.C., Singer, M., Trabasso, T.: Constructing inferences during narrative text comprehension. Psychological Review 101(3), 371 (1994)
7. Graesser, A.C., Millis, K.K., Zwaan, R.A.: Discourse comprehension. Annual Review of Psychology 48(1), 163–189 (1997)
8. Niehaus, J., Young, R.M.: A method for generating narrative discourse to prompt inferences. In: Proceedings of the Intelligent Narrative Technologies III Workshop, p. 7. ACM (2010)
9. Brewer, W.F., Lichtenstein, E.H.: Stories are to entertain: A structural-affect theory of stories. Journal of Pragmatics 6(5), 473–486 (1982)
10. Cheong, Y.-G., Young, R.M.: Narrative generation for suspense: Modeling and evaluation. In: Spierling, U., Szilas, N. (eds.) ICIDS 2008. LNCS, vol. 5334, pp. 144–155. Springer, Heidelberg (2008)
11. Bae, B.-C., Young, R.M.: Suspense? Surprise! or how to generate stories with surprise endings by exploiting the disparity of knowledge between a story's reader and its characters. In: Iurgel, I.A., Zagalo, N., Petta, P. (eds.) ICIDS 2009. LNCS, vol. 5915, pp. 304–307. Springer, Heidelberg (2009)
12. Ryan, M.L., Herman, D., Jahn, M.: Routledge Encyclopedia of Narrative Theory. Routledge (2005)
13. Rowley, J.: The wisdom hierarchy: representations of the dikw hierarchy. Journal of Information Science 33(2), 163–180 (2007)
14. Abell, P.: Narratives, bayesian narratives and narrative actions. Sociologica 1(3) (2007)
15. Good, I.J.: Good thinking: The foundations of probability and its applications. Univ. of Minnesota Press (1983)

Digital Museums of Cultural Heritages in Kyoto: The Gion Festival in a Virtual Space

Liang Li[1], Kyoko Hasegawa[1], Takahiro Fukumori[2], Wataru Wakita[1], Satoshi Tanaka[1], Takanobu Nishiura[1], Kozaburo Hachimura[1], and Hiromi T. Tanaka[1]

[1] College of Information Science and Engineering,
Ritsumeikan University, Japan
[2] Graduate School of Information Science and Engineering,
Ritsumeikan University, Japan

Abstract. We introduce studies on digital museums of cultural and artistic resources that originate primarily in Japan, conducted by Ritsumeikan University. These studies focus on digital archives of and exhibition techniques for the "objects" and "events" concerning the traditional cultural heritages in Kyoto, especially the Yamahoko Parade in the Gion Festival, using the latest technologies of high-precision 3D modeling, acoustic digital archiving, high-realistic sound filed recording and reproduction, visuo-haptic modeling, immersive display, and virtual reality.

1 Introduction

Digital museums, which use digital information technologies to measure, record, preserve, and display tangible and intangible cultural assets, have attracted increasing attention in the last two decades. The targets of digital museums have expanded from materials such as paintings, photographs, and books to three-dimensional (3D) objects such as Buddhist statues, sculptures, and architectural structures. In recent years, even intangible cultural assets such as dances, plays, and cultural events have been included as the targets of digital museum [1–3].

In this paper, we introduce studies carried out by four groups in our digital museum project at Ritsumeikan University. (1) K. Hachimura group constructed a CG content of the Virtual Yamahoko Parade and combine the motion and acoustics of the floats, crews, and spectators using virtual reality techniques. (2) S. Tanaka group created a visualization based on CG rendering of 3D point set data obtained from laser scanning of the original Funehoko. (3) T. Nishiura group digitally archived and reproduced the festival music signals (ohayashi) in the Gion Festival. (4) H. T. Tanaka group carried out digital archiving for large 3D woven cultural artifacts exhibition. They also developed a real-object-oriented visuo-haptic exhibition system for anisotropic reflection rendering of Ukiyo-e.

S. Yamamoto (Ed.): HIMI 2014, Part II, LNCS 8522, pp. 523–534, 2014.
© Springer International Publishing Switzerland 2014

2   Virtual Yamahoko Parade Experience System

This section describes the creation of the Virtual Yamahoko Parade and the development of the virtual experience system. The components of the VR contents were created as follows.

(1) Virtual Kyoto: The street model of "Virtual Kyoto" [4] was developed using various technologies and materials, such as geographic information system (GIS) data, cadastral maps, aerial photos, street photos, and landscape paintings. We used the model of part of Shijo Street (approximately 550 meters), which is extracted from Virtual Kyoto. It is reproduced along with the buildings and arcades on both sides of the street.

(2) CG floats: Six CG models of the floats (Naginatahoko, Kankohoko, Iwatoyama, Funehoko, Kitakannonyama, and Minamikannonyama) were created and introduced into the virtual environment. The CG models of Funehoko and Kankohoko were built from the 3D shape measurements of their miniatures (1:11 scale). The 3D CG models of Naginatahoko and Kitakannonyama were created from measured drawings. The CG models of Iwatoyama and Minamikannonyama were created by modifying the Minamikannonyama model. The textures of the floats were made by capturing photos of the floats during the festival.

(3) CG crews: Four kinds of CG parade crews belonging to Funehoko and Iwatoyama were created: hikikata who pull the floats; ondotori who direct the floats; kurumakata who control the traveling direction and the start-stop movement of the floats; and hayashikata who play ohayashi music on traditional Japanese instruments on the hayashibutai. We created CG models of the hikikata, ondotori, kurumakata, and hayashikata crews by 3ds max (Autodesk) and transformed them into Cal3D format to import to Vizard. Using a motion capture technique, we obtained the body motion data given to each character model performing actual actions. We captured a variety of the motions performed by the Funehoko crews who participated in our experiments. The textures of the costume for each character were created from photographs of the costumes actually used.

(4) Crowd simulation: Every year, over 150,000 spectators from all around the world visit Kyoto to watch the parade. To recreate the atmosphere of the festival, it is very important to reproduce the spectators who gather to watch the event. We arranged approximately 1,500 characters on both sides of Shijo Street in Virtual Kyoto in an attempt to represent the crowds. Idle motions and walking animations were randomly added to these characters.

(5) Music and sound: We employed a multi-point measurement technique to record and reproduce the parade music played with traditional instruments of drum, flute, and bell. On parade day, we also used the same technology to collect acoustic data by recording audio sources such as creaking sounds of the wheels of the floats, speaking voices of the spectators, and noises made by the crowds [5].

The Virtual Yamahoko Parade content (Figure 1) can be displayed on a large-scale immersive 3D display system with a cylindrical screen, installed at the College of Information Science and Engineering at Ritsumeikan University. Users

Fig. 1. The CG Yamahoko Parade

of the system can change their viewpoint in real time while viewing the Virtual Yamahoko Parade. The user interface devise is a gamepad or a Kinect motion sensor.

We also developed a "Virtual Yamahoko Parade Experience System," by which users are able to experience a virtual parade as if they are actually sitting on a float in the parade.

We collected route and acceleration data by using a GPS logger (BT-Q1000eX, Qstarz) and four acceleration sensors (WAA-006, Wireless Technologies, Inc.) during Hikizome, the rehearsal parade on July 13, and the actual parade on July 17, 2012. The sampling rates of the GPS logger and acceleration sensors were 5 Hz and 50 Hz, respectively. The data captured by the acceleration sensors were transmitted and recorded through Bluetooth technology to a laptop computer (CF-N9, Panasonic) attached under a wooden bench on the hayashibutai. The acceleration sensor recorded the accelerations on three perpendicular axes, the angular velocity around these axes, and time information. We also captured the front view from the hayashibutai with a 3D video camera (AG-3DA1, Panasonic) during the rehearsal parade. We did not set up the camera during the actual parade in order to protect the parade heritage.

We introduced a 6-DOF vibration system to reproduce the rolling and vibration. The system is driven by six electric actuators that provide translation in the three perpendicular axes combined with rotation around the three perpendicular axes of the 3D Cartesian coordinate system. The system takes six parameters for input: displacement of x, y, and z in millimeters, and pitch, roll, and yaw in radians. For the input into the vibration system, we transformed the acceleration and angular velocity data into displacement and angle data, respectively.

We integrated vibration, sound, and 3D vision to build the virtual Yamahoko Parade Experience System (Figure 2). We set up three 55-inch 3D monitors (LM9600, LG Electronics), which support line-by-line 3D signals with polarizing (passive) 3D eyeglasses, in front of the vibration system. We also set up five

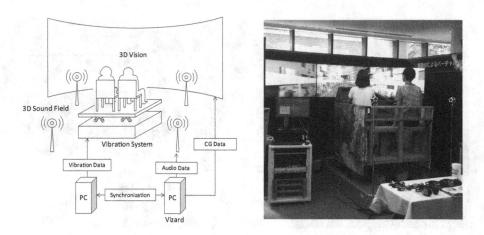

Fig. 2. The Virtual Yamahoko Parade Experience System

non-directional speakers (3D-032, Dr. Three Co., Ltd.) and a subwoofer (YST-SW010, Yamaha) to construct a 5.1 surround-sound environment.

3   Visualization of the Funehoko Float

The data obtained from laser scanning of a 3D object generally consists of a high-density 3D point set over the surface of the object. We have applied the new technique of particle-based rendering [6] to this 3D point set data. We then created a clear and high-quality transparent visualization of the outer form and internal structure of the Funehoko float from the Gion Festival.

Transparent visualization has the advantage of allowing the easily comprehensible representation of the Funeboko's internal structure, which would not be visible when looking at a photograph or the real thing. Previous transparent visualizations using 3D point set data followed two steps, first employing polygonization by joining up the points, and then sorting the polygons along the line of sight and rendering them transparently in order of depth. However, in the first step some of the points must be discarded, and in the second step if there is overlap between the generated polygons this often results in an incorrect visualization. In contrast, with the particle-based rendering method employed here, the point set can be used as is in its entirety in the visualization, and there is no need to sort points or polygons. An accurate transparent visualization can therefore be easily attained. Furthermore, with particle-based rendering, even if point set data for the various structural elements is collected separately, by simply combining the point sets the visualizations can be merged.

Laser scanning of the Funehoko float was conducted in 2010 and 2011, before, during, and after the Gion Festival. The main structure, axles, and wheels were scanned separately at different locations. The scanning equipment used was Leica's Scan Station 2. The subject was scanned multiple times from various angles, and the scanning data finally combined and organized with point set management software.

The shape of the subject according to the laser measurements was stored as 3D point set data. The point sets for the main structure, the axles, and the wheels can be viewed with Leica's 3D point set reading software, Cyclone Viewer Pro. The size of the point sets is approximately 10,000,000 points for the outer surface (including the surrounding fence); 1,000,000 points for the axle, and 1,000,000 points for each wheel.

We carried out the tasks of removing noise and unwanted sections of data, joining up the outer surface, axles, and wheels, and filling gaps in the point set using INUS Technology's point set processing software, Rapidform XOS. For the task of supplementing gaps in the point set, we manually constructed a polygon mesh for the missing areas and then created the additional points by resampling over these areas.

The procedure for visualization with particle-based rendering is as follows: (1) Generate or obtain 3D points distributed over the flat or curved surface to be visualized. (2) Divide the 3D point set from (1) into random groups. For each group, create an image by projecting particles onto a screen while conducting occlusion processing at the pixel level. We will refer to the number of groups as the "repeat level". (3) Take an average of the brightness values for each pixel across all groups to determine the final pixel brightness values.

By using particle-based rendering, color information for particles at different distances from the viewer can be shown in the correct proportions in the final image. As a result, transparent visualization of the internal 3D structure can be carried out with an accurate sense of depth. With previous CG techniques, internal 3D structure was visualized by (for example) ordering and reordering polygons along the line of sight and displaying them transparently according to depth. But there can be some uncertainty about the ordering of polygons, since they have their own discrete dimensions, and this can cause an inaccurate visualization or an increase in calculation time. With particle-based rendering, polygon reordering is replaced with a probabilistic processing method, and this problem is solved.

In principle, if all of the several hundred parts of the Funehoko were scanned and 3D point-set data obtained for them individually, it would be possible to perform particle-based rendering with this scanning data alone. However, we have taken a different approach here. To begin with, in the case of the axles, wheels, and main structure described above, we used laser scanning data. But for the other parts of the float, we resampled a polygon mesh created manually with modeling software to generate artificial point set data. Then we combined the two types of data and applied particle-based rendering with the entire data set.

The results of implementing particle-based rendering using 3D point sets corresponding to the outer surface, axles, wheels, and internal components of the Funehoko are shown in Figure 3. As shown in the figure, the outer shape and the internal 3D structure of the Funeboko have been clearly visualized. Since (unlike

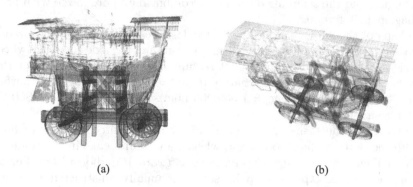

(a)   (b)

Fig. 3. Transparent visualization of the Funehoko: (a) repeat level 50 and (b) repeat level 100

when using polygonization) no points are discarded, an accurate visualization of the outer surface has been achieved. In Figure 3 (a), a repeat level of 50 was used, while a repeat level of 100 was used in Figure 3 (b); as the repeat level is increased, the transparency effect increases, while the outline of each element is emphasized.

4   High-Realistic Recording and Reproductions for the Sound Fields of the Gion Festival

The ohayashi of the Gion Festival is played with bells, flutes, and drums. The performers called the hayashikata, composed of approximately eight bell players, ten flutists, and two drummers, play the music following the beat of the drums (Figure 4).

To make high-quality measurements and high-fidelity reproductions of the acoustic sound field of the ohayashi in the Gion Festival, we recorded enhanced sounds of the instruments, ambient sounds, and sounds inside the floats during the parade.

In archiving the ohayashi of the Gion Festival, it is necessary to acquire high-quality sounds of the instruments at the time of recording and to avoid processing the recorded audio sources as much as possible so as to prevent target signals from being distorted. Specifically, it is essential to install the recording equipment, such as microphones, at the locations where the energy of the sounds of each instrument is secured at a maximum level during recording sessions. For this purpose, recordings in this project were conducted based on a multipoint measurement technique, in which the installation locations of the directional microphones (ECM-66B) were selected experimentally in order to enhance the sounds of each instrument. We installed the microphones in various locations on the condition that they would not be cumbersome for the performers. By installing microphones immediately beneath the drums and bells and placing pin microphones on the chest of the flute players, we secured the energy of the sounds of each instrument. We also set up acoustic absorbents throughout the room so as to avoid picking up undesired sounds such as vibration noise from the floor and walls. Furthermore, for the sake of acquiring high-fidelity sounds of the bells and drums that produce high sound pressure levels, we recorded them with a sampling frequency of 96 kHz and a quantization bit rate of 24 bits.

In an attempt to create high-fidelity reproductions of the ohayashi of the Gion Festival, we conducted high-quality recordings of ambient crowd sounds on the day of yoiyama, or the eve of the yamahoko parade, during the Gion Festival. We recorded ambient sounds while walking through the crowds and carrying nondirectional microphone equipment (SONY: PCM-M10). The recording was done with a sampling frequency of 48 kHz and a quantization bit rate of 16 bits.

We carried out a surround recording of the ohayashi inside a float as it was drawn through the city of Kyoto during the parade. There were constraints on placing the recording equipment because there are about thirty performers occupying this small space during the parade. We put five pieces of equipments (SONY: PCM-M10) under the beams where the performers were seated. We recorded the ohayashi at a sampling frequency of 48 kHz and a quantization rate of 16 bits to enable a long recording time with the equipment's small battery. We succeeded in capturing the surround sound of the ohayashi as well as the creaking and vibrating sounds made by the floats.

Fig. 4. Recording the ohayashi

5   A Digital Archiving for Large 3D Woven Cultural Artifacts Exhibition

In Gion Festival, the boat-shaped Funehoko float is especially noteworthy for its decorative woven cultural artifacts. The decorations used for the floats include embroidery of various materials-silk, gold thread, cotton, glass, felt-and their texture is quite complex. Cotton is stuffed into the embroidery which makes the fabric stand out in marked 3D relief pattern with complex reflection properties.

Moreover, because the 3D woven cultural artifacts are so large, approximately 1 × 3 m, the measurements must be done in sections to get an accurate reading. Therefore, in order to simplify the measurement and modeling, development of a new measurement system is needed. Also a development of a new system for digitally displaying multisensory full-scale, real-time, and interactive representations of the large 3D woven cultural artifacts is needed. Therefore, we digitally archived large 3D woven cultural artifacts used to decorate the Funehoko float in the Gion Festival.

5.1 Measurement and 3D Modeling of Large 3D Woven Cultural Artifacts

Left of Figure 5 shows our measurement system of large 3D woven cultural artifacts [7]. We installed a track on the floor and set up a 1-meter-high trolley the runs left and right on the track. We then mounted the laser scanner on top of the trolley (see left of Figure 5). This setup should permit stable 3D modeling while maintaining a constant distance of 1 m between the scanner and object (each shot is 300 × 200 mm) without in any way perturbing the object. The laser range scanner must be capable of sliding 5 m in the lateral direction and 1.5 m in the vertical direction. Thinking ahead of the joints when integrating the images, the 3D particle modeling was done at a resolution of 320 × 240 points while shifting 20 cm in the lateral direction and 15 cm in the vertical direction. After redundant points are eliminated and the interpolation processing is performed to fill holes, point cloud data is converted to ortho-images (see right of Figure 5), and subjected to image-based alignment in order to hold down costs of integration.

Finally, each ortho-images are aligned and integrated into a single image. Figure 6 shows integrated images. Each size of images is 5000 × 1500 pixels, and resolution is 0.7 mm per pixel.

5.2 Exhibition System of Large 3D Woven Cultural Artifacts

We developed a full-scale exhibition system of large 3D woven cultural artifacts (see left of Figure 7). The screen resolution is 5760 × 2160 pixels, and the resolution of the rendered model is 5000 × 1500 points. Stereoscopic viewing is achieved with the side-by-side method (split into upper and lower screens with 12-screen control). Also we developed a visuo-haptic exhibition system of large 3D woven cultural artifacts supporting direct touch with SPIDAR (see right of Figure 7). The accuracy of SPIDAR is very good near the center of the movable range of the grip, but deteriorates near the periphery of the grip range. Consequently, in landscape-oriented multiple display environments, the tensioned string remains taut and the object is sharply focused only in the central portion of the display. Moreover, the longer the string becomes, the more the initial tension must be increased so the string does not become slack, and this can cause the system to operate sluggishly. In the present system, we set up one screen that is within easy

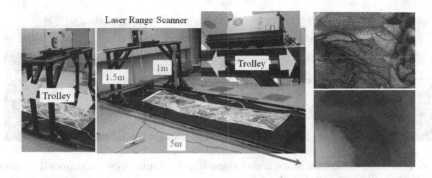

Fig. 5. 3D measurement system and ortho-images (color map and height map)

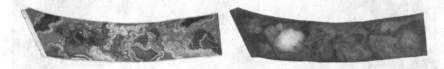

Fig. 6. Integrated color map and height map of large 3D woven cultural artifact

reach of the viewer at an angle to make it easier to operate. The SPIDAR is controlled in 1 KHz. The SPIDAR grip is connected to the each motor with attached encoder by tensioned string, and the position of the grip is calculated from the length of the string. By adjusting the tension of the string controlling each motor, force can be applied to any size or direction, which enables representation of the shape and tactile sense when touching a virtual object.

In future work, we plan to realize more real-time rendering and real-time deformation. Also we plan to develop a multi-finger haptic device and realize more real haptic interaction.

6 A Real-Object-Oriented Visuo-Haptic Exhibition System for Anisotropic Reflection Rendering of Ukiyo-e

The "ukiyo-e" is a typical example of a tangible cultural property from the modern Japanese era. Basically, an ukiyo-e is a "woodblock faithfully carved from a rough sketch and printed with coloring material." The coloring materials used for ukiyo-e are pigments obtained from plants, shells, and minerals. Mica, gold dust, and whitewash ("gofun") are used to impart a shiny, transparent, or three-dimensional appearance. A "baren" is used to print the pigments into the fiber of Japanese paper to impart color into the woodblock prints. Japanese paper is made from the "kozo" plant (paper mulberry), which has elongated fibers, whose irregular surface affects the way the surface of the paper reflects light. This imparts a complex anisotropic reflective property to the ukiyo-e, resulting to differing reflections depending on the direction of view. Also, different methods of printing are used for the ukiyo-e, so that it can display three-dimensionality

Fig. 7. Full-scale exhibition system and visuo-haptic display system supporting direct touch of large 3D woven cultural artifact

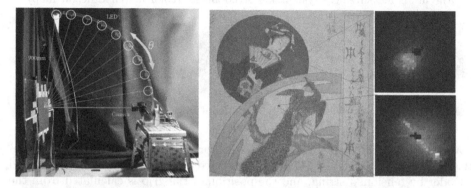

Fig. 8. Portable anisotropic reflection measurement system (PARMS) and anisotropic reflectance of the ukiyo-e

even though it is a flat-looking woodblock. One method used for printing is called "kara-zuri," wherein the paper is rubbed without using coloring material to result in an uneven surface, which combined with the texture of the Japanese paper, imparts a shadowy or three-dimensional appearance. In the same way, ukiyo-e painted using the "kira-zuri" method, which uses mica, reflects a glint of light when viewed at an angle, clearly showing the beauty of the mica used in the background. Thus, viewers can only appreciate the complex reflective properties of the ukiyo-e once they hold it in their hands and view it from different angles. The way ukiyo-e is displayed in art galleries and museums, however, make it difficult for viewers to actually hold and view it from different angles. Therefore, in this research, we studied and developed a digital exhibition system for experiencing the anisotropic reflective property of ukiyo-e.

We measured the BRDFs by PARMS [8] (see left of Figure 8). Right of Figure 8 shows the two type BRDFs. In the field where is pigment (green area), the anisotropic reflection is weak. The highlight centralize a point. In the field where is paper (red area), a strong anisotropic reflection phenomena can be observed. The highlight distribute along a line. These mean that we need to construct two shading models and blend them together to render the appearance of ukiyo-e.

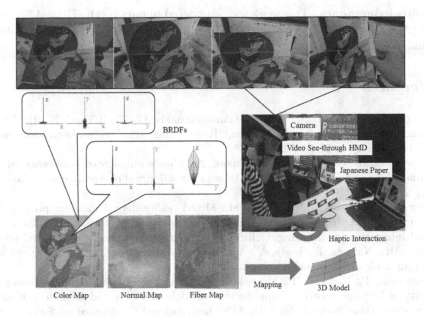

Fig. 9. Real-object-oriented ukiyo-e exhibition interface

We developed a real-object-oriented ukiyo-e exhibition interface (see Figure 9). As mentioned above, the ukiyo-e model uses two-dimensional images inferred from BRDF, surface texture information, and fiber characteristic information based on an analysis of HDR images of the ukiyo-e taken with light coming from different directions.

We used SONY HMZ-T2 for head mounted display (HMD). In this system, the viewer wears an HMD mounted with a camera, and when he/she looks at a real Japanese paper on his/her hand through the image on the camera, a CG of the ukiyo-e that corresponds to the shape of the Japanese paper is superimposed on the paper. In this study, we used AR Toolkit to infer the shape of the Japanese paper and perform superimposition. The Japanese paper has markers, and the NURBS curve was generated from the corner points of the markers in order to infer the three-dimensional shape of the Japanese paper. Next, the color map, normal map, and fiber map of the ukiyo-e were then mapped on the inferred 3-D surface to create a graphic rendering based on the BRDF information. Position of light source and viewpoint or viewing line direction were set at a fixed position, and shading of each fragment unit was performed based on the tilt and 3-D shape of the Japanese paper, and on the surface texture and anisotropic reflectance of the modeled ukiyo-e. This enables the viewer to experience the anisotropic reflective property of the ukiyo-e by tilting and bending the Japanese paper in different directions interactively.

Acknowledgements. This work was supported in part by the Digital Museum Project in the Ministry of Education, Culture, Sports, Science and Technology, Japan.

References

1. Magnenat-Thalmann, N., Foni, N., Papagiannakis, G., Cadi-Yazli, N.: Real time animation and illumination in ancient Roman sites. The International Journal of Virtual Reality 6, 11–24 (2007)
2. Papagiannakis, G., Magnenat-Thalmann, N.: Mobile augmented heritage: enabling human life in ancient Pompeii. The International Journal of Architectural Computing 2, 395–415 (2007)
3. Tanikawa, T., Narumi, T., Hirose, M.: Mixed reality digital museum project. Yamamoto, S. Ed.: Human interface and the management of information. Information and Interaction for Learning, Culture, Collaboration and Business, 248–257 (2013)
4. Yano, K., Nakaya, T., Isoda, Y.: Virtual Kyoto: exploring the past, present and future of Kyoto. Nakanishiya, Kyoto (2007)
5. Fukumori, T., Nishiura, T., Yamashita, Y.: Digital archive for Japanese intangible cultural heritage based on reproduction of high-fidelity sound field in Yamahoko Parade of Gion Festival. In: 13th ACIS International Conference on Software Engineering, Artificial Intelligence, Networking and Parallel/Distributed Computing, pp. 549–554 (2012)
6. Koyamada, K., Sakamoto, N., Tanaka, S.: A particle modeling for rendering irregular volumes. In: 10th EUROS/UKSim International Conference on Computer Modelling and Simulation, pp. 372–377 (2008)
7. Wakita, W., Tanaka, H.T.: Digital archiving of large 3D woven cultural artifacts. In: 33rd Annual Conference of the European Association for Computer Graphics, pp. 21–22 (2012)
8. Takeda, Y., Hara, J., Wakita, W., Sakaguchi, Y., Tanaka, H.T.: Development of a portable anisotropic reflectance measurement system for modeling and rendering of bidirectional texture functions. ACM SIGGRAPH 2012 Posters 38 (2012)

Polyhedron Network Model
to Describe Creative Processes

Tetsuya Maeshiro[1] and Midori Maeshiro[2]

[1] University of Tsukuba
[2] Federal University of Rio de Janeiro

Abstract. This paper proposes a description of creative process as a combination of emotive thinking and explicit knowledge thinking. We analyze music composition process as a creative process. Specifically, we define five facets to describe the music composition process to capture different aspects of composition. A facet is a perspective to view the musical piece. The perspective is different for composers and performers. Two musical pieces composed by a professional composer are described using the proposed model and analyzed. Results indicate the existence of two types of decision makings.

1 Introduction

This paper proposes a model to describe creative process as a combination of emotive thinking and explicit knowledge thinking. We analyze music composition process as a creative process. Specifically, we define the facets to describe the music composition process to capture different aspects of composition. A facet is a perspective to view the musical piece.

Human being is skillful at creating new concepts and ideas, and imagining non-existing conditions. These abilities are mainly related with sensitivity and emotion. On the other hand, computer system is adept at storing large amount of data. Although executions of describable operations and numerical computations are also advantages of computers, they are not relevant to this paper's topic. It is the author's assumption that during the thinking process by human beings, 40 to 50 % is related to sensitivity, treating nonverbal information and imagination, and the rest, 50 to 60 %, treats verbal concepts and explicit knowledge. The model presented in this paper assumes that sole use of either sensitivity or explicit knowledge does not enable the generation of new ideas, but simultaneous employment of both abilities are essential [1]. Conventional research on knowledge representation focused on the explicit knowledge. The proposed model is an attempt to unify the two kinds of thinking process.

This paper analyses the composition process of two musical pieces composed by a professional composer, treating the composition process as a sequence of decision makings. Causal relationships among decisions is non-sequential, although it is linear in temporal base. Decisions are basically parallel, with ramifications and convergences.

S. Yamamoto (Ed.): HIMI 2014, Part II, LNCS 8522, pp. 535–545, 2014.
© Springer International Publishing Switzerland 2014

Music composition process is adequate since (i) it is a creative process, and because of its artistic nature, sensitivity and emotion is strongly involved; (ii) there is a solid foundation of music theory, differing from other Arts fields such as paitings, sculptures and dances. Harmony of tonal music, for instance, involves mathematics of sound frequencies. The liberty and amount of sensitivity that is involved in music composition is higher than engineering process, industrial design and product design, for example, whith have strong theoretical bases. These are the reason to treat music composition.

Musical score is the de facto representation of musical pieces. Musical score encompasses every aspect of the musical piece, and it describes what to be performed, how to be performed, and composer's intentions. Everything is in the score, as some say. John Cage once said that by looking at the music sheet, one can judge the composer's talent, but not by listening to the performance of a musical piece. Music composition process involves a wide range of fields, and the list of fields depends on the music style. Even limiting to fields directly related to music, a composer should be familiar with many disciplines of musical theory inclluding Harmony, acoustics of musical instruments, and genre-dependent articulations of each musical instrument.

We treat the representation model of knowledge included in musical pieces. Many works on music analysis have been published, including the description model of music structure. For instance, Generative Theory of Tonal Music (GTTM) [3] is a model to describe the structure of musical pieces based on linguistic theory. Conventional works try to represent this type of knowledge as the static entity, usually treating as a structure of notes, chords and groups of these elements [3]. Typical structure is hierarchical, where the whole musical piece is positioned at the top of the hierarchy.

The representation model presented here focus on the creation process or composition process, from a blank music sheet to the final work. This is a "creation history" of musical piece. Obviously if the data on intermediate process is absent, the representation will only be about the final status of the music. However, automatic recording of intermediate process should not be a problem in near future thanks to the recent spread of Digital Audio Workstations (DAWs), as the composition task is increasingly executed on computers and not with paper and pencil.

The disclosure of description of intermediate composition process is useful for both composers and players. For composers, it is valuable to overview and clarify his own composition process to improve the composed opus, besides the benefit to reorganize his ideas. For players, the acquisition of background and underlying phylosophy is invaluable, because deeper understanding of musical piece is fundamental and crucial for good execution. Before the execution, every music player analyzes the musical piece he/she will perform. During the analysis, players investigate every note and their context, their raison d'être, and instructions on execution indicated by the composer.

The proposed method differs from conventional works because the musical piece is represented by a temporal sequence of decisions. Such a creation history is more valuable than static structures generated by conventional methods due to reasons discussed before.

2 Model

Decisions executed during music compositions are described using the Hyper-network model explained in this section. Relationships among decisions are also specified by the model.

The proposed model is extended from hypergraph [5], which has more representation power than conventional knowledge representation models that are based on graph [4]. The main difference is the capability to represent N-ary relationships and the property of duality. The proposed model follows basic definitions of semantic networks, where a node is connected to other nodes (1) to specify the nodes or (2) when nodes are related by some relationship.

The model to represent the decision making process, the hypernetwork model [7], is extended from the bipartite representation of the hypergraph [5]. The hypergraph model, on the other hand, has more representation capability than conventional knowledge representation models that are based on graph [4], such as semantic network [6], frame, and ER-model [8]. Conventionally used decision sequence representation is also a graph. Basically, the hypernetwork model follows basic definitions of semantic networks, where a node is connected to other nodes (1) to specify the nodes or (2) when nodes are related by some relationship.

A uniqueness of the hypernetwork model is the existence of three types of description elements, equivalent to the types of nodes. Graph and hypergraph models consist of nodes and links connecting the nodes. In decision sequence representation, a node represents a decision, and a link connects two or more decisions in sequence relationship. A link of the graph model can connect only two decisions, and a link of the hypergraph (hyperlink) connects any number of decisions. The bipartite representation converts the links into nodes, denoted relation nodes, hence two types of node exist: the vertex node and the relation node. The vertex node serves to represent decisions (entities), and the relation node to describe relationships among decisions. An analysis of knowledge property, however, indicates that a third type of node is necessary, the attribute node, to specify the properties of vertex nodes and relation nodes. Therefore, conventional representation models present at least two flaws: (1) relationships among multiple entities cannot be represented, and (2) representation is incomplete since attributes are not provided. The hypernetwork model resolves both problems.

In the context of decision representation, details or properties of a concept represented by a vertex node can be specified in two ways: by attachment of attribute nodes, or by relating to other vertex nodes through relation nodes. Combination of the two descriptions is also possible. The attribute node exists to specify any of three node types. Table 1 indicates the connectivity constraints among three node types. Two connections are prohibited: between vertex node and vertex node, and between relation node and relation node, constraint imposed from their role in hypergraph. Table 1 is symmetrical on diagonal axis

Table 1. Connectivity among vertex node, relation node and attribute node

	Vertex node	Relation node	Attribute node
Vertex node	—	Connect	Connect
Relation node	Connect	—	Connect
Attribute node	Connect	Connect	Connect

although the directionality of links depends on the context and what the network represents.

In order to represent decisions in music composition, we use the text description of decisions involved during the composition process. The text is written after each work stage defined by the composer himself, written by the composer himself. The number of stages depends on the composer's work style and musical piece being composed, as some pieces take years to be accomplished. Therefore, a stage is anything with varied work amount, number of created and edited notes, and working time durations. In other words, a stage corresponds to the amount of composition work between subsequent intermissions defined by the composer.

In each intermission and after the completion of composition, the composer reviews the modifications since the previous version of the music piece, enumerating every single alterations. Then the composer writes the Decision List Report, a text explaining each modification points, describing the decision type and the details. The decision type should be chosen from (a) Theoretical, (b) Selective, and (c) Intuitive. Theoretical decisions denote decisions based on Music theory. Empirical (heuristic) foundations are excluded because they are empirical and lack theoretical bases. The second type and the third type are used when multiple options exist. It is possible that a decision is theoretical and simultaneously either selective or intuitive, when multiple options exist. The selection of a theory is chosen from multiple possibilities or intuitively. Only one type is associated with decisions, however.

Moreover, it is important that the decision maker (composer) is experienced, and even if the decisions are superficially apparent as random choice, the choices are based on experience accumulated by the composer. Therefore, selective choices are non-random and intuitive, which are most of the times correct or adequate [2], completely different from novices' shots in the dark.

In order to homogenize the granularity of decision sizes, each decision description is analyzed to subdivide into smaller decisions or to join with other decisions depending on the explanation text. Two types of decisions exist, (1) Framework decisions and (2) Component decisions, differing on the extent affected by decisions. Framework decisions are global decisions, and affect the entire musical piece, such as tempo and instruments used. Component decisions are local decisions, modifying passages or a part of musical piece. Basically a component decision consists of a single modification on a single region of an instrument part. A region may contain any number of notes, between a single note, a single chord, or dozen of notes encompassing multiple measures. It may not involve any notes.

The next step is the generation of hypernetwork representation of extracted decisions. The hypernetwork model is explained in next section. The sizes of hypernetwork representation of all decisions are uniform, because the granularity of size of decisions are standardized in the previous step.

Then decisions are interconnected based on: Type-I: decision sequence, subdivided into Type-IA: Global order and Type-IB: Order within overlapped target region; Type-II: Overlap on target region (notes, measures, phrases, among others); Type-III: Identical element node (decision component); and Type-IV: Semantic relationship among element nodes (decision components). This connection process is semiautomatic using computer program. The Type-I connections generate sequence relationships among decisions. The second type of relationships, Type-II, connects decisions affecting at least one identical musical element. It connects multiple decisions that generate N-ary relationships, which are impossible to be generated using conventional representation models. The overlapped element is described in relationship entity, which also functions as a "concept" entity when a person reads the music score. Connections based on same musical element are used to connect multiple decisions if they contain identical elements. The hierarchical level of elements may differ in each decision. For instance, the composer refers to musical elements in other region to employ a variation of these elements. In this case, the hierarchical level of referred elements in decision structure will be different. In other cases, a same thematic element may be used multiple times, and the element description appearing in relevant decisions are linked.

The semantic connections, Type-IV, are based on semantic relationship among decision elements. The semantic relationship types used in our representation are: hierarchy of concept, hierarchy of target region, antonym (opposite concept), and synonym concept. Therefore, the identical connection is a special case of semantic connection.

The hierarchical relationship based on affected target region is generated automatically. Overlapped regions are excluded, as these are Type-II connections. Generation of antonym relationships is also automatic as it uses custom database which contains antonym concepts constructed manually from terms (words) present in decision descriptions.

A decision in a general form is a cause-result relationship. Multiple pre-status or precondition or facts and multiple post-status or postcondition are connected by a relationship that specifies the decision (Fig.1), thus a decision is an N-ary relationship, impossible to be represented by conventional knowledge representation models. A decision modifies the pre-status to generate the post-status. When adding new notes into a musical piece during composition, the pre-status is usually an empty set because it represents a blank sheet. Generally, the pre-status is varied because it depends on the recognition and interpretation of the composer.

It is possible to detection similar passages that is unable to be detected by other representation models. For instance, the passage shown in Fig.2 is the result of following decisions.

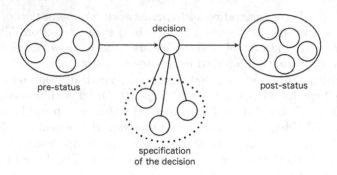

Fig. 1. Hypernetwork representation of a decision

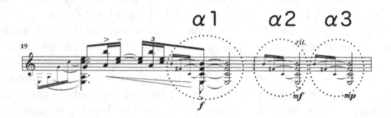

Fig. 2. Measures 19 – 20 of Music-Two

1. **D-1** After achieving the desired sharp boundary, the peak of the tension does not coincide with this boundary. Therefore, attach the tension peak to the bass boundary.
2. **D-2** Execute sudden shift to lower pitch to introduce unbalance.
3. **D-3** Introduce descending arpeggio with increasing sonority (f) to emphasize the unbalance that is deliberate.
4. **D-4** Repeat the descending gesture ($\alpha_1 \dots \alpha_3$) that causes an immediate release of tension in measure 20 before the formal recover of equilibrium in measure 21.

Fig.3 is the simplified representation of these decisions in cause-result relationship following the representation format of Fig.1. Decisions D-1 to D-3 are in sequence, while the decision D-4 is independent. Specifications of decisions are further specified, generating multi level structure. For instance, "descending arpeggio" of the decision D-3 is further specified because pitch and duration selections are also the results of composer's decision.

Fig.5 is a direct representation of measures 19 and 20 extracted from decisions using hypernetwork representation. Multiple viewpoints exist, where the three nodes (α_1, α_2, α_3) surrounded by a larger circle also function as a node of "tension release" and "re-tension" relationships. These decisions are the subdecisions

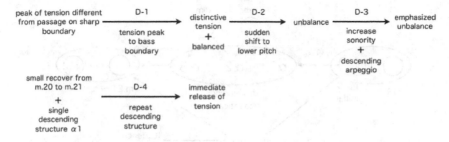

Fig. 3. Simplified representation of decisions D-1 to D-4

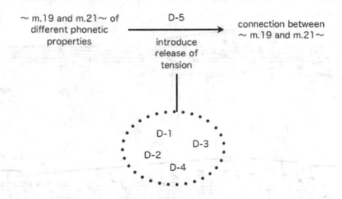

Fig. 4. Decision structure of decisions D1–D4

of a decision to release tension between until measure 19 and after measure 21 to achieve consistency of a single musical piece (Fig.4).

The description in Fig.5 is a conventional representation of musical structure and it focuses on the musical piece in its complete form, although it uses the hypernetwork model. On the other hand, the representation of decision structure (Fig.3) provides wider scope of background information, a new materials for performers to understand deeper the musical piece, resulting in better performance. These two structures are merged, and ability of viewpoint change allows better understanding of the musical piece.

The connection of elements based on similarity among decisions elucidates implicit relationships among musical elements, difficult and time consuming to be clarified by conventional music analysis methods. Fig.6 shows two regions, one of measures 19–20, and other of measures 32–34. These two regions were generated by identical decision, which is to introduce release of tension to the movement that the target passage connects, which are measures until 19 and measures after 21 in the first case, and measures until 32 and after 34 in the second case.

Detecting similar decisions is useful to analyze musical pieces and results in valuable information for the musical instrument players. Furthermore, similarity among decision sequences is more important than comparison of single decisions.

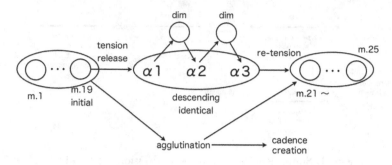

Fig. 5. Hypernetwork representation of relationships among elements involved in Fig.2

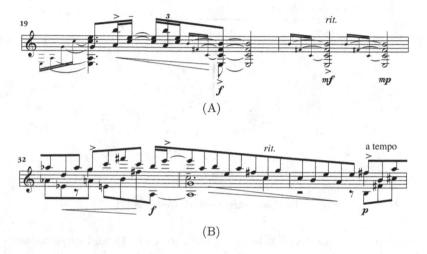

Fig. 6. Two passges that involve same decision, although their musical aspects are dissimilar

The computational cost of similarity detection among hypernetwork representations is nonpolynomial. However, we use a special purpose computer system, Starpack [9,10], customized to process hypernetwork representations. Starpack reduces the computational time to polynomial time by treating a set of decisions as a decision sequence.

3   Analysis and Discussions

We classify each decision element to the following five facets.

1. Decision type. Related to the process of decision making, and further classified to theoretical, selective and intuitive.
2. Concept. Composer's background idea, related to emotional aspect of decisions.
3. Structure. Related to music theory, which is explicit knowledge thinking.

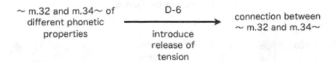

Fig. 7. Simplified representation of a decision behind the measure 33

4. Aesthetic. Mainly involving listeners, related to listening impression of executed music.
5. Playing technique. MAinly related to instrument players.

Two musical piecess, denoted Music-B1 and Music-B2, were analyzed. Music-B1 is for two violins, viola and violoncello, and consists of 39 measures. Music-B2, for clarinet Bb and fagotte, consists of 120 measures. composition of Music-B1 involved 41 main decisions. on the other hand, Music-B2 involved 16 main decisions. A main decision denotes a single decision that the composer makes as a unit. After the analysis of description of composition process by the composer, a main decision is subdivided into smaller decisions. Typically a main decision consists of 2 to 5 decisions.

Each decision is classified into one of five facets, besides the classification into theoretical and intuitive. Theoretical decisions use explicit knowledge, and intuitive decisions belong to sensitivity and emotional thinking process. Then the integration of all decisions offers a global view of a creation process that is a combination of emotional and explicit knowledge thinking processes.

Fig.8 shows the number of decisions extracted from Music B-1 and Music B-2. The number of decisions belonging to each facet is approximately similar. No decisions belonging to playing technique were detected, as technique related contents were not directly mentioned. However, playing techniques are indicated in musical score using conventional notations. It is interesting that playing technique is not involved in decisions to create musical piece, although this might be a particular case of analyzed musical pieces. since playing technique is annotated by the composer in music score, playing technique is important element in composed musical piece. However, it is not a factor to consider during the music creation process.

Another fact from Fig.8 is the weight on each facet that the composer devotes his attention. In this context, basic concept and musical structure have similar importance, i.e., emotional and explicit knowledge (verbal) thinking has approximately equal ratio. Specifically, the average value of emotional thinking is 50%, and verbal thinking is 60%, which are values very close to our initial assumption described in Introduction. This is a quantitative data that supports our basic assumption, and that both type of thinking process is involved in creative process of musical pieces.

Our previous analysis targeted stepwise composition process, where the composer wrote musical piece by small number of measures [7]. On the other hand, the composition process analyzed in this paper present different creation process,

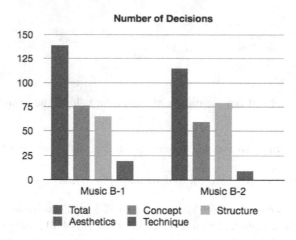

Fig. 8. Number of total decisions of Music B-1 and Music B-2. Number of decisions belonging to each of four facets except the decision type is also shown.

where the composer writes directly the best solution, with no significant modification of previously written parts. The composition involves very small after editing process, and passages written on the paper sheet is usually the definitive and final version with no further modifications. In this sense, it is more similar to the decision making process of experienced professional people [2].

Therefore, two types of decision making exist in musica composition process. The existence of a sequence of multiple decisions applied to the same passage is partially due to the lack of emergency in music composition task, which is fundamentally different from conditions encountered by firefighters, medical doctors and military commands. Such relaxation of constraints results in diversity of decision making process, and consequently of different creative process styles. Some composers do not postedit, while others executes a certain number of revisions.

This kind of information is missing in all available music sheets, but is of fundamental importance for instrument players. An interview survey to professional musical instrument players indicate that historic of every note and passage of musical piece is useful and helpful to understand the musical piece and generate images of musical piece to decide techniques and sonority to use when playing. In this context, an objective of the proposed description model is to provide representation of musical piece that musical instrument players are easy to understand. The five facets proposed in this paper are representations of a single set of facts and concepts. These facets are dependent to each other, and some elements of a facet are shared by other facet(s).

The proposed representation model is an attempt to represent two types of thinking, emotional and explicit knowledge, in order to analyze and understand the creative process. This paper focused on music composition process. The description was generated from a single person's creative process, but the explicit knowledge element can be implemented on computer systems, whose forte is a huge amount of storage. In the current stage, the interaction part should belong to human being. With this implementation, the proposed representation model can also be interpreted as the description of human computer interaction during creative processes.

References

1. Polanyi, M.: The Creative Imagination. Chemistry and Engineering News, 85–93 (April 25, 1966)
2. Klein, G.: Sources of Power: How People Make Decisions. MIT Press (1999)
3. Lerdahl, F., Jackendoff, R.S.: A Generative Theory of Tonal Music. MIT Press (1996)
4. Berge, C.: The Theory of Graphs. Dover (2001)
5. Berge, C.: Hypergraphs: Combinatorics of Finite Sets. North-Holland (1989)
6. Quillian, M.R.: Word concepts: a theory and simulation of some basic semantic capabilities. Behavioral Science 12(5), 410–430 (1967)
7. Maeshiro, T., Maeshiro, M., Shimohara, K., Nakayama, S.-i.: Hypernetwork model to represent similarity details applied to musical instrument performance. In: Jacko, J.A. (ed.) HCI International 2009, Part I. LNCS, vol. 5610, pp. 866–873. Springer, Heidelberg (2009)
8. Date, C.J.: An Introduction to Database Systems, 8th edn. Addison-Wesley (2003)
9. Maeshiro, T., Hemmi, H., Shimohara, K.: Ultra-fast Genome wide Simulation of Biological Signal Transduction Networks — Starpack. In: Frontiers of Computational Science, pp. 177–180. Springer (2007)
10. Hemmi, H., Maeshiro, T., Shimohara, K.: New Computing System Architecture for Scientific Simulations — Non CPU-oriented Methodology. In: Frontiers of Computational Science. Springer (2007)

3D CG Integral Photography Artwork Using Glittering Effects in the Post-processing of Multi-viewpoint Rendered Images

Nahomi Maki and Kazuhisa Yanaka

Kanagawa Institute of Technology, 1030 Shimo-ogino, Atsugi-shi, Kanagawa, 243-0292, Japan
{maki,yanaka}@ic.kanagawa-it.ac.jp

Abstract. Among various 3D display technologies, integral photography (IP) is one of the ideal 3D display systems because not only horizontal but also vertical parallax can be achieved through it without requiring users to wear special 3D glasses. Another advantage of IP is its applicability in material expression. In usual CG, in which rendering is carried out from one camera position, the glittering caused by the surface material is difficult to reproduce. As for users, they can perceive glittering when they move because each tiny convex lens on a fly's eye lens emits direction-dependent light. However, glittering is usually weak because the viewing zone of the IP display is not wide enough. Therefore, we propose a new method for implementing a glittering effect in the post-processing of images rendered for IP. A user can paint a large number of rendered images simultaneously and revise them with ease. We conduct experiments using a system that comprises a tablet PC with retina display and a fly's eye lens. When this method is applied to a motif of ice floating in air, which is part of an artwork entitled "Frozen Time," a strong glittering effect is obtained, especially when the tablet PC is held and tilted in various directions.

1   Introduction

Integral photography (IP) is an outstanding 3D display system through which not only horizontal but also vertical parallax can be achieved without requiring users to wear special 3D glasses. Thus, IP has an advantage that is similar to that of holography. However, IP is superior to holography in terms of the ease of electronic rewriting and color reproducibility. A simple IP system consisting of a liquid crystal display (LCD) and a fly's eye lens is shown in Figure 1. The light that changes directions is emitted from each minute convex lens, which forms a fly's eye lens (Figure 2). When the displayed image is seen from a fixed position with both eyes, a sense of depth is acquired as a result of binocular disparity. A sense of depth is also acquired through motion parallax when the position of the eye is moving even if the display is seen with only one eye.

Another advantage of IP is the glittering effect obtained if light goes into only one eye. This phenomenon could be attributed to binocular rivalry. Therefore, IP can also identify differences in materials. As a scene is rendered from a single camera position

S. Yamamoto (Ed.): HIMI 2014, Part II, LNCS 8522, pp. 546–554, 2014.
© Springer International Publishing Switzerland 2014

in non-stereoscopic CG, only a small part of the scene data is used. However, IP requires additional information from scene data because of its use of images rendered using a large number of camera positions. Therefore, various materials such as glittering material can be expressed by changing the angle from which a user views the image.

This advantage becomes remarkable especially when IP is carried out using a mobile device. A tablet device uses high-resolution LCD and can thus display high-quality 3D images. As such devices are small and lightweight, they can be carried anywhere at any time, thus allowing users to view 3D images without place and time restrictions. Furthermore, tablets are handheld devices and can thus be viewed from any direction. The binocular and motion parallax of an IP system facilitates an auto-stereoscopic view and allows the identification of materials. An advantage of the system is the transmission of 3D images through the Internet. Therefore, this system is a suitable device for producing media artwork.

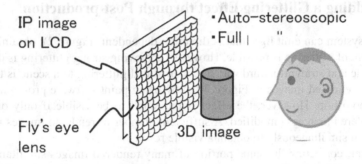

Fig. 1. Simple IP system

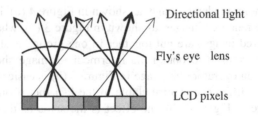

Fig. 2. Directional light

2   Method for Creating IP Images

The proposed method for creating IP images is an extension of an existing method [1–3]. We first describe the existing method as shown in Figure 3. When IP images are made using CG techniques, multi-viewpoint rendering shown in Figure 3 (a) is performed first. In this technique, the position and the angle of a virtual camera are changed regularly, and rendering is carried out from the camera position. Our original script controls the procedure. An MEL script can be utilized when Maya is used in rendering.

As shown in Figure 3 (b), the use of this method produces a rendered still image for every camera position. As the camera position moves on $n \times n$ grid points, n^2 rendered still images are obtained. With the typical value of n being 32, $n^2 = 1,024$ still images are obtained. Then, a single image called an "IP image," which is shown in Figure 3 (d), is synthesized from these images using an algorithm shown in Figure 3 (c). Subsequently, the IP image is displayed on a flat panel display such as an LCD. The displayed IP image is observed through a fly's eye lens, which is a two-dimensional array of small convex lenses. The fly's eye lens is called as such because of its similarity to the compound eye of insects. Then, an auto-stereoscopic image with both horizontal and vertical parallax can be observed.

3   Adding a Glittering Effect through Post-production

As an IP system can emit light that is direction dependent (Figure 2), obtaining a certain amount of glittering is possible. However, achieving strong glittering is difficult.

A simple and straightforward way to add artificial glittering to a scene is to modify one of the rendered images in Figure 3 (b) by using paint software programs such as Adobe Photoshop. However, the effect is too small to be visible if only one of the 1,024 rendered images is modified. A sufficient number of rendered images must thus be modified simultaneously to obtain a visible result.

However, correcting the same portion of many rendered images simultaneously is very time consuming for an operator. Thus, we introduce an intermediate image, which is a single image created by rearranging the original pixels of n' × n' adjacent rendered images.

A multi-viewpoint rendered image, as shown in Figure 4 (a), is created by connecting n × n discrete rendered images, as shown in Figure 3 (b), where n = 32. Then, n' × n' adjacent rendered images are put together in one group, as shown in Figure 4 (a). The pixels are rearranged to obtain the intermediate image shown in Figure 4 (b), where n' = 4. For an operator, the image in Figure 4 (b) is easier to handle than that in Figure 4 (a). This difference is attributable to the fact that if only one place is modified in the image in Figure 4 (b), the effect is the same as that when 16 places are modified in the picture shown in Figure 4 (a). The modified intermediate image in Figure 4(c) is then inverse-transformed to obtain the multi-viewpoint rendered image in Figure 4(d).

4   Experiment 1 (Coloring)

First, the effect in which the object appears colored only when seen from a certain direction was added using the aforementioned method.

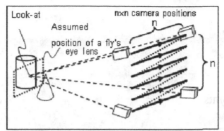

(a)   Multi-viewpoint rendering using our MEL script

n pixels

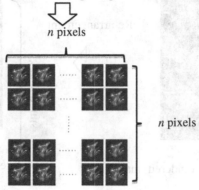

n pixels

(b) Images rendered from different viewpoints

To Fig. 4
From Fig. 4

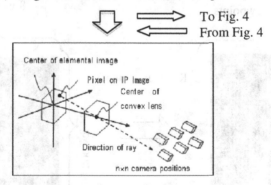

(c) Synthesis of IP image

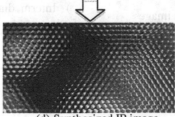

(d) Synthesized IP image

Fig. 3. Procedure of synthesizing an IP image

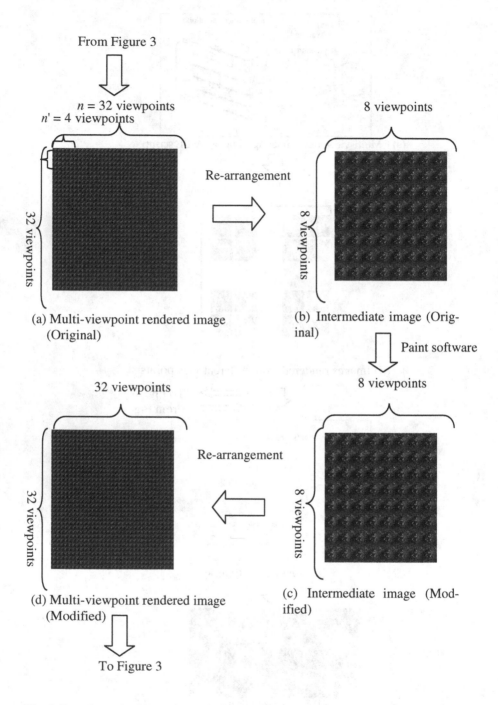

Fig. 4. Transformation into an intermediate image, modification, and inverse transformation

4.1   In the Case of an Intermediate Image Consisting of 2 × 2 Regions

To examine this effect, we conducted an experiment where $n = 32$ and $n' = 16$. In this case, the multi-viewpoint image is transformed into an intermediate image consisting of 2 × 2 regions, as shown in Figure 5 (a). The contrast in the lower left region of Figure 5 (a) increased. The contrast of the displayed image increases only when the displayed image is seen from the lower left.

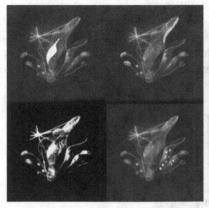

(a) Intermediate image consisting   (b) Synthesized and displayed IP image
   of 2 × 2 regions

Fig. 5. Case of $n = 32$ and $n' = 16$

4.2   In the Case of an Intermediate Image Consisting of 4 × 4 Regions

Figure 6 shows a case where $n = 32$ and $n' = 8$. In this case, the multi-viewpoint image is transformed into an intermediate image consisting of 4 × 4 regions, as shown in Figure 6 (a). The yellow component is enhanced in the four lower left regions, and the blue component is enhanced in three diagonal regions. Thus, the colors vary depending on the direction from which the image is viewed, as shown in Figure 5 (b).

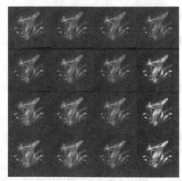

(a) Intermediate image cconsisting   (b) Synthesized and displayed IP image.
   of 4 × 4 regions.

Fig. 6. Case of $n = 32$ and $n' = 8$

5   Experiment 2 (Glittering)

The aforementioned method was applied to a picture of ice to produce a glitter effect.

Three columns from the right of the 4 × 4 domain image in Figure 7 were identified. The rightmost sequence was colored in white using paint software to represent the rightmost area of the ice. The same was done for the middle sequence, which represents the middle area of the ice that could glitter, and for the left sequence, which represents the leftmost area of the ice that could glitter.

As shown in the 4 × 4 image in Figure 7, the rightmost surface of the ice in the third image, the middle surface of the ice in the second image, and the left surface of the ice in the first image were all painted white to achieve a glittering effect. As a result, the different surfaces of the ice appear to glitter when the screen is tilted slightly.

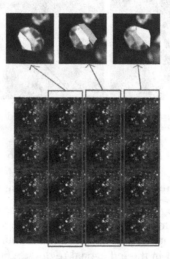

Fig. 7. Application of the glittering effect

6   Application to Artwork

We applied this technique to an artwork entitled "Frozen Time," which was derived from a short film called "Fossil Tears [4–5]." A star somewhere in the universe is expressed in the artwork. On this star, everything, even time, is frozen. The motifs are a crystallized fossil, a clock made out of opal, ice floating in the air, and others. We applied the aforementioned technique to achieve a glittering effect for each motif.

The obtained IP image was displayed on the 9.7-inch retina display (2048 × 1536 pixels) of a commercially available tablet computer and was observed through a commercially available minute fly's eye lens, which had a lens pitch of 1 mm. A ready-made fly's eye lens was used because the extended fractional view method was applied to synthesize the IP images. As a result, strong glittering was obtained. The glittering effect caused the ice to appear more crystallized than that when this technique was not applied. This result suggests the effectiveness of the technique.

Fig. 8. Artwork using the LCD of a tablet PC and a fly's eye lens: "Ice floating in the air" and part of "Frozen Time"

7   Discussion

We propose a technique for glittering a part of an object in the post-processing of rendered images.

A method that follows physical laws for making objects glitter is available. In this method, glittering is produced through the reflection and refraction on the surface of an object. The well-known ray tracing technique is suitable in creating the glittering effect through the proper placement of many light sources. However, this method has a drawback. As the viewing zone of IP systems is generally narrow, targets should have many surfaces whose normal vectors are slightly different from one another to make targets glitter within the narrow zone. However, setting the orientations of the surfaces in such a way that the reflected rays go within the narrow viewing zone is difficult, especially when many objects are present. In addition, the fact that the path of reflected light depends on not only the normal vector of the surface but also the z-coordinates of the surface increases the complexity of the problem. Another problem is the increase in rendering time in proportion to the number of surfaces. This method will become feasible if these problems are solved.

8   Summary and Conclusion

We proposed a novel technique for IP, in which visual effects such as glittering are applied artificially by modifying multi-viewpoint rendered images. We verified the effectiveness of the proposed method by applying it to an artwork entitled "Frozen Time."

The strong glittering we obtained caused the image of the ice to appear more crystallized than that when the technique was not applied. The effect was especially visible when the tablet PC was held and tilted in various directions. These results indicate the effectiveness of the proposed technique. Physically impossible and ever-changing visual effects, as well as previously impossible expressions, can be achieved using the proposed technology. The technique described in this paper is expected to be useful in extending the range of artistic expression using IP.

References

1. Yanaka, K.: Integral photography using hexagonal fly's eye lens and fractional view. In: Proc. SPIE 6803, Stereoscopic Displays and Applications XIX, 68031K, pp. 1–8 (2008)
2. Yoda, M., Momose, A., Yanaka, K.: Moving integral photography using a common digital photo frame and fly's eye lens. SIGGRAPH ASIA Posters (2009)
3. Yanaka, K.: Real-time rendering for integral photography that uses extended fractional view. In: Proc. SPIE 7237, Stereoscopic Displays and Applications XX, 723723, pp. 1–8 (2009)
4. Maki, N.: Fossil Tears (2012), http://vimeo.com/42954407
5. Maki, N.: 3DCG Animated Short Film "Fossil Tears". In: 4th Digital Contents Creation Group Meeting, Information Processing Society of Japan (2013) (in Japanese)

Steps towards Enhancing the User Experience in Accessing Digital Libraries

Carlo Meghini and Valentina Bartalesi

Istituto di Scienza e Tecnologie dell'Informazione "Alessandro Faedo"
– CNR Pisa, Italy
{carlo.meghini,valentina.bartalesi}@isti.cnr.it

Abstract. The advent of the Web has driven cultural institutions to publish digital representations of their assets online. The main problem of the cultural Web sites, and of their back-end Digital Libraries (DLs), is the limitation of the informative services offered to the user. DLs offer simple search functionalities which return a list of the information objects contained in the DL. No semantic relation among the returned objects is usually reported which can help the user in obtaining a more complete knowledge on the subject of the research. The introduction of the Semantic Web, and in particular of the Linked Data, has the potential of improving the search functionalities of DLs. Many cultural institutions have represented their metadata into *formal descriptions* encoded by means of formal languages such as RDF and OWL. Our study aims at exploiting the representations of the semantics of the objects contained in the new generation DLs in the in order to introduce a new search functionality. As output of a query, the new search functionality does not return just a list of objects but it presents a *narrative*, based on the objects of the library that are relevant to the query and on a set of semantic relations that connect these objects into something meaningful to the user. The paper presents the first theoretical achievements on a model for representing narratives.

Keywords: Narratology, Digital Libraries, Narrative, Storytelling, Semantic Networks, Ontologies.

1 Introduction

Digital libraries (DLs) are information systems that offer services over large sets of digital objects [28]. Nowadays, digital libraries are one of the most common types of information system that can be found in everyday life: they range from those serving large societies, such as the web or Europeana, to those serving single individuals, such as those managing the music or photo collections in our phones or tablets.

The current access functionalities to digital libraries are largely influenced by web search engines, whereby users express their information need in the form of a natural language query consisting of few words, and in response the digital

S. Yamamoto (Ed.): HIMI 2014, Part II, LNCS 8522, pp. 555–566, 2014.
© Springer International Publishing Switzerland 2014

library is expected to return a ranked list of relevant objects, in less than a second. This is in fact what happens in DLs such as Europeana. However, while this access functionality is serving well the users of the web, whose digital objects are rich text pages with graphics, images, links to other pages and possibly more, it performs very poorly on most digital libraries. The reason is that digital librarys contents are hardly designed to be consumed in the way web pages are: whether these contents are books (the traditional case), manuscripts, photographs, or videos, they are not meant to be read and navigated on the fly as web pages are. As a result, the user searching a digital library via the typical web-like query, typically obtains in response a ranked list of succinct metadata descriptors that in many cases disappoints the initial expectation.

This situation is somewhat paradoxical, because digital libraries possess metadata records that embody rich and articulated descriptions of their objects. However, such wealth of knowledge is not exploited when it comes to serving the digital library search facility.

In our study, we aim at overcoming the search functionality of current digital libraries by introducing narratives as first class citizens of digital libraries. The vision is that a user searching for Mozart in Europeana would obtain in response not the ranked list of objects concerning Mozart that the digital library knows about, as it is nowadays; but rather the user would obtain a narrative about Mozart, linking the relevant object in a story that would work as a contextualization of the objects themselves.

This paper presents a review of the works on narratives so far, and articulates our project in a detailed way, relating it to existing models both in the narrative and in the digital library fields. The paper is structured as follows: Section 2 reports the definition of narratology, a description of the background and illustrates the science of computational narratology; Section 3 reports related works. In Section 4 we present our idea of introducing narratives as a new functionality of DLs and we show the advantages that such functionality could produce. In Section 5 we introduce our methodology to create narratives. Finally, in Section 6 conclusions are reported.

2   Background

In literary theory, narratology is the study of narrative structure derived from literary criticism. It is a discipline in the humanities devoted to the study of the logic, principles, and practices of narrative representation [30]. An antecedent to the modern science of narratology could be found in Aristotles Poetics [2]. Aristotle considers narratology as being an imitation of a real action (praxis) that constitutes an argument (logos), providing the basis of the plot (mythos). The plot is formed by the events or fundamental units selected and ordered.

Despite its antecedents in classical theories of aesthetic, the theoretical principles of narratology derive from linguistic-centered approaches to literature defined by Russian formalists (in the earlier years of 20th century) and later developed through European structuralism. In general, Russian formalists consider narratology as based on the idea of a common literary language, or a universal pattern of codes that operates within the text of a work. The theoretical starting point is that narratives can be conveyed in many different communication forms using a wide variety of media, e.g. oral and written language, gestures, music, etc. In particular, Vladimir Propp [34] in his own work *Morphology of the Folk Tale* (1928) provides a model for folktales based on seven spheres of action and 31 functions of narrative. However, the body of this theory has had important developments in the mid-20th century. The foundations of narratology were found in such books of this period as Claude Lévi-Strauss's *Structural Anthropology* (1958) [23], which outlined a grammar of mythology; A.J. Greimass *Structural Semantics* (1966) [15], which proposed a system of six structural units called *actants*; and Tzvetan Todorovs *The Grammar of the Decameron* (1969) [46], which introduced the term *narratologie*. Gérard Genette [Genette, 1979] codified a system of analysis that examined both the actual narration and the act of narrating as they existed apart from the story or the content.

Since 1980, post-structuralist perspectives of narratology have been developed. In particular, two perspectives are proposed:

- Cognitive Narratology [17], which considers narratology a psychological phenomenon, and proposes a study of narrative aspects from a cognitive perspective.
- Contextualist Narratology which connects the phenomena encountered in narrative to specific cultural, historical, thematic and ideological context [Meister, 2011].

2.1 Fabula and Syuzhet

Russian Formalism distinguishes between the series of events, that is actions or occurrences taking place at a certain time at a specific location, that compose the story (fabula) and the particular way that story gets narrated (syuzhet). Fabula refers to the sequence of events of the narrative in chronological order; syuzhet is the way in which these events are presented in a narrative [34] [42]. The distinction between fabula and syuzheth has been used also by Chatman who makes reference to the two concepts as story and discourse, respectively [7]. In this way, there is a clear division between the content transmitted and the how this content is organized. Chatman [7] considers that the entities which take part to a narrative, along with the events, are the constituents of the story. Crawford [9] claims that a narrative is a high-level structure based on causality and not on time or spatial relations. He distinguishes characters from narrative events and also from world events.

A general agreement regarding the structures that define narratives has not been reached. For instance, McKee defines narratives as tree structures in which nodes are ordered in a chronological order [37]. Genette [13] identifies five concepts in narratology to describe the narrative structures: order, frequency, duration, voice and mood. Taking as starting point the Russian formalism, Bal [3] considers the fabula as the entities and the events created by the author to form the tale. The discourse is a selection of events from that fabula organized in a particular chronological order. Finally, the presentation is the concrete representation of the content (the text in a novel, for instance) that the author conveys to the audience.

2.2 Characters and Plots

In narratology, two entities are particularly important: characters and plots.

Characters are a fundamental constituent in a story. Aristotle considered that the most important element is the action [2], but it can be affirmed that characters appear in every type of tale. McKee [37] claims that it is not possible talking about the plot without characters and vice versa. Chatman [8] distinguishes the elements of a story in characters and elements in the scenario. Characters are usually humans or humanoid beings while the elements in the scenario are places and objects.

The terms plot refers to the events that build a story. In particular, the term refers to the relation that links an event to another in a pattern.

2.3 Computational Narratology

Computational narratology studies narratives from a computation perspective. In particular, it focuses on the algorithmic processes involved in creating and interpreting narratives, modeling narrative structure in terms of formal computable representations [26].

The Computational Narratology can assume different meanings according to different research contexts: (i) in the context of Humanities, computational narratology is defined as a methodological instrument for constructing narratological theories, extending narratological models to larger bodies of text, providing precise and consistent explication of concepts [29]; (ii) in a cognitive computing point of view, this terms refers to narrative texts, computer games, and more in general, software developed using semiotic, sociolinguistic and cognitive linguistic theories [16]; (iii) in a implementation and Artificial Intelligence (AI) perspective [6], computational narratology refers to the story generation systems, that is any computer application that creates a written, spoken, or visual presentation of a story. In particular, in AI this term refers to storytelling systems that is software to generate stories described in natural language, that implemented linguistic formalisms. Then, generation of narrative can be classified into two main categories: manual and automatic. In the manual generation, users usually collect tales through interviews, focus group, then aggregate them into a narrative. Although manual modeling can provide users with the most accurate and complicated narratological models, it is very time consuming and the quality of generated narratives is strictly associated with the capability of the narrator. In the other hand, automatic generation of storytelling only needs some input information to create narratives. An overview of automatic storytelling systems is reported in Section 3.

3   Related Works

The area of the theory of narratology that is related to our work is the one in the Artificial Intelligence field which concerns the development of storytelling systems aiming at reproducing a human-like narrative behavior or at creating interfaces or game environments using narrative as interactive method. During the development of such systems, narratological models are developed. Such models and, more in general, the computational narratology have been strongly influenced by linguistic and computational linguistics theories. In fact the development of the narratology in the Humanities has gone hand in hand with the growth to computational approaches to narrative.

Some of the early storytelling systems are TALE-SPIN [27], UNIVERSE [22], GESTER [32] and JOSEPH [20] which change the story grammars to create new stories. Story grammars represent stories as linguistic objects which have a structure that can be represented by a grammar. Lakoff [19] introduced the first story grammar for the Eskimo folktales. Rumelhart [38] proposed the first general grammar able to apply to a larger set of stories. Van Dijk [48], Thorndyke [45], Mandler and Johnson [25], Stein and Glenn [44] developed other general story grammars. However, such kind of storytelling systems produce stories compliant to their grammars but are not able to modify its knowledge to create different outcomes. Some other storytelling systems are MINSTREL [47], MEXICA [33] and BRUTUS [5]. They are hybrid systems which integrate several methodologies in order to implement an explicit computer model of creativity in writing. Recently, ontologies ware used to generate narratives. For example, MAKEBELIEVE [24] is an story generation system that uses commonsense knowledge in order to generate short stories from an initial one given by the user. The commonsense knowledge used in MAKEBELIEVE is selected from the ontology of the Open Mind Commonsense Knowledge Base [43]. The ProtoPropp storytelling system [14] uses an ontology of explicitly relevant knowledge, called the ProtoPropp ontology, and the Case-Based Reasoning (CBR) method over a defined set of tales. The aim is to create new stories from the existing ones that matches a given user query. In a recent storytelling system, FABULIST [36], the user supplies a description of an initial state of the world and a specific goal, and the system identifies the better sequence of actions to reach the goal.

As shown above, linguistic theories have conditioned computational narratology. For example, story grammars have been widely applied in computational narratology, as in Bringsjord and Ferrucci [5] and Lang [21]. The contributions of corpus linguistics to narratology are well-recognized [39], and recent advances in data text mining techniques allowed to test several literary hypotheses. For example, the system described in Elson et al. [12] is able to automatically retrieve conversational social networks from the dialogues included in 19th-century tales.

4 Narratives in DL

The advent of the Web and the increase of the number of tools to automatically create Web sites have driven cultural institutions (e.g., museums, archives) to publish digital representations of their assets online. The main problem of the resulting cultural Web sites, and of their back-end Digital Libraries (DLs), is the limitation of the informative services offered to the user. Although those DLs rely on broad knowledge bases, they offer simple search functionalities based on text free queries that return a ranked list of the information objects contained in the DL. No semantic relation among the returned objects is usually reported that can help the user in interpreting the obtained result and, more importantly, in obtaining a more complete knowledge on the subject of the research. The main reason for this behavior usually lies in the low level of formality at which the knowledge contained in the DLs is expressed. Such knowledge is mostly embodied in texts, images, or in multimedia objects, and extracting knowledge from these media is a notoriously difficult task.

The introduction of the Semantic Web [4], and in particular of Linked Data, has the potential of improving the search functionalities of DLs. In fact, thanks to the languages and tools developed in the context of the Semantic Web, many cultural institutions have moved to represent their vocabularies as formal ontologies and their metadata as formal descriptions couched in terms of those ontologies. This move has been achieved by means of formal languages such as RDF, used for metadata records, and such as OWL, used for formal ontologies.

The resulting new generation DLs allow implementing more effective search functionalities, due to the formal representation of the semantics of the objects contained in them. Our study aims at exploiting such representations in order to introduce a new search functionality for DLs.

The new search functionality that we envisage, does not return just a ranked list of objects in response to a query of the user, rather, it presents a narrative, based on the objects of the library that are relevant to the query and on a set of semantic relations that connect these objects into a narrative that is meaningful to the user. In addition, the use of narratives in DLs can be useful for two aspects: (i) for modeling and managing the provenance of the objects in a DL; and (ii) for enriching of the content of the DL with stories that connect the DL objects into meaningful units, i.e., narratives.

For what concerns the provenance, narratives could be important functionality (i) to improve the access to the knowledge of the DL objects; and (ii) for the preservation of such objects. The present provenance models are models with a very limited amount of formally represented semantics. In order to be general, such models end up using concepts such as process and states [31] that may be very helpful at the implementation level, because they can be applied to capture the provenance of any object; but offer very little help to the curators, who need to talk about specific types of process and state. As a result, the burden of mapping the actual processes taking place in each domain into the notion offered by these models, rests entirely on the curators themselves, partially defeating automation. We claim that the curators should be given more effective tools in

Fig. 1. The output of Europeana for the query *Versailles Conference*

order to represent the provenance of the objects they curate, and that narratives can be such a tool. In fact, the representation of provenance as a story is very intuitive because it directly reflects reality. Moreover, the types of events and actions that can occur in the provenance of the objects in a certain domain, can be easily identified, along with their parameters and along with the relationships that connect them. This implies that curators can be equipped with a tool for creating narratives endowed with a predefined set of elementary event and action types from which they can select for composing the provenance models of their curated objects. Such a tool would be much easier to use than current models, and as such would greatly improve the effectiveness of digital object curation.

For what regards the creation of story generation systems for the content enrichment, currently the DL search functionalities are centered on the metadata. A user query returns a ranked list of results, without specifying the relations among them. An example of a list of results is reported in Figure 1, which

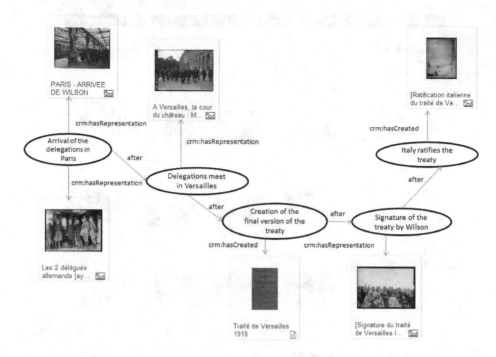

Fig. 2. An example of narrative of the *Versailles Conference*

shows the output of the Europeana[1] search functionality[2] for the query *Versailles Conference*.

In our hypothesis, the DL should return a semantic representation of the relations among the items of the resulting list using a narrative approach. At the same time, the digital curator would be able to create the narratives for the DL objects he/she would like to promote. For example, a narrative about the Versailles Conference can be defined by a digital librarian linking the information objects of the Versailles treaty (such as photographs of the people, the final declaration etc.) to an event which represents the Conference. Such event may be further divided in sub-events which will have to be properly placed on a temporal axis. An example of our idea of a narrative about the Versailles Conference is reported in Figure 2. We divided the main event of the Conference in several sub-events, to which we associated a digital object belonging to the Europeana DL. To illustrate our idea in an easy way, we used (*i*) the temporal relation *after* defined by Allen [1] to link an event to another; (*ii*) the relations crm:hasRepresentation and crm:hasCreated, defined in the CIDOC-CRM ontology [11] to link the events to the digital objects included in Europeana.

---

[1] http://pro.europeana.eu/web/guest/home
[2] http://eculture.cs.vu.nl/europeana/session/search

Figure 3 shows the narrative about the provenance of the *treaty of Versailles ratified by Italy*. The main event is divided into sub-events which reconstruct the provenance of the digital version of the treaty included in Europeana.

The DL could serve both narratives as output of a query about the Versailles Conference, thereby providing the user a semantic network telling a story. The same narratives could be re-used also in the context of a bigger narrative, for example one regarding the World War I.

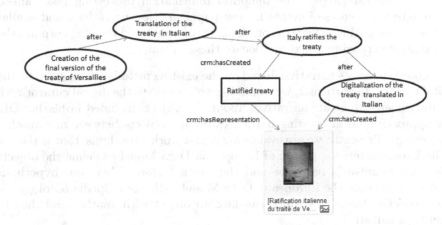

Fig. 3. An example of narrative of the provenance of the *treaty of Versailles ratified by Italy*

5   How to Create Narratives

Conventionally, the term *event* refers to an action or an occurrence taking place at a certain time at a specific location. The data models of the DLs are essentially focused on metadata. As such, these data models offer classes and properties for the description of objects (whether digital or not), and lack the expressive machinery to represents events and the relations between them that make up narratives. Various models have been developed for representing events on the Semantic Web, e.g. Event Ontology (EO) [35], Linking Open Descriptions of Events (LODE) [41], the F-Model (F) [40]. More general models for semantic data organization are CIDOC-CRM [11], the ABC ontology [18], the Europeana Data Model [10]. These general models aim at allowing the interoperability among the typical metadata records used for describing objects contained in museums and libraries. Such interoperability is a key enabling factor for aggregation DLs, that is DLs that collect metadata from a variety of sources in order to offer cross-source services. Europeana is a remarkable example of this kind of DLs. In order to achieve their interoperability goal, the models in question define classes and properties for modeling events and their relationships. The events these models describe include both historical events (e.g. deaths, births, wars) as well as the events concerning the objects collected in (e.g. deposit, changes of ownership, restoration). In order to populate the models with the events, two main methods are currently used:

- Using manually annotated corpora which include meta-tags for identifying the events presented in texts or in collections of objects included in DLs.
- Using Natural Language methodologies, that is Event Extractor systems in order to automatically detect the events included in texts. Such systems are trained on semantically annotated corpora. For example, in the last SemEval evaluation campaigns[3], the temporal information processing task[4] aimed to detect sequences of events in newspaper articles, narratives, and similar texts. The goal is to identify, on the basis of annotated training corpora, the events described in a text and locate these in time.

Our scope is to create narratives based on the existing metadata or defined by the digital curator. In particular, we would like to provide to the digital curator with the instruments to create narratives about the objects included in his/her DL. Our approach aims at creating narratives linking objects between one another using events. Presently, we are evaluating a first work hypothesis, that is the use of the Event-centered approach of Europeana Data Model to define the objects which can populate a narrative and their own *history*. Then, our hypothesis considers extending the Europeana Data Model with the DBpedia ontology[5] in order to define the events which can link an object with another and then to generate a narrative.

6   Conclusions and Future Work

In this paper we described how to exploit the representations of the semantics of the objects contained in the new generation DLs in order to introduce a new search functionality. As output of a query, the new search functionality of DLs does not return just a list of objects but it presents a *narrative*, based on the objects of the DL that are relevant to the query and on a set of semantic relations that connect these objects into a semantic network meaningful to the user. In this paper we presented a review of the works on narratives and described our project in a detailed way, relating it to developed models both in the narrative and in the digital library fields. We also presented the first theoretical achievements on a model for representing narratives. The creation of such model will be the next step of our project.

References

1. Allen, J.F.: Maintaining knowledge about temporal intervals. Communications of the ACM 26(11), 832–843 (1983)
2. Aristotele: Poetica. Laterza (1998)

---

[3] http://www.cs.york.ac.uk/semeval-2013/
[4] http://www.cs.york.ac.uk/semeval-2013/task1/
[5] http://wiki.dbpedia.org/Ontology

3. Bal, M.: Narratology: Introduction to the theory of narrative. University of Toronto Press (1997)
4. Berners-Lee, T., Hendler, J., Lassila, O., et al.: The semantic web. Scientific American 284(5), 28–37 (2001)
5. Bringsjord, S., Ferrucci, D.: Artificial intelligence and literary creativity: Inside the mind of brutus, a storytelling machine. Psychology Press (1999)
6. Cavazza, M., Pizzi, D.: Narratology for interactive storytelling: A critical introduction. In: Göbel, S., Malkewitz, R., Iurgel, I. (eds.) TIDSE 2006. LNCS, vol. 4326, pp. 72–83. Springer, Heidelberg (2006)
7. Chatman, S.: Characters and narrators: Filter, center, slant, and interest-focus. Poetics Today 7(2), 189–204 (1986)
8. Chatman, S.B.: Story and discourse: Narrative structure in fiction and film. Cornell University Press (1980)
9. Crawford, C.: Chris Crawford on interactive storytelling. New Riders (2012)
10. Doerr, M., Gradmann, S., Hennicke, S., Isaac, A., Meghini, C., van de Sompel, H.: The europeana data model (edm). In: World Library and Information Congress: 76th IFLA General Conference and Assembly, pp. 10–15 (2010)
11. Doerr, M., Ore, C.E., Stead, S.: The cidoc conceptual reference model: a new standard for knowledge sharing. In: Tutorials, Posters, Panels and Industrial Contributions at the 26th International Conference on Conceptual Modeling, vol. 83, pp. 51–56. Australian Computer Society, Inc. (2007)
12. Elson, D.K., Dames, N., McKeown, K.R.: Extracting social networks from literary fiction. In: Proceedings of the 48th Annual Meeting of the Association for Computational Linguistics, pp. 138–147. Association for Computational Linguistics (2010)
13. Genette, G.E., Lewin, J.E.: Narrative discourse: An essay in method. Cornell University Press (1983)
14. Gervás, P., Díaz-Agudo, B., Peinado, F., Hervás, R.: Story plot generation based on cbr. Knowledge-Based Systems 18(4), 235–242 (2005)
15. Greimas, A.J., McDowell, D., Velie, A.R.: Structural semantics: An attempt at a method. University of Nebraska Press Lincoln (1983)
16. Harrell Jr., D.A.: Theory and technology for computational narrative: An approach to generative and interactive narrative with bases in algebraic semiotics and cognitive linguistics. Ph.D. thesis, University of California, San Diego (2007)
17. Herman, D.: Narratology as a cognitive science. Image and Narrative 1, 1 (2000)
18. Lagoze, C., Hunter, J.: The abc ontology and model. Journal of Digital Information 2(2) (2006)
19. Lakoff, G.: Structural complexity in fairy tales. School of Social Sciences. University of California, Irvine (1972)
20. Lang, R.R.: A formal model for simple narratives (1997)
21. Lang, R.: A declarative model for simple narratives. In: Proceedings of the AAAI Fall Symposium on Narrative Intelligence, pp. 134–141 (1999)
22. Lebowitz, M.: Story-telling as planning and learning. Poetics 14(6), 483–502 (1985)
23. Levi-Strauss, C.: Structural analysis in linguistics and in anthropology. In: Semiotics-An Introductory Anthology, pp. 110–128 (1963)
24. Liu, H., Singh, P.: Makebelieve: Using commonsense knowledge to generate stories. In: AAAI/IAAI, pp. 957–958 (2002)
25. Mandler, J.M., Johnson, N.S.: Remembrance of things parsed: Story structure and recall. Cognitive Psychology 9(1), 111–151 (1977)
26. Mani, I.: Computational modeling of narrative. Synthesis Lectures on Human Language Technologies 5(3), 1–142 (2012)

27. Meehan, J.R.: Tale-spin, an interactive program that writes stories. In: IJCAI, pp. 91–98 (1977)
28. Meghini, C., Spyratos, N., Sugibuchi, T., Yang, J.: A model for digital libraries and its translation to rdf. Journal on Data Semantics, 1–33 (2013)
29. Meister, J.C.: Computing action: a narratological approach, vol. 2. Walter de Gruyter (2003)
30. Meister, J.C.: Narratology, synthesis. American Museum of Natural History (2012), http://ncep.amnh.org
31. Moreau, L., Clifford, B., Freire, J., Futrelle, J., Gil, Y., Groth, P., Kwasnikowska, N., Miles, S., Missier, P., Myers, J., et al.: The open provenance model core specification (v1. 1). Future Generation Computer Systems 27(6), 743–756 (2011)
32. Pemberton, L.: A modular approach to story generation. In: Proceedings of the Fourth Conference on European Chapter of the Association for Computational Linguistics, pp. 217–224. Association for Computational Linguistics (1989)
33. PÉrez, R.P.Ý., Sharples, M.: Mexica: A computer model of a cognitive account of creative writing. Journal of Experimental & Theoretical Artificial Intelligence 13(2), 119–139 (2001)
34. Propp, V.: Morphology of the Folktale, vol. 9. University of Texas Press (1973)
35. Raimond, Y., Abdallah, S.: The event ontology. Tech. rep., Technical report (2007), http://motools.sourceforge.net/event
36. Riedl, M.O., Young, R.M.: Narrative planning: balancing plot and character. Journal of Artificial Intelligence Research 39(1), 217–268 (2010)
37. Robert, M.: Story. substance, structure, style, and the principles of screenwriting (1997)
38. Rumelhart, D.E.: Notes on a schema for stories (1975)
39. Salway, A., Herman, D.: Digitized corpora as theory-building resource: New methods for narrative inquiry. New Narratives: Stories and Storytelling in the Digital Age. Lincoln: U of Nebraska P (2011)
40. Scherp, A., Franz, T., Saathoff, C., Staab, S.: F–a model of events based on the foundational ontology dolce+ dns ultralight. In: Proceedings of the Fifth International Conference on Knowledge Capture, pp. 137–144. ACM (2009)
41. Shaw, R., Troncy, R., Hardman, L.: Lode: Linking open descriptions of events. In: Gómez-Pérez, A., Yu, Y., Ding, Y. (eds.) ASWC 2009. LNCS, vol. 5926, pp. 153–167. Springer, Heidelberg (2009)
42. Shklovsky, V.: Art as technique. Russian Formalist Criticism: Four Essays 3 (1965)
43. Singh, P., et al.: The public acquisition of commonsense knowledge. In: Proceedings of AAAI Spring Symposium: Acquiring (and Using) Linguistic (and World) Knowledge for Information Access (2002)
44. Stein, N.L., Glenn, C.G.: An analysis of story comprehension in elementary school children: A test of a schema (1975)
45. Thorndyke, P.W.: Cognitive structures in comprehension and memory of narrative discourse. Cognitive Psychology 9(1), 77–110 (1977)
46. Todorov, T.: Grammaire du décaméron. Mouton The Hague (1969)
47. Turner, S.R.: The creative process: A computer model of storytelling and creativity. Psychology Press (1994)
48. Van Dijk, T.A., et al.: Recalling and summarizing complex discourse. In: Text Processing, pp. 49–93 (1979)

Switching the Level of Abstraction in Digital Exhibitions to Provide an Understanding of Mechanisms

Takuji Narumi, Hiroshi Ohara, Ryo Kiyama,
Tomohiro Tanikawa, and Michitaka Hirose

7-3-1 Hongo, Bunkyo-Ku, Tokyo, Japan
{narumi,ohara,kiyama,tani,hirose}@cyber.t.u-tokyo.ac.jp

Abstract. This paper proposes an approach for switching the level of abstraction for digital exhibition systems to provide an understanding of exhibit mechanisms. In conventional museum exhibitions, curators have tried to convey knowledge to visitors by displaying real exhibits. However, such conventional methods cannot effectively explain how a mechanism works. In contrast, digital media can be used to enhance delivery efficiency by providing interactivity to express the dynamic aspects of the exhibit. Based on this idea, we introduce the Digital Display Case system and interactive contents, whose level of abstraction can be changed at the Railway Museum (Japan). Our user study shows that switching the level of abstraction helps visitors understand the mechanisms of a rail car pendulum bogie.

Keywords: Level of Abstraction, Interactive Exhibition, Digital Museum, Digital Exhibition System, Digital Display Case.

1 Introduction

Recently, museums have demonstrated increasing interest in the use of digital technologies to provide supplementary background information about their exhibits. The conventional approach has been the placement of static displays, such as panels with text and figures, near the exhibited objects to convey relevant information. However, because the exhibit and the panel are often detached, this is an ineffective and problematic way to help visitors connect to the exhibit and its information. In particular, it is difficult for visitors to understand the dynamic mechanism of an exhibited artifact based on static information displayed on a panel.

For example, to convey the dynamic mechanism of railway bogies, the Railway Museum (Ohnari-Ku, Saitama, Japan) [1, 2] has been exhibiting authentic railway bogies alongside descriptions of figures, captions, cut-out models, and other materials intended to show visitors their active mechanism (Fig. 1). However, the museum argues that it has been difficult to understand the mechanism of a real moving bogie because it cannot be shown in static descriptions. Meanwhile, a video that describes the mechanism is not always effective. Because it is not an interactive system, most visitors simply pass by without watching the video to the end. Thus, an interactive

S. Yamamoto (Ed.): HIMI 2014, Part II, LNCS 8522, pp. 567–576, 2014.
© Springer International Publishing Switzerland 2014

exhibition system provides an effective way for visitors to relate to exhibitions, and more easily comprehend dynamic mechanisms.

The goal of our project is to construct a digital display case system [3–5] that enables museums to convey background information about exhibits effectively, using digital technology and virtual exhibits. While previous study [5] has shown that an interactive exhibition system which shows the movement of exhibits' mechanisms can convey their ingenuity effectively, it has also revealed that just showing the movement cannot provide a deeper understanding of the principle in the mechanisms.

Meanwhile, education researches have revealed that abstraction enhances learning of complex ideas [6]. Abstraction means extracting a particular essence and cutting out other elements, which helps in learning the principle of the exhibits' mechanisms. Therefore, the purpose of this study is the introduction of interactive switching of the level of abstraction, and to confirm its effectiveness. In this study, we chose the railway bogie as an example, and implemented a digital display case system with which visitors can interact. We conducted a field trial of the system at the Railway Museum and received feedback from the visitors and curators of the museum.

Fig. 1. Exhibition of the railway bogie

2   Related Work

Several studies have been conducted on exhibition systems that superimpose images on exhibits to provide background information. Virtual Showcase [7] superimposes images on exhibits using a half-silvered mirror, and allows multiple users to observe and interact with the augmented information in the display. Exfloasion [8] and MRSionCase [9] extend this concept, enabling presentation of floating images with different depths by constructing an imaging surface of two layers and placing half-silvered mirrors at the front and rear. These exhibition systems can effectively present information by superimposing it on the exhibit. However, it is difficult to convey dynamic information, such as mechanisms, since the exhibit stored in the system is static.

Other studies have examined systems that enable user interaction through the use of virtual exhibits or touch-enabled systems. Wakita et al. reported a system that allows direct interaction with virtual fabric using a space interface device for artificial reality (SPIDAR) haptic force display that presents force on the basis of data measured with a laser range scanner [10]. However, these systems are designed to realize the experience of touching static exhibits and the extent of the authors' knowledge. There are very few systems for exhibitions that allow users to manipulate the exhibit itself in order to understand its dynamic mechanism easily.

Recently, virtual experiment platforms have been designed and developed for students to understand the mechanism of motion systems [11]. Fan et al. [12] developed a system for students to perform mechanism motion experiments and to understand the composition of the mechanism and its motion principle through simulation.

The development of digital mock-up (DMU) technology and related studies is popular in modern manufacturing industry [13, 14]. DMU technology enables the design of products and the simulation of their behavior. Therefore, it is possible to improve the quality of products, reduce production costs, and shorten development periods. It is reasonable to infer that visitors will be able to understand the dynamic mechanism of exhibits more easily by applying DMU technology to exhibition systems.

3   Switching Method for the Level of Abstraction in Digital Display Case

3.1   Target of Abstraction and Abstraction Levels

We propose an approach for switching the level of abstraction interactively in a digital display case system (DDCS) [5], to provide an understanding of exhibit mechanisms. In this study, we showed a TR96 rail car pendulum bogie in the DDCS. The pendulum bogie enables the rail car to run at high velocities on tight curves by inclining the body of the rail car with the mechanism shown in Fig.2. We organized the level of abstraction into three stages; extraction, shape abstraction, and mechanism abstraction.

In the extraction stage, the parts which actualize the principle action of the mechanism are highlighted and others in the CG exhibit are made transparent. We called this an extracted model. In this case, two T links which actualize the pendulum mechanism are highlighted (Fig. 3). Since the real shapes of these elements are complex, visitors cannot always grasp the focus point of the model to understand the mechanism. Therefore, we made an abstract model by simplifying the shape of each element that composes the mechanism in the shape abstraction stage (Fig. 4). For example, when the movement of the mechanism is two-dimensional, three-dimensional (3D) shapes can be transferred into two-dimensional shapes while maintaining its movement. Some elements of mechanism are actualized by the combination of parts. These parts can be unified and replaced by one simple part while maintaining its function and movement. Fig. 4 shows the simplified results of the rail car and the T links. In this case, the T links, lifting link, and dampers are integrated into a simplified model.

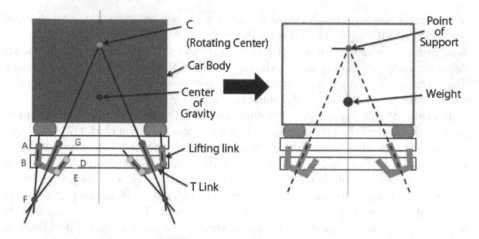

Fig. 2. The mechanism of TR96 Pendulum Bogie and its Principle

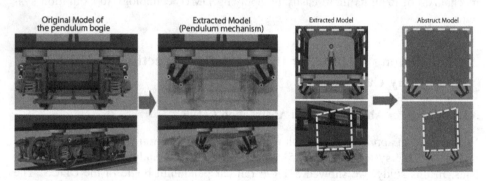

Fig. 3. Extraction of the Mechanism   **Fig. 4.** Shape Abstraction

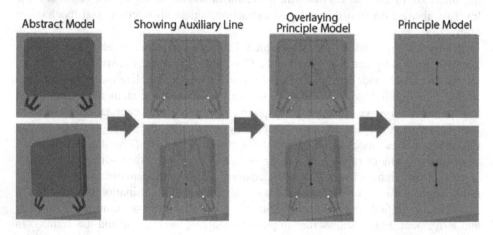

Fig. 5. Mechanism abstraction

There are variations in shape or mechanism, even when they have the same principle. For example, there are several types of springs, such as a coiled spring, a blade spring, and air suspension. However, all of them obey Hooke's law and have the same basic function, therefore, they can be simulated by just a spring model. In this way, the mechanism in an abstract model is translated into a principle model that represents the basic principle of the mechanism in the mechanism abstraction stage. It is difficult for visitors to understand how the principle model represents the function of the mechanism in the abstract model when the abstract model is translated into the principle model directly. Therefore, we introduced intermediate stages to assist in understanding the relationship between the abstract and the principle models. In the intermediate stages, the abstract model become transparent, and auxiliary lines and pointers help visitors understand the mechanism. Next, the principle model is overlaid onto these (Fig. 5). Finally, the abstract model, auxiliary lines, and pointers disappear, and only the principle model is shown.

3.2 Showing Forces and Comparison with a Normal Model without the Pendulum Mechanism

We implemented other visualization methods for helping visitors understand the effectiveness of the mechanism of the pendulum bogie. First, we visualized the forces acting on the car's body and a standing person in it. We showed the force of gravity, a centrifugal force, and a net force (Fig. 6 Left). Second, we introduced the interactive switching of various types of bogie. We used a normal bogie without the pendulum

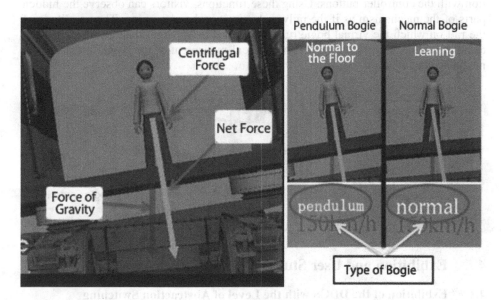

Fig. 6. Showing Forces and Comparison between a Pendulum Bogie and a Normal Bogie

mechanism for comparison, by locking the T link in the pendulum mechanism, preventing the body of the rail car from inclining. When the pendulum bogie runs at high velocities on a tight curve, the body of the rail car inclines, and the person in the car stands up straight on its floor. On the other hand, when a normal bogie runs at high velocities on a tight curve, the body of the rail car does not incline, and the standing person in the car inclines from the perpendicular (Fig. 6 Right). The comparison of the visualization result with and without the pendulum mechanism helps visitors understand the merit of the pendulum mechanism.

3.3   Digital Display Case

In this study, we use a DDCS [5] for exhibiting the interactive models with the proposed level of abstraction switching method and the visualization method described in 3.2. The DDCS comprises three 3D displays in the shape of a box. To view the exhibit, a user wears a pair of 3D glasses with a Polhemus sensor that measures the orientation and rotation of the receptor using magnetic fields generated by the transmitter. Based on the point of view measured by this sensor, the system calculates the computer graphics image to be displayed on each 3D display. This enables the visitor to view a virtual exhibit from many angles, as if it were actually inside the case (Fig. 7). Not only is the 3D model of the bogie shown but also its velocity along with the different types of bogies is shown. Dynamic computation to operate the system is performed by the open dynamics engine (ODE) [15], a physics engine, at 30 fps.

The user can interact with the exhibit by using a controller similar to a master controller of an electric train. We implemented the system to allow the visitor to operate the railway bogie with acceleration or deceleration and to switch the level of abstraction with the controller buttons. Using these functions, visitors can observe the hidden parts of the mechanism as if the railway bogie is real and running. The amplitude of the rail on which the virtual bogie runs, is defined to be larger than an actual rail because it is necessary to distend the mechanical movement of the bogie to convey the mechanism to visitors.

Fig. 7. Digital Display Case

4   Exhibition and User Study

4.1   Exhibition of the DDCS with the Level of Abstraction Switching

We exhibited the DDCS with the proposed level of abstraction switching method at the Railway Museum.

The exhibition period was 14 days (December 19–26, 2012, and January 9–14, 2013) and was open from 10:00 to 18:00. At the time of the exhibition, one or two docents assigned to explain the system generally remained near the digital display case.

4.2 User Study for Evaluating the Effectiveness of the Level of Abstraction Switching

We performed a user study to evaluate the effectiveness of the interactive switching method for the level of abstraction as an approach to provide a deeper understanding of exhibits' mechanisms. We exhibited two types of interactive model, switching the method every other day. The first method enabled the visitor to switch the level of abstraction (with abstract switching condition). In this condition, the users could abstract the model shown in the DDCS step by step. Fig. 8 illustrates each step and the pattern of level of abstraction switching with the abstract switching condition. The second method enabled the visitor to switch only the transparency of the parts that are unrelated to the principle of the mechanism (without abstract switching condition). This method was used in the previous study [3]. In this condition, the visitor could switch the model between 1 and 2 in Fig. 8. We asked the visitors to take a brief quiz on the mechanism of the pendulum bogie to determine their comprehension. Each cooperating visitor took the quiz twice, before and after experiencing the system. We compared how the percentage of questions answered correctly increased after trying the system between conditions. We prepared two types of quiz; one with sixteen questions for adults, and another with sixteen questions for children. This is because the difficulty of the quiz related to abstract concepts depends on age. Based on the one for adults, we simplified the quiz for children.

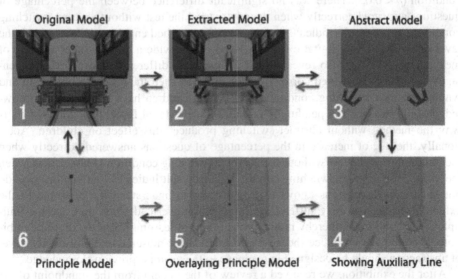

Fig. 8. The Pattern of Level of Abstraction Switching under the With Abstraction Switching Condition

4.3   Results and Discussion

Fig. 9 shows the average and standard deviation of the percentage of questions answered correctly under each condition. The number of cooperating adults was 19 for "with abstract switching" condition, and 10 for "without abstract switching" condition. The number of cooperating children was 14 for "with abstract switching" condition, and four for "without abstract switching" condition.

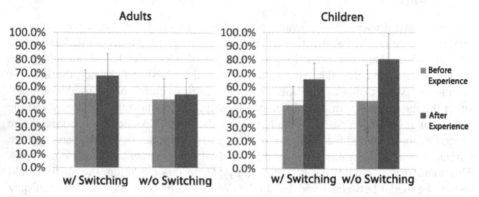

Fig. 9. Percentage of Questions Answered Correctly under each condition (Average and Standard Deviation)

We used the student's paired t-test for the percentage of questions answered correctly by each participant in "before-experience" and "after-experience" conditions. This test revealed that there is a significant difference between the percentage of questions answered correctly when the adults tried the test with the abstract switching condition ($p < 0.05$). There was no significant difference between the percentage of questions answered correctly when the adults tried the test without abstract switching condition. These results indicate that the proposed method enables adults to switch the level of abstraction in digital exhibitions and can provide a deeper understanding of mechanisms. The test also revealed that a significant difference between the percentage of questions answered correctly when children tried the test with both with and without abstract switching condition ($p < 0.05$). Children have less previous knowledge of physics, such as pendulum models and centrifugal force, than adults. This is why the method without abstract switching produces this effect on children. Additionally, the rate of increase in the percentage of questions answered correctly when the children tried the test without the abstract switching condition is larger than when they tried with abstract switching condition. This result indicates that visitors who do not have enough previous knowledge of physics to understand the principle of the exhibited mechanism may suffer from information overload when they see the multiple abstraction stage, thereby reducing the effect of learning from the digital exhibition. Therefore, to introduce the proposed method for museum exhibitions, the level of abstraction should be designed in response to the visitors' previous knowledge.

After the exhibition, we received a review of the system from the standpoint of the Railway Museum curators. The curators evaluated the visitors' reactions as very good, and reported that the exhibition was very effective in helping visitors understand the mechanism. On the other hand, they pointed out that they felt it was too difficult for visitors who were not familiar with physics to understand the principle of the mechanism, although they could grasp the way that the pendulum bogie works.

5 Conclusion

In this study, we propose an approach for switching the level of abstraction for digital exhibition systems to provide an understanding of exhibit mechanisms. We organized the level of abstraction into three stages; extraction, shape abstraction, and mechanism abstraction. The TR96 rail car pendulum bogie was chosen as an example of an exhibit with a complex mechanism. We introduced the DDSC and interactive contents whose level of abstraction can be changed to the Railway Museum (Japan). We performed a user study to evaluate the effectiveness of the interactive switching method for the level of abstraction that was based on the comparison of the effect of learning between the proposed approach and only showing the movement of the mechanism. The results of the user study indicated that the proposed method, which enables adults to switch the level of abstraction in digital exhibitions, can provide a deeper understanding of the mechanisms of a rail car pendulum bogie. However, the user study also showed that the proposed approach may not have a beneficial effect on providing a deeper understanding of mechanisms when the visitors are not familiar with physics.

Though the method was designed to convey the mechanism of pendulum bogies, we need to expand it to convey other railway mechanisms or other types of exhibit. We need a common framework for abstracting the principle of plural mechanisms. Moreover, to introduce the proposed method effectively, a design method for the level of abstraction based on the visitors' previous knowledge should be considered as a future work. For example, one possible solution is a method which decides how many abstraction stages the system should use to exhibit a mechanism, by using an age recognition system, based on computer vision techniques.

Acknowledgement. This research is partly supported by "Mixed Realty Digital Museum" project of Ministry of Education, Culture, Sports, Science and Technology (MEXT) of Japan. The authors would like to thank all the members of our project especially staff members of THE RAILWAY MUSEUM.

References

1. Japan Railway Museum, http://www.railway-museum.jp/
2. Narumi, T., Kasai, T., Honda, T., Aoki, K., Tanikawa, T., Hirose, M.: Digital Railway Museum: An Approach to Introduction of Digital Exhibition Systems at the Railway Museum. In: Yamamoto, S. (ed.) HCI 2013, Part III. LNCS, vol. 8018, pp. 238–247. Springer, Heidelberg (2013)

3. Kajinami, T., Hayashi, O., Narumi, T., Tanikawa, T., Hirose, M.: Digital Display Case: Museum exhibition system to convey background information about exhibits. In: Proceedings of Virtual Systems and Multimedia (VSMM), pp. 230–233 (October 2010)
4. Kajinami, T., Narumi, T., Tanikawa, T., Hirose, M.: Digital display case using non-contact head tracking. In: Shumaker, R. (ed.) Virtual and Mixed Reality, HCII 2011, Part I. LNCS, vol. 6773, pp. 250–259. Springer, Heidelberg (2011)
5. Kiyama, R., Kajinami, T., Ueta, M., Narumi, T., Tanikawa, T., Hirose, M.: Digital Display Case to Convey Dynamic Mechanisms of Exhibits. In: The 18th International Conference on Virtual Systems and Multimedia, pp. 299–306 (2012)
6. Dwyer Jr., F.M.: Adapting visual illustrations for effective learning. Harvard Educational Review 37(2), 250–263 (1967)
7. Bimber, O., Encarnacao, L.M., Schmalstieg, D.: The virtual showcase as a new platform for augmented reality digital storytelling. In: Proceedings of the Workshop on Virtual Environments 2003, vol. 39, pp. 87–95 (2003)
8. Nakashima, T., Wada, T., Naemura, T.: Exfloasion: Multi-layered floating vision system for mixed reality exhibition. In: 2010 16th International Conference on Virtual Systems and Multimedia (VSMM), pp. 95–98 (2010)
9. Kim, H., Nagao, S., Maekawa, S., Naemura, T.: MRsionCase: a glasses-free mixed reality showcase for surrounding multiple viewers. In: SIGGRAPH Asia 2012 Technical BriefsSIGGRAPH Asia 2012 Technical Briefs (SA 2012), Article 10, 4 pages (2012)
10. Wakita, W., Akahane, K., Isshiki, M., Tanaka, H.T.: A texture-based direct-touch interaction system for 3D woven cultural property exhibition. In: Koch, R., Huang, F. (eds.) ACCV 2010 Workshops, Part II. LNCS, vol. 6469, pp. 324–333. Springer, Heidelberg (2011)
11. Fritzson, P., Engelson, V.: Modelica - A unified object-oriented language for system modeling and simulation. In: Jul, E. (ed.) ECOOP 1998. LNCS, vol. 1445, pp. 67–90. Springer, Heidelberg (1998)
12. Fan, X., Zhang, X., Cheng, H., Ma, Y., He, Q.: A virtual experiment platform for mechanism motion cognitive learning. In: Shumaker, R. (ed.) Virtual and Mixed Reality, Part II, HCII 2011. LNCS, vol. 6774, pp. 20–29. Springer, Heidelberg (2011)
13. Gomes de Sa, A., Zachmann, G.: Virtual reality as a tool for verification of assembly and maintenance processes. Computers and Graphics 23(3), 389–403 (1999)
14. Xin, X., Gangfeng, T., Xuexun, G., Menghua, C.: The study of automobile chassis design and development based on Digital Mock-Up. In: 2011 International Conference on Electric Information and Control Engineering (ICEICE), pp. 2814–2817 (2011)
15. Open Dynamics Engine, http://www.ode.org

Information and Knowledge in Business and Society

Operations Research and Recommender Systems

Thomas Asikis and George Lekakos

Department of Management Science and Technology,
Athens University of Economics and Business, Athens, Greece
asikis.thomas@gmail.com, glekakos@aueb.gr

Abstract. Nowadays, Recommender Systems (RS) are being widely and successfully used in online applications. A successful Recommender System can help in increasing the revenue of a web-site as well as helping it to maintain and increase its users. Until now, research in recommendation algorithms is mainly based on machine learning and AI techniques. In this article we aim to develop recommendation algorithms utilizing Operations Research (OR) methods that provide the ability to move towards an optimized set of items to be recommended. We focus on expressing the Collaborative Filtering Algorithm (CF or CFA) as a Greedy Construction Algorithm as well as implementing and testing a Collaborative Metaheuristic Algorithm (CMA) for providing recommendations. The empirical findings suggest that the recommendation problem can indeed be defined as an optimization problem, which provides new opportunities for the application of powerful and effective OR algorithms on recommendation problems.

Keywords: Recommender Systems, Personalization algorithms, Operational Research, Metaheuristic.

1   Introduction

The number of possible choices in various sites that offer products or services increases rapidly day by day. Indeed, a typical user may have to make decisions such as: "With whom should I connect in a social network?", "What song should I hear on Soundcloud?", "Which product should I buy on Amazon?". Websites, offer a vast amount of possible choices to questions such as the above ones, so users need support in their decision making process in order to make the best possible selections [1].

Recommender Systems (RS) represent a type of information filtering systems that aim at predicting a user's items of interest in a large space of possible options, based on his previous preferences [2]. Typical recommendation approaches include collaborative, content based filtering and hybrid methods. Collaborative Filtering RS rely mostly on the behavioral similarity between users. Content Based Filtering RS focus on the similarities between item features that a user has favored in the past. In addition, several hybrid methods utilizing collaborative, content-based, demographic, and knowledge-based criteria have been developed in the last years [3]. In this article, the focus is on the collaborative approach due to its popularity, simplicity and intuition.

S. Yamamoto (Ed.): HIMI 2014, Part II, LNCS 8522, pp. 579–589, 2014.
© Springer International Publishing Switzerland 2014

Operations research (OR) provides methods and techniques that support the decision making process, by evaluating every possible alternative and estimating the potential outcome [4]. The main idea underlying the work presented in this paper is to exploit OR methods towards an optimized set of items to be recommended to the user.

Combinatorial Optimization is a method used in OR for the identification of optimal object/objects in a finite collection of objects [5]. It provides a suitable framework for the definition of a recommendation problem as an OR "Selection" problem. Recommender Systems aim at creating a selection of items that a user is most likely to respond positively (and eventually purchase or use the proposed item/items). In OR Selection problems, the aim is to select each item for the recommendation based on a choice criterion and evaluate the solution based on a specific evaluation criterion.

Along the above line of thinking, the objective of this paper is twofold: (a) to demonstrate that the recommendation problem can be defined and treated as an OR problem and (b) to design a well-performing recommendation algorithm based on OR techniques.

In the following, we firstly present extant related research and then we define the recommendation problem as an OR problem. At the next section we describe the implementation of a Collaborative-filtering Greedy-construction Algorithm (CGA) and a Collaborative Metaheuristic Algorithm (CMA) to determine if the combinatorial approach is suitable for the Social Recommender System Problem (SRSP). Finally, an empirical evaluation of the above algorithms is presented and the results are discussed in the final section of the paper.

2   Related Work

In this section we present some relevant RS techniques and discuss if they can be used to enhance the OR implementation in RS. In general, there are a lot of criteria that can be used for optimizing a recommendation. This provides us the flexibility to construct more reliable and accurate OR optimization methods. Trust is a concept that in general reflects the probability of someone doing an action, based on the actions performed from another person [6]. People are naturally grouped by trust. People who trust one another, usually can influence the behavior of each other and a high level of trust usually benefits all the parties in a transaction, by reducing the transaction cost between the seller and the buyer of an item. Moreover, trust can be aggregated and propagated though the members of a system. Those features have made trust one of the key components of some RS [7].

The advantages of the trust-based recommender systems can be found in a number of aspects: invulnerability to malicious attacks, greater control of the recommendation process, an explanation can be provided to users, for each item recommended to them. However, an important problem of trust-based algorithms, is data sparseness. Trust-based algorithms tend to face difficulty in sparse datasets [7] and their ability to produce good recommendations is limited.

On the other hand, features (mostly used in e-commerce recommenders where online purchases are enabled) such as the item's price may be used as a selection criterion. Such criteria are particularly useful for optimization problems that aim at maximizing product supplier's profits. Therefore the optimization problem can be rephrased as the following problem: How can we provide recommendations that match user's interests while ensuring the maximum profit for the provider? [8;12].

Novelty and diversity of recommendations can also serve as selection criteria as they may lead to quite effective recommendations [9]. Novel and diverse recommendations refer to items beyond the typical spectrum of items previously seen or consumed by the user and therefore they are perceived as an unexpected option that they user may have never considered in the past [10].

3   Defining Recommendation as an OR Problem

3.1   Problem Definition

A RS can be defined by the following:

$U = \{u_1, u_2 ...u_N\}$ a set of users.
$A = \{a_1, a_2 ...a_n\}$ a set of items.
$C_i = \{c_1, c_2 ...c_m\}$ the set of items that user i has already chosen.
$P_t = \{p_1, p_2... p_k\} \rightarrow$ the set of items that are selected to be recommended to U_t (recommendations).

From the above formalization we have:

$u_t \rightarrow$ the user who will receive the recommendations.
$C_t = \{t_1, t_2... t_m\} \rightarrow$ the set of items that U_t has already used.
$Ri = \{r_{ck} ... r_{cj}\} \rightarrow$ the set of ratings that a user i has given to an item c_j.
The above problem in combinatorial terms, can be expressed as follows:
   "Which is the optimal[1] set of items that we can recommend to a user?"

In order to operationalize the above problem in Operations Research terms, the following elements are defined:

Form of Problem Solution: The solution to the above problem is a selection of items from set A, that represents the set of items to be recommended (P_t).

Element of Solution: The element of solution is the single item r_j that will be recommended to the user.

Criterion of Choice: The criterion for selecting an item from A and use it as a recommendation in P_t. It can be expressed by a function of multiple criteria $f(c_1, c_2, ... c_3)$. Depending on the value of this function, it can be determined if the item can be used as a recommendation.

Evaluation Criterion: The criterion, which that will be used in order to evaluate the solution/recommendations provided to Ut. One of the most difficult and crucial tasks towards the solution of the recommendation problem is to define an evaluation criterion that could increase the quality of recommendations, without increasing the time

---

[1] Optimal means the set of items that will best match the user interests.

consumed for the algorithm execution. In general the evaluation criterion is used for evaluating the solutions produced from an algorithm. A metaheuristic can produce a vast number of possible solutions. The evaluation criterion is used by the metaheuristic to evaluate the solutions and choose the optimal one[15].

3.2   Algorithms

Collaborative-Filtering as a Greedy-Construction Algorithm (CGA). The first algorithm implemented is a Greedy Construction algorithm, which is based on the Collaborative Filtering. The algorithm has the following characteristics:

Criterion of Choice: The criterion upon which an item c from A will be selected and used as a recommendation in P_t for the user U_t is the "collaborative rating":

$$r'_{tc} = \bar{r}_t + \frac{\sum correl(U_t, U_i) * (r_{ic} - \bar{r}_i)}{\sum correl(U_t, U_i)} \tag{1}$$

Where:

r'_{tc}: is the predicted rating for the U_t for item c.
$\bar{r}_t$: is the average rating score of U_t.
$\bar{r}_i$: is the average rating of a user U_i.
$correl(U_t, U_i)$: is the correlation between users U_t and U_i, based on their known ratings.
r_{ic}: is the rating of item c from user i.

The algorithm is executed for a target user U_t from U, as follows:

1.   Pick the target user U_t from U.
2.   Calculate all correlations between U_t and the other users of U.
3.   Create neighbors of users that share correlation higher than 0.5, in a set $U_{similars}$.
4.   Based on those users, calculate the collaborative score for each item they have rated, and user U_t hasn't rated.
5.   Create the set A_{recs}, consisting of the above (step 4) rating
6.   For each item in A_{recs}: if it has score greater than 4, put the item in the recommendations set P_t.
7.   After putting all the appropriate items in P_t, recommend the items to the user.
8.   Evaluate the solution. Compare the average of the correlations the user had with all the users, with the one he has now.
9.   End.

Collaborative Metaheuristic Algorithm (CMA). This is the second algorithm that was developed and tested. CF can be used both as a metaheuristic and as a constructive algorithm. Constructive or Heuristic Algorithms, construct a solution from zero, building it element by element. To use a constructive CF, we created a solution from zero, adding items based on their collaborative score. To implement a collaborative model in a Metaheuristic Algorithm. An algorithm which uses already existent solutions, to find better ones. The basic elements of the CFA are the following:

Criterion of Choice: The criterion upon which an item c is selected from A for inclusion or exclusion to P_t is the following:

Inclusion Criterion:

$$g_c = \frac{0{,}5*d_t+0{,}4*correl'(U_t,U_i)+0{,}1*r_{ic}}{d_t+1+correl'(U_t,U_i)+r_{ic}} * random > y \qquad (2)$$

Exclusion criterion:

$$h_c = \frac{0{,}5*d_t+0{,}4*\frac{1}{correl'(U_t,U_i)}+0{,}1*\frac{1}{r_{ic}}}{d_t+\frac{1}{correl'(U_t,U_i)}+\frac{1}{r_{ic}}} * random > v \qquad (3)$$

Where:

$$d_t = \left| \frac{\sum_i^n correl(U_t,U_i)}{n} - \frac{\sum_i^n correl'(U_t,U_i)}{n} \right| = \left| \overline{correl(U_t)} - \overline{correl'(U_t)} \right| \qquad (4)$$

d_t : is the absolute difference between the initial average correlation the user had, and the current average correlation he has now.

$\overline{correl(U_t)}$: The initial average correlation of U_t with other users.

$\overline{correl'(U_t)}$: The current average correlation of U_t with other users.

$correl'(U_t, U_i)$: The new correlation between U_t and U_i, after the algorithm has removed and imported new items.

$correl(U_t, U_i)$: The initial correlation user U_t had with other users, before the start of the algorithm.

r_{ic}: is the rating of item c from user U_i.

$random$: A randomly generated number between 0 and 1. This variable is used to make the CMA a probabilistic algorithm. This is used to express the vagueness and randomness in human behavior.

y, v: Those are the intensification/diversity factors, in this article we are going to call them scope values, because they determine the scope of the solutions area that the algorithm is going to check. With higher values of y and v, less often the algorithm will allow a change to happen in P_t, be it either an import or removal.

Evaluation Criterion: The difference between the initial value of average correlation and the present value of average correlation, of the same user. The purpose of this criterion is to describe the user based on the average correlation he has with the users that are similar to him (correl(U_t,U_i)>0.5). Our aim is to reconstruct the target user's ratings, with new items and see if he still remains similar with the users that used to be highly correlated with him. Every time the algorithm produces a solution, we evaluate it based on the following:

$$min(d_t) = min\left(\left|Avg(correl(t,i))' - Avg(correl(t,i))\right|\right) \qquad (5)$$

The algorithm is being executed in the following way:

1. Calculate the initial average correlation $\overline{correl(U_t)}$ for U_t.

2.   Create U'^2_t.
3.   Calculate[3] a current average correlation value $\overline{correl'(U_t)}$, either randomly or based on U'_t.
4.   Calculate d_t. $d_{best}=d_t$.
5.   Set $P_{best}=P_t$.
6.   For counter = 0, counter<x*[4], counter++
    a.   Pick a user U_i from $U_{similars}$.
       i.   For each item of U_i
      ii.   Pick an item c that U_i has already rated
     iii.   Check if c belongs to C_t or P_t.
          1.   If it does, check if the removal criterion is fulfilled.
             a.   If it is remove the item from P_t.
             b.   Else do nothing.
          2.   If it does not, check if the removal criterion is fulfilled.
             a.   If it is, import the item in P_t.
             b.   Else do nothing.
    b.   After all removals and imports are done for P_t, calculate the new $\overline{correl'(U_t)}$.
    c.   Calculate d'_t .
    d.   Compare d'_t with d_{best} .
       i.   If $d'_t< d_{best}$. $d_{best}=d'$, $P_{best}=P_t$.
    e. $d_t=d'_t$.
7.   Propose the P_{best} as the new recommendation.
8.   End

The above Metaheuristic algorithm takes an imported set of chosen items or a set of recommendations, and sets it as Pt. Each time the metaheuristic executes a loop, it changes the contents of P_t and it compares the changes that happened on the average correlation value -Avg(Correl(U_t,U_i))- of the user. The random variable and the constants y and v are the tuning factors that decide if the algorithm is intensifying or diversifying the search. If y and v are low (around 0.4), the algorithm has a bigger scope in the solution area. This means that the algorithm is less likely to get stuck in a local minimum, but it is harder for it to find one.

The number of times the algorithm executes, is also another tuning factor for intensification. The more iterations the algorithm executes before proposing a solution, the more accurate the solution is. As the number of iterations increases, the program

---

[2] U'_t is the new user. This user can be "created" in various ways. It can be the input from another algorithm. We can create him also by removing/importing randomly solution elements from Pt.

[3] This value (average correlation) doesn't always need an U'_t to be calculated. It can be set with a random value between 1 and 0. We will explain the significance of this later on.

[4] X can be any positive number. It indicates the number of times we want the metaheuristic to execute. Each time the metaheuristic checks a new solution.

spends even more time in finding the solution. CMA is an algorithm that can use any set of choices as P_t, meaning that we can even import a random solution in it, and still expect it to produce better ones.

4   Empirical Evaluation

4.1   Dataset

The empirical evaluation of the above algorithms will be based upon the well-known dataset from epinions.com. This dataset consists of:

- A **set U** of 49.290 users.
- A **set A** of total of 139.738 items.
- In total 664824 ratings were given, as a set of $\Sigma R = r_1 + r_2 + \ldots + r_{664824}$
- Regarding trust, 487.181 statements were made.

This dataset has also been used to describe the ways of setting up a recommender system for new users, based on trust [11]. The dataset consists of 2 files. The first file provides the ratings data, to be used by the collaborative filtering. The data is represented as:

{User_id Item_id Rating}

- User_id is an integer, with positive values, which provides us the id of the user that gave the rating.
- Item_id is a positive integer also, which provides us the id of the rated item.
- Rating is a positive integer, ranging from 1 to 5. Its value provides us how much the user liked the item in ascending order. 5 means the user liked the item very much. 1 means the user didn't like the item.

4.2   Experimental Environment

In order to successfully test the algorithms' performance, we set up the experimental environment using the following:

— Java programming language for constructing and executing the algorithms.
— The datasets as well as the output data were stored in space delimited text files.
— Statistical processing was partially done by the Java applications and by the use of Microsoft Office Excel®.
— The hardware used for executing the above experiments, were 2 computers with following specs. A desktop with: Intel® i7 960 quad-core processor at 3.2 GHz, 6 GB of Ram and Windows 8 Professional OS. A laptop with: Intel® i7 2670QM quad-core processor at 2.2 GHz and 4 GB of RAM.

4.3   Algorithm Implementation and Tuning

The Collaborative-filtering Greedy-construction Algorithm (CGA), was implemented as it was described above. On the contrary, for the CMA implementation, some special tuning was performed. In order to decide the values of v and y, as well as the number of the algorithm iterations, we had to test it in some simulated datasets and some smaller samples of the Epinions Dataset. It is very important to note that as an input of the CMA after trying several scope values for this dataset - we determined that the following values should be used[5]:

- y=0.15, which means that the algorithm is likely to add new items in the recommendations set easily.
- v=0.9, which means that the algorithm will avoid deleting items often.
- Iterations' number = 50, which means that the algorithm will try 50 times to make the solution more accurate by changing the set of recommendations.

4.4   Results

We executed both algorithms for each user of the dataset, considered as the target user. Each time an algorithm was fully executed, it provided a set of recommendations for the target user. We evaluated the precision and recall of this set, using a test set consisting of the 30% of user ratings which we removed and treated as unknown to the algorithm. The results of the evaluation are summarized in the table below:

	CGA	CMA
Average Recall	0,004872652	0,00808811
Average Precision	0,441938921	0,572996974
Average F	0,008215866	0,012658391

Except from the average values, we checked how both algorithms performed throughout the dataset. The following charts (Fig 1, Fig 2) demonstrate that the CMA performed better, throughout the whole dataset, for all the evaluation metrics. Each chart represents the average score the algorithm achieved in the corresponding metric. The average total choices, show us how many items the user has rated, when he was used as target user. It must be noted that the collaborative approach cannot respond well to a cold start situation[13;14], where the target user has provided no ratings. For cold-start conditions a content-based metaheuristic algorithms is a more efficient solution.

---

[5] In a real-time applied recommender system, those values would be determined in a training set, and then applied to the production. Also this values, could be changed in real-time execution from the system.

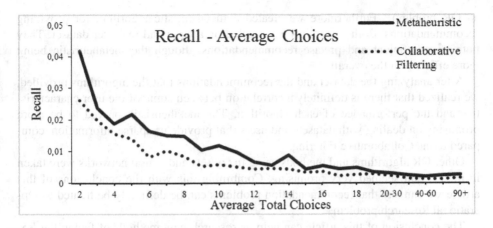

Fig. 1. Algorithm Comparison in terms of Recall

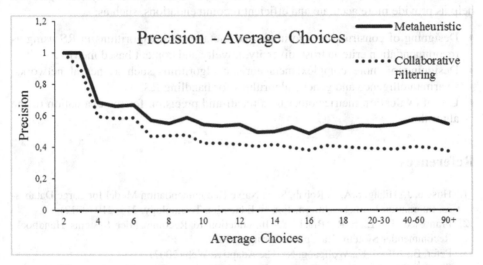

Fig. 2. Algorithm Comparison in terms of Precision

5   Conclusions and Future Work

Recommendation algorithms typically aim at predicting a set of items that the target user is most likely to be interested in. Even considering a highly accurate algorithm, there is no guarantee that the set of recommended items (produced by that algorithm) represents the optimum solution for the given recommendation problem. On the other hand, OR methods aim at optimizing the solutions to selection problems. Thus, the main idea underlying this paper is to utilize OR methods to find the optimum combination of items among the various "good" recommendation sets that can be produced.

We managed to implement the Collaborative filtering algorithm as a greedy constructive algorithm, thus demonstrating that Recommender systems can be treated as an OR problem. Furthermore we created a metaheuristic algorithm for providing recommendations. Both algorithms were tested on a large and real user dataset. They both gave efficient and precise recommendations, though the metaheuristic being more efficient in the overall.

After analyzing the dataset and the recommendations that the algorithms provided, we realized that there is definitely a correlation between some of the user characteristics and the performance of each algorithm. The metaheuristic proved to be more promising on dealing with datasets and users that provide us sparse information, compared to the Collaborative Filtering.

Other OR algorithms and methods using fuzzy sets and neural networks were taken in notice, and seemed very promising. Combining this with the conclusions of this article we can say that recommendation problems can be definitely be treated as Operational Research problem.

The conclusion of this article can help us research new methods of facing the RS. With the use of OR, we can definitely create new algorithms and systems that can help us provide more accurate and efficient recommendations, such as:

- Designing of constructive algorithms and metaheuristic algorithms in RS using as recommendation criteria trust, diversity, novelty and content based metrics.
- Designing of more complex metaheuristic algorithms such as neural networks, swarm intelligence and genetic algorithms for handling RS.
- Use of evaluation metrics other than recall and precision for the evaluation of the algorithms.

References

1. Hosein, J., Hiang, S.A.T., Robab, S.: A Naive Recommendation Model for Large Databases. Internation Journal of Information an Education Technology, 216–219 (2012)
2. Fransesco, R., Lior, R., Brach, S.: Introduction to Recommender Systems Handbook. Recommender Systems Handbook. Springer (2011)
3. Peter, B., Alfred, K., Wolfgang, N.: The Adaptive Web (2007)
4. Sharma, S.C.: Introductory Operation Research. Discovery Publishing House (2006)
5. Alexander, S.: Combinatorial Optimization. Springer (2003)
6. Gambetta, D.: Can We Trust Trust? Trust: Making and Breaking and Breaking Cooperative Relations (2000)
7. Qiu, Q., Annika, H.: Trust Based Recommendations for mobile Tourists in TIP. Hamiltou: [s.n.] (2008)
8. Fan, W.H., Cheng-Ting, W.: A strategy oriented operation module for recommender systems in E-commerce. Computers nad Operations Research (2010)
9. Paolo, C., Franca, G., Roberto, T.: Investigating the Persuasion Potential of Recommender Systems from a Quality Perspective: An Empirical Study. ACM Transactions on Interactive Intelligent Systems 2 (2012)
10. Saul, V., Pablo, C.: Rank and Relevance in Novelty and Diversity Metrics for Recommender Systems

11. Messa, P., Avesani, P.: Trust aware bootsraping of recommender systems. In: Proceedings of ECAI 2006 Workshop on Recommender Systems, pp. 29–32 (2006)
12. Chen, L.-S., Hsu, F.-H., Chen, M.-C., Hsu, Y.-C.: Developing recommender systems with the consideration of product profitability for sellers (2008)
13. Schein, A.I., Popescul, A., Ungar, L.H., Pennock, D.M.: Methods and Metrics for Cold-Start Recommendations (2002)
14. Lashkari, Y., Metral, M., Maes, P.: Collaborative Interface Agents (1994)
15. Gonzalez, T.F.: Handbook of Approximation Algorithms and Metaheuristics (2007)

E-Governance Transparency in Brazil – The Lack of Usability Is Detrimental to Citizenship

Cayley Guimarães, Leandro Daniel Reis Silva,
Diego Roberto Antunes, and Rodrigo Formighieri

Informatics Department, Federal University of Paraná, Curitiba - PR – Brazil
PRODEMGE, Belo Horizonte – MG – Brazil
profcayley@yahoo.com.br, leandro.daniel@hotmail.com,
drantunes@gmail.com, formighieri@bol.com.br

Abstract. Brazilian law requires that all cities with over 10.000 habitants divulge via Internet information regarding budgetary and financial information. Such information is an acquired social right that provides an arena in which to debate, demand for rights to be implemented, review policies and practices, among others, to guarantee that transparency and citizenship rights are respected. The transparency (government accountability) such mandatory e-governance (democratic, quality tools for State-Citizen interaction) information is still elusive. Only 14 percent of the cities required do so; and only 75 percent of those who divulge do it via Internet. This research surveyed the sites for availability and compliance with the law. It also analyzed the usability (both via Heuristic Evaluation - of 15 sites; and User Testing – with 5 users performing 4 tasks each on 3 different city sites). This research shows a direct link between the lack of usability and the lack of transparency and citizenship.

Keywords: E-Governance, Transparency, Usability, Citizenship.

1   Introduction

The Brazilian Federal Constitution from 1998 [4], in its 5th article, incise XXXIII says that: "[…] everyone has the right to receive from public agencies information of her particular, collective or general interest, that will be provided within the time frame of the law, under penalty of liability, except for those information whose secrecy is essential to the security of society and the State". Regulating Law 12.527 [22] states that all municipalities with a population of over 10,000 habitants must divulge via Internet information regarding budget and financial information. It is very important that an acquired social right be reflected in the country's carta magna. This gives the society an arena in which to debate their information needs; a basis from which to demand for rights to be implemented; an opportunity to review policies and practices among others, to guarantee that the citizenship rights are respected [21].

E-Governance, focused on the interaction between the State and the Citizen [18] is more than the automation of the processes, but a change in the manner which such interaction acquires quality, transparency, democratic participation and accountability

S. Yamamoto (Ed.): HIMI 2014, Part II, LNCS 8522, pp. 590–601, 2014.
© Springer International Publishing Switzerland 2014

[15]. The Brazilian government, thus, launched the Programa Brasil Transparente (PBT) – Transparent Brazil Program – establishing the implementation of such civil right [3]. Transparency is related to government accountability, and allows citizens to become aware of government spending, thus contributing to reducing corruption and bribery, among others.

Information dissemination along with visibility into government actions and disclosure of public resources spending allow people to partake in the political scenario by engaging in issues that affect them. Such engagement gives the citizens a tool with which to see that pubic funds are used properly and according to their needs [9]. Detailed transparency allows for real citizenship exercise [1]. Transparency is a vital factor in strengthening the relations between government and citizens, and should take the form of complete, objective, reliable, relevant information in systems that have usability, are reliable, easy to access and comprehend [13].

However, according to IBGE demographic census (2010) [8], of the 5.562 cities in Brazil, 55% of them should divulge their data, but less than 14% of those required do so; and only 75% of those who divulge do it via Internet. Most of the available sites lack information organization, search engine, usability and, most importantly, they do not comply with the law mandated by the PBT [3]. The lack of availability of information about State actions compounds with the lack of organization of civil society in Brazil (a vicious cycle) to result in very low political participation in the welfare of the general population: the State becomes tutor of people, who are, thus, deprived of actual citizenship [16]. Information and knowledge are among the means that allow for democratic relations; and democracy consolidation depends on the effective access and use, by citizens, of information about State actions [6]. Information democratization is essential to the human collective [11].

Information systems in general, and transparency information systems in particular, should be useful, and must present good information organization and interactivity with human beings so that citizens may interact socially, thus enhancing the quality of life and social interaction [20]. This concept of Human-Computer Interaction is akin to the idea of usability. Usability involves the ability of the system to allow the user to be able to achieve her goals. [2] list some desired characteristics of usability: easy of use; ability to transform goals into feasible successful operations and execution of tasks; error perception and recovery among others. Those characteristics can be engineered. And, in the case of this research, these characteristics can be verified. A site that lacks usability will not be conducive of success, given that users will face difficulties to perform the desired tasks; and, sometimes, the user will not be able to achieve her goals. It follows that government sites aimed at e-governance and transparency may not dismiss usability: it is paramount that citizens are able to obtain information. Otherwise, the site would not have served its purpose, and lack of citizenship ensues.

This research shows a direct link between the lack of usability of the required sites for transparency and the lack of citizenship. In order to show such link, the following methodological steps were performed: a survey of the existing requirements, and the compliance of the sites with them; a survey of existing availability of information on government sites; an analyses cross-referencing such surveys, emphasizing the discrepancies; user-centered heuristic evaluation and user test to characterize the information organization problems due to the lack of usability in existing sites and an analyses correlating usability problems with real-life needs of the users for their citizenship.

2   Usability, Transparency and Citizenship

Citizenship concept is inspired by the Greco-Roman days from ideas of democracy; popular participation in the collective destinies; sovereignty of the people and individual liberty. Currently, full citizenship is contained in the social, political and civil rights, and imply in the citizen's participation of society's destiny [14]. To that end, people should be provided with relevant information in order to make judgments. A person who practices democracy cannot lack knowledge and information lest the citizenship exercise results incomplete because the citizen wouldn't integrally express her liberty and will.

According to [20] the technological revolution brought about by the Internet allows for instantaneous communication through space and time providing access to a new social and political reality, bringing about a new scenario of various new political strategies. The installation and development of democracy in the electronic space are now fundamental requirements of the possibility to discuss democracy in the modern society; without such democratizations, there is no effective democracy [17]. Three phenomena bring the Internet closer to a virtual public domain: "connection environment", "complexity of contents" and "Interaction systems" [7]. These spheres empower the citizen to exercise her political rights. As for the first (connection) people have a privileged space in which to expose publicly their opinions and a place where they can obtain relevant information. As for the complexity, a dense network of data and content of all sorts is available. Such complexity is not without cost: the use and understanding of such content requires access, technology know-how, and usability. As for interaction, the citizen has direct access to forum, peers, politicians, government agencies etc. We are thus entitled to conclude that the new technologies change the way people communicate, interact and obtain knowledge and information about government actions [5].

Information systems may be defined as a set of interrelated components that collect, store, retrieve, process and disseminate information [10]. They affect people's daily lives, and their successful interaction with people is linked to its integration with the social environment in which it is immersed. It is necessary that information systems be useful and present usability for their users, to the extent that such systems increase information quality, transparency, and means to assess the actions and services from the government and public institutions, enhancing new forms of participation and influence from the people in public policies, changing the very structure of the political organization of the society [20]. Usability involves the system's ability to allow users to easily attain their goals of interaction with the system [19]. [2] lists characteristics required from a system to have good usability: easy to use; easy to understand; easy to perform the desired tasks; to succeed in the execution of tasks;

allow the user to perceive and correct errors. Thus, an information system lacking usability will not be successful in aiding the users to achieve their goals. In the case of this research, the lack of usability in sites of e-governance transparency prevents the user to access information for citizenship exercise.

According to [20], the Internet is part of people's lives, providing means with which they can exercise their citizenship and democracy: enhancing quality, transparency and accountability of actions and services by the government and public institutions; enhancing new ways of public participation and influence in government practices and policies; and modifying the very structure of the political organization within society. The creation and development of democracy in the electronic arena are fundamental requirements of the possibility to talk about democracy in the current society, without whom, there is no effective democracy [17]. Thus, it is mandatory that citizens are capable of obtaining the information they consider relevant, otherwise, they won't achieve their transparency goals.

3   Methodology

In order to show that the sites lacked usability, and therefore was not providing the citizen with adequate information for their needs about citizenship in the form of lack of transparency of government acts, this research conducted three phases of usability evaluation. First, the authors studied the PBT (CGU, 2013) for consistency, clarity, guidelines and compliance by the cities to the requirements. This phase consisted of document analysis and site overview.

Then, the authors analyzed 15 different sites thus composed: 5 sites from small cities (less than 50,000 inhabitants – Rondonópolis, Macaíba, Três Rios, Goanésia, Colinas do Tocantins), 5 sites from medium cities (between 50,001 and 500,000 inhabitants – Alegrete, Mossoró, Rio Grande, Macaé, Ilhéus) and 5 sites from large cities (over 500,001 inhabitants – Goiânia, Porto Alegre, Belo Horizonte, Belém, Manaus) from all regions of the country using Jakob Nielsen's Heuristic Evaluation. Brazil is geopolitically divided into five regions (also called macroregions – North, Northeast, Central-West, Southesast and South) by the Instituto Brasileiro de Geografia e Estatística (IBGE), composed by the States within them.

Finally, the authors conducted 15 traditional end-user studies with 5 users: each user performed 4 tasks (deemed important by the PBT (CGU, 2013)) each on a small, medium and large-sized city:

A) What is the amount for the ISS (Imposto Sobre Serviço – Tax on Services) collected in the month of January 2013? ISS being one of the major sources of income for the cities.
B) What is the net amount collected for the month of January 2013? This would give a ballpark figure of income and expenditure.
C) What is the highest salary within the Environmental Department? Political job positions in Brazil are notorious for their high salaries.
D) What are the communication channels to enquire about an specific information?

4   Results

4.1   Document Analysis

Law number 12527 regulates information access from incise XXXIII of article 5 from the Brazilian Constitution. Financial information is crucial for government Transparency. However, the law is incomplete, ambiguous, and vague. Several Income sources and expenditure transactions are not detailed, there is no specific orientation as to their nature, format of presentation, sources etc. – which opens a backdoor for those who do not won't to abide to the spirit of the law.

The vast majority of the sites that supposedly have the goal of divulging such information do not achieve them, be it because they lack structure, use proprietary software; require a lot of red tape for the common citizen to access among others. It was also observed that private contractors developed the existing sites. Most of the sites overviewed did not comply with the law even in the most basic information, such as address and contact. And all of the sites had some sort of usability problem that prevented the citizen to access the necessary information.

4.2   Heuristic Evaluation

The authors used Jakob Nielsen's heuristic evaluation [12], adopting the role of user to analyze each of the 15 sites, and found a total of 71 major errors. This means that if the same error appeared in different sites, such as "broken link", then it was counted only once, as a representative of that category (otherwise the number of errors would explode without any additional information). As per their severity (frequency of occurrence, impact for the user task, persistence and impact) 2 of those errors were considered simple to correct (Label and Font Size); 17 required special attention (change of page without the respective change of page label, different types of files and formats for research results etc.); 40 errors required mandatory correction (Information hierarchy, broken links, data entry validation, mandatory fields etc.) and 12 of them were considered catastrophic – errors that have to be corrected otherwise functionality would not ensue, such as lack of an information required by law. Unfortunately, these are not novel errors: Usability is a well-known and studied concept that should have been widely incorporated into all sorts of systems by now; and still, the same types of errors keep appearing in the most important ones, preventing the user to achieve her desired goal.

Next, some examples of such errors for each heuristic is presented:

— H1 – Visibility of the State of the System:

- The link "Other Information" on the site of the city of Três Rios and others: the page opens with only the title, with no content

— H2 – Correspondence between the System and the Real World – no apparent error found
— H3 – User Control and Liberty:

- For the site of the city Alegrete and others, it is impossible to navigate back to the home page
- For the city of Goiania, the link to "Salaries" took too long to process, and there was no way for the user to cancel the operation
- No "Contact us" link was found in several of the sites

— H4 – Consistency and Patterns:

- Most cities did not provide the required information on government employees
- Some links opened to other web pages, and some opened to files (usually PDF – no open source format)
- Use of acronyms, without explanation of their meaning

— H5 – Error Prevention:

- Overall, there is a lack of data-entry error treatment
- There are two sites related to Transparency for the city of Goianésia

— H6 – Help for the user to recognize, diagnose and recover from errors:

- Most links open to sites and/or files that are hidden. Once found, there is no direct way for the user to return to her point of origin

— H7 – Recognition, instead of Remembering:

- Lack of adequate information hierarchy and adequate labels for actions

— H8 – Flexibility and Efficiency of Use:

- Lack of links to access Money Allocation for infra-structure contracts

— H9 – Minimalistic Design and Aesthetics:

- The user has to navigate many links to access the Ombudsman page
- Most page are longer than the screen, and not adaptable to different platforms
- Results from a search are not formatted

— H10 – Help and Documentation

- In general, there is no help and/or documentation.

Figure 1 shows a graphic of the errors distributed among the heuristics (heuristic, number of errors and percentage). For example, for heuristic 1 (slice in light purple, there were 6 errors representing 9% of the total errors. Note that heuristic 5 – error prevention, had a total of 28% of the errors; along with heuristic 9 – Minimalistic design and aesthetics, with a total of 16%.

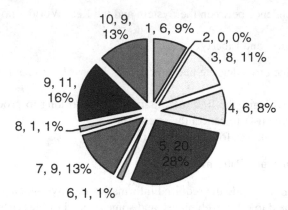

Fig. 1. Graph showing each heuristic (from center, clockwise), the number of errors and the percentage

4.3   End-User studies

The End-User studies followed traditional protocols (i.e. the participants were told what to do, not how; they were encouraged to Think-Aloud, they signed agreement forms). The sessions were not filmed though. At least two authors were present at each session (one as a facilitator and the others as observers). Five users participated in the Evaluation sessions: 3 females, and 2 males, aged from 26 to 61 years of age (average 45 years of age). All participants have graduate degrees in Medicine, Computer Science, Administration and Public Administration. Four participants work on the private sector (as mechanic, doctor, entrepreneurs) and one works in a government autarchy as a public administrator. The participants deal with public information on their daily lives, and their levels of education and computer skills are high. Albeit having profiles that would be considered skewed, the results below show that the participants still had problems overcoming the usability problems. The authors wonder what would happen if the participants were of a different (less sophisticated) profile.

User 1 – Tasks for a site from a Large City (Manaus – State Capital of Amazônia – North part of Brazil. Population: 1.8 Million):

A)   The user saw a link labeled ISS, but it turned out to be a link for business only. Back on the home page, the user navigated through **five different links**, without success. Lots of errors, and broken links appeared. The user complained about the design of the site. Back on the home page, the user chose the link for General Balance, but for 2013 there was only a note: "Information will be posted here". **The user gave up after 10:45 minutes without finding the information.**

B)   On the home page, the user found the link "Relatório de Responsabilidade Fiscal" (Fiscal Responsibility Report). The report was divided bi-monthly. The user found the information of the collected tax for the 12 months, and thought that those were the net balance. That is to say: **the user got the wrong information and took it to be the correct one**.

C) After 4 navigations, and **05:40 minutes, the user gave up** on the task.

D) The user found a "Contact Us" link, which was broken: "now, that's embarrassing, isn't it?" The user tried searching for a little longer, and a few links after gave up after **03:15 minutes.**

— *Tasks for a site from a Medium City* (Ilhéus – in the State of Bahia – Northeast part of Brazil. Population: 0.2 Million):

A) The user found a link for Income, but **there was no information available**.

B) There was no information about 2013. **The user gave up after 03:00 minutes**.

C) In order to find out the salary, the user had to know the name of the employee.

D) **The site didn't enable the Contact link**.

— *Tasks for a site from a Small City* (Colinas do Tocantins – in the State of Tocantins – Central part of Brazil. Population: 17,984):

A) The user found a link for Income, and found the information in **01:00 minute**.

B) The user found the information in **46 seconds**.

C) The user followed several links related to Environment, but did not find the information, and **gave up after 02:25 minutes**.

D) The user didn't find a link on the site for Transparency. The user went back to the site for the city and chose the contact link as a **possible** answer after 01:30 minutes.

User 2 – *Tasks for a site from a Large City* (Belém – State Capital of Pará – North part of Brazil. Population: 2.8 Million):

A) The user navigated through 4 links, and concluded that there was no such information. The user **gave up after 05:00 minutes**.

B) The user found the information in **30 seconds**.

C) The user used the search option that opened a file outside the system. The user used the browser back button to return to the home page. **The user gave up after 09:20 minutes**.

D) The user found the contact link, which had no e-mail or form, only a phone number, **after 01:50 seconds.**

— *Tasks for a site from a Medium City* (Macaé – in the State of Rio de Janeiro – Southeast part of Brazil. Population: 0.22 Million):

A) The user found a link for Income, but **there was no information available**.

B) There was no information about 2013. **The user gave up after 03:00 minutes**.

C) In order to find out the salary, the user had to know the name of the employee.

D) **The site didn't enable the Contact link**.

— *Tasks for a site from a Small City* (Goianésia – in the State of Goiás – Central part of Brazil. Population: 15,678):

A) The user found a link for Income, and found the information in **01:00 minute**.
B) The user found the information in **46 seconds**.
C) The user followed several links related to Environment, but did not find the information, and **gave up after 02:25 minutes**.
D) The user didn't find a link on the site for Transparency. The user went back to the site for the city and chose the contact link as a **possible** answer after 01:30 minutes.

User 3 – Tasks for a site from a Large City (Belo Horizonte – State Capital of Minas Gerais – Southeast part of Brazil. Population: 2.47 Million):

A) The user navigated back and forth through 10 links, and got "lost" several times. The user had to use the browser to return to the home page. The user concluded that there was no such information. The user **gave up after 10:00 minutes**.
B) The user found the information in **02:30 minutes**.
C) The user found a link for Salaries, but it only contained the minimum wage for each department. **The user gave up after 02:00 minutes**.
D) The user found the contact link, which had telephone and chat as options.

- Tasks for a site from a Medium City (Rio Grande – in the State of Rio Grande do Sul – South part of Brazil. Population: 0.17 Million):

A) The user found a link for Income, but was in doubt about the options. The random selected option opened a file outside the system: "too big". The user tried the browser search. **The user found the information after 01:45 minutes**.
B) The user repeated the steps from task A, and found the information at the end of the file in **02:50 minutes**.
C) The user was lost for **07:00 minutes** before a link took him to an expired page.
D) The "Online" link was broken. He then proceeded to navigate through the site to find a phone number after **05:00 minutes**.

— *Tasks for a site from a Small City* (Três Rios – in the State of Rio de Janeiro – Southeast part of Brazil. Population: 17,352):

A) The user found a link for Analytical Balance, which generated a PDF file. The user browsed the file for **01:50 minute** before giving up. The user then used the **search tool from the browser to find the information.**
B) The user browsed the PDF file found at the previous task and found the information in **01:36 minute**.
C) The site offered only two links: government and news. The user found some spreadsheets with only names and numbers, **but wasn't sure what they meant.**
D) The user found the "Talk to us" link under the "Services" menu, **but wasn't sure how to contact.**

User 4 – Tasks for a site from a Large City (Porto Alegre – State Capital of Rio Grande do Sul – South part of Brazil. Population: 1.47 Million):

A) The user spent 35 seconds looking through the menus before scrolling down to the link for Transparency, which opened a new window. Found the information in **01:35 minute**.

B)   The user found the total information in 20 seconds, and **mistook it for the net information.**

C)   The user navigated through 5 menus and had difficulties with acronyms for the departments. The user found the list of salaries, but in order to find the salary, the user had to select each employee. **The user gave up after 03:20 minutes.**

D)   Found the link "Information Service to the Citizen".

— *Tasks for a site from a Medium City* (Mossoró – in the State of Rio Grande do Norte – Northeast part of Brazil. Population: 0.23 Million):

A) The user found the information in **01:45 minute.**

B) The user found the information in 20 seconds.

   C) The user found the link for "Expenditure" but did not "see" the entire page. The user browsed 3 more links and **gave up after 07:28 minutes.**

   D) The user found the link "Contact us".

— *Tasks for a site from a Small City* (Macaíba – in the State of Rio Grande do Norte – Southeast part of Brazil. Population: 70,586):

A) The user navigated 6 links and found the information after **02:00 minutes.**

B) The user found the information in 15 seconds.

   C) The user found the names of the employees, **but didn't find to which department the employee belonged.**

   D) The user found the link "Ombudsman", and **considered that to be the only channel.**

User 5 – Tasks for a site from a Large City (Goiânia – State Capital of Goiás – Central part of Brazil. Population: 1.35 Million):

A)   The user browsed the site for **02:00 minutes**. The user found the "Income" link, **which opened to empty files.**

B)   Same as above: **the link opened to empty files.**

C)   The user browsed 3 links, and found the page for **the total only** of the salaries.

D)   The user **only found the link "Contact us".**

— *Tasks for a site from a Medium City* (Alegrete – in the State of Rio Grande do Sul – South part of Brazil. Population: 171,786):

A) The user browsed aimlessly through 7 links. The links were acronyms. **The user gave up after 06:30 minutes.**

B) The user found the information in 30 seconds.

C) The user browsed the site aimlessly and **gave up after 13:00 minutes.**

D) The user browsed the site for 02:45 minutes before going back to the home page. The user found a phone number and decided that that was the **only** communication channel after **05:00 minutes.**

— *Tasks for a site from a Small City* (Rondonópolis – in the State of Mato Grosso – Central part of Brazil. Population: 144,049):

A) The user found the information after **02:50 minutes**.
B) The user found the information in 30 seconds.
C) The user found a link with 8 employees. The user concluded that those were all the employees for the department. To find the salary, the user had to click on each employee. **The user gave up after 02:30 minutes**.
D) The user found the link for "Ombudsman" **only**.

5   Conclusions and Considerations

Transparency of government (money) transactions is a right that is guaranteed by the Brazilian Constitution, and regulated by law. This right is fundamental for full citizenship exercise. However, the government does not provide the municipalities with clear, precise information with which the cities should build their information systems to divulge financial statements. There are 5.562 cities in Brazil, 55% of them should divulge their data, but less than 14% of those required do so; and only 75% of those who divulge do it via Internet, as required by law.

Site overview, heuristic evaluation and end-user testing revealed that the sampled sites from small, medium and large cities of all regions of Brazil failed to provide the user with the desired information due to usability errors. This lack of usability is detrimental to full citizenship exercise. These usability errors are basic, and should not occur, especially on sites of great public importance.

Government and society must come together to fix such state of things in order to make Brazil a Transparent nation.

References

1. Araújo, L.R., Souza, J.F.: Aumentando a transparência do governo por meio da transformação de dados governamentais abertos em dados ligados. Revista Eletrônica de Sistemas de Informação 10(1), article 7 (2011)
2. Carroll, J.M., Moran, T.P.: Design Rationale: concepts, technique and use. LEA, New Jersey (1996)
3. CGU (2013), http://cgu.gov.br (accessed at December 12, 2013)
4. Brazilian Federal Constitution (1998), http://www.planalto.gov.br
5. Fishkin, J.S.: Possibilidades democráticas virtuais. In: Eisenberg, J., Cepik, M. (eds.). UFMG, Belo Horizonte (2002)
6. Gauderer, E.C.: Os direitos do pasiente: um manual de sobrevivência. R.J.: Record (1998)
7. Gomes, W.: Opinião política na internet (2001), http://www.unb.br (accessed at December 12, 2013)
8. IBGE: Census (2010), http://www.ibge.gov.br (acessed at December 12, 2013)
9. Lathrop, D., Ruma, L. (eds.): Open government: transparency, collaboration and participation in practice. O'Reilly Media (2010)
10. Laudon, K.C., Laudon, J.P.: Information Systems. Pearson, N.Y. (2004)
11. Moore, N.: Policies for an information society. ASLIB Proceedings 50(1), 20–24 (1998)
12. Nielsen, J.: Heuristic Evaluation (2013), http://www.nngroup.com (acessed at December 12, 2013)

13. OECD, http://www.oecd.org (acessed at December 12, 2013)
14. Pinsky, J., Pinsky, C.B. (orgs.): História da cidadania. Contexto, Paulo (2003)
15. Prado, et al.: Iniciativas de Governo Eletrônico. Revista Eletrônica de Sistemas de Informação 10(1), article 5 (2011)
16. Prata, N.V.: Informação e democracia deliberative: a dimensão informacional do processo de elaboração participative das leis. ECI/UFMG, BH (2007)
17. Rubin, A.A.C.: O lugar da política na sociedade contemporânea. In: Prado, J.L.A., Sovik, L. (eds.) Lugar Global e lugar Nenhum (2001)
18. Ruediger, M.A.: Governo eletrônico e democracia. Organizações & Sociedade 6, 25 (2002)
19. Scapin, D.L.: The need for a psycho-engineering approach to HCI. In: Abergo/Fundacentro, pp. 03–22 (1993)
20. Sorj, B.: Brasil@povo.com. Jorge Zahar Editor, São Paulo (2003)
21. Touraine, A.: New paradigm for understanding today's world. Polity, Cambridge (2007)
22. Law 12.527, http://www.acessoainformacao.gov.br (accessed at December 12, 2013)

Qualitative Study for the Design of Assistive Technologies for Improving Quality of Life of Visually Impaired

Yosuke Kinoe and Asuka Noguchi

Graduate School of Intercultural Communication, Hosei University
2-17-1, Fujimi, Chiyoda City, Tokyo 102-8160, Japan
kinoe@hosei.ac.jp

Abstract. This paper describes an effort to create a conceptual design of an assistive technology that aims to improve quality of life of people with low vision. We carried out a qualitative study including in-depth interviews with people of low vision.

The analysis revealed several key concepts to understand people's lived experiences of low vision including the ambiguity of their self-images and burdens in the interaction with the sighted people. The importance of building 'self-confidence of managing people's appropriate appearances' of low vision was emphasized. We created a conceptual design of a total assistive solution that supported people of low vision to perform each stage of a comprehensive cycle of the arrangement of their appearances. Our challenge continues to enhance a methodology for bridging a gap between qualitative research and the design of user experience.

Keywords: qualitative study, life story, low vision, assistive technology, quality of life.

1   Introduction

This paper describes an initial effort to create a conceptual design of an assistive technology that aims to improve quality of life of people with low vision. We adopted a qualitative study approach to clarify their *felt need*[1] [3] for the assistive technologies through a careful investigation of the *lived experience* [31] of people with low vision.

1.1   Living with Vision Loss

The visual impairment is divided into blindness and low vision. The WHO global report (2012) stated more than 285 million people are visually impaired worldwide, of

---

[1] Jonathan Bradshaw (1972) distinguished between different types of need: normative need is defined by experts, professionals such as doctors, policy makers; felt need is want, desire or subjective views of need which may or may not become expressed need; expressed need is demand or felt need turned into action [3].

S. Yamamoto (Ed.): HIMI 2014, Part II, LNCS 8522, pp. 602–613, 2014.
© Springer International Publishing Switzerland 2014

whom 39 million are blind and 246 million have low vision [41]. The majority of visually impaired have low vision, however, low vision is very poorly recognized by the community and its reality is rarely understood. Globally the principal causes of low vision include cataracts, age-related macular degeneration (AMD), and diabetic retinopathy [41]. It may also result from a brain injury, or cancer of the eye.

Low vision is emphasized on an aspect of 'vision that people hold,' rather than that has been lost. It can be defined as 'vision that, even when corrected by optical refractive correction, is not adequate for a person's needs' [20] and is typically appeared as a reduction in visual acuity and/or visual field. The visual performance of person with low vision is not same. There are various types of eye conditions that cause low vision including: central loss of vision, peripheral loss of vision, hazy vision, refractive errors, contraction of visual field, glare sensitivity, adjustment of eye movement, and color blindness. Loss of vision, even partial vision loss, leads significant consequences in various aspects of human life: mobility; communication and accessing to information; personal care such as toileting and dressing; daily living such as eating, cooking, time-keeping, cleaning and shopping; social activities; education; employment; recreational activities; and safety and freedom in everyday life.

On the basis of the WHO International Classification of Impairments, Disabilities, and Handicaps (ICIDH) [38], figure 1 illustrates different levels of vision loss [6]. This scheme describes the consequences of visual diseases and disorders at the level of the organ (e.g. impairment), the person (i.e. disability, reflecting the consequences of impairment), and the person as a social being (i.e. handicap, reflecting interaction with the surroundings). It should be noted that how the organ (e.g. eye) functions does not automatically determine how the person will function in their society.

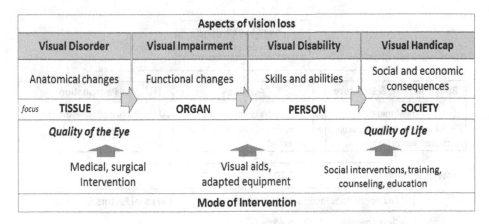

Fig. 1. Aspects of Vision Loss. (adapted from Corn, A.L. & Lusk, K.E., 2010, p.23)

1.2   Quality of Life and WHO ICF

Quality of life (QoL), as a concept, is frequently referred to in literature of various domains [32, 36] such as healthcare, rehabilitation, mental health, and nursing.

However, a definite definition of quality of life has not been obtained yet. For example, Hughes (1995) conducted a comprehensive review of 87 applied research literature, and found more than 40 different definitions of QoL [19].

The World Health Organization (WHO) has defined quality of life as 'an individual's perception of their position in life in the context of culture and value system in which they live and in relation to their goals, expectations, standards, and concerns' [39]. Quality of life has been defined as having both subjective and objective components. The objective component includes aspects of living conditions and social functioning such as employment, leisure, accommodation, and finance. The subjective component is frequently referred to as "well-being" or "life satisfaction."

Health has been defined in the WHO Constitution (1948) as 'a state of complete physical, mental, and social well-being and not merely the absence of disease or infirmity'. The functioning of an individual in a specific domain reflects an interaction between the health condition and the contextual: environmental and personal factors (Fig. 2). The WHO's International Classification of Functioning, Disability, and Health (ICF) is a framework that provides the concepts, definitions, categories and codes for functioning and disability as well as related Environmental and Personal Factors influencing them [40]. Body Functions are the physiological aspects of body systems, while Structures are the anatomical support. Actions executed by individuals are defined as Activities, and involvement in life situations is defined as Participation. Activities may relate to the interplay of multiple functions and structures. For example, essentials of jogging include the combination of orientation, balance, control of voluntary movement, muscle force, mobility of joints, structural support of bones and ligaments as well as Environmental Factors such as well-built pavements [40].

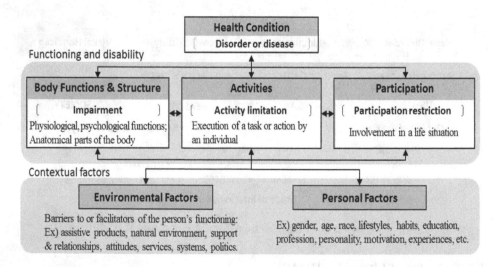

Fig. 2. WHO International Classification of Functioning, Disability and Health (ICF) [40]

1.3   Related Works: Assistive Technologies for Visually Impaired

Assistive device is located as a key component of the Environmental Factors of WHO's ICF. Assistive technology has a potentially important role to play in opening up new opportunities to disabled people and increasing the range of options open to them [17]. Various types of assistive devices and tools including conventional low-vision aids are available for people with visual impairments [1]; for example, spectacle magnifiers, stand magnifiers, large print books, audible kitchen aids, tactile scales, vibrating watches, and electronic vision enhancement systems (EVES). Recently, the wide range of advanced assistive technologies have been developed for visually impaired. Efforts include the use of various digital props, for example, an augmented cane using spatial sensors [34], intelligent way-finders for traveling [14, 26], assisting devices for shopping [24, 25], a head-mounted EVES [4], a remote infrared audible signage [16], robot-assisted navigators for traveling [27] and shopping [13].

Assistive technologies are expected to improve daily functioning of individuals with disabilities, particularly their performance of activities and pursuit of vocational, social, and community interests [29]. Historically, however, the development of assistive devices has tended to be characterized by a technology-centric approach [23]. The design of assistive technology generally did not take account of the types of their visual performances of the particular user class of low vision, instead, most assistive technology was mainly designed for its average population [18].

1.4   Our Approach

One of the most essential outcomes of assistive technology is increased quality of life of visual impairments. In the design of assistive technologies, it's essential to understand the specific needs of people with low vision in more detail, and their attitudes to visual impairment, and obtain an insight into 'hidden agendas' [33] that may not be immediately apparent.

In this paper, we examine *life-world*[2][30, 31] of people with low vision and investigate their felt-need as well as 'hidden agendas' for assistive technologies in everyday lives. We consider an integrated approach [22] that combines qualitative study and the design of assistive technologies for low vision. There exists a gulf between the outcome of field research and basis for the design of user experiences [9]. Our challenges involve methodological enhancements to bridge this gap in the research and design.

2   Qualitative Study

In order to carefully understand life-world of people with visually impaired and investigate various aspects of their potential requirements of assistive technologies, we

---

[2] "Only in the world of everyday life can a common, communicative, surrounding world be constituted. The world of everyday life is consequently man's fundamental and paramount reality." (Alfred Schutz and Thomas Luckmann, 1973).

adopted multiple qualitative research methods [8] that included structured interviews, semi-structured interviews [15], participant observation [35], and questionnaires. The triangulation of methods and data [7, 11] was taken into account.

The study started in Tokyo metropolitan area in 2010, with cooperation of a school for the blind and an association for supporting people with visually impaired. The participants were identified through the snowball sampling, a technique for gathering participants through the identification of initial subjects who can provide an escalating set of potential contacts by taking advantages of their social networks. This method is often used because the population under investigation is 'hidden' either due to low numbers of potential participants or the sensitivity of the topic [10].

We designed two different styles of the study that employed a different set of qualitative study methods. In the study 1, we employed a structured interview and e-mail interview. In the study 2, we adopted an in-depth interview. Two studies were carried out in parallel.

2.1 Study 1: Structured Interviews and Questionnaires

Method and Research Settings. We conducted a structured interview that contained three thematic categories: the conditions of the visual disorder, the conditions of everyday lives, and their felt-need. The topics of the interview were composed of eleven questions including: (a) their profiles and family structures, (b) current conditions of visual disorders and those secular changes, (c) the desires and challenges never to abandon, (d) troublesome circumstances with their everyday lives and the concerns with their social lives especially when interacting with other people, and (e) the concerns or troublesome circumstances related to the appearances of the selves including dressing. The interview session was divided into three sub-sections. First, we emphasized the establishment of a rapport with the participants, the informed consent process, and building a relationship of mutual trust. A structured interview was performed in the second section, by using a set of predefined research questions described above. In the last section, it was followed by an open-ended discussion. The interview session was carried out in December, 2013 in a small meeting room of public facility and lasted for approximately two hours.

Depending on the condition of participants' visual disorders, they were allowed to choose an e-mail interview [12] instead of a face-to-face interview. The questionnaires were composed of the same eleven questions used in the structured interview and were distributed to the candidates of respondents via e-mail. The participants were asked to describe their responses in free format. This study was carried out between October and November, 2013.

Participants. Sixteen participants out of twenty candidates of visually impaired who were identified through snowball sampling participated to the study. Seven respondents (female, aged between 34 and 62, average 46.3) joined a structured interview, and other nine respondents (six females and three males, aged between 18 and 39, average 27) joined an e-mail interview.

2.2   Analysis Results of the Study 1

All interviews were transcribed into texts. The responses in a free format obtained from e-mail interviews were arranged and incorporated into data. The analysis process included: (1) formatting and segmenting textual data; (2) open-coding (with ad hoc codes); (3) writing analytic memos for text segment; (4) performing content analysis by using contextual data such as individual visual performance; (5) re-coding with focus; (6) developing the concepts and core categories.

Observed Felt Needs Reflected the Visual Conditions and Living Environment. For example, some of participants with visual field contraction and participants of the blindness presented their needs of safely walking outside, timely noticing of an important sign from background, and efficiently handling of household affairs such as cooking and cleaning. The participants of low vision commonly presented examples of the difficulties in their everyday lives included finding out a person in a crowded place, reading a menu and texts in small or colored characters especially on a liquid-crystal display, writing texts with small characters, and playing with a ball game. On the other hand, working participants of low vision described needs of efficiently handling of administrative works such as documentation, making appropriate responses while meeting with others, and safe driving.

Difficulties in a Social Situation. The participants generally insisted that they were happy to enjoy the interactions with the sighted people in various situations as a friend, a colleague, or family. However, they simultaneously stated their difficulties in making smooth reactions and conversations with the sighted people particularly in a meeting or a party with large number of people.

The Appropriateness of the Appearances that Most People of Low Vision Care. In a general inquiry about their felt-needs for their daily living, only a few participants mentioned they expected a support for their dressing. On the other hand, for a specific inquiry about their appearances, thirteen of sixteen participants responded that they were paying much attentions to the appropriateness of the appearances and make-up.

2.3   Study 2: In-Depth Interviews

Method and Research Settings. Multiple qualitative research methods were employed in the study: semi-structured interviews, life story interviews [2, 28], participant observations, questionnaires, and open-ended discussions. The study was composed of the series of interview sessions that covered the variety of topics for understanding life-world of visually impaired. During the initial session, we emphasized the establishment of a rapport with the participant, and building a relationship of mutual trust. After the informed consent process, we started the series of interviews from descriptive topics such as (a) family structure, (b) a biographical sketch, and (c) current conditions and secular changes of visual disorders. While the interviews were iterated, the topics were gradually deepened into private topics related to *life story* such as their turning points or memorable experiences (both positive and negative), primary matters of interest including their wishes, and personal experiences of troublesome circumstances in everyday lives. Once the participants began their talk, we carefully avoided interrupting their narratives, particularly during life story interviews. The interview sessions of fourteen times were carried out between October, 2012 and November, 2013 and lasted approximately thirty five hours in total.

Participants. We met with three informants with low vision, "A," "B," and "C" (female, aged between 19 and 32 when interviewed) who participated the study 1. They were a graduate or students of a school for the blind in Tokyo metropolitan area.

Table 1. Profiles of the participants (In-Depth Interview)

#		Characteristics	Description
A	(a)	age, gender, occupation	early 20s, female, student (school for the blind)
	(b)	visual acuity (left / right)	0.06 / 0.08
	(c)	visual disorder	achromatopsia (congenital)
	(d)	visual sensitivity and perception	total color blindness; weak in dazzling light
	(e)	family (living with) / (living apart)	none / father, mother, younger brother
B	(a)	age, gender, occupation	late teens, female, university student
	(b)	visual acuity (left / right)	0.09 (corrected: left)
	(c)	visual disorder	developmental glaucoma (exposed 16 years old)
	(d)	visual sensitivity and perception	unable to see things in dim light; field of vision at 3%
	(e)	family (living with) / (living apart)	father, elder sister / elder sister
C	(a)	age, gender, occupation	early 30s, female, acupressure therapist
	(b)	visual acuity (left / right)	0.2 / 0.04 (corrected)
	(c)	visual disorder	cataract (congenital)
	(d)	visual sensitivity and perception	having difficulty in seeing things in dim light
	(e)	family (living with) / (living apart)	husband / father, mother, younger sister

2.4 Analysis Results of the Study 2

All interviews were transcribed into readable narrative texts. The transcripts were indexed with sequential number by the session number, time-code, and a speaker and were subdivided into key experiential units according to a topic mentioned there (segmentation). By combining a basic scheme of the Grounded Theory Approach [5, 37] and analysis procedure of the VPA Method [21], the narrative interviews were interpreted according to the spiral sequence of analysis stages: (1) open-coding with ad hoc codes (by developing categories of information) and writing analytic memos for text segment; (2) retrieving and comparing text segments to which the same codes were attached; (3) inter-connecting the categories; (4) selective coding with focus; (5) developing concepts and the core categories.

Difficulty in Understanding Individual Visual Performance of Low Vision. People of low vision assumed their families to well understand their visual conditions. On the other hand, most of their family members also believed that they well-understood it. However, it is very hard for the sighted people to understand the detailed conditions of individual visual performance of low vision even if they are family who live together or friends who meet to talk mostly daily.

Ambiguous Identity Swaying between the Sighted and the Blindness. The partici-pants A, B, and C from the in-depth interviews felt that the self-images of people of low vision seemed ambiguous. They revealed people of low vision were much sensi-tive to being *ordinary* in their actions. They were always carefully paying their atten-tions on maintaining their actions *natural*, so that the sighted people around them seldom could notice their visual impairments. For example, even close friends often forgot their impairments. People of low vision had an option: to unburden their visual performances, or to behave *naturally* as the sighted people did. The self-images of people of low vision seemed swaying between the sighted and the blindness.

Corrections by the Sighted People Often Caused Them to Fear Making Mistakes. All the participants reported they had uncountable embarrassing experiences with the sighted people in their daily lives. A and B mentioned similar failures in adjusting the appearances: wearing the front and back of the sweater adversely; seriously mismatch-ing in coordinating color of a cardigan and a skirt; walking with attaching a hanger to the belt of a coat. People of low vision usually suddenly noticed their failures when the sighted people pointed out the failure. They were sometimes depressed all day long once they noticed their failures of wearing inadequate clothes, as they were unable to correct it until went home. They sometimes felt an unexpected indignity caused with a correction by the sighted people, and seemed to feel a kind of mental burdens to partic-ipate to a social situation surrounded with the sighted people.

What Does "Royal" Mean? – aha! a Name of Color?! The participants A, B, and C preferred enjoying shopping, basically by themselves. They seldom went shopping either with their friends and family. When shopping, they lacked visual information that they couldn't obtain with their eyes but played an important role for making a decision to buy. For example, they first needed to know a floor plan of a shop and about in which shelf the target clothes would be found. When they reached in front of the shelf, they also needed to know type of clothes, its size, material and color, and about whether it well fitted to them. Unfortunately, a description on a tag of a product usually provided simple, abstract, and too limited information for a customer of vi-sually impaired to decide to buy it. They sometimes asked a staff to escort them while shopping, in most case, it was difficult to communicate smoothly and establish a com-fortable relationship with a shop staff who didn't know about individual detailed visu-al performance of a customer of low vision. The participants seldom used assistive devices for shopping because of its limited capability.

Reluctance in Using Assistive Technologies. Recently, numerous numbers of assistive technologies can be found. Even these tools indicated potential benefits, people of visual impaired often felt a kind of reluctance in using those technologies because those tools sometimes became a two-edged sword. For example, white cane, a spectacle magnifier with thick lens, and EVES are noticeable symbols for people of low vision and the blind. They were afraid that the utilization of an assistive tool demonstrated their impairments and sometimes prompted teasing, or also prompted other people too much to care them.

3   Discussion: Implications for Designing Assistive Prototypes

3.1   Focus on Daily Arrangement of the People's Appearances of Low Vision

The analysis result revealed that 'self-confidence of managing appropriate appearances' was a key for visually impaired to participate to social activities including interaction with the sighted people.

On the basis of the results of our qualitative studies, most participants frequently reported their experiences of failure of dressing and insisted they felt tense during meeting, talking, and dating with other sighted people because they were afraid to give people undesirable and unexpected impressions with their appearances. Although the management of the appearances can be considered as a very small piece of everyday life, it constitutes a foundation of an involvement in a social situation. 'Participation' is one of fundamental elements of QoL. Building 'self-confidence of managing appropriate appearances' is essential to maintain QoL of people with low vision.

3.2   A Call: Comprehensive Support for the Arrangement of the Appearances

The arrangement of the appearances is related to many other facets of daily living: for example, shopping; categorizing and storing clothes into a closet or a chest drawer; coordinating and wearing clothes appropriately for an interaction with other persons; undressing, washing, pairing and organizing clothes, and then preparing clothes for a next occasion. These elements are interconnected with each other and the series of them constitute a comprehensive cycle of the arrangement of the appearances. In order to enjoy 'satisfactory appearances,' it's necessary to success in each step. However, people of low vision often have difficulties or concerns in performing each step of the activities such as organizing clothes.

It's important to provide a total solution that aims to support people of low vision to perform each stage of a comprehensive cycle of the arrangement of the appearances. We focus on the design of smooth connections between the sequential elements of a comprehensive cycle. It aims at achieving the objectives to a reasonable extent with the organized and integrated function of individual components as a whole, rather than individually providing ad-hoc assistance of each stage.

The initial field evaluation on a conceptual design of a total support system was conducted by using a storyboard-based prototype and the analysis is still underway.

At the present, four participants of low vision joined the session. We found that overall responses were positive at least on a basic concept of a system. We also obtained their comments for the enhancements, their emphasis points, and their several unique practices (*bricolage*) of everyday lives, which were devised to cope with the difficulties they have in executing these activities. The results will be incorporated into next improvements in a spiral process of a system development.

4   Concluding Remarks

This paper described an effort of the initial phase of designing an assistive technology that aimed to improve quality of life of people with low vision. In order to investigate the felt-need for the assistive technology for people with low vision as well as their hidden agendas, we conducted a qualitative study by employing multiple qualitative research methods.

The qualitative study revealed several key concepts to interpret people's lived experiences of low vision: for example, the ambiguity of their self-images; both pleasures and burdens in the interaction with the sighted people; a reluctance in using a symbolic assistive device; and an unexpected indignity caused with a correction by the sighted kind people. The analysis results suggested that: frequent failures of managing the appearances inhibited people of low vision from an involvement in a social situation such as an interaction with the sighted people; building 'self-confidence of managing appropriate appearance' facilitated their social activities.

On the basis of the results from qualitative study, we created a conceptual design of a total assistive solution that aims to support people of low vision to perform each stage of a comprehensive cycle of the arrangement of the appearances thorough smooth connections between the sequential elements of the cycle.

Our challenge continues to enhance a methodology for bridging a gap between the outcomes of qualitative research and the design of user experience by investigating an appropriate harmonization among them.

Acknowledgments. This work was supported in part by JSPS Grant-in-Aid for Scientific Research (#23300263). We thank all the participants of our qualitative sessions, and the vice principal of a school for the blind in Tokyo metropolitan area, who devotedly supported our field studies. We also thank Ayako Uchitomi and our laboratory members 2010-2013.

References

1. AbleData: Your resource for assistive technology information,
   http://www.abledata.com/
2. Atkinson, R.: The Life Story Interview. Sage (1998)
3. Bradshaw, J.: A taxonomy of social need. In: McLachlan, G. (ed.) Problems and Progress in Medical Care, pp. 70–82. Oxford University Press (1972)

4. Broadbent, J., Culham, L.: Prescribing conventional devices for vision rehabilitation. CE Optometry 5(1), 12–16 (2002)
5. Charmaz, K.: Constructing Grounded Theory: A Practical Guide through Qualitative Analysis. Sage (2006)
6. Corn, A.L., Lusk, K.E.: Perspectives on Low Vision. In: Corn, A.L., Erin, J.N. (eds.) Foundations of Low Vision: Clinical and Functional Perspectives, 2nd edn., American Foundation for the Blind, NY (2010)
7. Denzin, N.K.: The Research Act, pp. 297–313. Aldine (1970)
8. Denzin, N.K., Lincoln, Y.S.: Introduction: The Discipline and Practice of Qualitative Research. In: Denzin, N.K., Lincoln, Y.S. (eds.) The SAGE Handbook of Qualitative Research, pp. 1–19. Sage (2011)
9. Dourish, P.: Implications for Design. In: Proc. ACM CHI 2006, pp. 541–550 (2006)
10. Faugier, J., Sargeant, M.: Sampling hard to reach populations. Journal of Advanced Nursing 26(4), 790–797 (1997)
11. Flick, U.: Managing Quality in Qualitative Research. Sage, London (2007)
12. Flick, U.: An Introduction to Qualitative Research. Sage (2014)
13. Gharpure, C.P., Kulyukin, V.A.: Robot-assisted Shopping for the Blind: Issues in Spatial Cognition and Product Selection. Intelligent Service Robotics 1(3), 237–251 (2008)
14. Giudice, N.A., Legge, G.E.: Blind Navigation and the Role of Technology. In: Helal, A., Mokhtari, M., Abdulrazak, B. (eds.) Engineering Handbook of Smart Technology for Aging, Disability, and Independence, pp. 479–500. John Wiley & Sons (2007)
15. Groeben, N.: Subjective Theories and the Explanation of Human Action. In: Semin, G.R., Gergen, K.J. (eds.) Everyday Understanding, pp. 19–44. Sage (1990)
16. Hatakeyama, T., Hagiwara, F., Koike, H., Ito, K., Ohkubo, H., Bond, C.W., Kasuga, M.: Remote Infrared Audible Signage System. International Journal of Human-Computer Interaction 17(1), 61–70 (2004)
17. Hersh, M.A., Johnson, M.A.: Disability and Assistive Technology Systems. In: Hersh, M., Johnson, M.A. (eds.) Assistive Technology for Visually Impaired and Blind People, pp. 1–50. Springer (2008)
18. Hersh, M.A.: Perception, the Eye and Assistive Technology Issues. In: Hersh, M., Johnson, M.A. (eds.) Assistive Technology for Visually Impaired and Blind People, pp. 51–101. Springer (2008)
19. Hughes, C., Hwang, B., Kim, J., Eisenman, L.T., Killian, D.J.: Quality of life in applied research: A review and analysis of empirical measures. American Journal on Mental Retardation 99(6), 623–641 (1995)
20. Jackson, A.J.: Epidemiology of Low Vision. In: Jackson, A.J., Wolffsohn, J.S. (eds.) Low-Vision Manual, pp. 1–26. Butterworth Heinemann (2007)
21. Kinoe, Y.: Redesign: Integration of Analytical and Creative Processes for Enhancing Software. In: Karwowski, W. (ed.) International Encyclopedia of Ergonomics and Human Factors, pp. 1229–1234. Taylor & Francis (2006)
22. Kinoe, Y., Ojima, C., Sakurai, Y.: Qualitative Study for Designing Peripheral Communication between Hospitalized Children and Their Family Members. In: Yamamoto, S. (ed.) HCI 2013, Part II. LNCS, vol. 8017, pp. 275–284. Springer, Heidelberg (2013)
23. Krishna, S., Colbry, D., Black, J., Balasubramanian, V., Panchanathan, S.: A Systematic Requirements Analysis and Development of an Assistive Device to Enhance the Social Interaction of People Who are Blind or Visually Impaired. In: Workshop on Computer Vision Applications for the Visually Impaired, Marseille, France (2008)

24. Kulyukin, V., Kutiyanawala, A.: Accessible Shopping Systems for Blind and Visually Impaired Individuals: Design Requirements and the State of the Art. The Open Rehabilitation Journal 3, 158–168 (2010)
25. Lanigan, P.E., Paulos, A.M., Williams, A.W., Rossi, D., Narasimhan, P.: Trinetra: Assistive Technologies for Grocery Shopping for the Blind. In: International IEEE-BAIS Symposium on Research on Assistive Technologies, Dayton, OH (2007)
26. Loomis, J.M., Golledge, R.G., Klatzky, R.L., Marston, J.R.: Assisting Wayfinding in Visually Impaired Travelers. In: Allen, G.L. (ed.) Applied Spatial Cognition: From Research to Cognitive Technology, pp. 179–203. LEA (2007)
27. Mori, H., Kotani, S.: Robotic Travel Aid for the Blind: Harunobu-6. In: 2nd European Conf. on Disability, Virtual Reality, and Assistive Technology, Sovde, Sweden, pp. 193–202 (1998)
28. Plummer, K.: Documents of Life 2. Sage (2001)
29. Scherer, M.J., Glueckauf, R.: Assessing the Benefits of Assistive Technologies for Activities and Participation. Rehabilitation Psychology 50(2), 132–141 (2005)
30. Schutz, A.: Reflections on the Problem of Relevance. In: Embree, L. (ed.) Collected Papers V - Phenomenology and the Social Sciences, pp. 93–199. Springer, Netherlands (1970)
31. Schutz, A., Luckmann, T.: The Structures of the Life-World, vol. 1. Northwestern University Press (1973)
32. Scott, I.U., Smiddy, W.E., Schiffman, J., Feuer, W.J., Pappas, C.J.: Quality of Life of Low-Vision Patients and the Impact of Low-Vision Services. American Journal of Ophthalmology 128(1), 54–62 (1999)
33. Silver, J.: The Psychology of Low Vision. In: Jackson, A.J., Wolffsohn, J.S. (eds.) Low-Vision Manual, pp. 103–115. Butterworth Heinemann (2007)
34. Sound Foresight Technology: UltraCane User Manual, http://www.ultracane.com/
35. Spradley, J.P.: Participant Observation. Wadsworth/Thompson Learning (1980)
36. Stelmack, J.A., Stelmack, T.R., Massof, R.W.: Measuring Low-Vision Rehabilitation Outcomes with the NEI VFQ-25. Investigative Ophthalmology & Visual Science 43(9), 2859–2868 (2002)
37. Strauss, A.L.: Qualitative Analysis for Social Scientists. Cambridge Univ. Press (1987)
38. World Health Organization: International Classification of Impairments, Disabilities, and Handicaps (ICIDH). WHO, Geneva (1980)
39. WHO QOL Group: The World Health Organization Quality of Life assessment (WHOQOL): Development and general psychometric properties. Social Science & Medicine 46(12), 1569–1585 (1998)
40. World Health Organization: International Classification of Functioning, Disability and Health (ICF). WHO, Geneva (2001)
41. World Health Organization Prevention of Blindness and Deafness Programme: Global data on visual impairment 2010. WHO/NMH/PBD/12.01 (2012)

Modeling Consumers with TV and Internet

Akifumi Nozaki and Kenichi Yoshida

Graduate School of Business Sciences, University of Tsukuba, Japan
{nozaki,yoshida}@gssm.otsuka.tsukuba.ac.jp

Abstract. The importance of web in marketing has been emphasized
and extensive studies have been carried out. On the contrary, there still
exist important marketing studies which follow traditional framework.
Although the importance of web marketing is undeniable, if we consider the wide spread of hard disk recorders and off-line viewing of TV
shows, we have to consider the advertisement effect of off-line viewing
using hard disk recorders. In this paper, we propose a framework of
consumer modeling to analyze the effect of off-line viewing. It follows
multi/cross-channel marketing framework. The important characteristic
of the proposed framework is that the stimulation of TV advertisement
is assumed to start consumer's behavior. We assume that the TV advertisements stimulate information flows in the social networks and affect
purchase behavior of consumers. Although the Internet, especially social
network on the Internet, is now playing important role to affect customers behavior during the process, the marketing theory still have to
settle TV advertisement as the main factor. To show the adequacy of the
proposed framework, this paper reports the effect of TV advertisement
on the phenomenon around WWW.

Keywords: Web marketing, TV advertisement, consumer modeling.

1 Introduction

The importance of web in marketing has been emphasized and extensive studies
have been carried out. For example, the prediction of box-office record using
twitter data [1] and evaluation of advertisement efficiency using web data [2]
are typical examples of success based on such studies. The diminishment in
TV program rating (See Fig. 1) also emphasizes the importance of this rapidly
leaping web marketing. Fig.1 shows the decreases of program ratings in each
Japanese TV broadcast channels. The total program rating has been decreased
from 37.4% to 31.4% during these 10 years in Japan [3].

On the contrary, there still exist important marketing studies which follow
traditional framework. Studies on consumer such as "AIDMA"[4] try to model
consumers' purchase behavior theoretically. Corporate marketers have used the
theoretical results of these studies in the business. In the standard theory, consumers first acquire product information through stimulation from outside. Articles on magazines and TV program are the typical examples of such stimulation.

S. Yamamoto (Ed.): HIMI 2014, Part II, LNCS 8522, pp. 614–621, 2014.
© Springer International Publishing Switzerland 2014

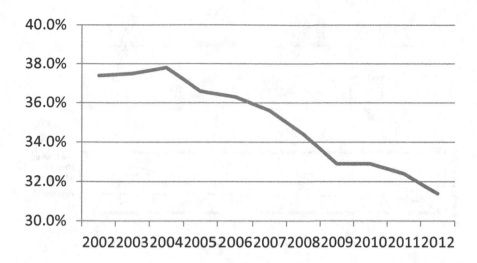

Fig. 1. Program Rating by Household in Japan [3]

Then, they will decide if they purchase the product based on the reputation of their familiar friends.

Since the wide spread of Internet has changed the customer behavior, simple theory cannot handle today's customer behavior. The information resources are spread into various types, and the customer behaviors become complex. This also emphasizes the importance of web marketing. Fig.1 is also used to accelerate this trend toward web marketing

Although the importance of web marketing is undeniable, if we consider the wide spread of hard disk recorders and off-line viewing of TV shows, the same Fig.1 might indicate the increase of total program rating. We have to consider the advertisement effect of off-line viewing using hard disk recorders. Note that the relative decrease of program rating during these 10 years is only 6%. If we consider the rapid spread of hard disk recorders and on-line viewing style of same 10 year period, the actual program rating might have increased.

In this paper, we propose a framework of consumer modeling. It follows multi/cross-channel marketing framework [5]. The important characteristic of the proposed framework is that the stimulation of TV advertisement is assumed to start consumer's behavior. We assume that the TV advertisements stimulate information flows in the social networks and affect purchase behavior of consumers. Motivation behind this framework is our intuition that the effect of TV advertisement is still the main factor in marketing. Although the Internet, especially social network on the Internet, is now playing important role to affect customers behavior during the process, the marketing theory still have to settle TV advertisement as the main factor.

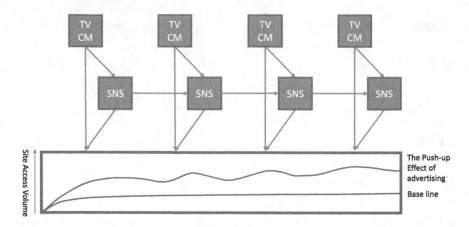

Fig. 2. Multi-Channel Model of Consumer Behavior

2   Multi-channel Model of Consumer Behavior

Fig.2 shows the conceptual image of our multi-channel model of consumer behavior. Important characteristic of it is that the TV advertisements are assumed to be the key factor of the model. We also assume that the information flow through social networks plays an important role in affecting consumers' purchase behavior. However, we believe that the key factor is TV advertisement. It first stimulates consumers. Then, social networks propagate its effect on sales.

Important data shown in Fig.2 are:

1. Data about advertising activities through TV broadcasting.
2. Information flow in social networks
3. Purchase log of Consumers

We plan to analyze the process which is stimulated by the TV advertisements. We will use 1) the broadcasting log of TV advertisements, 2) Twitter data which include the number of positive and negative reactions posted by consumers, and 3) the purchase log of panels. A consulting company makes us use their data on 2) and 3). The data is acquired using a toolbar installed in their web browsers. The current panel size is approximately 300,000. We also use user information such as gender, age, marital status, annual income, residence of panels.

Based on the above marketing data, we try to extract information flow in twitter. How the information is propagated through the panels? What are the common characteristics of the panels who are involved in the propagation? If they form clusters? If the brand of products gives the characteristics to the clusters? Analyzing these points is the target of our study. If we can clarify these points, we can design the best strategy to spent for TV advertising and WWW sites. Budget for the Japanese advertisement in 2012 was 58,913 billion yen, and TV advertisement is about 30% of them [6]. We can use the analyzing results to find best split of such large budget.

3   Preliminary Experiment

3.1   Comparison of Correlations

Our first experiment compares the correlation between purchase, WWW page view, amount of TV advertisement, and amount of keywords given to the search engines. Table 1 shows the results. Using the data acquired from panels (i.e., data gathered through the tool bar), keywords to the search engines and WWW viewing are analyzed. We concentrate on an online commerce site in this experiment. The site is a popular fashion commerce site in Japan. To make Table 1, we count how many times panels search the fashion site name through search engine ("search"). We also count the number of page views of the site ("visit") and number of page view of purchase pages ("purchase"). We also use weekly based amount of TV advertisements (GRP, "tspot"). Then, we calculate the correlations between weekly based numbers.

Table 1. Correlation between Data

	purchase	visit	tspot	search
purchase	100.0%			
visit	72.2%	100.0%		
tspot	36.9%	35.7%	100.0%	
search	67.6%	90.2%	48.7%	100.0%

As clearly shown in Table 1, "purchase (number of purchase page view)" and "visit (number of page view of the commerce site)" have high correlation. In addition, "search (how many times the site name was searched through search engine)" has high correlation with "purchase" and "visit". Using other data, we also confirm that "purchase" and "number of tweet" have high correlation (60.4%). However, "tspot (amount of TV advertisement)" has low correlation with them.

3.2   Analysis of Time Series Data

Simple comparison between correlations might miss lead inefficacy of TV advertisements, and exaggerate the importance of the Internet data such as data

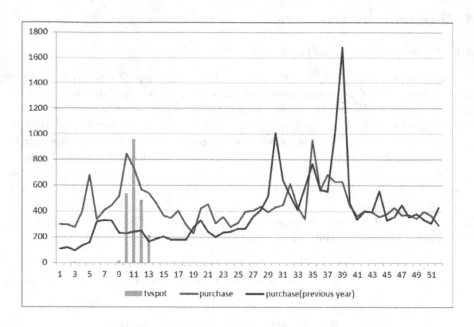

Fig. 3. TV spot and Purchase

from search engine. However, if we carefully analyze the time series of the same data, we can reach opposite conclusion. Figure 3 shows the phenomenon relates to such analysis.

Since "purchase" data is about fashion, seasonality is important characteristics of the data. To see this seasonality, Figure 3 shows the weakly based "purchase" data with "purchase" of previous year. It also shows the amount of TV advertisements "tspot". Although "purchase" shows clear seasonality (i.e, "purchase" shows similar trends and drifts every year), "tspot" also shows clear relation with "purchase". To confirm this, we made models which forecast "purchase" based on the past "purchase" and "tspot". Figure 4, 5 and 6 shows the results.

We used time series environment of weka [7], and made 3 models:

Model 1: Only from previous "purchase"
Model 2: Also use "purchase" of previous year to handle seasonality
Model 3: Also with "tspot"

The root mean square errors (RMSEs) are 69.244, 26.530 and 1.294 respectively. These RMSEs clearly show the seasonality of the data. They also show the efficacy of TV advertisement on "purchase". The important result here is that "TV advertisements still have large influence on purchase".

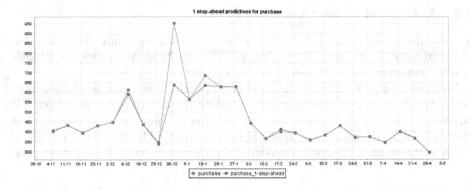

Fig. 4. Analysis based on only Purchase (RMSE=69.224)

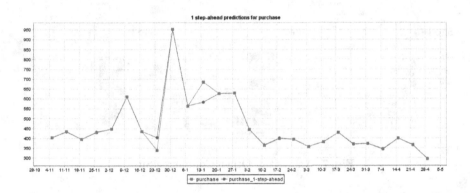

Fig. 5. Analysis with Previous Year Purchase (RMSE=26.53)

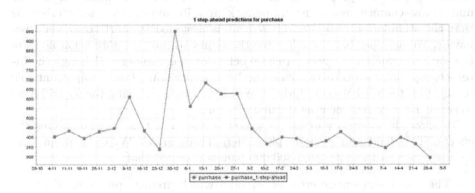

Fig. 6. Analysis with TV spot data (RMSE=1.294)

3.3   Analysis of Other Commerce Sites

The results shown in Fig. 4, 5, and 6 are based on the data about a single commerce site. To confirm the generality of the result, we also check the RMSEs of other commerce sites. Figure 7 shows the results.

Since site 3 is a small site, the number of purchase was not large enough to be analyzed. Thus we made models to estimate number of page views from TV advertisement. Model 1 tries to predict "number of page view" from past page view. Model 2 also uses "page view of previous year". Model 3 uses "volume of TV advertisement". The results also show the importance of TV advertisements.

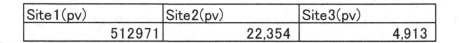

Site1(pv)	Site2(pv)	Site3(pv)
512971	22,354	4,913

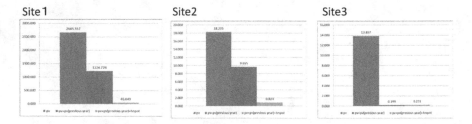

Fig. 7. Analysis of Other Commerce Sites

4   Conclusion

In this paper, we propose a framework of consumer modeling. It follows multi/cross-channel marketing framework and its important characteristic is that the stimulation of TV advertisement is assumed to start consumer's behavior. We assume that the TV advertisements stimulate information flows in the social networks and affect purchase behavior of consumers. Although the Internet, especially social network on the Internet, is now playing important role to affect customers behavior during the process, the marketing theory still have to settle TV advertisement as the main factor.

To show the adequacy of the proposed framework, this paper analyzes the effect of TV advertisement on the phenomenon around WWW. The experimental results based on the data from 300,000 panels revealed that:

- The root mean square error of a model which predicts purchase of a fashion commerce site from past purchase was 69.244 on our data. The volume information of TV advertisement can decrease the error down to 1.294.
- Similar results (importance of TV advertisement) were also observed on the page view of other commerce site.

- Although our prediction models show the importance of web advertisement, we found simple correlation analysis tends to underestimate the importance of TV advertisements. It tends exaggerate the importance of the Internet data such as data from search engine.

Acknowledgments. This work was partly supported by JSPS KAKENHI Grant Number 25280114.

References

1. Asur, S., Huberman, B.A.: Predicting the Future with Social Media, http://arxiv.org/abs/1003.5699, doi:10.1016/j.apenergy (March 27, 2013)
2. Uehara, H., Sato, T., Yoshida, K.: Analysing the Image Building Effects of TV Advertisements Using Internet Community Data 23(3), 205–216 (2008)
3. Tokyo Broadcasting System.inc/annual report 2002-2012
4. Hall, S.R.: Retail Advertising and Selling (1924)
5. Piercy, N.: Positive and negative cross-channel shopping behavior. Marketing Intelligence & Planning 30(1), 83–104 (2012)
6. Dentsu.inc, Advertising Spend in Japan, http://www.dentsu.co.jp/books/ad_cost/2012/
7. Time series analysis and forecasting with Weka, http://wiki.pentaho.com/display/DATAMINING/Time+Series+Analysis+and+Forecasting+with+Weka

The Relationships between the Products and Affective Evaluation Concerning Uniqueness

Yusuke Ohta and Keiko Kasamatsu

Department of Industrial Art, Graduate School of System Design,
Tokyo Metropolitan University, Tokyo, Japan
ota-yusuke@sd.tmu.ac.jp, kasamatu@tmu.ac.jp

Abstract. In this study, we focused on uniqueness of products, and it could be one of the *Kansei* value to increase attractiveness of products. We examined the affection and impression from characteristics of the unique products. As the result, it had a possibility that unique products could trigger positive emotion of humans, and it led to increasing with the attractiveness of the products. In addition, a product which made people feel unique was the function of products. However, it was considered that focusing on a shape in a uniqueness was effective for design of attractive product in order to makes impression of vaunty, attachment and pleasure. In the future, we will focus on more positive emotion, and examine the structure of positive emotion when user contacted with a unique product.

Keywords: Uniqueness, Affection, Product design.

1 Background

Recently, it has increased an interest that a necessary factor for new human centered design manufacturing. For manufacture, it has been gradually emphasized that incorporating *Kansei* value into products as one of the essential strategies for raising competitive edge of products in the consumer market. By paying attention to the *Kansei* value, a manufacture would be able to produce products that provide more satisfaction by incorporating attractive elements to the users, also able to keep developing attractive products by the supports of users. In particular, it gains momentum that focus to emotions or internal desire of human in discussion about an attractive product.

Norman (2001)[1] had described that it is important not only usability, but also design as well, and discussed about life of the people between an attractive product. He had described that the emotional side of design to cause a strong and positive emotion, and superior at all levels as Viscelal design, Behavioral design, Reflective design was critical for a product that supported and attractive that makes the life of the user wealthily. In addition, it is a critical factor to induce long-term use by color, shape, and material design of product, and strong influence to a sense of emotional attachment to the product[2]. Cho et al. (2009)[3] had described that the most important things is to consider that it should be satisfied the emotional desire of consumers in

S. Yamamoto (Ed.): HIMI 2014, Part II, LNCS 8522, pp. 622–630, 2014.
© Springer International Publishing Switzerland 2014

modern industries. Hassenzahl(2003)[4] had described that Hedonic quality was the internal desire of the user, and should be compatible with Hedonic quality and Pragmatic quality. The concept of user experience (UX) which related to that Hassenzahl model becomes pervasive. In those previous research, it was suggested that function and appearance had close relation with the design of product ever, and such product influences to a mind and a life of the user.

A movement such as focusing on human affection also could be seen at the manufacturing frontline. In order to produce a product that appeal to affection, it is considered that it is important for product manufacturers to understand how products affect consumers' emotions. Recently, the Volvo Car Group examined between design and emotion through the experiment using brain waves that was conducted to coincide with the launch of the Volvo Concept Coupe. Through this experiment, beautiful car design can tangibly evoke a powerful range of feelings that are on a par with the most basic of human emotions[5]. In this way, the product which satisfies the essential internal desire of consumers and the user and strong feelings make us fun, and our life wealthily around us.

Ohta et al. (2012) [6] considered that such products have a property to be common as a Kansei element "Uniqueness". Chang & Wu (2007) [7] investigated that the types and characteristics of household products elicit pleasurable responses. They identified five types of pleasurable form and 14 associated characteristics. The types of "novelty forms" include the characteristic of "unique appearance." Unique appearance means the creation of new shapes, unique colors, and creative materials. When the appearance of the product is unique, it causes to affect or make an opportunity of "Attention" or "Interest" in AIDMA[8] which expressed the process of the human consumption behavior. It may finally lead to a consumption behavior. In addition, according to Csikszentmihalyi (1992)[9], pleasure is characterized by a feeling of novelty.

It has been shown that the uniqueness of product appearance has a novelty value, and that a users could be attracted by the products that convey a sense of pleasure. It is considered that it has effective possibility and achieves pleasure and delight, and makes life wealthily to feeling from a uniqueness of product. Therefore, examining Uniqueness of products has the possibility to find a new Kansei value of the product. By utilizing its knowledge, a possibility that leads to proposing an attractive product could be expected.

2   Purpose

Ohta et al. (2012) focused on uniqueness of product appearance as one of the attractiveness, and clarified *Kansei* factors to constitute uniqueness in a product in the prior research. In the result, it was indicated that "Feeling of non-daily life" and "Smartness" were affected as factors to explain the uniqueness, and there was a strong and equilateral correlation between attractiveness and uniqueness. Therefore, it was considered that uniqueness could be suggested as one of the *Kansei* value to improve the attractiveness of the product.

Then, in this report, we examined the affection and impression for unique products to design unique and attractive products. In addition, we examined about the characteristics of a product that felt unique around us.

3   Method

3.1   Procedure

Participants were evoked a product which felt unique around themselves to investigate affection and the impression for a unique product. They answered product name, a point of felt uniqueness, owned or not and evaluated affection and an impression to product using the 7 point scale method. It had 6 opinions that Question items of "What point did you feel uniqueness?", and participants could chose only one item from "Function", "Shape", "Color", "Material", "Brand", "Others".

3.2   Evaluation Items

There were 21 valuations items, broken down as follows (Table 1). 14 affection items were selected (7 items of positive emotion and 7 items of negative emotion) referenced to R. Chitturi (2009) [10]. In addition, 4 items of uniqueness were selected as "Distinctive", "Novel", "Well-crafted" and "Vaunty" (Ohta et al., 2012). Moreover, 3 items of attractiveness items as "Attachment", "Pleasant" and "Attractiveness" were selected.

Table 1. 21 evaluation items

		Evaluation items
Affection items	Positive	Excitement
		Cheerfulness
		Delight
		Security
		Confidence
		Surprise
		Satisfaction
	Negative	Guilt
		Anxiety
		Sadness
		Disappointment
		Dissatisfaction
		Regret
		Anger
Uniqueness items		Distinctive
		Novel
		Well-crafted
		Vaunty
Attractiveness items		Attachment
		Pleasant
		Attractiveness

3.3   Participants

The participants were 348 students in university, the number of valid responses were 221, broken down as: 145 male and 76 female, response rate was 63.5% (Average: 19.1 age, standard deviation: 1.24 age).

4   Result

Figure 1 showed a ratio of owner who evoked uniqueness feeling products.

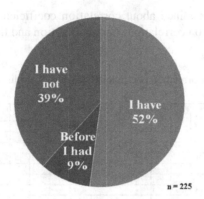

Fig. 1. A ratio of owner who evoked uniqueness feeling products

Figure 2 showed the average of the evaluation score for whole participant for the 21 evaluation items.

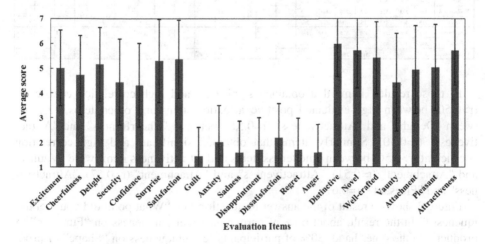

Fig. 2. The averages of the evaluation score for each evaluation item.

In items of affection, "Excitement", "Cheerfulness", "Delight", "Security", "Confidence", "Surprise" and "Satisfaction" got high evaluation. Particularly, the evaluation score of items as "Satisfaction", "Surprise" and "Delight" were high. On the other hand, "Guilt", "Anxiety", "Sadness", "Sadness", "Disappointment", "Dissatisfaction", "Regret" and "Anger" got a low evaluation. Particularly, the evaluation score of items as "Guilt", "Sadness" and "Anger" were low. 4 uniqueness and 3 attractiveness items were relatively high evaluation. Particularly, the evaluation score of items as "Distinctive", "Novel" and "Attractiveness" were high.

In the results of independent t-test, there was no significant difference between owner and not owner regarding evaluation score related to items of affection and impression.

In addition, it was examined about correlation coefficient between 21 evaluation items due to what affection correlations on the affection and the factor of uniqueness. Table 2 showed results.

Table 2. Correlation coefficient between 21 evaluation items

	Excitement	Cheerfulness	Delight	Security	Confidence	Surprise	Satisfaction	Guilt	Anxiety	Sadness	Disappointment	Dissatisfaction	Regret	Anger	Distinctive	Novel	Well-crafted	Vaunty	Attachment	Pleasant	Attractiveness
Excitement	1																				
Cheerfulness	.446**	1																			
Delight	.509**	.619**	1																		
Security	.187**	.199**	.278**	1																	
Confidence	.141*	.242**	.272**	.681**	1																
Surprise	.471**	.283**	.391**			1															
Satisfaction	.263**	.346**	.423**	.455**	.453**	.245**	1														
Guilt								1													
Anxiety	.172*			-.137*	-.176**		-.159*	.293**	1												
Sadness	.123							.418**	.429**	1											
Disappointment	.137*				-.272**		-.233**	.326**	.560**	.447**	1										
Dissatisfaction		-.196**				.025	-.281**	.241**	.414**	.209**	.660**	1									
Regret	.162*							.324**	.340**	.235**	.557**	.448**	1								
Anger					-.161*			.248**	.413**	.504**	.615**	.455**	.362**	1							
Distinctive	.289**	.247**	.203**	.115	.136*	.432**	.138*								1						
Novel	.346**	.225**	.204**	.070		.491**	.182**								.754**	1					
Well-crafted	.369**	.293**	.315**	.335**	.296**	.448**	.373**				-.143*				.535**	.501**	1				
Vaunty	.419**	.405**	.411**	.153*	.169*	.374**	.269**								.351**	.395**	.494**	1			
Attachment	.272**	.376**	.386**	.450**	.375**	.145*	.459**								.151*	.223**	.334**	.513**	1		
Pleasant	.394**	.474**	.455**	.025		.336**	.254**		.151*				.158*		.304**	.347**	.334**	.471**	.415**	1	
Attractiveness	.370**	.500**	.509**	.311**	.256**	.365**	.458**					-.210**			.435**	.398**	.504**	.541**	.572**	.668**	1

In those results, items that obtained significant and high correlation coefficient (r>0.50) between high evaluated positive affection items and other items were between "Delight" and "Attractiveness" (r=0.51), between "Cheerfulness" and "Attractiveness" (r=0.50). Similarly, items that obtained significant and high correlation coefficient (r>0.50) between uniqueness items and attractiveness items were "Vaunty" and "Attachment" (r=0.51), "Attractiveness" and "Attachment" (r=0.57), "Attractiveness" and "Pleasant" (r=0.67).

Figure 3 shows a result of the answer to question that "What point did you feel uniqueness?" In the result, about 60% of participants feel uniqueness on "Function" of product. On the other hand, 30% of participants feel uniqueness on "Shape" of product. "Color", "Material" and "Brand" were miners. The breakdown of "Other" was as follows: Design, Idea and Production method.

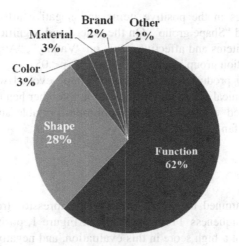

Fig. 3. Most uniqueness point of their products

Then, we focused on "Function" and "Shape", and compared with the differences on affection for function or shape. Figure 4 showed a result.

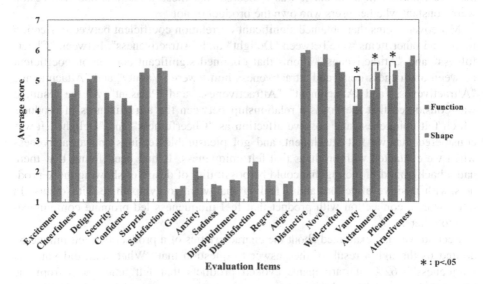

Fig. 4. Average of evaluation score of the difference of uniqueness point

Evaluation score of positive affection items got high, and negative affection items got low in participants who evoked product which felt uniqueness function ("Function group") and which felt uniqueness shape ("Shape group"). Evaluation of Uniqueness items and Affectiveness items got high score also.

The independent t-test was examined due to investigate regarding evaluation score according to the "Function group" and "Shape group". As the result, there were no significant differences in the positive items and negative affection items between "Function group" and "Shape group". On the other hand, significant differences were found in uniqueness items and affective items on "Vaunty", "Attachment" and "Pleasant" between "Function group" and "Shape group" (p<.05).

Meanwhile, a many products that "Function group" evoked were smartphone, vacuum cleaner, mechanical pencil and a stapler. On the other hand, many products that "Shape group" evoked were smartphone, umbrella, portable audio player, kitchenware, eraser, electric fan and pen case.

5   Discussion

At first, we had examined the affection and the impression from the product that makes people feel uniqueness. From the result of Figure 1, positive emotion items in Chitturi's research got a high score in this evaluation, and negative emotion items got low scores. Therefore, it was considered that positive emotion was felt when we contacted with products that felt uniqueness. Particularly, evaluation score of items as "Satisfaction", "Surprise" and "Delight" were high, it was considered that the results were common with D. Norman's description that an emotional design evoked strong positive emotion. In addition, it was indicated that these affections and impression were constant whether users who own the product or not.

Moreover, items that obtained significant correlation coefficient between affection items and other items were between "Delight" and "Attractiveness", between "Cheerfulness" and "Attractiveness". Items that obtained significant correlation coefficient between uniqueness items and attractiveness items were "Vaunty" and "Attachment", "Attractiveness" and "Attachment", "Attractiveness" and "Pleasant". As the result, it was considered that there was a relationship between the attractiveness of products which felt uniqueness and positive affection as "Cheerfulness" and "Delight". It was considered that we felt attachment, and got pleasurable feelings and attractiveness when we contacted with products that felt uniqueness. It had been found that there had a background of feeling that could be possibility of desire of showing those products with positive affection, and a feeling that want to sympathize with others. In other words, connection with product that feel uniqueness led promote communication to others.

Second, we had examined about the characteristics of a product that felt unique by around us through a result of the answer to question that "What point did you feel uniqueness?" 62% of participants evoked products that felt uniqueness from the "function" of product, and these answers were more than twice as much of "Shape". From this result, it was considered that many products around us felt uniqueness due to the function. Today, the using experience of product from users were very important[11], and it was considered that niqueness feeling from the function of product was related with satisfaction of UX.

In addition, it was examined the difference of evaluation between participants who evoked product which felt uniqueness function ("Function group") and which felt uniqueness shape ("Shape group"). The tendency of the evaluation were same as average of whole of participants. They felt positive affection more strongly than negative affection, and impression score got high also. There were no significant differences in affection items between "Function group" and "Shape group". On the other hand, significant differences were found on uniqueness items and affective items between "Function group" and "Shape group". Evaluation of "Vaunty", "attachment", "Pleasant" got higher when it contacted product that felt uniqueness in shape than contacted product that felt uniqueness in function. However, there were no significant differences between them on "Attractiveness". Therefore, it was indicated that there was no difference in feeling of affection evoked when we contact that felt the uniqueness for function or shape, and they felt positive emotion easily. Also, it did not influence on the attractiveness of the product. However, the product that felt uniqueness on shape made easier vaunt, in other words sympathize, pleasantly and felt attachment than the product that felt uniqueness on shape. Therefore, it was considered that focusing on a shape in a uniqueness was effective for design of attractive product in order to makes impression of vaunty, attachment and pleasure.

Meanwhile, at the product which was evoked a lot in this investigation, a smartphone has two types of the participants as "Function group" and "Shape group". The shape of product concerned with Viscelal design, and the function of product concerned with Behavioral design in the conditions of Norman's emotional design that makes user's life wealthily. In other words, it was suggested that a smartphone gave a feeling of positive uniqueness as in the Viscelal design and the Behavioral design, and it was superior to the Reflective design concerned with personal satisfaction such as attachment to use in this investigation. It was suggested that it had possibility of meeting a condition of emotional design that could life of the user makes wealthily from uniqueness side. It was considered that one of the factors that an innovative product such as a smartphone was supported in today that had those characteristics of uniqueness

6   Conclusion

In this study, we had focused on the uniqueness of the products that had the possibility of making our life wealthily, and it could be one of the *Kansei* value to increase attractiveness of products. In this report, we had examined the affection and impression for unique products for designing unique and attractive products. In addition, we had examined about the characteristics of a product that felt unique around us.

As the result, it was considered that people feel positive emotion when contacted with products that felt uniqueness. Particularly, it was suggested that there was a relationship between some positive emotion and attractiveness of a product. In addition, it was considered that the feeling of attachment, pleasurable and attractiveness were strongly related with the feeling from the uniqueness of products. Moreover, when a product which make us feel unique, most of the situations are because of the function factor but not shape factor. According to the difference of points of feeling uniqueness from the shape and function, there was no difference between affection and attractiveness of a product. However, a product that made us felt uniqueness from the shape which made us felt sympathize, pleasant, and attachment easily. Therefore, it was suggested that it was more effective to design the appearance of the product shapes if it was wanted to make such impressions product.

It is necessary that understanding about characteristics of user and product due to incorporating Kansei value as uniqueness in product design. To do that, it is necessary to understand processes of influence on affection when we felt uniqueness for product. In the future, we will focus on more positive emotion, and examine the structure of positive emotion when user contacted with a unique product. We wonder what is the feeling uniqueness for the product, or how influence gives us such products. We will examine and consider with attention in detail and suggest a method to utilize knowledge into product design.

References

1. Norman, D.: Emotional Design: Why We Love (or Hate) Everyday Things. Basic books (2003)
2. Hashimoto, E., Terauchi, F., Kubo, M., Aoki, H.: Construction of structure model expressing the relationship between Kansei factor of a product and affection. Bulletin of JSSD A Design Studies Study, Collection of Presentation of the Results of the Study Summaries (48), 226–227 (2001) (in Japanese)
3. Cho, H.S., Lee, J.: Development of a macroscopic model on recent fashion trends on the basis of consumer emotion. International Journal of Consumer Studies 29(1), 17–33 (2005)
4. Hassenzahl, M.: The Thing and I: Understanding the Relationship between User and Product, pp. 31–42. From Usability to Enjoyment, Funology (2003)
5. Volvo Car UK Press Releases,
   https://www.media.volvocars.com/uk/
   en-gb/media/pressreleases/136009/volvo-cars-world-first-
   experiment-reveals-the-emotive-power-of-car-design
6. Ohta, Y., Kasamatsu, K.: Proposal for a Kansei Index related to the Uniqueness of a Product. In: 4th International Conference on Applied Human Factors and Ergonomics, Proceedings, pp. 6984–6992 (2012)
7. Chang, W.C., Wu, T.Y.: Exploring Types and Characteristics of Product Forms. IJ Design 1(1) (2007)
8. Hall, S.R.: Advertising Handbook. General Books, CA (1986)
9. Csikszentmihalyi, M.: Flow: The Psychology of Happiness. Rider, London (1992)
10. Chitturi, R.: Emotions by Design: A Consumer Perspective. International Journal of Design 3(2), 7–17 (2009)
11. NIkata, K.: Kokoro wo Ugokasu Dezainn no Himitsu (Secret of design for move the hearts of people). Jitsumukyoiku-Shuppan, 132 (2013) (in Japanese)

Factors Influencing the Adoption of Cloud Computing by Small and Medium Size Enterprises (SMEs)

Shima Ramezani Tehrani and Farid Shirazi

Ryerson University, Toronto, Canada
shima.ramezanitehrani@ryerson.ca, f2shiraz@ryerson.ca

Abstract. The main objective of this study is to determine the factors influencing cloud computing adoption by Small and Medium sized Enterprises (SMEs). Based on two dominant theories in the field of diffusion of innovation, a conceptual model is proposed. In order to test the model empirically, an online survey was designed and launched. Decision makers of 101 SMEs agreed to participate in this survey. In order to evaluate the internal, convergent, and discriminant validity of the instrument, factor analysis and reliability tests were performed. Logistic regression is employed to test our hypotheses. The results of regression reveal that decision maker's knowledge about cloud computing is the main influential factor in decision making about its adoption.

1 Introduction

Small and Medium sized Enterprises (SMEs) significantly contribute to each nation's Gross Domestic Product (GDP) and its labor market. Therefore, proposing strategies and developing new systems are not only beneficial for SMEs, but also for the economy as a whole. According to Tan et al. [1], using appropriate Information and Communication Technologies (ICTs) helps SMEs become more efficient and productive; however, SMEs do not have access to enough resources (e.g. financial resources). Cloud computing, which is an alternative to deploying applications and systems on-premises, helps SMEs tackle many issues such as the high cost and risk that are involved in IT projects.

Similar to other innovations, in addition to costs and benefits, there are other factors that influence the decision to adopt cloud computing. Technology adoption is one of the biggest research streams in Information System (IS) field. So far, not many studies have investigated the adoption of cloud computing. Among these studies, few of them focused on the adoption of cloud computing by SMEs. In this research, we study the factors that influence the adoption of cloud computing by SMEs. In order to investigate the factors that influence the SMEs' decision to adopt cloud computing, a conceptual model has been proposed. This model is originated from two prominent theories of this field. These two theories are Rogers's Diffusion of Innovation (DOI) theory and Tornatzky and Fleischer's Technology, Organization, and Environment (TOE) framework. According to this model, twelve factors influence the adoption of cloud computing by SMEs. They are: *External Support, Competitive Pressure, Decision makers' cloud knowledge, Employee's cloud knowledge, information intensity,*

S. Yamamoto (Ed.): HIMI 2014, Part II, LNCS 8522, pp. 631–642, 2014.
© Springer International Publishing Switzerland 2014

Innovativeness, Relative advantage, Cost, Security and Privacy, Trialability, Complexity, and compatibility with company's norms and technologies.

The conceptual model is then empirically tested. An online survey is completed by IT decision makers of SMEs. The questionnaire consists of around 25 simple and easy to understand questions. A market research company is hired to invite SMEs to participate in this research. The collected data is quantitatively analyzed; in order to check the internal, convergent, and discriminant validity of the questionnaire, factor analysis and reliability checks are performed. Finally, the proposed hypotheses are tested using logistic regression.

1.1   Literature Review

SMEs are vital players of each market. One strategy which has been proven to enhance SMEs' ability to compete against larger companies is the use of appropriate technology [1]. Although adopting new technologies helps SMEs gain a competitive advantage, it usually involves high costs. Cloud computing, as a new computing paradigm, offers many advantages to companies, especially smaller ones. Flexibility, scalability, and reduced cost are just some of many advantages that cloud computing offers to SMEs.

To date, there is no universal definition for cloud computing. Perhaps the most accurate definition of cloud computing is the one offered by the National Institute of Standards and Technology (NIST). They defined cloud computing as "a model for enabling ubiquitous, convenient, on-demand network access to a shared pool of configurable computing resources (e.g., networks, servers, storage, applications, and services) that can be rapidly provisioned and released with minimal management effort or service provider interaction. This cloud model is composed of five essential characteristics, three service models, and four deployment models." [2]

Cloud computing has three different service models: Infrastructure as a Service (IaaS), Platform as a Service (PaaS), and Software as a Service (SaaS). IaaS, which is the basic level of cloud service, is the service of delivering infrastructure services to customers over a network (e.g. Internet). The second level of cloud computing or PaaS is a model of cloud computing by which customers have online access to all requested resources that are required to build their enterprise applications, including the business logic. The last and the most common cloud computing model or SaaS is application based services delivered to customers over a network. Users can access the software anytime and anywhere they desire as long as they have access to internet [3]. Cloud computing offers also four types of deployment models: private, public, community, and hybrid. Private cloud is a type of cloud computing in which the cloud service is exclusively offered to one particular organization. The public cloud, which is the most common deployment model, offers the service to general public. Cloud providers have the full ownership of the infrastructure; they have their own rules, policies, and pricing models. Community cloud offers services to a group of organizations in a community, which may share a set of similar interests such as a common mission, security requirements, policies, and compliance considerations. Finally, hybrid cloud is the combination of two or more previously explained models.

To date, the majority of the studies about cloud computing try to improve the reader's understanding and knowledge about cloud computing [4-5]. Other researchers aim to investigate the concept of cloud computing by studying only one type of cloud computing [6-8]. Some of the studies are focused on a particular system, such as ERP [9], e-learning applications [10], and Virtual Computing Lab (VLC) [11]. Other studies focus on the application of cloud computing in different fields of study, including construction [12], digital forensic investigation [13], the service industry [14], and biology [15]. Many other aim to identify the challenges related to using cloud computing [16-21]. Other studies have proposed different models and strategies (such as changes in policies, regulations, and laws) that can be used to face the issues related to cloud computing [22-26].

Diffusion of technologies is an interesting area of research; however, the diffusion of cloud computing has not yet received much attention from research perspectives. Low et al. investigated the influence of eight factors associated with the adoption of cloud computing in the high-tech industry in Taiwan. The regression analysis shows that while relative advantage has a significant negative influence on the adoption of cloud computing, top management support, firm size, competitive pressure, and trading partner pressure characteristics have a significant positive influence on the diffusion of cloud computing. Compatibility and complexity do not significantly influence the adoption of cloud computing [27].

Another study investigated the adoption of cloud computing by college students. They found that students' characteristics, first-hand experiences with the platform, and instructor support are factors that influence students' perception about ease of use [11]. Similarly, Taylor and Hunsinger [28] conducted research about the acceptance and usage of Google Docs[1] in a university setting. The results of analysis reveal that the person's emotional response is a factor that significantly influences the students' intention to use Google Docs. Many countries such as Australia, Japan, Malaysia, and Taiwan have invested heavily in cloud-related projects. This is another reason for which research about cloud computing is compelling [29].

2   Theory Review

The conceptual framework that is proposed in this research originated from two well-known theoretical frameworks in this field of study, which are Diffusion of Innovation (DOI) theory developed by Rogers [30-31] and the Technology, Organization, Environment (TOE) framework proposed by Tornatzky and Fleischer [32].

Diffusion of Innovation Theory (DOI) is a theory that tries to discover the factors that influence the spread of a new idea or technology in a society [31]. Rogers [30] defined diffusion of innovation as "the process in which an innovation is communicated through certain channels over time among the members of a social system". Any idea, process, product, or technology constitutes innovation, as long as it is perceived as new by individuals. Rogers [30] argues that each innovation has different

---

[1] Google Docs is a cloud service provided by Google.

attributes that influence its diffusion in society. Relative advantage, compatibility, complexity, trialability, and observability are the five key attributes of innovation. DOI does not take into account the environmental and organizational aspects of the context; therefore, in this study we used the Technology Organization Environment (TOE) framework, which takes into account other aspects of enterprises' context.

TOE framework, which is developed by Tornatzky and Fleischer [32], is originally an organizational psychology theory. However, it has extensively been used by IS researchers. According to TOE framework, three aspects of enterprises' context influence the decision to adopt an innovation at firm level. Based on this theory, the decision to adopt an innovation is influenced by technological, organizational, and environmental aspects of the enterprise. The technological aspect of the TOE framework refers to both the availability and characteristics of the technologies. The organizational context of TOE framework describes the characteristics and resources of the organization, such as its size, structure, and communication processes. The environmental aspect of this framework refers to structure of the industry, technological support infrastructure, and government regulations.

3 Research Model and Hypotheses

In order to study the adoption of cloud computing by SMEs, a conceptual model is proposed. According to this model, twelve variables influence the decision to adopt cloud computing, which are depicted in Figure 1. All factors except complexity have a positive influence on the adoption of cloud computing. A very important study by Tornatzky and Klein [33] reveals that relative advantage, complexity, and compatibility are the characteristics of innovation that have the most influence on the adoption of an innovation.

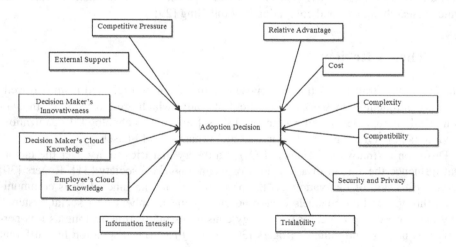

Fig. 1. Conceptual Model

3.1   Hypotheses

Based on the model, 12 different hypotheses have been proposed. Chau and Hui [34] argue that the size and structure of SMEs force them to rely on external parties. In this context, external support is defined as "The perceived importance of support offered by cloud providers". The first hypothesis is:

H1: Higher levels of perceived external support from cloud providers positively affects the likelihood of cloud computing adoption by SMEs

Competitive pressure is the level of competition among firms within the specific industry in which the company operates [35]. The following hypothesis is developed:

H2: Businesses that operate in more competitive environments are more likely to adopt cloud computing.

Having enough knowledge about an innovation is the first step in the adoption process. Therefore in the context of cloud computing, the following hypotheses have been developed:

H3: Decision Makers' knowledge about cloud computing is positively related to the decision to adopt cloud computing.

H4: Employees' knowledge about cloud computing is positively related to the adoption of cloud computing

Innovativeness is defined as "the level of decision makers' preference to try solutions that have not been tried out; and therefore are risky" [34]. Hypothesis 5 is:

H5: Decision Makers' innovativeness is positively related to the adoption of cloud computing.

According to Thong [35], information intensity is defined as "the degree to which information is present in the product or service of a business". The following hypothesis is related to this construct:

H6: Information intensity is positively related to the adoption of cloud computing

An advantageous technology is one that enables companies to perform their tasks more quickly, easily, and efficiently. Moreover it improves the quality, productivity, and performance of the company. The following hypothesis below is formulated:

H7: Decision makers' perception about the relative advantage of using cloud computing is positively related to cloud adoption

A technology that is difficult to understand, and whose use is considered to be complex, is less likely to be successfully adopted. Therefore, the following hypothesis is developed:

H8: The perceived level of complexity of the cloud computing has a negative impact on the adoption of cloud computing.

In this study, compatibility is defined as "the degree to which cloud computing is perceived as consistent with the existing values, past experience, and needs of companies". The related hypothesis is as follows:

H9: High levels of compatibility between cloud computing and a company's norms and technologies have a positive influence on cloud adoption.

We believe that the opportunity to use cloud computing on a trial basis positively influences the adoption of cloud computing; therefore the next hypothesis is:

H10: Higher level of trialability has a positive influence on the adoption of cloud computing

In this study, the cost of cloud computing is defined as "the degree to which decision makers perceive the total cost of using cloud computing to be lower than other computing paradigms". In the context of cloud computing the next hypothesis is:

H11. Decision makers who perceive cloud computing as being less costly than other computing paradigms are more likely to adopt cloud computing

In the context of cloud computing, security is defined as the security of the service, data centers, and media. It also takes into account the privacy and confidentiality of the companies' data. Therefore, in the context of cloud computing:

H12: The more secure that decision makers perceive cloud computing to be, the more they are willing to adopt cloud computing.

4   Research Methodology

Data collection procedure of this research is based on a survey. We developed a questionnaire which was reviewed and modified by a panel of experts, consisting of three IT professors and four PhD students. We used Qualtrics to develop our online questionnaire. The responses to our questions were captured on a 5 point Likert-type scale. The survey was sent to more than 500 decision makers. The response rate of 20% left us with 101 completed questionnaires. Both adopter and non-adopter companies were asked to participate in this survey. In order to assure the quality of the responses, several quality assurance (QA) questions were added to the questionnaire. The questions asked of participants were adapted mainly from papers already published in this field. In addition to the standard questions, we also developed some questions that are specific to the context of cloud computing.

In order to complete our research, the collected data needed to be analyzed. The statistical software used in this study is SPSS version 20. During the first stage, we used Factor Analysis (FA) to assess the construct validity of the theoretical model that is proposed. This method allows researchers to analyze the correlation between items and to determine a new set of variables that are highly correlated to each other. Reliability of the construct can also be checked by Cronbach's alpha; an alpha above 0.7 is considered adequate [37]. In order to test our hypotheses and predict the adoption of cloud computing, logistic regression is used.

5   Data Analysis Results

Our sample contained less than 5% missing values; therefore replacing them with the series mean is an appropriate method. A reliability test was performed on our pilot sample and some of the items which negatively influenced the reliability of the questionnaire were removed. Competitive pressure had an alpha lower than 0.7; therefore it was removed from further analysis. While a value of Cronbach's alpha of above 0.7 is acceptable, the inter-item correlation should be more than 0.3. [37] In this research, explanatory factor analysis (EFA), using the Principal Component extraction method based on constructs which yield Eigenvalues greater than 1 and the Varimax rotation method was performed.

Table 1. Final Results of Factor Analysis

	Component								
	1	2	3	4	5	6	7	8	9
RltAdv_effcny	.816								
RltAdv_prdt	.756								
RltAdv_eftv	.752								
RltAdv_fst	.738								
RltAdv_prfmc	.738								
RltAdv_Quik	.734								
RltAdv_advntg	.723								
RltAdv_Qlty	.723								
RltAdv_easy	.688								
RltAdv_tech	.598								
RltAdv_cap	.572								
CldKnw_Strct		.829							
CldKnw_models		.810							
CldKnw_gnrl		.800							
CldKnw_prcModel		.782							
CldKnw_type		.779							
CldKnw_cmpt		.735							
CldKnw_aver		.726							
CldKnw_bnft		.702							
Cost_Inv			.802						
Cost_CapEx			.717						
Cost_licsng			.679						
Cost_time			.676						
Cost_oprtng			.663						
Cost_prsnl			.655						
Cost_upgrd			.568						
Cost_mntnnc			.568						
ScPrv_cnfdtlty				.813					
ScPrv_Srvr				.790					
ScPrv_Mdia				.786					
ScPrv_data				.774					
ScPrv_cld				.759					
Cmpx_lng					.879				
Cmpx_tme					.865				
Cmpx_complct					.756				
Cmpx_gnrl					.716				
EmpCldKnw_bsc						.839			
EmpCldKnw_usg						.743			
EmpCldKnw_cmpr						.740			
InfoInt_rra							.872		
InfoInt_fst							.784		
InfoInt_Updt							.763		
ExtSup_CustSup								.773	
ExtSup_TechSup								.580	
ExtSup_CustHotln								.576	
INV_Impr									.873
INV_rsk									.793
Initial Eigenvalues	17.728	4.281	3.504	2.542	2.043	1.765	1.390	1.325	1.144
Variance	16.407	14.134	9.907	9.738	6.876	5.543	5.358	4.097	3.944

Extraction Method: Principal Component Analysis.   Rotation Method: Varimax with Kaiser Normalization.

According Hair et al. for 100 observations, the factor loadings of 0.55 and higher are significant. As such those constructs that had factor loadings lower than 0.55 were suppressed. One way to measure the appropriateness of the factor analysis is Bartlett's test of sphericity. The Bartlett's test was significant in this study, which proves the suitability of factor analysis. The Kaiser-Meyer-Olkin (KMO) criterion is another measure of Sampling Adequacy. Our model's KMO value was estimated as 0.839, which is considered excellent [38].

The preliminary results of factor analysis identified 11 different factors. This is consistent with our conceptual model. However, there is high cross loading among some of the constructs. After investigating the results of factor analysis, some of the items that have high cross loading or that have very low factor loading were deleted. In order to control the magnitude of factor reduction, items were deleted one by one.

As it can be seen in the table, nine different factors were identified. Together these nine factors account for 76% of total variance of all the variables in the research. In this study the composite values are calculated based on the average of variables in the scale [37]. The reliability of the final set of variables was checked again. Table 2 summarizes the final results of the reliability test. All items have high levels of Cronbach's alpha and inter-item correlation means.

Table 2. Reliability of Composite Scores

Construct	Number of Items	Inter-Item Correlation Mean	Cronbach's Alpha
Relative Advantage	11	0.641	0.951
Complexity	4	0.612	0.864
Security and Privacy	5	0.787	0.949
Cost	8	0.531	0.899
External Support	3	0.646	0.842
Decision Maker's Innovativeness	2	0.591	0.743
Decision Maker's Cloud Knowledge	8	0.725	0.953
Employee's Cloud Knowledge	3	0.638	0.838
Information Intensity	3	0.622	0.826

Means, standard deviations, and the results of normality tests of these new variables (composite values of each factor) are summarized in Table 3.

When performing logistic regressions, one of the important considerations is multicollinearity of the data. If multicollinearity exists among variables, the significance of the coefficient values is not properly predicted. In our sample, employees' Cloud Knowledge and decision makers' Cloud Knowledge have high collinearity. In the context of SMEs, the role of decision makers is more important; thus we elected to keep the decision maker's cloud knowledge and remove employees' cloud knowledge from further analysis. Logistic regression calculates the log likelihood value of each independent variable. The binary dependent variable has values of Yes (1) and No (0).

Table 4 is the classification summary of the model, which is one way to assess the model's goodness of fit. As it can be seen in the table, the model's classification accuracy is 79.2%, which means 79.2% of the time, the model correctly predicted the adoption decision.

Table 3. Descriptive Analysis for Composite Scores

Constructs	Descriptive Statistics			Skewness	Tests of Normality Kolmogorov-Smirnova	
	N	Mean	Std. Deviation	Statistics	Statistics	Sig.
Relative_Advantage	101	4.1989	.71613	-1.167	.075	.000
CloudKnowledge	101	3.9097	.86839	-.701	.144	.000
Cost	101	3.7339	.80325	-.209	.128	.176
Security_Privacy	101	4.1010	.78262	-1.509	.191	.000
Complexity	101	2.3168	.94729	.679	.142	.000
Employees' Cloud Knowledge	101	3.9264	.84143	-.683	.105	.008
Information Intensity	101	4.4059	.61933	-1.079	.208	.000
External_support	101	4.1584	.70015	-1.292	.132	.000
Innovativeness.	101	3.5000	.94340	-.902	.213	.000
Intention to Use	30	3.8556	1.09223	-0.846	.153	0.072
Valid N (listwise)	101					

Table 4. Classification Table

Observed		Adoption		Percentage Correct
		No	Yes	
Adoption	No	16	14	53.3
	Yes	7	64	90.1
Overall Percentage				79.2

Table 5 summarizes the results of our regression including the variables that are in the equation, their significance levels, their coefficients, and Wald values. Among eight independent variables, only Cloud Knowledge has a significant relationship with the adoption decision.

Table 5. Logistic Regression Results

	B	S.E.	Wald	df	Sig.	Exp(B)
CloudKnowledge	2.245	.659	11.607	1	.001	9.440
Cost_Reduction	-.241	.568	.181	1	.671	.785
External_Support	.122	.567	.047	1	.829	1.130
Relative_Advantage	-.434	.672	.417	1	.518	.648
Security_Privacy	-.310	.512	.367	1	.545	.733
Complexity	.121	.350	.119	1	.731	1.128
Information_Intensity	-.571	.544	1.103	1	.294	.565
Innovativeness	.465	.295	2.485	1	.115	1.592
Constant	-3.534	2.903	1.482	1	.223	.029

Based on the results, the probability of adopting cloud computing is higher for individuals who have greater knowledge about cloud computing. For an additional unit increase in cloud knowledge, the log odds of adopting cloud computing increases by a factor of 2.245. The high value of exponentiated beta means that for each unit increase in decision maker's knowledge about cloud computing, the chance of cloud computing adoption increases significantly.

6   Limitations and Future Studies

This research has some limitations, because of which the results cannot be generalized to all SMEs. Our main limitation is related to the sample size. Sample size becomes problematic because in order to get significant results, there should be at least 10 observations per each group of the dependent variable. Having eight different variables, our ideal sample size is 160, which is well beyond our actual sample size. Moreover, our sample is selected from North American companies. The results of this research are thus only applicable to SMEs located in North America. Moreover, the data is not restricted to a specific industry; this is problematic because each industry has its own characteristics and requirements. Performing further research in this field is highly recommended. Cloud computing is a new phenomenon; not many studies have been conducted in this field. The same study may be replicated using larger sample sizes, and in different industries. Performing a longitudinal study would also prove useful.

7   Conclusion

Similar to any innovation, the diffusion of cloud computing depends on various factors. In this research, we not only study the technical aspects of cloud computing, but also others such as environmental, organizational, and managerial factors. For this purpose, a conceptual model is proposed and empirically tested. The proposed model is developed based on two well-known theoretical frameworks in the field of technology adoption, which are: DOI developed by Rogers [30], and the TOE framework developed by Tornatzky and Fleischer [32]. Based on the research model, a set of hypotheses were proposed. In order to empirically test the model, we asked decision makers of SMEs to participate in an online survey. After the internal validity of the items was checked, factor analysis was performed. At this stage, some of the items were deleted. Removing these items left us with nine different factors.

Since this research is predictive in nature, regression analysis was used to test the hypotheses. Furthermore, our dependent variable is binary, therefore the most appropriate method of analysis is logistic regression. Based on the results, the only factor which significantly influences the adoption decision of cloud computing is the decision maker's knowledge about cloud computing. This knowledge is defined as the knowledge about the underlying structure of cloud computing, benefits of cloud computing, different types of cloud computing (SaaS, PaaS, and IaaS), various deployment models (public, private, or hybrid), and the pricing model of cloud computing.

This research contributes to both academia and business practice. First of all, the model proposed in this study is unique and has not been used in previous studies. Cloud providers can use the results of this study to increase the rate of adoption among SMEs. Based on the results of this study, cloud knowledge is the key factor in the diffusion of cloud computing. Cloud providers can use various mass media such as Facebook, LinkedIn, and Twitter to increase awareness about cloud computing.

References

1. Tan, K.S., Chong, S.C., Lin, B., Eze, U.: Internet-based ICT adoption: evidence from Malaysian SMEs. Industrial Management & Data Systems, 224–244 (2009)
2. Mell, P., Grance, T.: The NIST Definition of Cloud Computing. Gaithersburg: Computer Security Division Information Technology Laboratory National Institute of Standards and Technology (2011)
3. Fang, Z., Yin, C.: BPM Architecture Design Based on Cloud Computing. Intelligent Information Management, 329–333 (2010)
4. Youseff, L., Butrico, M., Da Silva, D.: Toward a Unified Ontology of Cloud Computing. In: Grid Computing Environments Workshop, GCE 2008, pp. 1–10 (2008)
5. Grossman, R.L.: The case for cloud computing. IT Professionals (2009)
6. Bhardwaj, S., Jain, L., Jain, S.: Cloud Computing: A Study of Infrastructure-as-a-Service. International Journal of Engineering and Information Technology, 60–63 (2010)
7. Repschlaeger, J., Wind, S., Zarnekow, R., Turowski, K.: A reference guide to cloud computing dimensions: Infrastructure as a Service Classification Framework. In: 2012 45th Hawaii International Conference on System Sciences (2012)
8. Kim, W.: Cloud computing adoption. International Journal of Web and Grid Services 7(3) (2011)
9. Saeed, I., Juell-Skielse, G., Uppström, E.: Cloud Enterprise Resource Planning Adoption: Motives and Barriers. In: International Conference on Research and Practical Issues of Enterprise Information Systems, pp. 99–122 (2011)
10. Doelitzscher, F., Sulistio, A., Reich, C., Kuijs, C., Wolf, D.: Private cloud for collaboration and e-Learning services: from IaaS to SaaS. Computing, 23–42 (2011)
11. Behrand, T., Wiebe, E.N., London, J.E., Johnson, E.C.: Cloud computing adoption and usage in community colleges. Behaviour & Information Technology 30(2), 231–240 (2010)
12. Liu, Q.: Cloud Computing in Construction An investigation into the potential implementation of cloud computing in China construction industry to mitigate Traditional IT application issues. Heriot-Watt University (2011)
13. Biggs, S., Vidalis, S.: Cloud Computing: The impact on digital forensic investigations. In: International Conference for Internet Technology and Secured Transactions, ICITST 2009, pp. 1–6 (2009)
14. Borangiu, T., Curaj, A., Dogar, A.: Fostering innovation in services through open education and advanced IT. In: International Joint Conference on Computational Cybernetics and Technical Informatics (ICCC-CONTI), pp. 437–444 (2010)
15. Talukder, A., Gandham, S., Prahalad, H., Bhattacharyya, N.: Cloud-MAQ: The Cloud-Enabled Scalable Whole Genome Reference Assembly Application. In: Seventh International Conference on Wireless and Optical Communications Networks (WOCN), pp. 1–5. IEEE, Bangalore (2010)
16. Dillon, T., Wu, C., Chang, E.: Cloud Computing: Issues and Challenges. In: 24th IEEE International Conference on Advanced Information Networking and Applications (AINA), pp. 27–33 (2010)

17. Khorshed, T., Ali, S., Wasimi, S.A.: A survey on gaps, threat remediation challenges and some thoughts for proactive attack detection in cloud computing. Future Generation Computer Systems 28(6), 833–851 (2012)
18. Subashini, S., Kavitha, V.: A survey on security issues in service delivery models of cloud computing. Journal of Network and Computer Applications, 1–11 (2011)
19. Katsaros, D., Mehra, P., Vakali, A.: Cloud Computing: Distributed Internet Computing for IT and Scientific Research. IEEE Internet Computing, 10–13 (2009)
20. Jensen, M., Schwenk, J., Gruschka, N., Iacono, L.: On Technical Security Issues in Cloud Computing. In: IEEE International Conference on Cloud Computing, pp. 109–116 (2009)
21. Zhang, Q., Cheng, L., Boutaba, R.: Cloud computing: state-of-the-art and research challenges. Journal of Internet Services and Applications, 7–18 (2010)
22. Li, X.-Y., Zhou, L.-T., Shi, Y., Guo, Y.: A Trusted Computing Environment Model in Cloud Architecture. In: Proceedings of the Ninth International Conference on Machine Learning and Cybernetics, pp. 11–14. IEEE, Qingdao (2010)
23. Khan, S., Zhang, B., Khan, F., Chen, S.: Business intelligence in the cloud: A case of Pakistan. In: 2011 IEEE International Conference on Business Intelligence in the Cloud: A Case of Pakistan, Cloud Computing and Intelligence Systems (CCIS), pp. 536–540 (2011)
24. Buyyaa, R., Yeoa, C.S., Venugopala, S., Broberga, J., Brandicc, I.: Cloud computing and emerging IT platforms: Vision, hype, and reality for delivering computing as the 5th utility. Future Generation Computer Systems, 599–616 (2009)
25. Ryan, P.S., Merchant, R., Falvey, S.: Regulation of the Cloud in India. Journal of Internet Law (2011)
26. Khalid, A.: Cloud computing and emerging IT platforms: Vision, hype, and reality for delivering computing as the 5th utility. In: International Conference on Signal Acquisition and Processing, ICSAP 2010 (p. Cloud Computing: Applying Issues in Small Business). IEEE (2010)
27. Low, C., Chen, Y., Wu, M.: Understanding the determinants of cloud computing adoption. Industrial Management & Data Systems 111(7) (2011)
28. Taylor, C.W., Hunsinger, A.: A Study of Student Use of Cloud Computing Applications. Journal of Information Technology Management, 36–50 (2011)
29. Lin, S.C., Yen, E.: Asia Federation Report on International Symposium on Grids and Clouds (ISGC). In: Proceeding of Science (2011)
30. Rogers, E.M.: Diffusion of Innovations, 4th edn. Free Press, New York (1995)
31. Rogers, E.M.: Diffusion of Innovations, 5th edn. Free Press, New York (2003)
32. Tornatzky, L.G., Fleischer, M.: The process of Technological Innovation. Lexington Books, Lexington (1990)
33. Tornatzky, L.G., Klein, R.J.: Innovation characteristics and innovation adoption-implementation: A meta-analysis of findings. IEEE Transactions on Engineering Management, 28–45 (1982)
34. Chau, P.Y., Hui, K.L.: Determinants of Small Business EDI Adoption: An Empirical Investigation. Journal of Organizational Computing and Electronic Commerce 11(4), 229–251 (2001)
35. Thong, J., Yap, C.: CEO characteristics, organizational characteristics and information technology adoption in small businesses. Omega, 429–442 (1995)
36. Thong, J.Y.: An integrated model of information systems adoption in small businesses. Journal of Management Information Systems 187 (1999)
37. Hair, J., Black, W., Babin, B., Anderson, R.: Multivariate Data Analysis. Pearson, lavoisier (2010)
38. Kaiser, H.F.: An index of factorial simplicity (1974)

Learning Effect Evaluation of an Educational Tool for Product-Service System Design Based on Learner Viewpoints

Kentaro Uei, Takashi Fujiwara, Akira Kazawa, Yutaro Nemoto,
Koji Kimita, and Yoshiki Shimomura

Dept. of System Design, Tokyo Metropolitan University, Tokyo, Japan
{uei-kentaro,fujiwara-takashi,kazawa-akira,
nemoto-yutaro}@ed.tmu.ac.jp, kimita@tmu.ac.jp,
yoshiki-shimomura@center.tmu.ac.jp

Abstract. Product-Service Systems (PSSs) are regarded as an attractive business concept for manufacturing industries to increase their competitiveness. To design PSSs, it is important to have points of view different from those of product design. To teach such new viewpoints, the authors have developed a business game named "EDIPS." However, the learning effects of this game have not been analyzed sufficiently. To analyze the learning effects, this study first organizes the earning contents of the game. By using the organized learning contents as criteria, the learning effects can be analyzed by using results of pre- and post-tests for learners.

Keywords: Product-Service Systems, Business game, Education.

1 Introduction

Due to advanced commoditization of product business and serious environmental problems, it has become difficult for manufacturing companies to keep up their competitiveness while using product-oriented business models. In this context, Product-Service Systems (PSSs) that combine products and services to create new added value are regarded as an attractive business concept [1–4].

In designing a PSS, it is important to focus on the value created by the whole system composed of a combination of products and services [3]. Therefore, the designers who will lead the manufacturing industries of the future must have a new mindset of amplifying value by providing a combination of products and services. For designers who have only learned traditional engineering, however, it is initially difficult to think in this manner. For this reason, many companies have not shifted their business models from product-oriented systems to PSSs. To promote the shift to PSS providers in the manufacturing industries, educational methods or tools that enable designers to easily and effectively learn this new way of thinking are required [5].

Against this background, the authors have developed an educational business game named EDIPS (Edutainment for Designing Integrated Product-service Systems) [6].

S. Yamamoto (Ed.): HIMI 2014, Part II, LNCS 8522, pp. 643–652, 2014.
© Springer International Publishing Switzerland 2014

This business game is a kind of "edutainment" tool that has the advantage of effective and enjoyable learning through active thinking in a simulated business environment. EDIPS is expected to effectively teach the philosophy of PSS design to players and change their mindset. The learning effects of EDIPS have been evaluated by using a questionnaire. The evaluation items in the questionnaire have been designed based on the learning content intended at a very early stage of the game's development. The results of the evaluation confirmed that EDIPS has specific educational benefits regarding the intended learning content. On the other hand, some learners pointed out that there are other educational benefits that conform to none of the provided evaluation items. This means that the past evaluation using the questionnaire is insufficient to evaluate the game's actual effect on learning.

In this study, the learning effects of EDIPS are analyzed from the viewpoint of the learner. In order to achieve this objective, we first extracted detailed learning contents from each basic rule of EDIPS and organized them. By using the organized learning contents as criteria, we analyzed the learning effects by conducting pre- and post-tests for learners. On the basis of the results of analysis, the learning effects of EDIPS are evaluated and discussed.

2 Product-Service System Design and Education

2.1 PSS Design

PSS aims to fulfill customer needs by creating added value by providing not only a product but also a combination of products and services [3]. To achieve this, a manufacturing company needs to deliver value to customers continuously by expanding the time domain to relate to customers by providing services not only at the time of the sales but also during the product's use, maintenance, and disposal phases. Thus, it is important for PSS designers to search for opportunities to deliver value to customers and provide appropriate services throughout the life cycle of the product [7]. Moreover, in PSS, the structure for delivering value varies according to the combination of products and services. Namely, PSS designers should also consider how to increase value by a combination of product functions and service activities.

2.2 EDIPS: A Tool for PSS Education

The authors have developed a business game, called EDIPS, that aims to help students effectively learn the new viewpoints identified in section 2.1. Figure 1 shows the conceptual structure of this game. The highest layer of Figure 1 indicates the game's educational objective. More concrete learning contents for achieving this objective are associated and deployed into sub-contents. The sub-contents, placed in the lowest layer of the learning contents, are connected with game mechanisms designed to teach these contents to learners. EDIPS was developed assuming that players will learn the contents by playing the game [6].

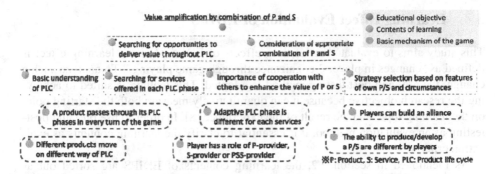

Fig. 1. Leaning contents and game mechanisms of EDIPS

EDIPS is a board game for five players (Figure 2). Each player assumes the role of either product provider or service provider and competes to earn the most points (i.e. money) to win. Product providers can earn points when they sell their own products (three kinds: red, blue, and yellow). Products sold by product providers pass through the following life cycle phases: installation, use, maintenance, and disposal. Service providers can offer four kinds of services of their own to target products and receive points according to the phase. From these rules, players can learn fundamental PSS strategies, such as offering services for products in the market in order to create high added value.

In addition, each player has a chance to become a PSS provider or to establish a PS alliance during the game. PSS providers can deal in both products and services by themselves. Therefore, PSS providers can effectively score many points by following their own strategy. On the other hand, product providers and service providers in an alliance can effectively score many points, as can the PSS provider, by dealing in their products and services following a cooperative strategy. These rules help players learn the importance of combining products and services to create added value.

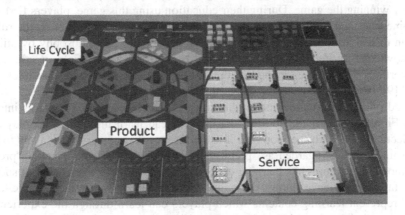

Fig. 2. EDIPS

3   Learning Effect Evaluation of EDIPS

This study aims to evaluate the learning effects of EDIPS. Here, a learning effect is defined as "changes in players' cognizance through game playing." To analyze such a change, the pre- and post-testing method is adopted. This method is suited to achieving the research objective because it can quantitatively measure both the starting point on the learning topic and the result of the experience [8]. In order to use pre- and post-testing as an evaluation method, it is essential to clarify the learning contents as evaluation criteria.

As mentioned in section 2.2, the learning contents of EDIPS are sorted out as shown in Figure 1. Since these contents were structured with a top-down approach in an early stage of the game development, these are expressed in abstract terms. Furthermore, current game mechanisms, which have been added and refined in a stepwise manner, are not exhaustive. This causes the evaluation criteria for learning effects to be insufficient. In order to evaluate the actual learning effects of EDIPS, therefore, it is essential to redefine the structure of the learning contents.

In this study, we first organized the learning contents of the game. Specifically, the learning contents were extracted from each basic rule of the game and categorized. This enabled us to clarify the evaluation criteria for the actual learning effects. Second, we conducted pre- and post-tests, which are composed of the same free-question items, for players. Using the results of the pre- and post-tests, we analyzed changes in players' cognizance after game playing. Based on the results of this analysis, we have clarified the game's educational benefits based on the learner's viewpoint.

3.1   Organization of Learning Contents of EDIPS

EDIPS aims to teach the philosophy of PSS design. Players are expected to learn the fundamentals of PSS and strategy for designing PSS by gaining experience and know-how for winning the game. During their education using this game, players first grasp the game rules and acquire knowledge in a phased manner by interpreting the rules in relation to real business. Moreover, they learn important PSS philosophy by utilizing the knowledge during game playing. Based on research in the field of educational engineering, such abilities gained in the above way can correspond to "intellectual skills" [9], which is one category of learning outcomes.

Based on the information above, this study categorizes learning contents into two types. First, we regard the abilities that players can learn through game playing as "intellectual skills." Furthermore, the knowledge that is necessary for players to learn intellectual skills is regarded as "preliminary knowledge." In this context, "preliminary knowledge" represents learning contents that players can learn without successful or failed experience during the game playing. On the other hand, "intellectual skills" represent learning contents which players can learn through the experience of utilizing preliminary knowledge to attain a purpose in a certain business environment.

To organize the learning contents of EDIPS, first, the rules of this game are listed and sorted out. Specifically, we extracted the rules by referring to the game manual (cf., [10]) and regarding one sentence of the game rules as a minimum unit. Since these rules basically represent some facts in actual business, we translated the extracted rules into the facts and sorted them out as preliminary knowledge. Finally, we estimated the intellectual skills that players can learn by utilizing the preliminary knowledge and organize them. Through this procedure, we clarify relationships among rules, preliminary knowledge, and intellectual skills.

Table 1 shows a part of the newly organized learning contents of EDIPS. As shown in Table 1, for example, "Utilizing one's own full manufacturing ability and selling skills in order to obtain high profits in the limited time and resources" is identified as an intellectual skill that players can learn through game playing. To learn this intellectual skill, players need to acquire four pieces of preliminary knowledge (e.g., "In order to sell products, it is necessary to manufacture the products at the factory and store them in a repository.") and to utilize them during game playing. Furthermore, Table 1 includes a relevant rule of the game for each piece of preliminary knowledge (e.g., "Product providers who conduct 'Production' transfer product cubes from the factory to one's own repository and pay 2 points per cube as costs."). Players learn each piece of preliminary knowledge by interpreting such rules in relation to the real business world.

Table 1. Organized learning contents of EDIPS (excerpt)

Intellectual skills	Preliminary knowledge	Rules of the game
(1) Utilizing one's own manufacturing and selling abilities fully in order to obtain high profits with limited time and resources	In order to sell products, it is necessary to manufacture the products at a factory and stored in a repository.	Product providers who conduct "Production" transfer product cubes from a factory to one's own repository and pay 2 points per cube as costs.
	There is an upper limit to the quantity of products that can be produced per unit of time.	In "Production" action, product providers can transfer up to four product cubes to one's repository.
	It is possible to obtain profits by selling manufactured products.	Product providers who conduct "Sales" move products in one's repository to the installation phase and earn points according to the price of the products.
	There is an upper limit to the quantity of products that can be sold per unit of time.	In the "Sales" action, product providers can move up to two products to the installation phase.
(2) Entering different product fields in order to enhance the robustness of product offering	It is possible to enter different product fields by introducing manufacturing technology with investment.	Product providers who conduct "Color addition" add a product color that they can deal.

3.2   Pre- and Post-Testing

To analyze changes in players' understanding before and after game playing, pre- and post-tests, which are composed of the same free-answer question items, are conducted. The free-answer question items are as follows:

Q1: From the manufacturer's point of view, what do you think are the important things in the design and development of a new business?

Q2: From the service provider's point of view, what do you think are the important things in the design and development of a new business?

In these question items, the organized learning contents that are shown in Table 1 are not implicated. This is to prevent respondents from reading too much into the learning contents from the question items. This enables us to analyze purely the changes in players' understanding.

The form of the free-answer questions is adopted in these question items. Also, the question items are abstract. By answering such abstract questions, respondents are stimulated to retrace their thinking and behavior during game playing. Then, by answering questions freely, honest answers can be extracted from respondents.

In addition, respondents' viewpoints are divided into those of manufactures (Q1) and service providers (Q2). This is because there are both roles of product providers and service providers in EDIPS. Therefore, by preparing players for both viewpoints, it is expected to prompt respondents to make themselves clear about their knowledge or experience using EDIPS.

3.3 Procedure for Analyzing Learning Effects

To analyze the learning effects of EDIPS, answers from pre- and post-tests are scored under evaluation criteria. The evaluation criteria include whether terms concerning the intellectual skills shown in Table 2 are included in the respondents' answer. Namely, there are sixteen criteria in this analysis. Hence, each respondent's answer is evaluated on a scale of zero to sixteen.

Table 2. Evaluation criteria for learning effects

	Intellectual skills
(1)	Utilizing one's own manufacturing and selling abilities fully to obtain high profits with limited time and resources
(2)	Entering different product fields to enhance the robustness of product offering
(3)	Advancing standards of products to enhance their value
(4)	Developing services to launch them to the market
(5)	Offering services to products to construct a PSS
(6)	Entering different product areas to enhance the robustness of service offerings
(7)	Offering services considering their compatibility with products to increase profits
(8)	Offering a PSS by combining products and services to enhance the value of products
(9)	Offering one's own services in combination with one's own products to increase competitiveness of the services
(10)	Offering one's own services in combination with an alliance partner's products to increase competitiveness of the services
(11)	Considering the circumstances of other companies to smoothly establish an alliance
(12)	Building a product reuse system to enhance efficiency of the product offering
(13)	Formulating strategies by considering market trends to increase the price of products
(14)	Formulating strategies while considering contingencies to gain steady profits
(15)	Understanding product life cycles to formulate appropriate sales strategies
(16)	Formulating strategies by considering reduction of environmental burdens to keep one's own societal value

Several analysts read each answer, discuss, and determine whether terms related to the criteria are included in the answer. The score is calculated by the number of criteria covered, as determined by the related terms included in respondents' answers. The answers for both Q1 and Q2 are scored in the above manner. Moreover, the results of the pre- and post-tests are compared. Increased scores are regarded as learning effects of EDIPS.

4 Evaluation Results

4.1 Settings

To evaluate the learning effects of EDIPS, several workshops were conducted. Workshop participants completed the pre- and post-tests mentioned in section 3.3. The participants were 21 engineering students and 2 engineers who work in manufacturing firms. They were acquainted with traditional engineering technology and product design, while they did not have much knowledge about PSS.

4.2 Analysis of Changes in Test Scores

Figure 3 shows scoring results of the pre- and post-tests. As shown in Figure 3, scoring results were totally increased after game playing. Specifically, the number of respondents who scored zero point decreased to four. The scoring averages in each test were calculated as follows: pre-test 0.7, post-test 1.9.

Figure 4 shows the number of respondents who scored for each intellectual skill. In the pre-test, answers related to (1): "Utilizing one's own manufacturing ability and selling skills fully to obtain high profits with limited time and resources" were most common. On the other hand, in the post-test, many respondents scored for intellectual skill (7), "Offering services considering their compatibility with products to increase

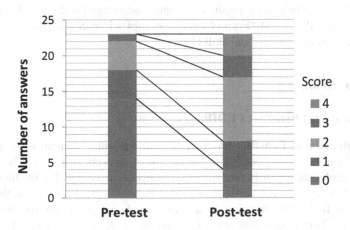

Fig. 3. Scoring results of pre- and post-tests

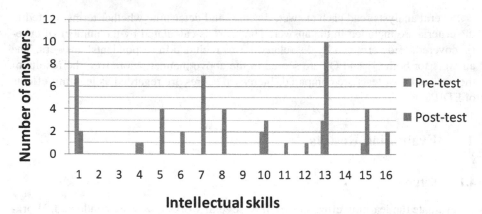

Fig. 4. Number of respondents who scored for each intellectual skill

profits from PSS," and intellectual skill (13), "Formulating strategies by considering market trends to increase the price of products." In addition, it can be confirmed that no respondent scored for intellectual skill (2), (3), (9), or (14).

4.3   Overall Evaluation

The score changes shown in Figures 3 and 4 indicate that EDIPS has specific leaning effects, as the post-test largely had higher scoring results than did the pre-test. Focusing on Figure 4, moreover, it can be said that EDIPS enables players to learn "Offering services by considering the compatibility of products to increase profits from PSS (intellectual skill (7))" and "Formulating strategies by considering market trends to increase the price of products (intellectual skill (13))." However, we could find out EDIPS has a lower learning effect on "Entering different product areas to enhance the robustness of product offering (intellectual skill (2))," "Advancing standards of products to enhance their value (intellectual skill (3))," "Offering one's own services in combination with one's own products to increase competitiveness of the services (intellectual skill (9))," and "Formulating strategies while considering contingencies to gain steady profits (intellectual skill (14))."

5   Discussion

5.1   Educational Benefits of EDIPS

Specific Educational Benefits. By comparing the learning content of each intellectual skill, it can be confirmed that the tendency of answers is different between pre- and post-test. As shown in Figure 4, many respondents scored for intellectual skills (7) and (13) in the post-test, while they scored for intellectual skill (1) in the pre-test. Intellectual skill (1) is the learning content of considering the ability required of product providers. This means that there is a strong tendency to answer the questions based on the viewpoint of the product provider. On the other hand, intellectual skill

(7) is the learning content of considering a combination of products and services, and intellectual skill (13) is the learning content of considering products and services in the market as a whole. This means that, in the post-test, there is a strong tendency to answer the questions based on the viewpoint of the service provider or the PSS provider.

Based on these results, we believe this game enables players to shift their mindset from product-oriented to service-oriented through game playing.

Remaining Issues. As mentioned in section 4.3, EDIPS has lower learning effects on intellectual skills (2) and (3). In organizing the learning contents of EDIPS, we estimated that players learned intellectual skill (2) from the action "Color addition" and intellectual skill (3) from the action "New standard." These two actions are associated with differences of products (e.g., category of products) and are expected to be conducted as a strategy for winning the game. For players, however, it is difficult to understand what strategies in real business are associated with these actions. This is because such product differences are translated into color of products in the game. Furthermore, it was not explained that each product color in the game represents differences in real products. This might cause the lower learning effects on intellectual skills expected to be learned from two actions above.

To enhance the learning effects for intellectual skills (2) and (3), a more concrete explanation about the relationship between components, rules, and real business should be given to players before or after using this game. This would prompt players to associate real business with the game playing.

5.2   Organized Learning Contents of EDIPS

After the workshops, we interviewed three respondents about their descriptions in the post-test. We asked them which rules of the game helped them to learn about the intellectual skills they obtained.

Through the interviews, we discovered that some respondents learned intellectual skill (7) from the rule related to the compatibility of products and services. In addition, some respondents mentioned that they learned intellectual skill (10) from the rule related to alliances and intellectual skill (13) from the event rule "Price change." In this event phase, prices of products and services vary, depending on the market condition. Comparing these results with the learning contents organized in this study, six of sixteen correspondence relationships between rules and intellectual skills were confirmed. Therefore, it can be estimated that the organized learning contents have a certain validity. Since all of the relationships were not confirmed in the interviews, the organized learning contents should be continuously verified in future works.

6   Conclusion and Outlook

In this paper, to evaluate the learning effects of EDIPS, we organized the learning contents of the game and analyzed the results of pre- and post-tests, using the organized learning contents as criteria. Based on the results, the effectiveness of EDIPS and remaining issues were discussed.

Future work should include improving the game based on the results of the pre- and post-tests. Moreover, the learning effects of EDIPS should be evaluated in greater detail by analyzing not only the results of pre- and post-tests but also the performance of "players" during game playing.

References

1. Tukker, A., Tischner, U.: Product-Services as a Research Field: Past, Present and Future. Reflections from a Decade of Research. Journal of Engineering Design 14, 1552–1556 (2006)
2. Shimomura, Y., Hara, T., Arai, T.: A Unified Representation Scheme for Effective PSS Development. CIRP Annals—Manufacturing Technology 58(1), 379–382 (2009)
3. Meier, H., Roy, R., Seliger, G.: Industrial Product-Service Systems-IPS2. CIRP Annals—Manufacturing Technology 59(2), 607–627 (2010)
4. Tischner, U., Verkuijl, M., Tukker, A.: First Draft PSS Review. SusProNet Report (2002)
5. Shehab, E., Tiwari, A., Vasantha, G.A., Lightfoot, H., Roy, R.: Industrial Product-Service Systems (IPS2): Think Tank. Decision Engineering Report Series, Cranfield University (2011)
6. Uei, K., Nemoto, Y., Shimomura, Y.: EDIPS: Effective and Enjoyable Product-Service System Design Education through Active Thinking. In: Proceedings of the 1st International Conference on Serviceology, ICServe 2013. The Society for Serviceology, Tokyo (2013)
7. McAloone, T.C., Andreason, M.M.: Design for Utility, Sustainability and Social Virtues, Developing Product Service Systems. In: Proceedings of the 8th International Design Conference, Dubrovnik, Croatia, pp. 1545–1552 (2004)
8. Ikejiri, R., Tsubakimoto, M., Fujimoto, T., Yamauti, Y.: Designing and Evaluating a Card Game to Support High School Students in Applying Their Knowledge of World History to Solve Modern Political Issues. In: International Conference of Media Education. Beijing Normal University (2012)
9. Gagne: Principles of Instructional Design, 5th edn. Wadsworth Publishing (2005)
10. Manual of EDIPS, http://www.comp.tmu.ac.jp/smmlab/research/doc/EDIPS_manual.pdf (accessed January 30, 2014)

Author Index